REPORTING WAR

What is the role of the journalist in wartime? When faced with the responsibility of bearing witness to the horror of modern warfare, how do reporters negotiate the competing demands of their employers, of governments and military sources, even of soldiers in the field of battle? How do they manage the tensions between objectivity, patriotism, and sympathy with the suffering of local people caught up in conflicts?

Reporting War examines the nature of contemporary war reporting in a range of locales, including Africa, the Balkans, the Middle East—especially Iraq—and southern Asia. The contributors, both practising and former journalists and leading academics, consider issues including the influence of censorship and propaganda, 24/7 rolling news, military jargon such as "collateral damage," embedded and unilateral reporters, and the visual imagery of war.

The book's major focus on the Iraq war encompasses media coverage of the run-up to war, the war itself, the anti-war movement in the UK, Europe, and the US, and the role played by news sources outside the mainstream, including the satellite channel Al-Jazeera and online reporting.

REPORTING WAR

Journalism in wartime

Edited by Stuart Allan and Barbie Zelizer

Routledge
Taylor & Francis Group

LONDON AND NEW YORK

First published 2004
by Routledge
2 Park Square, Milton Park, Abingdon, Oxon, OX14 4RN

Simultaneously published in the USA and Canada by Taylor & Francis Inc
270 Madison Avenue, New York, NY 10016

Routledge is an imprint of the Taylor and Francis Group

Typeset in Goudy by The Running Head Limited, Cambridge
Printed and bound in Great Britain by MPG Books Ltd, Bodmin, Cornwall

British Library Cataloguing in Publication Data
A catalogue record for this book is available from the British Library

Library of Congress Cataloging in Publication Data
Reporting war: journalism in wartime / edited by Stuart Allan and Barbie Zelizer.
p. cm.
1. War—Press coverage. I. Allan, Stuart, 1962– II. Zelizer, Barbie.
PN4784.W37R48 2004
070.4'333—dc22   2004 00287

ISBN 0–415–33997–9 (hbk)
ISBN 0–415–33998–7 (pbk)

CONTENTS

List of contributors   viii

INTRODUCTION

   Rules of engagement: journalism and war   3
   STUART ALLAN AND BARBIE ZELIZER

PART 1
War in the twenty-first century   23

  1 **Understanding: the second casualty**   25
     OLIVER BOYD-BARRETT

  2 **Information warfare in an age of hyper-militarism**   43
     RICHARD KEEBLE

  3 **A moral imagination: the media's response to the war on terrorism**   59
     SUSAN D. MOELLER

  4 **The PR of terror: how new-style wars give voice to terrorists**   77
     TAMAR LIEBES AND ZOHAR KAMPF

  5 **Researching US media–state relations and twenty-first century wars**   96
     PIERS ROBINSON

PART 2
Bearing witness   113

  6 **When war is reduced to a photograph**   115
     BARBIE ZELIZER

7 The Persian Gulf TV war revisited   136
DOUGLAS KELLNER

8 Tribalism and tribulation: media constructions of "African savagery"
and "Western humanitarianism" in the 1990s   155
SUSAN L. CARRUTHERS

9 Humanizing war: the Balkans and beyond   174
PHILIP HAMMOND

10 Prisoners of news values?: journalists, professionalism, and
identification in times of war   190
HOWARD TUMBER

11 Out of sight, out of mind?: the non-reporting of small wars and
insurgencies   206
PRASUN SONWALKAR

12 The battlefield is the media: war reporting and the formation of
national identity in Australia—from Belmont to Baghdad   224
MICHAEL BROMLEY

PART 3
Reporting the Iraq war   245

13 Militarized journalism: framing dissent in the Gulf Wars   247
STEPHEN D. REESE

14 War or peace?: legitimation, dissent, and rhetorical closure in press
coverage of the Iraq war build-up   266
NICK COULDRY AND JOHN DOWNEY

15 How British television news represented the case for the war
in Iraq   283
JUSTIN LEWIS AND ROD BROOKES

16 European news agencies and their sources in the Iraq war
coverage   301
TERHI RANTANEN

CONTENTS

17 Al-Jazeera and war coverage in Iraq: the media's quest for
    contextual objectivity   315
    ADEL ISKANDAR AND MOHAMMED EL-NAWAWY

18 Big media and little media: the journalistic informal sector during
    the invasion of Iraq   333
    PATRICIA AUFDERHEIDE

19 The culture of distance: online reporting of the Iraq war   347
    STUART ALLAN

    Index   366

CONTRIBUTORS

Stuart Allan is Reader in the School of Cultural Studies, University of the West of England, Bristol. He is the author of *News Culture* (Open University Press, 2nd edition, 2004) and *Media, Risk and Science* (Open University Press, 2002). His previous edited collections include, with Barbie Zelizer, *Journalism after September 11* (Routledge, 2002).

Patricia Aufderheide is Professor and Co-director of the Center for Social Media, School of Communication, American University, Washington DC. She is the author of many works of cultural criticism and commentary, including *The Daily Planet: a Critic on the Capitalist Culture Beat* (University of Minnesota Press, 2000).

Oliver Boyd-Barrett is Professor of Communication at California State Polytechnic University, Pomona. Recent books include *Approaches to Media* (co-edited with Chris Newbold; Edward Arnold, 1995), *The Globalization of News* (co-edited with Terhi Rantanen; Sage, 1998), and *The Media Book* (co-edited with Chris Newbold and Hilde Van Den Bulck; Hodder Arnold, 2002).

Michael Bromley is Head of Journalism at Queensland University of Technology, Australia, and has taught journalism in the UK and US. A former journalist, he has published widely on journalism and the media, and is a founding co-editor of the journal *Journalism: Theory, Practice and Criticism*.

Rod Brookes lectures at the Cardiff School of Journalism, Media, and Cultural Studies, Cardiff University. He is the author of *Representing Sport* (Arnold, 2002).

Susan L. Carruthers is Associate Professor of History at Rutgers University in Newark, New Jersey. She is the author of *Winning Hearts and Minds: British Governments, the Media and Colonial Counterinsurgency, 1945–60* (Leicester University Press, 1995), and *The Media at War: Communication and Conflict in the Twentieth Century* (Palgrave/Macmillan, 2000).

Nick Couldry is Senior Lecturer in Media and Communications at the London School of Economics and Political Science. His books include *The Place of Media Power* (Routledge, 2000), *Inside Culture* (Sage, 2000), *Media Rituals: a*

Critical Approach (Routledge, 2003), *Contesting Media Power* (co-edited with James Curran; Rowman and Littlefield, 2003), and *MediaSpace* (co-edited with Anna McCarthy; Routledge, 2004).

John Downey lectures in the Department of Social Sciences at Loughborough University. His publications include the co-edited *Technocities* (Sage, 1999). He is presently working on a book about communication, technology, and coercion.

Mohammed el-Nawawy is Assistant Professor, Department of Communication, Stonehill College, Easton, MA. He is co-author of *Al-Jazeera: the Story of the Network that is Rattling Governments and Redefining Modern Journalism* (Westview, 2003), and author of *The Israeli–Egyptian Peace Process in the Reporting of Western Journalists* (Greenwood, 2002).

Philip Hammond is Senior Lecturer in Media at London South Bank University. He is co-editor, with Edward Herman, of *Degraded Capability: the Media and the Kosovo Crisis* (Pluto, 2000).

Adel Iskandar is conducting doctoral research at the University of Kentucky. He is co-author of *Al-Jazeera: the Story of the Network that is Rattling Governments and Redefining Modern Journalism* (Westview, 2003) and co-editor of a forthcoming book on Edward Said.

Zohar Kampf is writing his PhD dissertation on the nature of political apology in the Department of Communication and Journalism at the Hebrew University of Jerusalem.

Richard Keeble is Professor of Journalism at Lincoln University. His publications include *The Newspapers Handbook* (third edition; Routledge 2001), *Ethics for Journalists* (Routledge, 2001), and *Secret State, Silent Press* (John Libbey, 1997).

Douglas Kellner is George Kneller Chair in the Philosophy of Education at UCLA. Recent books include *Grand Theft 2000: Media Spectacle and the Theft of an Election* (Rowman and Littlefield, 2001), *The Postmodern Adventure: Science, Technology, and Cultural Studies at the Third Millennium* (co-authored with Steve Best; Guilford, 2001), *Media Spectacle* (Routledge, 2003), and *From 9/11 to Terror War: the Dangers of the Bush Legacy* (Rowman and Littlefield, 2003).

Justin Lewis is Professor of Communication at the Cardiff School of Journalism, Media, and Cultural Studies, Cardiff University. Among his recent books is *Constructing Public Opinion: How Elites Do What They Like and Why We Seem to Go Along with It* (Columbia University Press, 2001).

Tamar Liebes is Professor and Chair of the Department of Communication and Journalism at the Hebrew University of Jerusalem. Among her books are *The Export of Meaning* (with Elihu Katz; Polity Press, 1992), *Reporting the Arab Israeli*

Conflict: how Hegemony Works (Routledge, 1997), and *American Dreams, Hebrew Subtitles: Globalization from the Receiving End* (Hampton Press, 2003).

Susan D. Moeller teaches media and international affairs at the Philip Merrill College of Journalism, University of Maryland, College Park. She is the author of *Compassion Fatigue: how the Media Sell Disease, Famine, War and Death* (Routledge, 1998). She is finishing a new book, *A Hierarchy of Innocence: how the Media Cover Good and Evil.*

Terhi Rantanen is Senior Lecturer in Media and Communications at the London School of Economics and Political Science. She is author of *The Globalization of News* (co-edited with Oliver Boyd-Barrett; Sage, 1998), *The Global and the National: Media and Communications in Post-Communist Russia* (Rowman and Littlefield, 2002), and *The Media and Globalization* (Sage, forthcoming).

Stephen D. Reese is Professor and former Director in the School of Journalism at the University of Texas at Austin. He is co-editor of *Framing Public Life: Perspectives on Media and Our Understanding of the Social World* (Lawrence Erlbaum, 2001) and co-author, with Pamela Shoemaker, of *Mediating the Message: Theories of Influence on Mass Media Content* (Longman, 1991).

Piers Robinson is Lecturer in Political Communication at the School of Politics and Communication Studies, University of Liverpool. He is author of *The CNN Effect: the Myth of News, Foreign Policy and Intervention* (Routledge, 2002).

Prasun Sonwalkar lectures in the School of Cultural Studies at the University of the West of England, Bristol. A former journalist, he has worked mainly on *The Times of India* and *Business Standard* and was Editor of the Zee News channel.

Howard Tumber is Professor of Sociology and Dean of the School of Social Sciences, City University, London. His recent books include *Reporting Crime: the Media Politics of Criminal Justice* (with Philip Schlesinger; Oxford University Press, 1994), *News: a Reader* (Oxford University Press, 1999), *Media Power, Policies and Professionals* (Routledge, 2000), and *Media at War* (with Jerry Palmer; Sage, 2004). He is a founder and co-editor of the journal *Journalism: Theory, Practice and Criticism.*

Barbie Zelizer is the Raymond Williams Professor of Communication at the University of Pennsylvania's Annenberg School for Communication. A former journalist, Zelizer's books include *Covering the Body: the Kennedy Assassination, the Media and the Shaping of Collective Memory* (University of Chicago, 1992), *Remembering to Forget: Holocaust Memory through the Camera's Eye* (University of Chicago, 1998), *Journalism after September 11* (with Stuart Allan; Routledge, 2002), and *Taking Journalism Seriously: News and the Academy* (Sage, 2004). She is a founding co-editor of the journal *Journalism: Theory, Practice and Criticism.*

INTRODUCTION

RULES OF ENGAGEMENT

Journalism and war

Stuart Allan and Barbie Zelizer

> The principles of reporting are put to a severe test when your nation goes to war. To whom are you true? To the principles of abstract truth, or to those running the war machine; to a frightened or perhaps belligerent population, to the decisions of the elected representatives in a democracy, to the exclusion of the dissenting minorities, to the young men and women who have agreed to put their lives at risk on the front-line? Or are you true to a wider principle of reasoning and questioning, asking why they must face this risk? Let me put the question with stark simplicity: when does a reporter sacrifice the principle of the whole truth to the need to win the war?
>
> Kate Adie, BBC war correspondent

"The very nature of war," Kate Adie (1998) once observed, "confuses the role of the journalist" (1998: 44). Confronted with the often horrific realities of conflict, any belief that the journalist can remain distant, remote, or unaffected by what is happening "tends to go out the window" in a hurry. Nevertheless Adie, at the time the BBC's chief news correspondent, offered no simple definition of what the role of the journalist should be "when faced with the consequences of battle and the muddle of war," admitting instead that "I don't have the answers, but I keep on asking questions" (Adie 1998: 54).

War reporting, as Adie's comments suggest, constitutes a litmus test of sorts for journalism more broadly. While the role of war correspondent has long been associated with a certain romantic lore, in actuality it is beset by an array of problems associated with allegiance, responsibility, truth, and balance. Such problems arise from time to time in the daily implementation of ordinary, everyday modes of journalism, of course, but their apparent lack of easy resolvability in wartime poses challenges that raise questions about the practice of journalism in more forms than just reporting war. "We knew we were placing ourselves in the bull's eye of a war," commented John Burns, chief foreign correspondent for *The New York Times*, about the Iraqi conflict. "And I don't think a journalist can sensibly claim to have an exemption in a war zone. [By] the very nature of what's about to

3

happen, there's a significant risk that you can be killed" (CBC-TV, November 23, 2003).[1] Journalists must be prepared to take that risk, but that does not make them heroes, in his view. "When we find ourselves in very difficult situations, it's of our own choosing," he added, but what is at stake is the need to "tell people as much of the truth as you can." Such observations, in our reading, suggest that traditional ways of thinking about the imperatives of war reporting and their implications more broadly for journalism need to be examined anew.

The distinction to be drawn between patriotism and militarism is central to the problems of reporting war. A reporter's sense of national identity, however defined, needs to be considered in a way that sheds light both on how it can underpin journalism's strengths while, simultaneously, recognizing the constraints it can impose on the integrity of practice. Vital here is the (usually tacit) assumption that covering the often harrowing nature of battle constitutes a higher order of journalism. War journalists are thought to do what all journalists do, only in a more heightened, vibrantly important fashion. To cover the story will entail, more likely than not, encountering conditions of an entirely different order than anything ordinarily associated with newswork. Images of the war reporter as adventurer or risk-taker, in the optimum sense, or as daredevil, fortune-hunter, or rogue, in the negative, help to fuel their celebration in novels, films, plays, and other fictional treatments. Similarly implicit here, however, is the notion that war reporters somehow "do journalism" better, that their experiences are more authentic, engaged, and noteworthy than those of other kinds of journalists. And yet, it is their very commitment to some rendering of national identity, even patriotism, that is likely to engender a change in journalistic work. It may entail a migration toward vague word choice, the absence of a broader perspective, the lack of explicit images, even the wearing of flag pins. When journalists under everyday conditions are seen to have strong sentiments for family, friends, or community, they are often taken off the story that involves them. When their sentiments for country are seen as strong in wartime, they are rarely removed from the story; rather, the expectation, at least in some quarters, is that they will simply change how they conduct themselves as journalists. The exceptional quality of this re-orientation deserves pause. It raises questions as to whether or not our ways of thinking about war journalism, as a mode of practice, have fallen short of the mark.

War reporting, in short, demands that notions of what constitutes good journalistic practice be realigned on the basis of different criteria than would typically seem appropriate, criteria thrown into sharp relief—at times violently so—by challenging circumstances. At the same time, war reporting's positioning as a litmus test for journalism also rests on an understanding of its capacity to influence public perceptions. Journalists are expected to function variously during war: to be present enough to respond to what is happening, yet absent enough to stay safe; to be sufficiently authoritative so as to provide reliable information, yet open to cracks and fissures in the complicated truth-claims that unfold; to remain passionate about the undermining of human dignity that accompanies war, yet

4

impartial and distanced enough to see the strategies that attach themselves to circumstances with always more than one side. In these and related ways, then, war reporting reveals its investment in sustaining a certain discursive authority—namely that of being an eyewitness. "I was there to witness," Adie recalled, "to repeat what I hear, to observe the circumstances, note the detail, and confirm what is going on with accuracy, honesty and precision" (Adie 1998: 46). Though Adie admitted that she needed faith that what she sought to communicate would not be in vain, it was not her mission to advocate particular forms of action. Nor was it easy to counter the deceptive nature of the battlefield. Witnessing was "the only way you can stand by your words afterwards, the only guarantee that you can give your listeners, or viewers, or readers. You saw it, you heard it, you are telling the truth as far as you know" (Adie 1998: 47).

This act of witnessing, of seeing for oneself the heart of the story, encapsulates the larger problem of determining what counts as truth in the war zone. It forms the basis of the journalist's relationship with diverse publics, where any one claim to truth will be interpreted in conjunction with varied—at times conflicting—normative criteria. Truth-telling, it needs to be acknowledged, is necessarily embedded in a cultural politics of legitimacy; its authority resting on presence, on the moral duty to bear witness by being there. Being there suggests that the violence, devastation, suffering, and death that inevitably constitute war's underside will somehow be rendered different—more amenable to response and perhaps less likely to recur—just because journalists are somewhere nearby. And yet the experience of a reporter's being there, so important for distant publics eager for news of the events of a war-torn region, is shaped quite systematically by a weave of limitations—political, military, economic, and technological, among others—that together may curtail the experience in drastic ways.

Anecdotal evidence from a range of wars bears this out, whereby a journalist's capacity to be present was limited, undermined, or even denied altogether when the battleground was placed off limits, the military barricade went up, the cameras broke down, or sources refused to talk. Moreover, a journalist's sense of citizenship, even patriotism, may call into question his or her perceptions of how best to conduct oneself as a reporter. All too often, journalists encounter those who demand to know: are you with us, or are you against us? It is at this point that individual journalists determine for themselves what their role should be, knowing that their ad hoc decision may have profound implications for how their audiences come to understand the nature of war and the consequences for its victims. In so doing, they know that even the most basic expectation of journalists in wartime—being there—is rarely realized entirely in the way they may have wanted, given the exigencies with which they must cope.

Perhaps nowhere did this receive as much attention as during the recent war in Iraq. The decision to embed reporters with the US and UK military forces—as a way of ensuring that journalists could "be there"—raised expectations that the ensuing coverage would be better, more comprehensive, fuller, and more reliable.

"The correspondent moving forward with a company or battalion of combat troops," Peter Preston (2003) argued, "will usually get the most vivid picture, with the most telling detail." Still, he added, such reports "may show little about the overall flux of the battle. Often he or she, lacking the broad view, will be too optimistic or pessimistic." The use of journalistic "embeds," moreover, generated fears that the military would secure the media in its pocket, creating unusual alliances and breaking down the autonomy with which journalism in wartime likes to assume it functions. "Embedding," commented Oliver Burkeman (2003) in Washington at an early point in the conflict, "has been an astounding PR success for the Pentagon." Reporters, he observed, "use the words 'we' and 'us' profusely, identifying themselves with the military, and while this has prompted concerns about objectivity among US commentators, it is not surprising, given their very personal stake in their unit's success."

In retrospect, such observations underscored yet another litmus test, one exemplified by various commentaries on war journalism made by reporters and media critics alike. Often missing in discussions about the relative successes and failures associated with reporting the Iraq war was a recognition of how the (at times acrimonious) debate about embedding—its perceived vices and virtues—was allowed to displace other lines of enquiry and critique. That is to say, to the extent that the microcosm of embedded reporters was allowed to stand in for the larger role of the news media, it became that much more difficult to discern and analyze the factors which characterized the overall coverage. Thus while embedded reports were a mainstay of the coverage, especially in the case of the 24-hour television news channels, other important factors shaping the war's representation remained under the radar of those tracking the progression of the war.

War in the era of 24/7 news

Television news, one opinion survey after the next indicated, proved to be the most used—and most trusted—news source for people in countries such as the US and Britain during the Iraq war. While the main network newscasts struggled to hold the attention of their viewers, however, audience figures suggested that the "rolling," "around-the-clock" news channels went from strength to strength in the early weeks of the conflict.

In the US, for example, the 24-hour news networks saw marked increases in their audience ratings. Much to the surprise of some observers, Fox News surpassed CNN as the top-rated news channel. The latter network, which came to prominence during the 1991 Gulf War (the breadth of its "blanket coverage" being unprecedented at the time), nevertheless claimed that it had a greater number of viewers watching overall. Still, the challenge posed by Fox was formidable by any measure. Explanations for its new-found popularity typically revolved around the stridently right-wing, pro-war stance informing its reporting and commentary, generally said to be more "in tune" with public opinion than CNN's more "neutral" stance. The openly partisan agenda of Fox—its logo "fair and balanced" being derided by critics as a misnomer—was discernible at a number of different levels.

"By the time US soldiers were headed across the desert to Baghdad," David J. Sirota (2004) maintained, "the 'fair and balanced' network, owned by media mogul Rupert Murdoch, looked like a caricature of state-run television, parroting the White House's daily talking points, no matter how unsubstantiated." For Jim Rutenberg (2003), writing in *The New York Times*, the "Fox formula" proved that there were significant ratings to be gained in "opinionated news with an America-first flair." Fox, he pointed out, represents a new approach to television journalism, one that "casts aside traditional notions of objectivity, holds contempt for dissent, and eschews the skepticism of government at mainstream journalism's core." MSNBC, occupying a distant third place in the ratings, has often been accused of "aping" a similar approach. "What Fox is doing, and frankly what MSNBC is also declaring by its product," Erik Sorenson, MSNBC's president, has acknowledged, "is that one can be unabashedly patriotic and be a good news journalist at the same time" (cited in Rutenberg 2003; see also Plunkett 2003; Wells and Cassy 2003).

Debates about the so-called "Fox effect" on "middle-of-the-road" journalism grew in intensity as the Iraq war unfolded. In any case, however, the growing popularity of 24-hour news, especially in the early days of the conflict, was difficult to dispute. Viewing figures gathered in the US for the first five days following the formal declaration of war indicated that CNN's audience was up by some 393 percent compared with the same week the previous year, while Fox News' ratings went up 379 percent, and MSNBC's improved by 651 percent (Deans 2003). While their audiences remained substantively smaller than those for the main terrestrial networks, ABC, CBS, and NBC, these figures were widely held to be indicative of a growing preference among viewers to turn to the 24-hour news channels for breaking developments, even in primetime.

In Britain, all three of the country's rolling news channels—BBC 24, Sky News, and ITV News Channel—witnessed significant increases in their viewing figures at the outset of the conflict. The near-constant flow of images was recurrently singled out for particular praise by some, many of whom drew favourable comparisons with the dearth of "colourful material" from the 1991 conflict. Steve Anderson, controller of ITV News and Current Affairs, remarked:

> The big difference this time around is technology has got better, lighter, easier to handle and it's cheaper. It's much more effective and so it's not unusual to go straight to live pictures out of, say, Basra. Often the pictures are mundane, but you can cut to it at the flick of a switch . . . Last Saturday we showed pictures of Iraqis down by the Tigris looking for downed pilots and firing into the water. It was a live event and we went with it—it was an incredible image, but in the end it didn't amount to anything.
>
> (cited in Doward 2003)

7

Rolling news, its advocates insisted, proved far more effective in bringing the war into people's homes than more traditional newscasts. Sky News' leading position in the ratings was frequently attributed to its oft-repeated claim to be the first to break stories. So-called "BBC insiders" refused to concede this point, however, and also insisted that the corporation engaged in more thorough fact-checking processes than its rivals, which took time.

All too often this incessant drive to be the first to break the story meant that due care and accuracy were sacrificed in the heat of the moment. Examples from the crisis in Iraq were all too plentiful, not least with respect to the array of claims made regarding chemical and biological weapons of mass destruction (WMDs). Reports broadcast on various rolling news networks in the US and UK also included, for example, claims that Iraqi "drones" would be dispatched to spread biological agents in the US; the Iraqi Republican Guard was planning to use chemical weapons on coalition forces in the defence of Baghdad; a grenade attack on a base in Kuwait was the work of terrorists (a US soldier was later charged); the early fall of the port of Umm Qasr; various "bioweapon" caches, including missiles containing sarin and mustard gas, had been found; the discovery of weapons-grade plutonium; the seizure of various mobile "bioweapons" laboratories; the defection of Tariq Aziz; the "uprising" in Basra, and so forth. These claims, among a myriad of others, were later acknowledged to be false, if not necessarily by the network which broadcast them in the first place (the Arab news network Al-Jazeera played a vital role in challenging such claims, for example). A further, particularly controversial example centred on the apparent "rescue" of Private Jessica Lynch from an Iraqi hospital. Once again, the key claims made were eventually shown to be untrue. "None of the absurd hype that surrounded the case came from her," the BBC's John Simpson (2003) remarked afterwards; "it was all the invention of the US Army spinners, and a credulous press desperate for some genuine heroics in a war which seemed disturbingly short of gallantry" (Simpson 2003: 313).

Some officials responded angrily to allegations of "propaganda" and "spin" where instances of false reporting occurred, insisting that such were the types of mistakes typically made in the "fog of war." Others blamed "over-enthusiastic reporters" for getting carried away. Seldom acknowledged, however, were the range of pressures brought to bear on journalists to influence the nature of the coverage. Here remarks made by CNN's Christiane Amanpour are telling. Interviewed on CNBC by Tina Brown, she was asked to comment on assertions that Bush administration officials had intimidated journalists, not least into feeling unpatriotic if they gave voice to criticism or dissent. She stated:

> I think the press was muzzled and I think the press self-muzzled. I'm sorry to say but certainly television and, perhaps, to a certain extent, my station [CNN] was intimidated by the administration and its foot soldiers at Fox News. And it did, in fact, put a climate of fear and self-censorship, in my view, in terms of—of the kind of broadcast work we did. I mean, all of us should have . . .

Here Brown interjected, asking: "And was there any story—was there any story that you couldn't do?" Amanpour replied:

> All—it's not a question of couldn't do it, it's a question of tone. It's a question of being rigorous. It's really a question of really asking the questions. All of the entire body politic in my view, whether it's the administration, the intelligence, the journalists, whoever, did not ask enough questions, for instance, about weapons of mass destruction. I mean, it looks like this was disinformation at the highest levels.
>
> (CNBC transcript, "Topic A with Tina Brown," broadcast September 10, 2003)

In using the term "disinformation," Amanpour proceeded to add, "I mean that we were all duped, everybody." In describing her unease with "the relationship between the media and the administration," she stated her belief that there was an intention "to deny what's actually going on" on the part of officials. In the case of her "perfectly routine" reports about the looting taking place, for example, she commented that "the Secretary of Defense basically accused people like me of selectively editing, of misrepresenting the truth."

Despite Amanpour being one of CNN's leading war correspondents, someone who had been "embedded" with the military during the conflict, her comments were promptly challenged by her network. Jim Walton, president of CNN Newsgroup, insisted that the network had not been subjected to undue influence. "Christiane is a valued member of the team and one of the world's foremost journalists," he said. "However, her comments do not reflect the reality of our coverage and I do not agree with her about this" (cited in *The Guardian*, September 16, 2003). Meanwhile a spokesperson for Fox News, Irena Briganti, responded by likening Amanpour to a "spokeswoman for al-Qaeda" (cited in *USA Today*, September 14, 2003), thereby effectively highlighting the very climate of self-censorship at issue.

In what is typically a fraught relationship between the arch rivals, both CNN and Fox News sought to reaffirm their self-proclaimed patriotism in different ways. Fox, like MSNBC, was typically upbeat about the war's progress. It ensured that a US flag always appeared in the corner of the screen, intended to "strike a chord" with viewers. It followed an aggressively partisan approach, where newscasters referred to US and British troops as "we," "ours," "heroes," and "liberators," and actively deflected criticism of the invasion. Evidently, if not surprisingly, the US military, according to Simpson (2003), "liked Fox's noisy, irreflective, triumphalist style, and couldn't understand why everyone couldn't be like that" (Simpson 2003: 369–70). CNN was calmer in contrast, somewhat less likely to be as deferential to government and military officials (evidence of "liberal bias," in the eyes of some Republican critics), and preferred to uphold a stricter line between news and editorial comment. Kathryn Kross, CNN's Washington Bureau Chief, maintained that "journalists serve their audience by being appropriately skeptical. If viewers are after cheerleading, they're looking in the wrong place. It doesn't mean we're not patriotic" (cited in Kurtz 2003).

A wide array of commentators have expressed their alarm about this apparent blurring of news and comment, not least with regard to the implications for reportorial standards. Greg Dyke, Director General of the BBC at the time, focused public attention on this problem in April 2003. Speaking at a journalism conference in London, he addressed the challenges confronting television news. "We must temper the drama and competition of live, rolling news with the considered journalism and analysis people need to make sense of events," he argued (*BBC News Online*, April 24, 2003). More than that, however, Dyke added: "Commercial pressures may tempt others to follow the Fox News formula of gung-ho patriotism but for the BBC this would be a terrible mistake." In acknowledging that Fox New's partisan pro-Bush stance had helped it to overtake CNN in average daily viewer ratings, he insisted that such "unquestioning" support for the White House was typical of the other US broadcast news media during the conflict. In a fragmented marketplace, he argued, no news operation was sufficiently strong or brave enough to stand up to government or military officials. Attempts to mix flag-waving patriotism with journalism, he feared, would inevitably undermine television news' credibility in the eyes of the public. "Essential to the success of any news organisation," he stated, "is holding the trust of its audiences."

Dyke returned to this theme when giving a speech at the International Emmys in New York in November 2003, where he accepted an award for broadcasting excellence. "News organisations should be in the business of balancing their coverage," he argued, "not banging the drum for one side or the other" (cited in *BBC News Online*, November 25, 2003). Citing research suggesting that only a tiny fraction of the commentators aired on US television were opposed to the war, he said: "I have to tell you if that was true in Britain, the BBC would have failed in its duty." In making the point that television news has a responsibility to broadcast a range of voices, he observed that viewing figures in the US for BBC News (namely BBC World and News 24) had effectively "doubled" in the last year. For Dyke, these figures showed that there was a growing audience for "impartial" news. "Telling people what they want to hear is not doing them any favours. It may not be comfortable to challenge governments or even popular opinion, but it's what we are here to do." BBC news reporting was hardly above criticism, of course, being consistently assailed from both ends of the political spectrum. Those on the right contended that it was "anti-war" in its coverage, while those on the left believed that it relied much too heavily on pro-war sources of information (echoes of this debate resounded throughout the Hutton inquiry and its aftermath).[2]

Much of the criticism of the British 24-hour networks' coverage of the Iraq conflict centred on their widely perceived tendency to present images without adequate context or explanation (effectively making them purveyors of "war porn" in the judgment of some). Differences between the three networks—BBC News 24, the ITV News Channel, and Sky News—in their coverage were most notable at a stylistic level, given that they each operate under strict conditions of "due impartiality" imposed by broadcast regulators. In sharp contrast with the so-called "Fox formula" (likened, by some, to an "either you're with us or against us" mentality), the three networks share similar space in the middle of the news spectrum. As Matt Wells (2003) has pointed out, not only do they have broadly similar news agendas, with correspondents situated in the same places, they also hold a "determinedly Western" perspective in common. During the conflict the "most frequent location of live two-way interviews," he observed, were "coalition command in Doha, military headquarters in Kuwait, the White House in Washington and Downing Street in London. Jerusalem, Amman, Cairo and Riyadh have barely had a look-in." The extensive use of such interviews, needless to say, underscored the networks' commitment to meeting the near-constant demands of live reporting (which appeared with less frequency on the terrestrial networks as the war went on—one major exception being the capture of Saddam Hussein).

For some critics, however, this approach to two-ways not only narrowed the range of views on offer, it also seemed to value immediacy for its own sake. "Television has become a 24-hour slog," argued veteran war reporter Jon Swain (2003), "with the result that while many of today's TV reporters may have all the traditional dedication and intrepidness of their predecessors, they cannot use it." In effect, he added, "[t]hey are tied to the satellite dish on the hotel roof ready to deliver 'live spots' and so are unable to explore in depth the stories they are supposed to be reporting" (see also Adie 2002).

Jon Snow (2004), anchor of Channel 4 News, has coined the phrase "Rooftop syndrome" to describe the ways "war correspondents are held hostage by the voracious appetite of 24-hour television news." One such victim, he contends, was the BBC's Rageh Omaar, "the face of the war in Baghdad," but whose rooftop appearances on the Information Ministry and the Palestine Hotel meant that he seldom had the opportunity to use his skills (see also Omaar 2004). Similarly pertinent here are the insights of Martin Bell (2003), recently retired from the BBC after more than 30 years in journalism. The 24-hour news services have special responsibilities, he believes, which are defined by F-words:

> They aim to be first and fastest with the news. Their nature, too often, is to be fearful, feverish, frenzied, frantic, frail, false and fallible. Some mistakes are bound to be made, as they always have been, by journalists seeking to discover the truth in the fog of breaking news; but those mistakes do not have to be as *systemic* as they have become in the rolling news business, when rumour masquerades as fact, and networks compete wildly with each other to get their speculation in first.
>
> (Bell 2003: 71; emphasis in original)

Bell is particularly troubled where the reporting of war and terrorism is concerned, but believes the point can be made more widely. In calling for a measure of self-criticism among journalists, as well as a code of practice (long overdue, in his opinion), he proceeds to issue an appeal for a return to first principles. The test of excellence, he argues, is not "We got it first!" but rather "We got it right!" (Bell 2003: 71).

One year after the invasion of Iraq commenced, answers to the question of how best to ensure reportorial standards of excellence are proving increasingly elusive. Nowhere are the imperatives shaping television news thrown into sharper relief than where the interests of public service collide with the private ones of shareholders. To the extent that the news agenda is determined by its potential for generating audience ratings (and therefore advertising revenue, in the case of commercial networks), newscasts will consistently prioritize stories revolving around drama, conflict, and controversy over and above (expensive, less "ratings-efficient") investigative journalism. War reporting is no exception to this general rule. The dynamics underpinning 24-hour news—especially when "going live"—raise significant issues regarding public perceptions about the nature of war.

Jack Straw (2003), the British Foreign Secretary, has even questioned whether the First and Second World Wars would have been won, had they been covered by these channels:

> Had the public been able to see live reports from the trenches, I wonder for how long the governments of Asquith and Lloyd George could have maintained the war effort. Imagine the carnage of the Somme on Sky and BBC News 24. But it is also worth speculating how much harder it might have been to maintain the country's morale after Dunkirk had live reports confronted the public with the brutal reality of German tactical and military superiority. Could the 'spirit of Dunkirk', so important to national survival, have withstood the scrutiny of 24-hour live news?
>
> (Straw 2003)

Straw himself was doubtful, but nevertheless made the important additional point that "in a democracy, the benefits of hour by hour and day by day reporting from the frontline far outweigh the disadvantages." And as he rightly pointed out, some correspondents on the frontline have "paid the ultimate sacrifice in pursuit of the truth" (24 in Iraq at the time of writing). Still, there can be little doubt that his interests as a Foreign Secretary necessarily contradict, at times, the interests of journalists committed to investigating the realities of warfare. Precisely how these contradictions are negotiated on the ground, of course, will have profound consequences for public trust in both government and journalism in times of war.

The chapters

Reporting War: Journalism in Wartime addresses the tensions, contradictions, and contingencies that shape the journalist's role in wartime. Recognizing that the aim of war coverage is frequently defined in relation to the urgent need to keep

12

diverse publics adequately informed, *Reporting War* surveys the ways in which this aim has been realized—or not—in the reporting of certain wars over recent years. Our contributors, both practising and former journalists as well as academics with a longstanding research interest in journalism, vary in perspective, academic discipline, and national origin, but they share the aim of recasting familiar assumptions about war reporting from a distinctive perspective.

Interwoven throughout the book are two main threads in thinking about the relative strengths and limitations of war reporting. First, the book tracks the forms and practices of reporting war across time. Focusing in the main on conflicts since 1990, it explores how the nature of war itself has been transformed, and how these changes have impacted upon the modes for journalistic engagement. These modes—typically characterized too narrowly around evolutions in technology—will be shown to prefigure a repository of adaptations by which journalists constitute themselves as responsible for bearing witness. Second, it considers the reporting of war in diverse locales. Ranging from Africa, the Balkans, the Middle East—especially Iraq—and southern Asia, the book attempts to discern both the general features and distinct specifics of reporting in comparative contexts. In so doing it asks, among other questions, in what ways do the US and British news media, in particular, bring to bear Western assumptions—political, cultural, and moral—about how and why war is waged.

Reporting War identifies and critiques an array of pressing issues associated with conflicts over recent years, always with an eye to what they can tell us about improving journalism today. Such issues include the influence of censorship and propaganda, "us" and "them" news narratives, access to sources, "24/7 rolling news" and the so-called "CNN effect," military jargon (such as "friendly fire" and "collateral damage"), "embedded" and "unilateral" reporters, visual images of war, tensions between objectivity, patriotism and humanitarianism, and online reporting, among others. Sustained attention is devoted to considering changes in journalistic forms and practices in the war in Iraq, and the ways in which they are shaping eyewitness reporting of that conflict. Taken together, then, the book's chapters raise important questions about how the exigencies of reporting war have challenged the practice of journalism, and what they may portend for the very future of journalism tomorrow.

Part 1—war in the twenty-first century

Truth, it is often said, is the first casualty of war. It is appropriate, then, that the first section of essays begins with Oliver Boyd-Barrett's "Understanding: the second casualty," where he argues that the public is poorly served by mainstream media reporting of war. In considering war reporting as a distinct genre of journalism, he identifies a range of "casualties" to truth and understanding, engendered by framing war through a narrative form that mainly serves government interests and the media colluding with them. Such "casualties" are apparent in the choices of which wars the news media decide to report; media representations of the

13

causes, durations and aftermaths of war; and a failure to contextualize conflict within metanarratives of empire and control. War-reporting-as-genre, he contends, obscures the nature of collusion between government and media, a collusion that previous research studies only partially explain.

Richard Keeble's "Information warfare in an age of hyper-militarism" commences with the provocative assertion that there was no war in the Gulf in 2003. Rather, he argues, a myth of heroic, spectacular warfare was manufactured, in large part, as a desperate measure to help provide a *raison d'être* for the (increasingly out-of-control) military industrial complexes in the US and UK—and to hide the reality of a rout of a hopelessly overwhelmed "enemy" army. The links between mainstream journalists and the intelligence services, this chapter suggests, are crucial factors in the manufacture of the myth. But it is not essentially a massive elite conspiracy, Keeble believes. Rather, the myth's origins lie deep within complex military, historical, and political forces. Moreover, as he shows, the manufacture of the "war" myth has profound implications for any study of the political and military origins of the conflict and media representations.

Susan D. Moeller, in "A moral imagination: the media's response to the war on terrorism," considers how the post-September 11 Bush administration has used a moral rhetoric to propel its "war on terrorism" policies, especially in Iraq, and how that "morality" has echoed through the US media. In arguing that war reporting is a subset of reporting on international affairs, she points out that many concerns that bedevil international coverage are exacerbated when journalists cover war. Considering the post-9/11 world, Moeller investigates issues of language, access, asking the right questions, and not only challenging the "spin" of the powers-that-be but also contesting the priorities set by those in power. To the extent that the Bush administration categorized its foreign policy agendas under the phrase "war on terrorism," she argues, it effectively stamped those policies with a moral imperative—an imperative, her analysis suggests, that the US media have been loathe to challenge.

In "The PR of terror: how new-style wars give voice to terrorists," Tamar Liebes and Zohar Kampf argue that September 11, 2001 may be considered a watershed in the gradual evolution of journalism's approach to terror. If until 9/11 terrorists could capture the news media's attention only via violent action, they have now been given a voice by which they act as regular, sought after sources. Rather than represent a front-page story recounting the merciless suffering inflicted on innocent victims, they now make statements, give interviews, and explain their motives, while journalists, following in their trails, speculate about their plans, ideologies, and psychological makeup. Analyzing the upgrading of terrorists to the cultural status of celebrities, Liebes and Kampf see live "disaster marathons" as the beginning of a process by which journalists relinquish control to terrorists and then pursue terrorists as legitimate news personas, disconnected from specific violent acts.

This section's discussion is rounded out by Piers Robinson in "Researching US media–state relations and twenty-first century wars." Wartime relations between the US media and government, he suggests, have traditionally been characterized by media deference to, and domination by, official viewpoints. In recent years, however, developments in communications technology (which reduce journalists' reliance upon official sources) and the ending of the Cold War (which recasts the ideological bond between journalists and policy-makers) have been thought to produce a more adversarial wartime media. Robinson critically assesses these claims, identifying two key developments which suggest otherwise—the professionalization of government media management strategies and the replacement of the ideology of the Cold War with the "war on terrorism." Both have strengthened US government dominance of the media agenda in wartime, suggesting that the thesis of significant change in the balance of power and influence between the US media and government during war cannot be supported yet. Now, as in previous wars, the media support US government war objectives.

Part 2—bearing witness

Barbie Zelizer's "When war is reduced to a photograph" examines how reporting war is characterized by a turn to the visual in providing accounts of the battlefield. Tracking the display of still photographs across recent conflicts, she argues that while war coverage typically shows more visuals, they do not necessarily contain more information. Rather, journalists gravitate toward the familiar, dramatic, aesthetic, and already meaningful in their depiction of war, thereby undermining the provision of newsworthy and critically important information in wartime. Zelizer discusses the characteristics of this turn to the visual, by which visuals are used to cement public interpretations of more recent conflicts in conjunction with wars experienced at other times and places and on different grounds. Muted are questions about the value of the parallel and the ends to which it is being used, suggesting that in the process of depicting war, visuals undermine the maintenance of a healthy body politic.

In "The Persian Gulf TV war revisited," Douglas Kellner returns to 1991 to discuss parallels between the Gulf War of then and that of now. Kellner indicates how the political economy of the US media facilitated the manufacturing of consent for US government policies. Kellner reflects on why the Gulf war was so popular with its audiences and how the Bush administration and Pentagon marshaled public support for the war, suggesting that the effects of television and the mainstream media are contradictory and may have unintended consequences. While in the spring of 1991, the Gulf War constituted a tremendous victory for the Bush administration and Pentagon, the event did not save Bush senior's presidency and eventually raised questions concerning whether he was really an effective leader. For Kellner, its short-term effects in temporarily boosting Bush senior's popularity, when set in relation to the sudden shift in public opinion concerning the war, point to the fickleness of audiences in a media-saturated society. These audiences, he believes, soon forget the big events of the previous year and immerse themselves in the latest media spectacle.

Attention turns to Africa in the next chapter, with Susan L. Carruthers's "Tribalism and tribulation: media constructions of 'African savagery' and 'Western humanitarianism' in the 1990s." Much Western news media reporting during the 1990s, she maintains, confirmed Africa's designation as a "hopeless continent": presided over by machete-wielding warlords, marshaling the blood-lust of child soldiers to barbarous, if not genocidal, ends. Accordingly, this chapter takes as its focus Western media constructions of conflict in Somalia and Rwanda, pondering both the so-called CNN effect, contrasting the attention paid to famine in Somalia with media inattention to Rwanda's genocide, and elaborating how a distorting "ethnic violence complex" structures Western news media accounts of the roots of African conflict. Carruthers explores journalism's role in producing a humane identity for the West, systematically erasing the latter's own profound implication in Africa's "failure." It is vital, she argues, that the language of Western intervention be interrogated for its obfuscation of the entrenched, and wrenching, processes through which the West continuously shapes Africa.

Philip Hammond's "Humanizing war: the Balkans and beyond" provides an interesting set of counterpoints. Pointing out that many commentators judge NATO's 1999 bombing of Yugoslavia to have been an "illegal but moral" war, abandoning the principle of non-interference in sovereign states in pursuit of the higher goal of upholding human rights, Hammond suggests that despite evidence to the contrary, Kosovo is still portrayed as a successful and ethical intervention. In Hammond's view, such claims rest on a number of falsehoods about the build-up to war and the nature of the conflict, including mainstream journalism's complicity in treating the West's public show of diplomacy as a genuine attempt at mediation and Kosovo as a one-sided campaign of "ethnic cleansing" and genocide. A predisposition to accept NATO propaganda and a search for moral absolutes in the Balkans, Hammond contends, offset the felt lack of cohesion and purpose in Western societies in the post-Cold War era. Today, even when the use of "humanitarian" rhetoric in the war on terrorism has met with some criticism, there persists an underlying agreement on the West's "moral duty" to intervene.

Howard Tumber's "Prisoners of news values?: journalists, professionalism and identification in times of war" argues that, in times of war, objectivity is a prized status where the principles of detachment are a key element in the social construction of the journalist's own sense of professional identity. The Falklands/Malvinas conflict, he suggests, was an excellent "bell jar" for examining the "performance" of the journalists who accompanied the British military and for assessing the ideal of objectivity in practical terms. Against this backdrop, he re-examines the experiences of the small group of journalists who reported the Falklands conflict of the early 1980s, before turning to the experiences of the much larger group of reporters "embedded" with the military in the recent Iraq war. Tumber's analysis addresses some of the reportorial choices made by journalists in both conflicts, especially where they were caught between identifying with their military protectors and adhering to their professional values.

In "Out of sight, out of mind?: the non-reporting of small wars and insurgencies," Prasun Sonwalkar draws attention to the conflicts routinely ignored by the media on national as well as international levels. He points out that the news media typically cover only a small share of the world's conflicts, even though terrorism and violence are usually defined as being inherently—and irresistibly—newsworthy and draws upon the findings of a case study of reporting in India, the two conflict zones of Kashmir and the northeast. A conflict is likely to receive coverage, he suggests, only if journalists see it as affecting what they perceive to be the "us" or "we" of news narrative, while a conflict revolving around "them" may be routinely ignored or accorded ad hoc coverage. Sonwalkar's interviews with senior Indian journalists reveal that Kashmir is seen as deserving of sustained coverage because it involves the Indian national "we" (Hindus, Muslims, the idea of secularism in India's constitution), while the northeast conflicts are consistently accorded low status, primarily because they involve India's sociocultural "they" (tribes, Christians, hill people).

Which war is represented in Australia's media arguably owes more to the cultural and historical location of war reporting than to the power of oligopolistic media ownerships over journalistic performance. This is the opening thesis of Michael Bromley's "The battlefield is the media: war reporting and the formation of national identity in Australia—from Belmont to Baghdad," which focuses on how journalists have shaped what war has meant to Australians and, in so doing, revalidated certain Australian national values originating in the foundation of the nation-state. Bromley argues that while much was made of the pro-invasion stand taken by media mogul Rupert Murdoch and his newspapers before the war in Iraq; journalists could be relied on a priori to invoke and evoke a mythology of war which tied military action seamlessly to Australian identity. They were therefore largely supportive of military action. Notwithstanding considerable public unease at Australia's involvement in the invasion, once military deployments were undertaken, journalists' automatic reference point was the ideal of the Australian "digger" (soldier) and the positive national characteristics embedded in it.

Part 3—reporting the Iraq war

This final section concentrates on the war in Iraq, still ongoing at the time of writing. It opens with Stephen D. Reese's "Militarized journalism: framing dissent in the Persian Gulf wars." He argues that "consensual patriotism" drives the marginalization of dissent, considering how news works through routine practices to generate specific frames of reference that anchor armed conflict, and its larger policy implications, within definitions largely controlled by the military. Specifically, Reese examines how a local television news organization covered communal responses to the Persian Gulf War of 1991 and how this extended into the more recent conflict. In rooting news coverage within professional routines and familiar and commercially appealing cultural themes, he argues, news coverage framed dissent so as to pit it against a favored patriotic "support the troops" position. The extent to which a military logic colors policy debate far from the war itself is considered in the light of more recent changes in the battlefield information environment of Gulf War II in Iraq, and the location of audiences within more globalized communities.

Nick Couldry and John Downey, in "War or peace?: legitimation, dissent, and rhetorical closure in press coverage of the Iraq war build-up," direct our attention to British newspaper coverage of the onset of war. Analyzing the discursive positions and rhetorical strategies adopted by seven national newspapers during a crucial week in the build-up to the 2003 Iraq war—the week of presentation of the Blix report (beginning January 27) to the United Nations Security Council—they show how these newspapers attempted to legitimize both war and peace. While various notions such as the manufacturing of consent, the public relations state, and the colonization of the public sphere emphasize the role of media in the reproduction of consent, the role of national newspapers in legitimating dissent was also key. Couldry and Downey also examine the limits of this legitimation of dissent in the build-up to the invasion of Iraq which they argue help to explain the pro-war shift in public opinion discernible at the beginning of the war.

Justin Lewis and Rod Brookes offer what is in many ways a complementary analysis, in "How British television news represented the case for the war in Iraq." Examining key features of the British television coverage of the war in Iraq, based on an analysis of over 1,500 news reports broadcast by the British Broadcasting Corporation (BBC 1), the Independent Television Network (for ITV), Channel 4, and Sky Television, they look at the overall shape of the coverage and then explore the degree to which news channels accepted or challenged pro-war assumptions during the war, notably about the threat of weapons of mass destruction and the enthusiasm of Iraq people for the US-led war. In so doing, Lewis and Brookes explore a number of controversial issues. Was the BBC's coverage anti-war as many alleged? Conversely, were the "embedded reporters" effectively "in bed" with the military? In answering these questions, they consider the relationship between media coverage and public opinion.

When the first US missiles hit targets in Baghdad on March 20, 2003, news organizations started hitting their targets around the world. Terhi Rantanen, in "European news agencies and their sources in the Iraq war coverage," discusses how the war coverage affected the daily routines of European news agencies, such as Reuters and Agence France-Presse. These agencies, she points out, are traditionally seen as the wholesalers of news to most media, and in a competitive global media environment, have become one of the many sources used by the media. In her chapter, Rantanen explores the measures the agencies took to cover the war and the sources to which they subscribed. She also studies how news agency editors evaluated their news sources, suggesting that they share a professional journalistic culture which goes beyond national boundaries. In the Iraq war, she argues, sources *outside* Europe were seen as less reliable, and this applied to *both* the US (such as the Associated Press) and Arab media (such as Al-Jazeera).

Adel Iskandar and Mohammed el-Nawawy make Al-Jazeera the primary focus of their chapter, "Al-Jazeera and war coverage in Iraq: the quest for contextual objectivity." Compared to its predecessors, Al-Jazeera represents a media revolution in the Arab world, the implications of which become particularly pronounced at times of war. Indeed, Al-Jazeera's success as a news organization with immense popular appeal, they argue, is a product of its novel brand of journalism. To describe the journalistic model within which the network operates, the authors introduce the concept of "contextual objectivity." Of particular interest in this concept are the tensions embedded within it, along with the media's reactions to its application in war reporting—not least with regard to how it complicates the work of journalists and media outlets alike. Iskandar and el-Nawawy argue that this concept possesses the potential to serve as a useful standard by which all networks may be judged, a thesis which they explore via a close look at Al-Jazeera's coverage of the war in Iraq.

Attention turns in the last two chapters to the Internet, beginning with Patricia Aufderheide's "Big media and little media: the journalistic informal sector during the invasion of Iraq." Describing the flourishing of grassroots reporting, opinion, and commentary on mainstream media during March and April 2003, when a vigorous public-opinion minority in the US, along with international voices, protested the US-led invasion of Iraq, she reports the findings of a research project at American University's Center for Social Media that surveyed the journalistic "informal sector" during the war. Aufderheide contrasts this phenomenon—which involved email, the Web, cable access, and public channels on satellite TV—with the suppression of dissent on the part of large, entertainment-oriented, US media companies. She proposes that the informal sector will continue to grow and that relationships will develop between mainstream media outlets and efforts in the informal sector, offering important evidence of a widely shared demand for more public participation in decision-making and widespread distrust of mainstream media reporting in crisis.

In drawing the book to a close, Stuart Allan's "The culture of distance: online reporting of the Iraq war" uses cultural theorist Raymond Williams' notion of the "culture of distance" to contextualize online journalism. Allan explores the Web-based mediation of witnessing and the distant suffering of others by addressing the use of the Internet as a news source during the conflict. He considers both the online reporting of Al-Jazeera (www.aljazeera.net) and the rise of warblogs, such as that belonging to Salam Pax, otherwise known as the "Baghdad Blogger" (dear_raed.blogspot.com). Attention focuses on the ways in which online reporting provides alternative spaces for acts of witnessing, a process which is shown to be uneven, contingent, and frequently the site of intense resistance. The culture of distance, Allan contends, is simultaneously a culture of othering. At stake, in his view, is the need to deconstruct journalism's "us and them" dichotomies precisely as they are taken up and re-inflected in news accounts where the structural interests of "people like us" are counterpoised against the suffering of strangers.

Conclusion

All in all, *Reporting War: Journalism in Wartime* has at its heart a commitment to exploring afresh the social responsibilities of the news reporter in public life during wartime. It is not chronological, in that it leaps back and forth in time. It is not comprehensive, in that it has not attended to every war that has occurred over recent years. Neither has it conclusively raised all of the relevant issues in the wars discussed in these pages. Even though the war in Iraq is still under way as we edit this book, our hope is nevertheless to offer a timely intervention. In so doing, we aim to contribute to a larger critical appraisal of both the guiding imperatives of journalism in wartime and the ways in which these imperatives impact more broadly across different modes of journalistic practice.

The echoes of war continue to resound long after the cacophony of battle has been silenced. In this book, we have endeavored to create a forum of contemplation around war reporting—past and present—so as to help create spaces for alternative voices to be heard. Our contributors, some of whom are former reporters, have undertaken this work as academics committed to the study of news and journalism, but also as citizens. "Citizenship," as one of the last century's finest war correspondents, Martha Gellhorn (1988: 408), pointed out, "is a tough occupation." She believed that as citizens we are obliged to make our own informed opinion and to stand by it. "The evils of the time change," she observed, "but are never in short supply and would go unchallenged unless there were conscientious people to say: not if I can help it" (Gellhorn 1988: 408). Dissent, based on morality and reason, is at the heart of what it means to be a citizen. And while the challenge of citizenship may be getting more difficult all of the time, there is nevertheless always room for optimism. "There has to be a better way to run the world," Gellhorn insisted, "and we better see that we get it" (Gellhorn 1988: 409).

Notes

1 A transcript of this interview is available on the Canadian Broadcasting Corporation webpage: http://www.cbc.ca/deadlineiraq/burns.pdf

2 The Hutton inquiry, named after Baron Hutton of Bresagh, was set up to investigate the chain of events which led to the Government weapons expert David Kelly apparently committing suicide after having been named as the likely source of a BBC report by Andrew Gilligan. In the BBC report, Gilligan had maintained that an intelligence dossier on Iraq had been altered under pressure brought to bear by the Prime Minister's office. The inquiry report largely exonerated the government, sparking allegations of a "whitewash" by critics. A copy is available online at: http://www.the-hutton-inquiry.org.uk/

References

Adie, K. (1998) "Dispatches from the front: reporting war," *Contemporary Issues in British Journalism*, the 1998 Vauxhall Lectures, Centre for Journalism Studies, Cardiff University.

Adie, K. (2002) *The Kindness of Strangers*, London: Headline.

Bell, M. (2003) *Through Gates of Fire*, London: Weidenfeld and Nicolson.

Burkeman, O. (2003) "US television," *The Guardian*, March 27.

Deans, J. (2003) "Fox challenges CNN's US ratings dominance," *The Guardian*, March 27.

Doward, J. (2003) "Sky wins battle for rolling news audience," *The Observer*, April 6.

Gellhorn, M. (1988) "Conclusion, 1988," *The Face of War*, London: Granta Books.

Kurtz, H. (2003) "For media after Iraq, a case of shell shock," *The Washington Post*, April 28.

Omaar, R. (2004) *Revolution Day: the Human Story of the Battle for Iraq*, London and New York: Viking.

Plunkett, J. (2003) "US TV news too liberal, say Americans," *The Guardian*, October 8.

Preston, P. (2003) "Here is the news: too much heat . . . too little light," *The Observer*, March 30.

Rutenberg, J. (2003) "A nation at war: the news media," *The New York Times*, April 16.

Simpson, J. (2003) *The Wars Against Saddam: Taking the Hard Road to Baghdad*, London: Macmillan.

Sirota, D.J. (204) "The Fox of war," salon.com, March 30.

Snow, J. (2004) "Get that man down from the roof at once," *The Observer*, March 7.

Straw, J. (2003) full text of Jack Straw's speech, *The Guardian*, April 1.

Swain, J. (2003) "Why the reporter is the last bastion of truth," *The Observer*, March 16.

Wells, M. (2003) "British 24-hour television," *The Guardian*, March 27.

Wells, M. and Cassy, J. (2003) "Media: ungag us," *The Guardian*, April 14.

Part 1

WAR IN THE TWENTY-FIRST CENTURY

1

UNDERSTANDING

The second casualty

Oliver Boyd-Barrett

War reporting as genre

War reporting as a distinct category of journalism, a genre, is a generally taken-for-granted feature of our information environment. This chapter explores the implications of the genre for our (mis)understanding of wars and of the periods of "peace" that allegedly separate them. In particular, I argue that the genre obfuscates the reasons why the media focus on some wars rather than others, often fail to capture both the deep-level and proximate causes of wars or explain their actual durations and aftermaths, and hide the extent of media manipulation by official monopolization of information flows. The genre is not well suited to covert and "designer" wars (such as the war on drugs). More importantly, I argue that the genre plays into the hands of power, and this is nowhere more apparent than the media's failure to identify the metanarratives or grand strategies that explain the links between different wars over extended periods of time. In effect, therefore, the genre of war reporting serves a propaganda purpose. Its generic character has been exploited by state and other propagandists in ways that cripple the capacity of media consumers to make useful sense of the world. A celebrated model of media complicity with propagandists in supposedly democratic societies, the "propaganda model" of Herman and Chomsky (1988), only weakly explains the absoluteness of complicity in times of war, and I extend this model to include the element of penetration of media by intelligence services in conjunction with the wars discussed here.

Knightley's study, *The First Casualty* (1975, reprinted 2002) offers a set of classic examples of war-reporting-as-genre. He traversed the Crimea, US Civil War, Boer War, World War I, Russian Revolution, Abyssinia, Spanish Civil War, World War II, Korea, Algeria, Vietnam, Gulf War I, and Yugoslavia, offering a series of massive, violent conflicts that nearly all involved organized, "regular" armed forces of distinguishable enemies, often nation-states, or of warring regions, ethnicities or social classes within nation-states whose legitimacy was contested.

Reporting war, especially combat, has always been typically dangerous, demanding great resourcefulness in gathering and transmitting information. Journalists may unthinkingly subscribe to or knowingly comply with the objectives, ideologies, and perspectives of one or another side to a conflict. Alternately, they must struggle to make sense of the "big picture" in resistance to information monopolies imposed by state and military. Such challenges and difficulties are the essence of war reporting, and these attributes figure into the genre of war reporting that results.

Problems of genre contour or boundary as the nature of conflict undergoes change are to be expected. Genres routinely exhibit transformations and yield hybrid forms in response to changing circumstances, artists' search for new expression, or changes in audience preferences and decoding skills. Genre is not only about text but is also a feature of the "routinization" of production that shapes audience reception and perception as much as it is shaped by them. Traditional conflicts between antagonists who are identifiable in terms of geography, ideology, character, and interest serve important production as well as textual functions. Classic warfare is the epitome of a "good story," high in tension and drama, with complex main plots and sub-plots played out within traditional binary oppositions of aggressor and victim, winner and loser. While expensive to cover, warfare is commercially rewarding for the media, since its threat and unfolding ignite insatiable audience appetite for news. Advertisers may initially fear the risk of juxtaposing products with unsavory and unsettling issues, but they soon benefit from higher audience numbers and from the potential for linking merchandise with the semiotics of patriotism. War provides a reason and a focus for news editors in their decision-making about deployment of resources, identification of sources and commentators, and news agendas. War provides a ritualistic challenge, testing, and evaluation, that call upon extraordinary resources and resourcefulness from media institutions, journalists, technicians, and other support workers. Their collective experiences feed the stuff of professional legend, confirming and renewing the narrative of what it means to be a "journalist." The genre draws from and feeds into other forms of media production, including motion pictures and television series, and all these in turn shape audience perceptions of and expectations about warfare and how the media should cover war.

Casualties of war reporting

Choice of war

The media are highly selective in their focus on wars and conflict. A war that does not attract media attention is not therefore unimportant, of low intensity or scale; nor is it necessarily of scant strategic importance to Western interests. While the United States prepared to invade Iraq in 2003 and the media, especially television news, beat the drums for war, there was equally if not potentially more serious tension brewing between the United States and North Korea. The evidence of actual or imminent, hostile, nuclear capability in the case of North Korea was more compelling than in the case of Iraq. Yet North Korea reporting was completely overshadowed by Iraq. War with Iraq suited the US administration's game-plan of reshaping the Middle East—a highly influential, controversial, "neoconservative" policy that had mixed pro-Israel, anti-Arab overtones at the service of control over world energy reserves, specifically, and US global hegemony, in general. Before the dangers of post-war destabilization of Iraq became apparent, the war promised to boost the likelihood of electoral success for the Republicans in 2004, and it offered stunning profits for the military-industrial complex from the sales of military equipment and reconstruction contracts.

Military and civilian casualties experienced by the US, Afghanistan and Iraq between 2001 and 2003 were grave, but tiny in comparison with those in the Democratic Republic of Congo (DRC) (formerly Zaire), where four million lives were lost between 1997 and 2003, more than any since World War II (Kiley 2003). Western interests in the Congo were considerable, but they had little motivation for publicity. Several gigantic European enterprises (notably Belgian and French) have large holdings in the Congo, and most of the country's external trade is with European states. The DRC is of especial interest to the US and Japan for its resources of coltan, used in computer chips and other electrical products. Vast oil reserves are believed to lie near Lake Albert in the province of Ituri, center of some of the most vicious bloodletting. US reporter Wayne Madsen provided congressional testimony in May 2001 that the US was using private military contractors in the DRC, and that American companies, including one linked to former President George Bush senior "were stoking up the conflict for military gain" (Lokongo 2002). Fighting continued until a tenuous truce in April 2003 and the formation of transitional government. In July 2003, the UN Security Council voted to impose an arms embargo on the DRC, but Britain and the US stood in the way of extending the embargo to include Rwanda and Uganda, which backed the militias that were slaughtering in eastern provinces (Kiley 2003). Wars, however grave, in which Western interests promote their goals through proxy participants, many of whom have only a partial understanding, at best, of the powers that support them (with or without the presence of covert Western forces or mercenaries), are less likely to command mainstream media attention than wars that directly engage the formal armed services of Western powers and that require manifest accountability to their respective governments.

Causes of war

Causes of warfare are typically problematic. I draw a distinction between *proximate* and *deep-level* strategic causes. At another level are broader, longer-term, non-strategic causes unlikely to be decipherable in their entirety by the actors involved, but which will be pried to the surface by historians. Proximate causes have curious relationships to deep-level causes. The "aggression" of one party, for example, may have been provoked by an apparent "victim," representing pre-emptive retaliation against the "victim's" maneuver toward its own, unspoken, deep-level ambitions. Proximate causes are generally those cited by the participants, often formulaic and often bogus. The opening gambits of warfare occur when journalists are *most* vulnerable to manipulation by official sources. In contemporary warfare officialdom seeks to monopolize communication flows by limiting journalistic access to sanitized information from official sources, by rationing transportation and communications facilities, excluding non-approved journalists from military protection and facilities, keeping journalists out altogether—as in Grenada (1983) and Panama (1989), corralling select numbers into press "pools"—as in the Falklands (1982), Grenada (1983), Panama (1989), Afghanistan (2001), and Gulf War I (1991–2) (Thrall 2000), or "embedding" them within military units—as in Gulf War II (2003).

Official controls are also most likely to work effectively in the opening stages of conflict. Issues of legality and morality may be under-articulated or unclear. Critiquing the US administration while troops initiate combat attracts accusations of lack of patriotism, even treason (especially if reporters attend diligently to information from the opponents' side), and endanger journalists' already restricted access to official sources and to the battlefield. This very moment when proximate and deep-level causes of war should be open to rigorous analysis is also the time when such analysis is most difficult and least popular. Dissection and disputation of causes can be a heady, intellectual, wordy, controversial exercise, at a time when the media are most of all preoccupied with covering the *action*, at the behest, they would say, of audience interest. Wars can and often do start with greatly insufficient attention to the possible multiplicity of real causes; if, when war *formally* begins, journalists have sacrificed *context*, the chances that they will recover it in time, before the issues become history, are not encouraging. The problems are compounded when journalists and audiences are ignorant as to the locations of battle, their cultures and societies, as was the case in Afghanistan in 2001, and Iraq, in both 1990–1 and 2003.

Confusion over the causes and preludes to war is a common failing in war reporting, which makes impossible an assessment by citizens about the *meaningfulness* of the very combat that is its focus. This was as true of the second Gulf War in 2003 as of the first in 1990. The intelligentsia was better informed the second time: they had studied the lies of the first war; were aware of the controversial impact of UN sanctions on the civilian population (especially children) and of the "no fly zones" imposed by the US and Britain, and many doubted the claims from Washington and London that Iraq posed an immediate threat to the US or was in possession of significant stockpiles of chemical, biological, or nuclear weapons. Such doubts fuelled unprecedented worldwide anti-war mass demonstrations. A second difference was the speed with which the rationale for war collapsed after initial combat, during the first weeks of occupation. Increasingly, it appeared that the case had been built on exaggerations and outright deceptions. This was no surprise to anyone who had followed many of the "alternative" news websites that provided day-to-day critical analysis drawn from a much wider diversity of sources than available through the mainstream US media, and from long before the war started as well as during and after the war. Among mainstream US media, however, the networks (terrestrial and cable news channels in the US) uniformly banged the drums for war long before the onset of invasion. During the war, television networks' news frames complied fully with US administration policy: they represented war as a necessary response to an immediate threat by Iraq, justifiable even without UN sanction, whose resulting consequences of death and destruction, both military and civilian, were inevitable sacrifices. Within that frame there was scope for mild disagreement among the Pentagon-vetted ex-military network commentators as to whether sufficient numbers of troops had been deployed and whether initial combat strategies were appropriate. But no network acknowledged the appropriateness of an entirely alternative frame—namely that Iraq did not pose a significant threat to the US, that the invasion did not have UN sanction but constituted an aggressive breach of Iraqi sovereign territory which the Iraqis were fully justified in defending, and that the consequences of war in terms of death and destruction amounted to war crimes attributable to the US and its allies (Boyd-Barrett 2003b). Unlike television news, the mainstream press captured a broader range of perspectives in the period leading up to the war and occasionally achieved significant exposures (including Defense Secretary Donald Rumsfeld's apparent acquiescence to Iraqi use of chemical weapons in its war with Iran in the 1980s), but there was a customary lack of outrage in face of growing evidence of subterfuge in the US administration's diplomacy and its case for war. Both before and during the war, the press was slow to acknowledge the extent to which it had been routinely duped by misinformation and fabrication (including the highly staged toppling of the statue of Saddam Hussein, and the Hollywood-style make-believe attention to the rescue of Private Jessica Lynch). Neither television nor the press seemed capable of assessing and listening carefully to non-government expert sources, including that of former UN weapons inspector Scott Ritter, who had argued that the UN had indeed detected and supervised the destruction of most weapons of mass destruction (WMD), and that any left in early 2003 would be inoperative.

Press controls and manipulation

War reporting is generally one sided. The media typically cover war from the point of view of the country in which they and their major owners and readers are based, reflecting the point of view of that country's government and its foreign policy elites. In part this reflects the difficulty that the media face in gaining protected access to other parties, and when correspondents dare to try to achieve such access they provoke charges of treason. Recent improvements in communications technologies have removed some of the physical impediments to multilateral coverage, but there is little evidence so far of these being seriously put to use by mainstream media for the purposes of achieving greater balance and a broader perspective. Western reporting of the wars in Afghanistan (2001) and Iraq (2003) were stories told by Western correspondents reporting from Western positions speaking to (mainly approved) Western political and military sources, mainly about Western military personnel, strategies, successes, and, less often, failures, and backed with comments from (often vetted) Western military "experts." This myopia might be attributed to media reluctance to be seen as relying on "unreliable," "censored," or "unverifiable" reports, a hypocritical position that is blind to media dependence on government or military sources of their own side for their most regular, professionally scripted or staged, and above all *safe* information, disinformation or lies.

When Gulf War I broke in 1990–1, the White House, putting into practice the lessons it had learned from the Falklands War and from the US invasions of Grenada and Panama during the 1980s, knew how to implement its strategy of "control by press pool." Several pools were organized, although few saw combat. Those journalists not selected for pools stayed in Dahrain, viewing televised briefings. Pool allocations were organized by the media themselves; big media rigged the process to suit themselves. Pool reporters were accompanied at all times by military escorts, had limited access to troops in the battlefield, and so were often unable to provide an independent first-hand view of combat. Military public affairs escorts warned pool members against violating guidelines, barred them from places "they should not be," and reviewed press stories before transmission back to the press corps, if necessary passing them up to the military command for approval. Independent journalists risked getting detained, lost, captured, or killed.

Afghanistan in 2001 was very different. Here, correspondents had exceptional freedom to roam the country, but they did so with little protection or other support from the military. The build-up of American and Alliance forces following September 11 generally occurred without media participation, and when America unleashed its first wave of attacks in October, "only a handful of journalists enjoyed a vantage point within Afghanistan" (Dalglish *et al.* 2003: 14). Forty journalists were allowed to join military forces on the USS *Enterprise* and two other warships, but these ships were incidental to the strikes and restrictions were imposed on what could be published. "In effect, most American broadcasters scratched out coverage from Pentagon briefings, a rare interview on a US aircraft carrier or a humanitarian aid airlift, or from carefully selected military videos or from leads." Reporters seldom had interviews with troops or secured positions near the front.

Gulf War II in 2003 introduced the Pentagon concept of the "embedded" reporter. Schechter (2003) argued that the media became part of a psychological warfare directed to the domestic US population. Its objective was to stifle dissent, garner unquestioning support, and rally around a common symbol. On the ground, the Pentagon (Dalglish *et al.* 2003) provided billeting, rations, and medical attention and some assistance with communications if necessary to as many as 1,000 journalists, 662 of whom were attached directly to armed service units. Reporters were discouraged from going out on their own. For the bigger story, the US administration set the agenda through its "messages for the day." These ensured consensus across the administration and set the media agenda. The work of embedded reporters was subsidized by the Pentagon, overseen by "public affairs" specialists, and linked to television networks that were dominated by military experts vetted by the Pentagon. Reporters were subject to 50 contractual conditions, including a long list of things on which they could not report, such as dead bodies. Stories had to be checked by the military. Reporters were *not* embedded, noted Schechter, with Iraqi families, humanitarian agencies, or anti-war groups. They sought few interviews with ordinary Iraqis, experts not affiliated with pro-administration think tanks, military people other than the retired sort, peace activists, or European and Arabic journalists.

Covert war

Some conflicts do not acquire the status of "war" in media eyes, though they may be as violent, devastating, and, above all, strategic, as formal military conflict. Conflicts in which the West has non-legitimate or illegitimate interests (in particular relating to the extension of capitalist markets) tend to invite covert Western intervention and escape critical media attention. Former CIA officer Ralph McGhee (quoted by Scott 1985) illustrated this when he averred that "where the necessary circumstances or proofs are lacking to support US intervention, the CIA creates the appropriate situations or else invents them and disseminates its distortions worldwide via its media operations" (McGehee 1981).

Pilger (2001) related the case of the overthrow of the nationalist leader of Indonesia, President Achmed Sukarno, by General Suharto in 1965–6. Suharto was dictator of Indonesia for the following 30 years. Sukarno's overthrow had unleashed a pogrom, supposedly against suspected Communists but claiming the lives of between 500,000 and a million people, including at least 80,000 in the island of Bali, a slaughter that the CIA described as one of the worst mass murders of the twentieth century (1968 CIA report quoted by Pilger 2001: 25). Britain and the US had agreed in 1962 on the need to "liquidate" Sukarno, who as founding father of the non-aligned movement of developing countries, had sought a "third way" between the interests of the two superpowers. He had nationalized US economic interests and kicked out the International Monetary Fund and the World Bank and used aid subsidies from the Soviet Union to confront the British in Malaysia. The USA, under the executive leadership of Marshall Green, US ambassador in Jakarta, with the help of Britain and Australia, spread anti-PKI and anti-Sukarno propaganda, organized and propagandized the student movement, equipped the army, handed over field communications networks, provided naval escorts for Suharto military, and furnished lists of communist operatives for the death squads (Kathy Kadane, quoted by Pilger 2001: 29). In covering Indonesia then and later, Western media, including Murdoch's *The Australian*, uncritically framed the Suharto takeover as a positive outcome in the battle against communism. Many journalists celebrated the slaughter of up to a million people as good news, while attacking those who accused Suharto of human rights violations.

The overthrow of Sukarno provided a model for American-directed death squads in Operation Phoenix in Vietnam in 1967 which assassinated 50,000, and for the US prosecution of civil war in Guatemala in 1968 from whence the model spread to the rest of Latin America, including the overthrow of Salvador Allende in Chile in 1973. More significantly yet, Suharto's triumph was capped in 1967 by a conference in Geneva sponsored by the Time-Life Corporation at which the world's leading transnational corporations (then as now, mainly American and British) met with Suharto's economic team. The conference planned Indonesia's transition, under a plan inspired by Ford Motor Co., in alliance with CIA front organizations, to a "market economy," and involved the parceling out of the Indonesian economy to Western interests along with significant tax concessions. The conference paved the way to the formation of the Inter-Government Group on Indonesia, which Pilger (2001: 39) described as the "real and secret" center of control of the Indonesian economy, and to the initiation of World Bank loans that Sukarno had sought to avoid, sinking Indonesia into a $270 billion debt load by 2000, even while the World Bank "lost track" of $10 billion of investments that went to Suharto.

Issues of covert war were of considerable importance throughout the Cold War and again during the "war on terrorism" (a war that, like the Cold War, also resembles what I call the "designer" war below). Saunders (2003) noted that the unofficial title for this war among top officials and ground-level operatives in the US military and CIA was World War IV. He wrote (pp. 1–2):

> Below the surface are dozens of operations, some secret and some simply unnoticed, conducted by the CIA, the FBI, the diplomatic corps and small, elite military squads . . . And much of the war is being fought by foreign governments that are willing and able to do things Americans wouldn't or couldn't . . . In some cases, that cooperation has led the United States to endorse and enable activities that are deeply unsavory, all in the name of stomping out terrorism.

He quoted Jonathan Stevenson, a senior strategist with the International Institute for Strategic Studies in London: "Counterterrorism is now 90% law enforcement and intelligence." In other words, we have a war that did not conform to the appearance of conventional warfare but was closer to intelligence and police work; operations were likely to be small and secret, sometimes illegal. Those who promoted this war called it a war on terrorism; though critics (Meacher 2003) argued that this claim was bogus, and that what the war was really about was the seizure of global power by the USA.

Designer war

It is the "unofficial" causes and purposes of war that tend to get marginalized by mainstream media in preference to the narratives relayed by official sources, the sources that dominate all sourcing for mainstream media. This applies to conventional wars and to conflicts or activities that may or may not be called wars.

The discourse over the "war on drugs" establishes an agenda in the Western media that focuses on: the scale of drug addiction in the US and elsewhere; the efforts of legal authorities to enforce drug laws; whether the war is being "won" or "lost;" and, less commonly, the impact of drug crime on prison populations and control. The *costs* of the war, rising from $1 billion in the Reagan years to nearly $20 billion a year by 2002 (Troshinsky 2002) are less readily caught by this agenda, which also obscures how money earmarked for the "drug war" is often spent in support of counter-insurgency and, not coincidentally, in the protection of oil pipelines, as in Colombia. The media agenda marginalizes darker issues associated with collusion between US government agencies and the drugs business, and the exploitation of the "war on drugs" as a pretext for different goals, including the access to minerals, protection of oil interests in Third World countries, financing covert operations and supporting unsavory but useful "assets" (Scott and Marshall 1998; Webb 1998; Cockburn and St Clair 1999; McCoy 2003). In Panama, for example, General Noriega was for many years favored by Washington; he was a CIA asset, carefully protected, among others, by George H.W. Bush senior when Bush directed the CIA from 1976 to 1978, and again when he became Vice President to Reagan. Noriega was helpful to Washington in the Iran/Contra scandal, when the planes flying personnel and supplies to fight the dirty war in Nicaragua—financed by Iranian money that paid for US supply of arms to Iran via Israel—returned to the US laden with drugs (feeding the "crack" crisis in impoverished, ethnic, inner-city zones such as South Central Los Angles). Noriega disappointed Washington when he refused to withdraw the treaty that his predecessor had signed with President Carter, under which control of the Panama Canal would revert to Panamanian control in 2000. The ostensible reason for the US invasion of Panama in 1989 was to protect the lives of US citizens (although, apart from some dubious incidents most likely provoked by US special forces, it is doubtful that any US lives were really at risk before the invasion, and to "restore" democracy (critics noted that Panama had never had a functioning democracy). The immediate outcome of the war was that Noriega was sent for trial on drugs charges to Florida. But the far more significant outcome was that the Panamanian military was liquidated, and a new US puppet government, in tune with US foreign policy and business interests, was installed.

In Afghanistan, the Taliban had been persuaded by the US administration to eradicate the opium trade, by means of a ban on opium cultivation in early 2001, which Washington rewarded with a $43 million grant. Yet following the US bombing of Afghanistan in 2001 and the routing of the Taliban, Afghanistan became the world's leading supplier of opium. If the proximate reason for the "war on drugs" is the volume of illegal drugs entering the US, two important "deep level" causes have to do with oil, and with the financing of covert paramilitary operations (as in Laos in the 1960s, and in both Nicaragua and Afghanistan in the 1980s). Consistent involvement in drug operations by the CIA (and other intelligence and para-military organizations) in all parts of the world have been reliably charted (Cockburn and St Clair 1999); such operations finance and help

provide a cover for covert military and political operations, bypass legal constraints, and provide substantial illicit earnings to the participants and their
political sponsors.

Durations and aftermaths

Poor media performance in exploring deep-level and even the proximate causes
of war is compounded by significant failures in their coverage of the underlying
political strategies during the course of wars, as well as of the factors that explain
the ending of wars—even stumbling over the issue of whether wars have actually
"ended." Sixty years after the end of World War II, for example, the USA continues to maintain military bases in many of the countries that it then fought, and to
incur substantial war "expenses." Many months after President G.W. Bush
declared hostilities were over in Afghanistan in 2001 and Iraq in 2003, US soldiers were regularly coming under enemy fire, clashing with local resistance and
suffering significant casualties. The impulse of politicians and hence mainstream
media to declare "victory" can have more to do with propaganda than with political reality. Even the admission of "failure" is suspect; Chomsky and Pilger
(quoted by Shah 2003) considered that the major US war aims in Vietnam were
in fact achieved.

In the fall of 1968, presidential candidate Richard Nixon and his associates
sabotaged the Paris peace negotiations, by covertly indicating to the South Vietnamese military rulers that an incoming Republican regime would offer them a
better deal than a Democratic one (Hitchens 2001). The South Vietnamese
withdrew from the Paris peace talks on the eve of the election, thus undermining
the electoral chances of Democratic Party hopeful, Vice President Hubert
Humphrey. Four years later, the Nixon administration concluded the war on the
same terms that had been on offer in Paris. In this period, many more hundreds of
thousands of lives were lost in Vietnam, Cambodia, and Laos, as were those of
20,492 American service personnel. The mainstream media mostly reported the
Paris negotiations at face value at the time and later showed scant interest in
Hitchens' revelations.

The ending of the war in Kosovo in 1999 again presented at least two levels of
explanation: proximate and deep-level causes. One proximate explanation for
why that war ended, argued Knightley (2002), was NATO's claim that the bombing had worked and that the Serbs had no stomach for further casualties and
destruction. Alternatively, some correspondents at the time believed that the war
ended because in the June peace talks, Russia (Serbia's ally) had urged Milosevic
to make a deal, threatening to cut gas supplies to Serbia.

A BBC documentary the following October noted that following Serbian
acceptance of the peace deal, the International Monetary Fund provided Russia
with nearly three billion pounds to pay off the interest on its foreign debts.
Knightley then went on to ask, some four years after the war, "what was the war
really all about?" (Knightley 2002: 508). Was it about ethnic cleansing of the

Kosovars? Probably not. Propaganda claims of 500,000 or more deaths proved fantastical: sober assessments placed the upper estimate for the number of people who had died in the Kosovo conflict at 3,000. Was the NATO bombing a US-inspired policy of punishing the Serbs? But if so, punishing them for what? Quoting a range of sources, Knightley variously suggested that the Serbs were punished for the humiliation that the West had suffered at their hands in Bosnia and for acting against the interests of US foreign policy. He quoted Russian dissident Alexander Zinoviev, who believed that the Serbs had threatened the policy of Western powers to force the creation of a single system of global governance to suit their own interests. Others suggested that Yugoslavia represented the gateway between the West and central Asia. This view, incidentally, resonated with the arguments of Brzezinski (1998), former National Security Adviser to President Carter who, in his book, *The Grand Chessboard*, made the case for US seizure of control of central Asia and subordination of the ex-Soviet republics, while noting that only a pretext on the scale of Pearl Harbor would mobilize popular opinion behind such an openly imperialist strategy. Some commentators, including Ruppert (quoted by Guerilla News Network, 2002) regarded Brzezinski both as mouthpiece for Project for a New American Century, which urged the invasion of Iraq, Syria, and Iran, and the radical reshaping of the Middle East, and as a harbinger of 2001, in that Brzezinski had expressly identified Afghanistan as the key piece of the jigsaw of the new Empire.

Consequences of war are equally poorly charted by media. As a prelude to the US use of the atomic bomb on Hiroshima and Nagasaki in 1945, the military leader of the Manhattan Project, General Leslie Groves, chose Hanford in eastern Washington as the site of the world's first large nuclear reactor. In the 47 years until its closure in 1990, this 570-square-mile complex experienced large releases of radioactivity, "particularly iodine-131 which rapidly contaminates air, vegetation, and milk supplies," and 441 billion gallons of contaminated liquids were directly disposed into the ground, enough, in the words of one source, to have "the potential to induce cancer in every person currently on the planet, 208 million times over" (Alvarez 2003: 31). A related issue, one rarely discussed by either the Pentagon or the media, concerns the use of depleted uranium (DU) in artillery shells and Tomahawk missiles launched against Iraq in Gulf Wars I and II, in Kosovo in 1998 and again in Afghanistan in 2001. Some 320 tons of DU were used in Gulf War I, one thousand or more tons in the second. DU is reprocessed nuclear waste from the manufacture of nuclear energy. It continues to emit low levels of alpha radiation. It is cheap, and contributes to high-density heavy metal shells that rip through tank armor like butter. They cause a radioactive and highly toxic dust on explosion. Shells that do not explode eventually release DU into the environment. Health implications are disputed within and outside of the Pentagon. Major Doug Rokke, who headed the US Army's DU Project after the Gulf War and advocated a ban on the manufacture and use of DU munitions, believes that many of the 221,000 veterans from Gulf War I on permanent disability (29 percent of that war's eligible veterans) were victims of

DU. Soldiers were ill-trained and ill-equipped to deal with radioactive munitions in Gulf War I. It seems that during Gulf War II soldiers took considerable precautions to avoid contamination, but Worthington (2003) noted that "any soldier now in Iraq who has not inhaled lethal radioactive dust is not breathing." Contamination was even more likely to affect citizens. In addition to the US troops, countless Iraqi and other civilians are believed to have suffered from a range of health problems attributable to DU (Hecht 2003; Traprock Peace Center 2003). Corroborating sources include the Royal Society, laboratories in Switzerland and Finland, radiation expert Dr Helen Caldicott, a 1993 Pentagon report, the US Army Environmental Policy Institute, the Uranium Medical Research Center in Afghanistan (sources quoted in Worthington 2003). Dr Asaf Durakovic, professor of nuclear medicine at Georgetown University and a former army medical expert found that 62 percent of sick veterans had uranium isotopes in their bodies and even semen. A *Christian Science Monitor* report (Peterson 2003) found high levels of radiation in the vicinity of DU bullets littered throughout Iraq. Few such sites had warning notices. DU has also been used in military practice maneuvers in many US states. The half-life of DU is 4.5 billion years, the age of our solar system.

Metanarratives of empire and control

Metanarratives such as that of the Cold War play out over lengthy periods, and their significance is often misunderstood. While the US and its allies were instrumental in the overthrow of Sukarno in 1965, for example, this was the culmination of a strategy of destabilization that started in 1953 (Scott 1985), when the US National Security Council agreed to prevent permanent communist control of Indonesia.

The principal metanarrative for understanding war in the first quarter of the twenty-first century is about the establishment of US capitalistic worldwide hegemony, so strong in 2003 that US defense spending exceeded that of the next 15 nations combined (Gwyn 2003), a hegemony that serves a plutocratic US elite, its allies overseas, the corporations and finance houses that generate their wealth, and the military establishment that protects it. The narrative stretches back at least to the presidency of Woodrow Wilson in the first quarter of the twentieth century, when Wilson advocated a doctrine of internationalism, a "crusade for hegemony that wore the mask of idealism, and fought, not for spoils, or glory, but to 'make the world safe for democracy,'" cf. Raimondo 2002). This in turn built on previous imperialistic escapades, including the US conquest of Spanish Cuba and the Philippines in the Spanish-American war of 1898 and the establishment of a US zone in Panama in 1904. Wilson argued in 1907 that "since trade ignores national boundaries and the manufacturer insists on having the world as a market, the flag of his nation must follow him, and the doors of the nations which are closed must be battered down" (Beams 2003). This narrative is also a story about the struggle between international capitalism and the nation state. To depict wars as struggles within and between nation states, as media persistently do, misses this fundamental dimension.

The metanarrative of hegemony takes different forms in different periods and is currently, in the form of the National Security Strategy pronounced by President Bush in September 2002, as robust as it has ever been. Although presented by the media as a *new* development in response to the events of September 11, 2001, much the same principles of preventive war supremacy had been enunciated in the past by Dean Acheson in 1963 (Barsamian 2003) and by George Kennan in 1948. Kennan noted that "we have about 60 percent of the world's wealth, but only 6.3 percent of its population. Our real task in the coming period will be to maintain this position of disparity" (Gwyn 2003). Stromberg (2002) noted that by the late nineteenth century, US leaders had "asserted a non-negotiable right of the US government to be "secure." US planning in 1943–4 for the post-war period determined that future US defense would require effective control of the Atlantic and Pacific Oceans, and that it could not allow rival power to control the Eurasian land mass.

US hegemony is not simply about political or military hegemony nor even *primarily* about these things. It is about economic hegemony and the US assertion to its right to impose capitalism worldwide. Though terms such as "democracy" have been frequently employed (as in William Kristol and Robert Kagan's 1996 call for a US "benevolent world hegemony"), it is "capitalism" that best explains the intensification of US overseas interventions since 1990. US supremacy also requires privileged access to the key resources on which its version of capitalism depends, and for the past one hundred years or more this has included access to cheap sources of oil. Western media typically fail to identify the relationship between the wars in which the US engages and this metanarrative of US supremacy. Most media coverage of the two Gulf Wars of 1990–1 and 2003 not only failed to place them within the grander narrative of US hegemony but also within the secondary narrative of oil supremacy. This secondary narrative is one of at least 30 years' duration and concerns US control of the Middle East and its oil—not so much for the *fuel*, as for the *power* that control of the fuel bestows over other regions and nations, notably Europe, Japan, and China.

The National Security Strategy, published in September 2002, claimed that the attacks of September 11, 2001 had "opened vast, new opportunities" (p. 28). This statement indicates a further narrative that the mainstream media have been slow to recognize and prioritize—the narrative of the "neo-conservative" influence in US foreign policy-making and, above all, what this influence signifies (a rejection, among other things of Kissinger policies of co-existence). The core of the neo-conservative movement came together with the formation in 1997 of the Project for the New American Century. This group, together with the Committee for the Liberation of Iraq, a PNAC spin-off, and the American Enterprise Institute, a conservative think tank that rented office space to PNAC, played a highly significant role in pushing for the 2003 invasion of Iraq and in promoting the cause of other interventions in the Middle East.

The metanarrative of US hegemony does not end with the acquisition of territory, military strength and trading power. Economic phenomena such as deflation, stagnation, financial looting, over capacity, and massive economic imbalances are reported by mainstream media as though these were quirky occurrences, either the side-products of a "bubble" economy or the symptoms of a temporary economic downswing. According to Beams (2003), they must be related to underlying pressures within the capitalist system, in particular the declining rate of profit in the period since World War II, a phenomenon that creates huge incentives for the seizure and/or "privatization" of resources that are locked into national monopolies or similar state-owned productive properties, even where these involve basic amenities such as water, education, health, or power. The US push for global domination, argued Beams, is "driven on as it is by the crisis in the very heart of the profit system, cannot bring peace, much less prosperity, but only deepening attacks on the world's people, enforced by military and dictatorial forms of rule."

War reporting and the propaganda model

Time and again the media align themselves with state propaganda, most intensely so in times of war. Herman and Chomsky (1988) developed a five-filter propaganda model to explain this phenomenon, and the model fits well with the sociology of mediated communication: corporate *ownership* and the profit orientation of the media; the influence of advertisers on media content; media's overwhelming dependence on *official* sources; media reporting routines that render them vulnerable to manipulation (e.g. the "beat" system and its slavish dependence on official sources); fear of "*flak*" by powerful sources; and sharing by many journalists of official ideologies of anti-communism or pro-global capitalism.

One consideration that Herman and Chomsky eschewed, however, was the direct purchase of media influence by powerful sources or the "buying out" of individual media and/or journalists by government authorities. Herman and Chomsky wanted to demonstrate that media complicity with propaganda did not require "conspiracy theory"—not quite the same thing, perhaps, as demonstrating that conspiracy does not happen. In the case of the media, this stand is peculiar to say the least, since there is irrefutable evidence of wide-scale CIA penetration of the media. The mid-1970s Senate (Church Committee) and House (Pike) investigations of the CIA exposed covert penetration of the media. The CIA published hundreds of books whose purpose was to undermine the Soviet Union and communism. Some were based on manufactured evidence. The agency owned dozens of newspapers and magazines worldwide. Carl Bernstein, of "Watergate" repute, wrote an article in 1977 revealing that over 400 US journalists had been employed by the CIA, ranging from freelancers to CIA officers working under deep cover. Journalists' support for the CIA ranged from intelligence gathering to serving as go-betweens with spies. Nearly every major US news organization had been penetrated, usually with the cooperation of top management. The Church Committee's final report had called upon the intelligence community to refrain from the use of journalists. In fact, the CIA merely curtailed the practice (Houghton 1996). The Reagan administration had no qualms about returning to old habits and included an illegal CIA-administered domestic propaganda war among covert operations in central America. A CIA memo quoted by Cockburn and St Clair (1999: 32) explained that the agency maintained "relationships with reporters from every major wire service, newspaper, news weekly and TV network" and that in many instances "we have persuaded reporters to postpone, change, hold or even scrap stories that could have adversely affected national security interests or jeopardized sources or methods." This was confirmed by the *Guardian* newspaper in 1991 (quoted by Pilger 1998: 496), whose correspondent Richard Norton-Taylor disclosed that some 500 prominent Britons were paid by the CIA through the corrupt, now defunct, Bank of Commerce and Credit International, including 90 journalists, many of whom were in "senior positions." Nor was it likely that such corruption would be reserved for non-US journalists. In 1996, the Council on Foreign Relations suggested that the CIA be freed from some policy constraints on covert operations, such as the use of journalists and clergy as cover. CIA Director John Deutch argued that American journalists "should feel a civic responsibility to step outside their role as journalists" (Cockburn and St Clair 1999: 90). A 1997 law, the Intelligence Authorization Act, actually permitted reinstatement of the practice, subject to presidential approval; in any case, the CIA had reserved the right to use the practice, noting, as Deutch stated before Congress, that it already had the power to use US reporters as spies. Following the mid-1970s, furthermore, many propaganda functions were transferred by the CIA and Congress to privately funded organizations, through conduits such as the Ford Foundation and similar bodies; examples included The Asia Foundation, Congress for Cultural Freedom, and the National Endowment for Democracy (Brandt 1997), and many of these finance supposedly free media operations. Elsewhere (Boyd-Barrett, forthcoming), I explore the implications of such penetration for war reporting in Iraq of 2003 and other conflicts.

Conclusion

My purpose here has been to dissect the limitations of war-reporting-as-genre. My examples are intended to demonstrate that with respect to some of the most important international conflicts in the past half century or more, the media's reporting of war has been almost guaranteed to misinform and obfuscate. Herman and Chomsky's acclaimed "propaganda model," which helps account for media complicity with propaganda, does not sufficiently address evidence of direct state penetration and the covert control of supposedly independent, privately-owned media, a phenomenon that may provide additional explanation for the media's continued adherence to a patently faulty genre. For the media have typically failed on numerous counts: to probe stated proximate causes of conflict, to prise out deep-level causes, to avoid complicity with state propaganda machinery, to follow and make accurate sense of strategic changes in the courses of war, and to fully determine the factors explaining the ending of wars, and the aftermaths and other implications of war. On each of these counts, war reporting remains in the service of propagandistic purposes.

References

Alvarez, R. (2003, August 18) "The legacy of Hanford," *The Nation*, vol. 277, no. 5, pp. 31–5.

Barsamian, D. (2003, May) "An interview with Noam Chomsky," *Monthly Review*, retrieved August 30, 2003 from www.monthlyreview.org/0503chomsky.htm

Beams, N. (2003, July 10, 11) "The political economy of American militarism," *World Socialist Web Site*, retrieved August 30, 2003 from www.wsws.org

Bernstein, C. (1977, October 20) "The CIA and the media," *Rolling Stone*.

Boyd-Barrett, O. (2003a) "Doubt foreclosed: US mainstream media and the attacks of September 11, 2001," pp. 35–49 in N. Chitty, R. Rush and M. Semati (eds), *Studies in Terrorism: Media Scholarship and the Enigma of Terror*, Penang: Southbound Press.

Boyd-Barrett, O. (2003b) "Imperial news and the new imperialism," *Third World Resurgence*, 151–2, pp. 44–8.

Boyd-Barrett, O. (forthcoming) "Casualties of genre," paper prepared for the 2004 conference of the Center for Global Media Studies, Seattle.

Brandt, D. (1997) "Journalism and the CIA: the mighty wurlitzer," *NameBase NewsLine*, no. 17, April–June, retrieved August 30, 2003 from www.namebase.org/news17.html

Brzezinski, Z. (1998) *The Grand Chessboard: American Primacy and Its Geostrategic Imperatives*, New York: Harper Collins.

Chomsky, N. (2003) *Middle East Illusions*, Lanham, MD: Rowman and Littlefield.

Cockburn, A. and St Clair, J. (1999) *Whiteout: the CIA, Drugs and the Press*, New York: Verso Books.

Dalglish, L., LaFleur, J., and Leslie, G. (2003) *Homefront Confidential: How the War on Terrorism Affects Access to Information and the Public's Right to Know*, 4th edition, Arlington, VA: The Reporters Committee for Freedom of the Press.

Gwyn, R. (2003, January 1) "Dawn of imperial America," *Toronto Star*.

Hecht, S. (2003, March 30) "Uranium warheads may leave both sides a legacy of death for decades. Los Angeles Times accessed through Common Dreams News Center," March 30, 2003, at http://www.commondreams.org/views03/0330-02.htm

Herman, E. and Chomsky, C. (1988) *Manufacturing Consent: the Political Economy of the Mass Media*, New York: Pantheon Books.

Hitchens, C. (2001) *The Trial of Henry Kissinger*, New York: Verso.

Houghton, K. (1997) "Subverting journalism: reporters and the CIA," *Committee for the Protection of Journalists*, www.cpj.org/attacks96/sreports/cia.html

Kennan, G. (1948, February 24) PPS/23: "Review of Current Trends in U.S. Foreign Policy," in *Foreign Relations of the United States*, vol. I, pp. 509–29.

Kiley, S. (2003, August 17) "Chaos and cannibalism under Congo's bloody skies," *The Observer*.

Knightley, P. (2002) *The First Casualty: the War Correspondent as Hero and Myth-Maker from the Crimea to Kosovo*, Baltimore, MD: Johns Hopkins University Press.

Kristol, B. and Kagan, R. (1996) "Toward a neo-Reaganite foreign policy," *Foreign Affairs*, July/August, retrieved August 30, 2003 from www.ceip.org/people/kagfaff.htm

Lokongo, A. (2002) "Media coverage of the Congo invasion: In the Footsteps of Western Interests?," *Media Development*, issue 1, www.wacc.org.uk/publications/md/md2002-1/lokongo.html.

McCoy, A. (2003) *The Politics of Heroin: CIA Complicity in the Global Drug Trade*, Lawrence Hill and Co.

McGehee, R. (1981, April 11) "The CIA and the White Paper on El Salvador," *The Nation*, vol. 255, no. 4, p. 423.

Meacher, M. (2003, September 6) "This war on terrorism is bogus," *The Guardian*, retrieved August 30, 2003 from www.guardian.co.uk

Peterson, S. (2003, May 15) "Remains of Toxic Bullets Litter Iraq," *Christian Science Monitor*, retrieved May 15, 2003 from *Christian Science Monitor Online*, http://www.csmonitor.com/2003/0515/p01s02-woiq.html

Pilger, J. (1986) *Heroes*, London: Jonathan Cape.

Pilger, J. (1998) *Hidden Agendas*, New York: Random House.

Pilger, J. (2001) *Heroes*, Cambridge, MA: South End Press.

Pilger, J. (2002) *The New Rulers of the World*, London: Verso.

Raimondo, J. (2002, October 9) "Iraq: First Stop on the Road to Empire," *Antiwar.com*, retrieved October 30, 2003 from www.anti-war.com

Rampton, S. and Stauber, J. (2003) *Weapons of Mass Deception: the Uses of Propaganda in Bush's War on Iraq*, New York: Penguin.

Saunders, D. (2003, September 6) "The Fourth World War: gestation of a new American Imperialism," *The Toronto Globe and Mail*, Vancouver.indymedia.org.

Schechter, D. (2003) *Embedded: Weapons of Mass Deception: How the Media Failed to Cover the War in Iraq*, New York: News Dissector/Mediachannel.org

Scott, P.D. (1985) "The United States and the overthrow of Sukarno," 1965–7, *Pacific Affairs*, 58, summer, pp. 239–64.

Scott, P.D., and Marshall, J. (1998) *Cocaine Politics: Drugs, Armies, and the CIA in Central America*, Berkeley, CA: University of California Press.

Shah, A. (2003, January 21) "War, propaganda and the media" in *Global Issues*, retrieved August 30, 2003, from www.globalissues.org/HumanRights/Media/Propaganda/Vietnam.asp?Print=True

Stromberg, J. (2002, October 12) "The old cause: what is 'new' in the new Bush doctrine?," *Anti-war.com*, retrieved October 30, 2003 from www.antiwar.com

Thrall, T. (2000) *War in the Media Age*, Cresskill, NJ: Hampton Press Inc.

Traprock Peace Center (2003) "Gulf War Casualties and 'Depleted' Uranium: an Educational Campaign Providing Resources on Radioactive, Chemical and Biological Weapons," Traprock Peace Center, http://traprockpeace.org/depleteduranium.html

Troshinsky, L. (2002, August 15) "'US drug war alliances futile,' says expert," United Press International, United States Congress Senate Select Committee to Study Governmental Operations with Respect to Intelligence Activities (1975) *Final Report of the Select Committee to Study Governmental Operations with Respect to Intelligence Activities, United States Senate: Together with Additional, Supplemental, and Separate Views*, 6 vols, KF 31.5, G7 1976.

United States House Select Committee on Intelligence and Senate Select Committee on Intelligence (2003) *Report of the Joint Inquiry into the Terrorist Attacks of September 11*, Washington DC.

Vann, B. (2002, February 20) "US militarism targets South American oil," *World Socialist Web Site*, retrieved August 30, 2003 from www.wsws.org

Vann, B. (2003, June 27) "*New York Times* reporter Judith Miller accused of 'hijacking' military unit in Iraq," *World Socialist Web Site*, retrieved August 30, 2003 from wsws.org/articles/2003/jul2003/

Webb, G. (1998) *Dark Alliance: The Contras and the Crack Cocaine Explosion*, Seven Stories Press.

Worthington, A. (2003, May 3) "Death by slow burn: how America nukes its own troops," *The Idaho Observer*.

2

INFORMATION WARFARE IN AN AGE OF HYPER-MILITARISM

Richard Keeble

The daily press and the telegraph, which in a moment spread inventions over the whole earth, fabricate more myths . . . in one day than could have formerly been done in a century.

Karl Marx 1871

There was no war in the Gulf in 2003. Rather, a myth of heroic, spectacular warfare was manufactured, in large part, as a desperate measure to help provide a *raison d'être* for the (increasingly out-of-control) military industrial complexes in the US and UK—and to hide the reality of a rout of a hopelessly overwhelmed "enemy" army. The links between mainstream journalists and the intelligence services are crucial factors in the manufacture of the myth. But it is not essentially a massive elite conspiracy. Rather, the myth's origins lie deep within complex military, historical, ideological, and political forces which it is crucial to identify. Moreover, the manufacture of the "war" myth has profound implications for any study of the political and military origins of the conflict and press representations.

The war problematic

The US/UK invasion was supposedly over Iraq's WMD—yet none were ever found. US/UK jets had been bombing Iraqi targets regularly since the end of the 1991 conflict so there was no clear start to the conflict. And with the president of the defeated state melting away into thin air there was no clear end. Casualties on both sides mounted as hostilities continued after the end of the so-called war. Thus the bombing of Baghdad on March 20 became the manufactured "start" of the "war" narrative; and there were two contrived endings: the symbolic toppling of the Saddam statue before the world's media on April 9 and the statement by President Bush before a gathering of US troops on May 1 that the "major combat operations" were over.

The "greatest battles since World War II" were predicted and celebrated in the press, just as during the 1991 Gulf conflict. But again there was no real warfare:

no credible enemy. In a matter of days the world's mightiest military power inevitably crushed a ragtag army of conscripts and no-hopers. As defence expert John Keegan (2003) commented in the *Daily Telegraph* of April 8: "In truth, there has been almost no check to the unimpeded onrush of the coalition, particularly the dramatic American advance to Baghdad: nor have there been any major battles. This has been a collapse, not a war." Agence France-Presse (AFP) photographer Cris Reeves, with the US marines, saw hardly any action at all. "It was like two weeks of camping for me with 20-year-old marines. I was 48 so I was exhausted" (Guillot 2003).

War is about killing. We know precisely how many Americans and British soldiers died. Some 115 US troops were killed in combat and 23 in accidents and so-called friendly-fire incidents (though from May 1 to November 1, 2003 the toll was 221 as the "war" dragged on); 19 British troops died in combat with 25 killed in "non-hostile situations" (Beaumont and Graham 2003). All of these casualties were profiled and listed in "rolls of honour" in the mainstream press (Epstein 2003). According to John Pilger (2003), as many as 10,000 Iraqi civilians were killed during the invasion—with thousands more injured. But the precise figure of how many thousands of Iraqis perished, were maimed, or psychologically damaged (in the lead-up to the invasion, during the invasion, and in the aftermath) we will never know. So silence shrouds the essential horror.

The war's most heroic story, the saving of Private Jessica Lynch, turned out to be a completely manufactured drama (Kampfner 2003) while a Sky News "exclusive" about a cruise missile launch from a Royal Navy submarine proved to be a hoax. The outrageous victory claims of the Iraqi minister of information, Mohammed Saeed al-Sahhaf (dubbed "Comical Ali" by the Western media), as US troops captured Baghdad airport were only matched, given the scale of the slaughter, by the US/UK's fantastic claims over their supposedly precise weapons (Mayrhofer 2003).

The controversial comment of the French postmodern theorist, Jean Baudrillard (1991), about the 1991 Gulf conflict—"there was no war"—appears equally relevant to the 2003 conflict. The mainstream media, in effect, manufactured the myth of war. Jack Lule (2002: 277) argued that myth is best understood as "a societal story that expresses prevailing ideas, ideologies, values and belief." Accordingly, a tidy narrative of quick and relatively easy "warfare" (built around myths of national glory, macho heroism, monstrous villainy and "precision weaponry") was manufactured in the British mainstream press while the reality was an illegal, unnecessary assertion of brute force (Mailer 2003).

Militarism "out of control"

The war myth emerges from the fact that the force deployed by the US/UK bears no relation to the threat posed. The US and UK are essentially fighting phantoms of their own making: thus the threats are grossly exaggerated, fictionalized. The US budget plans for 2004 incorporate defence spending of more than $400 billion (alongside a record White House deficit of $455 billion)—and that does not include the extra billions expected for the occupation of Iraq. This represents more than all the military spending of the rest of the world and more than twice the spending of the next 15 of the world's powers. Moreover, the US has military bases in three-quarters of the countries of the world and 31 percent of all wealth. Robert Harvey talks of the "United States of the World" (2003: 13–36). This is a military colossus (backed by the UK) of a kind never before seen since the Roman empire—and it is running out of control. As the late historian, E.P. Thompson (1982), argued, there is a technological imperative driving the US and UK toward warfare and testing new military systems.

The boom in military spending, begun during the Korean War years of the 1950s, continued relentlessly during the Cold War. By 1990, more than 30,000 US companies were engaged in military production, roughly 3,275,000 jobs were in the defense industries and 70 percent of all money spent on research and development was directed at defense work (Drucker 1993: 126). With the demise of the Soviet Union, the United States became desperate in its search for new enemies (Keeble 1997). Grenada (1983); Libya (1986); Panama (1989); Iraq (1991, 1993, 1998 and 2003); Somalia (1992–3); Serbia (1999) (Hammond and Herman 2000); and Afghanistan (2001) were all puny powers rapidly crushed by the overwhelming firepower of the American colossus in a series of manufactured, media-hyped militarist adventures (Webster 2003).

In the UK, the arms industry is worth more than £5 billion a year, amounting to 20 percent of global weapons sales. It employs up to 150,000 people, the UK standing as the world's second largest manufacturer after the US with 32 percent of the market. Yet arms deals remain remote from public scrutiny, being run by the Defence Export Services Organization, "a secretive group within the Ministry of Defence, controlled by the arms companies themselves and with a history of actively conniving at bribery" (Leigh 2003) .

Thus the US/UK responses to the September 11 attacks, with the launch of the endless "war on terrorism," the attacks on Afghanistan and Iraq, and the threats to the "rogue" states, Syria, Iran, and North Korea, are not distinctly new strategies but accelerating long-standing strategies of military imperial adventurism (Curtis 2003a, 2003b). Al-Qaeda, blamed for the September 11 atrocities and a series of later attacks on Western interests, is a shadowy, elusive grouping against whom traditional, war fighting strategies (involving major battle confrontations) are inappropriate. And so the US/UK is left manufacturing a spectacle of traditional "warfare." As US novelist Don DeLillo commented: "I'm almost prepared to believe that the secret drive behind our eagerness to enter this war is technology itself—that has a will to be realized. And that the administration is essentially a Cold War administration looking for a clearly defined enemy which was not the case after September 11. Now there is a territorial entity with borders and soldiers in uniform."[1]

Moreover, given the integration of the media industries' interests with those of the military industrial complex and the importance of the media's role in supporting the state's militarism, it is worth identifying the media-military-industrial complex as another factor behind the manufacture of the "war" myth (Keeble 1997: 26; McChesney 2002).

Secrecy feeds the myth-making

Secrecy also feeds the myth-making. Alongside the "democratic" state in both the US and UK there exists a secret and highly centralized state occupied by the massively over-resourced intelligence and security services (MI5, MI6 and GCHQ, the Cheltenham-based signals spying centre), secret armies, and undercover police units. Since the 1980s a raft of legislation, such as the Official Secrets Act, the Regulation of Investigatory Powers Act, the Anti-Terrorism, Crime and Security Act 2001, has reinforced their growing powers (Morgan 2003). Mark Almond (2003), lecturer in modern history at Oriel College, Oxford, has highlighted the extent to which intelligence has reached into the heart of the Blair government: "More than any predecessor, Blair has relied on a kitchen cabinet in Downing Street but one made up of a cabal of diplomats and intelligence officials rather than ambitious, if unelected party apparatchiks. Hence the focus on globalization rather than domestic issues. Blair has liberated British politics from the influence of politicians." Professor David Beetham (2003) has similarly highlighted the "secret, warfare" state which has totally undermined the democratic system.

But examining the activities of the intelligence services remains incredibly difficult. A few researchers and journalists—such as Stephen Dorril (2000), author of a seminal history of MI6, David Leigh and Richard Norton-Taylor of the *Guardian*, Martin Bright and Nick Cohen of the *Observer*, Paul Lashmar and Chris Blackhurst, of the *Independent*, freelance Phillip Knightley, and Robin Ramsay, editor of the alternative journal, *Lobster*, have managed to penetrate the fog that envelops all the work of the spooks—but only slightly.

Spooks and hacks: close encounters of a strange kind

While it might be difficult to identify precisely the impact of the spooks (variously represented in the press as "intelligence," "security," "Whitehall," or "Home Office" sources) on mainstream politics and media, from the limited evidence it looks to be enormous. As Roy Greenslade, media specialist at the *Guardian*, commented: "Most tabloid newspapers—or even newspapers in general—are playthings of MI5."[2] Bloch and Fitzgerald (1983: 134–41) report the editor of "one of Britain's most distinguished journals" as believing that more than half its foreign correspondents were on the MI6 payroll. In 1991, Richard Norton-Taylor revealed in the *Guardian* that 500 prominent Britons paid by the CIA and the now defunct Bank of Commerce and Credit International, included 90 journalists (Pilger 1998: 496).

In their analysis of the contemporary secret state, Dorril and Ramsay (1991:

x–xi) gave the media a crucial role. The heart of the secret state they identified as the security services, the cabinet office and upper echelons of the Home and Commonwealth Offices, the armed forces and Ministry of Defence, the nuclear power industry and its satellite ministries, together with a network of senior civil servants. As "satellites" of the secret state, their list included "agents of influence in the media, ranging from actual agents of the security services, conduits of official leaks, to senior journalists merely lusting after official praise and, perhaps, a knighthood at the end of their career."

Following the passing of the 1989 Security Service Act, links between the media and MI5 and MI6 grew closer, according to James Adams (1994: 94–8). Phillip Knightley, author of a seminal history of the intelligence services, even claimed that at least one intelligence agent is working on every Fleet Street newspaper.[3]

During the controversy that erupted following the end of the "war" and the death of the arms inspector Dr David Kelly (and the ensuing Hutton inquiry) the spotlight fell on BBC reporter Andrew Gilligan and the claim by one of his sources that the government (in collusion with the intelligence services) had "sexed up" a dossier justifying an attack on Iraq. The Hutton inquiry, its every twist and turn massively covered in the mainstream media, was the archetypal media spectacle that drew attention from the real issue: why did the Bush and Blair governments invade Iraq in the face of massive global opposition? But those facts will be forever secret. Moreover while the Gilligan affair might appear to have reinforced the liberal notion of adversarial state–media relations, in fact, as Rogers (1997: 64) argued, "this focus obscures the extent to which the media have actually supported and colluded with the secret state." Significantly, the broader and more significant issue of mainstream journalists' links with the intelligence services was ignored by the inquiry.

Yet during the Hutton period, a myth emerged that the 2003 invasion of Iraq was the first conflict to be justified on (dodgy) evidence supplied by the intelligence services. Yet even during the Vietnam conflict, intelligence on the strength of the Vietcong was faked to make the case for war more plausible (Ramsay 2003). Similarly, the US attack on Libya in 1986—deliberately aimed to effect "regime change" by assassinating President Gaddafi—was justified by President Reagan on dubious intelligence (dutifully reported in the mainstream media) of Libyan responsibility for the bombing of a disco in West Berlin, frequented by US servicemen. Intelligence misinformation before the 1991 Gulf massacres constantly "over-sexed" Iraq's alleged nuclear capability since opinion polls in the States showed fears of President Saddam Hussein as a "nuclear monster" were most likely to win support for the military option (Reich 2002). Even during the 1991 Iraqi conflict much of the reporting was based on intelligence-driven disinformation. For instance, while Iraqi soldiers were deserting in droves and succumbing to one massacre after another, all the British media highlighted intelligence predictions of the "largest ground battle since the Second World War." Images of enormous berms, sophisticated Iraqi defences and trenches of burning oil filled the media. But in the end there was nothing more than a 100-hour rout. Colin Powell, in his account of the 1991 war, estimated that 250,000 Iraqi soldiers were eliminated (Powell 1995).

Similarly since the September 11 atrocities in the United States, the London-based mainstream media have been awash with intelligence-inspired leaks stressing the dangers of terrorist attacks in Britain. Even the *Independent*, most critical of the US/UK rush to military action, gave credibility to dubious "intelligence" sources. On September 16, 2001, for instance, Lashmar and Blackhurst reported that at least three terrorist cells linked to Osama bin Laden were at large in Britain. An "intelligence source" was quoted as saying: "There is no reason why what happened in America couldn't happen in Britain or any European country." This is terrifying stuff. But how much is fiction? (Bright 2002). Similarly in September 2002 the *Daily Express* was awash in intelligence-inspired scare stories. "Nuclear attack in just months" it thundered on September 9; "Anthrax threat on our streets: Britain on alert for Saddam suicide squads" it reported the next day. A climate of fear is manufactured allowing the apparatus of the national security state (surveillance cameras, email snooping, arrest without trials, and demonization of asylum seekers) to expand. On September 15, 2002, drawing on intelligence disinformation linking Iraq to nuclear weapons, the *Sunday Express* editorialized: "War brings evil but we believe the country must not be frightened from doing what we pray will save the world from the greater evil of nuclear bombs. We see no alternative but to help demolish the Iraqi regime."

On March 18, 2003, before the major air assault on Baghdad began, the *Sun* typically reported: "According to intelligence reports Republican Guard units have been equipped with chemical warfare shells to make a desperate last stand south of Baghdad. A source said: 'They clearly have given some chemical capability to some forces.'" On April 2 the *Sun* "revealed" that Saddam Hussein had issued a coded chemical attack on US/UK troops. Coalition intelligence chiefs, it reported, interpreted a reference to "catching breath" in a speech by Saddam Hussein "as a signal for lethal chemicals or nerve gas to be unleashed against US forces massing south west of Baghdad." There were similar reports throughout the mainstream press.

Dodgy dossiers and the epistemological implications

The problem with intelligence is that it can never be double-checked. By definition, it remains secret and exclusive. It could all be fiction (and often is). All too often journalists are seduced by the attractions of secret exclusive information. When politicians further doctor the evidence from the intelligence services, as appears to have happened before the Iraqi conflict, for their own warmongering purposes (with the creation of a new intelligence agency, the Office of Special Plans, by US Defense Secretary Donald Rumsfeld, to manufacture evidence of Iraqi possession of WMD) we have entered the realm of hyper myth.

As Dorril (2003: 4) commented:

The reality is that intelligence is the area in which ministers, and the MI6 info ops staff behind them can say anything they like and get away with it. Intelligence with its psychological invite to a secret world and with its unique avoidance of verification, is the ideal means for flattering and deceiving journalists.

The former foreign secretary, Lord Howe, told the Scott arms-to-Iraq inquiry: "In my early days I was naïve enough to get excited about intelligence reports. Many look, at first sight, to be important and interesting and significant and then when we check them they are not even straws in the wind. They are cornflakes in the wind" (Norton-Taylor 2003).

Another problem with intelligence is that anyone attempting to highlight its significance is accused of lacking academic rigour and promoting "conspiracy theory." Certainly underlying the myth of "warfare" lie complex cultural, military, and ideological forces. But given the close links between politicians, journalists, and the intelligence services some conspiratorial elements have to be acknowledged to be behind mainstream media's coverage of the Iraqi crisis.

With the emphasis on intelligence, the focus of journalism shifts from objective, verifiable "facts" to myth: in effect, there is a crucial epistemological shift. As General Richard Myers, chairman of the joint chiefs of staff, admitted: "Intelligence doesn't mean something is true. You know, it's your best estimate of the situation. It doesn't mean it's a fact. I mean, that's not what intelligence is" (Stephen 2003). Similarly, the historian Timothy Garton Ash stressed: "The trend in journalism as in politics, and probably now in the political use of intelligence, is away from the facts and toward a neo-Orwellian world of manufactured reality" (2003). The assumption of Iraq possessing WMD was based entirely on unverifiable intelligence reports as is so much of the reporting of the "war on terror."

The crucial role of embedded journalists in the manufacture of the "war" myth

Most of US/UK imperialism advances essentially in secret. Both countries have deployed forces virtually every year since 1945—most of them away from the glare of the media (Peak 1992). But at various moments the US/UK chooses to fight overt, manufactured "wars." We, the viewers and readers, have to see the spectacle. It has to appear "real." During the first Gulf "war," the pooling system was used to keep correspondents away from the action (Keeble 1997: 109–26; McLaughlin 2002: 88–93). And since most of the action was conducted over the 42 days from the air, with journalists denied access to planes, the reality of the horror was kept secret.

In contrast, during the 2003 conflict, journalists were given remarkable access to the "frontlines." And those frontline images and reports from journalists who were clearly risking their lives, aimed to seduce the viewer/reader with their facticity; the correspondents were amazed at their "objectivity." Yet beyond the view of the camera and the journalist's eye-witness, with the war unproblematized, the essential simulated, mythical nature of the conflict lay all the more subtly and effectively hidden. Moreover, military censorship regimes always serve essentially symbolic purposes—expressing the arbitrary power of the army over the conduct and representation of "war."

Significantly defence minister Geoff Hoon claimed: "I think the coverage . . . is more graphic, more real than any other coverage we have ever seen of a conflict." Most of the critical mainstream coverage highlighted the information overload. But, as David Miller (2003) commented: "It is certainly true to say that it is new to see footage of war so up-close but it is a key part of the propaganda war to claim that this makes it 'real.'"

Some 600 US and 128 UK journalists, including journalists from the *Western Daily Press*, *Scotsman*, *Manchester Evening News*, *Ipswich Evening Star* and *Eastern Daily Press*, and one from the music network MTV, were "embedded" with military units. According to Phillip Knightley (2003): "The idea was copied from the British system in World War I when six correspondents embedded with the army on the Western front produced the worst reporting of just about any war and were all knighted for their services. One of them, Sir Phillip Gibbs, had the honesty, when the war was over, to write: 'We identified ourselves absolutely with the armies in the field.' The modern embeds, too, soon lost all distinction between warrior and correspondent and wrote and talked about 'we' with boring repetition."

As the *Times* media commentator, Brian MacArthur, reported (2003): "Embeds inevitably became adjuncts to the forces." Audrey Gillan, with the Household Cavalry for the *Guardian*, was one of the few to accuse the military of censorship. She reported that soldiers complained of being like mushrooms— kept in the dark with you know what shovelled on top of them—but she could not use this phrase for fear of upsetting the brigade HQ.

Some 5,000 journalists were in the Gulf region to cover the hostilities. Two thousand were in Kuwait and on ships with the US and UK naval task forces in the Arabian Gulf; 290 were in Baghdad; 900 in northern Iraq with Kurdish fighters: the rest were in Jordan, Iran, Bahrain, and at the Allied Central Command in Doha, Qatar (Milmo 2003). Here there was little consistent challenge to the dominant military agenda. On one occasion *New York* magazine writer Michael Wolff (2003) dared to break ranks and ask the provocative questions: "Why are we here? Why should we stay? What's the value of what we're learning at this million-dollar press center?" He was soon to pay the price for his daring. Fox TV attacked him for lacking patriotism and after right-wing commentator Rush Limbaugh gave out his email address, in one day Wolff received 3,000 hate messages.

Unprecedented access to the "front lines" was the carrot, but the stick was always on hand. Fifteen non-Iraqi journalists were killed, two went missing and many unilateral non-embeds were intimidated by the military. Had there been the same death rate for journalists during the Vietnam war, there would have been 3,000 killed.[4] As John Donvan (2003) argued, "coalition forces saw unilaterals as having no business on their battlefield." Unilateral Terry Lloyd, of ITN, was killed by marines who fired at his car; Reuters camera operator Taras Protsyuk and José Couso, a cameraman for the Spanish television channel Telecino, died after an American tank fired at the fifteenth floor of the Palestine hotel in Baghdad while Tarek Ayoub, a cameraman for Al-Jazeera, died after a US jet bombed the channel's Baghdad office. Two journalists working for RTP Portuguese television, Luis Castro and Victor Silva, were held for four days, had their equipment, vehicle, and video tapes confiscated and were then escorted out of Iraq by the 101st Airborne Division. How many Iraqi journalists perished in the slaughters we will never know. For most of the Western mainstream media they are non-people.

The nature of the Fleet Street consensus

For the 1991 conflict all Fleet Street newspapers backed the military response together with 95 percent of columnists. For the 1993 and 1998 attacks on Iraq the consensus fractured with the *Guardian*, *Independent*, and *Express* coming out against the attacks. Then for the NATO attacks on Serbia in 1999 virtually all of Fleet Street backed the action, even calling for the deployment of ground troops (which not even the generals dared adopt as policy). There was one exception—the *Independent on Sunday*—and its editor, Kim Fletcher, left the paper just weeks after the end of the conflict. But there was far more debate among columnists. A survey I conducted showed 33 out of 99 prominent columnists opposed military action against Serbia. For the attacks on Afghanistan and the toppling of the Taliban, the whole of Fleet Street backed the action—but again there was a wide-ranging debate among columnists and letter writers (Keeble 2001).

In 2003, with significant opposition to the rush to war being expressed by politicians, lawyers, intelligence agents, celebrities, religious leaders, charities, and human rights campaigners—together with massive street protests—both nationally and internationally, the breakdown in Fleet Street's consensus was inevitable. Yet still for the invasion of Iraq, the majority of Fleet Street backed the action (though columnists and letter writers were divided). The *Independents* (the daily and Sunday), carrying prominently the dissident views of foreign correspondent Robert Fisk, were the most hostile. Following the massive global street protests on February 15, the *Independent on Sunday* editorialized: "Millions show this is a war that mustn't happen."

The *Guardian* did not criticize military action on principle but opposed the US/UK rush to war and promoted a wide range of critical opinions. The *Mirrors* were also "anti" in the run up to the conflict (perhaps more for marketing reasons since the Murdoch press was always going to be firmly for the invasion) with the veteran dissident campaigning journalists John Pilger and Paul Foot given prominent coverage. But then, after editor-in-chief Piers Morgan claimed his papers' stance attracted thousands of protesting letters from readers, their opposition softened. And the *Mails* managed to stand on the fence mixing both criticism of the rush to military action with fervent patriotic support for the troops during the conflict.

The demonization of "Saddam"

The media's focus on the "monstrous," "evil," global power of Saddam Hussein has since 1990 been an essential ingredient of the propaganda strategy to manufacture the credible enemy. The Iraqi president has clearly been an appalling dictator—as critics have been stressing since the 1970s (though the CIA played significant roles in the two coups that brought Hussein's Ba'athists to power in 1963 and 1968). But in the 1980s, when Iraq was closely allied to the West during its eight-year war with Iran, Fleet Street's coverage of Hussein was rare and generally positive. Even the reporting of the chemical bombing of Kurds in Halabja on March 16, 1988 was notable for its restraint. And the Iranians, not "Saddam," were blamed (Casey 2003).

The demonization of "new Hitler," "madman," "monster" Saddam, the "butcher of Baghdad" only began in earnest following the Iraqi invasion of Kuwait in August 1990. And this hyper-personalization of the conflict has remained a constant feature of the press coverage ever since—even in newspapers critical of the US attacks of 1993, 1996, 1998, and 2003. It serves to simplify an enormously complex history and direct all blame at one man.

During the 1991 massacres, Fleet Street constantly focused on Iraq's army as being "1 million-strong," the "fourth largest in the world," "full of battle hardened fanatics" following the 1980–8 war with Iran. In reality, the Iraqi army was war-weary, full of bare-footed conscripts desperate to surrender, quickly destroyed in a massive 42-day assault. In this context, the stress on "global terrorist" Saddam in the propaganda was crucial in the manufacture of the credible enemy (Keeble 1998).

By 2003, Iraq was a completely dysfunctional state, destroyed following more than a decade of UN sanctions and constant weekly bombings by the US/UK—hardly covered in the mainstream media—and with a profoundly unpopular regime. Thus, the focus on the demonized personality of "Saddam" throughout the media was all the more important in the creation of the war myth. On March 19, as Iraqis prepared to defend Baghdad, the *Sun* reported on Saddam Hussein: "Fiend to unleash poisons." Another report described him as a "monster." The following day the *Sun* reported Lt Tim Collins calling for "Our boys to 'rock the world' of Saddam's evil diehards." Saddam was planning to poison Iraq's water system "as a last act of savagery." In the *Daily Star* of March 28, the Iraqi president was described as "an evil dictator," a "brutal tyrant" while an unnamed military source is quoted as saying: "There appear no depths to which Hussein will not stoop." As the US troops approached Baghdad, on April 4, the *Mirror* framed its coverage entirely around the personality of "tyrant" Saddam. "What will he do?" asked its front page headline. "As US troops reach Baghdad, the world waits for Saddam to play his final, despotic card." Significantly, the *Mail's* logo for its coverage of the conflict was "War on Saddam." On March 30, the *Sunday Telegraph* editorialized, highlighting his unique barbarism:

Saddam's record means that the coalition forces must be ready for any-thing. This, after all, is a dictator who planned during the last Gulf War to chain American PoWs to the front of his tanks; a murderer who—uniquely in the history of depravity—has turned chemical weapons on his own people.

On March 20, Julian Borger, in the *Guardian*, grappled with the contradictions. On the one hand, he reported: "In terms of technology and sheer might, this coming conflict is likely to be one of the most unequal in history." Yet, to reaffirm the myth of war, there is always the Saddam demonization card to play. So Borger continued: "But the Iraqi leader's proven readiness to embrace desperate and unconventional measures makes him potentially a far more dangerous foe than any the Pentagon has taken on in recent years."

Significantly, the *Observer*, in outlining its support for military action in its leader of January 19, framed its entire argument around the demonized personal-ity of "Saddam." First it referred to the "nature of Saddam Hussein's regime and the call by many Iraqi exiles and dissidents for him to be overthrown." The war was not about oil. "For the second motive for displacing Saddam is the danger he poses to the wider world." And it concluded: "If Saddam does not yield military action may eventually be the least awful necessity for Iraq."

The manufacture of the precise, clean, humanitarian war

Central to the manufacture of the war myth is its representation as clean, precise, and humanitarian. All the US/UK overt major military interventions since Viet-nam, up to 2003 were largely risk free, taking less than 1,000 US troops' lives. All resulted in appalling civilian and enemy soldier casualties. Yet the propaganda—in Orwellian style—has constantly stressed the precision of the weapons and claimed the raids were for peaceful purposes: to introduce democracy and free-dom. Casualty figures were always covered up (or dubbed in the militaryspeak "collateral damage"). According to Cummings (1992: 121) the 1991 conflict appeared not as "blood and guts spilled in living colour on the living room rug" but through a "radically distanced, technically controlled eminently 'cool' post-modern optic." Kellner (1992: 386) described it ironically as "the perfect war." During the "humanitarian" NATO attacks on Serbia in 1999, hundreds of civil-ians were killed (Chomsky 1999; Hammond 2000). A leaked government report later revealed that only 40 percent of RAF bombs hit their targets while the hit-rate for the high explosive, 1,000 lb bomb was just three out of 150, or 2 percent (Plavsic 2000).

During the 2003 invasion of Iraq, the press constantly reaffirmed this same pro-paganda stress on precision, yet reached new heights of exaggeration. As the *Sun* of March 20 reported beneath the headline: "The first 'clean' war": "A senior defence source said last night: 'Great attention to precision-guided weapons means we could have a war with zero casualties. We are a lot closer toward that ideal. We may be entering an era where it is possible to prosecute a humanitarian war.'" In effect, could not the military's rhetoric about precision and smart weapons have betrayed its ultimate ambition—to destroy war itself?

Even the *Guardian*, one of the most critical of the US/UK rush to invade Iraq, reported on March 19: "The last Gulf War may have marked the introduction of space age weapons—from laser-guided bombs to cruise missiles smart enough to know which set of Baghdad traffic lights to turn left at—but as collateral damage figures later proved, the technologies were still largely in their infancy."

Following the Ameriyya shelter bombing by an American Stealth jet during the Gulf massacres of 1991 (when hundreds of Iraqi women and children perished) most of Fleet Street blamed "Saddam," described it as a propaganda coup for the Iraqi leader or claimed it was inevitable (Keeble 1997: 166–72). All of this was part of a strategy to deflect blame for the atrocity away from its perpetrators. Similar strategies appeared during the 2003 invasion. For instance, after a bomb fell on a Baghdad market on March 26 most of Fleet Street followed the military agenda and questioned whether the Iraqis (incredibly) had fired the missile. In the *Mail* of March 27, the headline focused on "the propaganda coup Saddam had hoped for" while correspondent Ross Benton reported: "It was the first major incident of 'collateral damage' since the war began but allied officials said they could not confirm that the bombs were dropped by US or British warplanes." The *Sun* on the same day headlined "Who's to blame?" and reported: "If the market blasts were caused by off-target Allied bombs, it will be a propaganda gift to Saddam." The *Guardian*, alongside a moving eye-witness account by Suzanne Goldenberg of the aftermath of the bombings, highlighted US "confusion over blame for raid." But the *Mirror*, fiercely anti-war at the time, discounted US denials and condemned it as "the worst civilian outrage since the war began a week ago." No paper listed nor profiled the 14 Iraqis reported killed: they were the nameless victims of the carnage.

Even in those newspapers critical of the US/UK invasion, the dominant images reflected the military agenda of marginalizing the reality of the slaughter. For instance, a special issue of the *Independent Review* of April 9, 2003 was devoted to images from the conflict. But out of 14 photographs, just three focused on Iraqi casualties while another showed blurred images of bodies on a road after a "friendly fire" attack on a convoy of US and Kurdish forces. The pro-Blair *Times'* section 2 issue of April 10 carried 49 images: out of these just five showed casualties (but pictures of 24 British soldiers killed and the coffins of another six were also carried). Similarly the *Sun*'s "24 page souvenir" of April 15 displayed 43 images—all of them predictably celebrating US/UK military heroics, with no casualties shown and Iraqis almost invisible. Again pictures of "the brave men who died for freedom" were carried. The *Observer* of April 13 carried an eight-page "war in pictures" supplement: out of 50 images, just six focused on casualties. The unnamed dead were always Iraqi.

The manufacture of heroism in a post-heroic age

Modern war-fighting strategies have virtually eliminated the possibilities of heroic action. Technology has taken the place of men (and the occasional woman). Soldiers now largely press buttons and watch the consequences on a video. Electronics and space-based technologies are all-important. Luckham commented (1984: 2): "We are now entering a stage in which the manufacture of warfare is overtaking man and expropriating his culture. Automated warfare and the nuclear bomb have deprived man of his capacity to strive for glory, recognition or safety through combat."

Slaughtering thousands of conscripts, soldiers, and civilians in appalling massacres is hardly heroic. Yet society desperately needs its heroes. And so the spectacular "war" provides the perfect theater for the manufacture of heroism. Thus, the patriotic pops are full of celebrations of "Our boys" and their heroic deeds. Typically, the *Sun*'s leader of March 21 highlighted Prime Minister Tony Blair's "sombre and emotive" broadcast hailing the "heroism of Our boys and girls." On March 24, it listed the 31 US and British soldiers killed under the headline: "How the tragic heroes perished."

During the 1991 Gulf massacres there was virtually no hand-to-hand combat, and so in an attempt to revive the heroic images of World War II, the press constantly used cartoon representations and photographs of troops in training. In 2003, no such devices were necessary. The "frontline" shots were enough to promote the myth of "real" battle.

The most blatant manufacture of heroism surrounded the exploits of Private Jessica Lynch which gripped the world's media on April 3, 2003. Under the strapline, "An incredible story of heroism as teenage PoW snatched back," the *Sun* reported on the "daring midnight raid." "Army supply clerk Jessica, 19, was plucked to safety by US special forces from a hospital used as a base by Saddam Hussein's death squads." And it went on to quote Brigadier General Vince Brooks: "America doesn't leave its heroes behind. Never has, never will." Along with the rest of the mainstream media, the *Guardian* framed its coverage around the title of the Hollywood blockbuster *Saving Private Ryan*. Under the headline "Saving Private Lynch: how special forces rescued captured colleague," it reported on the "daring midnight raid." But in the end, all was found to be fiction. There was no gun battle—simply because there were no Iraqi soldiers in the hospital at the time, as Kampfner (2003) revealed in the *Guardian*.

Given the prominence of media hype in current conflicts it is inevitable that a few critical journalists will deconstruct certain events and expose their manufactured dimension. Even the *Sun*, on April 15, exposed the story of the heroic "Stay lucky" soldier pictured wearing a helmet riddled with bullet holes as a prank. But focusing on individual hoaxes is very different from highlighting the whole "war" as a construct.

The essential task

A few months before his death in September, Edward Said (2003) identified the way in which the dominant discourse in the US/UK before the invasion of Iraq fabricated an "arid landscape ready for American power to construct there an ersatz model of free market 'democracy.'" But he concluded with typical optimism: "Critical thought does not submit to commands to join in the ranks marching against another approved enemy. Rather than the manufactured clash of civilizations we need to concentrate on the slow-working together of cultures that overlap, borrow from each other and live together." Indeed, while US/UK militarism appears out of control my analysis here argues that it is built on lies, misinformation, and myth. And by exposing the lies and the myth, by joining with the global movement for peace and human rights, we can all help put a brake on the US/UK military juggernaut.

Notes

1 Quoted in "Notes from New York, a profile of DeLillo," by Duncan Campbell, *The Observer*, May 4, 2003.
2 Quoted in Seamus Milne (1994) *The Enemy Within: the Secret War Against the Miners*, London: Verso; reprinted by Pan in 1995: 262.
3 Phillip Knightley interviewed London, September 25, 2003.
4 Christiane Amanpour, chief international correspondent for CNN, quoted in Jessica Hodgson (2003) "Mother of all war journos," *The Observer*, November 2.

References

Adams, James (1994) *Secret armies: the full story of SAS, Delta Force and Spetsnaz*, London: Hutchinson.
Almond, Mark (2003) "So how will he be judged?" *The Guardian*, May 15.
Baudrillard, Jean (1991) "The reality gulf," *The Guardian*, January 11.
Beaumont, Peter and Graham, Patrick (2003) "Iraq terror spirals out of control as US intelligence loses the plot," *Observer*, November 2.
Beetham, David (2003) "The warfare state," *Red Pepper*, June.
Bloch, Jonathan and Fitzgerald, Patrick (1983) *British Intelligence and Covert Action*, London: Junction Books.
Bright, Martin (2002) "Terror, security and the media," *Observer* online, July 21, http://observer.guardian.co.uk/libertywatch/story/0,1373,758265,00.html (accessed July 22).
Casey, Leo (2003) "Questioning Halabja: genocide and the expedient political lie," *Dissent*, New York, summer: 61–5.
Chomsky, Noam (1999) *Lessons from Kosovo: the New Military Humanism*, London: Pluto.
Cummings, Bruce (1992) *War and Television*, London: Verso.
Curtis, Mark (2003a) "Partners in imperialism: Britain's support for US invasion," www.zmag.org May 10 (accessed May 11).
Curtis, Mark (2003b) *Web of Deceit: Britain's Real Role in the World*, London: Vintage.
Donvan, John (2003) "For the unilaterals, no neutral ground," *Columbia Journalism Review*, May/June www.cjr.org/year/03/3/donvan.asp (accessed July 12, 2003).

Dorril, Stephen (2000) MI6: Fifty Years of Special Operations, London: Fourth Estate.

Dorril, Stephen (2003) Spies and Lies, Free Press, April.

Dorril, Stephen and Ramsay, Robin (1991) Smear, London: Fourth Estate.

Drucker, Peter E. (1993) Post-capitalist Society, Oxford: Butterworth-Heinemann.

Epstein, Edward (2003) "How many Iraqis died? We may never know," San Francisco Chronicle, May 3.

Garton Ash, Timothy (2003) "Fight the matrix," The Guardian, June 5.

Guillot, Clare (2003) "Nassiriya: le soldat Reeves face à la foule en colère," Le Monde; April 17.

Hammond, Philip (2000) "Reporting 'humanitarian' warfare: propaganda, moralism and NATO's Kosovo war," Journalism Studies, vol. 1, no. 3, pp. 365–86.

Hammond, Philip and Herman, Edward S. (eds) (2000) Degraded Capability: the Media and the Kosovo Crisis, London: Pluto.

Harvey, Robert (2003) Global Disorder, London: Constable.

Kampfner, John (2003) "The truth about Jessica," The Guardian, May 15.

Keeble, Richard (1997) Secret State, Silent Press: New Militarism, the Gulf and the Modern Image of Warfare, Luton: John Libbey.

Keeble, Richard (1998) The Myth of Saddam Hussein: Media Ethics, Kieran, Matthew (ed.), London, Routledge, pp. 66–81.

Keeble, Richard (2001) "The media's battle cry," Press Gazette, October 5.

Keegan, John (2003) "Saddam's utter collapse shows this has not been a real war," The Daily Telegraph, April 8.

Kellner, Douglas (1992) The Persian Gulf TV War, Boulder/San Francisco/Oxford: Westview Press.

Knightley, Phillip (2003) "Turning the tanks on the reporters," Observer, June 15.

Leigh, David (2003) "Greasy palms in pinstripe pockets," The Guardian, September 16.

Luckham, Robin (1983) "Of arms and culture," Current Research on Peace and Violence IV, Tampere, Finland, pp. 1–63.

Lule, Jack (2002) "Myth and terror on the editorial page: The New York Times responds to September 11," Journalism and Mass Communication, Columbia, pp. 275–93.

MacArthur, Brian (2003) "Changing pace of war," The Times, June 27.

McChesney, Robert (2002) "September 11 and the structured limitation of US journalism," in Stuart Allan and Barbie Zelizer (eds), Journalism after September 11, London: Routledge, pp. 91–100.

McLaughlin, Greg (2002) The War Correspondent, London: Pluto Press.

Mailer, Norman (2003) "We went to war just to boost the white male ego," www.timesonline.co.uk/article/0..482-662789.00.html (accessed August 12, 2003).

Mayrhofer, Debra (2003) "What's in a name?" www.mwaw.org April 15 (accessed May 12, 2003).

Miller, David (2003) "Embedding propaganda," Free Press, special issue, June.

Milmo, Cahal (2003) "Reporting for duty," The Independent, March 18.

Morgan, David (2003) "Climate of fear," Morning Star, June 12.

Norton-Taylor, Richard (2003) "The BBC row has been got up to obscure the ugly truth," The Guardian, June 28.

Peak, Steve (1982) "Britain's military adventures," London, The Pacifist, vol. 20, p. 10.

Pilger, John (1998) Hidden Agendas, Verso: London.

Pilger, John (2003) "The big lie," Daily Mirror, September 22.

Plavsic, Dragan (2000) "NATO's war: the truth comes out," Socialist Review, September.

Powell, Colin (1995) *Soldier's Way*, London: Hutchinson (with Joseph Persico).

Ramsay, Robin (2003) "Lying about Iraq," *Lobster*, no. 45, summer.

Reich, Stephanie (2002) "Slow motion holocaust," *Covert Action Quarterly*, no. 72, pp. 22–8.

Rogers, Ann (1997) *Secrecy and Power in the British State: a History of the Official Secrets Act*, London: Pluto Press.

Said, Edward (2003) "A window on the world," *The Guardian Review*, August 2.

Stephen, Andrew (2003) "America," *New Statesman*, August 4.

Swain, Jon (2003) "Why the reporter is the last bastion of truth," *Observer*, March 16.

Thompson, Edward P. (1982) *Notes on Exterminism: the Last Stage of Civilisation, Exterminism and the Cold War*, London: Verso, pp. 151–63.

Webster, Frank (2003) "Information Warfare in an Age of Globalization," Daya Kishan Thussu and Des Freeman, eds, *Information Warfare in an Age of Globalization: War and the Media*, London: Sage, pp. 57–86.

Wolff, Michael (2003) "I was only asking," *The Guardian*, April 14.

3

A MORAL IMAGINATION

The media's response to the war on terrorism

Susan D. Moeller

Once upon a time there lived a mandarin in China. Sequestered in his palace his sleep was untroubled, even when a calamity befell a hundred million of his people. Destruction of that immense multitude held little interest for him; he snored "with the most profound security." Then, late one evening his lapdog nipped him on his littlest finger. The court doctor came to minister to him and told him that if the injury grew worse over the night, he might well have to amputate the finger. Oh, how his sleep was disturbed then. The dull pain of the bite and the greater agony of wondering whether he would have to suffer the loss of his little finger kept him awake through all the dark hours.

The eighteenth-century French philosopher Denis Diderot and the eighteenth-century Scottish political economist Adam Smith both told versions of this tale of the Chinese mandarin (Smith 1976; Ginzburg 1994). The inherent drama of the fable is in the mandarin's complete moral disregard of the value of the lives of his subjects. Yet, as Diderot and Smith and generations of moral philosophers since them have explored, there are ways—there must be ways—to make the lives of distant strangers of value to us.

One plausible manner in which to do so is through what has been called "enlightened self-interest." A broader and more long-term understanding of self-interest, for example, might have influenced that self-centered despot to comprehend that the deaths of so many of his subjects could not but negatively affect his own luxurious lifestyle. His sleep might then have been troubled as he contemplated his future loss of living standards and he might have applied himself to figuring out what could best ameliorate the situation. Perhaps among those possible remedies might have been some that would not just protect his own resources, but that might prevent future losses of life: the building of a dam, if the calamity was a catastrophic flood; the institution of mandatory grain reserves, if the calamity was caused by a plague of locusts.

When contemplating action, noted the Nobel Prize-winning physicist Richard Feynman, the core political question is: "Should I do this?" Yet, in order to determine whether a certain action "should" be taken, Feynman argued that another question has to first be addressed: "If I do this, what will happen?" The first question, "what will happen?" may have an answer that can be arrived at empirically. The answer may be knowable. In an example that Feynman gives, for instance, it may be evident that the enactment of a certain economic policy will cause a depression. But it may not inevitably follow that a depression is something to be avoided at all costs. The answer to the question "Should I do this?" is a matter of judgment.

> You see, only knowing that it is a depression doesn't tell you that you do not want it. You have then to judge whether the feelings of power you would get from this, whether the importance of the country moving in this direction is better than the cost to the people who are suffering. Or maybe there would be some sufferers and not others. And so there must at the end be some ultimate judgment somewhere along the line as to what is valuable, whether people are valuable, whether life is valuable.
>
> (Feynman 1998: 44–6)

War reporting is a subset of reporting on international affairs. Many of the concerns that bedevil international coverage are even more problematic when journalists cover war. Lives are not only perceptibly "valuable" during times of conflict, as in Feynman's formulation, but lives are waged and lives are lost depending on the policies and strategies that are chosen. Ergo, the journalistic problems of language, of access, of asking the right questions, of not only challenging the "spin" of the powers-that-be, but contesting the priorities set by those in power, take on extraordinary significance. This chapter considers how the post-9/11 Bush administration has used a moral rhetoric to propel its "war on terrorism" policies, especially in Iraq, and how that "morality" has echoed through the American media.

The moral high ground

US politicians cannot afford to be seen as putting self-interest above concern for the community. Not for Americans has been the unvarnished self-interest of the mandarin, however much reality suggests that Americans are no more exceptional in the exercise of policy than other nations. "An Iraq invasion without UN sanction would be a pre-emptive attack by the world's only superpower," wrote the editors of the *Los Angeles Times* on March 14, 2003 in an editorial headlined "The right way in Iraq." "It would probably be successful in the initial military phase—but at what cost? A pre-emptive strike can be justified if the threat is imminent and unavoidable. With neither of those conditions proven, a pre-emptive attack yields the moral high ground. The US would be cast as the global bully, seeking to arrogate the installation of governments in other lands" (*Los Angeles Times* editorial 2003: 14).

The ethos of American policy has been that self-interest may be a driving factor in the formation of behavior, but by itself is not sufficient cause for action. A higher motivation must be claimed—such as President Bush's "crusade" against terrorism or his commitment to "rid the world of the evil-doers," as he called for in the days after September 11. Values must lie alongside interests. Moral intention, in other words, is assumed to be essential to Americans' high regard of themselves. Philosophers, politicians, and the public alike assume a tie between public policy and moral obligation.

At any given point in history, however, certain policies which have been deemed to be moral, in hindsight look less so.[1] The impetus for action which appeared to be concern for others has been revealed to be a mandarinesque self-interest, with very little of it "enlightened." During the nineteenth century, for example, journalist John L. O'Sullivan wrote an editorial supporting the annexation of Texas in the July/August issue of the *United States Magazine and Democratic Review*. The article persisted through history, for in it O'Sullivan argued that it is "the right of our manifest destiny to over spread and to possess the whole of the continent which Providence has given us for the development of the great experiment of liberty and federaltive [sic] development of self government entrusted to us."[2]

The doctrine of "manifest destiny" helped generations of Americans rationalize the institution of policies that were racist at best and genocidal at worst. Yet the argument for "manifest destiny" was couched in moral language and cited Providence as the ultimate originator of the doctrine—territorial expansion was not only inevitable and divinely ordained, but would bring "liberty, civilization and refinement" to the "masses of mankind."

Although the phrase "manifest destiny" was coined in the mid-nineteenth century, the nation—and before that, the colonies—had always thought of itself as a place apart, not just geographically, but morally. The new world was to be in the words of John Winthrop in 1630, a "city upon a hill," and those who lived in it were to be "blessed" by "the Lord our God . . . in the land whither we go to possess it." Those who came to America, and those who have helped to define these United States have incorporated into their visions a destiny not imitative of the destinies of other nations or other empires. As O'Sullivan wrote six years before his "manifest destiny" editorial,

> Our national birth was the beginning of a new history, the formation and progress of an untried political system, which separates us from the past and connects us with the future only; and so far as regards the entire development of the natural rights of man, in moral, political, and national life, we may confidently assume that our country is destined to be the great nation of futurity.

> (O'Sullivan 1839)

"America," he argued, "is destined for better deeds." Here, in an essay that early laid out his thoughts on "manifest destiny," we hear not only the call of duty but a religious charge of responsibility. "What friend of human liberty, civilization, and refinement, can cast his view over the past history of the monarchies and aristocracies of antiquity, and not deplore that they ever existed?" he asked.

> What philanthropist can contemplate the oppressions, the cruelties, and injustice inflicted by them on the masses of mankind, and not turn with moral horror from the retrospect? . . . We must onward to the fulfillment of our mission—to the entire development of the principle of our organization—freedom of conscience, freedom of person, freedom of trade and business pursuits, universality of freedom and equality. This is our high destiny, and in nature's eternal, inevitable decree of cause and effect we must accomplish it. All this will be our future history, to establish on earth the moral dignity and salvation of man—the immutable truth and beneficence of God.
>
> (O'Sullivan 1845)

People of conscience must be morally affronted by the abuses and injustices sanctioned by "monarchies and aristocracies," dictators, and warlords, O'Sullivan argued. Americans have a responsibility to protect the oppressed and to enforce the basic rights of all human beings. But in what cause were these words applied?

Minus the more flowery rhetorical flourishes, this passage could have been seamlessly included in President George W. Bush's address to the joint session of Congress on September 20, 2001, when he outlined "our war on terror." That war began, he said,

> with al-Qaeda, but it does not end there. It will not end until every terrorist group of global reach has been found, stopped and defeated . . . This is not, however, just America's fight. And what is at stake is not just America's freedom. This is the world's fight, this is civilization's fight, this is the fight of all who believe in progress and pluralism, tolerance and freedom.

Bush ended his speech with the same invocation of God that O'Sullivan had made:

> The course of this conflict is not known, yet its outcome is certain. Freedom and fear, justice, and cruelty, have always been at war. And we know that God is not neutral between them. Fellow citizens, we'll meet violence with patient justice, assured of the rightness of our cause and confident of the victories to come. In all that lies before us, may God grant us wisdom and may he watch over the United States of America.
>
> (US Newswire, September 20, 2001)

Why such language? It offers moral justification. Historian Jackson Lears wrote in a *New York Times* opinion:

The proposed war against and rebuilding of Iraq has brought the sentimental, self-satisfied sense of Providence back into fashion. One might
have supposed that an attack on our country would have rendered
utopian agendas unnecessary—as it did for most Americans during
World War II. But while a war on terrorism may not need Providence to
justify it, a war to transform the Middle East requires a rhetoric as
grandiose as its aims. The providentialist outlook fills the bill: it pro-
motes tunnel vision, discourages debate and reduces diplomacy to
arm-twisting.

(Lears 2003: A25)

The war on terrorism

The Cold War framed the world into an "us" versus "them" arena. Not only relations with the Soviet Union, but also international affairs in Africa, Asia, and
central America were referenced through the concern that countries in those
regions might be susceptible to communism. The fear of "losing" countries to the
Soviets gave birth to the domino principle and the notion of proxy states—policies that prompted the American engagement with countries such as Vietnam,
Nicaragua, and Ethiopia.

The meaning of the Cold War went well beyond the James Bond stereotyping
of who were the good guys and the bad guys. The Cold War defined who Americans could support and who they could not—anyone who was a friend of the
USSR was no friend of the USA's. The "enemy of my enemy is my friend" logic
made for some very uncomfortable bedfellows, but it helped immensely in clarifying who Americans should care about, in defining who mattered.

Then the rattling of the Iron Curtain in the 1980s, which culminated in the
tumbling of the Berlin Wall in 1989, changed not only the political landscape in
Europe but the perception of global politics. Entire regions fell off the political
and media radar. Nasty conflicts in out of the way places no longer mattered as
proxy wars; brutal struggles for power were dismissed by both politicians and the
press as internecine tribal or ethnic or religious conflicts without external ramifications (Moeller 1999: 287). There were few perceived over-arching reasons as
to why outsiders should care about Sub-Saharan Africa, Southeast Asia, or even
eastern Europe any more. No dominant vision—or even snappy moniker—
appeared to unify what was happening, despite a call by many that
"humanitarianism" compelled engagement. Indeed, there was a general retreat
from international affairs on the part of both the Bush senior and Clinton White
Houses as well as the media.

Then came September 11. "Every nation in every region now has a decision to
make," said President George W. Bush in his speech on September 20. "Either
you are with us or you are with the terrorists" (US Newswire, September 20,
2001). Within just weeks, Bush's new "war on terror" frame became the default
test used to discover who were America's global "friends" and "enemies." The war

on terrorism became the window through which all international events were viewed—a situation that emphasized places and events that had (or were purported to have) connections to "global terrorism," but that left others that didn't neatly fit the terrorism frame out of public view.

Newsrooms scrambled to cover both domestic and foreign terrorist-related events—a scramble made all the more ungainly because all but a few media outlets were woefully understaffed with reporters expert in international affairs, a consequence of the past years' closing of overseas bureaus and cutbacks on time and space devoted to foreign news in order to save money and boost profits. Understaffing—and the prior undervaluing of international coverage—made it more difficult for news organizations to cover the assumptions behind the "war on terror" frame, and parenthetically made it more difficult for them either to nimbly cover the changing terrorism story (from Osama bin Laden and al-Qaeda, to anthrax, to the axis of evil, to Iraq and Saddam Hussein, to WMD, etc.), or to cover foreign stories unrelated to the terrorism arc.

Three months after the attacks on the World Trade Center, on the 60th anniversary of the attack on Pearl Harbor, President Bush defined his conception of terrorism before more than 8,000 sailors and marines and their families assembled on the vast deck of the nuclear-powered aircraft carrier, the USS *Enterprise*. "We're fighting to protect ourselves and our children from violence and fear. We're fighting for the security of our people and the success of liberty," Bush said. "We're fighting against men without conscience but full of ambition to remake the world in their own brutal images" (US Newswire, December 7, 2001).

Bush described these men as "a movement, an ideology that respects no boundary of nationality or decency . . . They celebrate death, making a mission of murder and a sacrament of suicide." And he compared the 9/11 "terrorists" to the enemies of World War II: "They have the same will to power, the same disdain for the individual, the same mad global ambitions. And they will be dealt with in just the same way . . . Like all fascists, the terrorists cannot be appeased; they must be defeated" (US Newswire, December 7, 2001).

Naming not just the 9/11 conspirators, but a much larger conception of "the enemy" as "terrorists" and naming America's cause as a "global war against terrorism"—rather than a more limited effort to eradicate al-Qaeda or to capture Osama bin Laden—was an attempt by President Bush to forestall and even pre-empt media and public criticism of such ancillary agendas as overthrowing Saddam. The Bush administration succeeded at labeling its foreign policy objectives as part of a war against terrorism, thus making it very difficult for political opponents or media commentators to challenge the president without coming off as not only "soft" on defense, but as cavalier about the lost American lives of 9/11.

The Bush administration's tactics that effectively proscribed dissent were familiar ones from the Israeli–Palestinian conflict. The only way to be "for" terrorism is to redefine terrorism as something else, to change not just the language but the focus and context of the debate. In the Israeli–Palestininan skirmishing for the moral high ground there, Israeli officials have long cited Palestinian "terrorism" as their rationale for their policies, which have included helicopter missile attacks against Palestinian buildings, "targeted assassinations," closures of Palestinian towns and villages, and razing of the homes of alleged militants. Hamas and Islamic Jihad spokespeople have claimed that Israeli "state terror" has forced them into such strategies as suicide bombings and other attacks on Israeli soldiers and civilians. Both sides emphasize context. Both sides assert that their actions are retaliatory; that they are not the perpetrators, but instead the victims. Both sides also contest who are the civilians—in other words who are the legitimate targets of attacks: Israel argues that the settlers are civilians, while many Palestinian militants consider the settlers who have built homes on land seized in the 1967 war to be combatants in effect, because they have been the leading edge of the Israeli occupation and have been protected by the Israeli military. *New York Times* reporter Serge Schmemann wrote,

> One side invokes the murder of Israeli innocents by human bombs, the other speaks of the injustices suffered by the Palestinians . . . This mingling of acts of murder with a desire for freedom has enabled the leaders on both sides to befuddle their people and their supporters, portraying suicide bombers as martyrs in a just struggle of national liberation, or casting the destruction of the institutions and symbols of Palestinian statehood as a war on terrorism.
>
> (Schmemann 2002: section 4: 1)

The challenge with such terms as "innocence" and "terrorism" is that their meaning is in the eye of the beholder. President Bush's post-9/11 call for a broader war on terrorism had its contemporary antecedents with similar rationales: in this case Bush characterized those who perished on September 11 as "innocents" and those who killed them as "terrorists." And the media responded as they always have at the start of a national crisis—they rallied in support of the president and appropriated his characterization of the situation. At the end of October 2001, for example, the then-CNN chairman Walter Isaacson wrote a memo to his staff that ordered them to balance the broadcast images of civilian devastation in Afghanistan with reminders of the American lives lost at the World Trade Center and the Pentagon. Isaacson suggested language for his anchors, including: "The Pentagon has repeatedly stressed that it is trying to minimize civilian casualties in Afghanistan, even as the Taliban regime continues to harbor terrorists who are connected to the September 11 attacks that claimed thousands of innocent lives in the US." It "seems perverse," Isaacson said, "to focus too much on the casualties or hardship in Afghanistan" (Kurtz, October 31, 2001: C1).

But like the Israeli and Palestinian labeling, pro-al-Qaeda and pro-Saddam forces familiar to viewers of Al-Jazeera also described as "innocent civilians" those who died in Afghanistan or Iraq as a result of American bombing. Post-September 11, there is a larger recognition that innocence is conferred, rather than inherent, that innocence needs to be asserted; it is not unequivocally self-apparent. During World War II, those who were killed in Nanking or in the Blitz or in the concentration camps were just called "civilians." Their innocence was implicit in their status as civilians. Saying "innocent civilians" would have been redundant. Today the innocence of the victims on each side of the war on terrorism is loudly proclaimed—just as it has been in the Israeli–Palestinian conflict. Affirming one's innocence may confer no protection, but it allows one to lay claim to the moral high ground.

Chosen words

"Terrorist" and "terrorism" have long been charged words because the terms are used as political epithets, but they are rarely defined. There are political sensitivities about the usage of these terms and phrases that the media rarely acknowledge. When Secretary of State Donald Rumsfeld says that North Korea is a "terrorist regime," for example, few journalists define that phrase—or contrast the kind of terrorism attributed to North Korea with the terrorism attributed to al-Qaeda. All terrorism is conflated, a conflation that has helped leave the impression in American minds, for example, that Saddam Hussein was in part responsible for the attacks of 9/11.

Americans want to believe that they hold the moral high ground. And they are abetted in their belief by media that do not always explain that that ground is contested—and that the language used to make the moral case is typically loaded. "After 10 months of strife," reporter Cameron Barr of the *Christian Science Monitor* wrote a month and a half before September 11, "the Israeli–Palestinian conflict is increasingly defined by 'terrorism'—both the act and the epithet" (Barr 2001: 1). But, he continued, "perhaps no word in modern political usage is more controversial than 'terrorism.' The United Nations spent 17 years trying to come up with a universally accepted definition, and failed." Walter Laqueur, in a recent article "Left, right and beyond: the changing face of terror," observed that terror "is not an ideology or a political doctrine, but rather a method—the substate application of violence or the threat of violence to sow panic and bring about political change" (W. Laqueur 1996; Purdum 2002: section 4: 1). In his earlier book *Terrorism*, Laqueur noted that "it is not the magnitude of the terrorist operation that counts, but the publicity." The terrorist is inseparable from his or her beholder. As reporter Melvin Maddocks has said, "A terrorist without an audience is inconceivable" (Maddocks 1980).

"Terrorism is theater," wrote terrorism expert Brian Michael Jenkins.

> All terrorist acts involve violence or the threat of violence. A terrorist act ordinarily would be considered a crime—murder, kidnapping, arson. Most terrorist acts would also violate the rules of war . . . What sets terrorism apart from other violence is this: terrorism consists of acts carried out in a dramatic way to attract publicity and create an atmosphere of alarm that goes far beyond the actual victims. Indeed, the identity of the

victims is often secondary or irrelevant to the terrorists who aim their violence at the people watching.

(www.csmonitor.com)

After September 11, 2001, a number of media outlets took it upon themselves to give their readers and viewers a hasty history course in terrorism. "The word originated during the French Revolution when enemies of the state were guillotined in the Reign of Terror," reporter Jim Auchmutey reminded the readers of the *Atlanta Journal-Constitution*. "'Those hellhounds called terrorists . . . are let loose on the people,' British politician Edmund Burke wrote in one of the earliest usages cited by the Oxford English Dictionary" (Auchmutey 2001: 1D).

Geoff Nunberg, on National Public Radio's interview program "Fresh Air," (Bogaev and Nunberg 2001) traced the changing meaning of the term, noting that in the late nineteenth century some like the Russian revolutionaries who assassinated Tsar Alexander II in 1881 viewed it as "a justified political strategy," and even Jack London believed that terrorism could be a "a powerful weapon in the hands of labor."

> By the mid-twentieth century, terrorism was becoming associated more with movements of national liberation than with radical groups and the word was starting to acquire its universal stigma . . . most of the Third World movements that resorted to political violence in the 1950s and 1960s didn't call themselves terrorists. They preferred terms like freedom fighters or guerrillas or mujahaddin. Terrorism became a condemnation, a word used only by the colonial powers. That's the point when news organizations like Reuters started to become circumspect about using the word to describe groups like the IRA and the African National Congress . . .

By the 1980s, Nunberg noted, terrorism began to be applied more generically "to all manners of political violence," including acts such as the fatwah against Salman Rushdie, which Nunberg observed "was far from an act of indiscriminate violence; more like state-sponsored contract killing." *New York Times* editor A.M. Rosenthal even attacked Christopher Hitchens for "refusing to describe the fatwah against Salman Rushdie as terrorism." "By then," Nunberg commented, "the word 'terrorism' had acquired a kind of talismanic force, as if refusing to describe something as terrorism was the next thing to apologizing for it" (Bogaev and Nunberg 2001).

But these thoughtful attempts to locate the meaning of the word "terrorism" did not typically wrestle with the consequences of the Bush administration's usage of the term "terrorism" and its choice to aggregate its foreign policy decisions under the rubric "war on terrorism." Anne-Marie Slaughter, the dean of the Woodrow Wilson School at Princeton University, and the former J. Sinclair Armstrong Professor of International, Foreign, and Comparative Law at Harvard

Law School, was one of the few to early point out the effect of that choice. "From a legal perspective, the difference between calling what has happened war and calling it terrorism is considerable," she wrote in the *Washington Post* the Sunday after 9/11. "Terrorism is a matter for the courts and prosecutors. War is up to our military forces. But which best describes what we face now?" (Slaughter 2001).

Those rare media institutions which did caution about the usage of the word "terrorism" were pilloried for their lack of patriotism. Media columnist Howard Kurtz reported on a Reuters internal memo written by Stephen Jukes, the wire service's global head of news, after the 9/11 attack. "We all know that one man's terrorist is another man's freedom fighter and that Reuters upholds the principle that we do not use the word terrorist," said Jukes in a conversation with Kurtz. "To be frank, it adds little to call the attack on the World Trade Center a terrorist attack."

"We're trying to treat everyone on a level playing field," Jukes said, "however tragic it's been and however awful and cataclysmic for the American people and people around the world . . . we don't want to jeopardize the safety of our staff. Our people are on the front lines, in Gaza, the West Bank and Afghanistan. The minute we seem to be siding with one side or another, they're in danger." "We're there to tell the story," Jukes told Kurtz. "We're not there to evaluate the moral case." Despite the reasonableness of Jukes' responses, Kurtz chided him for his (and Reuters') "value-neutral approach"—as if fairness and balance were not vaunted journalistic values, especially in the coverage of international issues (Kurtz, September 24, 2001: C1).

Before 9/11, a number of media outlets in addition to Reuters had a policy in place about the use of the words "terrorism" or "terrorist." The Associated Press, according to its spokesman Jack Stokes, uses a variety of terms and does permit the use of the word "terrorist" for those in non-governmental groups who carry out attacks on the civilian population (Gelfand 2002). Other news organizations have shunned the words in reference to the Israeli–Palestinian conflict, aware of the politicization of the words, but have had no compunctions about using the terms in other circumstances. Roger Buoen, the assistant managing editor of the *Minneapolis Star Tribune*, for example, explained in a pre-9/11 statement to his paper's ombudsman that the paper tried to avoid "characterizing the subjects of news articles" in order to let readers make up their own minds on the evidence presented. "In the case of the term 'terrorist,'" he wrote, "other words—'gunman,' 'separatist,' and 'rebel,' for example—may be more precise and less likely to be viewed as judgmental." And Buoen also noted that the paper was especially concerned about perceived bias in its Mid-east coverage: "We also take extra care to avoid the term 'terrorist' in articles about the Israeli–Palestinian conflict because of the emotional and heated nature of that dispute. However, in some circumstances in which nongovernmental groups carry out attacks on civilians, the term is permitted" (Gelfand 2002).

The dilemmas of talking about "terrorism" do not stop with problems of definition. A few news outlets observed problems of labeling as "terrorist" even those groups which the US government has identified as terrorist. As Todd Purdum of *The New York Times* noted, "With rare exceptions, like Iraq, the United States government's official definitions of terrorist entities focus on organizations and individuals, not governments. Israel, as American officials often note, is a democracy accountable to the norms of international law. The practical effect is that only the Palestinians, who lack a state, are generally labeled terrorists" (Purdum 2002).

Officials use language with calculated intent—administrations previous to President Bush also spoke with care. Back in the waning days of the Carter administration, for example, the president indulged in "one of the clarifying acts of foreign-policy-through-semantics," as Maddocks wrote, when he declared that it was "terrorists" rather than the government of Ayatollah Khomeini who were responsible for the hostage-taking (Maddocks 1980: 23). A less successful attempt by a president to justify his actions through considered word choices was President Clinton's attempted side-stepping of the term "genocide" in reference to Rwanda. The State Department was caught out in that case by the media—the advantage for the administration of denying that "genocide" had taken place was too obvious. "How many 'acts of genocide' does it take to make a genocide?" was just one of the questions asked of the State Department spokesperson (Moeller 1999: 290–1).

President George W. Bush has had enormous success in agenda-setting. After September 11, it was a short step for many media to first source the terms of "the war on terror" and "terrorist" to the president and other administration officials, then as the terms slipped into common usage to begin applying the terms to the Bush foreign policy goals without attribution. The US media generally acquiesced with the deliberate terminology chosen by the administration.

By contrast, before, during, and after the Iraq war, British news outlets were more willing to challenge the White House's interpretation of events. In the aftermath of Bush's May 1 speech proclaiming "victory" in Iraq, for example, the *Guardian* pointed out that the Bush administration had used the term "terrorist" as a conscious element in its foreign policy—with groups or countries it wants to condemn, noted the *Guardian*, it applies the term terrorist, with groups it is interested in allying itself to, it ignores a prior label of terrorist. "Growing US pressure on Iran takes many forms, much of it questionable and some of it deeply hypocritical," observed the leader article in the *Guardian* on May 20. "A campaign of public accusation is now in full flood; in the past few days alone, National Security Adviser Condoleezza Rice has reiterated her view that Iran harbours al-Qaeda terrorists, while another official claimed it is stockpiling chemical weapons. Pressure is applied," the article continued, through such means as "US collaboration with the Iraq-based, Iranian opposition Mujahedeen," which also is a way that "the Bush administration seeks to convince the world that Iran, like Saddam's Iraq, constitutes a threat that may one day have to be extinguished by force." The irony of all that, said the *Guardian*, is that "Iran, for example, helped the US pursue al-Qaeda fugitives from Afghanistan; there is no evidence of collusion with al-Qaeda now. But Tehran is justifiably outraged by US sponsor-ship of the Mujahedeen, who Washington itself has long labelled terrorists" (*Guardian* leading article 2003).

Asking the questions

In September 2003, celebrity journalist Tina Brown on her CNBC cable show "Topic A with Tina Brown" asked CNN reporter Christiane Amanpour whether journalists had been limited in what they could cover during the American war in Iraq: "It's not a question of couldn't do it, it's a question of tone," replied Amanpour.

> "It's a question of being rigorous. It's really a question of really asking the questions. All of the entire body politic in my view, whether it's the administration, the intelligence, the journalists, whoever, did not ask enough questions, for instance, about weapons of mass destruction." And then Amanpour added that part of the cause of the journalists' fail-ures and/or reticence was that they had to contend with "disinformation at the highest levels."

> (www.mediaweb.co.za)

A hundred and fifty years ago, in the era when "manifest destiny" was first enun-ciated, there was no precedent of an investigative press that could critically examine the statements and contentions of public officials, that could challenge a foreign policy that seemed to have little basis in fact or that seemed geared only to rally the audience for partisan political ends. Now, in the first decade of the twenty-first century there has been little incentive to do so, despite the rich precedents of journalists challenging the powers-that-be in decades past. In the current profit-driven deadline news business there has been little inclination to examine the operating assumptions of foreign policy when the effects of that policy have been so demanding of coverage. It has made sense that over the last several years, coverage of breaking news—such as the US troop engagement in Iraq—is what blankets the news, while coverage of the motivations behind for-eign policies has been minimal. It has been easier to embed with the troops, and give a-day-in-the-life style coverage, than do enterprise reporting.

As a result, during the Iraq war and the immediate "aftermath," many journal-ists toed the administration's and Pentagon's line in Iraq, foregoing their own investigation of events. *New York Times* Pulitzer Prize winning reporter John Burns noted his disgust over the media coverage of Iraq in an interview included in an edited collection of journalist interviews, *Embedded: the Media at War in Iraq, an Oral History*. "Now left with the residue of all this, I would say there are serious lessons to be learned. Editors of great newspapers and small newspapers and editors of great television networks should exact from their correspondents the obligation of telling the truth about these places," Burns said. "It's not impossible to tell the truth." More information could have been gotten out about the Bush administration's stated rationale for American involvement, and even about the Iraqi regime, he argued (Burns 2003).

Increasingly more journalists and pundits have been speaking out, charging that during the pre-war period and the "hot" conflict in Iraq most of "the media largely toed the Bush administration line in covering the war and, by doing so, failed to aggressively question the motives behind the invasion," as USA Today media critic Peter Johnson wrote (Johnson 2003). "For some reason or another, Mr Bush chose to make his principal case on weapons of mass destruction, which is still an open case," noted New York Times reporter Burns (Burns 2003: 161). But by the end of the Iraq conflict in the late spring of 2003, it was not so much that the media accepted the administration's rationale for its policies—in fact by then many journalists, especially editorial and opinion writers were downright skeptical of the linkages Bush had drawn between other nations' purported WMD and the concomitant terrorist threat to the US, for example. By then, it was not that journalists remained uncritical of the statements emanating from the White House, the Pentagon, and the State Department, as that they still were too accepting of how international issues and events were prioritized.

Too often the recognition that the administration gave to terrorism and purportedly related issues, such as WMD, received comparable recognition from the media—even if journalists criticized the administration's "spin." In effect the media continued to confirm the Bush administration's political and diplomatic agenda-setting. Through overly stenographic reporting on the president, the media amplified the administration's voice—so when Bush said to the country that Americans are vulnerable to WMD in the hands of terrorists, the media effectively magnified those fears, even while they challenged the prior assumption that Iraq had been an "imminent threat." "The nation is being trained to consider terrorism only in its most apocalyptic forms," Mark Leibovich of the Washington Post noted in May 2003. "Many sociologists, scenario planners and counterterrorism experts believe the government and the media are too focused on extreme menaces—namely the terrorist attacks that involve weapons of mass destruction" (Leibovich 2003). Again, it had been President Bush who set the tone for the apocalyptic approach. As his carrier speech on May 1, 2003 detailed:

> The liberation of Iraq is a crucial advance in the campaign against terror. We've removed an ally of al-Qaeda, and cut off a source of terrorist funding. And this much is certain: No terrorist network will gain weapons of mass destruction from the Iraqi regime, because the regime is no more . . .
>
> (United Press International 2003)

Home Security Secretary Tom Ridge underlined that fear when he moved the US terror alert back to Orange later that same month. Ridge noted that while there was no specific threat against the US that had prompted the heightened status, "weapons of mass destruction, including those containing chemical, biological or radiological agents or materials, cannot be discounted," he said (Langley 2003).

Framing the news

During the Cold War, policy makers, NGOs, and the media had prioritized the rights of states—concern over the ability of certain states to trigger Armageddon caused the plight of the individual, however poignant or horrific, to pale in comparison. After the Cold War, and the lessening of the global nuclear threat, they all shifted to emphasize individuals and to highlight minority group identity.

Human rights became a core measure by which the American media evaluated international actors and events in the world community. As Harvard professor Michael Ignatieff has written, "We are scarcely aware of the extent to which our moral imagination has been transformed since 1945 by the growth and practice of moral universalism, expressed above all in a shared human rights culture." The language of human rights became a familiar and essential component of global communications and international diplomacy. It found its way into both the media's assessment of "foreign" affairs and governments' justifications for their actions. It did not become so central a feature of policy that it overrode security interests, but it became impossible, at least for Western powers, to appraise their foreign policy—whether relating to trade issues or military engagement—without considering the human rights repercussions.

For a window of time during the 1990s, the American mainstream media, while often mediocre in their coverage of the world, went beyond merely reacting to foreign policy. The entrée of humanitarianism and human rights allowed the media to pry open the decision-making process and ask tough questions. Investing in human rights coverage permitted the media to do what historian Thomas Laqueur has recommended: expand "the moral imagination that allows us to regard the suffering of distant humans as making the same sort of claim on us as the suffering of proximate ones" (T. Laqueur 2001: 131–5).

The power of the media to highlight human rights abuses and to draw attention to how political was the process of assessing those abuses, brought into prominence the hypocrisy of the Bush senior's administration's decision to head to Somalia rather than to Bosnia, for example, and the Clinton administration's ducking of responsibility for the Rwandan genocide. Human rights came to be understood as a political component of foreign policy, not merely as part of a humanitarian agenda. Despite the rhetoric, it became clear that human rights would be protected only if it served American interests—variously defined—to do so.

Just as the presidents in the 1950s and 1960s were consumed by not "losing" countries to Communism on their watch—a fear that resulted in the escalation of the Vietnam War—in the 1990s, Presidents Bush and Clinton were fearful of American troops losing their lives overseas. As a result the presidents avoided

72

military engagement in situations that threatened to turn into Vietnam-like "quagmires," and were more sympathetic to purely humanitarian relief efforts where victims could be rescued without danger. The US government became conditionally willing to use military action to rescue foreign victims and clothed its limitations as well as its proclivities in the rhetoric of human rights. In truth, the de facto policy of a zero tolerance for American casualties was a better predictor of American engagement than human rights policy, but even so, that compassionate rhetoric handed journalists a platform from which to critique public policy. Since the goals of human rights, humanitarianism, and civil society were stated goals of the administrations, journalists now had an "obligation," not just an "interest" in reporting on how well those ideals were being upheld.

Through the "election" and first months in office of President George W. Bush, that responsibility continued. September 11 brought it to an abrupt end. Overnight President Bush adopted language (and policies) limiting domestic civil liberties and human rights using the justification of his declared "war on terrorism." "Ours is a great land," Bush said in a speech in November 2001, "and we'll always value freedom. We're an open society. But we're at war. The enemy has declared war on us. And we must not let foreign enemies use the forums of liberty to destroy liberty itself" (US Newswire, November 29, 2001). Civil liberties and human rights seemed expendable in the face of "higher" priorities—and the multilateral coalition used to fight the war against the Taliban, which included groups and nations with poor records on human rights, such as the Afghan Northern Alliance and Uzbekistan, further distanced the administration from considering human rights to be at the core of its foreign policy. (Although ironically, as a number of commentators have remarked, the war in Iraq could have—should have—been justified by the Bush administration on human rights grounds alone. "[I] never believed Saddam had any weapons of mass destruction that threatened us," *New York Times* columnist Tom Friedman wrote after the discovery of the multitude of mass graves, "but . . . this war could easily be justified by his mass destruction of his own people") (Friedman 2003: A25).

Without human rights as an inescapable formal foreign policy instrument, the media lost much of their capacity to see into policy and probe for answers. Yet, as philosopher Akeel Bilgrami has noted, not taking a moral stance toward the state, not holding it accountable for more than rational self-interest may encourage the state to be "morally insensitive." "It may be," he suggested, "that if we showed all these moral responses toward them, we would encourage in them a greater sensitivity to moral issues and standards" (Bilgrami 2002). There is practical value in moral accountability.

The responsibility to tell stories is not a light one—it does not begin or end with a facile relating of information. Before 9/11, the American media covered the battles of Mogadishu, Srebrenica, and Kigali, among other places, but also documented the failures of American foreign policy by holding the government and international organizations morally as well as politically accountable for their actions. They did so not by resorting to political persuasion or even by being actively adversarial. They held the political actors liable by being eyewitnesses to events, by communicating bluntly what they saw and heard, by publicly juxtaposing a statement made previously with a comment made later. In those instances, the media not only cultivated a moral imagination in their audience but also understood that they had a responsibility to do so—the human rights of distant strangers were reported on because the well-being of those strangers was understood to be relevant to Americans.

If the media were delegates to the mandarin, representing the concerns of his subjects, what arguments would they have at their disposal to convince him to become engaged by the trials of people he had never seen? They could try to cultivate a moral imagination in him sufficient to acquaint him with others' pain and torments. In his awakened awareness of the vulnerability of his own comfort he could find cause to alleviate the suffering of those others. The virtue in empathy is that it is both a welcome gloss over the cold habit of self-interest as well as a meaningful and practical end in itself.

In the real aftermath of 9/11, challenging the terrorism frame is itself an act of moral imagination. The "if-you're-not-with-us-you're-against-us" attitude of President Bush's war on terrorism is a new variant of "manifest destiny": American "destiny" is "manifest." Or else, just as the "Cold War" label seduced the media and entire nations into believing that it explained everything, even though it omitted much and distorted more, so too the terrorism frame threatens a nuanced understanding of the world. Both dangerous simplifications of the world order were articulated by politicians who then accused those who didn't believe of being unpatriotic—even those who only wanted to challenge the application, not the need for such policies.

The war on terrorism substitutes moral rhetoric for a moral imagination. "History has driven us toward moral enlightenment—and then left the final choice to us," wrote author Robin Wright. "Religious motivation isn't necessary. Simple self-interest will do" (Wright 2003). Enlightened self-interest. Self interest of the kind that would convince a mandarin to care for those "hundred millions of his people."

Notes

1 Of course there also remain campaigns that have retained their moral flavor, even in historical hindsight—such as the American Civil Rights campaign, as articulated by such Christian preachers as the Rev. Martin Luther King, Junior.

2 In a recent book, author Linda Hudson argued that it was not O'Sullivan, but a nineteenth-century political writer named Jane McManus Storm Cazneau who wrote the anonymous "Annexation" article (Hudson 2001).

References

Auchmutey, J. (October 21, 2001) "The power of language," *The Atlanta Journal and Constitution*, p. 1D.

Barr, C.W. (July 31, 2001) "In Mideast, one weapon of choice is a loaded word," *Christian Science Monitor*, p. 1.

Bilgrami, A. (2002) "Accountability: the philosophical background," ICRC's *Forum: War and Accountability*, Geneva, p. 15.

Bogaev, B. and Nunberg, G. (October 5, 2001) "History of the term terrorism," Fresh Air, NPR.

Burns, J. (2003) "The moral compass of Iraq" in Bill Katovksy and Timothy Carlson (eds), *Embedded: the Media at War in Iraq, an Oral History*, Guilford, CT: Lyons Press, pp. 160, 161.

Feynman, R. (1998) *The Meaning of It All: Thoughts of a Citizen-Scientist*, Reading, MA: Perseus Books, pp. 44–6.

Friedman, T. (May 14, 2003) "Two right feet," *The New York Times*, p. A25.

Gelfand, L. (February 3, 2002) "Newspaper careful in use of label 'terrorist,'" *Minneapolis Star Tribune*, p. 27A.

Ginzburg, C. (Autumn 1994) "Killing a chinese mandarin: on the moral implications of distance," *Critical Inquiry*, vol. 21, no. 1, pp. 46–60.

The Guardian leading article (May 20, 2003) "Self-fulfilling prophecy: US threats make matters worse in Iran," *The Guardian*, London, p. 21.

Hudson, L.S. (2001) *Mistress of Manifest Destiny: a Biography of Jane McManus Storm Cazneau, 1807–1878*, Austin: Texas State Historical Association.

Johnson, P. (September 15, 2003) "Amanpour: CNN practiced self-censorship," *USA Today*, p. 4D.

Kurtz, H. (September 24, 2001) "Peter Jennings, in the news for what he didn't say," *The Washington Post*, p. C1.

Kurtz, H. (October 31, 2001) "CNN chief orders 'balance' in war news; reporters are told to remind viewers why US is bombing," *The Washington Post*, p. C01.

Langley, A. (May 20, 2003) "US terror alert raised to second highest level: intelligence assessments indicate al-Qaeda in operational period," State Department.

Laqueur, T. (2001) "The moral imagination and human rights" in Michael Ignatieff, *Human Rights as Politics and Idolatry*, Princeton, NJ: Princeton University Press, pp. 131–5.

Laqueur, W. (September/October 1996) "Postmodern terrorism," *Foreign Affairs*.

Lears, J. (March 11, 2003) "How a war became a crusade," *The New York Times*, p. A25.

Leibovich, M. (May 1, 2003) "Fear factoring: nervous about the terrorist threat, people imagine the worst," *The Washington Post*, p. C1.

Los Angeles Times editorial (March 14, 2003) "The right war in Iraq," *Los Angeles Times*, p. 14.

Maddocks, M. (January 17, 1980) "'Terrorist': a bomb-thrower of a word," *Christian Science Monitor*, p. 23.

Moeller, S. (1999) *Compassion Fatigue: how the Media Sell Disease, Famine, War and Death*, New York: Routledge.

O'Sullivan, J.L. (November 1839) editorial, *United States Magazine and Democratic Review*.

O'Sullivan, J.L. (July/August 1845) "The great nation of futurity," *United States Magazine and Democratic Review*.

Purdum, T. (April 7, 2002) "What do you mean, 'terrorist'?," *The New York Times*, Week in Review Desk, section 4: p. 1.

Schmemann, S. (April 7, 2002) "The world: beyond reason, the method of this madness," *The New York Times*, Week in Review Desk, section 4: p. 1.

Slaughter, A. (September 16, 2001) "A defining moment in the parsing of war," *The Washington Post*, p. B04.

Smith, A. (1976) *Theory of Moral Sentiments* in A.L. Macfie and D.D. Raphael (eds), Oxford: Clarendon Press, vol. 3, no. 3.4, pp. 136–7.

United Press International (May 2, 2003) "Bush speaks to nation aboard warship."

US Newswire (September 16, 2001) "Transcript of President's September 16 remarks upon arrival on South Lawn."

US Newswire (September 20, 2001) "Text of President Bush's September 20 speech as prepared for delivery to Congress."

US Newswire (November 29, 2001) "Transcript of remarks by the President to US Attorneys Conference in Washington."

US Newswire (December 7, 2001) "Transcript of remarks by President Bush on *USS Enterprise*."

Wright, R. (September 11, 2003) "Two years late, a thousand years ago," *The New York Times*, p. A25.

www.csmonitor.com/specials/terrorism/lite/expert.html

www.mediaweb.co.za/ArticleDetail.asp?ID=2572

4

THE PR OF TERROR

How new-style wars give voice to terrorists

Tamar Liebes and Zohar Kampf

Media coverage of terror has slid in and out of the coverage of war, largely because recent wars have been preceded and followed by episodes of terror. A loosely linked chain was created in the wake of September 11, whereby al-Qaeda's attack led the US to declare war against the regime in Afghanistan, and then against Iraq, motivated, in part, by the allegation that Saddam Hussein had supported the September 11 terrorists. Similarly, the outbreak of Palestinian violence in 2000 and the bloodshed which followed, led to the so-called "a-symmetrical" or "low-intensity" war which the Israeli army had declared against the terrorists. In all three wars, the lines between terrorists and "harborers" were blurred, with the two becoming interconnected symbols in an "axis of evil."

The logic of fighting evil regimes with the aim of abolishing terror is fraught with internal contradictions not only for politicians and generals, but also for journalists. Consider how the inability of winning against terror in Afghanistan and Iraq altered the framing of war itself. Starting as an almost naïve proclamation of the triumph of good against evil, the aftermath has altered the story and the ways in which it is covered. Terror, seeping in, stained the victory with daily doses of bloodletting, re-framing reality as an explosive, here-to-stay routine. The high-spirited coverage of war, now seen as unfinished, has transformed into the nagging coverage of the confused, chaotic, violent routine of the aftermath of war.

The process reminds us once again that distinct, relatively short, media events—such as operation "shock and awe," and, *mutatis mutandis*, the Twin Tower attack—invite journalists to mobilize and join in the crisis, or the high-powered action, as players rather than spectators—embedded with the army in Iraq, and connecting with the traumatized public after September 11. But once the glamour of the event fades, its overriding power exhausted, the media are left to themselves to search for and compete over the best follow-up stories.

We argue that the unfinished story of September 11, reinforced by the inconclusive aftermath in Afghanistan and Iraq, has sent media off on their own search for terrorists. Uncontrolled and undefeated, they remain the mysterious, evasive power, which may raise its head at any time, anywhere around the globe, remaining a constant threat. This multi-branched story, with its significant serial character, plays on the public's deep seated anxiety, on the prurient desire to get acquainted with these behind-the-scene heroes, but no less on the ambition of journalists and their sense of adventure. While terrorists have to hide from the military forces pursuing them, interaction with the media is of mutual interest, resulting in various versions of hide-and-seek. Thus, in parallel to the (widely criticized) patriotism that characterized US media coverage of the wars in Afghanistan and in Iraq, the same media have developed new genres of covering terrorists, quite apart from the coverage of terror attacks, which may even be characterized as "unpatriotic."

This chapter argues that September 11 changed the image of terror and the journalistic approach to terror. Thus, following September 11, which effectively demonstrated the power of new-style international anarchic terror, terrorists have come to be labeled enemies, rather than criminals. And, if until September 11 terrorists could capture media attention only via violent action, following it the terrorists have been given voice. We argue that there has been a gradual shift whereby terrorists have become regular, sought after sources, achieving a status in which they speak for themselves, are listened to, explain their motives, and, to some extent, set the news agenda. Rather than a bloody blot on the front page representing the merciless suffering inflicted on innocent victims, they now make statements, give interviews, and negotiate with governments, while opinion editorial writers and commentators, following their trail, speculate about their plans, their ideologies, and their psychological makeup.

In what follows we analyze this change, bring evidence to substantiate it, propose possible causes, and discuss some of the ethical issues it raises. First we point to the processes that changed the character of both terrorist and media organizations during the 1990s, and the ensuing new genres of reporting terror. Live disaster marathons signal the beginning of journalists relinquishing control to terrorists, followed by the media's regular pursuit of terrorists as legitimate news personas, disconnected from specific violent acts. We bring initial evidence for this transformation from television news channels and from the inside pages of the printed press. Second, we offer four possible reasons for the upgrading of terrorists to the cultural status of celebrities. Third, we define and illustrate new-style genres of covering terror. These quasi-news soft formats include unmediated showing of "home movies," interviewing by proxy stories of search and find missions, centering on the journalists heroic endeavors; and psychological profiles of (live or dead) terrorists, provided by families, friends, and colleagues. In both the coverage of war, and in the new formats of covering terror, journalists end up compromising professional norms, as access is controlled by the sources (the army/ the terrorists).

The media in pursuit of terrorists

Whether terror is directed to achieve political aims, to create public pressure on decision-makers for negotiating an ad hoc case, or to spread diffuse shock and fear, it relies on the media for realizing its aims. Until recently, most media researchers agreed on the way in which news media cover demonstrators, rioters, and protest movements, and, all the more so, terrorists. They argued that whereas politicians and representatives of the elite are free to address the media at any time (crossing the threshold through the "front door"), the only chance of radical groups to invade the screens is via the "back door," that is, by the use of violence (Gitlin 1980; Wolfsfeld 1991). Hence, a trap emerged in which groups such as the anti-Vietnam movement in the US, Aldo Moro's kidnappers in Italy, and the Palestinians during the 1980s found themselves. The more violence they created, the greater the chance of crossing into the screens and being viewed by the public. The chance, however, was also greater for the coverage to be more nega-tive, and therefore act as a boomerang.

Two processes during the 1990s radically changed the character of both terror itself and the way in which it was covered. Until that time, terrorist groups such as the IRA, the Red Brigade or the PLO, even if they had international connec-tions, were perceived as an internal national phenomenon, handled in the domestic field. Governments treated terrorists by controlling their appearance— more precisely, their non-appearance[1]—on local media. This was done by legislation, by putting pressure on national media, or by negotiating and reaching an understanding with media institutions over limiting exposure to terrorists. Media institutions followed suit, adopting internal directives for limiting cover-age (Weimann 1999).[2] The situation in which both terror and media were operating within the nation's boundaries made it possible for governments to limit the terrorists' capacity to exploit the media for creating public anxiety, enhancing their bargaining power while holding hostages, or communicating with their own supporters.

This contained situation changed when connections among terrorist organiza-tions in various countries tightened, making terror into an international network. At the same time, revolutionary communication technologies created a new media ecology, transforming the journalistic profession and its locus. Thus, the (insufferable) ease of transmitting live from various sites disintermediated editors by interrupting news editions with "breaking news." The realization of the public's right to know by the accepted journalistic practices suffered another blow by the establishment of new competing media channels, broadcasting around the clock and viewed beyond the state's borders, with each quoting everyone else, and with every channel doing its best to keep zapping viewers from escaping. A significant example is the taking root of the marathonic live format throughout and following terrorist attacks, which in effect cancelled the editor's role, and, with it, the striving for fair, precise, and responsible news, and the obligation for not publishing, knowingly or carelessly, untrue or inexact information. The genre of disaster marathons caused public criticism of journalists for playing into terror-ists' hands, that is, for inadvertently doing them a service (Liebes 1998).[3]

Whereas live marathonic broadcasts make for controversial journalism, their format does not deviate from the principle of covering terror only when it acts.

The significant upgrading of terrorists' status in the media, apparent following September 11, should be seen as the result of the acknowledgment of terrorists as another regular beat on the editorial map. This legitimacy means that they are regularly monitored, that their reactions to relevant events are sought out, that their threats are given central space, and that journalists take risks to reach their hiding places for an "inside" look and an exclusive scoop. Terrorists in Afghanistan, Baghdad, and Gaza have no more need to act in order to appear (or, rather, to exist)—they have been acknowledged as an institutional news source. The meaning of this change (to which we were introduced as television viewers and newspaper readers) is that terrorists, who had been perceived as despicable criminals, with no legitimacy for appearing as news persona, have turned into a new sector of celebrities in popular culture. As we demonstrate in what follows, journalists seek out terrorists to discover their face "behind the news," in an attempt to understand their motives, environment, and vision, and to present them to press and television audiences in the West.

Such a change can be expected to be found in the "soft" genres of news, such as in-depth interviews, human stories, and profiles of celebrities. Thus, we looked at two kinds of journalistic genres in the printed and electronic press. In the press we chose the *New York Times* weekly magazine as a suitable host for clusters of intimate stories, exposing the profiles of news personas. On television we observed the appearances of superstar Osama bin Laden on interviews and on "home-movies".

By locating items on the basis of a key word search, we found all the appearances of the words "terror/terrorist" in the *New York Times Magazine* between the years 1996 and 2003.[4] Choosing September 11 as the watershed (keeping in mind, however, that the process had started earlier and speeded up significantly from this point on), we assumed that before this date soft items featuring terror would focus on the personal stories of the victims, not of the perpetrators. Following September 11, we expected that personal stories featuring terrorists would be added, and that these stories would be disconnected in time (and place) from the terrorist events.[5]

Our findings confirmed our expectations. In the six years prior to September 11, "terror" stories in the *New York Times* supplement focused only on the victims and their suffering, with no attempt to look at terror through the eyes of the terrorists themselves.[6] In the 15 months following September 11 we found six human interest stories, such as interviewing groups, elaborating motives, or interviewing relatives, all of which focused on the profiles of terrorists.

The results of our examination of bin Laden's appearances on television show that in the five years prior to September 11, he was interviewed three times (on Al-Jazeera, CNN, and ABC). From September 11, 2001 to the end of 2002, he scored 15 appearances. As interviewing the world's most wanted person was close to impossible, 14 of these interviews were in the form of unmediated "home movies" (the equivalent of free advertising). As we elaborate in what follows, it is ironic that America's number one enemy, a sought after criminal, who was responsible for the most destructive (physically and symbolically) terrorist attack directed at the US, became a superstar for whom major ethical principles of journalism were being compromised.

Possible reasons for the upgrading of terrorists to superstars

The automatic, universal adoption of the genre of breaking news—that is, live marathonic broadcasting during, and in the wake of, a multi-victim attack—facilitates the upgrading of terrorists to superstars. This format is shaped by technological developments that allow for the simultaneous live transmission from multiple loci, in effect getting rid of the function of editing and thereby abandoning the broadcast to the terrorists. Exactly at a moment of crisis in which the government is weakened, and a space opens for media to take the lead, television, taken by complete surprise, has no tools with which to make use of this opportunity. In a media ecology that dictates broadcasting live, leaving no time for acting professionally, the switch from "chronology" to "history" (Carey 2002) may cause journalists to lose their privileged status. On September 11, instead of taking the lead, anchors and reporters gave up on their distanced position and joined the public to watch the performance with bewilderment and amazement. Thus, the various channels ended up competing with one another over promoting the terrorists' message (Blondheim and Liebes 2002). Bin Laden's attack, constructed as an unfinished story, in which the crucial question of "who has done it" was left open, meant that days later the media were engaged in the mystery of finding out more about the event's heroes, wondering who bin Laden was and where he could be found. The process of media's crowning bin Laden as mega-star was boosted by the US government. The world's only superpower declared war against the man.[7]

Second, the ecological change in the environment of media, with news channels such as CNN and Sky broadcasting to different target audiences the world over, pushes for less identification and a more independent position toward the channel's home country. Moreover, the existence of satellite channels, broadcasting from and to Arab states, and considered "democratic," allow CNN-like news channels more flexibility in giving voice to terrorists. "Quoting" from channels such as Al-Arabia, Abu Dhabi or Al-Jazeera, whose more empathetic stance toward terrorism offers an address for terrorists to send tapes and grant interviews,[8] softens the criticism against the Western channels as giving legitimacy to terrorists. Moreover, in parallel to the internationalization of news channels, the international connections among terror organizations have tightened, increasing the universal relevance of stories about terrorist attacks and their protagonists. When a terrorist attack occurs elsewhere it is less problematic to relate to terrorists as protagonists and, at the same time, interest in terror stories, terrorist tactics, intentions, and personalities, is ensured.

Third, there is the change in the intellectual atmosphere in the postmodern era, which (in spite of the overriding importance of competition over audiences) can also justify the change in journalistic practices (Ezrachi 2002). The new historiography heralds the end of the grand narratives of the postcolonial era, narratives well known for their being a "white mythology," aimed at repressing various others. Its demise points to a need to offer alternative grand narratives to the repressed (Weinrib 2003). The first step is raising the heretofore depressed awareness of those whose voice is not heard. In this spirit, media scholars such as Nick Couldry (2001) see in the World Trade Center attack a statement of the repressed, those pushed to the margins by the institutions of media, and left in a state of symbolic inferiority. According to this perception it is possible to prevent future attacks by listening to the voice of the repressed, and thus contributing to the creation of more equality between the worlds. Based on the notion that a genuine act of communication emerges out of interruption rather than out of harmony, thinkers such as Levinas, Derrida, and Lyotard insist on the importance of communicating with alterity rather than with sameness (Pinchevski 2003). By talking to people who are like oneself only reinforces one's own perceptions by their reactions. Levinas argues that attention has to shift from the content of conversation to the communication act or, in other words, from what was said to the fact of saying. The spirit of these perceptions softens the traditional view, according to which journalists should be careful not to appear to be conducting negotiations with terrorists, or, worse, giving them a platform for propaganda.

Last, the increasing personalization of politics (of which the media are a main culprit) and, with it, the incessant search for new superstars (Kellner 2003), creates the right atmosphere for the protagonists of terror to become international celebrities. Status conferral, as Lazarsfeld and Merton were aware of, is indifferent to whether whoever appears is an honorable hero or a lowly villain. Villains, notably gangsters, are well known heroes (albeit tragic) in the heart of American popular culture (Warshow 1979). Moreover, in the era of multiculturalism, the judgment of celebrity as villain or hero itself increasingly lies in the eye of the beholder (as seen in the split reactions of the American public in the Clarence Thomas affair, or in the O.J. Simpson trial). And regardless of what the judgment is, curiosity only speeds up when a celebrity is discovered as a villain at heart.

Ways of abandoning journalistic norms in the media coverage of terrorists

A look at the various tactics and formats of covering terrorists reveals different types of deviations from heretofore accepted journalistic practices. As mentioned above, one blatant practice, endorsed by news directors, is the *unmediated showing of mysteriously arrived terrorists' tapes*. The reality in which any pictures of mega terrorists are regarded as major "scoops" allows for scrapping the most elementary criteria demanded for other news items: when/where/by whom was the tape recorded? is this the person we claim it is? is he still alive? This handing over of full control to terrorist sources, and (totally or partially) relinquishing the journalists' professional role, amounts to providing unpaid advertising to terrorists, a service that would never be given to domestic political leaders.

Terrorist-made videotape vignettes often belong to the genre of "home movies," possibly aimed as teasers to chasers, a "proof" that the terrorists are alive and doing well. The latest video to date, as *Washington Post* writer Philip Kennicot told us (September 11, 2003), "arrived right on schedule . . . to mark the second anniversary of September 11" and features "a pastoral walk in the woods, a dreamscape . . . by the perverse logic of dreams, all the more threatening." Another sub-genre of self-produced terrorist tapes consists of a formal public address, in which terrorists directly appeal to "fan" and/or "enemy" audiences, encouraging the first and threatening the latter (as in bin Laden's tapes congratulating terrorists in Iraq, warning the US troops, or in the suicide bombers' announcements of personal wills).[9]

In the format labeled "quasi interview," journalistic control is compromised by delegating the job not quite to the terrorists themselves but to proxies (trusted by terrorists) who have access, as in the case of CNN's collaboration with Al-Jazeera, elaborated on below.

However, when journalists do venture into enemy territory, in an attempt to create direct contact with subjects in their hiding places, they risk compromising professional principles in different ways. One danger is that the risky, adventurous route of "getting there," managed by the terrorists, ends up filling the whole frame. Accepting the terrorists' offer, and thereby abiding by their rules, makes the journalist dependent and somewhat vulnerable along the way, and the relationship that develops between him and his sources becomes the real story. The game of treasure hunt takes over and overshadows whatever story the journalist was out to get. The reporter becomes the hero of the story, but so do his hosts, who, instead of repeating their hate mantras, reveal themselves as considerate, generous, and human. Even if journalists do attempt to carry out their journalistic work, the shift in the balance of power once they get there, and their precarious, somewhat threatened and semi-hostage position makes them feel grateful to their hosts and does not encourage adversarial positions.

In addition to the repeated airing of terrorist home videos, the intervewing by proxy, and the journalist's "being there," other genres increasingly found on the weekend magazines (and their television equivalents) are "soft" stories, of the kind that can be shown at any time. These items present a range of *personalizing*, *humanizing*, and *biographical stories*, sociologically or psychologically oriented. The product of making contact with would-be or imprisoned terrorists, or with families, childhood friends, foes, teachers, and colleagues of terrorists, laced these stories with information received from sociologists, psychologists, and criminologists. Zooming in on the profile of terrorists who have died, or vanished, or both, they invade one life speculating about how did he transform into a terrorist, what was it that caused him to abandon everything, who was he influenced by, and what could have saved him. Personalization thus skirts around the political issues of terrorist actions and ideologies, choosing the easy, popular way of exposing the tragedy of one man, one family or one football team in stories disconnected from the acts of destruction and their ramifications.

Interviewing by proxy

Among the forms of the coverage of terrorists discussed, interviews, even if second hand, still present an attempt to carry out journalistic work, however constrained. Before examining the question of interviewing by proxy, the fundamental issue of whether terrorists should be given voice at all needs to be confronted. Whereas a case can be made for distinguishing between terrorists acting for the legitimate cause of fighting occupation, it is difficult to justify interviews with a hiding terrorist, promoting acts of mass destruction, based on the belief that there is no possibility of compromise between Islam and the infidels (the Americans, capitalism, Western culture).[10] Whereas news reports on terrorists within the mandate of surveillance (on clues to the identity of perpetrators, on progress of the chase, etc), devoting television prime time to the pre-advertised exclusive scoop of listening to bin Laden, means that *the system to whose eradication he dedicates his life is giving him the stage* (Blondheim and Liebes 2002). Arguments such as "know your enemy" or the need to "release pressure" in order to avoid an explosion, relevant to local conflicts with limited goals (the Palestinians in Israel, the IRA in Britain), do not hold in the case of diffuse and total terror (Blum-Kulka, *et al.* 2003). Second, even if the White House claim that bin Laden makes use of being interviewed for transmitting operational orders is not particularly convincing, there is nothing like appearing on American networks for *strengthening his power among his supporters*. And third, for CNN's original target audience, the fact of incorporating bin Laden in familiar formats (with its careful distribution among "different voices") means more than the unmediated broadcast of his repetitive mutterings to his cohorts in a foreign language, and it may even *create an illusion of lessening the threat*, while contributing to its increase. And last, taking into account his consistent effort never to incriminate himself directly or be discovered, and his use of Western channels to strengthen himself *vis à vis* his supporters, there is *no hope that bin Laden (or his cohorts) would cooperate* in the way in which other interviewees are expected to do.

But even if the principle according to which the interviewing of terrorists is a legitimate journalistic mission is accepted, the professional compromises that media are pushed to make exactly in such ethically borderline cases are questionable. Note that the more dangerous the terrorist, the more painful the concessions.

As stated above, Osama bin Laden's appearance on CNN on February 1, 2002 in what the network called "an interview" is a good example of demonstrating the risk to journalistic ethics in interviewing by surrogate. The show features segments of an interview granted to Tayseer Alouni, an Al-Jazeera reporter, three months earlier, to which CNN was allowed to add written "omnibus"-style questions. That CNN's bosses were aware of the problematics of interviewing by proxy can be seen by their avoidance of the issue in their (misleading) introduction to the program: "Accused terrorist mastermind Osama bin Laden said 'the battle has moved to inside America' *in the only television interview he's granted since the September 11 attacks—now airing for the first time."*

Missing in this framing is the fact that the "scoop" was by then old news (also reported by *The New York Times* in December 2001), and that Wolf Blitzer (or any other CNN reporter) was not holding the microphone.

The professional issues demonstrated by this case study allow for the reexamination of the definitions of terms such as "scoop," "news value," and "news interviews." Specifically, the dubiousness of the interview under scrutiny can be put in the form of a number of ethical issues:

First, as the *Los Angeles Times* pointed out (October 18, 2001), the interview was planned "even as (CNN) executives added that they don't know whether he is dead or alive," that is, they were giving up on the fundamental practice of being able to grant their audiences the basic knowledge of whether or not the interviewee is the person CNN claims he is. The question—is this the real bin Laden?—takes on particular relevance after the known practice of the appearance (mostly on audio tapes) of "doubles" of Saddam Hussein and Mullah Omar, following the Iraq war. As no Western journalists could ever meet with bin Laden following September 11 (and as very few saw him before), there would always be a doubt as to the authenticity of tapes emerging from somewhere.

Reactions of the competing news channels to the interview expressed mixed feelings of "criticism, curiosity and envy," making it quite clear that given the opportunity they would do the same. Expressing the belief that at war journalists should be patriotic (a belief reaffirmed by US journalists during the Iraq war), and voicing a softer version of Condoleezza Rice's concern with the channel's handing airtime to bin Laden for communicating with his own supporters, CBS News President Andrew Heyward stated that "CNN should not be seen bargaining with terrorists" or "as providing a platform for propaganda." In a similar spirit, the interview was called "a slap in the face of the American people" and was compared to "interviewing Adolf Hitler or Emperor Hirohito, who ordered the attack on Pearl Harbor."[11]

Further, competing news channels criticized the interview's newsworthiness, illustrating the confusion around this term (ironically the first critic was Al-Jazeera's Director General, who decided not to air the interview for reasons of lacking "newsworthiness"). Strictly, the criterion for judging an interview as "newsworthy" consists of whether any new, significant information was gained by talking to the interviewee. CNN's own definition for the journalistic scoop they were offering viewers can be found in Blitzer's opening promo: "Late October, in the only television interview with Osama bin Laden since the September 11 attacks, broadcast here for the first time, *he makes clear that the war of terror is not finished.*" As what is highlighted as the new information in the quote could not be of great surprise for CNN audiences, the interview's news value must lie in the first part of Blitzer's introduction. These words hold the promise of seeing bin Laden for the first time since the September 11 attack. The offer to look at bin Laden's face connects directly with the viewers' awed curiosity about the hidden protagonist of the September 11 trauma, a collective nightmare which had remained an unfinished narrative, with only occasional glimpses at the putative villain, who, regardless of the price on his head, remained free, unreachable, and enigmatic. This need to see bin Laden is what Peter Bergen, a CNN terror analyst, means when he states: "Frankly, if he was reading out of the telephone book it would be newsworthy." If he is right, this may be an example of the trade off between the status attributed to the interviewee and the amount of new information gained. The more status, the less crucial the new information.

That the interview stands for the kind of journalism in which it is the "authentic" encounter with the persona that counts, not the words, is confirmed by CNN's method of interviewing. Carried out by giving a list of written questions to Al-Jazeera's Tayseer Alouni, it was rightly criticized as unprofessional. Giving up on the direct questioning, CNN's competitors argued, means losing the possibility of surprising the interviewee, and/or challenging him.[12] Moreover, by losing the most essential journalistic instrument they also gave up on the hope that he could be led to answering the questions considered crucial for the American public. In other words, they did not even have the opportunity to be seen as carrying out negotiations with the terrorists. Yet, when it concerns "the most wanted man in the world" and "if it's this or nothing" (Andrew Heyward, CBS news president, *Los Angeles Times*, October 18, 2001), CBS as well as MSNBC were also ready to make an exception.

This brings us back to the point that for the US audiences, the message obviously lies in the pictures, not in Blitzer's translated choice of quotes. Nobody would expect bin Laden to admit to being in charge of the September 11 attacks (after all, there is a price on his head). And, unsurprisingly, he does make sure to restrict his own role in the attack to that of a supporter and believer, appointing God (whom he mentions no less than 36 times) as the active leader of the attack.

Last, there is the problem of the proxy's identity, which public criticism of CNN has failed to question. Not surprisingly, Alouni, working for a channel known all along as empathetic to bin Laden ("Al-Jazeera is not bin Laden's formally, but he clearly is its star," says Fouad Ajami, *New York Times Magazine*, November 11, 2001), was chosen for being trusted by bin Laden. His arrest in September 2003 as an al-Qaeda supporter indicates that the doubts about his acting as a CNN messenger may have been justified, and that Blitzer's complements for his creating "good professional rapport" with bin Laden were at most only half true (that is, the rapport was good, but not quite professional).[13]

Other formats presenting the terrorist persona on global news media raise similar ethical issues to the ones highlighted by the CNN–Alouni interview, giving them more weight. Stories in which personal biographies are drawn, motives sought out, and experts on the human psyche and on environmental circumstances consulted, all contribute to the process of personalizing terrorists and the upgrading of their status, turning them into a new class of celebrities fraught with internal contradictions. Threatening, mysterious, and enigmatic yet sometimes all too human, struck by fate, and deeply committed to the cause, they have become the best show in town. This means that journalists are prepared to take personal risks to seek them out and talk to them in person.

"Getting to know you": the new genres of covering terror

In a world turning into a frontier, in which people lose their sense of personal security, with personalized politics in which the strongest man in the world is chasing villains in the old Western style, the media also join the chase. Both the security forces and the journalists pursue terrorists to the end of the world. The military are looking for their heads; the media want to hear what they have to say.

Whereas, as we have shown, the handing over of the interviewing of terrorists to mediators raises serious professional problems, embarking on the risky road of making direct contact with terrorists (or their sympathizers) tends to compromise professional practices in a different way. In the pursuit of terrorists, journalists sometimes become occupied with the journey of getting there and with their own heroic endeavors along the way. Having gotten there, as the balance of power shifts—with journalists finding themselves as quasi-hostages and terrorists playing hosts—control slips again, and the journalists risk being compromised by their subjects, or, worse, falling in love with them.[14]

The case of ABC's John Miller's interview with bin Laden (May 1998) shows how the story of "getting there" can make the journalist into a hero, and, more important, how it seems to influences the tone and content of the interview. Highlighting the story of how "Miller and his crew were led by armed Islamic militants by foot through the mountains of southern Afghanistan to meet bin Laden at a secret hideaway," the questions he ends up posing allow his interlocutor to present himself in a favorable light. Rather than directly challenge his interviewee, Miller attributes the questions about bin Laden's terrorist activities to the American authorities, thereby distancing himself from the accusations, and making them sound more tentative.[15] This can also be seen in his use of subjective, "soft," verbs for describing the degree of conviction held by the authorities—they "believe," they "paint him as a terrorist leader," "investigat(ing) a suspicion . . . " Whereas in the case of ordinary news interviews (Clayman 1992) such mitigating techniques could be deployed for creating a neutral/objective, appearance, in the setting of bin Laden's interview, conducted as it were in his hideaway, surrounded by militants with drawn guns, it is more feasible to see them as used for ensuring the journalist's survival behind enemy lines.

The first question posed by Miller (as quoted by the ABC network Internet site), focusing on bin Laden's heroic past, is most flattering: "Mr bin Laden, to Americans you are an interesting figure: A man who comes from a background of wealth and comforts who ends up fighting on the front lines. Many Americans think that's unusual."

In case the point about bin Laden's sacrificing his comfortable life for a cause was missed, Miller goes even further, comparing bin Laden to a no lesser character than US president Teddy Roosevelt, ending with "you are like the Middle East version of Teddy Roosevelt." Interviewing by proxy could not be more flattering than the way in which ABC's correspondent carries out his job. Whether overawed by his getting an interview, or by the need to get back, Miller does not exactly give a hard time to his interviewee. Much less flattering were bin Laden's cohorts granting interviews to journalists for settling internal accounts. Thus, Jaffar Omar Talib, we are told [*New York Times*, March 10, 2002], "dismisses bin Laden as lightweight," and an interview with Abu Abbass, Achille Lauro's kidnapper, starts with: "To hear Abu Abbass tell it, terrorists like Osama bin Laden give terrorists like him a bad name."

(*Newsweek*, November 4, 2002)

A recent example of a feature story, in which talking to terrorists is framed by the writer as a journalistic feat, and which tends to romanticize its subjects, is Scott Johnson's *Newsweek* cover story (October 10, 2003), featuring a terrorist group called "the Army of Muhammad." Johnson turned out to be particularly lucky as his interview was carried out a few days prior to the group's blowing up the UN headquarters in Baghdad. Trying out names—"guerrillas" on the cover, "resistance fighters" in the story's headlines—Johnson's photograph features three men, waving their "AK-47s," their eyes peeping out of cracks in the *kaffiyehs* hiding their faces. The cover announcing an "Exclusive: *inside* Iraq's resistance," and underneath: "A *behind–the-lines-look*." The headlines in the inside pages make sure we would not miss the point by repeating the scoop: "*Inside* an enemy cell."[16]

Johnson became the real hero of his story only a few days later, when "his" terrorists made the headlines. Similarly, Suleiman A-shafi, Israel's Channel II journalist, and a Palestinian himself, interviewed Hammas leader Ismail Abu Shnev, in an item which opened the evening news show on the next day, following Shnev's killing that morning. And Daniel Pearl became a tragic hero as he was killed by his interviewee in the meeting they had arranged.

Significant as it may be, undertaking the risky route for meeting with a star terrorist is relatively rare. The more common type of coverage, less taxing for reporters, aims at getting the public acquainted with "ordinary" terrorists. The bulk of the *New York Times Magazine* corpus we examined consists of reports focusing on the story of one terrorist, a human being like us, who, because of an unhappy psychological disposition, or a difficult childhood, or pure bad luck, was caught up in a tragic situation. Some of these stories reconstruct the terrorists' profiles after their death, while others investigate the lives of terrorists in hiding or in prison.

In the following example, a feature shown on *60 Minutes* (CBS, May 28, 2003) tells the story of a suicide bomber. Framing the event as a melodrama for which only fate is to blame, it illustrates the problematics of this increasingly popular genre of journalism. Bob Simon, out to investigate the phenomenon of women suicide bombers in Palestinian society, stumbles on a perfect case in point. It is an attack on a supermarket in Jerusalem in which two girls died. One, an 18-year-old Palestinian, and the suicide bomber; the other, a 17-year-old Israeli, and the victim. The Palestinian, we are told by Simon, was a good-looking, successful pupil, engaged to be married—"no different from the neighbor's daughter"—who became a terrorist, surrendering to forces larger than herself. The victim, on the other side, sent by her mother to buy food before the Sabbath, entered the neighborhood supermarket when chance caught up with her. The story reverberates with familiar echoes of "if only . . .," "she was not supposed to go by this bus," "she happened to be late that morning," spoken by broken-hearted mothers, the day after. The parallel narratives proceed by interviewing family members (the bomber's father, the victim's mother), highlighting the photographs of the two beautiful girls, which fate so tragically brought together.

The problems with this emotionally moving narrative lie exactly in the powerful neat symmetrical structure, which has given up on distinguishing between perpetrator and target and represents the two girls as arbitrary victims of fate. Typical to this kind of story, the journalists' search for a motive focuses on the personal lives of the would be terrorists. Repeatedly, the reason for becoming a terrorist lies somewhere in the person's psychological make-up, and/or in a constitutive event in his or her biography. Thus, responsibility is shifted from the perpetrator to either internal or external reasons over which he or she has no control. This psychologized approach fits the character of personalized human stories. It also prevents a structural analysis.

The closest this genre gets to discussing social and political factors is when a psychologist invited to interpret the motivation of the story's protagonist touches on the larger context by mentioning environmental influences. This skirting on the political, without straying too far from the personal, can be demonstrated by another 60 Minutes report (May 5, 2003). This time Bob Simon attempts to construct a profile of a suicide bomber with the assistance of a Palestinian psychiatrist and an Israeli psychologist, two experts on the human psyche. Even when the report is defined in terms of exploring an issue, not in the more usual terms of telling the story of one person, the experts chosen are specialists concerned with the workings of the (individual) mind, thus framing the issue as psychological (or psychoanalytic). Nevertheless, in offering two alternative explanations, the Palestinian psychiatrist, in what may be seen as a deviation from his field of expertise, does introduce the idea of a change in the social environment in which teenage Palestinians grow up. Proposing a strictly psychological explanation, Dr Eyad Sarraj characterizes the personality of a would-be terrorist: "They are usually very timid people, introvert, their problem was always communication in public, or communicating their feelings." However, in his alternative explanation, Sarraj shifts the emphasis from the individual psyche to external social pressures. Describing a process of changing fashions in Palestinian society, in which teenage role models have undergone a dramatic change, he compares the time of his own growing up with the present, touching on the political: "In all my teenage time my symbols were body-building and movie stars, and singers, and people like that. Then it changes . . . the guerrilla, the fighter; then it was the stone thrower, and today it is the martyr."

A slightly different variation of journalistic missions aimed at uncovering the roots of the phenomenon takes reporters into the field in an attempt to investigate the home roots of celebrity terrorists (now dead, in hiding, or in prison) by visiting their "natural" environment, and meeting the families in which they grew up. One such story is based on interviews with family members of Zacarias Moussaoui, al-Qaeda topnotch, now in prison (*The New York Times*, February 9, 2003). Under the title (reminding us that) "Everybody has a mother," Moussaoui's brother offers the familiar psychological interpretation to the "causes of (his brother's) anger." He also happens to be promoting a book he is finishing on the subject. The abundance of profile stories of Muhammad Atta offered by the press, disclose dubious scoops such as an interview with his father entitled "he never had a kite" (*Newsweek*, September 25, 2001), psychological descriptions of the "double life of a suicide pilot" as "the shy, caring, deadly fanatic" (*Guardian*, September 23, 2001), and the familiar motive of "the seeds of rage," suggesting an ideological explanation.[17]

The symmetry between villain and victim, the strong element of arbitrary fate, and the shifting responsibility to external sources, on the one hand, and the project of getting acquainted with the terrorist's personal biography, on the other, all contribute to creating empathy between the reader/viewer and the story's protagonist. The focus on psychological and environmental interpretations effectively cut off the perpetrator from his or her action and, worse, from the suffering caused. Moreover, these profile stories, usually reserved for the stars of popular culture, gradually upgrade terrorists to a new status in the exhibitionist culture of spectacle (Kellner 2003). The paparazzi-style pursuit of terrorists may be seen in the attempts to interview anyone who knew them (recall interviews with Mullah Omar's personal driver, *Newsweek*, January 21, 2001), and in stories equating the notorious fame of terrorists with that of other popular culture stars. One example of the latter is the extensive coverage of the Hebron "invincible" football team, in which six members became suicide bombers, causing a situation in which "the team has started to lose" (*Newsweek*, July 7, 2002). The interlacing in the story's narrative of the engagement in popular sport and the engagement with terror—from its being the best team, through its losing, and ending with the wish of a father of one suicide bomber that "the Jihad soccer team will one day be born again"—blurs the boundaries between the protagonists' identity as football players, with whom it is easy to identify, and their identity as suicide bombers, with whom it is more difficult. Described by the way they look (one has "a baby face," another has "brooding eyes"), their mobilization by a mosque called "Jihad," their participating in the Hammas terrorist movement, and their participation in a football team ("squad" in the story) with the same name, there is no mention that "Jihad" means "a sacred war," and the translation of *Shaheeds* (suicide bombers) into "martyrs" ("the Jihad mosque became an factory of martyrs") refers only to the Muslim meaning of "saint" without the action involved.

Common to in-depths interviews with hidden terrorists (as in *Newsweek's* feature "Muhammad's Army") or with their relatives (as in interviewing Muhammad Atta's father), or in the drawing up of psychological profiles with the help of professionals, is looking at terrorists as disconnected from their acts, thus creating a distance between the character responsible for terror and the suffering he causes. In his book *Modernity and the Holocaust*, Zygmunt Bauman (1989) explains the way in which all the moral scruples of Nazis carrying out orders during the holocaust were pushed aside by the distance created between the act—executed within the framework of the bureaucratic system and facilitated by modern technology—and the devastation it caused. This distancing cancels the moral meaning of the killers' actions and contributes to the erasing of the humanity of the victims by their remaining invisible. We argue that the genre of interviewing, and other personalizing formats used—ones that lay terrorists on the psychologist's couch, or that venture into the field to talk to their families—are aimed at exposing their fundamental humanity. These genres also lead readers and viewers to empathize with the story's heroes, creating a short circuit between the person we get to know intimately and his/her responsibility for the suffering he/she caused and is planning to cause. In other words, positioning viewers *vis à vis* bin Laden, or likewise protagonists, as having a face, and making them understand their motives and their world view, disconnects terrorists in time and place from the acts they had committed. It also neutralizes journalists' capacity to play "devil's advocate." They end up allowing their interviewees to create ambiguity regarding their responsibility for executing the atrocities which make them into sought after media stars.

Whereas Bauman points to the strategy of erasing the humanity of the victims (to facilitate their being treated inhumanely), current television creates an opposite problem by showing the human faces of the perpetrators of mass killings who cannot be confronted with their crimes or their victims because journalists relinquish their basic tools to do so. The fundamental conflict of interest that exists between interviewer and interviewee, with subjects maneuvering between a rhetoric of avoiding responsibility, directed at the channel's target audiences, and another rhetoric of "*aleihoom*," disintermediating that audience directed to their own fans.[18] Thus, distancing reinforces the status of terrorists as a new kind of celebrity of popular culture. In bin Laden we watch an authentic and charismatic visionary who, in spite of not taking any direct responsibility for September 11, makes use of the opportunity to "balance" the picture by justifying the mass killing and promising more. Appearing on CNN he can show his status in the eye of the enemy to millions of potential fans, watching directly or from the wings.

Finally, to return to the question of the paradox of media enthusiastically supporting the government and the military at war (and accused of exaggerated patriotism) that switch roles to undermine government policy by turning the enemy into a super star. First, what is common to an embedded journalist and one who chases terrorists is the sense of being there. Conveying to viewers the authenticity of the experience has long overtaken ideals such as objectivity, accuracy, and responsibility. Second, the timing and the rhythm of covering war is dictated by the government and the military. Stories of getting acquainted with the persona of terrorists (in between attacks), however, are initiated by journalists, who are (at least in part) in charge of the timing and the pace. Third, pursuing terrorists provides journalists with an opportunity to prove that they are not always patriotic. Once left on their own, they can return to their journalistic role.[19] It may also be the result of obeying the internal logic of popular exhibitionist culture, which results in the treating of different subjects by similar formats. Thus, as from "our" side the story of war and disaster is told as personalized, human experience (tragic, heroic, or both), the coverage of terrorists is also motivated by the search for heroes, villains, and victims. True, the terrorist is seen from "our" perspective (as contestants or victims), but the enemy's courage, daring, and determination can be admired. And in the context of an unfinished story, in which the scoring of points continues, it will always have high ratings.

Notes

1 According to Kern, Just, and Norris (2003), the importance of the local angle in news reporting on terrorism during the 1970s and the 1980s led to paying little attention in the case of the American media to most of the terror attacks around the world. Citing Weimann and Winn (1993) they reveal that between 1968–80 less than 20 percent of terror attacks were reported by the three main American television networks. The numbers declined further in the 1990s, when international terror attacks occurred less frequently.

2 Thus in the case of the IRA (from the 1970s until the mid-1990s), the use of laws prohibiting the interviewing of terrorists on media in Britain created a constant rift between the government and media organizations (Wilson 1997); likewise, in the Israeli case, interviewing Palestinians was legally prohibited until the beginning of the Oslo process.

3 One case in point is the public criticism in Israel following a 72-hour long live broadcast of Israel's public television channel in the wake of a series of terrorist attacks on buses, carried out by the Hamas in March 1996. Academics and left-wing politicians accused the channel of exacerbating the impact of the attacks, and playing into the hands of the opposition to the Oslo peace process, both by the obsessive occupation with the events and by the "whining" delivery style of its anchor.

4 The years in which this option is accessible in the *New York Times* Internet site.

5 In stories of journalists' pursuit of terrorists, we did not include journalistic missions aimed at exposing essential information for investigative reporting (such as the one conducted by Daniel Pearl), concerned with raising a warning about environmental risks.

6 Overall, the word "terror" appeared 301 times—156 between January 1, 1996 and September 10, 2001, and 145 times between September 11, 2001 and August 31, 2003. The word "terrorist" appeared 250 times—76 between January 1, 1996 and September 10, 2001, and 174 between September 11, 2001 and August 31, 2003. In the first period, only one item may be considered fitting for the category of the personalization of terror. It is Jeffery Goldberg's story of his voyage to Haqqania Madrasa (*The*

New York Times, June 25, 2000), a militant Muslin seminary in Pakistan, in which he interviewed future Taliban soldiers and leaders.

7 A recent example of serving terrorists' causes is the Israeli media's launching of a live marathon following a suicide bomber's attack in an Ultra Orthodox neighborhood in Jerusalem on August 2003. In the attack's aftermath, television could fatalistically foretell Israelis that this is "the end of the *Hudna* (a reconciliation period between Israel and the Palestinians)," and, we add, the victory of terror.

8 Whether Al-Jazeera's allocating "so much airtime" to bin Laden, and making him into a celebrity, is due as claimed by el-Nawawy and Iskandar (2002) to his promoting advertising sales, or whether it is also the result of empathy for his cause, there is unanimous agreement that bin Laden is the channel's star.

9 Tapes recorded by suicide bombers on the eve of their mission, designed for the recruitment of new candidates, and for blocking the way for last minute regrets.

10 The basic claim that "terror" against occupation is legitimate, while terror against ideology or for ideology (as in the bin Laden case) are not, can be found in the debate over the definition of terror, in the US media and in Arabic countries such as Egypt, Jordan, and Saudi Arabia (*Haaretz*, September 11, 2003). This distinction was adopted also by the *Washington Post* for the labeling of members of the Palestinian Hamas group as "militants" and members of al-Qaeda as "terrorists" (a distinction criticized by pro-Israeli Media Watch camera.org). The explanation of the *Washington Post*'s Ombudsman (September 21, 2003) for the differences was that "Hamas conducts terrorism but also has territorial ambitions, is a nationalist movement and conducts some social work. As far as we know, al-Qaeda exists only as a terrorist network."

11 Voiced by the President of the Media Research Center in Alexandria Va, this criticism could be reinforced by bin Laden's first statement in which he announces that "the battle has moved inside America. We will work to continue this battle, God permitting, until victory, or until we meet God."

12 As Eric Sorenson, president of NSNBC, said sending out questions "takes out the element of surprise, and rehearsed answers are not as honest as spontaneous ones." In the same spirit, Fox channel's spokesman announced "the only way we would do it is if we could have a sit down interview with bin Laden" (*Los Angeles Times*, October 18, 2001).

13 The claims against Alouni's interview (for example, the insult from a governmental source "he looked like a wimp,") concentrated on his failure to make bin Laden answer the crucial questions (*The New York Times*, December 12, 2001). Further, Alouni's extra deferential attitude may be evident in his repeatedly addressing bin Laden with the differential "Sheikh." A typical example of his representing bin Laden's interests might be seen in the following question: "al-Qaeda is facing now a country that leads the world militarily, politically, technologically. Surely, the al-Qaeda organization does not have the economic means that the United States has. How can al-Qaeda defeat America militarily?"

14 Sometimes, an invitation is extended by the terrorists, as in the case of a *Daily Telegraph* reporter in Pakistan, who received a fax one week before the first anniversary of September 11 on the attack, and was brought, eyes tied up, via a number of safe places, to a flat in which he was introduced to a suitcase stuffed with al-Qaeda correspondence. A few days later the source was arrested.

15 From a discourse perspective, Miller changes his footing (Goffman 1981) from claiming authorship for his question to taking the role of animator in which he represents a third party.

16 Johnson managed the scoop, he tells us, through the assistance of "a well-connected intermediary," asked to "help in connecting some fighters." It is clear that in the competition between the military and the media in pursuit of terrorists, the media wins.

For obvious reasons intermediaries for arranging interviews are easier to find than collaborators (i.e. intermediaries for arranging capture).

17 "In the streets where the terrorists came of age, many young Egyptians profess admiration for America. But the seeds of rage are here too" ("Muhammad Atta's neighborhood," *Newsweek*, December 16, 2001).

18 Recall Dan Rather's interview with Saddam Hussein, heavily criticized by the government, or Blitzer's interview with bin Laden analyzed above.

19 This of course reminds us that interviews are based on the assumption of the interviewee's willingness to cooperate with the interviewer. Interviews with criminals are unusually carried out in the law courts that have their methods for trying to extract true answers from defendants.

References

Bauman, Z. (1989) *Modernity and the Holocaust*, Cambridge, England: Polity Press.

Blondheim, M. and Liebes, T. (2002) "Live television's disaster marathon of September 11 and its subversive potential," *Prometheus*, 20: 3.

Blum-Kulka, S., Kampf, Z., and Liebes, T. (2003) "Talking with the enemy?: interviews with Palestinians during the second Intifada" in Y. Shlesinger and M. Muchnik (eds), *Lamed Le ILASH* (Hebrew), Studies in Modern Hebrew, Jerusalem: Tzivonim Publishing.

Carey, J. (2002) "American journalism on, before and after September 11" in B. Zelizer and S. Allan. (eds), *Journalism after September 11*, London and New York: Routledge.

Clayman, S.A. (1992) "Footing in the achievement of neutrality: the case of interview discourse" in P. Drew and J. Heritage (eds), *Talk at Work*, Cambridge: Cambridge University Press, 163–98.

Couldry, N. (2001) *A Way Out of the (Televised) Endgame*, online, available www.open-democracy.net/debates/article-8-39-11.jsp (accessed August 20, 2000).

el-Nawawy, M. and Iskandar, A. (2002) *Al-Jazeera: How the Free Arab News Network Scooped the World and Changed the Middle East*, MA: Westview, Cambridge.

Ezrachi, Y. (2002) "There is no objective journalism," *Hayin Hashvi'it* (Hebrew), vol. 39, pp. 38–40.

Gitlin, T. (1980) *The Whole World is Watching: Mass Media in the Making and Unmaking of the New Left*, Berkeley, CA: University of California Press.

Goffman, E. (1981) "Footing" in *Forms of Talk*, Philadelphia, PA: University of Pennsylvania Press, pp. 124–60.

Kellner, D. (2003) *Spectacle Culture*, New York: Routledge.

Kern, M., Just, M. and Norris, P. (1993) "The lesson of framing terrorism" in P. Norris, M. Kern, and M. Just (eds), *Framing Terrorism: the News Media, the Government and the Public*, New York: Routledge.

Liebes, T. (1998) "Television's disaster marathons: a danger for democratic processes" in T. Liebes and J. Curran (eds), *Media, Ritual and Identity*, London: Routledge, pp. 71–84.

Pinchevski, A. (2003) "Interruption and alterity: dislocating communication," PhD dissertation: McGill University.

Warshow, R. (1979) "Movie chronicle: the Western" in G. Mast and M. Cohen (eds), *Film Theory and Criticism*, New York and Oxford: Oxford University Press.

Weimann, G. and Winn, C. (1993) *The Theater of Terror: the Mass Media and International Terrorism*, New York: Longman Publishing/Addison-Wesley.

Weimann, G. (1999) "The theater of terror: a tough challenge to democracy" in R. Cohen-Almagor (ed.), *Basic Issues in Israeli Democracy* (Hebrew), Tel Aviv: Sifriat Poalim.

Weinrib, E. (2003) *History—Myth or Reality?* (Hebrew), Tel Aviv: Open University.

Wilson, R. (1997) *The Media and Intrastate Conflict in Northern Ireland*, available online http://cain.ulst.ac.uk/dd/papers/media.htm (accessed August 20, 2000).

Wolfsfeld, G. (1991) *Media, Protest, and Political Violence: a Transactional Analysis*, Columbia, SC: The University of South Carolina.

5

RESEARCHING US MEDIA–STATE RELATIONS AND TWENTY-FIRST CENTURY WARS[1]

Piers Robinson

For those of us seeking to understand the relationship between the state and media during wartime, the Iraq war is potentially a unique case. The unprecedented scale of domestic and international public opposition, the failure to obtain unequivocal UN authorization and the distinctive justifications used to "sell" the war, including the alleged WMD threat and humanitarian justifications related to Saddam Hussein's record of tyranny, created an ambiguous and controversial political environment. In addition, the presence of 24-hour news, the Internet and satellite broadcasting appeared to destabilize wartime media–state relations. An important question raised for those who have attempted to assess the relative balance of power between the US media and the state during wartime is whether we have witnessed an empowered wartime media or, conversely, continued domination of the news agenda by official viewpoints.

With this question in mind, I start by setting out an overview of our empirical and theoretical understanding of media–state relations during previous wars. There are reasons for thinking why we may be witnessing a more powerful and influential media, including the impact of *real-time* and *24-hour news*, *transnational media organizations* (so-called "global" media) and the *Internet* as well as post-Cold War geopolitical circumstances, but there are also many reasons to suggest that the impact of such changes is far less than is often assumed to be the case. Setting out the research imperatives necessary to test the thesis that there has been a significant change in the balance of power between government and media during wartime, I argue that in the absence of appropriate research and substantial empirical evidence, we cannot yet claim that there has been a significant change in the balance of power and influence between the US media and the state during wartime.

Manufacturing consent for war

An extensive literature on the media's reporting of war highlights the consistency between media agendas and the agendas of governments (see for example Glasgow University Media Group 1985; Hallin 1986; Herman and Chomsky 1988; Bennett 1990; Bennett and Paletz 1994; Mermin 1999; Wolfsfeld 1997). This research consistently suggests that when it comes to matters of national security and war, media rarely report outside the bounds of what Daniel Hallin (1986) described as elite-legitimated controversy. So, for example, in his seminal study of the Vietnam War, *The Uncensored War* (1986), Hallin examined the widely held belief that the news media played an oppositional role to official US policy. Contrary to orthodox thinking, he found that critical reporting only surfaced after the Washington political establishment became divided between the "hawks," who believed victory should be achieved at all costs, and the "doves," who believed the price of victory was not worth paying. Moreover media rarely, if ever, reported outside the bounds of this debate to argue that the war was fundamentally wrong or immoral. Similarly, in relation to the post-Cold War 1991 Gulf War, Bennett and Paletz's edited collection *Taken by Storm* (1994) highlighted the failure of journalists adequately to criticize official policy. In his summation chapter Paletz wrote:

> Insufficient dedication to the freedom of the press, fear of provoking government outrage, shared frames of reference with governing elites, and the pursuit of sales and ratings are among the factors that help explain the acquiescence to government curbs, no matter how reluctant, of media executives.
>
> (Paletz 1994: 284)

Five reasons are frequently put forward in the literature on media–state relations for explaining media deference to the state in wartime: reliance upon government information sources, Cold War ideology, the "rally round the flag" effect, political flak, and the corporate nature of mainstream US news media. I will outline each in turn.

First, journalists rely overwhelmingly on government sources when constructing the news (Hallin 1986: 63–70; Herman and Chomsky 1988; Bennett 1990: 109; Wolfsfeld 1997; Mermin 1999). The need to supply a steady and rapid flow of "important" news stories, combined with the vast public relations apparatus of government and powerful interests more broadly, means that journalists tend to become heavily reliant on public officials when defining and framing the news agenda.

Second, during the Cold War the ideology of anti-Communism acted as a control mechanism by providing journalists with a template with which to "understand" global events, as well as providing political elites with a powerful rhetorical tool with which to criticize as unpatriotic anyone who questioned US foreign policy (Hallin 1986: 8–58; Herman and Chomsky 1988: 29).

Third, owing to nationalism and the desire to "support our troops," the so-called "rally round the flag" effect (Mueller 1973) occurs during wartime. This phenomenon can be understood to limit critical reporting through journalists' and editors' own patriotic response to military action as well as the desire among media outlets to reflect the patriotism displayed by the public.

Fourth, when controversial material is aired it generates a disproportionate degree of "flak" from individuals connected with powerful interests including government "spin doctors." Such criticism serves to caution editors and journalists against putting out news stories that are "too" controversial.

Fifth, the "size, ownership and profit orientation of mass media" (Herman and Chomsky 1988: 3), and their shared "common interests . . . with other major corporations, banks, and government" (Herman and Chomsky 1988: 14) creates a clash of interest between the media's supposed role as a watchdog of the government and the interests of government and business elites (Bennett 1990: 109; Herman and Chomsky 1988: 3, 14). Via institutional factors including strategic interventions by owners of media conglomerates, recruitment processes that select and reward journalists who see the world in a way congenial and relatively unchallenging to elite interests, routine self-censorship on the part of journalists and editors, and, perhaps most importantly, the internalization of a US elite ideological framework, news stories that run contrary to vested interests are, on balance, less likely to surface than those consistent with the worldview of major conglomerates.[2] While the importance of economic factors for the shaping of media output are sometimes downplayed or dismissed as conspiratorial, there does exist remarkable proximity between US foreign policy objectives and US business interests, as shown by Jonathan Mermin in his 1999 study of US media coverage of post-Vietnam US military interventions:

> One powerful interest that has a major stake in US foreign policy and does have access to the news is business. But business, as a rule, has found US foreign policy to be quite consistent with its interests. In the Cold War, Washington supported anti-Communists against Communists—real and imagined—the anti-Communists being the side more interested in economic engagement with the United States in terms favourable to American business. In the post-Cold War era, a major organizing principle of US foreign policy has been to secure investment opportunities, market access, and oil for American business. The objectives of US foreign policy therefore continue to match the interests of American business.
>
> (Mermin 1999: 28–9)

The relative explanatory weighting accorded to each of these factors in terms of shaping wartime coverage is open to debate. There does, however, exist considerable agreement within the literature that all these factors play a role in shaping media output both during times of war and, more generally, with respect to US media coverage of international affairs.[3] Also, the research discussed should not be taken to suggest that media deference to the government in wartime is absolute, only that, on balance, news media tend to reflect the government line during war.

Wartime media–state relations in the twenty-first century

In recent years, with the rise of the 24-hour news cycle and media outlets such as CNN in the 1980s, substantial debate has emerged regarding the power of news media to shape government decision-making in respect to international affairs— the so-called "CNN effect" (see Robinson 2002). Two key lines of argument have been put forward to support the thesis that media possess greater power and independence during times of international crisis. These are technological developments that, in general terms, appear to have challenged the government dominance as news source and changed geopolitical circumstances surrounding the end of the Cold War. Hence, in terms of the explanatory framework identified earlier, the continued applicability of the first two factors explaining wartime media deference (i.e. reliance on government information sources and Cold War ideology) have been brought into question. Of the other three factors (rally round the flag, flak, and the corporate nature of US media) there is, of course, little reason to believe these have substantially altered over recent years in terms of increasing the autonomy and influence of media during international crises.

Technological developments

At the forefront of debate during the 1990s was the apparent ascendancy of the 24-hour news channel and the associated proliferation of advanced news-gathering equipment facilitating real-time television coverage,[4] the rise of transnational media organizations (global media) and the Internet. The net effect of these technological developments, according to many analysts, was government loss of control over the information environment and a news media that was, at least potentially, more likely to be adversarial and "off-message" (e.g. Annis 1991; Nye 1999; Rothkopf 1999; Shapiro 1999; Volkmer 1999; Deibert 2000; and Herrera 2002). The working assumption here was that media became less dependent upon government information sources when defining and framing the news agenda and more likely to include alternative viewpoints. For example, Nye claimed that:

> The free flow of broadcast information in open societies has always had an impact on public opinion and the formulation of foreign policy. But now the flow has increased in volume and shortened news cycles . . . The so-called CNN effect makes it hard to keep items that might otherwise warrant a lower priority off the top of the public agenda. Now, with

the added interactivity of groups on the Internet, it will be harder than ever to maintain a consistent agenda.

(Nye 1999: 26)

Specifically, with respect to the 24-hour news cycle, James Hoge claimed that today's pervasive media increase the pressure on politicians to respond promptly to news accounts that by their immediacy are incomplete, without context and sometimes wrong (Hoge 1994). In relation to real-time television coverage, Preston argued that:

Newsgathering technology (ever-smaller ENG [electronic news-gathering] cameras, portable satellite dishes for sending back images . . . and capacity for field editing) increased viewer engagement with . . . war by enabling journalists . . . to film clandestinely in places that would otherwise remain unpublicised; through the ability to send material quickly or even live; and through the increase in volume of stories and footage

(Preston: 1996: 112)

The key assumption underpinning these claims was that the ability to report in real-time, 24 hours a day enabled the media to report events without mediation by government press briefers. With respect to the transnationalization of media organizations, Brown argues that it "challenges the ability of states to control information flows" (Brown 2003a: 88) and, according to Shaw (2000), this "diffusion of information through the increasingly global media cannot be contained within the bounds that even the most powerful state leaders would prefer" (Shaw 2000: 33). Volkmer (1999: 4–5) took this analysis one step further by arguing that CNN International is actually facilitating the emergence of a global public sphere. Finally, the Internet was argued by many to have both expanded the availability of alternative information for journalists and the public and to have empowered non-elite voices. For example, analyzing the David and Goliath struggle between the indigenous Chiapas guerrilla army and the Mexican state, Kellner claimed that "From the beginning, the peasants and guerrilla armies struggling in Chiapas, Mexico used computer data bases, guerrilla radio, and other forms of media to circulate news of their struggles and ideas" (Kellner 1998: 182). The problem with such claims, however, is that there are many reasons to suppose that technological advances have had little impact on the range of sources used and substantive viewpoints expressed in mainstream US media.

24-hour news and real time coverage

It is unclear that 24-hour news and real-time coverage provide any greater range of views, depth of analysis or understanding than traditional media outlets. Much of the content of 24-hour channels[5] is in fact highly repetitive with the same news segments being repeated on an hourly basis. Actual live coverage interrupts this hourly cycle only when a significant event occurs at which the media are present. So, for example, during the 2003 Iraq war the hourly bulletin cycle would often be interrupted for live coverage of "US/UK" press briefings and statements by leading political figures. Furthermore, as Thussu argued, the drive to deliver audiences to advertisers in a fiercely competitive market can lead 24-hour news "to sensationalization and trivialization of often complex stories and a temptation to highlight the entertainment value of news" (Thussu 2003: 118). For example, the fall of Baghdad to US forces was epitomized by live coverage of the statue of Saddam Hussein being pulled to the ground by a group of Iraqi men. The event was enthusiastically reported by some Western journalists through comparison with the collapse of Communist regimes in Eastern Europe. These comparisons were, however, dubious for two reasons. First, the now seminal images generated by coverage of the fall of Communism throughout Eastern Europe showed massive numbers of people protesting/celebrating as opposed to the several hundred Iraqis seen pulling down the statue of Saddam in central Baghdad. Second, the overthrow of the Communist regimes was via popular public protest, not armed intervention by a foreign power. More significantly, the statue was pulled down with practical help from US soldiers. Hence it is a matter of controversy whether the pulling down of the statue was orchestrated by US soldiers. Certainly, sober review of the footage shows that, beyond the several hundred Iraqi men working with the US marines to pull down the statue, the surrounding area was sparsely populated with Iraqi civilians who remained passive when the statue fell. More generally live coverage of the fall of Baghdad was often at the expense of more measured assessments regarding both Iraqi support for the US forces and the actual degree of control that US forces had achieved. As we are now all too well aware, the ability of US/UK forces to maintain even minimal levels of security within Iraq has caused a sober reassessment among journalists and policy-makers regarding initial claims of victory and liberation. In short, 24-hour news and real-time reporting may create the impression of greater transparency, accuracy, and diversity; but the superficial nature of such coverage can actually limit the overall depth and quality of reporting.

Transnational (global) media

With respect to transnational or global media, the claim that these are either affecting the ability of governments to control information or creating a global public sphere has been predicated upon the assumptions that significant numbers of US citizens are indeed utilizing such media, and that the content of these media outlets actually reflects a truly global range of viewpoints. However, it is far from clear the extent to which audiences have abandoned traditional terrestrial (and national) based media in favor of transnational media outlets. As Carruthers (2000: 202) argued, "some social theorists . . . point to the stubborn preference of many audiences for national, regional or more local news." More importantly, the extent to which such outlets are genuinely "transnational" or "global" in terms of content is highly questionable. For example, Volkmer's claim of an emerging global public sphere is based mainly upon CNN International's (CNNI) "World report," a bulletin that features reporters from around the world. This bulletin, however, represents only one small part of CNNI's[6] overall output while CNN broadcasts to US citizens retain a US-centric perspective (Wallis and Baran 1990; Thussu 2000). Hence Volkmer's thesis would appear to be overstated. Also, with respect to the 1999 Kosovo war, Thussu (2000: 345) found that CNN "reported uncritically . . . [and] . . . tended to follow the news agenda set up by the US military . . . [while] few alternative views were aired." In short, Carruthers would appear correct in arguing that "the content of the 'globalized' media broadly reflects the interest, concerns, and values of elites, and generally of First World elites" (Carruthers 2000: 202).

It is also worth noting here the continued vulnerability of "alternative" global media, such as the Arab satellite television station Al-Jazeera to political flak (the third factor used to explain media deference in war time). During the 2003 Iraq war considerable flak was directed at Al-Jazeera as it frequently incurred criticism from the US government for allegedly biased reporting. Interestingly, the New York Stock Exchange withdrew Al-Jazeera's accreditation soon after the war had started, supposedly "as part of a general reorganization of space for media out-lets."[7] So, while the presence of Al-Jazeera might on the one hand suggest the creation of a greater pluralization of viewpoints in the global media milieu, the channel is still vulnerable to punishment and flak when it is perceived to have "over-stepped" the boundaries of "acceptable" reporting.

The Internet

While the Internet appears to facilitate a more plural media sphere, its impact in terms of influencing both mainstream news coverage and pressure group mobiliza-tion has been far from clear. In terms of influencing mainstream news coverage, the extent to which on-line information sources have been integrated into processes of news-gathering has received insufficient attention from empirically based academic research[8] and it might well be the case that journalists and editors remain predisposed to rely upon what are perceived to be more "credible" sources of information such as government officials and other elite voices. This is arguably even more likely to be the case during wartime when misinformation and propaganda on the World Wide Web is likely to be at a peak. In respect of the mobilization of interest groups, there is reason and evidence to indicate that the empowering potential of the Internet is far less than is often argued to be the case. For example, with respect to the quality of on-line political expression (a much vaunted component of arguments surrounding the positive impact of the Internet on deliberative democracy), Wilhelm (2000: 98) found that:

> The data support the conception of online political forums as facilitating self-expression and monologue, without in large measure the "listening,"

responsiveness, and dialogue that would promote communicative action, such as prioritising issues, negotiating differences, reaching argument, and plotting a course of action to influence the political agenda . . . If a democratic discussion is defined as at least in part by the quality of the conversation, then the newsgroups analysed in this study are not very deliberative . . . Rather than listening to others, more times than not persons opposed to a seed message used it to amplify their views.

(Wilhelm 2000: 98)

In terms of facilitating the mobilization of non-elite protest groups such as the "Stop the War Coalition," much research to date indicates that the Internet at best serves only as an additional form of communication rather than as a revolutionary tool of mobilization (see for example Froehling 1997; Cleaver 1998; Hill and Hughes 1998; Pickerell 2000; and Romano 2002). Indeed, it is plausible that, rather than strengthening grassroots activism, reliance on Internet communication might lead to less committed activists and ephemeral political protest. Indeed, some of the latest research indicates that political mobilization via the Internet is effective only in certain relatively limited circumstances and that there exists little substitute for securing access to traditional mainstream media.[9] The central problem here, often ignored in the literature, is that a proliferation of Internet-based issue groups might simply contribute to the creation of a fractured public sphere in which many issue areas are actively discussed but in which few develop the necessary critical mass in order to start to affect both mainstream broadcast media, public opinion and politicians. In sum, while many analysts continue to make a great play of Internet era pressure group activity, such as the anti-globalization movement and the anti-war movement (e.g. the US-based Campaign for Peace and Democracy and the UK-based Stop the War Coalition), little hard evidence is available to indicate these have been any more effective at mobilization than protest groups from earlier eras such as the anti-apartheid movement of the late 1970s and 1980s. The question remains as to whether the Internet really has changed the power and influence of non-elite movements.

Overall then, there are many reasons to question the thesis that new technology has increased either the diversity of sources and viewpoints in the news (let alone the quality and depth of coverage) or the ability of protest movements to influence mainstream media and political debate. If these claims regarding the transformative power of new technology are to be substantiated, much more research is necessary. In the first instance, with respect to the 2003 Iraq war, Hallin's conceptual spheres can be drawn upon in order to assess the extent to which the different media outlets operated beyond the bounds of "elite legitimated controversy" (Hallin 1986), such as debate over tactics, likelihood of military victory, and the need for UN backing, into a "sphere of deviance" (Hallin 1986) in which the fundamental legitimacy of the war was openly questioned. Important issues here surround the extent to which both traditional mainstream media (such as ABC, CBS, and NBC) and new media (such as

CNN) reported within the reference frames of the US government, focusing on the humanitarian arguments in favor of war and the threat of WMDs; or, alternatively, reflected the reference frames of anti-war opinion, focusing instead on issues such as the alleged illegality or immorality of the action, as well as "hidden" causes such as US geostrategic and economic motives for the war. As part of this analysis it is also necessary to identify the extent to which US media drew upon new media sources (for example Al-Jazeera and Internet sources) and how that information was presented. If real-time, 24-hour news coverage and the Internet have indeed significantly challenged the ability of governments to control information flows, we would expect to observe greater plurality of viewpoints in the new media outlets compared to traditional outlets and extensive use of new media sources across all media outlets.

With respect to the Internet and protest movements, research is necessary to establish the extent to which the US anti-war movement utilized the Internet *relative* to other forms of communication when both organizing protest and expanding debate to a wider public audience. It is also important to analyze both how, and to what extent, the anti-war movement utilized the Internet in order to influence mainstream media coverage. Overall, it needs to be established whether or not the Internet actually facilitated more effective communication between activists, thereby enabling protest, and whether or not the anti-war movement was able to utilize the Internet in order to secure adequate representation within mainstream news media.

New media technology versus "spin"

Even if over time new communication technologies have increased the potential power of media outlets, the increasingly professional government media management techniques (Thrall 2000; Vickers 2000; Brown 2002, 2003a) might have counteracted these technological developments with sufficient effectiveness to maintain government dominance as a news source. Here the first factor, a reliance on government information sources that is in part due to the "vast public relations apparatus of government," might have become even more powerful and significant in terms of shaping the news.

It was during the Falklands conflict in 1981 that the British government demonstrated the effectiveness of fostering sympathetic reporting by placing journalists alongside combatants. Learning in part from the British experience during the Falklands, in the 1991 Gulf War the US military adopted the pool system allowing selected journalists to front line units while other journalists were channelled toward the memorable set-piece press briefings. It was largely during these briefings that the use of dramatic images of "smart" bombs and sanitized language (such as the use of the terms "collateral damage" and "surgical strikes") ensured media coverage did not relay too much of the grim reality of war (see for example Baudrillard 1991; Philo and McLaughlin 1993; and Bennett and Paletz 1994).

Since the 1999 Kosovo conflict, attempts to manage the information environment during wars and crises have accelerated. Coalition military operations in Kosovo, Afghanistan, and the 2003 Iraq war have been accompanied by sustained and highly organized attempts to influence media agendas by promoting coverage of some issues rather than others and to influence the framing of stories in ways that support the government's cause. As Brown (2003a: 93) argued, at least some of the impetus for these attempts during the 2002 war in Afghanistan came from the UK government's Director of Communications and Strategy, Alistair Campbell:

> [Campbell's] solution was to create Coalition Information Centres (CICs) in Washington, London and Islamabad that would coordinate the release of information, attempt to control the news agenda and rebut opposition claims in exactly the way that the Clinton–Blair 'war room' model operated in domestic politics.

Other activities inherent in the "war room" model include the use of press releases, media appearances, press conferences, and speeches. In strategic terms, these activities seek to encourage the development of common media frames over time. In tactical terms they serve to minimize coverage of damaging or hostile stories and to discredit oppositional counter-narratives. Some of the routine consequences during the 2003 Gulf War of such attempts at "perception management" would appear to include the repeated and premature announcements concerning suspected WMD sites as the US/UK military advanced into Iraq, over-optimistic announcements concerning a popular uprising against Saddam's forces in Basra and premature claims regarding the taking of the border town of Umm Qasr during the first weeks of the conflict. A more dramatic and exceptional example of media-management was the recovery of the US soldier Jessica Lynch that involved a military operation coordinated and exploited in order to facilitate dramatic and positive news coverage. Ruthlessly exploited by the US military at the time as a tale of daring heroism, press briefers at Central Command (Centcom) in Doha, Qatar, presented the rescue as occurring under hostile conditions and exaggerated the circumstances under which Jessica Lynch was captured to create the impression she had fought to the last bullet. In reality, as Lynch herself has admitted, she did not fire a single shot during her capture and she was in fact well cared for by Iraqi doctors and nurses.[10]

Overall, the jury is still out as to the extent to which the ascendancy of these coordinated and sustained approaches to wartime media management have counteracted the *potential* effects of new media technologies discussed earlier. Accordingly, there is need to identify the key government information management strategies and actual outputs (press briefings, etc.) over the course of recent wars, including strategic attempts to develop common framings over time, tactical activities designed to minimize damaging coverage and/or to discredit counter-narratives, the techniques used to coordinate US and UK information management strategies and the involvement of embedded journalists. Mapping of government information strategies and outputs would enable a unique and unprecedented comparison of the relationship between government information and media output. Framing analysis of war coverage, as outlined earlier, could be combined with the analysis of media management strategies in order to provide a profile of media–state power relations over the course of a conflict and to identify the degree of autonomy maintained by the media in the face of government information management strategies. Specifically, the extent to which media coverage either followed government information strategies or, conversely, preceded, and influenced them needs to be demonstrated empirically, allowing assessments to be made regarding the balance of power between government and media at different points of a conflict and the degree of media influence (the so-called CNN effect) upon policy formulation.[11]

Geopolitics and the "death" of ideology?

With the collapse of the USSR and the bipolar order, it was often assumed during the 1990s that "journalists were freer not just to cover the stories they wanted but to criticize US foreign policy as well" (Robinson 2002: 7; Entman 2000). With respect to the explanatory framework set out earlier, the constraints that Cold War ideology placed upon media coverage of international events appears to many analysts to have become irrelevant in the post-Cold War era. Indeed, at least during the early 1990s, many commentators argued that the "new humanitarian" wars fought in, for example, northern Iraq (1991) and Somalia (1992–3) were driven by media coverage (the so-called CNN effect) operating in the geopolitical vacuum created by the collapse of the Cold War anti-Communist consensus (Hoge 1994; Mandelbaum 1994; and Entman 2000). While many of these commentators decried the influence of media on foreign policy-making and stressed the need for elite control of the foreign policy agenda, over the course of the 1990s new norms of humanitarian intervention became reflected in a foreign policy community more sensitive to the notion of humanitarian war. This in turn reflected the internationalist and Wilsonian temperament of many US Democrats. A similar change was observed within the British foreign policy-making community as it reacted to proclamations of an ethical foreign policy by the Blair government. By the end of the 1990s, with the NATO air war against Serbia, the notion of humanitarian war was established among a large part of Western policy-making elites.[12] In short, if the early 1990s witnessed a more influential media that helped to persuade policy-makers to engage in humanitarian intervention, by the late 1990s the concept had become a policy tool that Western leaders employed in order to justify armed intervention in the internal affairs of another state. This was seen most clearly in the NATO air war against Serbia. Although this was primarily an act of coercive diplomacy that had the unintended effect of exacerbating a humanitarian crisis, it was promoted and justified to Western publics, quite successfully, as a humanitarian war.[13]

With the events of September 11, 2001 and the Bush administration's subsequent declaration of a "war on terrorism" the geopolitical landscape has been further, and dramatically, transformed. Humanitarian concerns have been, and are likely to continue to be, secondary to US objectives aimed at containing and eliminating the al-Qaeda network. This was seen during the war against Afghanistan when the humanitarian crisis that occurred following US attacks was clearly of secondary importance to the US goal of destroying the Taliban government and disrupting/destroying the al-Qaeda terrorist network. Perhaps of greater significance, the "war on terrorism" frame provides journalists, particularly in the US, with a template with which to understand global events and a powerful rhetorical tool with which to justify a more aggressive and interventionist foreign policy agenda. For example, this has already been seen during the build-up to and war against Iraq. The US government worked hard to associate Saddam Hussein with al-Qaeda in the eyes of the US public, even in the absence of any firm evidence, while mainstream US media reported this claim uncritically leaving some Americans actually unsure of the difference between Hussein and bin Laden.[14] In addition, the humanitarian war discourse of the 1990s has functioned as a further legitimating device employed by both British and US political elites when justifying military action in Afghanistan and Iraq. In particular the British Prime Minister Tony Blair advocated war on grounds of both national security owing to a perceived threat from Iraq's WMD program and the claim that regime change could be justified in humanitarian terms in order to save the Iraqi people from Saddam Hussein. Importantly, however, as David Clark (former Foreign Office Special Adviser) recently pointed out,[15] such a claim is spurious because the situation in Iraq did not meet the criteria (i.e. large-scale human suffering that cannot be averted by other means) by which humanitarian war is justified.[16]

Overall, it is tempting to conclude that the threat of Communism, which helped create an ideological bond between journalists and policy-makers during the Cold War, has been effectively replaced by the "war on terrorism," combined in some instances with a liberal "humanitarian" discourse that has created a consensus between journalists and policy-making elites. Hence the second factor, Cold War ideology, in our explanatory framework might still be just as relevant today except that it has been replaced by the "war on terrorism." Consequently, ideological mechanisms remain very much in place, with the result that dissent and criticism during the "war on terrorism" will possibly be just as muted as during the Cold War.

This point notwithstanding, if scholars are to advance the thesis that the Cold War's ending has had a substantial impact on media–state relations, it would be useful to apply the issues outlined here retrospectively to a consideration of earlier conflicts and military interventions, such as the Vietnam War and US involvement in central America during the 1980s. So doing would enable an analysis of the degree of change and continuity in media–state relations, particularly as they relate to the changing geopolitical circumstances and developments in media technology.

Conclusion: wartime media–state relations—change or continuity?

While research has consistently demonstrated that the media have tended to remain deferential to government positions during times of crisis and war, the media have been, and continue to be, regularly attacked for being too critical of wartime/crisis policies, often through claims that new media technology is affecting the balance of power between media and state. For example, the US war in Vietnam was fought when television ownership had become widespread among the US public. Following the US defeat and withdrawal many sought to explain military failure in terms of the "Vietnam syndrome," whereby domestic populations were unable to tolerate casualties owing, at least in part, to graphic and decontextualized television news coverage. Richard Nixon argued:

> The Vietnam War was complicated by factors that never before occurred in America's conduct of a war . . . More than ever before, television showed the terrible human suffering and sacrifice of war. Whatever the intention behind such relentless and literal reporting of the war, the result was a serious demoralization of the home front, raising the question whether America would ever again be able to fight an enemy abroad with unity and strength of purpose at home
>
> (Nixon 1978: 350)

As we now know from Hallin's (1986) *Uncensored War*, the notion of an anti-war media during Vietnam is largely a myth. The same exists with respect to the CNN effect of the 1990s. At the time of the interventions in Iraq (1991) and Somalia (1992) the claim that the media were responsible for these "humanitarian" wars was widespread throughout foreign policy and humanitarian circles. Again, such claims were made in the context of an ongoing debate over the rise of 24-hour global news media and changing geostrategic realities. And yet subsequent research has demonstrated that the CNN effect was largely exaggerated and that the actual influence and power of mass media was far more circumscribed than suggested by widely held assumptions regarding the CNN effect (Gowing 1994; Strobel 1997; and Robinson 2002). Substantive military intervention, even during the 1990s, remained driven by geostrategic reasoning rather than any kind of media pressure or CNN effect.

Such examples should be sobering for those who make claims of significant change in media–state relations. So too should be the fact that only two of the five factors put forward to explain media deference during war time—Cold War ideology and media reliance on government sources—*could* be argued to have changed. Even with respect to these factors, however, there are many reasons to suggest continuity rather than change. In particular, it seems likely that any empowering effects of new media technology may well have been counteracted by reinforced government media management strategies. Little change in the areas of political flak, nationalism, and the corporate nature of the US news media suggests that the media have "served the military rather well" (Carruthers 2000: 271–2), acting now, as in previous wars, in support of US government war objectives.

Yet, as I have discussed, there remains a persistent discourse surrounding new communication technology and the post-Cold War political environment, which suggests that the contemporary media are more powerful and influential than their predecessors. Perhaps more than a few academics and commentators are guilty of wishful thinking, or at least engaging in research that is predicated upon the assumption of change rather than continuity.[17] There is need, then, to focus more closely on the reasons that change continues to haunt our discussions of war reporting, even when evidence suggests the contrary.

Notes

1 Thanks to the editors Stuart Allan and Barbie Zelizer, as well as Peter Goddard and Marion Lloyd, for feedback on earlier drafts. Some of the material, in particular that which identifies future research agendas, is drawn from an ESRC research grant proposal, award reference RES-000-23-0551, developed by the author, Peter Goddard (University of Liverpool) and Philip Taylor and Robin Brown (Institute of Communications, University of Leeds).

2 For useful introductions to the processes by which institutional factors limit critical journalism see Klaehn (2002) and Herman (2000).

3 For a detailed review of the overlap between the claims of Herman and Chomsky (1988) and other key scholars see E. Herring and P. Robinson (2003), "Too polemical or too critical? Chomsky on the study of the news media and US foreign policy," forum on Chomsky, *Review of International Studies* vol. 29, no. 4: pp. 553–68.

4 The phrase "real-time" should be understood to refer both to the actual live reporting of events and the use of "on the spot" footage obtained through the use of electronic news gathering equipment (ENG) and other such portable newsgathering equipment. This equipment allows journalists to report live or almost live without relying upon government sources.

5 For example see US-based CNN, UK-based Sky News, and BBC News 24.

6 According to Volkmer (1999: 160) "World report" is run for 15 minutes daily as part of the show *International Hour*, at 6.30 and 9.30 GMT Tuesday to Friday and has two omnibus editions on a Sunday.

7 See "The untouchables," *The Guardian*, March 31, 2003.

8 As a guide, to date I have reviewed well over 50 academic texts that analyze the impact of new information communication technologies (NICTs) and have yet to find an examination of the impact of online information sources upon news-gathering.

9 See, for example, Bruce Bimber (2003), *Information and American Democracy*, Cambridge University Press: Cambridge.

10 For further details see "The war we never saw: the true face of war," Channel 4, June 5, 2003, "The truth about Jessica," *The Guardian*, Thursday, May 15, 2003, and "Lynch: military played up rescue too much," CNN, Saturday, November 8, 2003: downloaded from http://edition.cnn.com/2003/US/11/07/lynch.interview/index.html, download date November 12, 2003.

11 Inferences developed from research would need to be triangulated with primary interviews with journalists, policy makers and press briefers, and secondary sources (such as memoirs, public statements and academic accounts) in order to build up a thorough picture of media–state relations during the war.

12 See in particular the speech by British Prime Minister Tony Blair to the Economic Club of Chicago, Hilton Hotel, Chicago, USA, Thursday, April 22, 1999, available online at www.fco.gov.uk

13 For further details on this case of intervention see Robinson 2002: pp. 93–110.

14 For opinion poll data on US beliefs in an al-Qaeda/Hussain link and Bush's linking of the two see "Hussein link to 9/11 lingers in many minds" by Dana Milbank and Claudia Deane, *Washington Post*, Saturday, September 6, 2003, p. A01.

15 David Clark, "Iraq has wrecked our case for humanitarian wars," *The Guardian*, Monday, August 11, 2003.

16 For further reading on humanitarian war and intervention see O. Ramsbotham and T. Woodhouse (1996) *Humanitarian Intervention in Contemporary Conflict*, Cambridge: Polity Press and Blackwell.

17 For further details on problems surrounding theorizing change and the tendency to exaggerate media impact see Philip Hammond (2000) "Lessons of the first draft of history," *Media Culture and Society*, vol. 22, pp. 847–51; Piers Robinson (2000) "Media power and world politics: problems of research design," *Media, Culture and Society*, vol. 22, no. 2, pp. 227–32; and Robin Brown (1998) "It's got to make a difference, hasn't it?: communication technology and practice in world politics," paper presented at the British International Studies Association Annual Conference, University of Sussex, December 14–16, 1998.

References

Annis, S. (1991) "Giving a voice to the poor," *Foreign Policy*, 84, pp. 93–106.

Baudrillard, J. (1991) "La Guerre du Golfe n'a pas eu lieu," *Libération*, March 29, 1991. For an English translation, see Baudrillard (2000) *The Gulf War Did Not Take Place*, translated with an introduction by P. Patton, Sydney: Power Publications.

Bennett, W.L. and Paletz, D.L. (eds) (1994) *Taken by Storm: the media, Public Opinion and US Foreign Policy in the Gulf War*, Chicago, IL: University of Chicago Press.

Bennett, W.L. (1990) "Toward a theory of press state relations in the United States," *Journal of Communication*, vol. 40, no. 2, pp. 103–25.

Bimber, B. (2003) *Information and American Democracy*, Cambridge: Cambridge University Press.

Brown, R. (1998) "It's got to make a difference, hasn't it? Communication technology and practice in world politics," paper presented at the British International Studies Association Annual Conference, University of Sussex, December 14–16, 1998.

Brown, R. (2002) "The US and the politics of perception management," *Journal of Information Warfare*, vol. 1, no. 3, pp. 40–50.

Brown, R. (2003a) "Spinning the war: political communications, information operations and public diplomacy in the war on terrorism" in D. Thussu and D. Freedman (eds), *War and the Media: Reporting Conflict 24/7*, London: Sage.

Brown, R. (2003b), "Clausewitz in the media age: rethinking the military media relationship" in M. Just, M. Kern and P. Norris (eds), *Framing Terrorism*, London: Routledge.

Carruthers, S.L. (2000) *The Media at War: Communication and Conflict in the Twentieth Century*, Macmillan: London.

Cleaver, H.M. Jr (1998) "The Zapatista effect: the Internet and the rise of an alternative political fabric," *Journal of International Affairs*, vol. 51, no. 2, pp. 6,211–40.

Deibert, R. (2000) "International plug 'n' play: citizen activism, the internet and global public policy," *International Studies Perspectives*, vol. 1, no. 3, pp. 255–72.

Entman, R. (2000) "Declarations of independence: the growth of media power after the Cold War" in B.L. Nacos, R. Shapiro, and P. Isernia (eds), *Decision Making in a Glass House: Mass Media, Public Opinion and American and European Foreign Policy in the 21st Century*, London: Rowman and Littlefield Publishers, pp. 11–26.

Froehling, O. (1997) "The cyberspace 'war of ink and internet' in Chiapas, Mexico," *Geographical Review*, vol. 87, no. 2, pp. 291–307.

Glasgow University Media Group (1985) *War and Peace News*, Milton Keynes: Open University Press.

Gowing, Nik (1994) "Real-time coverage of armed conflicts and diplomatic crises: does it pressure or distort foreign policy decisions?" Harvard: Joan Shorestein Barone Center, working paper, pp. 91–4.

Hallin, D. (1986) *The Uncensored War*, Berkeley, CA: University of California Press.

Hammond, P. (2000) "Lessons of the first draft of history," *Media Culture and Society*, p. 22.

Hammond, P. and Herman, E. (eds) (2000) *Degraded Capability: the Media and the Kosovo Crisis*, London: Pluto Press.

Herman, E. (2000) "The propaganda model: a retrospective," *Journalism Studies*, vol. 1, no. 1, pp. 101–12.

Herman, E. and Chomsky, N. (1988) *Manufacturing Consent*, New York, NY: Pantheon.

Herrera, G.L. (2002) "The politics of bandwidth: international political implications of a global digital information network," *Review International Studies*, vol. 28, no. 1, pp. 93–122.

Herring, E. and Robinson, P. (2003) "Too polemical or too critical? Chomsky on the study of the news media and US foreign policy," Forum on Chomsky, *Review of International Studies*, vol. 29, no. 4, pp. 553–68.

Hill, K.A. and Hughes, J.E. (1998) *Cyberpolitics: Citizen Activism in the Age of the Internet*, Rowman and Littlefield Publishers INC: Lanham, Boulder, New York, Oxford.

Hoge, J. (1994) "Media pervasiveness," *Foreign Affairs*, vol. 73, pp. 136–44.

Kellner, D. (1998) "Intellectual, the new public spheres, and techno-politics" in C. Toulouse and T.W. Luke (eds), *The Politics of Cyberspace*, Routledge: New York and London, pp. 167–86.

Kennan, G.F. (1993) "Somalia, through a glass darkly," *The New York Times*, September 30.

Klaehn, J. (2002) "A critical review and assessment of Herman and Chomsky's 'propaganda model,'" *European Journal of Communication*, vol. 16, no. 4, pp. 147–82.

Mandelbaum, M. (1994) "The reluctance to intervene," *Foreign Policy*, vol. 9, pp. 3–8.

Mermin, Jonathan (1999) *Debating War and Peace*, Princeton, NJ: Princeton University Press.

Mueller, J. (1973) *War, Presidents and Public Opinion*, New York: John Wiley.

Nacos, B.L., Shapiro, R., and Isernia, P. (eds) (2000) *Decision Making in a Glass House: Mass Media, Public Opinion and American and European Foreign Policy in the 21st Century*, London: Rowman and Littlefield Publishers.

Nixon, R. (1978) *The Memoirs*, New York: Grosset and Dunlap.

Nye, J. (1999) "Redefining the national interest," *Foreign Affairs*, vol. 78, no. 4, pp. 22–35.

Paletz, D.L. (1994) "Just deserts" in W.L. Bennett and D.L. Paletz (eds), *Taken by Storm: the Media, Public Opinion and US Foreign Policy in the Gulf War*, Chicago, IL: University of Chicago Press, pp. 277–92.

Philo, G. and McLaughlin, G. (1993) *The British Media and the Gulf War*, Glasgow: Glasgow University Media Group.

111

Pickerell, J. (2000) "Environmentalists and the Net: pressure groups, new social movements and new ICTs" in R. Gibson and S. Ward (eds), *Reinvigorating Democracy? British Politics and the Internet*, Ashgate: Aldershot, pp. 129–50.

Preston, A. (1996) "Television news and the Bosnian conflict" in J. Gow, R. Paterson and A. Preston (eds), *Bosnia by Television*, London: British Film Institute.

Ramsbotham, O. and Woodhouse, T. (1996) *Humanitarian Intervention in Contemporary Conflict*, Cambridge: Polity Press and Blackwell.

Robinson, P. (2000) "Media power and world politics: problems of research design," *Media, Culture and Society*, vol. 22, no. 2.

Robinson, P. (2001) "Theorizing the influence of media on world politics: models of media influence on foreign policy," *European Journal of Communication*, vol. 16, no. 4, pp. 523–44.

Robinson, P. (2002) *The CNN Effect: the Myth of News, Foreign Policy and Intervention*, Routledge: London and New York.

Romano, D. (2002) "Modern communications technology in ethnic nationalist hands: the case of the Kurds," *Canadian Journal of Political Science*, vol. 35, no. 1, pp. 127–49.

Rothkopf, D. (1999). "The disinformation age," *Foreign Policy* vol. 114, pp. 82–96.

Shapiro, Andrew (summer, 1999). "The Internet," *Foreign Policy*, no. 115, pp. 14–27.

Shaw, M. (2000) "Media and public sphere without border," in B.L. Nacos, R. Shapiro, and P. Isernia (eds), *Decision Making in a Glass House: Mass Media, Public Opinion and American and European Foreign Policy in the 21st Century*, London: Rowman and Littlefield Publishers, pp. 27–40.

Strobel, W. (1997) *Late Breaking Foreign Policy*, Washington DC, WA: United States Institute of Peace.

Taylor, P.M. (1997) *Global Communications, International Affairs and the Media Since 1945*, Routledge: London and New York.

Thrall, A. (2000) *War in the Media Age*, Cresskill, NJ: Hampton.

Thussu, D.K. (2000) "Legitimizing 'humanitarian intervention'? CNN, NATO and the Kosovo crisis," *European Journal of Communication*, vol. 15, no. 3, pp. 345–61.

Thussu, D.K. (2003) "Live TV and bloodless deaths: war, infotainment and 24/7 news" in D.K. Thussu and D. Freedman (eds), *War and the Media*, London: Sage, pp. 117–32.

Vickers, R. (2000) "Blair's Kosovo campaign: political communications, the battle for public opinion and foreign policy," *Civil Wars*, vol. 3, no. 1, pp. 55–70.

Volkmer, I. (1999) *News in the Global Sphere*, Luton: University of Luton Press.

Wallis, R. and Baran, S. (1990) *The Known World of Broadcast News: International News and Electronic Media*, London: Routledge.

Wilhelm, A. (2000) *Democracy in the Digital Age: Challenges to Political Life in Cyberspace*, Routledge: London and New York.

Wolfsfeld, G. (1997) *The Media and Political Conflict*, Cambridge: Cambridge University Press.

Part 2

BEARING WITNESS

6

WHEN WAR IS REDUCED TO A PHOTOGRAPH

Barbie Zelizer[1]

Journalism's images of war disturb. Among the most powerful visuals known to humankind, they are haunted by the stubborn inevitability and proximity of death. Combining the cool mechanics of the camera with the hot passions of wartime, they offer visual statements about circumstances much of the world prefers not to see: shattered bodies and mangled buildings, triumphant soldierly gestures, hopes and broken spirits nestled inside devastation somehow too deep for the camera to record. Journalism's images of war both show what has been and offer glimpses of what might be. And for those who have never experienced war firsthand, journalism's images of war provide what may be the only depiction of what sadly has become one of the reigning circumstances of the contemporary age.

But journalism's images of war do not emerge from a vacuum. They are shaped through a turn to the visual—a journalistic emphasis on images that typically takes place during wartime. Crafted through a maze of practices and standards, both explicit and implicit, by which photographers, photographic editors, news editors, and journalists decide how war can be reduced to a photograph, journalism's images of war have come to represent an elaborated template for imagining and assessing the wars of the twenty-first century. Such images reflect what the camera sees by projecting onto that vision a set of broader assumptions about how the world works. The ways in which this happens, however, raise questions about the degree to which images, particularly photographs, are well suited to shaping the public's encounter with war.

When war is reduced to a photograph, the camera provides images that show far more than just the scene at hand. Images that are composite, more schematic than detailed, conventionalized, and simplified work particularly well in this regard. Used as pegs not to specific events but to stories larger than can be told in a simple news item, journalism's images become a key tool for interpreting the war in ways consonant with long-standing understandings about how war is supposed to be waged—notions about patriotism, sacrifice, humanity, the nation-state, and fairness that come as much from outside journalism as from within. War is presented as often heroic and reflective of broader aims associated with nationhood, clean and at times antiseptic, and involving human sacrifice for a greater good. Whether or not this actually reflects how war is waged is beyond the mission of journalism's images of war. For a range of visual cues, or familiar templates for using images, helps journalists depict circumstances that are fraught with unpredictability, stressful judgment, emotionalism, inconsistency, and high stakes, facilitating journalism's depictions of war but not necessarily in ways that support the image's workings as a tool of news relay. Relying on particular images, cues, and themes that have proven themselves over time, journalism's images of war gravitate toward the memorable—as established through frequently depicted, aesthetically appealing, and familiar images—as much as toward the newsworthy. What does this mean for the health of the body politic, which depends on images of war to provide presumably reliable visual depictions of war-stricken zones?

When compared with times of peace, wartime often produces both more pictures, more varied pictures, and pictures whose display is justified on a wide range of attributes—such as memorability, drama, or vividness. The use of pictures depends not so much on explicit and articulated standards but on informal strategies among journalists about how best to use them (Zelizer 1993; Rosenstiel 2003; Glaser 2003). As reporters, editors, photo-editors, and photographers, journalists agree on a myriad of interpretive strategies—regarding who depicts the war, what is depicted, how it is depicted, and in which ways—that are shaped against the larger restrictions through which pictures can be displayed. In wartime, informal strategies among journalists thereby shape the turn toward the visual, whereby it is agreed, though not necessarily articulated, that photographs depict certain aspects of the war but not all.

For only certain aspects of war are ever seen in the images of war. Lacking depiction are those sides of war which do not fit the prevailing interpretive assumptions about how war is to be waged. In most wars, there are few or no images of human gore, one's own war dead or POWs, military operations gone badly, or the effect of one's own war on civilians of the other side. In certain conflicts, such as those in which the West is involved, this is more pronounced than in others. Lacking depiction too have been a range of conflicts that missed being seen almost totally—wars in East Timor, Sudan, Somalia, Liberia, and Zaire, to name a few.

And yet wartime's turn to the visual offers a way for news organizations to accommodate the prominence of visual representation as a way of engaging with war. The turn to the visual has a number of predictable attributes in war journalism which have come to characterize our expectations of war as we begin the twenty-first century. Examined here primarily in the US media and largely in conjunction with the most reported wars of the past five years, the turn to the visual nonetheless can be found in a far broader range of military conflicts and geographic contexts, all of which have come to inhabit public depictions of the contemporary era. In suggesting that journalists regularly gravitate toward certain kinds of visual depictions in their visualization of recent wars, the turn to the

116

visual raises questions about the ways in which images function in wartime. More specifically, it queries the role played by visuals in relaying a strategically crafted depiction of war and in undermining the maintenance of a healthy body politic.

The turn to the visual in war

How journalism depicts war has always been considered against a more complicated set of assumptions about the ways in which images, particularly photographs, work. Photography's specific attributes—its materiality, ease of access, frozen capture of time, an affective and often gestalt-driven view of the world that is thought to bypass the intellect and communicate directly with the emotions—highlight its power and durability. Photographs are thought to work through a twinning of denotative and connotative force, by which the ability to depict the world as "it is"—commonly associated with photographic verisimilitude, realism, indexicality, and referentiality—is matched with a symbolic power to couch what is being depicted in a broader, generalizable frame that helps us recognize the image as consonant with broader understandings of the world—typically associated with universality, generalizability, and symbolism (Hall 1974; Sekula 1984). The two forces are rarely presumed to work equally in journalism, where the former is privileged over the latter. Denotation and the truth-value of the photograph, more than connotation, are thought to be critical, because journalism needs photographic realism to enhance its ability to vouch for events in the real world. In reality, however, connotation is as important, if not more, than denotation.

During the recent war in Iraq, for instance, the pictures of Saddam Hussein's statue being dismantled in April of 2003 in Baghdad's Firdous Square (Delay 2003; Hicks 2003) were called by the *Boston Globe* a depiction of "the first feel-good moment of the war" (Gilbert and Ryan 2003: D1) and appraised as a referential depiction of the statue being brought down. They were also, however, seen as images earmarking the beginning of revolution, in a manner long attributed to similar photographs from Eastern Europe from the 1950s onward. One such well known photograph depicted the statue of Stalin being dismantled by student protesters in Budapest of 1956 (reprinted in Swain 1992). Positioned in the center of the page on some newspapers and atop the masthead on others, the context surrounding the Baghdad photograph was as important in establishing its importance as the sheer target of what it depicted. Furthermore, when later contextualized against wide-angle views of what then appeared to be a relatively empty Firdous Square, populated by some 200 people who were mostly US troops and journalists, that appeared the following day, accusations arose that the photograph had been staged rather than simply shot at random (Lichfield 2003; Fisk 2003). Reports that the square was sealed off from the crowds, that foreign troops (using a US armoured vehicle) pulled down the statue rather than local people, that pro-American free Iraqi forces were brought into the square rather than a naturally evolving crowd (Brown 2003) were all claims that helped establish the seemingly referential depiction as problematic and the historical parallel with eastern Europe as erroneous. Connotation was everything.

Turns to the visual like this one in relaying war news have been historically complicated, for they occur against the backdrop of a professional inattention to images. For most journalists, news images have always taken a backseat to words. Since the photograph's inception in the mid-1800s, pictures have long been seen as the fluff of journalism, the stuff that illustrates but is adjunct to verbal description. Even today, with an array of imaging technologies like moving pictures, television, cable, and the interactive displays of the Internet, there still remain insufficient standards for how to use an image in news, where to put an image, whether to credit an image, how to title an image, or how to connect an image with the text at its side (Zelizer 1995). It is no surprise that journalists find themselves depending on a repertoire of informal cues by which they decide what to depict and in which way.

And yet, it is to images that journalism turns in times of war. There are three main attributes that characterize the turn to the visual in wartime, each of which caters to a news image's memorability:

1   There are more images in wartime than in times of peace.
2   Images function more in wartime like non-journalistic modes of visual representation than in times of peace.
3   Images gravitate more in wartime toward familiar depictions of the past than in times of peace.

War and the frequency of images

The bursting of wartime journalism with images should raise no eyebrows, for such has been the case since the earliest displays of news images. Images have always taken over the spaces available to them when war rears its head, in ratios disproportionate to how journalists cover the world in more peaceful times. No surprise, then, that photography helps establish the truth claims of journalists seeking to provide authoritative accounts of the war. As prizewinning photographer Don McCullin said of his photographs of the wartorn regions of Vietnam and Lebanon, "Many people ask me 'why do you take these pictures?' . . . It's not a case of 'There but for the grace of God go I'; it's a case of 'I've been there'" (McCullin 1987: 11). Displaying a similar sentiment, Dorothea Lange hung the following words of Francis Bacon on her darkroom door: "The contemplation of things as they are, without substitution or imposture, without error or confusion, is in itself a nobler thing than a whole harvest of invention" (quoted in Lyons 1966: 67).

Such has long been the aspiration though not always the practice. Images of war extend from a tradition in which artists in the early years of the illustrated press "had little compunction about distorting the real facts of the event," whose battles they rarely saw (Voss 1994: 136). The photographic images of the Crimean War were not much better, generally portraying British triumphs, placid views far from the frontlines, and circumstances in which everything looked "ship-shape and everyone happy" (Knightley 1975: 15). The US Civil War brought with it a stark realism associated with photography and moved away from the romanticized tenor of drawings, introducing what came to be known as the "first living room war" (Goldberg 1991: 20) and couching war's representation in terms of realist discourse and authenticity rather than imagination and interpretation. World War II was documented by more photographers than any previous military conflict, and the rapid transmission of their depictions of battlefields by wire helped make the war-news reader during the 1940s "far closer to events on the battlefield than his [sic] grandfather, regardless of the actual distance he might be removed from active fighting" (Mathews 1957: 193). A peculiarly autonomous sense about the process of capturing a scene through photographs existed in these pre-television times. As World War II photographer Margaret Bourke-White said of a shot she made of a dead family killed in a German air raid, "a protecting screen draws itself across my mind and makes it possible to consider focus and light values and the techniques of photography, in as impersonal a way as though I were making an abstract camera composition" (cited in Goldberg 1986: 245).

The introduction in later wars of more sophisticated imaging technologies—in particular, the moving image and its evolving technologies of documentary, television, cable, and digitalization—raised questions as to whether or not photographs would continue to matter in war's visualization. Accounts of newsgathering practices widely held that the Korean War was the first covered by television, that the Vietnam War introduced graphic images of war, that the Gulf War of 1991 advanced cable images 24 hours a day, and that the 2003 war in Iraq embraced broadband Internet and its associated digital devices—websites containing live video, photography collections, audio reports, animated weaponry displays, and interactive maps—that offered a "more intimate and multi-faceted view of the war than . . . possible ever before" (Harmon 2003: C4). Through it all, the still photograph persisted as a viable mode of recording, even though fundamental questions lingered regarding its use.

In each war, photographic depiction flourished, though it depended on what the military and political forces, and sometimes editors, allowed the public to see. During the Spanish American War, the *Journal* put out as many as 40 editions in one day, much of which were characterized by a "lavish use of photographs and illustrations" (Moeller 1989: 68). The photographs of Larry Burrows during the Vietnam War earned him the title of "the greatest war photographer there has ever been" (Hopkinson cited in Knightley 1975: 408), despite the fact that his much-publicized doubts about the role of the photographer and the war itself were at odds with his capacity to jump into settings and take photographs without hesitation. The photographs of Eddie Adams, Ron Haeberle, and Malcolm Browne produced still shots far more memorable than the corresponding nightly television footage, with Haeberle's images of the massacre at My Lei displayed as still visuals on television.

Certain wars fell short of photographic centrality. Depiction of the Falklands War totaled a meager 200 individual photographic shots, mostly cleansed portrayals of antiseptic warfare and virtually no human corpses, creating an "illusion of a clean war" (Taylor 1991: 112–13), while the Gulf War of 1991 was shaped through the less than satisfying visuals of cable television, where television cameras stood still as viewers watched a shaky setting accommodate an incoming SCUD missile, and helmeted television reporters hopped in front of live cameras as they tried to dodge the firing around them (Zelizer 1992). At the side of such video footage, photographs were "censored into invisibility, void of images of real violence and suffering" (Robins 1993: 325), and when they did appear—such as a much-discussed shot of an Iraqi soldier immolated in his vehicle published in the *Observer* of London—US editors refused to publish them.

Yet by more recent wars, wavering decisions over what kinds of images to publish made way for a more frequent and prominent display of images. While conflicts in both Africa and Asia generated little world interest because in one view the "bone-thin men behind barbed wire in the Balkans, on the doorstep of the West, resonate[d] more deeply . . . than the many horrors of Asia and Africa" (Lane 1992: 27), pictures nonetheless appeared. Africa, in particular conflicts in Rwanda and Burundi, persisted in the public imagination as a "dark continent, where nothing happens except coups, massacres, famines, disease and drought" (Douglas 1994: 15). The Balkan violence of the 1990s was so unevenly visualized that it paradoxically earned both the status of "Europe's first television war" (Marshall 1994: A16) and the name of "the war that can't be seen" (Cohen 1994: E4), whose stories and pictures were "lost in the fog of second-hand reporting" and whose journalists "were unable to get there" (Rohde 1995: A1). At the same time, observers claimed that the stream of photographs depicting people who looked like "one's neighbors" were responsible for generating support for the war (Douglas 1994: 15).

Following the events of September 11, newspapers and newsmagazines raised the number of photographs by, in some cases, twice the usual number of images published (Zelizer 2002). This continued to be the case in the two wars that followed—Afghanistan and Iraq. The war in Afghanistan was visualized through images that implied a certain romanticized nostalgia for a reclaimed civilization, with shots of newly unveiled women or women appearing for the first time in public places (Nalkur 2002), liberated crowds, and breathtaking colorful landscapes topping the coverage. During the 2003 war in Iraq, a turn to the visual involved newspapers turning over whole pages and sections to images that were larger, bolder, more colorful, and displayed prominently. Likened by Tom Brokaw to "drinking from a fire hydrant" and by Dan Rather to a "literal flood of live pictures from the battlefield" (quoted in Hilbrand and Shister 2003: A1, A20), early images of Iraq were plentiful across the media. During the first few months of the invasion, an informal count of the images appearing in the *New York Times* revealed that the *Times* displayed two to two and a half times the number of photographs than that displayed before the war—40 or 50 images rather than 20. Newspapers featured double-page photographic spreads and quarter-, half-, and full-page photographs; television networks displayed galleries of still photographs to background music while tracking the experiences of single war photographers as part of their nightly line-up. Photographic marginalia cluttered news organizations' websites, offering updated visual digests of that day's events on the battlefield. In each war, then, the message seemed clear: photographs matter.

But how do photographs matter? On the face of things, the move toward more visual relays fits what the news is supposed to do in wartime—give the public more information when more information is needed. But often images instead provide what is already known, familiar, and sensical. During the war in Iraq, for instance, one *New York Times* article showed not one but three pictures of Iraqis uncovering the graves of their relatives (pictures appended to Fisher 2003: A10). A different image focused on the horror on the face of an American servicewoman, as she watched Al-Jazeera images of captured and killed soldiers which significantly were not shown, forcing audiences to supply the context against which to explain the image ("An American servicewoman watched images from Al-Jazeera . . . ," 2003: B6). The *Philadelphia Inquirer* published a full page spread of five images under the joint title "Portraits of war: conflict, capitulation." The captions appended to each picture were broad and lacking in discreet detail, as in "Iraqis welcome members of Britain's Second Royal Tank Regiment," with no names, no definite location, and no time in which the photograph had been taken (pictures appended to "Portraits of war" 2003: A21). In a setting in which every column-inch is precious, all of this is worth considering. While it is generally agreed that more photographs appear than in peacetime, more images of wartime do not necessarily mean more information about war.

War and the aesthetic appeal of images

The turn to the visual is exemplified by images that look less like typical news relays and more like non-journalistic images. War images are typically bigger, bolder, more colorful, more memorable, more dramatic, prettier, shocking, and more aesthetically pleasing or noteworthy than the relays received otherwise. What they are not necessarily is newsworthy.

The impulse toward aesthetic, dramatic, pleasing, or shocking images has long been part of photography's practice in journalism and exemplified by images that typically win prizes and generate professional acclaim, like Eddie Adams' shot of a streetside execution of a Vietcong soldier by the chief of the South Vietnamese police (Adams 1968). The aesthetic for war images, however, has itself changed, as over time war has tended to be depicted in changing aesthetic patterns. In Peter Howe's words,

> the first war photographers really didn't photograph war at all. Because of the bulk of their equipment and the length of time it took to make an

exposure, they were limited to battleground landscapes, posed pictures of fighters, simulated combat, and portraits of soldiers prior to battle.

(Howe 2002: 14)

Early emphasis on distant battlefields, exemplified in conflicts like the Spanish American War, gave way by the time of the Korean War to large numbers of close-ups of individual soldiers. Along the way, differing degrees of attention were paid to pictures of wartime suffering, deaths of soldiers and civilians, and broad landscapes. Parts of the aesthetic cycled irregularly over time: Vietnam displayed a return to printing studio portraits of the dead, as favored during the Spanish American War (Moeller 1989); pastoral landscapes, seen in early shots during the Spanish American War of the 1890s, re-emerged in areas known for breathtaking physical terrain, like the war in Afghanistan in 2001. The degree of comprehensiveness embodied by images also wavered, as certain wars tended to accommodate a more wide-ranging repertoire of photographs than in earlier wars, such as World War I, while others signaled a move backward in clamping down on the display of certain targets of depiction associated with wartime, as in the Falklands War.

The aesthetic draw of the image also generates numerous examples of shifting the target of photographic representation so as to secure a "better" picture. Connected here is a long tradition of altering photographic images—dramatizing a look of menace by blackening skin or altering the position of figures and structures so as to enhance overall composition. The decision in March 2004, for instance, to delete clearly visible body parts in UK newspaper pictures of the bombings in Madrid (Luckhurst 2004) exemplified the underside of the urge to publish only those pictures that fit aesthetic expectations.

At the same time, accommodating the aesthetic draw of an image produces images that are not always clear or focused, as one might expect from a news photograph. In the recent war in Iraq, one newspaper ran a story titled "As sandstorm rages, Iraqis seized" and displayed an AP photograph of Iraqis being detained (Bouju 2003: 3). While the photograph's caption noted that the detention was taking place "in the glare of Humvee headlights," it did not clarify that the headlights' glare obscured the detainees from the news audience's vision; nor did that ill vision stop the newspaper from printing the photograph as the largest, most prominent image on the page.

In the years since color photographs became a part of mainstream news, color becomes a central way of signaling aesthetic appeal. Photographs of the war of Afghanistan in particular played to color, from the vividness of the fabrics swathing the dispossessed women and children to the breathtaking landscapes pitching voluminous mountain-caps against bright blue skies. No wonder, then, that readers' letters proclaimed the photographs of Afghanistan in positive superlative terms: one reader to the *Los Angles Times* proclaimed the photographs of Afghanistan "not sensational or sentimental, just beautiful. (They get) right in the middle of things and shoot at the precise moment when reality unfolds. Nothing in (the) images is mere background" (Coonradt 2001: B12). Another noted that the photographs of Afghani children were "a glorious testament to the timeless beauty of innocence and to the common admiration of this human condition among Earth's inhabitants" (Takase 2001: A12). At a time in which the incursion into Afghanistan was only a month or so under way and thousands of refugees had already gone homeless and hungry while others had lost their lives in brutal battles, the laudation of photography's aesthetic appeal gives pause to the image's role in documenting the conflict.

During the war in Iraq, color remained at the forefront of the photograph's aesthetic appeal. The *Chicago Tribune* featured a front-page image of the back profile of a soldier outlined against an amorphous orange background, making it appear as if he were disappearing into an unidentifiable abyss (DiNuzzo 2003). As the US forces moved into Basra in March of 2003, *The New York Times* featured a half-page portrayal of a woman carrying potable water ("Hauling water" 2003: B1). The picture, striking for that same peculiar orange haze that was typical of many images from the region owing to the impact of dense sand in the air, was significantly lacking in definitive detail: the *Times* mentioned nothing about where precisely the photograph was taken other than on the outskirts of Basra, nothing about the women other than that they carried potable water, and nothing about what lurked behind the orange haze.

In fact, the orange haze appeared to be the striking reason for choosing the photograph and others like it. On a day in which accompanying news stories documented attacks against Iranian opposition groups in Iraq, exchanges of fire in Mosul, and the plundering of the Iraqi National Museum, this artistic choice to lead the section on the war displaced an informationally rich one. In the words of the *Chicago Tribune*'s art critic:

> If you have the capacity to dazzle in newsprint, you make pictures to take advantage of it [and] color rescues [these photographs]. It is bright, upbeat, conveying an atmosphere of Operation Happy Trails even when the content of the shots is dark, treating death.

In this sense, "eye-popping colour draws us from the truth" (Artner 2003: 4). As news, then, the aesthetic appeal of images works against the information that such depictions can provide.

At times, the aesthetic appeal of war images turns too to explicitly non-journalistic modes of visual representation. One article in the *Philadelphia Inquirer* in March of 2003 about the false surrender of Iraqi troops was illustrated by a reprint of the Goya painting, *The Third of May 1808*, in which he depicted the execution of Madrid residents at the hands of Napoleonic forces (pictures appended to Lubrano 2003: C1). With the decision to include it came another decision not to include a photograph that depicted more directly what was happening in Iraq, suggesting that the image's aestheticization works too against its newsworthiness in wartime.

War and the familiarity of images

Journalism's images of war offer pictures that are consonant with already existing notions of what wartime is. As media critic Frank Rich said of coverage of the recent war in Iraq, the public knew what was coming: "Iraqis are the better seen-than-heard dress extras in this drama, alternately pictured as sobbing, snarling or cheering" (Rich 2003: section 2: 15). While such displays suit editors' desire to keep newspapers "family friendly" and offset their fears of an advertiser backlash, news photography nonetheless offers what becomes a default visual setting for many of the contested and conflicted wars of the twentieth and twenty-first centuries. The turn to the visual, then, offers a turn to familiar images that couche war's representation in already resonant ways. As one column in the *Chicago Tribune* phrased it, "it's as though all wars become, at some level, the same war; all reaction that of a common humanity" (Leroux 2003; section 2: 1).

The interpretive assumptions guiding the display of pictures thus often have to do with images that withstand the test of time. Journalists rely on photographs to offer aspects of war that words cannot, and often they accomplish this by weaving memorable scenes from the past into their pictures of the present. Images of past wars offer a fertile repository from which journalists can seek cues on how to do their work, for recycling familiar images has journalists often following standards that are not particularly newsworthy and upset or possibly undermine the journalistic value of their coverage. With photographs, then, historical precedent offers an accessible context for wars in need of definition. For journalists, this makes sense: in times of war, earlier wars in other times and places offer a quick way to decide how to use photographs.

Thus, Robert Capa's iconic tribute to Republican Spain, hailed as a death-in-action shot which depicted a soldier of the Spanish Civil War at the moment of his impact from a bullet (Capa 1936), in fact thematically recycled an image taken at the siege of Verdun in 1916 during World War I. That earlier shot, taken from film footage by an anonymous cameraman, showed a French officer being shot to death as he led a counter-attack straight into the field of a German machine-gun (pictured in Stepan 2000). Reminiscent of a long-standing tradition in which soldiers ran directly into the field of fire, the photograph not only portrayed the trench warfare of Verdun but became emblematic of the collision of "nineteenth century notions of courage" with "modern reality" (Stepan 2000: 30).

Problematic, however, are the decisions about what constitutes news that ensue. In that journalists only have so many column-inches and minutes in which to present their notions about how the world works, each decision to incorporate the past is accompanied by one to incorporate the present to a lesser degree. In other words, war coverage often hinges on a vehicle that works against the grain of "good" journalism yet adheres precisely to the grain of "good" memory work. For instance, depicting September 11 (Franklin 2001) and the war in Afghanistan (Chenelly 2001) through images that recalled a World War II photograph of the flag-raising atop Mount Suribachi (Rosenthal 1945) relays little of the circumstances of the later wars, though the parallel does instantiate the messages of heroism, patriotism, human sacrifice, and the importance of the nation-state that accompanied the earlier photograph. Additionally, the act of hoisting the flag, the traditional symbol of victory, earlier depicted as achievable through a backdrop of anonymity, "clean" warfare, and group effort, moves on into caricatures, advertisements, and popular culture, as seen in one caricature of the 2003 war in Iraq (McCoy 2003), suggesting that even if the associations are irrelevant to the later wars, the use of the image as parallel depictions establishes a connection that lasts.

Moreover, journalism's journey to the past in wartime is uncharted territory. There are no standards, no guidelines, no explicit directives about what in the past best works in the present, for whom, and to which ends. Simply stated, who is to say which past makes sense? Should the 2003 war in Iraq be seen against the first Gulf War, Somalia, or Vietnam? And yet, journalists look to the past, in all of its forms, as one way to reinstate the normal. This means that wars not necessarily alike can receive a similar visual treatment in the news simply because the form of the war's coverage is rendered similar. The past thus intrudes into the present of news photographs by acting as a carrier for symbolism and connotative force. Bringing systematic messages about what matters, this involves a slew of recycled associations that link new wars with familiar experiences of patriotism, civic pride, heroic sacrifice, and the durability of the nation-state. Photographs are used to drive these associations home. Thus, connecting backward in time is signified by a visual trajectory of journalism's images that extend across wars in different times and places.

The depiction of war over time gravitates in clear directions. Often journalism's images of war are clear even before they are presented as news. Memorable, dramatic, and symbolic, they cut and depict events in a way that helps the public not only make sense of them but also remember them in the years that follow. War images capture the essence of war in a way that illustrates some vivid emotion or bring home what appear to be fundamental truths. In one media critic's view, the "heroic, often unrepresentative images" of war are useful in that they "deliberately recall [other] photographs and famous cinematic sequences" (Kakutani 2003: E1, E5). Much of the power of depicting new wars thus comes from earlier times.

There are three ways in which journalists cue a linkage between an image of war and the past—through words, through parallel pictures, and through substitutional depictions (Zelizer 1998).

Functioning as carriers of meaning that direct interpretations of the images at their side (Barthes 1977, 1981; Hall 1974), words offer a way to connect what is depicted with the intention by which it is shown. The parallel between a contemporary war and a war of earlier times is here enunciated primarily in words and only secondarily in the image itself. Articulation is generally found in the words surrounding the photograph—captions, titles, headlines, and accompanying bodies of text—that guide audiences in the image's interpretation. Using words as directed cues for interpretation is built into the ways in which journalists create familiar standards for describing war to the public. Calling East Timor "Indonesia's Tiananmen" ("The Tiananmen in East Timor," 1992: A20) or "another Cambodia" (Kondrake 1979) explains complicated wars through association. In a column titled "The real echoes from Vietnam" alongside an image of Saigon, *Newsweek* correspondent Jonathan Alter addressed the circumstances of war-torn Iraq in 2003 by discussing the implications of having "a moment early last week [when] it felt like 1967" (Alter 2003: 41). Some images are contextualized against an unspecific past, couched in broad terms, such as a shot from *The Economist*—depicting weeping women in Bosnia—that was entitled "Out of the past" with no details that identified the shot as contemporary or tracked which past was being referenced ("Weeping women" 1991). Other times the past is invoked more specifically, as when *The New York Times* asked "Does the world still recognize a holocaust?' in an article about a 1993 execution of Muslims in the Balkans (pictures appended to Darnton 1993). Other parallels are struck through recalling the circumstances of a photograph's taking, as in likening the image of Mohammad Aldura, a 12-year-old Palestinian boy shot to death in the midst of a battle between Israeli soldiers and Palestinians during the Intifada of 2000 (Abu-Rahma 2000), and, once again, Eddie Adams' iconic shot (Adams 1968) of the shooting of a Vietcong soldier by the South Vietnamese Chief of Police in 1968 (Roskis 2000). Parallels are also shaped by region or locality. Conflicts in Burundi were labeled as "the next Rwanda" (Gillett and des Forges 1994), while battles in Russia and Moldova were called "the next Bosnia" ("The next Bosnia" 1992: 43). On March 31, 2003, in its first issue after the recent war in Iraq began, *Time* magazine titled its cover photograph "Gulf War II." In each case, the implication that earlier wars could offer an appropriate backdrop against which to interpret contemporary battles sets up an associative framework by which the more recent wars are seen through the filter of the earlier ones. The use of words as guides, then, pushes audiences to a position by which they are required to engage with the war that came before while dealing with the more recent military conflict. As *Time* put it, "the shock of recognition is acute . . . Surely these pictures . . . come from another time" (Walsh 1995: 46–7).

A second way of cueing the past through images is by simply repeating the thematic portrayal of earlier wars, visually marking the past but offering no verbal cues. Ranging from the predictable—the heroic gestures of soldiers—to the grotesque—stark depictions of human corpses, journalism's images of war rework recognizable and familiar themes of representation in visually depicting new wars. Pictures are used as parallels in ways that mark the associations surrounding certain wars as antecedents to later ones. The Tianenmen Square shot of a man stopping a cordon of Chinese tanks in June 1989 with nothing more than a shopping bag symbolized individual courage standing firm before the armed might of the state (Widener 1989), but it also recalled a 1968 shot of a plumber in Prague, who, on coming face to face with the Soviet tanks about to overrun the Czech city, stood in front of the tank, tore open his shirt, and shouted at the tank commander to shoot him (Bielik 1968). A 1987 dpa (Deutsche Presse-Agentur) image of the beginnings of the first Intifada in Israel—in which a crew of kaffiyaed men and boys, led by a flag-bearer carrying the Palestinian flag, was sprawled across a Nablus plaza readying themselves to throw rocks ("The Intifada" 1987)—was likened to the Delacroix painting *Liberty Leads the People*, which depicted a storming crowd bearing forward a flag during the French Revolution (Stepan 2000: 158–9). Malcolm Browne's much-celebrated image of a Buddhist monk immolating himself in the streets of Saigon of 1963 to protest the Vietnam war (Browne 1963) resurfaced in photographs of a Kurdish teenage girl, Necla Kanteper, who set herself on fire in 1999 in the London streets following the capture of the Kurdish guerrilla chief Abdallah Ocalan (picture appended to Gillan 1999: 3), and of an Indian national, Mandeep Singh Sodhi, who set himself on fire in 2000 in front of the state legislature to protest police harassment ("India Suicide" 2000); each symbolized human sacrifice for a greater good. Robert Capa's shot of a dead German soldier falling into a building from an outside balcony, that appeared in *Life* on May 14, 1945 (Capa 1945), was echoed in numerous shots from Iraq in 2003 that emblemized the same visual trope of the faceless, anonymous, bloodless death of the enemy soldier (i.e. Hill 2003). A World War II image taken by W. Eugene Smith of a US GI holding a fly-covered baby removed from a cave filled with hundreds of corpses (Smith 1944; Figure 6.1)—hailed by *Life* magazine as one of the score of photographs that "people most readily remember" ("Moments remembered" 1960: 91)—was recycled into a similar shot taken in Beirut during the city's onslaught during the mid-1980s (Faddoud 1985) and later into a much-publicized photograph of a US soldier holding an Iraqi child (Sagolj 2003; Figure 6.2), where it was slated by the *Detroit Free Press* already in 2003 as an image that would be "embedded in history" (Hinds 2003: H1).

A third kind of stopover in the past employs an image of previous wars that is both articulated and visible. This kind of image implies the most direct connection between different wars, in that it directly substitutes photographs of recent wars with earlier war photographs. These acts of substitutional representation extend a broader disjunction, often evident in news, between the place of the news-text and the place of the image at its side. In this regard, images of earlier wars reappear as direct visual cues to more recent events. Pictures are used either as partial substitution, when pictures of the past are positioned alongside images of the war being covered, or as total substitution, when pictures of the past are used in place of any image of the war being covered. In both cases, the editorial decision to use a photograph of the past takes away column-inches from the war being covered. Such visual substitutions bring back a wide range of wars from the past and, in cases of partial substitution, they establish a definitive visual corollary between the war of then and the war of now. Following September 11, the *Philadelphia Inquirer* displayed a pair of images—one of which depicted the collapsed World Trade Center towers, the other of which showed the 1941 assault on Pearl Harbor—which drew a visual parallel between the two events despite

Figure 6.1 A US GI holds a fly-covered baby, photograph by W. Eugene Smith, first published in *Life*, August 28, 1944 (courtesy of Getty Images)

Figure 6.2 US marine doctor with Iraqi girl, photograph by Damir Sagolj, April 2003 (courtesy of Reuters)

the fact that other historical parallels with other events might have been more suitable (pictures appended to Infield 2001: A11; discussed in Zelizer 2002). A *Time* column on the so-called victory in Afghanistan was accompanied by two photographs—one of Afghanistan and one of Somalia (pictures appended to Krauthammer 2001: 60–1). A *Boston Globe* article about the toppling of the statue of Saddam Hussein in Baghdad in 2003 was illustrated with additional photographs depicting other seemingly similar moments from earlier points in time—the razing of the Berlin Wall, the lone protester in Tienanmen Square, and workers jumping off a statue of Lenin in Riga before Latvia seceded from the Soviet Union (pictures appended to Gilbert and Ryan 2003: D1). *The New York Times* ran one essay entitled "Watching Iraq, and Seeing Vietnam," in which pictures of Saigon and Baghdad were positioned side by side (Whitney 2003: section 4: 1; Figure 6.3) and another in which pictures of dead soldiers in the streets of Baghdad and Mogadishu were lined up side by side alongside the suggestion that the image would help turn the tide against the later war as it had done in the earlier one (Kifner 2003 section 4: 1). Other times the photograph of the past completely displaces the contemporary photograph. A *New York Times* piece about civilian casualties, written at the onset of the war in Iraq in 2003, was illustrated by one image of dead civilians in Kosovo in 1999 and two photographs of structural devastation in Kosovo in 1999 and Kabul, Afghanistan in 2001, but no image at all of what was then already transpiring in Iraq (Eviatar 2003: D7, D9). A *Time* article republished a picture of a Kurdish refugee fleeing Iraqi persecution

Figure 6.3 "Watching Iraq, and Seeing Vietnam," *The New York Times*, November 9, 2003 (courtesy of *The New York Times*)

129

in 1991 as a bridge between one article about Saddam Hussein in 2003 and another querying the US betrayal of Iraqis during the earlier Gulf War (picture appended to McGeary 2003: 57), the picture offering a visual bridge by which the more recent article could be understood. An article about urban warfare in Baghdad during the war in Iraq positioned a drawing of what soldiers in the street would look like alongside a photograph of a tank unit patrolling Mogadishu, Somalia, ten years earlier ("A nation at war" 2003: B12). *Newsweek* featured an image of Saigon in a column on Iraq (Alter 2003: 41). In all of these cases, the distance between the war of today and that of earlier wars is collapsed via its visual representation. The image of then substitutes for the image of today.

When war is reduced to a photograph

What does the turn to the visual in wartime tell us? Wartime reportage involves making quick decisions under fraught circumstances. In that regard, the availability of cues—whether they have to do with frequency, aesthetic appeal, or familiarity—help reporters, photographers, photo-editors, and news editors make judgments about which photographs should depict a given circumstance of war. All of this matters because it is not the photograph's referentiality—its ability to present the world as is—that endures in journalism's turn to the visual. Despite the fact that photographers and journalists have long stipulated that the referential force matters in news photographs, it is the photograph's symbolic or connotative force—its ability to contextualize the discrete details of a setting in a broader frame—that facilitates the durability and memorability of a news image. Given the lack of standardization about how to use photographs, the marginalization of photography as an autonomous mode of news relay, and the importance of informal cues in directing journalistic practice, the turn to the visual makes sense as a way of directing the engagement with news photographs. Such cues are often not the best, most complete, or most representative mode of depiction, so that what is seen in war is often not what is depicted in its photographs.

This means that journalism's images of war provide a strategically narrowed way of visualizing the battlefield. When a news photograph is deemed "memorable," there is reason to believe that modes of appraisal other than newsworthiness are being invoked. Journalism's images force the public to see war but in a way that only partly reflects the war being depicted. Coverage, then, takes its cue from a turn to the visual that offers war's core visual representation in the news, regardless of how well it does so as part of journalism's own role in documenting war.

The ramifications of this are disturbing. Lost in the depictions tracked here are the important visual aspects of each individual war and the socio-political differences that differentiate wars from each other. Pictures in this sense are supported by their own lack of standardized usage in news, where they often are used to shape public consensus precisely because the standards for regulating their use are uneven. Is it any surprise, then, that images facilitate the accomplishment of political and military ends, mobilizing public support for strategic action in wartime? With the turn to the visual serving up the material by which this is accomplished, there is need to think more critically about what such ends suggest for the viability of a healthy and contested public sphere.

The ends that are at stake are numerous and varied. One might only think about the pictures not seen—of the recent war in Afghanistan and, at the time of writing, the ongoing war in Iraq. The fact that in times of war, journalism shifts to a mode of photographic relay that proceeds basically without directives other than informal impulses toward frequency, aesthetic appeal, and familiarity allows for unusual, even faulty news judgment. It allows for pictures of the memorable, frequent, dramatic, aesthetically appealing, powerful, and familiar over the newsworthy, and it encourages pictures in a way that facilitates faulty comparisons across events. Most important, it allows journalists to strike parallels between wars for no better reason than the surrounding mandates for interpreting them resemble each other. Those faulty comparisons are problematic. How alike are the wars positioned here as visual parallels? They are not very alike at all. Yet depicting new wars in ways that link them with old practices of depiction forces a spectator position on the public that may have less to do with the war itself and more to do with the parallel being struck. The public sees many pictures of war, but what it sees is not necessarily what it needs to see. Seen are shards of wartime presented in a way that forces certain public responses and mutes questions about the ultimate value of both the depictions and the parallels being displayed, for whom and to which ends.

When war is reduced to a photograph, then, its usage depends on journalism being less journalistic than it needs to be. What clearer note is needed to signal the dangers that photographs pose to the maintenance of a healthy body politic in wartime?

Notes

1 Thanks to Lauren Feldman and Bethany Klein for collecting photographs studied for this chapter. Parts of the chapter were presented at the Shorenstein Center on the Press, Politics, and Public Policy at Harvard University, University of Southern California, the Conference on the Media at War at the University of California at Berkeley, Middle Tennessee State University, the New Hampshire Humanities Council, the New School University, Grand Valley State University, and Wabash College. Special thanks to the Annenberg School for Communication at the University of Pennsylvania and to Harvard University's Shorenstein Center, where I was a fellow during the spring of 2004, for technical help in completing this chapter.

References

Abu-Rahma, Talal, "Shooting of Mohammad Aldura," September 30, 2000, image taken as a video still for French TV2.

Adams, Eddie, "General loan shooting of Vietcong soldier," February 2, 1968, Saigon, Vietnam, image taken for AP/World Wide Photos.

Alter, Jonathan, "The real echoes from Vietnam," Newsweek, April 14, 2003, p. 41.

"An American servicewoman watched images from Al-Jazeera . . . ," *The New York Times*, March 24, 2003, p. B6, image taken for Getty Images.

Artner, Alan G, "The war, in color," *Chicago Tribune*, April 10, 2003, section 5: pp. 1, 4.

Barthes, Roland, "The rhetoric of the image," in *Image/Music/Text*, New York: Hill and Wang, 1977.

Barthes, Roland, *Camera Lucida*, London: Hill and Wang, 1981.

Bielik, Ladislav, "The end of the Prague spring," August 21, 1968, Bratislava, Czechoslovakia, image taken for *Smena*.

Bouju, Jean-Marc, "Iraqis detained," *Chicago Tribune*, March 27, 2003, p. 3, image taken for the Associated Press.

Brown, John, "'They got it down': the toppling of the Saddam statue," *Counterpunch*, April 12, 2003, posted at http://www.counterpunch.org/brown04122003.html

Browne, Malcolm, "Reverend Quang Duc in flames," June 12, 1963, Saigon, Vietnam, image taken for AP/World Wide Photos.

Capa, Robert, "Death of a loyalist soldier," September 15, 1936, image taken for *Vu*.

Capa, Robert, "Dead German soldier," May 14, 1945, image taken for *Life*.

Chennelly, Joseph, "New way," *Time*, December 24, 2001, p. 61, image taken for US Marine Corps.

Cohen, Roger, "In Bosnia, the war that can't be seen," *The New York Times*, December 25, 1994, p. E4.

Coonradt, Peter, "Afghan coverage" (letter to the editor), *Los Angeles Times*, November 22, 2001, p. B12.

Darnton, John, "Does the world still recognize a holocaust?" *TheNew York Times*, April 25, 1993, section 4: p. 1.

Delay, Jerome, "Statue of Saddam Hussein falls," *The New York Times*, April 10, 2003, p. 1, image taken for Associated Press.

DiNuzzo, Nuccio, "An army soldier clears a building," *Chicago Tribune*, March 27, 2003, p. A10, image taken for *Chicago Tribune*.

Douglas, Susan, "A three way failure," *Progressive*, July 1994, p. 15.

Eviatar, Daphne, "Civilian toll: a moral and legal bog," *The New York Times*, March 22, 2003, pp. D7, D9.

Faddoud, Joseph, "Rescuer cradles injured baby," May 22, 1985, image taken for Agence France-Presse.

Fisher, Ian, "Threat gone, Iraqis unearth Hussein's nameless victims," *The New York Times*, April 25, 2003, pp. A1, A10.

Fisk, Robert, "Baghdad: the day after," *The Independent*, April 11, 2003, p. 1.

Franklin, Thomas E., "Flag raising after September 11," Bergen Record-AP, image taken September 2001.

Gilbert, Matthew and Suzanne C. Ryan, "Snap judgments: did iconic images from Baghdad reveal more about the media than Iraq?" *Boston Globe*, April 10, 2003, p. D1.

Gillan, Audrey, "'We came here not to get out alive: we're ready for anything'; Kurdish protesters besieged in London say they will die for the cause," *The Guardian*, February 17, 1999, p. 3.

Gillet, Eric and Alison des Forges, "The next Rwanda," *The New York Times*, August 11, 1994, p. A23.

Glaser, Mark, "Photojournalism gets boost online," *Online Journalism Review*, posted August 7, 2003.

Goldberg, Vicki, *Margaret Bourke-White: a Biography*, New York: Harper and Row, 1986.

Goldberg, Vicki, *The Power of Photography*, New York: Abbeville Press, 1991.

Halbwachs, Maurice, *The Collective Memory*, Chicago, IL: University of Chicago Press, 1980.

Hall, Stuart, "The determinations of news photographs," in Stanley Cohen and Jock Young (eds.), *The Manufacture of News*, London: Sage 1974.

Harmon, Amy, "Improved tools turn journalists into a quick strike force," *The New York Times*, March 24, 2003, pp. C1, C4.

"Hauling water," *The New York Times*, April 17, 2003, B1, image taken for Reuters.

Hicks, Tyler, "Statue's head dragged through Baghdad streets," *The New York Times*, April 10, 2003, p. 1, image taken for *The New York Times*.

Hilbrand, David and Gail Shister, "A flood of images into homes," *Philadelphia Inquirer*, March 27, 2003, pp. A1, A20.

Hill, James, "Iraqi soldier killed," *The New York Times*, March 27, 2003, image taken for *The New York Times*.

Hinds, Julie, "Photographic memory," *Detroit Free Press*, April 11, 2003, pp. H1, H4.

Howe, Peter, *Shooting Under Fire: the World of the War Photographer*, New York: Artisan, 2002.

"India suicide," January 11, 2000, image taken for Associated Press/Press Trust of India.

Infield, Tom, "Tuesday's terror evoked echoes of Pearl Harbor," *Philadelphia Inquirer*, September 13, 2001, p. A11.

"The Intifada," West Bank, December 12, 1987, image taken for Dpa.

Kakutani, Michiko, "Shock, awe and razzmatazz in the sequel," *The New York Times*, March 25, 2003, pp. E1, E5.

Kifner, John, "Good as a gun: when cameras define a war," *The New York Times*, November 30, 2003, section 4: pp. 1, 5.

Knightley, Philip, *The First Casualty*, New York and London: Harcourt Brace and Jovanovitch, 1975.

Kondrake, Morton, "Another Cambodia," *New Republic*, November 3, 1979, pp. 13–14.

Krauthammer, Charles, "Only in their dreams," *Time*, December 24, 2001, pp. 60–1.

Lane, Charles, "When is it genocide?" *Newsweek*, August 17, 1992, p. 27.

Leroux, Charles, "Still images, moving words," *Chicago Tribune*, March 27, 2003, section 2: p. 1.

Lichfield, John, "Single pictures that capture history's turning points," *The Independent*, April 10, 2003, p. 10.

Lubrano, Alfred, "Even war has rules," *Philadelphia Inquirer*, March 30, 2003, section c: p. 1.

Luckhurst, Tim, "Altered images," *The Independent*, March 16, 2004, np.

Lyons, Nathan, *Photographers on Photography*, Englewood Cliffs: NJ: Prentice-Hall, 1966.

McCoy, Glenn, "Victory flag raising" (political cartoon), *Philadelphia Inquirer*, April 21, 2003, p. A2.

McCullin, Don, "Notes by a photographer," in Emile Meijer and Joop Swart (eds), *The Photographic Memory: Press Photography—Twelve Insights*, London: Quiller Press, and the World Press Photo Foundation, 1987, pp. 11–26.

McGeary, Johanna, "Target: Saddam," *Time*, April 14, 2003, pp. 51–7.

Marshall, Tyler, "Faced with a TV war, Europeans switch off," *Los Angeles Times*, March 19, 1994, p. A16.

Mathews, J.J., *Reporting the Wars*, Minneapolis: University of Minnesota Press, 1957.

"Moments remembered," *Life*, December 26, 1960, pp. 91–102.

Moeller, Susan D., *Shooting War: Photography and the American Experience of Combat*, New York: Basic Books, 1989.

Nalkur, Sonal, "Images of liberation in the coverage of Afghan women," unpublished masters' thesis, Annenberg School for Communication, 2002.

"A nation at war," *The New York Times*, March 27, 2003, p. B12.

"The next Bosnia," *The Economist*, June 6, 1992, pp. 43–4.

"Portraits of war: conflict, capitulation," *Philadelphia Inquirer*, March 23, 2003, p. A21.

Rich, Frank, "The spoils of war coverage," *The New York Times*, April 13, 2003, section 2: pp. 1, 15.

Robins, Kevin, "The war, the screen, the crazy dog, and poor mankind," *Media, Culture and Society* 15 (1993).

Rohde, David, "Evidence indicates Bosnia massacre," *Christian Science Monitor*, August 18, 1995, p. A1.

Rosenstiel, Tom, "War in Iraq: covering the news," Washingtonpost.com, posted April 10, 2003.

Rosenthal, Joe, "Flag raising atop Mount Suribachi," image taken on February 23, 1945.

Roskis, Edgar, "Replaying the pictures," *Le monde diplomatique*, December 2000.

"Rwanda killers leave a village of the dead," *The New York Times*, May 14, 1994, p. C3.

Sagolj, Damir, "US marine doctor with Iraqi girl," *Detroit Free Press*, April 11, 2003, p. H1, image taken for Reuters.

Sekula, Alan, "On the invention of photographic meaning," in *Photography Against the Grain*, 1974; reprint, Halifax: Press of the Nova Scotia College of Arts and Design, 1984.

Smith, W. Eugene, "Baby found in cave," August 28, 1944, location unknown, image taken for *Life* magazine.

"Somalia: the mire," *The Economist*, September 11, 1993, pp. 62–3.

Stepan, Peter (ed.) *Photos that Changed the World: the 20th Century*, Munich, London and New York: Prestel, 2000.

Swain, Nigel, *Hungary: The Rise and Fall of Feasible Socialism*, London, 1992.

Takase, Richard M., "Refugee children" (letter to the editor), *Los Angeles Times*, November 26, 2001, p. A12.

Taylor, John, *War Photography: Realism in the British Press*, London: Routledge, 1991.

"The Tiananmen in East Timor," *The New York Times*, January 21, 1992, p. A20.

van der Deen, David, "Watching for a judgment of real evil," *The New York Times*, November 12, 1995.

Voss, F.S., *Reporting the War*, Washington, DC: Smithsonian, 1994.

Vulliamy, (ed.) *Seasons in Hell: Understanding Bosnia's War*, New York: St Martin's Press, 1994.

Walsh, James, "Unearthing evil," *Time*, January 29, 1995, pp. 46–7.

"Weeping women," *The Economist*, August 10, 1991, image taken for WHOM.

Whitney, Craig R., "Tunnel vision: watching Iraq, seeing Vietnam," *The New York Times*, November 9, 2003, section 4: p. 1.

Widener, Jeff, "Massacre in Beijing," June 5, 1989, People's Republic of China, image taken as a video still.

Zelizer, Barbie, "CNN, the Gulf War, and journalistic practice," *Journal of Communication* 42, winter 1992, pp. 66–81.

Zelizer, Barbie, "Journalists as interpretive communities," *Critical Studies in Mass Communication*, vol. 10, no. 3, 1993, pp. 219–37.

Zelizer, Barbie, "Journalism's 'last' stand: wirephoto and the discourse of resistance," *Journal of Communication*, vol. 45, no. 2, 1995, pp. 78–92.

Zelizer, Barbie, *Remembering to Forget: Holocaust Memory through the Camera's Eye*, Chicago, IL: University of Chicago Press, 1998.

Zelizer, Barbie, "Photography, journalism, and trauma," in Barbie Zelizer and Stuart Allan (eds), *Journalism after September 11*, London and New York: Routledge: 2002, pp. 48–68.

7

THE PERSIAN GULF TV WAR
REVISITED

Douglas Kellner

The 1991 war against Iraq was one of the first televised events of the global village in which the entire world watched a military spectacle unfold via international satellite and cable networks.[1] In retrospect, the Bush administration and the Pentagon carried out one of the most successful public relations campaigns in the history of modern politics in its use of the media to mobilize support for the war. The mainstream media in the United States and elsewhere tended to be a compliant vehicle for the government strategy to manipulate the public, imperiling democracy which requires informed citizens, checks, and balances against excessive government power, and a free and vigorous critical media (see Kellner 1990, 1992, and 2001). Indeed, if the media do not adequately inform citizens, provide a check against excessive government power and corruption, and adequately debate the key issues of the day, democracy is undermined.

Moreover, the US media, especially CNN, completely dominated global coverage of the event. CNN had cameras and reporters in Baghdad throughout the war, a large crew in Israel, and live coverage of all US military and government press conferences. Thus its images, discourses, and material tended to shape global coverage of the event. This meant that the Bush administration and the Pentagon were able to control the flow of representations and framing of events, and thus to manage the global media spectacle of Gulf War I.[2]

In this chapter, I first discuss the production of the text of the "crisis in the Gulf" and then "the Gulf War." This will involve analysis of disinformation and propaganda campaigns by the Bush administration, the Pentagon, and their allies, as well as dissection of the constraints produced by the so-called pool system. I also indicate how the political economy of the media in the United States facilitated the manufacturing of consent for US government policies. Then I critically engage the meanings embedded in the text of the war against Iraq and the reception of the text/event by the audience. The latter process will take on the question of why the Gulf War was popular with its audiences and how the Bush administration and the Pentagon marshaled public support for the war.

Disinformation and propaganda

The 1991 Gulf War can be read as a text produced by the Bush administration, the Pentagon, and the media that propagated images and discourse of the crisis and then the war to mobilize consent and support for the US military intervention. Analysis of the text of the "crisis in the Gulf" indicates that from the beginning the mainstream news institutions followed the lines of the Bush administration and the Pentagon.[3] Mainstream media in the US are commercial media subject to intense competition for audiences and profits. Consequently, mainstream television, newspapers, and news magazines do not want to alienate consumers, and thus are extremely cautious in going against public opinion and the official government line. The mainstream media also favor official government sources for their stories, especially in times of crisis. Thus, they tend to be conduits for US government policies and actions, though there are significant exceptions (see Kellner 1990).

In response to the Iraqi invasion of Kuwait in early August 1990, the US government began immediately first to build consensus for the US military intervention and then to promote a military solution to the crisis, and the mainstream media were compliant accomplices. When the Bush administration sent a massive troop deployment to the region, the mainstream media applauded these actions and became a conduit for mobilizing support for US policy. For weeks, few dissenting voices were heard in the mainstream media, and television reports, commentary, and discussion strongly privileged a military solution to the crisis, serving as a propaganda vehicle for the US military and national security apparatus that was facing severe budget cutbacks on the very eve of the invasion. No significant television debate took place over the dangerous consequences of the massive US military response to the Iraqi invasion, or over the interests and policies that the military intervention served. Critics of US policy were largely absent from the mainstream media coverage of the crisis, and little analysis was presented which departed from issues presented by the Bush administration.

The Bush administration controlled the media discourse in part through disinformation and propaganda and in part by means of control of the press via the pool system. A military pool system was set up which restricted media access to soldiers and the battlefield; members representing different media like the press, radio, and television were organized into "pools" and taken to chosen sites. They were accompanied at all times by military personnel, called "minders," who restricted their access and tightly controlled their movements. The reports were then sent to Dhahran, Saudi Arabia, where a Joint Information Bureau censored the reports that then became common material available to those media outlets that had joined the pool. This was the tightest control over the press in any war in US history and assured that positive images and reporting of the war would take place.[4]

In the early days of "the crisis of the Gulf," the Bush administration carried through a highly successful disinformation campaign by means of their control and manipulation of sources that legitimated the US military deployment in Saudi Arabia on August 8, 1990. During the first days of the crisis, the US government constantly claimed that the Iraqis were mobilizing troops on the border of Saudi Arabia, poised to invade the oil-rich kingdom. This was sheer disinformation and later studies revealed that Iraq had no intention of invading Saudi Arabia and did not have large numbers of troops on the Saudi border in a threatening posture.[5]

The disinformation campaign that legitimated the US sending troops to Saudi Arabia began working through the *Washington Post* on August 7, 1990, the same day Bush announced that he was sending US troops to Saudi Arabia. In a front page story by Patrick Tyler, the *Post* claimed that in a previous day's meeting between the US *chargé d'affaires*, Joseph Wilson, and Iraqi President Saddam Hussein, the Iraqi leader was highly belligerent, claiming that Kuwait was part of Iraq, that no negotiation was possible, that he would invade Saudi Arabia if they cut off the oil pipes which delivered Iraqi oil across Saudi territory to the Gulf, and that American blood would flow in the sand if the US sent troops to the region.

A later transcript of the Wilson–Hussein meeting revealed, however, that Hussein was cordial, indicated a willingness to negotiate, insisted that he had no intention of invading Saudi Arabia, and opened the doors for a diplomatic solution to the crisis. The *Post* story was taken up by the television networks, wire services, and press, producing an image that there was no possibility of a diplomatic solution and that decisive action was needed to protect Saudi Arabia from the aggressive Iraqis. Such a story line legitimated the sending of US troops to the Gulf and provided a perfect justification for Bush's intervention in the region.

Editorial columns in the *Washington Post* the same day supported the imminent Bush administration deployment. Mary McGrory published a column titled "The beast of Baghdad," which also assumed that Iraq was set to invade Saudi Arabia and which called upon Bush to bomb Baghdad! Precisely the same line appeared in an opinion editorial piece by the *Post*'s associate editor and chief foreign correspondent Jim Hoagland who kicked in with a column: "Force Hussein to withdraw" (p. A19). As certain as McGrory of Iraq's imminent invasion of Saudi Arabia, Hoagland opened by proclaiming that "Saddam Hussein has gone to war to gain control of the oil fields of Kuwait and ultimately of Saudi Arabia. The United States must now use convincing military force against the Iraqi dictator to save the oil fields and to preserve American influence in the Middle East." According to Hoagland, Saddam Hussein "respects only force and will respond to nothing else."

The rest of the article consisted of false analysis, questionable analogies, and bellicose banality. Hoagland claimed that the "Iraqi dictator's base of support is too narrow and too shaky to withstand a sharp, telling blow." Yet some six weeks of the most intense bombing in history were unable to dislodge Hussein whose support, or staying power, was obviously much stronger than Hoagland could imagine. Hoagland also believed that "he [Hussein] is so hated at home that his defeat, even by foreign forces, will be greeted as deliverance by his own nation and by much of the Arab world." As it turned out, both Iraq and the Arab world were deeply divided over Hussein and the sweeping generalities that Hoagland proclaimed were totally off the mark.[6]

Thus, the Bush administration and *Washington Post* disinformation and propaganda concerning the Iraqis' readiness to invade Saudi Arabia worked effectively to shape media discourse and public perception of the crisis and to legitimate Bush's sending US troops to Saudi Arabia. In particular, Patrick Tyler's front-page story concerning Hussein's meeting with Joe Wilson and Iraq's alleged refusal to negotiate a solution or leave Kuwait provided the crucial media frame through which debate over the advisability of sending US troops to Saudi Arabia was discussed.[7] On August 7, in a PBS McNeil–Lehrer discussion of the proper US response to Iraq's invasion of Kuwait, co-anchor Judy Woodruff stated: "Iraq's leader Saddam Hussein was quoted today [in the *Post* story—D.K.] as saying the invasion of Kuwait was irreversible and permanent." Later on in the same show, former National Security Adviser (and Iran/Contra felon) Robert McFarlane quoted the story as evidence that Hussein was not going to leave Kuwait, and that therefore US military intervention in Saudi Arabia was necessary. And in a discussion with Arab-American leaders as to whether a US military intervention was justified, Woodruff interjected: "the US chargé in Baghdad did have a two-hour meeting with Saddam Hussein yesterday which by all accounts was very unsatisfactory as Saddam Hussein insisted that he was going to stay in Kuwait and made what were reported to be veiled threats against other nations in the area"—all disinformation that Bush administration officials fed to the *Post*, which was then disseminated by other mainstream media.

In his early morning television speech on August 8, which announced and defended sending US troops to Saudi Arabia, Bush claimed that "the Saudi government requested our help, and I responded to that request by ordering US air and ground forces to deploy to the kingdom of Saudi Arabia." This was false as accounts of the Saudi–US negotiations later indicated that the United States pressured the Saudis to allow US military intervention into their country (Woodward 1991: 241ff; and Salinger and Laurent 1991: 110ff). Bush repeated the dubious claim that "Iraq has massed an enormous war machine on the Saudi border," and his administration emphasized this theme in discussion with the media, which obediently reproduced the argument. At 9:24 a.m. on August 8, for instance, Bob Zelnick, ABC's Pentagon correspondent, dutifully reported that the Pentagon informed him that Iraqi troop presence had doubled since the invasion of Kuwait, that there were now more than 200,000 Iraqi troops in Kuwait with a large force poised to invade Saudi Arabia.

Yet it is not at all certain how many troops Iraq actually deployed in Kuwait during the first weeks of the crisis. All pre-invasion reports produced by the Bush administration indicated that Iraq had amassed over 100,000 troops on the border of Kuwait. Initial reports during the first few days after the invasion suggested that Iraq actually had between 80,000 and 100,000 troops in Kuwait, more than enough for an occupation, as the Bush administration liked to point out and as the mainstream media diligently reported; once the US forces were on their way to Saudi Arabia, the Iraqi forces allegedly doubled and reports claimed that there were at least 100,000 Iraqi troops amassed on the border of Saudi Arabia. But these figures invariably came from Bush administration or Pentagon sources, and sources critical of the US claims concerning the number of Iraqi troops deployed revealed a quite different figure.

St Petersburg Times reporter Jean Heller published two stories (November 30 and January 6) suggesting that satellite photographs indicated far fewer Iraqi troops in Kuwait than the Bush administration claimed (the January 6 story was republished in In These Times, February 27, 1991: 1–2). Heller's suspicions were roused when she saw a Newsweek "Periscope" item that ABC's "Prime time live" had never used several satellite photographs of occupied Kuwait City and southern Kuwait taken in early September. Purchased by ABC from the Soviet commercial satellite agency Soyez-Karta, the photographs were expected to reveal the presence of a massive Iraqi troop deployment in Kuwait, but failed to disclose anything near the number of troops claimed by the Bush administration. ABC declined to use them and Heller got her newspaper to purchase the satellite photographs of Kuwait from August 8 and September 13 and of Saudi Arabia from September 11. Two satellite experts who had formerly worked for the US government failed to find evidence of the alleged build-up. "'The Pentagon kept saying the bad guys were there, but we don't see anything to indicate an Iraqi force in Kuwait of even 20 percent the size the administration claimed,' said Peter Zimmerman, who served with the US Arms Control and Disarmament Agency during the Reagan administration" (Heller 1991: 2).

Both satellite photographs taken on August 8 and September 13 showed a sand cover on the roads, suggesting that there were few Iraqi troops on the Saudi border where the Bush administration claimed that they were massed, threatening to invade Saudi Arabia. Pictures of the main Kuwaiti airport showed no Iraqi planes in sight, though large numbers of US planes were visible in Saudi Arabia. The Pentagon refused to comment on the satellite photographs, but to suggestions advanced by ABC (which refused to show the photographs) that the pictures were not high enough quality to detect the Iraqi troops, Heller responded that the photograph of the north of Saudi Arabia showed all the roads swept clean of sand and clearly depicted the US troop build-up in the area. By September, the Pentagon was claiming that there were 265,000 Iraqi troops and 2,200 tanks deployed in Kuwait which posed a threat to Saudi Arabia. But the photographs reveal nowhere near this number and, so far, the US government has refused to release its satellite photographs.

Interestingly, Bob Woodward (1991) noted that the Saudis had sent scouts across the border into Kuwait after the Iraqi invasion to see if they could detect the Iraqi troops that the United States claimed were massed for a possible invasion of their country. "The scouts had come back reporting nothing. There was no trace of the Iraqi troops heading toward the kingdom" (Woodward 1991:

258–9). Soon after, the US team arrived with photographs of the Iraqi troops allegedly massed on the Saudi border, and General Norman Schwarzkopf explained to the Saudis that the Iraqis had sent small command-and-control units ahead of the mass of troops, which would explain why the Saudi scouts failed to see them (Woodward 1991: 268). Former CIA officer Ralph McGehee told journalist Joel Bleifuss: "There has been no hesitation in the past to use doctored satellite photographs to support the policy position that the US wants supported" (*In These Times*, September 19, 1990: 5). Indeed, Emery (1991) reported that King Hussein of Jordan was also sent pictures of tanks moving along roads near the Saudi/Kuwaiti border which had been shown to the Saudis, and that King Hussein claimed that the Saudis had "pressed the panic button" when they saw the photographs. King Hussein was skeptical and "argued that if Saddam Hussein had wanted to invade the Saudis, he would have moved immediately, when the only thing between him and the Saudi capital was a tiny and untested—if expensively equipped—Saudi army" (Emery 1991: 25).

This was how the disinformation campaign worked to legitimate US deployment of troops in Saudi Arabia: high Bush administration officials called in journalists who would serve as conduits for stories that Iraq refused to negotiate a withdrawal from Kuwait and that they had troops stationed on the borders of Saudi Arabia, threatening to invade the oil-rich kingdom. The Pentagon and Bush administrations also released information at press conferences concerning the Iraqi threat to Saudi Arabia and Iraq's unwillingness to negotiate, and these "official" pronouncements supplemented the unofficial briefings of reporters. In turn, editorial writers and commentators on television networks took up these claims which they used to bolster arguments concerning why it was necessary for the US to send troops to Saudi Arabia.

The Hill and Knowlton propaganda campaign

Hence, a successful disinformation campaign was undertaken by the Bush administration and Pentagon to legitimate sending US troops to Saudi Arabia. Beginning in early October, a sustained propaganda campaign was underway that legitimated the US use of military power to force Iraq out of Kuwait. This propaganda offensive involved demonization of the Iraqis for their "rape of Kuwait" and the demonization of Saddam Hussein as "another Hitler" and the incarnation of evil.[8] This campaign was inspired by a British campaign during World War I, repeated by the US when it entered the war, on the "rape of Belgium" which stigmatized the Germans as rapists and murderers of innocent children— charges later proven to be false.

The demonization of Hussein and the Iraqis was important because if they were absolutely evil and a threat on a par with Hitler and the Nazis, no negotiation could be possible and a diplomatic solution to the crisis was excluded. To help stigmatize the Iraqis, a Kuwaiti government group financed a propaganda campaign, undertaken by the US public relations firm Hill and Knowlton, which invented Iraqi atrocities in Kuwait, such as the killing of premature babies who were allegedly taken out of incubators and left to die on the floor. In October 1990 a tearful teenage girl testified to the House of Representatives Human Rights Caucus that she had seen Iraqi soldiers remove 15 babies from incubators and leave them to die on the floor of the hospital. The girl's identity was not revealed, supposedly to protect her family from reprisals. This story helped mobilize support for US military action, much as Bush's Willie Horton advertisements had helped him win the presidency by playing on primal emotions. Bush mentioned the story six times in one month and eight times in 44 days; Vice-President Dan Quayle referred to it frequently, as did General Norman Schwarzkopf and other military spokespersons. Seven US senators cited the story in speeches supporting the January 12 resolution authorizing war.

In a January 6, 1992, opinion editorial piece in The New York Times, John MacArthur, the publisher of Harper's magazine, revealed that the unidentified congressional witness was the daughter of the Kuwaiti ambassador to the US. The girl had been brought to Congress by Hill and Knowlton, which had coached her and helped organize the congressional human rights hearings. In addition, Craig Fuller, Bush's former chief of staff when he was Vice-President and a Bush loyalist, was president of Hill and Knowlton and was involved with the PR campaign, as were several other former officials for the Reagan administration who had close relations with the Bush administration.

Thus, the Kuwaiti government developed a propaganda campaign to manipulate the American people into accepting the Gulf War and the Bush administration used this campaign to promote their goals. Hill and Knowlton organized a photograph exhibition of Iraqi atrocities displayed at the United Nations and the US Congress and this was widely shown on television. They also assisted Kuwaiti refugees in telling stories of torture, lobbied Congress, and prepared video and print material for the media.

On January 17, 1992, ABC's "20/20" disclosed that a "doctor," who testified that he had "buried fourteen newborn babies that had been taken from their incubators by the soldiers," was also lying. The "doctor" was actually a dentist and later admitted to ABC that he had never examined the babies and had no way of knowing how they had died. The same was true of Amnesty International which published a report based on this testimony. (Amnesty International later retracted the report, which had been cited frequently by Bush and other members of his administration.) ABC also disclosed that Hill and Knowlton had commissioned a "focus group" survey which brought groups of people together to find out what stirred or angered them. The focus group responded strongly to the Iraqi baby atrocity stories, and so Hill and Knowlton featured them in its PR campaigns for the Free Kuwait group.

In addition to carrying out a massive propaganda campaign, the US government also instituted a sustained effort to control information and images through the pool system (see above) and few of the US broadcasting networks sought out critical or alternative views. Few significant anti-war voices were heard in the mainstream media during the first months of the troop build-up in Saudi Arabia. A study by the media watchdog group FAIR reported that, during the first five months of television coverage of the crisis, ABC devoted only 0.7 percent of its Gulf coverage to opposition to the military build-up. CBS allowed 0.8 percent, while NBC devoted 1.5 percent, or 13.3 minutes for all stories about protests, anti-war organizations, conscientious objectors, and religious dissenters. Consequently, of the 2,855 minutes of television coverage of the crisis from August 8 to January 3, FAIR found that only 29 minutes, or roughly 1 percent, dealt with popular opposition to the US military intervention in the Gulf.[9]

The small amount of images of anti-war demonstrators and opinion that appeared in the mainstream media during the crisis in the Gulf often juxtaposed anti-American demonstrations in Arab countries that frequently burned US flags with images of US demonstrations. Such a juxtaposition coded anti-war demonstrators as Arabs and as irrational opponents of US policies. US demonstrators were portrayed as an unruly mob, as long-haired outsiders; their discourse was rarely cited and coverage focused instead on the chanting of slogans, or images of marching crowds, with media voice-overs supplying the context and interpretation. Major newspapers and newsmagazines also failed to cover the burgeoning new anti-war movement. Thus, just as the media symbolically constructed a negative image in the 1960s of anti-war protesters as irrational, anti-American, and unruly, so too did the networks present the emerging anti-war movement of the 1990s in predominantly negative frames.

Not only was the discourse of the anti-war movement ignored, but also "none of the foreign policy experts associated with the peace movement—such as Edward Said, Noam Chomsky or the scholars of the Institute for Policy Studies—appeared on any nightly news program" (FAIR press release, January 1991). A Times-Mirror poll, however, that was recorded in September 1990 and January 1991 discovered "pluralities of the public saying they wished to hear more about the views of Americans who oppose sending forces to the Gulf" (Special Times-Mirror News Interest Index, January 31, 1991). Furthermore, soldiers who were alarmed at their deployment in the Saudi desert and objected to the primitive living conditions there were silenced, in part by Pentagon restrictions on press coverage and in part by a press corps unwilling to search for dissenting opinions.

And yet on the eve of the war, more than 50 percent of the American public opposed a military solution to the crisis. Perhaps images of families being separated and young troops being sent to the Saudi desert produced a negative response to the possibility of a war in the region that could take many US lives. Quite possibly, despite the lack of critical discourse on the media, many individuals could still think for themselves and produce anti-war opinions against the grain of the dominant pro-military solution government and media discourse. And maybe the memory of Vietnam and US military misadventures produced apprehensions over a war in the Persian Gulf. But the disinformation and propaganda campaigns were successful in that they persuaded the majority of nations in the UN and the US Congress to support a declaration legitimating the use of force to expel Iraq from Kuwait. And once the war began, the Bush administration was quickly able to mobilize support for its positions.

The media propaganda war

When the US began military action against Iraq on January 16, 1991, the mainstream media became a conduit for Bush administration and Pentagon policies and rarely allowed criticism of its actions, disinformation, and mishaps during the war. Television served primarily as a propaganda apparatus for the multinational forces arrayed against the Iraqis and as a cheerleader for their every victory. Anchors like Dan Rather of CBS and Tom Brokaw of NBC went to Saudi Arabia and, along with the network correspondents there, seemed to totally identify with the military point of view. Whenever peace proposals were floated by the Iraqis, Arab states, or the Soviet Union, the networks quickly shot them down and presented the Bush administration and Pentagon positions on every aspect of the war (see note 8).

The media framed the war as an exciting narrative, providing a nightly miniseries with a dramatic conflict, action, and adventure, danger to allied troops and civilians, evil perpetuated by villainous Iraqis, and heroics performed by American military planners, technology, and troops. Both CBS and ABC used the logo "Showdown in the Gulf" during the opening hours of the war, and CBS continued to utilize the logo throughout the war, coding the event as a battle between good and evil. Indeed, the Gulf War was presented as a war movie with beginning, middle, and end. The dramatic bombing of Baghdad during the opening night and exciting Scud wars of the next days enthralled a large television audience and the following weeks provided plenty of excitement, ups and downs, surprises, and complex plot devices. The threats of chemical weapons, terrorism, and a bloody Iraqi ground offensive seemed to produce great fear in the television audiences and helped to mobilize support against the villainous Iraqis. The ground war in particular produced a surge of dramatic action and a quick resolution and happy ending to the war (at least for those rooting for the US-led coalition).

Television also presented the war visually with dramatic techno-images, playing repeatedly the videos of hi-tech precision bombing and the aerial war over Baghdad and the Patriot/Scud wars over Saudi Arabia and Israel. The effects of the war on American families was a constant theme, and patriotism and support for the troops was a constant refrain of the commentators. The military released videotapes of hi-tech precision bombing which were replayed repeatedly, similar to replays of heroics in a sports event. Indeed, sports metaphors were constantly used and the pro-war demonstrators who chanted "USA! USA!" rooted for the American side as sports fans, as if the Gulf War were the Super Bowl of wars. The military and media kept daily tally of the score of Iraqi tanks and equipment eliminated, though the sanitized war coverage contained no "body count" figures and images of wounded or dead soldiers were strictly forbidden. The winnability and justification for the war were stressed and the narrative was oriented toward a successful conclusion that was presented as a stunning victory.

It was obviously in the television networks' interests to attract the audience to their programming, and competition revolved around presenting the most patriotic, exciting, and compelling coverage. To properly explicate this dimension of the text of the Gulf War, one needs to focus on the production of the text within the framework of the political economy of commercial television. First, the sources of the news on the mainstream media were generally limited to the Bush administration and the military. This was partly the result of the pool system that restricted media access to the theater of battle and that exercised censorship over every image and report filed. Yet the networks themselves also restricted the range of voices that appeared. A survey by FAIR of the television coverage of the first two weeks of the war revealed that of the 878 news sources used by the three major commercial networks, only 1.5 percent were identified as anti-war protesters—roughly equivalent to the amount of people asked to comment on how the Gulf War disrupted their travel plans. In the 42 nightly news broadcasts, only one leader of a peace organization was interviewed, while seven Super Bowl players were asked their views of the war.[10]

On the other hand, in report after report, television portrayed pro-war rallies, yellow ribbons, and the wave of patriotism apparently sweeping the country. The networks also personalized the US troops and their families, thus bonding the public to the troops in the desert, helping manufacture support for the US military policies. In these ways, the audience was mobilized to support every move of the Bush administration and the Pentagon and, as the war went well and relatively fast, the country was swept along in a victory euphoria, as if it was winning the Super Bowl of wars and was thus number one in the world. Such imagery and discourse helped create support for a war that barely 50 percent of the public and Congress desired on the eve of Bush's bombing of Baghdad.

Furthermore, the audience was terrorized into support for the US troops by a series of propaganda campaigns, masterfully orchestrated by the Bush administration and the Pentagon. Early in the crisis, reports were leaked that Iraqi chemical weapons were being brought to the field of battle, and throughout the war there were many reports of the threat of Iraqi chemical weapons. In addition, there were almost daily reports on the threats of terrorism manipulated by the Iraqis. When the Iraqis paraded US POWs on television, there were claims that they were torturing coalition troops. Such reports created a mass hysteria in sectors of the audience, which were positively bonding with the troops. Moreover, after the Iraqi Scud attacks on Israel and Saudi Arabia, there were reports of thousands of people buying gas masks and vignettes of families producing sealed rooms in their home in the case of chemical attack. Obviously, such hysteria helped mobilize people against the Iraqis and make them desire their military defeat and punishment.

On the whole, television and the mainstream media arguably served as propaganda arms for US government policy. The media endlessly repeated Bush administration "big lies," such as its alleged efforts to negotiate a settlement with the Iraqis when it was actively undermining the possibility of a diplomatic settlement. And the media repeated every propaganda line of the day, amplifying Bush administration claims concerning alleged torture and mistreatment of US POWs (later revealed to be highly exaggerated), that an Iraqi infant formula milk factory destroyed by US bombing was really a military installation producing chemical/biological weapons, that a civilian sleeping shelter was really a military command and control center, or that Iraqi "environmental terrorism" was responsible for the Persian Gulf oil spill and other ecological devastation.[11]

The US mainstream media projected the image of the war most desired by the Pentagon and the Bush administration; i.e. that it was fighting an eminently clean and successful hi-tech war. From the beginning, the bombing of Iraq was portrayed as efficient and humane, targeting only military facilities. Over and over, despite pictures from Iraq that revealed the contrary, the Pentagon and the Bush administration stressed the accuracy of their bombing strategies and the oft-repeated images of the precision bombs, with video cameras built into their heads, presented an image of pinpoint accurate bombing. Likewise, the frequent pictures of Patriot missiles apparently knocking out Iraqi Scud missiles created the impressions of a highly effective hi-tech war. Later, the Pentagon itself admitted that only 7 percent of the bombs used were so-called "smart bombs" and admitted that over 70 percent of its munitions missed their targets, but the dominant images of a hi-tech war presented an impression of a highly efficient technowar. It was also later revealed that a large percentage of US casualties resulted from "friendly fire," from the bombing of one's own troops.

The lack of significant critical voices in the mainstream media during the crisis in the Gulf and then the Gulf War also can be explained by reflection on the political economy of the media and the system of media production in the United States. The broadcast media are afraid to go against a perceived popular consensus, to alienate people, and to take unpopular stands because they are afraid of losing audience shares and thus profits. Because US military actions have characteristically been supported by the majority of the public, at least in their early stages, television is extremely reluctant to criticize what might turn out to be popular military actions.[12]

The broadcast media also characteristically rely on a narrow range of established and safe commentators and are not likely to reach out to new and controversial voices in a period of national crisis. The media generally wait until a major political figure or established "expert" speaks against a specific policy and that view gains a certain credibility as marked by opinion polls or publication in "respected" newspapers or journals. Unfortunately, the crisis of democracy in the United States is such that the Democratic party has largely supported the conservative policies of the past decades and the party leaders are extremely cautious and slow to criticize foreign policy actions, especially potentially popular military actions. The crisis of liberalism is so deep in the US that establishment liberals are afraid of being called "wimps" or "soft" on foreign aggression, and thus often support policies that their better instincts should lead them to oppose.

Warrior nation

The result of the propaganda blitz and war hysteria was a warrior nation that turned many in the television public into fanatic supporters of the Bush administration war policy. The pro-war consensus was mobilized through a variety of ways in which the public identified with the troops. Television presented direct images of the troops to the public through "desert dispatches" that produced very sympathetic images of young American men and women "in harm's way" and serving their country. Television news segments on families of the troops also provided mechanisms of identification, especially because many of the troops were reservists, forced to leave their jobs and families, making them sympathetic objects of empathy and identification for those able to envisage themselves in a similar situation. There were also frequent television news stories on how church groups, schools, and others adopted US troops in Saudi Arabia as pen pals, thus more intimately binding those at home to the soldiers abroad. People were also bound to troops through rituals of display of yellow ribbons, chanting and waving flags in pro-war demonstrations, and entering into various pro-war support groups.

The media generated support for the war, first, by upbeat appraisals of US successes and then by demonizing the Iraqis that made people fervently want a coalition victory. Initial support was won for the war effort through the media-generated euphoria that the war would be over quickly, with a decisive and easy victory for the US-led coalition. Then, the audience got into the drama of the war through experiencing the excitement of the Scud wars and the thrills of technowar war with its laser-guided bombs and missiles and videotapes of its successes. The POW issue, the oil spills and fires, and intense propaganda campaigns by both sides also involved the audience in the highly emotional experience of a television war. The drama of the war was genuinely exciting and the public immersed itself in the sights, sounds, and language of war.

The media images of the hi-tech precision bombing, (seeming) victories of Patriot over Scud missiles, bombing of Iraq, and military hardware and troops helped to mobilize positive feelings for the US military effort in much of the audience. Military language helped normalize the war, propaganda and disinformation campaigns mobilized pro-war discourse, and the negative images and discourses against the Iraqis helped mobilize hatred against Iraq and Saddam Hussein. Polls during the first weeks of the war revealed growing support for the war effort, displaying a widespread propensity to believe whatever the media and military were saying. A *Times-Mirror* survey of January 31, 1991, indicated that 78 percent of the public believed that the military was basically telling the truth, not hiding anything embarrassing about its conduct of the war, and providing all of the information it prudently could. Seventy-two percent called the press coverage objective and 61 percent called it for the most part accurate. Eight out of ten said the press did an excellent job. Fifty percent claimed to be addicted to television watching and said that they could not stop watching coverage of the war. Fifty-eight percent of adults under 30 called themselves "war news addicts" and

21 percent of these "addicts" said they had trouble concentrating on their jobs or normal activities, while 18 percent said they were suffering from insomnia.

It was, however, the total media and social environment that was most responsible for mobilizing support for the US war policies. From morning to evening, the nation was bombarded with images of military experts, vignettes of soldiers at home and abroad, military families, former POWs, and others associated with the military. Military figures, images, and discourse dominated the morning talk shows, the network news, discussion programs, and the 24-hour-a-day CNN war coverage, as well as saturation coverage on C-Span and many other cable networks. On home satellite dishes, the channels were saturated with live transmissions concerning the war, as the networks prepared or presented their reports from the field, and one satellite transponder provided hours per day of live military pool footage from Saudi Arabia for use by the networks—propaganda provided by the military free of charge. Television news pre-empted regular programs for weeks. The result was a militarization of consciousness and an environment dominated by military images and discourses.

Some concluding reflections

The analysis in the last sections suggested how the US corporate media helped mobilize support for the Gulf War. After the successful ground war, Bush's approval ratings shot up to a high of 90 percent. But more detailed analysis of poll data indicated that there was not the seemingly overwhelming bipartisan support. Solop and Wonders' (1991) review of published poll data indicated that those most supportive of President Bush and his war policies were Republican white males who had conservative attitudes. Females, blacks, liberals, and Democrats were less supportive. Moreover, the study by Eveland, McLeod, and Signorielli (1994), based on interviews during and after the war revealed that there was less overall support for the war than would be expected given the degree and type of media coverage relating to public opinion about the war. Both during and after the war, more than 50 percent of the respondents said they were "neutral" or disagreed with the statements in the "I support the war" scale. In addition, during the war only 6.6 percent of the respondents said that they strongly agreed with statements describing support for the war; this figure fell to 2.8 percent in the survey conducted one year later (Eveland, McLeod, and Signorelli 1994).[13]

Although saturation television coverage was strongly propagandistic and seemed to help mobilize audience support for the war, continued coverage of turmoil in the region, especially images of the suffering of the Kurds and other Iraqis at the end of the war, soured segments of the audience on the war and perhaps on military intervention, which did not seem to have achieved the promised positive results. Thus, ultimately, the media may have contributed to turning large portions of the public against military solutions to the problems of the Middle East and elsewhere in the world. It may be that the nightly images of the soldiers in the desert and then the images after the war of continued suffering and turmoil might have raised questions concerning the wisdom of US military intervention.

In addition, the fact that the war was experienced by much of the audience as a dramatic spectacle meant that it could be soon forgotten and overwhelmed by Hollywood, television, and other subsequent spectacles of the culture industry. By the summer of 1992, Bush's presidency was in serious trouble and, as it turned out, patriotic images and discourse from the war were unable to save him in the 1992 election. Revelations of the positive and supportive Reagan/Bush policies before the war toward Iraq suggested that Bush and his cohorts had constantly miscalculated in providing aid and diplomatic support to the Iraqi regime from the early 1980s to the eve of the invasion of Kuwait (see Friedman 1993).

In 1992, in a series of articles in the *Los Angeles Times*, Murray Waas documented how George Bush himself actively promoted US trade with Iraq and helped block attempts to criticize Iraq or impose sanctions on it from the Reagan administration until weeks before the Iraqi invasion of Kuwait. Classified documents show that Bush, first as Vice President and then as President, intervened repeatedly over a period of almost a decade to obtain special assistance for Saddam Hussein—financial aid as well as access to hi-tech equipment that was critical to Iraq's quest for nuclear and chemical arms. In Waas' summary:

> In June 1984 Vice President Bush telephoned the president of the Export-Import Bank to urge approval of a $500 million loan guarantee for Iraq to build an oil pipeline. Ex-Im, which had been reluctant, approved.
>
> In February 1987 Vice President Bush telephoned the Ex-Im president to press for $200 million in loan guarantees. Economists warned the bank that Iraq could not repay the loans, but the bank approved the guarantees.
>
> In March 1987 the Commerce Department approved export licenses for shipment to Iraq of dual-use technology, useful for scientific or military purposes. Over the next few years exports of this kind totaled $600 million, and much of the equipment may have gone into aerial spying and other military uses.
>
> In August 1988 a cease-fire ended the Iran–Iraq war. But the American tilt toward Iraq continued. Some intelligence was being provided as late as May 1990.
>
> In 1989 Bush, now President, signed a national security order directing government agencies to improve ties with Iraq.
>
> In October 1989 Secretary of State James A. Baker telephoned Secretary of Agriculture Clayton Yeutter and urged him to approve $1 billion in new loan guarantees to Iraq despite fears that the credits were being misused. In November Yeutter approved the guarantees.
>
> In January 1990 President Bush signed an executive order finding that it would not be "in the national interest" for the Ex-Im Bank to stop loan guarantees to Iraq.

In April and again in June 1990 the Commerce Department proposed restrictions on hi-technology exports to Iraq. An interagency group chaired by Robert M. Gates, then Deputy National Security Adviser to Bush, rejected the proposals.

In July 1990 the Senate voted overwhelmingly to cut off loan guarantees to Iraq because of Saddam's human rights violations, including the gassing of a Kurdish village. The administration condemned the vote.

On July 31, 1990, with 100,000 Iraqi troops massed at the Kuwait border, Assistant Secretary of State John Kelly went to Capitol Hill and testified against ending loan guarantees to Iraq.

On August 2, 1990, Iraq invaded Kuwait.[14]

Moreover, the fact that Saddam Hussein continued to rule with an iron fist in Iraq and that his neighbors continued to feel threatened after the Gulf War raised questions as to the success of Bush senior's policy and whether the war really accomplished any significant long-term goals, other than temporarily boosting Bush's ratings in the polls and producing a positive image of the US military after the shame of defeat in Vietnam. In the chaotic aftermath of the Gulf War in which the US failed to intervene to helped the uprising against Hussein's regime and in the light of his reassertion of his power and domination, the extreme hyperbole of the construction of Saddam Hussein and his regime as absolute evil to some extent backfired since the Evil One was not removed from power in the aftermath of the war. Although Bush urged the Iraqis to overthrow Hussein, once the US declared an end to the fighting and Iraqi rebels rebelled against Hussein's regime, the US remained on the sidelines. General Schwarzkopf himself stated in a PBS television interview on March 27, 1991, that he had preferred to continue fighting to "annihilate" completely the Iraqi military which was violently suppressing the insurgent forces against Hussein as Schwarzkopf spoke. The continuation of Saddam Hussein in power, the destructive environmental effects of the war, the so-called Gulf War syndrome that has disabled over 160,0000 US troops, the need for Bush junior to "finish the job," and the current chaos and instability of Iraq reveal Gulf War I to have been in retrospect a Pandora's box of evils that produced a brief euphoric high with a long hangover.[15]

Consequently, saturation television coverage of dramatic political events is a two-edged sword: it might shape public opinion into supporting the US intervention, as it obviously did during the Gulf War. But repeated images of a drawn-out stalemate, or images of death and destruction in a fighting war, or representations of protracted suffering as long-term effects of the war, could be turned against the political group and its leaders who produced such destruction. The very ubiquity of the broadcasting media and now the Internet, and the central role of the media in contemporary politics, renders media spectacle a complex and unpredictable political force (Kellner 2003a). Lust for pictures to attract audiences led the networks into a race to get into Iraq and to interview its leaders and to show its people. Images of continual and increased suffering of the Iraqi people and others in the area as a result of US military interventions in the 1991 and 2003 Iraq wars have helped produce negative images of the US throughout the world and might ultimately lead people to see that war is no way to solve political conflict, and that it produces overwhelming destruction, suffering, and death.

Hence, a multiperspectival approach that captures different aspects of a complex phenomenon like mainstream media coverage of US interventions in the Middle East should also analyze the contradictions of audience reception of the media texts and potentially contradictory images and effects, as well as analyzing media texts and their conservative, systems-maintenance functions. Although my analysis has focused primarily on the ways that US media coverage of the 1991 Gulf War supported the policies of the Bush administration and the Pentagon, analysis of the reception by audiences of the multiple Middle East crises, the Gulf War, and its aftermath might have ultimately helped undermine Bush senior and the conservative hegemony of the Reagan/Bush senior years, contributing to the latter's defeat in 1992. Perhaps Bush senior went overboard in demonizing Hussein, and his regime's continued rule of Iraq served to rob Bush senior of claims of genuine victory. Likewise, although Bush junior's administration appeared to have won a smashing military triumph in the 2003 war against Iraq, its consequences and aftermath could undo the regime of the son, as the contradictory aftermath of Gulf War I helped to undo the presidency of the father (see Kellner 2004).

In any case, the effects of television and the mainstream media are contradictory and may have unintended consequences. While in the spring of 1991, the Gulf War constituted a tremendous victory for the Bush administration and the Pentagon, the event did not save Bush senior's presidency and eventually raised questions as to whether he was really an effective president. Its short-term effects in temporarily boosting Bush senior's popularity and the sudden shift in public opinion concerning the war and Bush also point to the fickleness of audiences in a media-saturated society, who soon forget the big events of the previous year.[16]

And yet the woefully one-sided coverage of the Gulf crisis and war by the mainstream media calls attention once again to the need for alternative media to provide essential information on complex events like the Gulf War. During the war, those of us who opposed it got information from computer databases, such as PeaceNet, or progressive publications like *The Nation, In These Times, The Village Voice,* and *Z Magazine*. Locally, in addition to holding teach-ins at universities, critics of the war attempted to make use of public access television and radio to criticize the Bush administration's war policy and refusal to negotiate a diplomatic solution. Democratizing our media system will require a revitalization of public television, an increased role for public access television, the eventual development of a public satellite system, and the production of progressive computer databases, websites, list-serves, and weblogs (Kellner 1990 and 1995). Because politics are more and more acted out on media screens, without the reconstruction of television and the mass media, the prospects for democratization of US society and polity are dim.

Notes

1 In this chapter, I draw on my book *The Persian Gulf TV War* (Kellner 1992), and later studies of the event in Kellner 1995 and Best and Kellner 2001.

2 Following the publication of my *Persian Gulf TV War* (Kellner 1992), I was invited all over the world to lecture on the event and interviewed officials from British, French, Belgium, German, Finnish, Swedish, and many other state television networks; all of the people I interviewed affirmed that CNN tended to control the media flow and frames in depiction of the war. Things were quite different, however, in the 2003 war on Iraq that had many Arab television networks present in Iraq, as well as many European and other global networks that framed the event quite differently from the US networks.

3 By the "mainstream media" in the United States, I mean the major national television networks, including ABC, CBS, CNN, NBC, and CBS; the national weekly news magazines *Time, Newsweek* and *US News and World Report*; and national newspapers such as *The New York Times, The Wall Street Journal, USA Today,* and *The Washington Post.* These mainstream media are corporate media, owned by an ever-shrinking and more powerful number of transnational corporations. See the contrast between mainstream and alternative media that I develop in Kellner 1990 and the analysis of corporate media in Kellner 2003a.

4 Following the example of British censorship of the press during the Falkland Islands/Malvinas war, the US tightly controlled press access during the Grenada foray and instituted the pool system during the Panama invasion; for detailed analysis of how it worked during the Gulf War, see Kellner 1992: pp. 80ff.

5 See the discussion below and Kellner 1992, pp. 17ff for documentation of this claim.

6 Hoagland's remarkable misreading of Iraq was duplicated by the Bush administration's neo-conservatives who claimed prior to the US/UK war against Iraq in 2003 that Iraqis would welcome their "liberators" with open arms and that the US would easily be able to reconstruct the country and lead it to democracy (see Kellner 2004).

7 Through computer data base searches, I discovered how this story was taken up by the television networks and most major newspapers, and was used in many later summaries of the story to explain why Bush *had* to send US troops to Saudi Arabia; see the documentation in Kellner 1992.

8 A study undertaken by the Gannett foundation indicated that there were over 1,170 articles linking Hussein with Hitler (LaMay *et al.* 1991, p. 42). This comparison obviously presupposes a false analogy in terms of the military threat to the region and the world from the Iraqi army—whose threat was hyped up from the beginning. Iraq's 17 million population can hardly compare with Germany's 70 million and its military was significantly less threatening than Hitler's military machine, which was the most powerful in the world in the 1930s. Nor could Iraq, which depends on oil for over 95 percent of its exports, be compared with an industrial powerhouse like Germany. It is also inappropriate to compare a major imperialist superpower with a regional power, Iraq, that itself is the product of colonization.

It might also be noted how the Bush administration and media personalized the crisis, equating Iraq with its leader. Whereas in coverage of the 8-year war between Iran and Iraq, in which the US covertly supported Iraq, references were to "Baghdad" and "Iraq," during the Gulf crisis and war it was usually "Saddam Hussein" who was referred to as the actor and source of all evil (I am grateful to Richard Keeble for this insight.)

9 FAIR, press release, January 1991.

10 Cited in Joel Bleifuss, *In These Times*, March 20, 1991, p. 5.

11 In fact, allied bombing was also responsible for much of the ecological damage; see the documentation in Kellner 1992 and Clark 1992.

12 There was also organized right-wing pressure against networks or mainstream publications that criticized the Bush administration or the Pentagon; such pressure was increased in the Afghanistan and 2003 Iraq war, so that during these events the US broadcasting media were even less critical of the second Bush administration and Pentagon (see Kellner 2003b).

13 Muller documented that within a month and a half after the Iraqi surrender only a small majority of 52 percent believed that the US intervention was largely or totally successful and that, by June 1991, the number fell by another 8 percent (1994, p. 277). Other polls which tracked public opinion between the end of the war and summer 1991 showed declines of 14 percent and 19 percent in support for the proposition that the war had been worth fighting (Mueller 1993, p. 214).

14 See Murray Waas, *Los Angeles Times* (May 7, 1992). Another *Los Angeles Times* story by Murray Waas and Douglas Frantz, "Bush tied to '86 bid to give Iraq military advice," described how: "As Vice President during the Ronald Reagan administration, George Bush acted as an intermediary in sending strategic military advice to Iraqi President Saddam Hussein at a critical point in the Iran–Iraq war, according to sources and classified documents." A recent book by Chambers Johnson *The Sorrows of Empire* (2004: 223ff) documents how the CIA helped install Saddam Hussein into power, provided military assistance to Iraq during the 1980s war with Iran, and provided loans and material that enabled him to develop his weapons programs, including chemical and biological weapons.

15 On the Gulf War syndrome, see Hersh 1998. See also Phil Hirschkorn and Richard Roth, "Gulf War veterans suing companies for chemical exports" (CNN, January 17, 2003) who report: "About 209,000 Gulf War veterans have filed claims with the Veterans administration, and 161,000 of them are receiving disability payments."

16 David Halberstam claimed that the Gulf War "was a war without real resonance . . . when it was over, it was over, leaving remarkably little trace" (2001, pp. 16). In some ways, this may be true domestically, but it helped create resentment of US military power that had resonance in enraging Jihadist forces who have targeted the US with terrorism attacks, and it also failed to eliminate the regime of Saddam Hussein, tempting the second Bush administration into what is now appearing as a major disaster.

References

Best, Steven and Kellner, Douglas (2001) *The Postmodern Adventure*, London and New York: Routledge and Guilford Press.

Chomsky, Noam (1989) *Necessary Illusions*, Boston: South End Press.

Clark, Ramsey (1992) *War Crimes: A Report on United States War Crimes Against Iraq*, Washington: Maisonneuve.

Emery, Michael (1991) "How Mr Bush got his war: deceptions, double-standards and disinformation," Westfield, NJ: Open Magazine pamphlet series; originally published in the *Village Voice*, March 5, 1991, pp. 22–7.

Eveland, W., McLeod, E., and Signorielli, N. (1994) "Conflict and public opinion: rallying effects in the Gulf War," *Journalism Quarterly*, 1994, vol. 71, no. 1, pp. 20–31.

Friedman, Alan (1993) *Spider's Web*, New York: Bantam Books.

Halberstam, David (2001) *War in a Time of Peace: Bush, Clinton, and the Generals*, New York: Scribner.

Heller, Jean (1991) *In These Times*, February 27: 1–2.

Herman, Edward and Chomsky, Noam (1988) *Manufacturing Consent*, New York: Pantheon.

Hersh, Seymour (1998) *Against All Enemies: Gulf War Syndrome: the War between America's Ailing Veterans and Their Government*, New York: Simon and Schuster.

Johnson, Chalmers (2004) *The Sorrows of Empire*, New York: Metropolitan Books.

Kellner, Douglas (1990) *Television and the Crisis of Democracy* Boulder, CO: Westview.

Kellner, Douglas (1992) *The Persian Gulf TV War*, Boulder, CO: Westview.

Kellner, Douglas (1995) *Media Culture*, London and New York: Routledge.

Kellner, Douglas (2001) *Grand Theft 2000*, Boulder, Co.: Rowman and Littlefield.

Kellner, Douglas (2003a) *Media Spectacle*, London and New York: Routledge.

Kellner, Douglas (2003b) *From 9/11 to Terror War: Dangers of the Bush Legacy*. Lanham, MD.: Rowman and Littlefield.

Kellner, Douglas (2004) "9/11, Spectacles of terror, and media manipulation: a critique of Jihadist and Bush media politics" in *Critical Discourse Studies*, vol. 1, no. 1.

LaMay, Craig, *et al.* (1991) *The Media at War*, New York: Gannett Foundation Media Center.

Mueller, J. (1993) "American public opinion and the Gulf War" in S.A. Renshon (ed.), *The Political Psychology of the Gulf War: Leaders, Politics and the Process of Conflict*, Pittsburgh, PA: University of Pittsburgh Press, pp. 199–226.

Mueller, J. (1994) *Policy and Opinion in the Gulf War*, Chicago, IL: University of Chicago Press.

Rogin, Michael (1987) *Ronald Reagan: the Movie*, Berkeley, CA: University of California Press.

Salinger, Pierre, and Laurent, Eric (1991) *Secret Dossier: the hidden agenda behind the Gulf War*, New York: Penguin Books.

Solop, F.I. and Wonders, N.A. (1991) "Reaction to the Persian Gulf crisis: gender, race, and generational differences," paper presented at American Association of Public Opinion Research.

Woodward, Bob (1991) *The Commanders*, New York: Simon and Schuster.

8

TRIBALISM AND TRIBULATION

Media constructions of "African savagery" and
"Western humanitarianism" in the 1990s

Susan L. Carruthers

Africa and/as "a problem from hell"

For Western news organizations the scramble from Africa began many years ago, with bureaus closed and permanent staff slashed in favor of cheaper local stringers. From this landscape of neglect—a continent routinely overlooked all bar its southern tip—Rwanda and Somalia stand out as sites of intense (if also belated and short-lived) Western media coverage in the 1990s. True, there were brief flurries of attention to famine in Sudan, "warlordism" and grotesque carnivals of carnage in Sierra Leone and Liberia, to the violent re-emergence of the Congo from Zaire, and the forcible break-up of refugee camps along Rwanda's borders in 1996. But nothing matched the density of cameras and volume of commentary afforded the Western interventions to "Restore Hope" in Somalia (1992–3), and to bandage the aftermath of Rwanda's genocide (1994). Moreover, both episodes have had a lingering afterlife in western Europe and North America. Since September 11, 2001, US commentators have turned to these troubled expeditions for a variety of object lessons—whether they seek to expatiate on the dangers of such missions' premature termination (Somalia) or delayed dispatch (Rwanda). Indeed, the former is frequently identified as an explanation, if not an excuse, for the latter.

Rwanda's neglected genocide thus figures prominently in the Pulitzer-winning *A Problem from Hell*, Samantha Power's highly publicized indictment of America's failure to put its "never again" utterances on genocide into practice (Power 2002). In liberal critiques of this kind, Rwanda, as icon of indifference to human suffering on an epic scale, is emblematic of the immorality of "isolationism," with the US *débâcle* in Somalia explaining (if only in part) America's refusal to act in timely fashion in Rwanda. But since 9/11, the meaning of Mogadishu—where "hope" expired in a ferocious fire-fight between US Rangers and Somali militia—has also been incorporated into a larger explanatory scheme that attempts both to account for al-Qaeda's attacks and to legitimate the ways in which the Bush administration has chosen to wage its pre-emptive and retaliatory "war on terror." In recent months, the failed UNOSOM mission has haunted accounts not only of how Rwandan lives were subsequently squandered but also how America rendered *itself* vulnerable through its undignified scurry from Somalia (Cain 2003). Refusing to sustain even limited casualties in the interests of nation-building in Africa, America found itself losing over 2,000 lives on home soil. These two phenomena were not unconnected, or so the new received wisdom goes—one fount of which may be traced to *Black Hawk Down*, Mark Bowden's bestseller from which Ridley Scott dramatically reconstructed Hollywood's "Battle of Mog" (Bowden 2002). Where the book intimates, the movie more boldly underscores chains of connection between the horn of Africa and the Twin Towers, between Aidid and bin Laden, implying that the premature US pull-out inspired those seeking to spook a timorous Uncle Sam (Bowden 2002: 428; Carruthers 2003: 178–9).

This lesson in the perils of pusillanimity now underpins the Bush administration's public account of how terrorists are emboldened—not, as some critics of US global policy might have it, by the arrogance of American power wielded overwhelmingly and unilaterally, but rather by the sole superpower's squeamishness when it comes to incurring casualties. Hence cut-and-run must be replaced with "shock and awe." Reading from a script that might have been ghosted by Bowden, President Bush bolstered his September 7, 2003, call for $87 billion to prosecute the "war on terror" by summoning the spectre of another scuttle—this time from Baghdad rather than Mogadishu: "We have learned that terrorist attacks are not caused by the use of strength. They are invited by the perception of weakness. And the surest way to avoid attacks on our own people is to engage the enemy where he lives and plans" (Bush 2003). Present in all but name, Somalia is clearly the case in point as Bush seeks to animate American energies for combating another "problem from hell." Rwanda and Somalia are not, then, finished stories safely laid to rest in the files and photographic archives—to the extent that the past ever is beyond retrieval by hungry hunters for serviceable lessons or salutary warnings.

This chapter concentrates on journalism from the first half of the 1990s. More particularly, it examines *appraisals* of media coverage offered from a range of academic and other vantage points (Livingston and Eachus 1995; Murison 1996; Wall 1997; Philo *et al.* 1998; Livingston and Eachus 1999). These critiques fall into two broad camps: one focused on the conditions under which the West "intervenes"; the other on the inadequacies of what the media offers as knowledge about Africa. In this division of labor (somewhat schematically overdrawn here), media studies, NGO activists, and international relations scholars tend to concentrate on Western policy processes and outcomes, while Africanists, anthropologists, and political geographers deconstruct the poverty of media imagery and analysis of complex crises. Juxtaposing these two distinct scholarly mappings of the terrain, I propose an alternative, more bi-focal, lens through which to view media representations of Africa and their wider significance for identity politics and practical policy alike.

Recent revisitations of Rwanda and Somalia, sketched on a thumbnail above, are germane to the broader argument advanced here: that more must be done to place "the West" and "Africa" in the same analytic frame, to make explicit what often remains (as in Bush's September 2003 speech) only intimated.[1] In other words, this chapter suggests how, in writing Africa so largely out of global news while simultaneously attenuating itself from the deep roots of ostensibly localized anarchy, tribalism, or state implosion, the West continually constitutes itself in unacknowledged relation to Africa. As Bush's version of terrorists' emboldening suggests, sub-Saharan Africa continues to feed the West's subconscious, providing a mythic (often biblically-inflected) imaginary for the nature and location of good and evil, hence enabling identities to be fashioned around the profound polarity of "Western civilization" and "African barbarism." If Europe "is literally the creation of the Third World," as Frantz Fanon asserted, then Africa surely looms large in the production of the West, whose material and mental dependencies on Africa are often denied and/or projected as unidirectional needs and claims made by "them" of "us" (Fanon 1967: 81). Exploring this obfuscated mutuality may help us better understand both the character of the West—particularly its self-proclaimed "humanitarian interventions"—and the global underpinnings of ruptured social relations in Africa.

Media reporting and intervention: the "CNN effect" considered

Two distinct bodies of work, overlapping at their margins, have explored Western media depictions of African implosion (state failure, "ethnic violence," famine, and genocide). This section explores the variety of positions falling within the first broad church, concerned primarily with the West rather than Africa. Here the focus rests on relationships between media and policy elites—and between media and aroused Western publics—in trying to fathom the conditions under which the "international community" acts, whether in Africa or elsewhere. Much of this debate has centred around the so-called CNN effect (or "curve"), a coinage of the early 1990s that sought to capture the impact of real-time television images on foreign-policy processes. Sparked by media attentiveness to the Kurdish crisis that immediately followed the 1991 Gulf War, various commentators probed whether the emergence of 24-hour global news channels has effected a revolution in foreign policy-making (at the state and multilateral levels), and of cosmopolitan consciousness across state boundaries (Gowing 1994; Shaw 1994, 1996; Neuman 1996; Strobel 1997; Robinson 1999, 2001, 2002). Africa is at once prominent in, yet only incidental to, this dissection of media power—centred on the potency of televised imagery—which transposes many Vietnam-era concerns onto the ostensibly new post-Cold War era of "humanitarian intervention." In other words, at stake in the CNN effect debate is an adjudication of media capacity to interrupt the smooth course of policy deliberation and, for better or ill, inject emotion and empathy into decision-makers' calculus.

In a sense, *where* the media might force Western policy-makers to intervene is immaterial as much of the debate treats "intervention" as an effect of different variables "pushing" and "pulling," largely abstracted from specificities of context. That said, Africa nevertheless provides proponents with their paradigmatic case of the CNN effect: Somalia. By this account, Operation "Restore Hope" was galvanized by real-time images of wide-eyed Somali children whose distended bellies offered a rebuke to complacent, well-upholstered Westerners. Guilt-stricken American citizens thus prodded the Bush administration into an international-ized relief mission, launched—under the television cameras' intense, and somewhat discombobulating, gaze—in December 1992 as US SEALs stormed ashore the beaches of Mogadishu (Sharkey 1993; Keenan 1994: 142–3, 147; Stech 1994). Equally, however, elucidators of the "effect" postulate that tele-vision's mobilization of emotions is short-term and shallow: "fickle" in the preferred epithet of Nik Gowing (Gowing 1994). CNN may exert a near instan-taneous "agenda-setting effect" but since its ability to do so rests on manipulation of public sentimentality, it fails to generate sustained support for prolonged and costly interventions of the kind its coverage seems designed to elicit. Hence as soon as CNN starts to relay images of Western casualties incurred in the name of restoring hope (or "providing comfort," or delivering "infinite justice") public support collapses, and policy-makers face equally irresistible pressures to pull troops out precipitately. Somalia appears to crystallize this dynamic, as the opera-tion was apparently terminated in October 1993 in direct response to images screened in America of "bloated corpses of US soldiers being dragged through the dusty streets of Mogadishu," and "more shocking still . . . of a soldier with rope tied around his ankles and his arms, splayed in the sign of the crucifix" (Pilking-ton 1993). These images, according to a number of Clinton staffers (including National Security Adviser Anthony Lake), generated an immediate announce-ment of the mission's termination, leaving one Congressman to conclude that "pictures of starving children, not policy objectives, got us into Somalia in 1992. Pictures of US casualties, not the completion of our objectives, led us to exit Somalia" (Minear, Scott, and Weiss 1996: 46; Gowing 1994: 67).

At least three parties have exhibited a keen interest in dissecting the potency of global media and their putative power to mobilize responses to distant suffer-ing: policy elites, students of "humanitarian intervention," and media scholars. Policy elites, ruffled by the emergence of 24-hour news channels that seemingly corrode the autonomy of executive processes, have intervened in a well-publicized debate carried on both in and about the media. Some are keen to deny that news organizations do more than effect a superficial disarrangement of prior-ities, mandating (at most) intensified "spinning," but rather more attest the distorting impact of new global media in mobilizing transnational publics in ways that detrimentally compress response times, at worst rendering foreign policy decision-making "epiphenomenal to news decision making" (Livingston and Eachus 1995: 415). Most famously, Realist *eminence grise* and architect of Cold War containment, George Kennan, ruminated in *The New York Times* on television images' denial of space "for what have traditionally been regarded as the responsible deliberative organs of our government, in both the executive and legislative branches" (Kennan 1993). His criticism explicitly rejected any notion that this development might be technologically determined: a function of shortened news-cycles and real-time footage that are the necessary stocks-in-trade of global news channels. Rather, Kennan and others (including the former UK Conservative Foreign Secretary Douglas Hurd) have lambasted what they see as declining journalistic abidance by professional codes of objectivity and neutralism in favor of a crusading approach, simultaneously adversarial and advocatory: a lamentable "do something" journalism that has flourished as post-Cold War conflicts—in which the West ostensibly has no particular stake—have proliferated (Seib 1998: 44–5).

The critique of media "power without responsibility" is well-worn, dusting down old charges against American journalists in Vietnam of abandoning objectivity, espousing anti-war partisanship, and showing rather too much graphic footage of what modern weapons do to human flesh to permit the war's sagacious managers to prosecute it to a successful conclusion (Hallin 1989). While many reporters (Halberstam 1972; Arnett 1995; and others) have disputed the accusation of back-stabbing, some nevertheless endorse the notion that unvarnished reportage did indeed play a determining role in undermining popular support for the war in Vietnam—but by "showing it as it was" rather than through actively oppositional reporting (Carruthers 2000: 112). In a similar fashion, some of those who have found themselves the more recent target of attacks on "do something" journalism have been keen to corroborate a CNN effect of sorts, while investing it with humanitarian potential and hence with a different moral valence than those who identify a "curve" they are keen to decry. Former BBC reporter and MP Martin Bell, for instance, has made a number of interventions on behalf of a "journalism of attachment" that takes specific aim at Hurd's revulsion for "real-time" television: "The mandarins' objection is not just to the power but to the impertinence of the upstart medium, which challenges their monopoly of wisdom, and rushes in where the pinstripes fear to tread" (Bell 1995: 137–8, 1997, 1998).

A more laudatory reading of the CNN effect, in at least its initial catalytic phase, unites such journalists with many advocates of "humanitarian intervention": a second group (including both non-governmental organization workers and international relations scholars) that has been attentive to media reporting of "distant crises" (Rotberg and Weiss 1996; Shaw 1996; Ignatieff 1998; Wheeler 2000). Here again, the specificities of conflict in Africa—the character and consequences of UN interventions—have often been less salient than broad claims about the emergence of a "global civil society" that mitigates the reluctance of states to contravene the principle of sovereign inviolability when confronted with instances of grave humanitarian disaster in foreign locales (Clarke 2002: 94–5; Shaw 1996). For some, television is to be congratulated for constituting "macropublics of hundreds of millions of citizens . . . nurturing public controversies beyond the boundaries of the nation-state" (J. Keane 1996: 172–3). Both the immediacy and indelibility of images of human suffering lead to a contraction of sympathies confined to local kinship communities, while expanding our capacity for empathy with "distant suffering" wherever it occurs. According to civil society optimists, such as John Keane, however questionable some forms of media fascination with violence may be, television's focus on human distress nevertheless "contains a hidden, potentially civilizing dialectic" (1996: 172–3, 182–3; Boltanski 1999).

Those who credit television with enhancing Westerners' eagerness for "saving strangers" find both encouraging and dispiriting evidence in Africa (Wheeler 2000). To the extent that Operation "Restore Hope" was animated by this new cross-border solidarity with human suffering, and insofar as the benevolence of its intentions is accepted, then Somalia may offer some cause for optimism. But the disastrously conflicted character of the mission, which quickly "crept" from a militarized food assistance operation to a manhunt for General Aidid in which all Somalis were treated as potential enemies, squeezed public enthusiasm for the deployment in the US and beyond (Dowden 1995: 93; Stech 1994). Hence wearied or confused would-be humanitarians were all too susceptible to images of "their" casualties being dragged through the streets of Mogadishu, seizing upon the shocking images aired in early October 2003 as decisive evidence that it was time for US troops to depart. Moreover, the disaffection engendered by a mission that palpably destroyed hope directly contributed to US failure to intervene in order to prevent a thoroughly foreseeable genocide in Rwanda in April/May 1994. After the stunning events of October 2003, purportedly the "worst day" of Clinton's life (at least pre-Lewinsky), post-Vietnam aversion to "quagmires" was compounded by fear of another "Mog" (Gowing 1994: 67; Dauber 2001). The most immediate manifestation of this hybrid "Vietmalia syndrome" was Presidential Decision Directive no. 25, which established restrictive criteria governing, and indeed tightly circumscribing, any future US intervention overseas (Shattuck 1996: 173). Accordingly, when Rwanda's genocide began in April 1994—after months of well-documented preparatory propaganda and planning—Clinton's response involved a scrupulous avoidance of the descriptor "genocide" (which would have mandated an international response), and a steadfast desire to station US troops as far from the site of slaughter as possible (Destexhe 1995; Prunier 1997).

During the genocide's initial phase, the UN's chief concern was to rescue its own (predominantly white) personnel, and effect as speedy an exit from Rwanda as possible. Many journalists—to the extent that they had hitherto populated the "boringly" placid country—followed suit (Hilsum 1995). Six weeks of killing of the most intimate face-to-face variety, went largely unreported, or certainly barely televised, by Western media (Lorch 1995; Livingston and Eachus 1999). Live satellite broadcasting facilities were not established in the border town of Kigali until late May (Minear, Scott, and Weiss 1996: 64). By then the story had moved on—or at any rate a second story had emerged which became confused in much press reporting with the insufficiently told story of genocide: namely, a massive exodus of refugees, fleeing the anarchic compound of genocide and civil war, as the Rwandan Patriotic Front advanced into the country from Ugandan exile to replace the government of assassinated President Habyarimana. Latching onto a now-familiar icon of wounded innocence—the refugee—the international media began to cover this story intensively, focusing on the relief operations of various NGOs in establishing a city-sized encampment at Goma, and the onset of a deadly cholera epidemic among its rapidly swelling population (Rosenblatt 1996). At this point, Washington announced a contribution to the UN's relief effort, arguably impelled by images of humanity in extremis that cried out for action (Minear, Scott, and Weiss 1996: 65).

Given this dilatory response on the part of both media and policy-makers who preferred to extract their bodies from harm's way and avert their gaze from genocide, advocates of "intervention" question how television's affective properties can be enhanced such that quickly animated sympathies and salvific impulses do not wither prematurely, or collapse into self-protectionism at the first sign of humanitarianism claiming "our" lives while trying to save "theirs" (Girardet 1995; Rotberg and Weiss 1996). Where some take issue with the calibre of Western reporting—its ready recourse to visual and verbal cliché—others critique the patchiness as well as the paucity of coverage. While certain "emergencies" become constituted as media spectacles (as the Rwandan post-genocide relief operation did) others, sometimes just as costly to human life, unfold unobserved. Why, for example, was a devastating famine in Sudan during 1992, which claimed more lives than its counterpart in Somalia during the same period, almost wholly ignored (Livingston 1996; Natsios 1996)? Why is media attention to distant distress so selective and so short-lived? Do news organizations wrongly presume indifference, apathy, or "compassion fatigue" on the part of their consumers (Moeller 1999)? How far do, or should, humanitarians' and journalists' agendas converge?

Communications scholars share an interest in at least some of these same questions, albeit with a different—and less practical—stake in the answers. Media research has long concerned itself (in a certain branch, at least) with mapping the multivalent flows of influence between media, state, and audience; and with questions of how news is selected, filtered, and framed. Over the past decade, several scholars have devoted themselves to a more systematic analysis of the CNN effect than the frequently impressionistic formulations of those often holding an immediate, personal investment in asserting that new(s) media either do, or emphatically do not, lead policy-making. In order to dissect the purportedly "pushing" and "pulling" properties of real-time news, analysts have not only scrutinized apparent instances of the effect's efficacy (Somalia, in particular, but also Rwanda, former Yugoslavia and the 1991 Kurdish crisis) but have also examined why CNN fails to cover many similarly "meretricious" instances of grave humanitarian catastrophe around the world. In so doing, scholars have sought to dispel an often implicit assumption of CNN-effect proponents: that the news media

now supplant more conventional intelligence or diplomatic channels of emergency "early warning."

But they have gone considerably further, finding little to substantiate a "strong
CNN-effect" thesis (Gowing 1994; Livingston and Eachus 1995; Livingston
1996; Robinson 2002). Taking Somalia as the paradigm to be unpicked, several
critics have contested both parts of the equation that pictures got "us" in and out
of that imbroglio. In one of the most detailed studies of the multi-level interactions between policy-makers (in and beyond the US government) and media,
Steven Livingston and Todd Eachus argue compellingly that journalists' attention to Somalia was focused by the advocacy efforts of US government officials
and aid workers, whose persistence finally convinced reluctant news organizations to commit resources to the story once an estimated 300,000 to 500,000
Somalis had already died of famine by mid-1992 (Livingston and Eachus 1995:
417). Earlier Red Cross attempts to organize press briefings and tours in the
autumn of 1991 had been notably unsuccessful (Gassman 1995: 155). Real-time
news media—roving the world for sensational stories (as they are sometimes
imagined to do)—certainly could not be credited with forcing Somalia's famine
to the top of the policy-making agenda. On the contrary, serious and sustained
media reportage began only *after* the Bush administration had committed itself to
a militarized relief operation: a decision which Livingston and Eachus attribute to
a more conventional piece of diplomatic traffic in the form of a telegram dispatched by the US ambassador to Kenya, to which the president was perhaps
particularly susceptible having visited a US CARE shelter in Sudan in the mid-
1980s (Livingston and Eachus 1995: 425–6; Natsios 1996: 163–8).

Scholars continue to debate the precise determinants of Bush's decision to
mount Operation "Restore Hope": the admixture of altruism and aggrandizement
that may have prompted Bush to anticipate lingering benefits from being seen to
"do something," with the luxury of leaving extrication entirely to his successor. At
any rate, although the question is only sometimes reduced to one-dimensional
causative terms, few would claim that television pictures "caused" the intervention (Robinson 2001). The cameras' massed presence in Mogadishu was much
more an *effect* of militarization than the reverse. As several commentators point
out, "Restore Hope" was nothing if not an event orchestrated for media consumption—but in which discordant elements soon overwhelmed an increasingly
conductorless score (Keenan 1994; Stech 1994). When things fell apart, with the
US-led forces engaged in a reciprocally brutal game of tag with Somali "warlords,"
most journalists exited the country, just as they would do in Rwanda some months
later. From a peak of 600—to observe the SEALs' arrival—the press corps dwin-
dled to a mere half dozen, none of them American (Pilkington 1993). So,
whatever impact the infamous images of October 1993 made, it is worth noting
that they were neither relayed in real-time nor were they the product of express
journalistic intent to challenge the operation. The footage of brutalized Rangers to
which so much has been imputed was in fact shot by a Somali driver, bequeathed a
Hi-8 camcorder by the departing Reuters crew after three colleagues were beaten

to death by enraged Somalis in the aftermath of a US helicopter attack in July 2003 (Lyman 1995: 126).

Did the image of the "crucified" Ranger, however acquired and with whatever delay between recording and transmission, destroy "Hope"? This remains a more complex case to determine. Arguably not, however. According to some well-informed accounts, a decision to withdraw was already on the cards if not yet publicly announced. In a sense, the pictures may have provided the pretext for termination. The final pull-out, it is sometimes noted, did not in fact occur for several months, begging questions as to whether a more resolute presidency could have weathered the immediate storm over the October episode had it been minded to continue an operation for which there remained residual US public support (Gowing 1994: 69; Natsios 1996, 163; Stech 1994: 244). For many such scholars, then, the conclusion to be drawn is that policy-makers retain primacy over the policy process—susceptible to the "push" of potent imagery only during moments of irresolution, and even then often responding to televisual prompting in superficial ways, making what Gowing calls "pseudo-responses" to media-generated crises (Gowing 1994).

Ancient hatreds, modern humanitarians

Media scholars generally heed the *content* of this coverage only insofar as certain policy outcomes may hypothetically be more likely in response to specific framing practices. Piers Robinson, for example, proposes that "empathy framed coverage," which "tends to focus on the suffering of individuals, identifying them as victims in need of 'outside' help," may be more likely to generate (inter)governmental action than "distance framing" that "tends to minimize pressure for intervention" by emphasizing the roots of catastrophe in "ancient ethnic hatreds" (Robinson 2001: 943). Attention to *how* African news is reported forms a segue from the first group of analysts to the second: a point of intersecting interest in news media characterization of events in Africa, and its practical consequences. But where the former discuss the affective properties of content (as trigger of/inhibitor to Western intervention), the latter elucidate the descriptive and analytic purchase of Western media tropes. Commonly, such scholars lament the failure of journalists to offer adequately informed and nuanced accounts of African crises (Myers, Klak and Koehl 1996; Wall 1997; McNulty 1999; Fair and Parks 2001; Pottier 2002). In particular, many Africanists take issue with Western media's unthinking elevation of "tribalism" to explanatory primacy in accounting for warlordism in Somalia and genocide in Rwanda. Not only does this ethnocentrism (or indeed racism) omit the West's own implication in the roots of African state failure, economic collapse, and societal disintegration but it also has profound consequences for what types of action—or inaction—become thinkable in response. For some the problem is that ethnicized explanations mandate Western neglect of situations attributed to endemic animosities; for others that such flimsy conceits legitimize self-interested interventions with unavoidably injurious consequences.

163

If Somalia forms "exhibit A" in the CNN effect debate then Rwanda provides a more pressing point of concern for Africanists anxious to deconstruct the impoverishment of Western news analysis. Nowhere did the ready resort to "ancient ethnic hatreds" more powerfully pre-script coverage than in Rwanda. The genocide of 1994 was reduced to a simple tale of Hutu slaughtering their Tutsi neighbors: the latest iteration of an ongoing cycle of bloodletting since time immemorial (Murison 1996; Myers, Klak, and Koehl 1996; Wall 1997; McNulty 1999). This prevailing narrative assigned clear-cut moral and ethnic identities to Tutsi victims and Hutu perpetrators. Violence may have been reported as "black-on-black" but media-made morality was etched in black and white: good Tutsi, evil Hutu. Paradoxically, however, in their eagerness to maintain these categories and to affirm the purity of refugee victimhood, many journalists reporting the post-genocide exodus into Tanzania and Zaire failed to appreciate that those filling the camps around Rwanda's borders included several thousand who had *enacted* the genocide—not, as reporting often implied, an indistinguishable mass of "innocents" fleeing in fright (de Waal 1994: 25; F. Keane 1996: 186). Concentrating on the "big story" of Western humanitarianism, the selfless altruism of relief workers, and the spareness of human suffering at its most raw and seemingly undifferentiated, much reportage failed to note how the camps became havens for the exiled *interahamwe* militia, which would (in time) form a serious challenge to the new RPF regime (de Waal 1998; Fair and Parks 2001). Rather, refugees were required to serve as mute totems: "Good people to whom bad things happen," as one journalist later characterized the role (Minear, Scott, and Weiss 1996: 64).

As a corrective to such ill-informed, inaccurate or downright tendentious accounts, many Africanists have sought to dismantle the attribution of violence to "ethnic hatreds"—whether with reference to Rwanda's genocide, the anarchic conditions of Somalia, the marauding gangs of machete-wielding child soldiers in Liberia, Sierra Leone, or other locations in what Madeleine Albright dismissively denoted as the "hopeless continent." Such scholars (and advocates of a more self-reflective humanitarianism) stress the constructedness of social identities in Africa, as elsewhere, together with the complex local and global determinants of violence that give the lie to any suggestion that tribalism underlies African crises. Some question, with regard to Rwanda's genocide, whether Hutu and Tutsi constitute distinct ethnicities at all (Mamdani 1996; McNulty 1999). All, however, share an understanding of ethnicity's potency as a manipulable resource—a rich and renewable seam of energy to be mined—in struggles over power and privilege, representation, and resources. In the words of Johan Pottier:

> Rwanda's bloodbath was not tribal. Rather it was a distinctly modern tragedy, a degenerated class conflict minutely prepared and callously executed . . .
> The power of shamelessly twisted ethnic argument for the sake of class privilege was demonstrated most shockingly in the blatant imaginings about history that galvanized Rwanda's "Hutu Power" extremists. These

extremists killed Rwanda's Tutsi and sent their bodies "back to Ethiopia" via the Nyabarongo and Akagera rivers. The imagined origins of "the Tutsi", along with their (poorly understood) migrations and conquest of Rwanda, were evoked by power-crazed Hutu politicians to instill "ethnic hatred" in the very people they themselves oppressed: the victims of oppression were spurred on to kill a minority group which the oppressors had labelled the "real enemy".

(Pottier 2002: 9)

The point here is more profound than that an intense barrage of hate propaganda—transmitted largely by radio—primed Rwanda's genocide, turning neighbours into killers (Chrétien 1995; F. Keane 1996; Kirschke 1996; Des Forges 1999). While analyses of radio's role may say something significant about how genocide is organized, and how dispersed the locus of responsibility (with broadcasters included among those subsequently indicted for crimes against humanity at Arusha), they do not necessarily suffice to dislodge "ethnic hatred" from its explanatory pedestal. What is required, Pottier and others suggest, is an account that does more than substitute "manufactured" hatreds for "authentic" (and supposedly ancient) ones, leaving matters at that (Appadurai 1998). As Jan Nederveen Pieterse puts it "Ethnicity, although generally considered a cause of conflict, is not an explanation but rather that which is to be explained. The terminology of ethnicity is part of the conflict and cannot serve as the language of analysis" (1997: 71).

What constitutes sufficient explanation—and which interests are inflected through the idiom of ethnicity—will be returned to later. Since most media deliver only stories saturated in essentialism, several commentators probe the roots of this explanatory impoverishment. Why do Western journalists so routinely "get Africa wrong"? Should this be put down to narrowly professional shortcomings within news organizations or ascribed to media's broader ideological situatedness? For some critics, the answer lies primarily in the long-term erosion of foreign news services, which has hit Africa particularly severely since agency staffers and permanent correspondents were already so over-stretched and thinly spread. As a result of this depletion of accumulated knowledge, more news organizations rely—at least for crisis coverage—on "parachute" journalism: star reporters simply airlifted into and out of the latest location of humanitarian disaster (Pedelty 1995). Wholly ignorant of local conditions, and harried by over-abundant deadlines (with rolling news increasing journalists' on-camera airtime and correspondingly diminishing their opportunities for off-camera investigation), these parachutists predictably plunder a stock of well-worn clichés, stereotypes, and pre-scripted storylines: of African tribalism, implacable enmities, unspeakable evil, maniacs with machetes, and benefactors in blue berets.

In journalists' telling, this reliance on certain easily grasped conventions arises less because it conserves their time than because it fails to make a drain on ours: with Western audiences conceived as intolerant of complexity, especially in places of which they know, and care, rather little (Behr 1992). Hence CNN's insistence that Rwanda's genocide could not have been covered while it unfolded in April/May 1994, as that would have required simultaneous coverage alongside Nelson Mandela's inauguration as South African premier. Rather, it had to appear sequentially—after the massed press corps moved from Johannesburg to Kigali en route "home" (without which coincidence, by implication, the refugee situation might have received considerably less attention). Why not both simultaneously? "[S]howing two African topics at the same time . . . might confuse their audience": viewers presumed incapable of grasping that "good news" from Africa might unfold synchronously with something conforming to the more familiar catastrophic mold (Gassman 1995: 157). Similarly, journalists are often wont to attribute their eagerness to establish clear-cut points of identification for sympathy and targets for blame to a deficiency in viewers' ability to grasp complexity, or a deficit in public patience to fathom it. Circumstances not being obligingly simple but attention-spans being so truncated, journalists must necessarily reach for stock characterizations. Hence the concentration in post-genocide Rwanda on the figure of the refugee: a late twentieth-century icon of innocence—as long, of course, as refugees remain encamped at Goma and not Sangatte ("over there" and not, like the *fin de siècle* hate figure—the "bogus asylum seeker"—making more pressing claims on/of us "over here").

According to Pottier, journalists' ignorance also renders them susceptible to manipulation by African elites eager to promote their own particularist versions of contemporary events, together with an appropriately (re)configured account of history (2002). But perhaps this "tainting" is a less significant phenomenon (since rather few journalists seriously trouble to seek out indigenous sources, and some insist on their skepticism toward "native informants" (Meisler 1992)) than journalists' embeddedness within particular cultural, political, and economic matrices which endlessly replenish the reservoir from which easy "ethnic" explanations are retrieved, while filtering out alternative accounts. After all, journalists who reflect retrospectively on their African days tend not to do much better a job of explaining the deep roots of the continent's crises, however much remission from deadlines they may enjoy for rumination. Hence in journalistic memoirs such as Scott Peterson's *Me Against My Brother*, "Heart of Darkness" motifs are just as evident as in more instantaneous analyses (and equally of a piece with the tropology of Hollywood's imperial "rescue fantasies," such as the recent Bruce Willis vehicle, *Tears of the Sun*). Whether, then, in news reports, movies, memoirs, or travelogue, Africa remains cast as a continent of epic odyssey and spiritual quest—a place that has "always known violence and war"—resulting in epiphanic but invariably bathetic lessons about humanity, and the capacity for evil lurking in all of us (Peterson 2001: xiii). "[I]n Africa," Peterson muses with an audacity that would surely be inconceivable applied to any continent other than Africa, "there is a Jungian balance between remarkable good and intense evil. But it may be more of a Manichean battle between the forces of light and dark, because as worthy of spiritual celebration as the good may be, the degree of evil is also extraordinary" (2001: xiv). His account of Somalis' bloodlust as a function of these "ancient nomadic warriors" having been catapulted "by default into a new era" could have been lifted straight from accounts of Kenya's Mau Mau "emergency" in the 1950s, which similarly explained Kikuyu "atavism" as a crisis of modernization as backward tribes struggled with, and against, the disruptive impact of "progress" on ossified traditions and irrational beliefs (Peterson 2001: 6; Carruthers 1995: 128–93).

To note the persistence of egregious Othering in Western constructions of Africa is not to highlight anything either new or neglected (Hawk 1992; Nederveen Pieterse 1992). Africa—as dark continent—has long functioned as foil to the West's virtuous self-conception as cradle of civilization and progenitor of the Enlightenment. Too often, however, emphasis is placed on correcting Western "misperceptions" of Africa. Crucially, we need to go beyond a dissection of these enduring Western figurations, probing the ideological work of the identity-practices involved. How does the West constitute *itself* in relational terms to Africa? What politics are enabled by construing "evil" as a qaat-chewing warlord, a kleptocrat outfitted in leopard-skin, an ululating child toting an AK-47?[2] What functions, in other words, do particular representations of Africa perform for "us"? If decontextualization and excessive ethnicization in news reporting result more from media's *structural* position within a particular set of power relations than from narrowly *procedural* shortcomings, then making sense of how Africa is—and is not—covered requires an account of news-media's role in simultaneously normalizing and obscuring the current global order. The task is thus to make visible the ways in which news-media efface the systemic underpinnings of local crises such that the West effectively "disappears" from reporting on the roots of African "failure," while Western virtuousness is affirmed as the civilized correlative to barbarism (Salter 2002).

Conclusion: an intervention on "intervention"

Clearly this is a larger undertaking than the conclusion of an essay can accomplish, yet a necessary step beyond much of the literature that deals with media reporting, African crises, and Western intervention. Indeed, the argument advanced here is that the very language of "intervention" constitutes a barrier to understanding the constitutive role that Africa plays in the West's self-conception, and the profound part that the West plays in Africa's predicament. This is not, however, a position commonly espoused. For many liberal commentators, the problem is rather that accounts emphasizing the endemic character of "ethnic violence" too easily generate neglect of grave humanitarian need, and a resolute skepticism over the virtues and value of intervention. If conflict is represented as irremediable—embedded in the genetic make-up of tribes—then wary Westerners may well believe that their interpositions could at best but mitigate the aftermath of violent tribalism. Peacekeeping forces might conceivably hold aroused ethnic enmities in abeyance, but unless they remain permanently present such situations will always threaten to collapse back into barbarism. So, why "go there" when intervention promises to be protracted, or, if temporary, then recurrently required to staunch the inevitable reanimation of murderous passions? For liberals of this stripe, the issue is how to build support for sustained overseas commitments, and for timely interventions that do not simply exacerbate dependence, corruption, autocracy, or population displacement (de Waal 1998). The proposed solution is a media that builds support for militant human rights interventionism, cultivating Western willingness to expend blood and treasure in the name of human solidarity—an agenda that facilitated liberal enthusiasm for "humanitarian bombing" of Serbia during NATO's Kosovo campaign, recently leading some (notably Michael Ignatieff) into highly supportive postures toward the "liberationist" pretensions of current US foreign policy (Kaldor 1999; Ignatieff 2000, 2003; Wheeler 2000).

For some on the left, on the other hand, the trouble with Western journalism is that it legitimizes intervention *too* readily. Mel McNulty, for example, argues that "Misinterpretation of these crises [in Rwanda and Zaire] as ethnically-driven facilitated Western interventionary responses, the rationale for which may be summarized as 'they are mad, we are sane, we must save them from themselves,' and served, whether deliberately or accidentally, to make a bad situation worse" (1999: 268). She goes on to impute a fair degree of deliberation to the West, which while making a show of its charity being imposed upon, calculatedly threw a "cloak of humanitarian concern" over an intervention that served "military-strategic interests" in the Great Lakes region (McNulty 1999: 268). The precise nature of these interests—and the extent to which they may be ascribed to others besides the French (whose *Opération Turquoise* was widely criticized as an intervention on behalf of the *génocidaires*)—remains unclear, however.

What, then, *is* the character of this interventionism? Does not a concentration on sporadic, short-term militarized operations, which may be fairly readily attributed to specific national neocolonial agendas, obscure the wider and more enduring role of Western institutions in establishing, maintaining, and adjusting the global neoliberal framework within which Africa is deeply embedded? "Intervention"—whether invoked by its advocates or its detractors—perpetuates an assumption that the West's typical posture toward Africa is one of either benign or malign neglect, punctuated by brief intrusions of intense activity, altruistic or self-interested depending on the interpreter's perspective (Feher 2000; Chandler 2002). Missing here is more than acknowledgment of the deep colonial backstory. After all, several accounts (including contemporaneous media reports) have inserted Belgian imperial "divide and rule" tactics into their analyses of Rwanda's genocide: with the consolidation of antagonistic ethnicities attributed to Belgian machinations in instituting a *kipende* system that crystallized ethnic difference (giving it both documentary shape and somatic form), and materially privileging the minority Tutsi population.

Excavation of the colonial roots of current crises is undoubtedly necessary. But historical correctives must not occlude the constant influence in (and over)

Africa of Western institutions, whose structural violence is displaced and implicitly disavowed by fetishizing the grotesquery of African barbarism. Emphasizing colonial distortions—in the absence of an account of contemporary, and constant, Western involvement in Africa—may serve to suggest that wholesale influence ended with the onset of formal independence. Hence the widespread assumption that Africa is not just a "hopeless" continent but also "forgotten"—so disastrously under-performing, so riddled with corruption and conflict as to have been shut out from, and left behind by, the unstoppable forces of globalization. Yet while these "invisible" influences may frequently drop from our line of vision, institutions at the heart of the global neo-liberal project have not dropped Africa from theirs. Africa has certainly not been immune from the dislocating processes of "accumulation by dispossession" that characterize the "new imperialism" as outlined by David Harvey (Harvey 2003). How often, though, is Rwanda's genocide linked to the consequences of a catastrophic collapse of world coffee prices (triggered by Washington's intransigence) that "sentenced many poor to unprecedented levels of despair, making them vulnerable to manipulation by politicians in search of extreme solutions to their country's (and their own) growing insecurity" (Pottier 2002: 21)? More generally, local struggles over resources—which may become similarly "ethnicized"—must be understood as occurring within larger frameworks of global markets, IMF interventions, international arms trading, and crossborder cultural circuits: hence, as Paul Richards has shown, the exposure of child soldiers in Sierra Leone to Stallone videos and Western news media, both of which influenced the performative dimensions of their military tactics (Richards 1996). By heeding such phenomena we may begin to insert the West into accounts of Africa's predicament, and Africa into our understandings of how the West sustains more than merely its humane self-conception.

Notes

1 "The West" is a problematic descriptor on at least two counts. The geographic catch-all implies a degree of homogeneity that fails to capture the diversity of the region so labeled, while implying grid coordinates that do not fully map the location of the global north. These qualifications notwithstanding, a dispersed but powerful entity, "the West," continues to use that self-descriptor, and to construe itself in "civilizational" terms under this banner. I use it here (henceforth without quotation marks) as both a shorthand convenience but also to invoke—and critique—that self-conception. Similarly, "Western media" functions as an abbreviation for mainstream English language journalism of primarily the United States and United Kingdom (and their respective "global" news organizations), which of course also homogenizes the variety of opinion and outlets to be found in both states and beyond.

2 Take, for example, the following passage from William Shawcross' *Deliver Us from Evil: Warlords and Peacekeepers in a World of Endless Conflict*, which, while critical of the corruption and confusion surrounding certain UN interventions, reserves a particular vernacular of opprobrium for its African "devils": "The Nigerian presidential Gulfstream was furnished in dictator-chic style, with beige leather seats, gold-plated seat buckles and other fittings, and gold taps in the lavatory . . . There was a small VIP

section at the front of the plane where Annan sat, a large television screen before him. I wondered how many really bad people had sat in that seat" (Shawcross 2000, p. 271).

References

Appadurai, A. (1998) "Dead certainty: ethnic violence in the era of globalization," *Public Culture*, vol. 10, no. ii, pp. 225–47.

Arnett, Peter (1995) *Live from the Battlefield*, London: Corgi.

Behr, E. (1992) *Anyone Here Been Raped and Speaks English? A Correspondent's Life Behind the Lines*, Harmondsworth: Penguin.

Bell, M. (1995) *In Harm's Way: Reflections of a War Zone Thug*, London: Hamish Hamilton.

Bell, M. (1997) "TV news: how far should we go?," *British Journalism Review*, vol. 8, no. i, pp. 6–16.

Bell, M. (1998) "The truth is our currency," *Press/Politics*, vol. 3, no. i, pp. 102–9.

Boltanski, L. (1999) *Distant Suffering: Morality, Media and Politics*, Cambridge: Cambridge University Press.

Bowden, M. (2002) *Black Hawk Down: a Story of Modern War*, New York: Signet.

Bush, G.W. (2003) "In Bush's words: 'we will do what is necessary' in the fight against terror," *The New York Times*, September 8, pp. A10.

Cain, K.L. (2003) "The legacy of Black Hawk down," *The New York Times*, October 2, p. A27.

Carruthers, S.L. (1995) *Winning Hearts and Minds: British Governments, the Media and Colonial Counter-insurgency, 1945–60*, Leicester: Leicester University Press.

Carruthers, S.L. (2000) *The Media at War: Communication and Conflict in the Twentieth Century*, Basingstoke: Macmillan/Palgrave.

Carruthers, S.L. (2003) "Bringing it all back home: Hollywood returns to war," *Small Wars and Insurgencies*, vol. 14, no. i, pp. 167–82.

Chandler, D. (2002) *From Kosovo to Kabul: Human Rights and International Intervention*, London: Pluto Press.

Chrétien, J.-P. (1995) *Rwanda: les médias du génocide*, Paris: Karthala.

Clarke, J.N. (2002) "Revisiting the new interventionism," *Peace Review*, vol. 14, no. i, pp. 93–100.

Dauber, C. (2001) "'The shots seen 'round the world': the impact of the images of Mogadishu on American military operations," *Rhetoric and Public Affairs*, vol. 4, no. iv, pp. 653–87.

Des Forges, A. (1999) *Leave None to Tell the Story: Genocide in Rwanda*, New York: Human Rights Watch.

Destexhe, A. (1995) *Rwanda and Genocide in the Twentieth Century*, London: Pluto Press.

de Waal, A. (1994) "African encounters," *Index on Censorship*, vol. 6, pp. 14–31.

de Waal, A. (1998) *Famine Crimes: Politics and the Disaster Relief Industry in Africa*, Bloomington, IN: Indiana University Press.

Dowden, R. (1995) "Covering Somalia—recipe for disaster" in E. Girardet (ed.), *Somalia, Rwanda and Beyond: the Role of International Media in Wars and Humanitarian Crises*, Dublin: Crosslines Global Report.

Fair, J.E. and Parks, L. (2001) "Africa on camera: television news coverage and aerial imaging of Rwandan refugees," *Africa Today*, vol. 48, no. ii, pp. 35–57.

Fanon, F. (1967) *The Wretched of the Earth*, Harmondsworth: Penguin.

Feher, M. (2000) *Powerless by Design: the Age of the International Community*, Durham: Duke University Press.

Gassman, P. (1995) "TV without government: the new world order?" in E. Girardet (ed.), *Somalia, Rwanda and Beyond: the Role of International Media in Wars and Humanitarian Crises*, Dublin: Crosslines Global Report.

Girardet, E. (ed.) (1995) *Somalia, Rwanda and Beyond: the Role of International Media in Wars and Humanitarian Crises*, Dublin: Crosslines Global Report.

Gowing, N. (1994) "Real-time television coverage of armed conflicts and diplomatic crises: does it make or break government policy?," Harvard: Joan Shorenstein Barone Center working paper, pp. 94–1.

Halberstam, David (1972) *The Brightest and the Best*, New York: Random House.

Hallin, D. (1989) *The "Uncensored War": the Media and Vietnam*, New York: Oxford University Press.

Harvey, D. (2003) *The New Imperialism*, Oxford: Oxford University Press.

Hawk, B. (ed.) (1992) *Africa's Media Image*, Westport, CT: Praeger.

Hilsum, L. (1995) "Where is Kigali?," *Granta*, vol. 51, pp. 145–79.

Ignatieff, M. (1998) *The Warrior's Honor: Ethnic War and the Modern Conscience*, London: Chatto and Windus.

Ignatieff, M. (2000) *Virtual War: Kosovo and Beyond*, London: Chatto and Windus.

Ignatieff, M. (2003) "The Burden," *New York Times Magazine*, January 5, vol. 22–7, no. 50, pp. 53–4.

Kaldor, M. (1999) *New and Old Wars: Organized Violence in a Global Era*, Stanford: Stanford University Press.

Keane, F. (1996) *Season of Blood: a Rwandan Journey*, Harmondsworth: Penguin.

Keane, J. (1996) *Reflections on Violence*, London: Verso.

Keenan, T. (1994) "Live from . . . " in J.-L. Déotte *et al.* (eds), *Visites aux armées: tourisms de guerre*, Basse-Normandie: FRAC.

Kennan, G.F. (1993) "Somalia, through a glass, darkly," *The New York Times*, September 30, 1993, p. A25.

Kirschke, L. (1996) *Broadcasting Genocide: Censorship, Propaganda and State-sponsored Violence*, London: article 19.

Livingston, S. (1996) "Suffering in silence: media coverage of war and famine in the Sudan" in R. Rotberg and T. Weiss (eds), *From Massacres to Genocide: the Media, Public Policy and Humanitarian Crises*, Washington, DC: Brookings Institution.

Livingston, S. and Eachus, T. (1995) "Humanitarian crises and US foreign policy: Somalia and the CNN effect reconsidered," *Political Communication*, vol. 12, pp. 413–29.

Livingston, S. and Eachus, T. (1999) "Rwanda: US policy and television coverage" in H. Adelman, and A. Suhrke (eds), *The Path of a Genocide: the Rwanda Crisis from Uganda to Zaire*, New Brunswick, NJ: Transaction Publishers.

Lorch, D. (1995) "Genocide versus heartstrings" in E. Girardet (ed.), *Somalia, Rwanda and Beyond: the Role of International Media in Wars and Humanitarian Crises*, Dublin: Crosslines Global Report.

Lyman, R. (1995) "Occupational hazards" in E. Girardet (ed.), *Somalia, Rwanda and Beyond: the Role of International Media in Wars and Humanitarian Crises*, Dublin: Crosslines Global Report.

Mamdani, M. (1996) "From conquest to consent as the basis of state formation: reflections on Rwanda," *New Left Review*, vol. 216, pp. 3–36.

171

McNulty, M. (1999) "Media ethnicization and the international response to war and genocide in Rwanda" in T. Allen and J. Seaton (eds), *The Media of Conflict: War Reporting and Representations of Ethnic Violence*, London: Zed Books.

Meisler, S. (1992) "Committed in Africa: reflections of a correspondent" in B. Hawk, (ed.) *Africa's Media Image*, Westport, CT: Praeger.

Minear, L., Scott, C., and Weiss, T. (1996) *The News Media, Civil War and Humanitarian Action*, Boulder, CO: Lynne Reinner.

Moeller, S. (1999) *Compassion Fatigue: How The Media Sell Disease, Famine, War and Death*, New York: Routledge.

Murison, J. (1996) *Fleeing the Jungle Bloodbath: the Method in the Madness*, Edinburgh: Centre of African Studies, occasional paper no. 65.

Myers, G., Klak, T., and Koehl, T. (1996) "The inscription of difference: news coverage of the conflicts in Rwanda and Bosnia," *Political Geography*, vol. 15, no. i, pp. 21–46.

Natsios, A. (1996) "Illusions of influence: the CNN effect in complex emergencies" in R. Rotberg and T. Weiss (eds), *From Massacres to Genocide: the Media, Public Policy and Humanitarian Crises*, Washington, DC: Brookings Institution.

Nederveen Pieterse, J. (1992) *White on Black: Images of Africa and Blacks in Western Popular Culture*, New Haven, CT: Yale University Press.

Nederveen Pieterse, J. (1997) "Sociology of humanitarian intervention: Bosnia, Rwanda and Somalia compared," *International Political Science Review*, vol. 18, no. i, pp. 71–93.

Neuman, J. (1996) *Lights, Camera, War: Is Media Technology Driving International Politics?* New York: St Martin's Press.

Pedelty, M. (1995) *War Stories: the Culture of Foreign Correspondents*, London: Routledge.

Peterson, S. (2001) *Me Against My Brother: at War in Somalia, Sudan and Rwanda*, New York: Routledge.

Philo, G., Hilsum, L., Beattie, L., and Holliman, R. (1998) "The Media and the Rwanda crisis: effects on audiences and public policy" in J. Nederveen Pieterse (ed.), *World Orders in the Making: Humanitarian Intervention and Beyond*, Basingstoke: Macmillan, 1998, pp. 211–29.

Pilkington, E. (1993) "Shots that shook the world," *The Guardian*, October 11, 1993.

Pottier, J. (2002) *Re-imagining Rwanda: Conflict, Survival and Disinformation in the Late Twentieth Century*, Cambridge: Cambridge University Press.

Power, S. (2002) *A Problem from Hell: America and the Age of Genocide*, New York: Basic Books.

Prunier, G. (1997) *The Rwanda Crisis: History of a Genocide*, London: Hurst.

Richards, P. (1996) *Fighting for the Rain Forest: War, Youth and Resources in Sierra Leone*, Oxford: James Currey.

Robinson, P. (1999) "The CNN effect: can the news media drive foreign policy?," *Review of International Studies*, vol. 25, no. 1, pp. 301–9.

Robinson, P. (2001) "Operation Restore Hope and the illusion of a news media driven intervention," *Political Studies*, vol. 49, pp. 941–56.

Robinson, P. (2002) *The CNN Effect: the Myth of News, Foreign Policy and Intervention*, London and New York: Routledge.

Rosenblatt, L. (1996) "The media and the refugee" in R. Rotberg and T. Weiss (eds), *From Massacres to Genocide: the Media, Public Policy and Humanitarian Crises*, Washington, DC: Brookings Institution.

Rotberg, R. and Weiss, T. (eds) (1996) *From Massacres to Genocide: the Media, Public Policy and Humanitarian Crises*, Washington, DC: Brookings Institution.

Salter, Mark (2002) *Barbarians and Civilization in International Relations*, London: Pluto Press.

Seib, P. (1998) *Headline Diplomacy: how News Coverage Affects Foreign Policy*, Westport, CO: Praeger.

Sharkey, J. (1993) "When pictures drive foreign policy," *American Journalism Review*, vol. 15, no. x, pp. 14–19.

Shattuck, J. (1996), "Human rights and humanitarian crises: policy-making and the media" in R. Rotberg and T. Weiss (eds), *From Massacres to Genocide: the Media, Public Policy and Humanitarian Crises*, Washington, DC: Brookings Institution.

Shaw, M. (1994) "Civil society and global politics: beyond a social movements approach," *Millennium: Journal of International Studies*, vol. 23, no. iii, pp. 421–34.

Shaw, M. (1996) *Civil Society and Media in Global Crises: Representing Distant Violence*, London: Pinter.

Shawcross, W. (2000) *Deliver Us from Evil: Warlords and Peacekeepers in a World of Endless Conflict*.

Stech, F. (1994) "Preparing for more CNN wars" in J. Petrie (ed.), *Essays on Strategy XII*, Washington, DC: National Defense University Press.

Strobel, W. (1997) *Late-Breaking Foreign Policy: the News Media's Influence on Peace Operations*, Washington, DC: United States Institute of Peace.

Wall, M.A. (1997) "The Rwanda crisis: an analysis of news magazine coverage," *Gazette: the International Journal for Communication Studies*, vol. 59, no. ii, pp. 121–34.

Wheeler, N.J. (2000) *Saving Strangers: Humanitarian Intervention in International Society*, Oxford: Oxford University Press.

9

HUMANIZING WAR

The Balkans and beyond

Philip Hammond

A notable feature of the propaganda surrounding the war on terrorism has been the tendency of coalition leaders to fall back on what Michael Ignatieff calls the "dominant moral vocabulary" of the 1990s (*The New York Times*, February 5, 2002): the discourse of humanitarianism and human rights. Washington reportedly spent hundreds of thousands of dollars hiring advertising and public relations consultants to "humanise the war" in Afghanistan (Channel 4 News, November 6, 2001), though the results were bizarre. President George W. Bush invited American children to donate a dollar to the Red Cross while his airforce deliberately bombed the organization's facilities in Kabul and Kandahar; and Afghan children had trouble distinguishing the aid packages from the cluster bombs, both dropped by US planes. By the time the invasion of Iraq started in March 2003 political leaders seemed to have all but forgotten about searching for WMD, let alone combating international terrorism, instead promising to "liberate" the Iraqi people. It is as if the war on terrorism cannot be justified on its own terms, and has to be invested with some higher "moral" purpose in the form of humanitarianism or upholding human rights.

This adoption of humanitarian rhetoric by the Bush administration has dismayed many former enthusiasts of ethical interventionism. In Europe, criticism is tinged with anti-Americanism and distaste for the Republican Party, as in Timothy Garton Ash's concern that "the association with Bush's America is tarnishing [the] liberal internationalist project" (*Guardian*, September 19, 2002). Yet there are similar worries in the US. Richard Falk, for example, laments a fall from the "golden age" of the 1990s: since 9/11, humanitarianism has been used to provide "a cover for imperial objectives," offering "post hoc rationalizations for uses of force otherwise difficult to reconcile with international law" (*Nation*, July 14, 2003). David Rieff is also bothered by the cynical instrumentalism with which humanitarianism is treated, noting that Secretary of State Colin Powell described NGOs in Afghanistan as "an important part of our combat team" (2002: 236). More broadly, having advocated military intervention in the Balkans throughout the 1990s, Rieff is now worried that talk of humanitarianism provides an automatic justification which elides the human costs of war (Rief 2002: 284). Yet while many critics have challenged the high-flown moral claims made about the war on terrorism, the possibility of a more benign imperial relationship between the Great Powers and weaker states is usually still assumed.

The discourse of humanitarianism and human rights was promoted throughout the 1990s by journalists and commentators as an organizing principle for a post-Cold War world order (Herman and Peterson 2002), nowhere more conspicuously than in media coverage of the former Yugoslavia. As they sought to encourage Western intervention in Bosnia, reporters and intellectuals developed the "moral vocabulary" which was later given an official stamp of approval by NATO during the 1999 Kosovo conflict, and which has since been used as a standby justification for intervention anywhere from Afghanistan to Liberia. This chapter looks back at the pre-9/11 "golden age" and suggests that those who now complain that US imperialism is destroying international order should reflect on how 1990s humanitarianism and human rightsism did the same. The moralistic media consensus which developed in favor of intervention in the Balkans was premised on the notion that Western action to uphold human rights should override established principles of international law, particularly that of non-interference in the internal affairs of sovereign states. This development has been driven by the felt need of Western societies to discover some new moral purpose in the post-Cold War world, despite the disastrous consequences of intervention for those on the receiving end of their benevolence.

The doctrine of "illegal but moral" intervention

Many assessments of the Kosovo war concede that—as an unprovoked attack unauthorized by the UN—NATO bombing was illegal. It is widely maintained, however, that war was nonetheless morally justified. The arguments made to support this are: that bombing was a last resort, launched only after diplomatic efforts to resolve the conflict between the Yugoslav government and ethnic-Albanian separatists had failed; and that NATO had to act because of both the severity of the actual emergency and in order to avert an even worse catastrophe. On the first count, the Independent International Commission on Kosovo (whose members included Falk and Ignatieff) concluded that while "the intervention was . . . not legal," it was "legitimate because it was unavoidable: diplomatic options had been exhausted" (IICK 2000: 289). Regarding the second point, a post-war enquiry by the British parliamentary Foreign Affairs Committee argued that while the bombing may have been of "dubious legality," it was "justified on moral grounds" because there was a "humanitarian emergency . . . before NATO intervened, and . . . a humanitarian catastrophe would have occurred . . . if intervention had not taken place" (UKFAC 2000). Similar arguments were made by Prime Minister Tony Blair during the bombing in a major speech setting out a new "doctrine of the international community" (April 23,

1999). Their continued repetition is a remarkable illustration of the propaganda role played by the mainstream Western media in reporting Kosovo.

Contrary to what some still claim, there was no real diplomatic effort to resolve the Kosovo crisis. The closest the Western powers came to an attempt at mediation was the Organization for Security and Cooperation in Europe's (OSCE) Kosovo Verification Mission (KVM), which monitored a ceasefire in 1998–9. The intervention of the OSCE was never likely to resolve the crisis, since it encouraged secessionist Kosovo Albanians to believe that internationalizing the conflict was their best strategy. The ceasefire was also inherently flawed because it was entirely one-sided, restricting the Yugoslav security forces but allowing the Kosovo Liberation Army (KLA) to "get organised, to consolidate and grow," in the words of KLA commander Agim Ceku (*Moral Combat: NATO at War*, BBC2, March 12, 2000). Furthermore, the powerful Western countries who seemed to be backing the mission were actually subverting it. America's hawkish Secretary of State, Madeleine Albright, chose William Walker as head of the mission, a diplomat with a history of excusing US-approved atrocities in central America (Johnstone 2002: 239). As KVM monitor Roland Keith later observed, Walker was "part of the American diplomatic policy . . . which had vilified Slobodan Milosevic, demonised the Serbian administration and generally was providing diplomatic support to . . . the KLA leadership" (*Moral Combat*, March 12, 2000).

Walker's key contribution was his reaction to an alleged massacre at the village of Racak on January 15, 1999. He was shown around 40 dead bodies, which the KLA claimed were civilian victims of a Serbian atrocity. Without waiting for any investigation of the incident, Walker called US Balkans envoy Richard Holbrooke and NATO commander General Wesley Clarke by cellphone from the scene, and declared to the world's media that the Serbs had committed a "crime against humanity" and an "unspeakable atrocity." Questions were immediately raised about the incident in the German and French press, offering quite a different interpretation. The Yugoslav authorities had announced in advance that there would be an operation in Racak in response to recent KLA killings in the area, and invited OSCE monitors and Western journalists to observe it. Having visited the scene and viewed footage of the operation taken by a local Associated Press television crew, some European journalists suggested the dead may have been KLA guerrillas killed in a fight with Yugoslav forces. The UK and US media, however, proved unwilling to ask any questions whatsoever about the incident. Renaud Girard, one of the French reporters who contested the official version of the "Racak massacre," was rounded on by Anglo-American journalists who complained: "You're killing our story."[1]

The orchestrated outcry over Racak led directly to the Rambouillet "negotiations" the following month. The talks, brokered by the NATO powers, presented an ultimatum to Yugoslavia: sign a preordained "agreement" or face bombing. The idea was to get the Kosovo Albanian delegation to sign, but make the terms so unacceptable to the Serbs that they would refuse, thereby precipitating bombing. As State Department spokesman James Rubin later explained, the aim was "to create clarity . . . as to which side was the cause of the problem . . . and that meant the Kosovar Albanians agreeing to the package and the Serbs not agreeing to the package" (*Moral Combat*, March 12, 2000). Embarrassingly, the ethnic Albanians initially refused to sign up, since the agreement did not offer full independence for Kosovo; whereas the Yugoslav side accepted the political agreement, though arguing that it should be implemented by UN rather than NATO troops. Since the "negotiations" were designed to produce exactly the opposite outcome, the terms were changed in order to make them impossible for Yugoslavia to accept: Kosovo's future as part of Serbia was left uncertain, a NATO force was insisted on, and an appendix was inserted giving NATO troops unrestricted access to the whole of Yugoslavia, including territorial waters and airspace, and immunity from local law. At the talks, British Foreign Secretary Robin Cook openly invited the ethnic Albanian delegation to sign so that airstrikes could be carried out (BBC Ceefax, February 21, 1999).

At least some journalists were fully aware of America's intentions at Rambouillet: a senior State Department official told them that "the bar was set too high for the Serbs to comply" because "they need some bombing" (Kenney 1999). Yet no-one saw fit to report this deliberate provocation of war, instead maintaining that Yugoslavia had been offered what NATO's then Secretary General, Javier Solana, called a "balanced and fair peace agreement." Most British journalists proved incapable of describing the Rambouillet process accurately until months after the war ended, when it no longer mattered. It was not until March 2000 that the BBC's up-to-the-minute online news service reported that the negotiations had been "designed to fail" (Mason 2000). Even as the Rambouillet talks were underway, Western states were using the OSCE mission as cover for their own intelligence operations. Predictably, this too was not reported until a year later, when the US Central Intelligence Agency admitted its agents had been among the OSCE monitors, "developing ties with the KLA and giving American military training manuals and field advice on fighting the Yugoslav army and Serbian police" (*Sunday Times*, March 12, 2000). Far from being "exhausted," diplomacy had not been attempted. Rather, there was a public show of diplomacy which provided a pretext for war.

In a speech a year after the bombing, NATO Secretary General Lord George Robertson asked "was the intervention in Kosovo moral?" He suggested that "the only possible answer is 'yes,'" because "By March of 1999, Serb oppression had driven almost 400,000 people from their homes." According to Robertson, "this was ethnic cleansing—plain and simple": "before the air campaign . . . the atrocities being committed by Serb forces against the Albanians were organized, systematic, and dictated by a centrally directed strategy" (Robertson 2000). Robertson's claims rest on a narrative developed during the war by NATO propagandists and compliant journalists which entails an extreme distortion of events.

It is true that the conflict had created around 400,000 refugees and "internally displaced persons" during the year preceding the bombing, although by March

1999 many had returned home "in places where there is no violence, and especially where KVM has a continuing presence" (UNHCR 1999a). In contrast to Robertson's retrospective assertion that "this was ethnic cleansing—plain and simple," contemporaneous assessments suggested different reasons for the flight of refugees, including "clashes between Government security forces and the KLA, kidnappings, street violence and, more recently, military exercises by the Yugoslav army" (UNHCR 1999a). German Foreign Ministry reports in early 1999 stated that:

> explicit political persecution linked to Albanian ethnicity is not verifiable . . . actions of the security forces [are] not directed against the Kosovo-Albanians as an ethnically defined group, but against the military opponent and its actual or alleged supporters.[2]

The refugees included around 55,000 who fled to other parts of Serbia or to Montenegro (UNHCR 1999b), the vast majority of whom were undoubtedly Kosovo Serbs. Particularly since the start of the one-sided ceasefire, the main cause of violence was KLA activity. Just before the bombing the US Committee for Refugees (1999) reported: "Kosovo Liberation Army . . . attacks aimed at trying to 'cleanse' Kosovo of its ethnic Serb civilian population." UNHCR said, "Over 90 mixed villages in Kosovo have now been emptied of Serb inhabitants and other Serbs continue leaving, either to be displaced in other parts of Kosovo or fleeing into central Serbia." The Yugoslav Red Cross estimates there are more than 30,000 non-Albanian displaced currently in need of assistance in Kosovo, most of whom are Serb.

At the time, even NATO privately acknowledged the real cause of continuing conflict. According to minutes of the North Atlantic Council, the KLA was "the main initiator of the violence," and had "launched what appears to be a deliberate campaign of provocation" (*Moral Combat*, March 12, 2000). This was at the very moment when Western intelligence agencies and private US military training companies were providing assistance to the KLA.

NATO did not go to war because of "systematic" atrocities and large numbers of refugees. Rather, NATO promised that the bombing would *prevent* a refugee crisis. On the first day of the war, James Rubin insisted that if NATO had not acted, "you would have had hundreds of thousands of people crossing the border." The following day Blair declared: "fail to act now . . . and we would have to deal with . . . hundreds of thousands of refugees" (BBC, March 25, 26, 1999). It was only after the bombing began, and hundreds of thousands did indeed flee, that the war was quickly re-presented as a response to the refugee crisis. As a senior NATO official later explained: "Following the fiasco of the lightning strikes, the refugees provided us with a new objective for the war" (*Le Nouvel Observateur*, July 1, 1999). This was possible because journalists proved quite willing to reverse the chronology of events to claim: "This is why NATO went to war—so the refugees could come back to Kosovo" (BBC, June 16, 1999).

This was when the claims about "ethnic cleansing" and "genocide" became important: it had to be maintained that the huge refugee exodus from Kosovo was due to a premeditated campaign of atrocities which the Serbs would have carried out regardless of whether NATO intervened. Bang on cue, documents outlining a secret Serbian plan for "ethnic cleansing"—codenamed Operation Horseshoe—were revealed by Germany's Foreign Minister, Joschka Fischer, on April 6, 1999. After the war, German Brigadier General Heinz Loquai, a former OSCE adviser, exposed the supposed blueprint for genocide as a fake concocted by the German intelligence services (*Sunday Times*, April 2, 2000). At the time, however, the theme of "genocide in Kosovo" was taken up with enthusiasm by the media. Every UK news organization discovered "echoes of the Holocaust" (*Sun*, April 1, 1999), relishing each atrocity story. In an article which her own newspaper, the *Guardian*, did not publish until after the war, Audrey Gillan recounted in the *London Review of Books* (May 27, 1999) how UNHCR spokesman Ron Redmond

> spoke to the press of bodies being desecrated, eyes being shot out. The way he talked it sounded as if there had been at least a hundred murders and dozens of rapes. When I pressed him on the rapes, asking him to be more precise, he reduced it a bit and said he had heard that five or six teenage girls had been raped and murdered. He had not spoken to any witnesses.

Gillan went on to describe how a BBC reporter then "reeled off what Ron Redmond had said, using the words 'hundreds,' 'rape,' and 'murder' in the same breath." It would be extraordinary if no crimes or atrocities were committed in Kosovo, since it was engulfed by civil war as well as under NATO bombardment. The suggestion of exceptional "genocidal" violence, however, was simply Western propaganda designed to justify the further violence of NATO bombing.

Media hysteria fed off wild official statements estimating the death toll in Kosovo at anything from 10,000 to 100,000 or higher. However, post-war forensic investigations have so far failed to corroborate such numbers. By February 2003, after more than three years of investigations, a total of 4,019 bodies had been found, according to the UN's Kosovo Office of Missing Persons and Forensics. In addition, there are 164 people who the UN classifies as missing "considered dead," plus around 800 bodies exhumed from sites in Serbia where they had apparently been concealed during the war. This would bring the total to around 5,000, although it should also be borne in mind that these numbers do not distinguish between civilians and soldiers, nor between Albanians and Serbs. More bodies will probably be found, but in 2003 the UN suggested that a "generous estimate for the mortal remains still unaccounted for and to be recovered during this year in Kosovo, would be between 500 and 700."[3] There were many tragic deaths, but there was not a new Holocaust.

Despite all the evidence to the contrary, the belief persists that Kosovo was a successful and "moral" war. Hence in 2003 many of those who opposed war with

Iraq were at pains to emphasize their prior support for NATO bombing. "We supported the war in Kosovo," announced the *Independent* in an anti-war editorial (February 7, 2003), and the *Guardian's* Jonathan Freedland criticized the build-up to war while writing that "US power can sometimes be a force for good in the world: that's why I supported the Kosovo campaign" (February 5). Repelled by Bush, liberal commentators demanded more of the moralizing that had justified the Kosovo campaign. Johann Hari, for example, wrote that:

> We do not need Bush's dangerous arguments about "pre-emptive action" to justify this war. Nor do we need to have the smoking gun of [weapons of mass destruction]. All we need are the humanitarian arguments we used during the Kosovo conflict.
>
> (*The Independent*, January 10, 2003)

Similarly, James Rubin suggested that: "if Tony Blair had been the explainer of the rationale for war in Iraq . . . as opposed to some of the comments coming out of the Pentagon, we'd be in much better shape in terms of global public opinion" (*Iraq: A Just War?*, Channel 4, February 28, 2003).

Yet while the propaganda for war with Iraq was undoubtedly clumsy, it was no more inept than in Kosovo, which also featured bogus diplomacy and dodgy documents. In 1999 the propaganda tended to be taken at face value because many journalists and commentators were predisposed to welcome war. It fitted the "moral" worldview which developed in the 1990s, epitomized by Western perceptions of the former Yugoslavia.

Reinventing the West in the Balkans

The various explanations of the break-up of Yugoslavia offered in news reports reflected and informed broader debates over the 1990s about how the West should respond. Journalists were among the foremost advocates of "moral" responses to the Yugoslav crisis, often challenging other explanations and policies. Yet beneath the apparent differences there was considerable agreement. The debate about the Balkans was also a debate about the West's self-image, and revealed more about how Western elites were attempting to reinvent themselves for the post-Cold War era than about events on the ground.

Early reporting tended to view the crisis as a continuation of the recent fall of Communism in eastern Europe. A 1991 survey of US coverage noted that much reporting "persisted in inaccurately forcing the Yugoslavian civil war into a black-and-white Cold War framework" (Kavran 1991). The *Los Angeles Times* (July 8, 1991) described the secession of Croatia as "a battle between hard-line communists and free-market democrats," for example; and the *Independent* (July 4, 1991) explained that Serbia was one of the "last redoubts" of Communism and totalitarianism, whereas Slovenia and Croatia, both "Westernised and prosperous," represented "democracy." If the "breakaway" republics were Westernized democracies struggling to escape Communist tyranny, then it made sense for Western governments to offer support, as local politicians were quick to recognize. Croatian President Franjo Tudjman, for example, was angling for international backing when he described the conflict as "the same that has been going on in Eastern Europe for the past three years: democracy against communism" (*European*, August 18, 1991).

Yet Western triumphalism following the Cold War was short lived: the unity of the West could no longer be taken for granted in the absence of the Soviet enemy, and the sense of cohesion and purpose which the old politics of Left and Right had given to domestic politics was now lost. In 1991 Croatia's historic ally Germany led the European Community in recognizing Slovenian and Croatian independence, effectively challenging US policy. In 1992 America sought to re-establish its leadership, pushing for recognition of Bosnian independence in a reversal of its previous support for the integrity of the Yugoslav federation. In both Croatia and Bosnia, as had been predicted, the result was bitter civil war. While the relatively painless secession of Slovenia may have looked like another former Communist nation making a transition to democracy, these protracted and bloody conflicts demanded a different explanation. An influential essay by Samuel Huntington recast the East/West division as a "clash of civilisations," arguing that "the Velvet Curtain of culture has replaced the Iron Curtain of ideology as the most significant dividing line in Europe." The world was riven by civilizational "fault lines," one of which ran "almost exactly along the line now separating Croatia and Slovenia from the rest of Yugoslavia." Those on the wrong side—Orthodox Christians and Muslims, in the case of Yugoslavia—were "much less likely to develop stable democratic political systems" (1993: 30–1). Again this was a theme taken up by local leaders, Tudjman suggesting that Serbs and Croats were "not just different peoples but different civilisations" (*European*, August 18, 1991), and Slovenian minister Petar Tancig contrasting the "violent and crooked oriental-bizantine heritage" of Serbia and Montenegro with the "more humble and diligent Western-catholic tradition" of Slovenia and Croatia (quoted in Johnstone 2002: 137). Media coverage echoed these ideas. Peter Jenkins wrote, for example, that "There were two Europes for many centuries before the Cold War was thought of: Western Christendom, Catholic and baroque, and Eastern Orthodox Europe which, in the Balkans, merged into the Ottoman Empire and the world of Islam" (*The Independent*, November 12, 1992). This perspective suggested that Yugoslavia was torn by "ethnic" conflicts which had a long history, but that some ethnic groups were close to, if not part of, the West.

Other proponents of "ethnic" explanations for Yugoslavia's break-up, however, made no such distinctions. Robert Kaplan's (1994) development of Huntington's idea drew the division, not between different civilizations, but between the civilized world and various zones of anarchy: "places where the Western Enlightenment has not penetrated," which are populated by "re-primitivized man" and under constant threat of "cultural and racial war." This was the spirit in which the *Telegraph's* Defence Editor, John Keegan (1993: xi), argued that:

The horrors of the war in Yugoslavia, as incomprehensible as they are revolting to the civilised mind, defy explanation in conventional military terms. The pattern of local hatreds they reveal are unfamiliar to anyone but the professional anthropologists who take the warfare of tribal and marginal peoples as their subject of study . . . Most intelligent newspaper readers . . . will be struck by the parallels to be drawn with the behaviour of pre-state peoples . . .

Descriptions of the war as an inexplicable outbreak of tribal antagonisms drew on a tradition of Western writing about the Balkans as an inherently unstable region of "ancient passions and intractable hatreds" (Kaplan quoted in Hansen 1998: 132).

All these explanations of the conflict in Yugoslavia offered a self-flattering view of the West—as a beacon of democracy and civilization—and portrayed Yugoslavs, particularly the Serbs, as barbarians. However, many argued that the view of the Balkans as characterized by "ancient ethnic hatreds" provided a convenient excuse for Western governments. Indeed, President Bill Clinton was reputedly deterred from taking decisive military intervention in Bosnia by his reading of Kaplan's work. BBC correspondent Allan Little suggests that the consensus about Bosnia was:

That the Balkan tribes had been killing each other for centuries and that there was nothing that could be done. It was nobody's fault. It was just, somehow, the nature of the region. It was a lie that Western governments at that time liked. It got the Western world off the hook.

(Little 2001)

There is not such a straightforward correlation between "tribal" explanations and a non-interventionist stance as this suggests, but Western policy was certainly incoherent and leaders no doubt felt reluctant to commit themselves to politically risky military action. It is not true, of course, that Western governments did nothing: in addition to their decisive diplomatic support for secessionists, they imposed sanctions on the Serbs, gave covert military support to Croats and Bosnian Muslims, and sent "peacekeeping" troops. Yet many journalists—most, according to Little—wanted the West to go further, calling for tough military action. Another BBC correspondent, Martin Bell, coined the phrase "journalism of attachment" for a new style of reporting which would "not stand neutrally between good and evil, right and wrong, the victim and the oppressor" (Bell 1998: 16). In the US, an analogous argument in favor of "advocacy journalism" was made by high-profile reporters such as CNN's Christiane Amanpour (Ricchiardi 1996).

Where "tribal" explanations seemed to suggest that all sides were as bad as each other, advocacy journalists wanted to apportion blame; where proponents of Balkanism talked of the war's complex historical roots, they maintained the conflict was easy to understand. For Amanpour it was "black and white . . . there was a clear aggressor and clear victim" (quoted in Ricchiardi 1996). For Little, the war was "very simple and straightforward": it happened because "Milosevic was a megalomaniac dictator" (*Guardian*, January 6, 2003). If events did not fit this simplistic framework, they were distorted or disregarded. Western journalists consistently downplayed or ignored attacks by Croats and Bosnian Muslims, so that Serbian attacks appeared to be evidence of a one-sided war of aggression. Nik Gowing (1994: 35) points out, for example, that the Croat siege of Mostar was "virtually unreported," despite suffering at least as bad as the plight of Sarajevo. Indeed, when Western politicians, journalists, and celebrities came to visit the siege of Sarajevo they invariably saw only the Muslim-held centre of the city, and ignored the Serb-populated areas. Although Sarajevo was a supposedly demilitarized "safe area," Bosnian government forces in the city were accused by UN General Francis Briquemont of provoking the Bosnian Serbs "on a daily basis" (quoted in Binder 1994-5: 73). This pattern was repeated elsewhere, such as at Gorazde, where an April 1994 NATO airstrike against Bosnian Serbs was presented as a response to the Serbian assault on the town, in which thousands were said to have been killed or wounded. It later transpired that the attack—deliberately provoked by Bosnian Muslim forces from within the "safe area"—caused "closer to 200 than 2,000 casualties," mostly soldiers, and that the extent of the fighting had been exaggerated by UN officials. General Sir Michael Rose revealed that the visible destruction of the town had largely resulted, not from the Serbian shelling, but from previous Bosnian Muslim attacks which had driven 12,500 Serbs from the area (Bogdanich and Lettmayer 2000).

Through a selective and one-sided style of journalism which Gowing (1997: 25-6) has called the "secret shame" of the media in Bosnia, the war was portrayed as a simple battle of Good versus Evil. As senior BBC correspondent John Simpson (1998: 444-5) subsequently wrote: "a climate was created in which it was very hard to understand what was really going on, because everything came to be seen through the filter of the Holocaust." The Serbs were depicted as Nazis committing genocide against innocent Bosnian Muslim civilians. Reporters even discovered Nazi-style "death camps" in Bosnia in 1992—though typically they noticed only the Serb camps, when according to the Red Cross in autumn 1992 the Bosnian Muslims actually had more camps (12 compared to eight), with nearly as many detainees (1,061 compared to 1,203) (Johnstone 2002: 71). The equation between Serbs and Nazis which reporters—and the PR firm employed by the Bosnian government, Ruder Finn—attempted to create in the public mind invoked moral absolutes in a way that resonated powerfully with contemporary sensibilities. Mick Hume (1997: 18) suggests that the war thereby provided "a twisted sort of therapy, through which foreign reporters [could] discover some sense of purpose—first for themselves, and then for their audience back home," as journalists undertook a "moral mission on behalf of a demoralised society." As Ignatieff (2003: 42) admits: "The Western need for noble victims and happy endings suggests that we are more interested in ourselves than we are in the places, like Bosnia, that we take up as causes."

Advocacy journalists provided a valuable service for Western politicians, elaborating the "moral vocabulary" through which leaders could articulate a sense of purpose and mission. As former President Ronald Reagan noted in a 1992 speech, the end of the Cold War had "robbed much of the West of its uplifting, common purpose" (*Sunday Times*, December 6, 1992). The solution he offered—speaking on the day his successor, George Bush senior, was sending the Marines to Somalia on a "humanitarian" mission—was "a humanitarian velvet glove backed by a steel fist of military force." Among Reagan's specific proposals were a new role for NATO and "sharply focused bombing" of the Serbs. When NATO leaders proposed something similar in 1999, they used the same moralistic rhetoric which had been developed by advocacy journalists in Bosnia. Blair, for example, in an echo of Bell's "journalism of attachment," described the Kosovo bombing as "a battle between good and evil; between civilization and barbarity; between democracy and dictatorship" (*Sunday Telegraph*, April 4, 1999).

As noted above, the moral arguments of advocacy journalists were often pitched against "tribal" explanations of the conflict, chiefly because these were thought to hinder the clear identification of human rights abusers necessary for decisive intervention, but also because the most vociferous advocates of intervention were liberal, left-of-centre writers, for whom talk of backward Balkan tribes smacked of essentialism. While thousands of Islamic fighters came from abroad to support Alija Izetbegovic's Muslim state—including Mujihadeen veterans of America's proxy war in Afghanistan (O'Neill 2003)—Western reporters and intellectuals celebrated Bosnia as a model of multiculturalism and tolerance. As Hansen (1998: 172) suggests, Bosnia was understood as an "ideal Western self"— a romanticized embodiment of the values which the West was supposed to represent. Westerners projected onto Bosnia their own notions of "multiculturalism," variously understood to be an American or European ideal. Rieff, for example, went to Bosnia in search of the "'Americanization' of the European future," convinced that the US is "the most successful multicultural society in history" and that "Western European countries are becoming multiracial and multiethnic" (1995: 35, 10). For Europeans, who considered themselves already multicultural, "Bosnia became a 'little Europe' which must be saved from the evils of nationalism" (Johnstone 2000: 143–4).

Bombing Yugoslavia in 1999 was justified in the same terms. In a series of speeches Clinton explained that "it's about our values" (March 23, 1999), making it clear that these were "moral values" (May 31) and "American values" (June 1). Robin Cook described the conflict as a battle between "two Europes competing for the soul of our continent." Yugoslavia represented "the race ideology that blighted our continent under the fascists," while NATO's vision of "the modern Europe" was of "a continent in which the rights of all its citizens are respected, regardless of their ethnic identity" (*Guardian*, May 5, 1999). Yet the professed multiculturalism of Western societies was less evident in the mass expulsions and deportations of ethnic Albanian refugees from NATO countries in the year following the conflict, accompanied in Britain by a media panic over "bogus asylum-seekers." And although Blair declared at the end of the war that "we intend to start building [the] new Europe in Kosovo" (June 10), neither is multiculturalism much in evidence in Kosovo itself, where most of the non-Albanian population have been violently driven out. By October 2001, the OSCE reported that, since NATO's victory in June 1999, there had been more than 5,000 terrorist attacks, over 1,000 murders and more than 1,000 abductions.[4]

As in Bosnia, amid all the talk of tolerance, the Serbs were demonized, sometimes in the crudest terms. In the *Telegraph* Patrick Bishop suggested that "'Serb' is a synonym for 'barbarian'" (March 26, 1999), while Steve Crawshaw wrote in the *New Statesman* (May 31, 1999) that "millions of Serbs" were "liars on a grand scale" who had "gone mad." The *Independent*'s Marcus Tanner (May 11, 1999) asked: "Do Albanians look like Serbs?"

> No . . . The Serbs often have black or dark brown hair and are generally darker and more heavily built than Albanians. Their appearance is fairly typical of southern Slavs. By contrast, the Kosovars look Celtic to a British eye. They have curly hair, which is often blonde or rust coloured, and their skin tends to be very pale and covered in freckles. Their eyes are often green or blue and their build is much more slender than that of the Serbs. They have longer heads. It is not surprising that they look so different as they belong to different races that have very rarely intermarried.

Tanner's clumsy attempt at racial typology was clearly intended to make Kosovo Albanians more appealing to white British readers while portraying the Serbs as suspiciously thick-set and swarthy. Even more bluntly, the *Sun* (April 14, 1999) described the Serbs as "animals," who were "an affront to humanity," and urged that they be "shot like wild dogs." As a study commissioned by the Holocaust Educational Trust noted: "the utilization of anti-Slav stereotypes during the Kosovo crisis arguably evoked the use of similar stereotypes . . . during the Nazi era," when the German media portrayed the Serbs as subhuman (Cica 2001). Such imagery was also employed during the Bosnian war, when, for example, the *Independent*'s leader-page cartoon depicted Bosnian Serbs as apes in combat gear (May 29, 1992).

Despite the apparent differences between exponents of "tribal" explanations and advocates of "ethical" intervention to uphold human rights, all sides in the debate assume the superiority of the West—whether this is understood in civilizational or moral terms. As Ignatieff (2000: 213) notes:

> While the language of the nation is particularistic—dividing human beings into us and them—human rights is universal. In theory, it will not lend itself to dividing human beings into higher and lower, superior and inferior, civilized and barbarian. Yet something very like a distinction between superior and inferior has been at work in the demonization of human rights violators.

Ignatieff warns against "an absolutist frame of mind which, in defining all human rights violators as barbarians, legitimizes barbarism" (Ignatieff 2000: 213), but seems to have adopted just such a mindset himself, arguing that "force and the threat of it are usually the only language tyrants, human rights abusers and terrorists ever understand" (*The New York Times*, September 7, 2003).

Dulce et decorum est?

Advocacy journalists and others campaigning for "moral" intervention in Bosnia presented themselves as critics of their governments. Many saw NATO's bombing of the Bosnian Serbs as "too little, too late" to reverse the West's failure to intervene with sufficient force, and even the Kosovo war did not go far enough for some. Rieff (1999: 10) bemoans the "limited" and "hesitant" character of the 1999 bombing, for example, while Ignatieff (2000: 215, 213) criticizes the contemporary view of war as a "surgical scalpel," advising that we should instead see it as a "bloodstained sword" and resolve that "when the sword is raised, it must be used to strike decisively." It may seem odd that those most preoccupied with morals and ethics should express such bloodthirsty sentiments. It is not just that moral self-righteousness leads to demands for violence. Humanitarian intervention has also failed to resolve the underlying problem it was attempting to address.

When advocacy journalists and committed intellectuals went to Bosnia in search of a cause, they hoped to offset the lack of moral purpose and cohesion in their own societies. The aspiration was that human rights might "fill the morality gap" (Klug 1997). Yet although episodes of NATO bombing and some high-minded rhetoric may temporarily alleviate the problem, the television spectacle of "virtual war" does not engage wider public enthusiasm or allegiance. Ignatieff worries that "commitment is intense but also shallow"; Rieff complains that the public regarded the Kosovo war with "indifference" and lethargy (quoted in Chandler 2003). Their suggested remedy is for governments to work harder to persuade people of the need to sacrifice lives for human rights goals. If war seems cost-free, the arguments about its moral necessity will not be properly had out. Hence Rieff's dissatisfaction with "humanitarian" justifications for intervention as too glib: failing to emphasize "the horror of what such an intervention will involve, *assuming* it is justified, is the gravest mystification" (2002: 284, original emphasis). Better to be explicit about the destruction and killing and persuade the public of its necessity. Similarly, Mary Kaldor (2000: 61) is critical of the attempt in Kosovo "to wage war without risking casualties." Instead, she urges a "readiness to die for humanity," though she graciously adds that this dying need not take place "in an unlimited way."

Yet there are no other terms in which advocates of intervention can make their case other than the moral vocabulary of human rights: they simply have no other political project. The result is that, despite some unhappiness with Bush's appropriation of their rhetoric, they are beginning to do for the war on terrorism what they did in the Balkans: denouncing the West's moral failings while pushing for ever-greater interference in other countries in the name of human rights. Falk complains that:

> the Bush administration has been doing its best to wreck world order as it had been evolving, and . . . part of the wreckage is the abandonment of legal restraints on the use of international force, the heart and soul of the UN Charter.
>
> *(Nation*, July 14, 2003)

Yet if anyone wrecked the UN system it was the advocates of "human rights intervention" who put the West's moral duty to intervene above the principle of sovereign equality. Ignatieff argues that upholding sovereign equality means "defending tyranny and terror" (*The New York Times*, September 7, 2003): this was the complaint of ethical interventionists throughout Falk's "golden age" of humanitarian intervention. It was what led many, including Falk himself, to approve the Kosovo bombing as "illegal but moral." The alternatives for the future, Ignatieff suggests, are leaving the UN Charter as "an alibi for dictators and tyrants" and letting the US go its own way, or reforming the UN so it will more readily use force "to defend human rights" multilaterally (*The New York Times*, September 7, 2003.). Or as Todd Gitlin (2003) puts it: "not empire, but human rights with guns."

Between those who advocate military force to promote human rights, and those who seek to legitimize a limitless war on terrorism with humanitarian rhetoric, we face an uninviting choice. It may be easy to see through the cynical justifications of the "war on terrorism," but the underlying consensus in favor of "moral" intervention still needs to be challenged.

Notes

1 Renaud Girard, interview with Diana Johnstone, January 25, 2000.
2 This and other similar German government documents are posted at emperorsclothes.com/articles/german/Germany.html
3 UNMIK Office of Missing Persons and Forensics, press release, February 3, 2003 (www.unmikonline.org/press/2003/pressr/pr917.htm)
4 See www.osce.org/kosovo/documents/reports/minorities/

References

Bell, Martin (1998) "The journalism of attachment," in Matthew Kieran (ed.) *Media Ethics*, London: Routledge, pp. 15–22.

Binder, David (1994–5) "Anatomy of a massacre," *Foreign Policy*, no. 97, Winter, pp. 70–8.

Bogdanich, George and Martin Lettmayer (2000) *Yugoslavia: the Avoidable War*, documentary film, USA: Frontier Theatre and Film.

Chandler, David (2003) "Culture wars and international intervention: an "inside/out" view of the decline of the national interest," unpublished paper.

Cica, Natasha (2001) *Truth, Myth or Genocide?*, research paper, London: Holocaust Educational Trust.

Gitlin, Todd (2003) "Goodbye, new world order: keep the global ideal alive," *Mother Jones*, July 14 (www.motherjones.com/commentary/columns/2003/29/we_478_01.html)

Gowing, Nik (1994) *Real-Time Television Coverage of Armed Conflicts and Diplomatic Crises*, Cambridge, MA: Harvard University.

Gowing, Nik (1997) *Media Coverage: Help or Hindrance in Conflict Prevention?* New York: Carnegie Corporation.

Hansen, Lene (1998) *Western Villains or Balkan Barbarism?*, PhD dissertation, University of Copenhagen.

Herman, Edward S. and David Peterson (2002) "Morality's avenging angels: the new humanitarian crusaders" in David Chandler (ed.) *Rethinking Human Rights*, Basingstoke: Palgrave.

Hume, Mick (1997) *Whose War is it Anyway?* London: Informinc.

Huntington, Samuel P. (1993) "The clash of civilizations?," *Foreign Affairs*, vol. 72, no. 3, Summer, pp. 22–48.

Ignatieff, Michael (2000) *Virtual War*, New York: Metropolitan Books.

Ignatieff, Michael (2003) *Empire Lite*, London: Vintage.

IICK (2000) *The Kosovo Report*, Oxford: Oxford University Press.

Johnstone, Diana (2000) "The French media and the Kosovo war" in Philip Hammond and Edward S. Herman (eds) *Degraded Capability: the Media and the Kosovo Crisis*, London: Pluto.

Johnstone, Diana (2002) *Fools' Crusade: Yugoslavia, NATO and Western Delusions*, London: Pluto.

Kaldor, Mary (2000) "Europe at the Millennium," *Politics*, vol. 20, no. 2, May, pp. 55–62.

Kaplan, Robert D. (1994) "The coming anarchy," *The Atlantic Monthly*, vol. 273, no. 2, pp. 44–76.

Kavran, Olga (1991) "Cold War lives on in Yugoslavia reporting," *Extra!*, November/December (www.fair.org)

Keegan, John (1993) *A History of Warfare*, London: Pimlico.

Kenney, George (1999) "Rolling thunder: the rerun," *The Nation*, June 14, pp. 48–51.

Klug, Francesca (1997) "Can human rights fill Britain's morality gap?," *Political quarterly*, April–June, vol. 68, no. 2 (accessed electronically).

Little, Allan (2001) "The West did not do enough," *BBC Online*, June 29 (http://news.bbc.co.uk/hi/english/world/from_our_own_correspondent/newsid_1413000/1413764.sm)

Mason, Barnaby (2000) "Rambouillet talks 'designed to fail,'" *BBC Online*, March 19 (http://news.bbc.co.uk/hi/english/world/europe/newsid_682000/682877.stm)

O'Neill, Brendan (2003) "Cross-border terrorism: a mess made by the West," *Spiked*, July 24 (www.spiked-online.com/Articles/00000006DE7B.htm)

Ricchiardi, Sherry (1996) "Over the line?," *American Journalism Review*, September (accessed electronically).

Rieff, David (1995) *Slaughterhouse: Bosnia and the Failure of the West*, London: Vintage.

Rieff, David (1999) "A new age of liberal imperialism?," *World Policy Journal*, vol. 16, no. 2, Summer, pp. 1–10.

Rieff, David (2002) *A Bed for the Night: Humanitarianism in Crisis*, London: Vintage.

Robertson, Lord George (2000) "Law, morality and the use of force," May 16 (www.nato.int/docu/speech/2000/s000516a.htm)

Simpson, John (1998) *Strange Places, Questionable People*, London: Macmillan.

UKFAC (2000) *Fourth Report*, May 23 (www.publications.parliament.uk/pa/cm199900/cmselect/cmfaff/28/2802.htm)

UNHCR (1999a) "UN inter-agency update on Kosovo humanitarian situation report 82," March 4 (www.reliefweb.int/w/rwb.nsf/0/29291b9f2df28d62c125672b004a07fa?Open-Document)

UNHCR (1999b) "Kosovo crisis update," March 30 (www.unhcr.ch/cgi-bin/texis/vtx/home/+2wwBmDevEudwwwwMwwwwwwwwhFqnN0bItFqnDni5AFqnN0bIcFqEQd5d VdagGo5o5aupmwBnaTwGqrDzmxwwwwwww/opendoc.htm)

US Committee for Refugees (1999) "Fighting heats up Kosovo winter; fresh displacement," March (www.refugees.org/news/crisis/kosovo_u0399.htm)

10

PRISONERS OF NEWS VALUES?

Journalists, professionalism, and identification in times of war

Howard Tumber

The battle for information and the contest over the winning of public opinion is a feature common to all conflicts. Attempts by the US government and the military to control and manage news during the invasion phase of the 2003 Iraq conflict involved a number of different measures and procedures. Using familiar techniques of censorship, misinformation, obfuscation, and psychological operations to varying degrees, the US was able to frustrate journalists and news organizations in their search for information. But it is the process of embedding journalists with military units that is the subject of discussion here and its implications for the future reporting of conflict.

The embedding of reporters within the military was a key event of the communications set-up of the 2003 conflict. Unlike the Falklands conflict in 1982 when journalists were "embedded"[1] with the British Task force almost by accident, during the war in Iraq there was a deliberate plan set out by the US Department of Defense in consultation with news organizations for journalists to be "situated" within various parts of the military. The thinking behind this "innovation" had been developing for some time. Ever since the Vietnam War, governments and the military had experimented with different methods of "controlling" and "managing" the media. The information policy adopted by the British Government and the military during the Falklands conflict was poorly organized and lacked planning. There was an absence of agreed procedure or criteria, no centralized system of control, and no coordination between departments (see Morrison and Tumber 1988: 189–90). But whatever impromptu measures the British introduced at the time, together with *post hoc* justifications, were clearly based on the myth of Vietnam, that somehow the media and television in particular were to blame for the US losing the war. US defense officials, using the experience gained during the Falklands conflict, have since tried various measures—pooling arrangements, stationing reporters in military units—in different operations over the last 20 years. Embedding in various guises has been used before, both in World War II and Vietnam, and in a limited way in more recent times in Haiti in 1994, Somalia in

1992–5, and Bosnia in 1995 (see Porch 2002). The protests by news organizations following the lack of media access operating in Gulf War I and the restrictions experienced in recent conflicts in Kosovo in 1999 and Afghanistan in 2001 led the Pentagon to reassess the reporting rules for the current conflict (see Tumber and Palmer 2004).

The embedding process in Gulf War II was planned well in advance of the invasion of Iraq in March 2003. A number of briefings took place in Washington between Pentagon officials and news organizations to discuss the process and journalists began attending military training courses in November 2003.[2]

Falklands War as precedent

To understand some of the occupational problems experienced by the journalists embedded with the military during Gulf War II it is helpful to revisit some aspects of the reporting of the Falklands conflict. On April 2, 1982, Argentinian forces invaded the Falklands Islands, a group of small islands held under British sovereignty but territorially disputed by the Argentine government. On April 3 the United Nations Security Council called for an end of hostilities, the withdrawal of Argentinian troops, and the peaceful resolution of the dispute. The British Government, supported by parliament, proposed to send a Task Force of British ships to the Falklands. On April 5 the first ships began to sail. Naturally the media began to clamour for places aboard the Task Force and the scramble to gain a berth extended to the international media as well as the British. In the event only 30 media personnel (including journalists, broadcasters, photographer camera operatives, sound people, and engineers) all representing British news organizations were allowed to go. No members of the foreign media were given access (see Morrison and Tumber 1988).[3] The British media assigned to the Task Force included a number of "veteran" correspondents but also some young and relatively inexperienced journalists.

The Falklands conflict was an excellent "bell jar" not only for examining the "performance" of the journalists who accompanied the British military in their "liberation" of the islands, but also for assessing ideas of objectivity and impartiality.

For the journalists in the Falklands, their future was structurally entwined with that of the troops. Matters that became important to the troops also mattered to the journalists, including contact with families back home. The result was that journalists not only shared the moods of the troops through collective experience, but also began to identify with them by being part of the whole exercise. Consequently, although some of the journalists disagreed with the decision to send the Task Force to the South Atlantic, once it seemed that conflict was inevitable, they felt an affinity with the troops, a mutual determination to see the venture through to the end (Morrison and Tumber 1988: 97).

For example, one of the Task Force journalists, Patrick Bishop, then of the *Observer* newspaper commented shortly after the end of the conflict:

The situation was that you were a propagandist; and that's how it turned out. So there wasn't any need to put pressure on anyone to write gung-ho copy because everyone was doing it without any stimulus from the military. And that's how most of the reporters felt. They were all very patriotic and "positive" about the whole thing. So the military didn't have to lean on them.

(cited in Morrison and Tumber 1988: 98)

Among the journalists in the Falklands a shift took place in the values that questioned the virtue of remaining untouched and unmoved toward those they lived with. There was simply no escaping the military's embrace. As Mick Seamark, then of the *Daily Mirror*, and another of the journalists accompanying the military, commented shortly after he returned to the UK:

On this occasion you were always part of it. You couldn't get off, you couldn't say at the end of one day: "Let's go and have a drink somewhere, away from the story." You were part of the story in that sense. The journalists certainly began to feel that they belonged.

(cited in Morrison and Tumber 1988: 98)

This belonging began to change the journalists' language. As David Norris, then of the *Daily Mail*, relayed on his return from the Falklands: "I found I was referring to 'us' collectively when we were on shore" (cited in Morrison and Tumber 1988: 98). Even Gareth Parry, of the liberal *Guardian*, mentioned that, with the approach of danger, his attitude changed from originally saying "British" to (after a few weeks) "us" or "we."

What in effect happened was that the process of involvement and identification by the journalists had little to do with their individual private views and feelings about the conflict or the attitudes of their news organizations. The dynamics of the situation were so strong that they overwhelmed all this. As Morrison and Tumber suggested:

What was happening to the journalists was that their professional need to cover a story in a detached way was slowly being swamped by the very real, human need to belong, to be safe. The comradeship and closeness demonstrated by the troops, which the journalists so admired, were not just the random product that any occupational association throws up, but the response to having to work closely together especially during military exercises and having to solve tasks as a group. At the same time the enclosed world of a group of men (*and all the media personnel were men as were most of the military*) living together means that the need for emotional expression, fulfillment, and release, the talking over of worries, fears or any of a myriad small problems which beset individuals,

became totally restricted to colleagues, thus giving a remarkable closeness in relationships.

(Morrison and Tumber 1988: 99)

The evidence of this emotional embrace by the journalists was clear in the comments made by the journalists after they returned to Britain. For example, Robert
McGowan, then of the *Daily Express*, reflected:

> I think you'll find that most of the journalists made lifelong friends with
> some of the units. I certainly have. What is more, if the setting is very
> dangerous, time spent in close proximity to others who are sharing the
> same experiences submerges the individual's personal characteristics.
> The other person becomes "you": he knows what you are going through.
> There is a transparency to feelings and relationships not commonly
> found in civilian settings.
>
> (cited in Morrison and Tumber 1988: 100)

In the Falklands conflict, the difficulties the journalists faced in performing their
own professional duties obliged them to make allies of the military, driving them
further into cooperation. For the journalists there was no escape from the military's embrace. There was no possible chance of physically distancing themselves
or of gaining psychological respite by returning to a hotel to write their stories. As
Morrison and Tumber described:

> The journalists not only merely observed their subjects, but lived their
> lives and shared their experiences, and those experiences were of such
> emotional intensity that the form of prose which journalists use to take
> the reader into that experience—the "I was there" form—provided not
> only a window for the reader, but also a door for partiality irrespective of
> any desire to remain the detached professional outsider.
>
> (Morrison and Tumber 1988: 95–6)

The experience of the correspondents during the Falklands raises a number of
issues about the responsibilities of journalists in times of conflict. News values,
which serve journalism as an occupation well in peacetime or amid some other
country's war, do not necessarily serve the individual journalist well in the midst
of his/her own country's war. When correspondents are "embedded" among their
own country's military, their (journalism's) professional values of impartiality and
objectivity can look wrong or misplaced.

It is much easier for producers and editors, situated miles away, to hold on to
the central idea of objectivity, even as their colleagues in the field find the concept less easy to grasp. Of all the journalists in the Falklands, the broadcasters
most successfully retained their independence. This was partly because the principles of "balance" and "impartiality" were more firmly entrenched within that

193

medium than in print journalism. In addition these journalists were better able to weather pressure toward partiality because, compared with the press, they were more regularly in touch with their home offices (see Morrison and Tumber 1988: 102–3, 105).

For the journalists in the Falklands, events conspired to make them totally involved and, although analytically impartiality and objectivity are not regarded as the same, for practical purposes, given the dynamics of the situation, to lose impartiality in those circumstances was journalistically to lose objectivity. "Only by remaining completely impartial and unmoved by events would it have been possible to hold a totally objective account" (Morrison and Tumber 1988: 104).

For these journalists the entire experience had brought them to understand the nature and purpose of the campaign, the behavior of the military, and the conduct of the war, as participants rather than observers. The journalists had entered a different, closed world and their values shifted with them.

Revisiting the Falklands some 20 years later, the comparisons with the experiences of the journalists "embedded"[4] with military forces during the 2003 invasion of Iraq are compelling.

Embedded in 2003

Keith Harrison, of the Wolverhampton (UK) *Express and Star*, reporting from Umm Qasr, the southern port in Iraq, in 2003 admitted to the quickness of the socialization process. His account provided a feel of his and other correspondents' experiences:

> It's been less than a week, but already the experiences of the war have had a startling effect on everyone taking part—and those reporting on it. In our combat kit, we look and sound like soldiers, which is a tribute to the Army's embedding system, in which journalists are trained and attached to military units for the duration of a campaign. We answer to the Commanding Officer, we follow orders, we share the rations, we eat where the soldiers eat and we sleep where they sleep. The Royal Logistic Corps—where they go, we go. The military language that first seemed like talk from another world is now our mother tongue. Terms like "sitrep" (situation report) and "be advised" have not so much crept into our language as carried out a military coup. Place is now location. Car is always vehicle. Pardon has become "say again." ETD, ETA, and IAD— estimated time of arrival/departure and immediate action drill—are now used almost constantly as we communicate with the soldiers and officers of the RLC. We know that dobhi is laundry, gash is rubbish and "chogie" is an affectionate term for the local workers. We say ablutions, not toilets, and put up with flies, food and facilities that we would have sniffed at just three short weeks ago. Sniffing at the toilets today would be extremely unwise. The novelty of the American MRE (Meals Ready to

Eat or Meals Rejected by Everyone) has long since worn off, but at least we're now experts in heating the food with the chemical packs involved. We're becoming indoctrinated and recognise the sights and sounds of army life instantly. We've endured no fewer than 30 air raids since war began. Many have been false alarms—others have carried the chilling threat: "Incoming ballistic missile! Take cover! Missile in air!" . . . Hours earlier, when we left our US base, we were given lengthy and frankly disconcerting farewells from those staying behind in reserve. As our vehicle was being prepared, TV pictures showed an Iraqi bunker being blown to smithereens at close range by a US tank and I found myself cheering along like a bloodthirsty Dallas cowboy.

(Harrison 2003)

It is hardly surprising then that the reports and language used by the journalists embedded with the troops would echo these developing attachments.

Some of the "unilaterals"[5] believed that it became complicated for the embedded reporters to report uncompromisingly on the actions of their units. "Once you bond with these guys, once reporters have come to like these guys, they're not going to report how horrible anybody can be in war, how they were laughing as they shot people" (broadcast network correspondent cited in Cook 2003).

Jeff Gralnick, a journalist with experience in Vietnam warned of the dangers facing the embedded reporters and likened them to the fate of hostages with their captors:

But that is not, as we know, why you've opted to be embedded. Not for combat. Not that. You're all going over to report. Truth. Honesty. The real story. But that is going to be difficult because once you get into a unit, you are going to be co-opted. It is not a purposeful thing, it will just happen. It's a little like the Stockholm Syndrome.

You will fall in with a bunch of grunts, experience and share their hardships and fears and then you will feel for them and care about them. You will wind up loving them and hating their officers and commanders and the administration that put them (and you) in harm's way. Ernie Pyle loved his grunts; Jack Laurance and Michael Herr loved theirs; and I loved mine. And as we all know, love blinds and in blinding it will alter the reporting you thought you were going to do. Trust me. It happens, and it will happen no matter how much you guard against it.

Remember also, you are not being embedded because that sweet old Pentagon wants to be nice. You are being embedded so you can be controlled and in a way isolated.

Once you're in the field, all those officers and commanders you now hate, because you love your grunts, you will hate even more because they will have total control over where you can go, what you can see and what you can do. Vietnam was easier, we came and went—serial embedees—

essentially uncontrolled which made for a great deal of reporting the Pentagon would rather have buried. And this embedding plan, which is being adopted now like war summer camp, has been put together by guys, now senior officers, who were burned or felt burned by the press as juniors 35 or so years ago. Fool me once . . .

(Gralnick 2003)

Gralnick also warned of the need to remember that the experience of reporting as an embedded reporter was only one small part of the jigsaw:

One more thing to remember. War is a macro kind of thing. Units in the field and their grunts are the micro parts of it. So if you are in the field with a unit where bad things happen, you are seeing only what is around you. Nothing else. You have no idea how the war is going, only how your war is going, so never turn what you have in front of you into something that ends with cosmic conclusion about the war and policy themselves. Many of us 35 years or so ago—hawk reporters or dove—did just that and many of us regret it to this day.

(Gralnick 2003)

For some of the journalists the socialization process had begun some four months earlier (in November 2003) when they attended one of a series of Pentagon-held week-long training seminars for journalists at a Marine Corps base in Quantico, Virginia.[6] The seminar provoked the journalists into assessing their relationship with the military and even made news itself. The issue that arose was how to ensure "separation."

Upon arrival at the camp, journalists received military issue equipment such as backpacks, helmets, flak-jackets, and NBC (nuclear, biological, chemical) suits, which they then used in training exercises (DeFoore 2003). According to *Washington Times* staff photographer Gerald Herbert "at first they enjoyed getting their hands on the new 'toys'" (cited in DeFoore 2003) but a few of the journalists quickly realized the dangers of donning all the military gear.

DeFoore outlined the story:

After a demonstration on weaponry, one of the participating photographers took a picture of UPI reporter Pam Hess wearing full battle fatigues and holding an M-16 while a marine at her side gave instructions. When the picture ran in *The International Herald Tribune* the next day, some boot campers began to worry about how they were being perceived by the outside world. Some feared the picture would fuel suspicions that American journalists are working in concert with the American military, a danger made all the more real by the murder of *Wall Street Journal* reporter Daniel Pearl last year in Pakistan.

(DeFoore 2003)

Spencer Platt, *Getty News* staff photographer, an attendee at the training camp, commented:

> I don't think in any sense we should wear anything that confuses us as members of the military, this is a new war and journalists are targets. If the concept gets out there that we're working for the military, it's going to make our jobs much more difficult.
>
> (cited in DeFoore 2003)

DeFoore continues the story,

> On the final night of boot camp the journalists learned they were about to become the subjects in a massive photo-op organized by the military. The thought of marching five miles in full gear with still and TV cameras documenting their every move spooked many of the journalists there. So before the big event, many decided to present themselves in more of an independent light when the time came for their pictures to be taken.
>
> (DeFoore 2003)

Gerald Herbert, a *Washington Times* staff photographer and another attendee, was concerned about the implications:

> All of a sudden the media were trying to spin the media. That question was nagging me all week long and came to a head that day: at what point are we observing and at what point are we participating? Some of the journalists used white tape and black markers to designate themselves as press, while others wore jeans and one guy even drew a peace symbol on his shirt. In the back of your mind you're wondering how much is too cosy and when do you become your subject. It's a very difficult line and it's still something people are trying to sort out. How much do you assimilate into [the military's] mode and how much do you maintain a profile of visual separation?
>
> (cited in DeFoore 2003)

It is evident that the possibilities of identification can begin outside of the "action" phase of any conflict. Some news organizations (and journalists groups) are becoming increasingly aware and concerned about issues of physical safety and psychological welfare and are paying for their reporters to attend specialist courses outside of the military sphere. The special ones conducted by the military in the period leading up to the invasion of Iraq clearly helped to initiate a socialization process. These courses only lasted a few days and it was easy for journalists to escape from their embrace but it is clear that early signs of identification began.

Jules Crittenden a reporter for the *Boston Herald* embedded with the US

Army's 3rd Infantry Division, had previously covered other conflicts. For him *"action is an attractive flame"*:

> As for us, the reporters, action is why we came. No news is no news. There are some earnest souls here with a sense of indignation, but a lot of those I've met are what my network affiliate pal called the "war tourists." Ours is a business that takes us where intense things are happening, and calls on us to try to convey that intensity. The execution of that task is a drug that can become a meaning unto itself. Here, in other foreign assignments and back in the States, I have been privileged to enter the intimate places of people's lives, when they are stripped bare by adversity. Most of what we write ends up in the recycling bin, to be pulped for another news cycle, but I'll be content to exit life knowing that I was able to see something of what this world can be like and share a little of it with others.
>
> (Crittenden 2003)

Crittenden admitted though that the

> combat was rarely more than moderate for us. It offered us the thrill of close brushes with death, but it was the Iraqis who did all the dying when A Company, "The Assassins," rolled up in their tanks flying the Jolly Roger flag.
>
> (Crittenden 2003)

The following comments from Crittenden indicated both his closeness to the troops and his praise for those reporters trying to remain independent:

> But it is beginning to look like A Company is almost out of the action, with others due to step in. My job here recording the lives of these soldiers at war is nearly done, and it will be time to say goodbye. There is the question of whether I can hop a ride with whoever gets sent to finish the regime in Tikrit. There is the question of going there independently. God bless those reporters who will, but that is expected to be very hostile territory where the chances of being killed will be high. Receiving fire is one thing, but depending on the good will of bandits and mujahideen, at the risk of ending up like one of those crumpled bodies by the side of the road, is unappealing. Several independent reporters I've spoken to say they won't do it. I'm sure others will.
>
> (Crittenden 2003)

For Crittenden the intimacy extended to receiving souvenirs of Saddam Hussein's palaces. Here he related an exchange with a US Colonel:

"You gotta love this. This is like Patton in that German palace at the end of World War II," said Lt. Col. Philip de Camp, commander of the 4/64 Armor battalion, with a big toothy grin. He was sitting in one of Saddam's chairs, with one of Saddam's gold-plated AK-47s in front of him on one of Saddam's big conference tables strewn with American military maps and other articles of a warfighting battalion's business.

De Camp handed me one of the battalion's battle coins, with the "Tuskers" elephant head emblem on it and the motto "We Pierce."

"You earned it," de Camp said.

(Crittenden 2003)

Crittenden went on to romanticize his experience with the troops:

I'll walk away with other souvenirs. The rare privilege of becoming close to a good group of soldiers and riding with them into battle. The names and faces of all those soldiers and everything we shared in a little more than a month. The experience of riding with a conquering army into the capital of my nation's enemy, into that enemy's own yard. The memory of this strange tour of Mesopotamia, the Cradle of Civilization. Too bad civilization grew up and left home. We missed all the old ruins but saw a lot of new ones.

(Crittenden 2003)

For some of the reporters, like their predecessors in the Falklands, their experiences living alongside the military were reflected in their copy. Chris Ayres of the *Times* recognized his emotions and the impossibility of remaining detached. In writing about Marines shooting Iraqis who failed to stop at a checkpoint, he wrote:

To the Marines—and to me—there was nothing gung-ho about it. It was simply survival. Of course, I was hardly objective: as a journalist embedded with a frontline artillery unit, my chances of avoiding death at the hands of suicide bombers were directly linked to the Marines' ability to kill the enemy.

(cited in Mangan 2003)

In both the Falklands conflict and in Gulf War II the journalists' adoption of military jargon, however strenuously they sought to excise it from their vocabulary, indicates how efficiently they were being assimilated.[7] As war progressed in Iraq, some correspondents became very involved.

The story of Sanjay Gupta is an interesting one in the context of the journalist at war. Gupta, a CNN medical correspondent, received a brief to deal with chemical weapons stories. But he was then invited to travel with a mobile military unit known as the "Devil Docs" and, as the only trained neurosurgeon among a group of military doctors, there were times when he was pressed into medical action. He worked on a number of patients, not only US military but also a two-year-old Iraqi boy and an Iraqi soldier (Huff 2003; see also Bauder 2003).

Gupta outlined his position: "I knew I was going into a place where people were going to be injured, I didn't volunteer for this. I made it quite clear my mission was journalism not medicine" (cited in Huff 2003). But as he later said:

> Today, one of the other doctors said they were flying someone in with a significant head wound, "would you mind taking a look?" he said. Sure enough it was a penetrating wound to the brain. I knew this person was not going to survive a flight to Kuwait.
>
> (cited in Huff 2003)

Compare Gupta's position with the hypothetical one posed in a discussion held in 1989 and raised again by Amitai Etzioni on his website during Gulf War II (see Etzioni 2003). "In a future war involving US soldiers, what would a television reporter do if he learned the enemy troops with which he was travelling were about to launch a surprise attack on an American unit?" The question involved a hypothetical conflict between the north Kosanese and the US supported south Kosanese. Both Peter Jennings, the ABC anchor, and Mike Wallace, correspondent of 60 Minutes, responded that getting ambush footage for the evening news would take priority over warning the US troops.

At first, though, Jennings responded that "if he was with a north Kosanese unit that came upon Americans, I think I personally would do what I could do to warn the Americans." Wallace countered that other reporters, including himself, "would regard it simply as another story that they are there to cover. I'm a little bit at a loss to understand why, because you (Jennings) are an American, you would not have covered that story" (cited in Etzioni 2003). When Wallace was asked "Don't you have a higher duty as an American citizen to do all you can to save the lives of soldiers rather than this journalistic ethic of reporting fact?" he responded: "No, you don't have a higher duty . . . you're a reporter." This argument convinced Jennings, who conceded, saying "I think he's right too, I chickened out" (Etzioni 2003).

Wallace was apparently mystified when Brent Sowcroft, the former National Security Adviser, argued in relation to the hypothetical, that "you're Americans first, and you're journalists second."

In contrast to Wallace, Gupta's position became that of a participant. In his case he had his "other" professional values to fall back on. His Hippocratic oath and medical professional values enabled him to participate with a "clear" conscience. His decision was "automatic" and did not involve a deliberation or "professional" dilemma. Other journalists did not have "an other" to fall back on unless it is some wider moral and ethical cultural system.

Observing or participating?

The idea of objectivity can be regarded in two distinct ways. In the first instance, objectivity is conceptualized as an impossible goal. "Objective reporting" is associated with ways of gathering news (knowledge about places, people, and events) and conveying them in a detached, impersonal way free of value judgments. Nevertheless, the act of reporting itself places limitations (such as space, time, and pertinence) on the ability to report the whole known truth. It follows, therefore, that the necessity of selection and the hierarchical organization of a story, suggests more of a subjective rather than objective outcome (Bovee 1999: 114–16, 121; Bourdieu 1996: 21). In addition, the structural environment of the institutions of reporting is also restricted by economic and political factors that lead to a subjective outcome (Schudson 1978). In the second instance, objectivity is used as a strategic ritual, allowing for the defense of the profession (Tuchman 1972; Bovee 1999: 123–4). The procedures of the verification of facts, the separating of "facts" from "analysis," the presenting of conflicting possibilities and supporting evidence, the judicious use of quotation marks, the structuring of information in an appropriate sequence and the criterion of common sense in assessing news content, while enabling the claim to objectivity (which functions as a shield from criticism), do not guarantee objectivity. Instead, they only allow an operational view of objectivity (Tuchman 1972: 662–79; see also Tumber and Prentoulis 2003).

Objectivity is a prized status within journalism. The institutionalized and thus professional phase of journalism started with the elevation of objectivity to the dominant ideology within the profession (Trice 1993: 60). Objectivity became the foundation for the social responsibility claims of the journalistic identity. In war corresponding the principles of detachment are a key element in the social construction or formation of identity. But it is here that problems emerge. Correspondents face criticism in two ways. By following the tradition of detached reporting, journalists are censured or condemned for their dispassionate stance often in the form of accusations of a lack of patriotism and for eschewing the perceived national interest. At the same time the "journalism of attachment," the human, emotional face of war corresponding, has been criticized for opening the door to mistaken accounts of the conflicts, and for being "self-righteous" and "moralizing" (Ward 1998; McLaughlin 2002: 166–8; Tumber and Prentoulis 2003).

The conditions of detachment are also important because they are a facilitator of objectivity, and it is in this regard that governments and military practices attempt to ensure that the "objective" coverage of stories is often restricted or negated during international conflicts.

In the Falklands and Iraq a clear clash occurred between two competing sentiments. On the one hand the journalists carried the occupational ideology of impartiality and objectivity while the military rucksacks on their backs symbolically carried more than the single source of their provision: in effect, where did their commitments lie—to traditions of journalistic practice or to those who could and did protect them, the military? (See Morrison and Tumber 1988; Tumber and Palmer 2004.)

In Gulf War II the conditions for the journalists were different from those during the Falklands and the nationalities of the correspondents were not restricted as they had been during the Falklands. But elements of the situation were very similar.

To repeat the question posed by Gerald Herbert of the *Washington Times*; "at what point are we observing and at what point are we participating?"

Are the acknowledgments of their predicaments by journalists during the Falklands and Ayres in Gulf War II "admissions of irrevocably compromised journalistic integrity, or evidence of a degree of self awareness that others responsible for covering the conflict might do well to emulate?" (Mangan 2003).

In conflict situations like the Falklands and Gulf War II, journalists enter a realm of professional uncertainty. The values that "normally" ensure a "protective distance give way to affinity values born of proximity." Journalists become emotionally involved with the troops with whom they are located—and want "their" side to win.[8]

Few people can stand aside in the face of anguish and suffering, especially when those who need help have been companions, hosts, and mentors. In the Falklands conflict, Max Hastings, who had already covered 11 wars, understood the ambiguities of the war reporter's role; and resolved the tension between observer and participant by openly deciding, at least on one occasion deliberately, to assist the efforts of the Task Force by his writing. There was no self-delusion on Hastings' part about what this meant in terms of standard journalistic practice (Morrison and Tumber 1988: 113). Hastings, on his own admission, was partial in his approach in that he made a conscious decision not to report anything detrimental to the war effort, but such partiality did not exclude him from being objective.

Writing about the Falklands conflict, Morrison and Tumber suggested that a reasonably well-defined role (in this case) within British journalism—the participatory journalist—had evolved. Furthermore, in certain circumstances the participant is likely to be more critical than their erstwhile "objective" colleague, the observer.[9] The journalist as observer works within a system of news values placing and judging events providing for a degree of predictability in news selection. The journalist as observer, therefore, is more secure and is protected by the accredited acceptance of understandings of the profession and news organizations than the participant, who, while not operating entirely outside such values— must still "make" the news—intercedes with their own individual personal judgment of events related to emotions unconnected to journalism itself. An extra dimension is added to the news gathering process which in extreme cases leaves the participant vulnerable to challenge. The responsibility for the story or story selection, therefore, is for the participant a greater individual act than it is for the observer where it is dispersed among collective values. Thus the participant, having dismissed a story not on the grounds of newsworthiness, but from personal values, sees the accepted story as their own *property*. Because of the exclusivity of the story, the personalized decision, the direct emotional as opposed to occupational connectedness, the journalist cannot withdraw behind the blinds of news values and news expectations to defend his story, but confronts it as a moral or emotional commitment (Morrison and Tumber 1988: 130).

The problem for the participant journalists, wedded to the events around them, is how to respond when events force a choice between professional commitment and participatory loyalties. For the journalists in the Falklands,

> freed as prisoners of news values, the deliberate allowing of affection to influence operations, there is no reason to assume that the witnessing of disasters would have resulted in a linear move to the position of "analytical observer." The very affection which formed the basis of sympathetic reporting could equally have formed the basis for outright critical onslaught at the slaughter of men with whom they identified. Thus, rather than move back into the traditional camp, the participant role may simply have been extended to include righteous wrath.
>
> (Morrison and Tumber 1988: 130)

In these situations as Morrison and Tumber argued:

> The participant, governed by emotions of a different kind from those of the observer, is potentially the much more uncontrollable of the two types. Having already overturned accepted news judgment to pursue feelings of their own, the participant is free to move their affections where they will. Thus, whilst the observer would not overlook a military setback, their reports would still be bound by the developed options of "impartiality and objectivity" and constrained by efforts at fairness. Not so, however, the participant with their loosened attachment to such values. The very feelings that prohibited copy reflecting badly on the troops could easily move to expose weakness, incompetence, or the mere fact that the war was unwinnable, all done in the name of the men whom he so fondly regarded and with whom affinity is felt. From such feelings the crusader is made.
>
> (Morrison and Tumber 1988: 130)

This last point is crucial for the US Defense Department officials and military who were instrumental in the planning and implementation of the embedding process. If military success is achieved then the dangers of having to deal with "uncontrollable" participant journalists are minimized. It is on this basis that future planning and honing of the embedding process is ongoing by Pentagon officials (see Tumber and Palmer 2004, ch. 4). But for news organizations and the public the dangers of embedding are all too evident. The enmeshing and identification of journalists within the military can lead to problems in the integrity of the information supplied. For the observer, being a "prisoner of news values" bound by the rules and procedures of an occupation, ensures a protective safety.

The problem is to maintain those values in a social world (the military) where the plausibility structure supporting those values remains sufficiently intact.

For the large news organizations operating in Gulf War II, unlike the situation during the Falklands conflict, the potential problem of identification arising from the embedding process was mitigated through the presence of their other "unilateral" journalists working in the region and other reporters stationed at the media center at Centcom headquarters in Doha, Qatar. This allowed for alternative stories and perspectives about the war in addition to those from correspondents embedded with military units. The problems for the "unilateral" journalists were the physical dangers they encountered not only from Iraqi attack but also from so-called "friendly fire."[10] The portents for news coverage of future wars and conflicts are not good. Governments and military will plan more embedding formats with all the associated risks for "objective" reporting, increase warnings to non-embedded journalists about their safety, and continue the usual policies of censorship, misinformation, and delay in confirmation of events. For the future, the struggle for news organizations will be in resisting these increasing pressures and, for journalists, a continuation of the current reassessment about the nature of witnessing, truth, and objectivity.

Notes

1 Embedded was not a term used during the Falklands conflict. Because the organization of the placing of reporters on board the Task Force ships was done quickly and haphazardly, little thought was given to the process, and hence its naming, by military and defense officials.
2 For details see Tumber and Palmer 2004.
3 The study involved interviewing all the journalists who sailed with the task force to cover the war (see Morrison and Tumber 1988).
4 Approximately 500+ journalists were "embedded" with the military during the 2003 war in Iraq. The United States Government allowed journalists to accompany forces in the field, on ships, and at departure airfields.
5 The term given to those reporters not "embedded" with the military.
6 Over 50 members of various news organizations attended the course which included staged hostile environment scenarios and instruction on chemical weapons protection (DeFoore 2003, see also Tumber 2002).
7 In Gulf War II some journalists "escaped" from the "embedding process" and left their units. In some cases it was a difficult decision because news organizations were prevented from sending in replacements (the no substitute rule). Toward the end of the war the numbers leaving their units increased considerably.
8 Hollywood often portrays the journalist as making an emotional choice. In the feature film *Under Fire*, Nick Nolte playing the part of a photojournalist on assignment in Nicaragua for an American news organization is asked by one of the Sandinistas, "Whose side are you on?" "I don't take sides, I take pictures" is his response. Later in the film his "objective" stance changes to partisanship when he agrees to help the "rebels" by faking a photograph purporting to show that the dead rebel leader is still alive (Tumber 1997).
9 The "participant" role has been discussed further in the context of the "journalism of attachment" see Tumber 1997 and 2002; Carruthers 2000, p. 240; McLaughlin 2002, p. 166; Seib 2002, p. 68; Tumber and Prentoulis 2003, p. 225.

10 For details of incidents and subsequent investigations see News Safety Institute 2003; Tumber and Palmer 2004, ch. 3.

References

Bauder, D. (2003) "CNN reporter performs surgery in Iraq," www.EditorandPublisher.com April 3.

Bourdieu, P. (1996) *On Television and Journalism*, London: Pluto.

Bovee, W.G. (1999) *Discovering Journalism*, Westport, CN, and London: Greenwood Press.

Carruthers, S.L. (2002) *The Media at War*, Basingstoke: Macmillan Press.

Cook, J. (2003) "Military, media meet off battlefield to debate war coverage," www.chicago tribune.com August 18.

Crittenden, J. (2003) "Embedded journal: leaving Iraq," www.Pointer.org. April 14.

DeFoore, J. (2003) "Photo-news access vs. independence: thoughts on media boot camp," www.pdonline.com March 26.

Etzioni, A. (2003) "Reporters first, Americans second?" www.Amitai-notes.com March 21.

Gralnick, J. (2003) "Lessons to survive by," www.Tvweek.com March 21.

Harrison, K. (2003) "War reporting: diary of a journalist with the army," www.Timeson-line.co.uk March 24.

Huff, R. (2003) "CNN's own 'Devil Doc' scrubs up for duty again," www.Nydailynews.com April 9.

Mangan, L. (2003) "Them and us: the singular language of the embeds," *Media Guardian*, April 7, p. 5.

McLaughlin, G. (2002) *The War Correspondent*, London: Pluto.

Morrison, D.E. and Tumber, H. (1988) *Journalists at War*, London: Sage.

News Safety Institute (2003) "Dying to tell the story," News Safety Institute.

Porch, D. (2002) "No bad stories," www.Nwc.navt.mil/press/review/2002/winter/art5-w02

Seib, Phillip M. (2002) *The Global Journalist: News and Consciousness in a World of Conflict*, Lanham, MD, and Oxford: Rowman and Littlefield.

Schudson, M. (1978) *Discovering the News: a Social History of American Newspapers*, New York: Basic Books.

Trice, Harrison M. (1993) *Occupational Subcultures in the Workplace*, Ithaca and New York: ILR Press.

Tuchman, G. (1972) "Objectivity as a strategic ritual: an examination of newsmen's notions of objectivity," *American Journal of Sociology*, vol. 77, pp. 660–79.

Tumber, H. (1997) "Bystander journalism, or journalism of attachment," *Intermedia*, vol. 25, no. 1, pp. 4–7.

Tumber, H. (2002) "Reporting under fire: the physical safety and emotional welfare of journalists" in B. Zelizer and S. Allan (eds), *Journalism after September 11*, London: Routledge.

Tumber, H. and Palmer, J. (2004) *Media at War*, London: Sage.

Tumber, H. and Prentoulis, M. (2003) "Journalists under fire: subcultures, objectivity and emotional literacy," in D.K. Thussu and D. Freedman (eds), *War and the Media*, London: Sage.

Ward, Stephen J. (1998) "Answer to Martin Bell: objectivity and attachment in journalism," *The Harvard International Journal of Press/Politics*, vol. 3, no. 3, pp. 121–5.

Zinsmeister, K. (2003) "Different worlds," Nationalreview.com April 7.

11

OUT OF SIGHT, OUT OF MIND?

The non-reporting of small wars and insurgencies

Prasun Sonwalkar

Recent developments in Iraq, Afghanistan, Kosovo, East Timor, or older conflicts in Northern Ireland, Catalonia, and Kashmir, have been popular "news pegs" for media academics and journalists alike. But there is something striking about this calendar of conflict: these seem to be the only conflicts that are deemed worthy of sustained coverage by the news superpowers based in the West. There is a distinct sense of these being "our" wars, because "we" are interested or involved, while "their" wars—the numerous wars and conflicts that are taking place right at this moment in much of the developing world involving much violence and terrorism—do not really matter much. As Weimann and Winn concluded after analyzing conflict data involving hundreds of groups and over 5,000 events between 1968 and 1986, "less than one-third of all terrorist events are actually reported" (1993: 71).

This chapter attempts two things: one, by focusing on the many wars and conflicts that the media routinely render invisible, it makes a case for greater media and scholarly attention to this vast unreported world; and two, it presents a case study located in India where the conflict in Kashmir is routinely privileged in the discourse of the English-language national press, but the host of insurgencies and conflicts in India's northeast, involving much violence and terrorism, are routinely neglected. Using the case study, I show how dominant socio-cultural values contribute to the marginalization of wars and conflicts involving minorities in news discourse, even if they involve much violence and terrorism. This seems to be evident not only along the more familiar West–Rest dimension but also *within* multicultural nations such as India.

At the very basic level, the trope of "war and media" or "conflict and media" is predicated on a "presence" in media content. This takes the form of analyses of state-centric reportage, how specific wars were covered by specific national media systems, propaganda, military–media relationship, psychological operations, human rights perspectives, or changes in professional practices (embedded journalists), among others. This chapter seeks to present a contrary view by exploring the nether world of "absence" of news in media content about most wars and conflicts within and across nations. There is much that can be mined by effecting a shift from "presence" to "absence."

The thesis of "symbolic annihilation" that was hitherto viewed in terms of the marginalization of news about women (Tuchman 1972) and other minorities can also be applied to the coverage of wars and conflicts that involve swathes of population in the developing world. There are countless wars and conflicts raging across Africa, Asia, and elsewhere that figure only in small print in research statistics of think tanks or when citizens of Western countries fall victims there. The selectivity evident in scholarship and media content, preferring wars and conflicts involving Western powers, has obvious implications in an increasingly interconnected world, where the movement of humans, material, and money across continents to finance terror is no longer a difficult proposition—as the events of September 11 showed. The need to bring most—if not all—wars and conflicts into the international public sphere has never been more important than now. One can no longer be sure where or when a terrorist will strike, and why. The distinction between "our" terrorists and "their" terrorists can scarcely be maintained any longer.

At least in theoretical terms, the value of human lives lost in wars in Africa or Asia and elsewhere cannot be lower than those lost on September 11. The absence of news, or according low priority to the many "invisible" wars and conflicts, means that they do not figure in the public agenda, within national public spheres, or at the international level. The media is a key factor in conflict resolution efforts, but one first needs to be aware of something before public opinion is created and authorities compelled to "do something." As Wolfsfeld observed: "The very fact that policy makers and citizens are encouraged to think about some challenges rather than others is, by itself, likely to affect the allocation of public resources and how people relate to the political world" (1997: 13).

Selectivity is built into the processes and dynamics of news production. This is evident at various levels: when the Western media routinely ignore wars and conflicts in the developing world, and also *within* national settings when elite-controlled media systems, equally routinely, ignore conflicts involving minorities. Violence and terrorism have long been privileged as key news values, but they remain hostage to the defining news value of cultural proximity. Wars and conflicts are not intrinsically newsworthy; they need to be culturally proximate enough to become news, in international as well as national settings. Even a high degree of violence as part of serious conflicts may not always qualify as news if it does not involve the "right" perpetrators or victims in the "right" geographies of culture. For every conflict that is well covered or analyzed, there are countless that remain unreported, ignored, or marginalized. It is nonetheless true that conflicts in the developing world may figure intermittently on the international media's radar, and more often within national settings, but there still remain scores of wars and conflicts that do not make it to the news columns or television bulletins even *within* national settings.

Journalists are invariably drawn from the "national mainstream" and circularly cater to this section of society and its value system. Thus, events and issues that do not fall within the paradigm of interest to this section are unlikely to be considered by journalists as newsworthy. Even if wars and conflicts involving the "other" meet the "most salient, operational news value of violence" (Hall 1981: 237), they may still not resonate in the media. Journalists breathe the same dominant socio-cultural air of the "national mainstream," and this cannot but influence their work, notwithstanding the demands and claims of being professional, objective, or ethical in their routines.

The fact remains that, despite the real and stated commitments to multiculturalism in democratic societies, at the grassroots level, the existence of a socio-cultural binary of "us" and "them" or "we" and "they" is very much a reality and can scarcely be denied. This is true not only in Western societies but also within multicultural countries such as India. But this socio-cultural binary is not a given; it is created historically during processes of nation formation when majorities and minorities are manufactured. The binary also shifts according to focus, locale, and perspective (Shils 1975; Elliott 1986; Elias 1994), and deeply influences news production. I argue that at its most fundamental level, news must essentially be about *us*, and that even though the contours and constituents of "us" usually remain amorphous, journalists always have a clear conception of what will interest "us." As Alistair Hetherington, former editor of the *Guardian*, put it, the instinctual news value of most journalists simply is: "Does it interest me?" (1985: 8).

In communications research, race has been the prime node through which "othering" in news discourse is examined. Several studies have highlighted the way reporting, particularly in tabloids, panders to racial prejudices and attitudes. Racism has become so commonsensical that it has almost become banal, to use Billig's term (1995). As Hall argued, there is a racist "common sense" that pervades British society: "Since (like gender) race appears to be 'given' by Nature, racism is one of the most profoundly 'naturalized of existing ideologies'" (1990: 9). The non-white sections of population come to be routinely seen as the "they" of British society; a position that is so ingrained as to be unquestionable. Announcing a special series on British Islam, soon after September 11, the *Guardian* asked in a full-page insertion with a veil in the background: "How much do we know about them?" The paper obviously did not feel the need to identify who it considered to be the "we" and "them." The question precluded the possibility that British Muslims might also be its readers.

Hartley (1992) analyzed a similar situation with regard to the representation of Aboriginals in Australia, and he suggested that journalistic strategies of inclusion and exclusion had become so ingrained and naturalized that they had become part of the "common sense" or what Shils (1975) calls the "central value system" of a society. In India, a similar situation is evident in relation to "caste." The domination of the upper caste or Brahminical order of things, or the events and issues involving the Hindi-speaking people, is so pervasive as to make it commonsensical and natural.

Another node of "othering" is at the level of nation, which is also a selective project. The discourse of nations and nationalism is premised on several assumptions about common myths and historical memories, a common, mass culture, a historic territory, common legal rights, and duties of members, etc. The "we"/"they" dynamic is central to nation formation and in the case of young nations, to nation building. It assumes a version of hegemony by which one view of society is made to appear as the "natural" order of things, beyond rational questioning, which may completely delegitimize or even obliterate alternative versions. As Nag observed:

> Nations have always been concerned about "us" against "them." Nations are obsessed with "self" and discriminate the "other." The construction of the national self has always been only vis-à-vis the "other." The basis of such construction is differentiation. The "self" consisted of people who share common cultural characteristics and such commonalities could be measured only by contrasting against those who do not.
>
> (Nag 2001)

Nossek referred to the socio-cultural binary, but in a discussion about the coverage of *foreign* political violence:

> [When] political violence is reported and covered, there is already a prior definition by the journalist of the event as some kind of political violence—say, war, terrorism or a violent demonstration—that predates the reporter's own professional definition. Thus, professional norms become secondary to the national identity of the correspondent covering the story for the newspaper. The definition requires the journalist to decide instantly whether or not it is *our* war or *theirs*, *our* terrorism or *theirs*, etc. The definition, and the immediate stance adopted as a result, will influence whether the event is selected as news and the way it is covered.
>
> (Nossek forthcoming; emphasis added)

But this binary may well be conceptually applied *within* national settings, where journalists decide instantly whether events and issues, and also wars and conflicts, are "ours" or "theirs." Applying the binary to this Indian case study, I demonstrate how prolonged insurgencies in the northeastern part of the country do not always qualify as news while similar events and issues in Kashmir are routinely privileged in the discourse of the English-language national press based in New Delhi. The focus here is less on the better-known Kashmir conflict than on the weakly resonating insurgencies in the ethnic cauldron of India's northeast.

I first present an overview of lesser known wars and conflicts across the globe and then outline some basic characteristics of the Indian press and emphasize its

209

centrality in modern India. The subsequent section looks at key features of the two conflict zones. Then interviews with senior Indian journalists reveal the salience of the binary and the differences and disjunctures in their perceptions toward the two conflict zones. Both bear similarities in terms of the nature and intensity of violence, secessionist goals, foreign involvement, use of sophisticated arms, degree of local alienation, challenge to the nation-state, etc. In other words, Kashmir and the northeast demonstrate "comparable message potential" (Entman 1991: 9) for news coverage. The account is also based on my experience of covering the northeast conflicts and Kashmir for *The Times of India* and other publications over a decade.

Invisible wars and conflicts

Evidence suggests that a veritable "third world war" may well be going on in the developing world. According to Scherrer, "warfare and mass violence is not going on between East and West, nor between North and South, but occurring at this very moment inside some 60 states in four continents" (1999: 53). Since 1945, more than 250 major wars have taken place, mostly in the developing world, and very few of them were inter-state conflicts. According to the Stockholm International Peace Research Institute (SIPRI), of the 57 major armed conflicts in 45 countries during 1990–2001, only three were inter-state: Iraq–Kuwait, India–Pakistan and Eritrea–Ethiopia; the rest were internal wars and conflicts over territory or resources.

Scherrer's study reveals a rich menu into which analysts of ethnicity and nationalism can tap: underneath the structure of most nation-states there is an "extraordinary multitude of between 6,500 and 10,000 nations, nationalities, and peoples as ethnic entities of diverse size" (1999: 54). His "Register of violent conflicts, 1985–94" lists 102 examples. Over half a century, Gurr (1993) has been tracking the careers of as many as 300 politically active ethnic and religious groups engaged in conflict. According to *Conflict Barometer 2002*, as many as 173 violent political conflicts were carried out during the year: "Ongoing political conflicts of 2002 are most frequently carried out on the conflict issues of national power, territory and autonomy" (HIIK 2002: 5).

Ethno-national wars and conflicts are considered "among the most important security problems in the world today" (Brown 2001: xi). According to Chenoy, "Ethnic and religious conflicts threaten to tear apart more societies today than any other issue" (2002). These involve many "nations without states"—or "Trojan nationalisms" (Appadurai 1996: 165)—and their struggles to win statehood, autonomy, self-determination, etc. From the state's viewpoint, these are branded as 'insurgency,'" "separatism," or "secessionism," a terminology also reflected in the dictum that "one man's terrorist is another's freedom fighter." At the international level, the careers of only a few such ongoing conflicts figure in the media on a consistent basis, though not all resonate to the same degree. The usual suspects are Northern Ireland, the Basque separatism in Spain and Catalonia, Kashmir, Tamil separatism in Sri Lanka or conflicts in the Middle East. However, they constitute but a fraction of the number of ongoing conflicts, given that an overwhelming majority of the 189 members of the United Nations are non-homogenous and internally diverse nation-states, and that many face conflict situations in various forms.

The power geometry of international relations ensures that conflicts involving major actors such as the United States, western European states, or NATO are extensively covered by the news superpowers based in the West. But the situation is different in relation to the large number of ongoing conflicts in the developing world; many of them now involve challengers with an international reach. In Britain, the only media focus on "invisible" conflicts is the Channel 4 series, *Unreported World*, though it does not deal only with conflicts and routinely records low viewership owing to its late night telecast.

The international media largely ignored the tinderbox situation in Afghanistan when the Taliban took over in 1996, but provided blanket coverage only after September 11 happened. The Western media woke up to realities in Afghanistan only when "we" were attacked. Until then, only a few journalists such as Robert Fisk reported on the depredations of the fundamentalist regime in a country that had already been ravaged by the Soviet occupation. By late 2003, in another example of Western news superpowers pursuing the foreign policy of their governments, attention quickly shifted from Afghanistan to Iraq, amid pious declarations that this time the West would not "let Afghanistan down." Except for stray news, Afghanistan had soon ceased to be a story in much of the Western media.

Centrality of the press in India

In this chapter, the focus is on the Indian press, and in particular, the influential New Delhi-based English-language press that is considered India's "national press." It occupies a privileged position in the country's mammoth press industry, partly because it was the language of the colonial rulers, and because English continues to be the language of communication of the government and of the most influential sections of Indian society. As early as 1954, Windmiller observed that "India's English language press is the only national press and it is paramount in the world of Indian journalism" (1954: 315).

As Smith observed, by 1947—when India became independent—the press had matured in the acid bath of the freedom struggle: India "had already acquired a sophisticated press, experienced in agitation, but also knowledgeable in the arts of the government" (1980: 159). Gandhi and Nehru considered a free press to be crucial to the success of India's tryst with democracy.

At the beginning of the twenty-first century, the privately-owned print media reflects India's kaleidoscopic diversity, and "offers a product line that is dizzying in its diverse array of languages, ownership structures, and topics" (Viswanath and Karan 2000: 92). As Jeffrey observed, "No other country—indeed no other continent—in the world has a newspaper industry as complex and highly developed as India's" (1993: 2004). It is competitive and pluralist and is not dominated by any single group or ideology; India is also the biggest market for English-language publications outside Britain and the US (Sonwalkar 2002). Newspapers are published in over 100 languages, including in English and 18 major official languages (each spoken by millions), 81 other languages/dialects and some foreign languages.

The English-language press based in New Delhi "[identifies] itself with the fears and anxieties of the Indian state" (Mudgal 1995: 78), but it is also credited with playing "a stabilizing role in national politics, promoting national integration and secular values, avoiding extremes and sticking to the middle path" (Joshi 2002). It reflects the opinion of influential readership and plays an agenda-setting role; it "delineates the priorities of the country and conditions the expectations of the most powerful segments of the Indian population: the political, intellectual and business elite" (Haque and Narag 1983: 35).

English-language newspapers are published from several metropolitan centres but some "stand out as India's quality press" (Viswanath and Karan 2000):

- *The Times of India* (established 1838)
- *The Statesman* (1875)
- *The Hindu* (1878)
- *Hindustan Times* (1924)
- *Indian Express* (1932).

According to industry estimates, these newspapers account for over 60 percent of the overall circulation of English-language newspapers in the country. Reports published in these newspapers often figure in parliamentary debates and influence policy positions and politics. They co-exist with a vibrant English-language financial press, and mass circulation English-language magazines such as *India Today*, *Outlook*, *Filmfare*, etc. devoted to news and current affairs, entertainment, and lifestyle. Journalists and editors working in the English-language press are the most known across the country. New Delhi is the hotbed of political journalism, where "the media is more pervasive than anywhere else in the country" (Jha 1992: 145).

Conundrum of Indian conflicts

Since India's independence, secessionist demands have been raised in three areas: Punjab, Kashmir, and the northeast states. The demand for "Khalistan" for the majority Sikhs of Punjab hogged national and international headlines during the 1980s, but by the early 1990s the Indian state had militarily and politically neutralized the insurgency. But the might of the state continues to be challenged in Kashmir and the northeast where the idea of secession retains much local valence. Three wars have been fought since 1947 in which Kashmir has been a direct or indirect factor, two between India and Pakistan in 1947–9 and 1965, and one between India and China in 1962. The 1962 war was fought mainly in the northeast when the Red Army overran the Indian state of Arunachal Pradesh and entered Assam, before pulling back.

Kashmir and the northeast figure prominently in India's official list of "problem areas" (UMHA 2003). Kashmir is part of the federal state that is officially called "Jammu and Kashmir," while the northeast region is a conglomeration of seven states: Assam, Arunachal Pradesh, Mizoram, Manipur, Tripura, Nagaland, and Meghalaya. The state of Jammu and Kashmir is India's only Muslim-majority province, and by the logic of British India's partition in 1947 into Hindu-majority India and Muslim-majority Pakistan, it should have become part of the Islamic state of Pakistan. But Kashmir's former Hindu ruler opted to join India in the face of invasion by Pakistani troops immediately after independence, and modern democratic India has since tenaciously held on to the picturesque valley as the prime symbol of its commitment to secularism. Its presence in India is also sought to serve as a symbol of assurance that a Muslim-majority province can thrive in a Hindu-majority India, which anyway has more than twice as many Muslims as in Pakistan.

The Kashmir conflict involves two of the largest religious communities in South Asia: Hindu and Muslim, who have a mixed history of close interaction and attrition over the years. Their issues dominate mainstream public discourse in India. Kashmir has been the most contentious issue between India and Pakistan. As Bose (1999) observed,

> Both countries have chosen to make possession of Kashmir central to the *raison d'etre* of their respective national existences—"secular" nationalism in the case of India, Muslim nationalism in the case of Pakistan. The result of this competition are maximalist, zero-sum claims to Kashmir which are fundamentally irreconcilable with each other.

Both sides hold on to their respective positions with equal tenacity. Among the factors driving India's position is the not unrealistic apprehension that

> Kashmir's exit from the Indian Union would set off powerful centrifugal forces in other parts of the country. [The] stakes for both states involve far more than territorial claims: the question of control of Kashmir goes to the very basis of the state-building enterprise in South Asia.
>
> (Ganguly 1996)

Unlike the Hindu–Muslim–Aryan dynamics that underpin the Kashmir conflict, the northeast is inhabited by a melting pot of tribes of Mongoloid and other ethnic stock, many of whom have converted to Christianity or retain animist faith. It also has a large non-tribal population that shares many of the anxieties and insecurities of tribes *vis-à-vis* the vast Hindu–Muslim dominated Indian mainstream. The region is culturally and ethnically closer to neighbouring southeast Asia than to south Asia. The seven states in the region have been in

Table 11.1 Northeast insurgency casualties, 1992–2001

	Civilians	Security forces	Militants
Assam	2,459	611	1,371
Arunachal P.	31	9	31
Mizoram	6	13	1
Nagaland	603	235	882
Tripura	2,082	296	255
Meghalaya	63	50	27
Manipur	1,371	649	830
Total	6,615	1,863	3,397

Source: Ajay Sahni, "Survey of conflicts and resolution in India's northeast," in *Faultlines*, vol. 12.

the grip of more than one form of conflict: secessionist insurgency, separatism within India, struggles for local autonomy, inter-, and intra-tribal clashes, locals versus "outsiders," locals versus immigrant Muslims from Bangladesh, language tussles, boundary clashes among the seven states, etc. The recent calendar of casualties in the region runs into thousands (see Table 11.1).

The conflicts are played out within the overall context of the region's historically tenuous links with mainland India. Its people bear a deep sense of alienation from the rest of the country; the feeling is strong that "India," "New Delhi," and the "Central Government" are solely interested in the region for its tea, oil, and other natural resources. Until 1972, it was India's External Affairs Ministry that administered two of the region's seven states, Nagaland and Arunachal Pradesh. A key fact central to the "otherness" of the region is that British rule spread there nearly a hundred years after the British had subjugated the rest of India which had implications for its participation in the freedom struggle and subsequent integration in modern India.

Owing to prolonged unrest, the northeast is often referred to as "India's Ulster" or as a potential "East Timor" (Dutt 1999). At least 50,000 people have been killed in insurgent violence since 1947, of whom 25,000 alone perished in violence linked to the Naga insurgency, which is as old as the Kashmir conflict. Since World War II—when Kohima (capital of Nagaland) and Imphal (capital of Manipur) were prominent theaters of battle between the Allied powers and the Japanese—"the political scene in north-east India . . . has never been placid" (Singh 1987: 22). Tribes were apprehensive of the vast Hindu–Muslim population in the rest of India, and they had heard that Hindus revere the cow, that they would ban cow slaughter and deprive them of their food: beef. The sense of "otherness" was constructed at various levels, including religious, ethnic, and cultural (including culinary).

In human geographical terms, the region is literally peripheral to the project of modern India (see Figure 11.1). Less than one percent of the northeast's boundary is contiguous with mainland India, while the remaining 99 percent form India's international borders with China, Bangladesh, Myanmar, and Bhutan. Kashmir

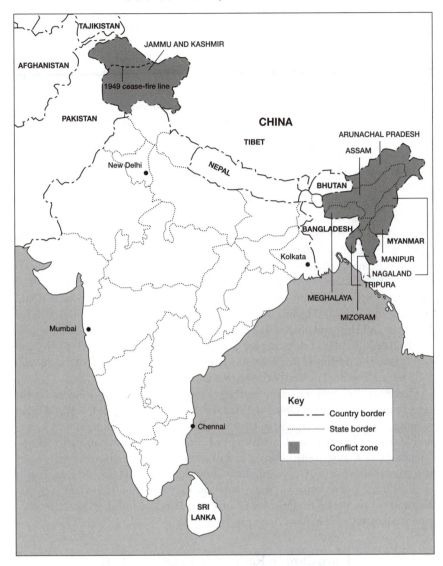

Figure 11.1 Kashmir and northeast conflict zones in India (courtesy of Indo-Asian News Service)

and the northeast are located at opposite ends of the Himalayan range. The northeast covers a land area of 255,037 square km (approximately the combined size of the United Kingdom and Ireland). The northeast's political representation is 24 in the lower house of parliament (Lok Sabha: the House of the People) that has 545 members.

The "otherness" of the northeast is acknowledged in Indian public discourse. The Constitution recognizes that the region is "special" and needs statutory

215

protection; a clutch of laws and regulations has been enacted for the purpose, and new states were created to meet tribal aspirations. But as the Planning Commission, a federal government department, puts it: "The Northeast tends to be seen as a distant outpost, some kind of land's end" (1997: 2). Federal civil servants are loathe to serve in the region.

On the other hand, Kashmir has an evocative resonance in the mists and myths of early Hinduism; it is also widely known for its pacific brand of Islam: Sufism. Unlike the northeast, Kashmir has inspired much poetry and Bollywood themes over the years. The low status of the northeast is driven by an "absence of cultural and psychological integration with the mainstream" (Datta 2000). In mainland India, inhabitants from the northeast with Mongoloid features are viewed as strangers or foreigners. As Horam (1988: 64) observed: "As soon as a Naga crosses north-east India and ventures westwards, he is mistaken for a Thai, Cambodian, Chinese or Japanese and treated as a foreigner . . . Even Indians fail to recognize them as Indians."

The region's "otherness" invokes themes such as civilized (mainstream)–barbaric (northeast), developed–undeveloped, cultured–uncultured, etc. The pejorative attitude toward tribes is ingrained in the mainstream psyche dominated by the Hindu–Muslim dynamic. The situation is not dissimilar to what Hartman and Husband observed in the British context; that there are elements in the British cultural tradition that are derogatory to non-whites (1981: 274). Most conflicts in the northeast involve tribes who have close knowledge of the difficult hilly terrain and are known for their fierce martial prowess.

Modern India's determination to preserve territorial boundaries inherited at the time of independence prompted the state to deploy the army, air force, and other security forces in the northeast in large numbers. Owing to prolonged unrest, several laws have been enacted, many dubbed "draconian" by human rights groups. Violations of human rights during counter-insurgency operations often worsen the ground situation but, as journalists admit during interviews, they are hardly deemed worthy of reporting in the newsrooms in New Delhi. Issues and events in Kashmir or other areas that involve or affect the Hindu–Muslim problematic continue to be privileged in news discourse.

Journalists on Kashmir and northeast India

Wide-ranging disjunctures in the perceptions of journalists toward Kashmir and the northeast emerged in the interviews conducted for this study. Part of a wider study to highlight and explain differences in the resonances of the two conflict zones in the Indian national press, the responses were noteworthy for two reasons: there was a remarkable unanimity among journalists that the northeast region had a low status in the news agenda, and the terminology of the socio-cultural binary ("we" and "they") was clearly reflected. None of them said they were prejudiced toward the region and its peoples, but even while stating that conflicts in the region were "serious" and that they deserved more attention, they admitted that there was a strong feeling in newsrooms that "there is no interest among readers; somehow the region, its peoples and issues do not seem to matter to us" (YV).

DD, a journalist and human rights activist working in Nagaland, said:

> Some time ago, we wanted to release a document, *Where Peacekeepers Have Declared War*, detailing events in Nagaland and Manipur as part of the army's counter-insurgency operations. We organized a press conference at the Press Club of India in New Delhi. More than 40 people turned up, including seniors of the rank of assistant editors and associate editors, but the next day not a line appeared in the papers. The national press is not interested in the Naga issue.

According to YV, the instinctual feeling about the northeast among journalists is that "whatever happens there, somehow does not affect us and our readers." Kashmir, on the other hand, is routinely seen as "something that deeply affects us" (VVPS). Journalists see tribes in the northeast as "primitive," which carries the implication that the non-tribal section of India's population is "modern." DAT, a New Delhi-based special correspondent of *The Times of India*, was not even aware if the paper had a correspondent in the northeast, because he did not remember the last time the paper had any report from the area (it was later discovered that the paper did have a correspondent there).

DPS said he often had to struggle to get his northeast-related stories published in his paper. His seniors would ask: "Who is bothered, why do you bother?" He said he once had to explain to his colleagues that "Kuki" was not a biscuit but the name of a major tribe of Manipur, where hundreds of people had been killed in clashes with Nagas. Indian culture, he said, was still largely considered Aryan culture while the Mongoloids of the northeast were considered alien. He would like to see the region covered extensively, like Kashmir, but he said he felt helpless owing to "complete lack of interest" among his seniors and colleagues.

Three journalists explained how the low status of tribes and the northeast region is part of the cultural air in which they operate:

> Right from an early age, we are not made aware of our country's ethnic diversity. We only know of Bengalis in eastern India, nothing beyond. Most of us will not be able to tell a Naga from a Mizo. The attitude towards the tribes is that they are a necessary evil, so all we have to do is to hold on to them and their territory by force. The feeling is that we are superior—the concept of Aryan supremacy. The image is that people there drink, eat all kinds of meat, they are amoral Christians who believe in polygamy and who fight bitterly. In sum, it is a society we don't need to know much about. The Indian army is there; give them two slaps and they will be quiet.
>
> (NM)

Prejudices are very deep even among highly paid officers. The attitude is that they are jungle people, and the same is the attitude among media men. There is discrimination by rulers, ministers, bureaucrats, and intelligence agencies. My colleague wanted to go to the northeast for his honeymoon; he became a major target of ridicule in our newsroom. The northeast holds no appeal; also, it is too distant. It is remote to me culturally, I do not relate to their languages, culture, or race. They are all chinks.

(VVPS)

The northeast's low status is fed into the sub-conscious right from childhood in north India. In folktales, at least in eastern Uttar Pradesh where I come from, it is portrayed as a region of women from where one never comes back, or as a region that is not worth going to. On the other hand, Kashmir has the opposite place. It is a place that everyone aspires to visit before dying. So when something happens or goes wrong there, the people are disturbed. The poetry of great [Hindi] poets such as Dinkar or Pant resonates with Kashmir imagery. Kashmir is considered the crown, the most important part of the body. The northeast too has the same importance, but there is no awareness of this.

(RBR)

The responses underline the importance of "cultural proximity" *within* nation-states. The media do not function in a socio-cultural vacuum. Media images of a particular section of society or region cannot be very different from the general (dominant) values prevalent in society. The pejorative attitude toward the northeast and its tribes affects the coverage of all events and issues, including those involving much violence and terrorism. As the responses indicate, a particular ethnicity (Aryan), language (Hindi) and region (north and central India) come to be routinely privileged in the news discourse of the national press. They also reiterate the low status of tribes who are traditionally seen as lying outside the fold of the Hindu caste system. As DD remarked, "such perceptions among journalists amounts to news apartheid. This is not talked about. They won't even accept that there is underlying racism in this."

SC said prejudices about the region and its people affected coverage of insurgencies. Human rights abuses, if they occur elsewhere and involve people from groups considered "mainstream" would trigger sustained coverage over days, but invariably go unreported and unnoticed when they occur in the northeast. As he said:

It is difficult to interest colleagues in northeast news. It is a battle. The over-riding view undoubtedly is Delhi-centric; it is the perspective of north and central India. The northeast suffers in this environment, even if there is violence there. For 20 years we had no one (correspondent) in the northeast. Sometimes the correspondent from Calcutta or Patna

218

used to cover it. Due to its complexity, the attitude of newspapers is: this is a beehive, why should we put our hands in it, why should we bother? We don't know, we don't cover.

In such an environment, on the rare occasions that news from the region is published, it is invariably marked by errors: incorrect names of state capitals or names of important tribal politicians/actors or incorrect mention of constitutional provisions for the region. According to AJP, "among journalists, there is no stake in the northeast. They often go wrong on facts; worse, nobody notices it."

The Kashmir conflict, with its relatively simpler Hindu–Muslim–Pakistan dimension, is considered "sexy" (DAT) to cover and ensures prominent exposure to journalist output. The conflicts in the northeast are numerous and complex; it is impossible to report them without basic knowledge about the kaleidoscope of tribes, religions, languages, and the plethora of constitutional and legal provisions for the region. News reporting demands that events are conveyed in a simple and easy to understand manner, which may preclude lengthy explanations. As HC, a veteran journalist who covered the northeast in the 1950s, remarked, journalists like to take the easy route by ignoring complex events and issues.

ZA, former northeast correspondent on *The Times of India*, hinted at an Orientalist frame that governed coverage of the region:

> The general attitude in newsrooms towards northeast developments is one of apathy. Since many are from states other than the northeast, they don't relate to developments there, and prefer to ignore the region. However, when it comes to what's called juicy, sexy or exotic stories, they are displayed prominently. For example, when I did a story on the matriarchal Khasi society in Meghalaya coming under pressure, it was not only used as a front-page story, it was also reproduced in *The New York Times* and the *International Herald Tribune*. One has to sell his northeast stories harder in the newsroom than stories from other regions.

The northeast has better chances of figuring on the radar of the national press if news reports are seen as "juicy, sexy, or exotic" by the Indian mainstream. There is clearly no reason to believe that the notion of Orientalism is confined only to the West–Middle East dimension. As the interview responses indicate, this sense of the "other" can also be constructed *within* the Orient.

The routine non-coverage or low coverage of the northeast in the national press adds to the local sense of ennui in the region. AB, editor of an Assamese daily, said:

> There is a complete alienation from the system. It is a chaotic situation. Secret killings are adding to the problems. The young are attracted to the rebels because they have seen the judiciary, national press, parliament; they have all failed. They choose to remain silent on our issues,

219

when so many get killed. They do not play the role they should; they are responsible for this chaotic situation here. The rulers and the intellectuals based in New Delhi have no time for us; nobody bothers. The Delhi press also supports them. At least write some facts. At least reflect 50 percent of the situation here. Now not even five percent is reflected in the Delhi press. There is no democratic reaction in other parts of the country to events happening here, because no news from here is published. They don't know, so they don't react, so no pressure is put on the government. Assam is seen as distant, as a forest area, as if people here are not civilised or cultured.

Journalists interviewed in the northeast cited several instances of major events involving much violence and killing going unreported in the national press; they even questioned the idea that the New Delhi-based press should be considered "national" in any sense of the term. One rebel sympathiser told me in some frustration that even when groups resort to terrorism to force authorities in New Delhi to take notice of sometimes legitimate grievances, there is no reaction or resonance because it goes underreported in the national press.

Insurgents often change tactics by targeting the minority Hindi-speaking people in Assam, which leads to much concern and action in New Delhi. Hindi is India's national language, and New Delhi is located in what is called the "Hindi heartland" or the "Hindi belt" of north and central India—it has the largest representation in the Indian parliament. The attacks on Hindi-speaking people attract media coverage—the latest was the killing of over 50 Hindi-speaking people in Assam in November 2003—because they amount to an attack on "us," as perceived by journalists. But other incidents of violence and terrorism usually go unreported since they do not involve the "right" people or the "right" geographies of culture.

Conclusion

If acts of violence and terrorism were so irresistibly newsworthy, as the interlocking discourses of violence/terrorism/conflict and the media suggest, the host of insurgencies in northeast India should have resonated at least as much as the single insurgency based in Kashmir, if not more. Violence and terrorism have been long privileged in the production of news, while the trope of the margins has been mostly confined to the politics of representation. Research has rarely examined the *non*-coverage of events and issues involving the minorities or the margins. This gap assumes more salience owing to the fact that the movement of men, material, and money to finance terror knows no national borders, as events in Iraq, Afghanistan, and Turkey show. If news discourse is seen as being by the elite, for the elite, and of the elite, the exclusion of minorities' life situations is likely to be institutionalized in newsrooms.

As the example of northeast India shows, even when insurgent outfits resort to terror to attract the attention of authorities to sometimes legitimate causes, their activities may not resonate in the media. Not only are most events involving violence and terrorism in the region not covered, but also, when they are, they invariably lack historical and political contexts. Within multicultural national settings, the key variable in the sustained coverage of wars and conflicts is the socio-cultural environment in which journalists operate. Reifying this in the form of the "we"–"they" binary, I suggest that only those conflicts that involve or affect the "we" are likely to be accorded sustained media attention; those affecting or involving the "they" are unlikely to figure in news discourse.

A conflict has to be consonant with the socio-cultural background of journalists for it to be deemed newsworthy. An event of terrorism or violence is first subject to the question: who is involved or who is affected? Thus, contrary to Gans' contention that during their professional work journalists "leave their conscious personal values at home" (1980: 182), I suggest that war and conflict reporting is a matter of constant tension between journalists' socio-cultural background and professional norms such as objectivity, impartiality, and fairness. As some interviewees stated, tribes in the northeast are not "people like us" or that they "do not share our way of life." As American journalist John Phillip Santos said, "The overarching challenge is to rid our journalism of any vestige of an 'us and them' attitude, of an unspoken regard of any community as 'others'" (Allan 2001: 257).

The northeast insurgencies are among the many invisible conflicts raging at this moment across the world. In an age of globalization of terror, such selectivity of news reporting can have serious implications. Professionals and media scholars need to devise ways to focus on such invisible wars and conflicts without jeopardizing commercial compulsions. Readers and television viewers need to be made aware of the many potential sources that can bring war and terror home.

References

Allan, S. (2001) *News Culture*, Buckingham: Open University Press.

Appadurai, A. (1996) *Modernity at Large: Cultural Dimensions of Globalisation*, Minneapolis, MN: University of Minnesota Press.

Billig, M. (1995) *Banal Nationalism*, London: Sage.

Bose, S. (1999) "Kashmir: sources of conflict, dimensions of peace," *Economic and Political Weekly*, March 27.

Brown, M.E. (2001) "Preface" in *Nationalism and Ethnic Conflict*, Michael E. Brown *et al.* (eds), MIT Press: Cambridge, MA.

Chenoy, A.M. (2002) "Militia mentality," *The Times of India*, September 17.

Datta, S. (2000) "Northeast turmoil: vital determinants," *Strategic Analysis*, March, vol. XXIII, no. 12, pp. 2,123–33.

Dutt, J.K. (1999) "An East Timor in India?," *The Statesman*, November 12.

Elias, N. (1994) *The Established and the Outsiders: a Sociological Enquiry into Community Problems*, London: Sage.

Elliott, W.A. (1986) *Us and Them: a Study of Group Consciousness*, Aberdeen: Aberdeen University Press.

Entman, R.M. (1991) "Framing US coverage of international news: contrasts in narratives of the KAL and Iran air incidents," *Journal of Communication*, vol. 41, no. 4, pp. 6–27.

Ganguly, S. (1996) "Explaining the Kashmir insurgency: political mobilization and institutional decay," *International Security*, vol. 21, no. 2, fall 1996.

Gans, H. (1980) *Deciding What's News*; London: Constable.

Gurr, T.R. (1993) *Minorities at Risk: a Global View of Ethnopolitical Conflicts*; United States Institute of Peace Press.

Hall, S. (1981) "The determination of news photographs," in S. Cohen and J. Young (eds), *The Manufacture of News: Deviance, Social Problems and the Mass Media*, London: Constable.

Hall, S. (1990) "The whites of their eyes: racist ideologies and the media," in M. Alvarado and J.O. Thompson (eds), *The Media Reader*, London: British Film Institute.

Hartley, J. (1992) *The Politics of Pictures: the Creation of the Public in the Age of Popular Media*, London: Routledge.

Haque, M. and Narag, S. (1983) "The coverage of two Indian Elections by three prestigious dailies," *Media Asia*, vol. 10, no. 1, pp. 35–43.

Hartman, P. and Husband, C. (1981) "The mass media and racial conflict," in S. Cohen and J. Young (eds), *The Manufacture of News: Deviance, Social Problems and the Mass Media*, London: Constable.

Hetherington, A. (1985) *News, Newspapers and Television*, London: Macmillan.

HIIK (2002) *Conflict Barometer 2002*, 11th annual conflict analysis, published by Heidelberg Institute of International Conflict Research, University of Heidelberg.

Horam, M. (1988) *Naga Insurgency*, New Delhi: Cosmo.

Jeffrey, R. (1993) "Indian language newspapers and why they grow," *Economic and Political Weekly*, vol. XXVIII, no. 38, September 18; pp. 2004–11.

Jha, P.S. (1992) "The media and the metropolis: the role of media in creating urban consciousness in Delhi," *Asian Journal of Communication*, vol. 2, no. 3, pp. 130–56.

Joshi, M. (2002) "Gujarat and the media," *The Times of India*, May 7.

Mudgal, V. (1995) "Media, State and Political Violence: the Press Construction of Terrorism in the Indian Punjab," unpublished PhD thesis, University of Leicester.

Nag, S. (2001) "Nationhood and displacement in the Indian subcontinent," *Economic and Political Weekly*, December 22.

Nossek, H. (forthcoming) "Our news and their news: the role of national identity in the coverage of foreign news," in P. Sonwalkar, A. Sreberny, and H. Nossek (eds), *News Media and Political Violence*, Cresskill, NJ: Hampton Press.

Planning Commission (1997) *Transforming the Northeast: Tackling Backlogs in Basic Minimum Services and Infrastructural Needs*, high level report to the Prime Minister, Planning Commission, Government of India, March 7.

Scherrer, C.P. (1999) "Towards a comprehensive analysis of ethnicity and mass violence: types, dynamics, characteristic and trends," in H. Wiberg and Christian P. Scherrer (eds), *Ethnicity and Intra-State Conflict: Types, Causes and Peace Strategies*, Aldershot: Ashgate.

Shils, E. (1975) *Centre and Periphery: Essays in Macrosociology*, Chicago, IL: University of Chicago Press.

Singh, B.P. (1987) *The Problem of Change: a Study of North-east India*, Delhi: Oxford University Press.

Smith, A. (1980) *The Geopolitics of Information: how Western Culture Dominates the World*, New York: OUP.

Sonwalkar, P. (2002) "'Murdochization' of the Indian press: from by-line to bottom-line," *Media, Culture and Society*, vol. 24, no. 6, pp. 821–34.

Tuchman, G. (1972) "Objectivity as strategic ritual: an examination of newsmen's notions of objectivity," *American Journal of Sociology*, vol. 77, pp. 660–79.

UMHA (2003) website of the Union Ministry of Home Affairs, Government of India, http://mha.nic.in/scen.htm accessed August 28, 2003.

Viswanath, K. and Karan, K. (2000) "India," in *Handbook of the Media in Asia*, Shelton A. Gunaratne (ed.), London: Sage.

Weimann, G. and Winn, C. (1993) *The Theatre of Terror: Mass Media and International Terrorism*, London: Longman.

Windmiller, M. (1954) "Linguistic regionalism in India," *Pacific Affairs*, vol. 27, no. 4, December 1954, pp. 291–318.

Wolfsfeld, G. (1997) *Media and Political Conflict: News From the Middle East*, Cambridge: Cambridge University Press.

12

THE BATTLEFIELD IS THE MEDIA

War reporting and the formation of national identity in Australia—from Belmont to Baghdad

Michael Bromley

In memoriam: 28 Australian journalists and newsworkers killed in combat situations, 1900–2003[1]

The invasion of Iraq by the so-called "coalition of the willing," led by the USA in March and April 2003 was arguably the most reported military conflict in history. More than 3,000 correspondents, ranging from backpack journalists working alone with wireless digital equipment to television anchors and their production crews, were assigned to cover events across the Middle East. Such intensity of focus on limited military action which, unlike the "total war" experiences of most of the twentieth century, involved non-combatant Western domestic populations only indirectly, had been building since at least the Vietnam War, reaching a previous historical peak during the earlier Gulf conflict of 1991 (Tiffen 1992b: 44). This reflected two apparently contradictory long-term general trends. On the one hand, those holding power were made more accountable to the public, and the capacity to call them to account has increased exponentially (Tiffen 1992a: 118–19). Part of this was exhibited in the extent to which public life was shaped by the routines, rituals, demands, and expectations of journalism (Blumler and Gurevitch 1996: 127–8). As a consequence, individual journalists were less easily controlled; for example, the appointment of official war correspondents, particularly during the World Wars of 1914–18 and 1939–45, and the censorship inherent in the system, foundered on the work of journalists like Wilfred Burchett, whose eye-witness account of the effects of the bombing of Hiroshima in 1945 was unsanctioned by Pacific Command, and James Cameron, who angered the British government by reporting the brutality of Republic of Korea forces during the Korean War in the 1950s.

Parallel to this growing claim to a freedom to report, the ethos and means of public communication diffused far more widely and deeply in society (Hartley

2000: 41). Thus, the myths, images, and ideas of war were shaped for the past 150 years by both highly professionalized, technocratic journalists *and* the accounts captured in letters, diaries, photographs, etc. of ordinary people (McCrum 2001). On the other hand, the management of public communication ("spin") gave rise to the notion of "the public relations state" (Deacon and Golding 1994: 5–6). States and the military tried especially to curtail journalists' freedoms in and around combat zones, and to neutralize the inquisitive, perhaps even mischievous, roving reporter, exemplified by the logistical and psychological controls exerted on British correspondents during the Falklands War in 1982 (Morrison and Tumber 1988). A system of "pooling" enforced by the US in and around the Gulf in 1991 contributed decisively to the ways in which combat was presented in the media. Moreover, the professionalization of the military worked to eliminate unofficial first-hand combatants' accounts, although not always successfully (McCrum 2001).[2] As a result, *how* wars are reported became a highly contested extension of the military action, and possibly even of greater importance than much of the combat itself, presenting "an increasingly important second front" (Tiffen 1992b: 44, 55).

Australia's involvement in the 2003 invasion of Iraq resonates with many of these broader issues. Australians (originating in white, European colonization and settlement) fashioned a sense of national identity through participation in war around the foundation of the State at the beginning of the twentieth century. Reporting and recollecting war were crucial to this project. The deployment of military personnel in 2003, therefore, had enormous potential symbolic significance, and the main mechanism for realizing this potential was the way in which Australia's journalists recorded events for the public at home. This juxtaposition of combat and the reporting of combat helped unravel the conundrum of Australia's minimum military contribution to the "coalition," and how that was massaged into a major international intervention.

Australia and the "coalition"

Australia's military participation in the invasion of Iraq was a "token" effort (Broinowski 2003: 2): the total presence—navy, air force and army together—in all of the Middle East was never more than 2,100 out of 300,000–400,000 coalition troops.[3] At least one in eight Australian forces had already been withdrawn by mid-May, and most were back in Australia a month later (Fickling 2003a).[4] The "war" was over as far as Australia was concerned when the Prime Minister, John Howard, provided ritual closure to Operation Falconer, attending street parades of returning military personnel in Sydney and Perth on June 18 and 20, and the Chief of the Australian Defence Forces (ADF) was delivering valedictories to the episode—even though both American and British troops were still dying in Baghdad and Basra.[5]

The size of the Australian military intervention in Iraq was matched by its ethereal quality. Possibly up to a third of the Australian personnel were drawn from the highly secretive, so-called special forces (Defence Ministry 2003; Marcus 2003). At the outset, Howard insisted that Australia would send no infantry or other types of "ground troops." This reflected a more general shift to a higher reliance on secretive special forces in the ADF, their numbers having doubled in the five years to 2000 (Ferguson 2003), making Australia's army more specialist and less citizen-based. "In modern warfare," Howard said in a radio interview, "a lot more can be achieved with highly mobile technologically proficient but small numbers of troops" (Radio 4BC 2003). At the same time, Australian politics have also become more controlled and secretive, and increasingly reliant on media management (Phillips 2003).[6] As a consequence, according to the former diplomat Alison Broinowski (2003: 10–11), Australians were "confused" and "unclear" about the country's involvement in the invasion of Iraq. In September, 67 percent of 1,200 people surveyed for an *Australian* newspaper poll believed that the government had misled them on the issue of Iraq's possession of WMD (a key argument in support of the invasion), and 36 percent felt that the deception was deliberate (ABC Online 2003b). Furthermore, during the actual fighting in Iraq, the Australian government and military maintained an almost total silence on operational matters.

The role of journalists in interrogating Australia's participation in this military conflict might have been expected to assume a particular importance, then. As *The Australian's* media commentator pointed out

> if journalism is the first brush stroke of history we ought to do our damnedest to get it right—and that means very deliberately *not* taking the word of governments or their agencies such as the military at face value.
>
> (Day 2003—emphasis in original)

Many Australian journalists complained that they were prevented from doing their jobs by military and civilian officials who imposed stringent restrictions on reporting (Cohen 2003; Mottram 2003). An Australian parliamentary analysis agreed that "Australians [were likely to] receive an overwhelming amount of information from American sources . . . but little information about Australia's contribution to the conflict" (Miskin, Rayner, and Lalic 2003).

The role of journalism and the media

The Australian media assigned about 60 journalists and crew to the invasion. Of these, perhaps fewer than a third actually spent time in Iraq before May 1 (Crikey.com 2003). Paul McGeough (2003), working for the Fairfax chain of newspapers, made a contested claim to being the only Australian reporter (one of between 150 and 250 foreign correspondents) to cover the entire conflict from Baghdad. Only four reporters were "embedded" with fighting units (out of about 600 journalists so accredited by the US military). About twice as many were located in the expensively-constructed Central Command media centre near Doha, Qatar, where 700 were accredited and many complained bitterly of the deficiencies of the briefings (Media Watch 2003a). Even in this climate, Australian military secretiveness seemed to be excessive (Callinan 2003). On March 31, David Marr, presenting ABC Television's Media Watch program (2003b), claimed, "there have been no reports from Australian forces in action. None." The program produced what were claimed to be the notes made by an Australian journalist during a media call with ADF pilots and crew on March 25:

> Journalist: How many pilots have we got up there?
> Pilot: A few.
> Journalist: How many missions have you flown so far?
> Pilot: Enough.
> Journalist: Are you doing air attacks or flying in a support role?
> Pilot: Both.
> Journalist: Can you expand on that?
> Pilot: No.
>
> (Media Watch 2003e)

A majority of Australian correspondents and their news crews were actually scattered elsewhere in the Middle East—"distant from the action . . . milling about" (Wright 2003). The most prolific sources of information on Australia's involvement in Iraq were said to be the military briefings taking place in the Australian federal capital, Canberra. The popular Australian perspective on the invasion of Iraq is likely to have been impacted, therefore, not just by the media per se (Keeble 1997), but by the media operating at a considerable distance from any direct experience of Australian participation (a dimension perhaps captured in Nicholson's cartoon—see Figure 12.1).

The invasion of Iraq appeared to many Australians to be no more than a "symbolic war," therefore (George Munster Forum 2003). In this way, it was fought in the Australian media as much as, if not in some ways more than, on the ground. As international tension mounted early in 2003, a former editor-in-chief of the Sydney Morning Herald newspaper identified the media and journalism as equally culpable with politics for widespread public cynicism and disbelief, which could be countered only by journalism based on "moral courage" (Bowman 2003). Yet the media seemed predisposed to only one view of the conflict. Roy Greenslade's (2003) revelation that all 175 newspapers owned by the global media proprietor Rupert Murdoch, including seven of the 12 national and metro dailies in Australia, espoused editorially his personal support for the invasion of Iraq, was widely cited in Australia (Jackson 2003a).

Figure 12.1 "So this is what war is really like!" Nicholson cartoon for *The Australian*, March 20, 2003 (courtesy of the artist)

The Australian media

Australia's media are arguably the most oligopolized in the Western world (Pilger 2002; Simms 2002). They are predominantly owned by three corporations, Murdoch's News Limited, Fairfax, and Kerry Packer's Publishing and Broadcasting Limited (PBL). This hyper-concentration of ownership and control has been associated with forms of tabloidization, curtailing the capacity of Australian newspaper journalism to provide "an accurate, timely, high quality, engaging, unbiased and uninterested [*sic*] flow of information and ideas" Hilmer (2001). Overseas reporting appears to have been particularly affected by this. Peter Manning, a former director of news and current affairs at the Channel 7 television network, has complained of a failure to consistently report international events, and of a lack of analytical depth in such journalism (*The Media Report* 2001), while the *Sydney Morning Herald* journalist and former foreign correspondent, Christopher Kremmer, noted in October 2002 the reliance placed by the Australian media on overseas media to supply them with foreign news (George Munster Forum 2002). From 1990, particularly in television, the emphasis in international coverage has been on "soft" stories (Putnis 1996: 2). Quantifiable declines in foreign correspondence have been difficult to demonstrate, although van Druten (2003: 1, 41–50, 56, 64–5) traced the reduction of the ABC's staffing in Europe over a decade from eight correspondents and two producers to four correspondents, and from December 2003, to three correspondents.

Newspapers

In 2000 News Limited controlled 68 percent of major daily newspaper circulations, nearly 60 percent of Saturday papers sold, more than three-quarters of Sunday sales, almost half of the market in suburban weekly newspapers, and nearly a quarter of the regional press. Fairfax newspapers accounted for 21.5 percent of the major daily sales, more than a quarter of Saturday circulations, nearly a quarter of Sunday sales, 18 percent of the suburban press, and 15 percent of regional papers. Only three other companies (APN News and Media and Rural Press with 30 percent and 15 percent respectively of regional sales, and West Australian Newspaper Holdings with about 10 percent of both the metro daily and suburban markets) have significant press holdings, which in total amount to sales of no more than about 1.35 million of about 13 million newspapers sold (2–3 million national and metropolitan dailies, 620,000 regional dailies, 3.5 million Sundays, and 6.4 million suburban titles). Although concentration of ownership and control has been a feature of the Australian press since the second decade of the twentieth century, the trend accelerated markedly after the mid-1980s. Between 1987 and 2000 News Limited alone closed ten newspapers (Lewis 2001: 101–6).

Television

PBL runs Channel 9, Australia's largest national television network, with more than a 30 percent share of the free-to-air audience, and nearly a quarter of all television audiences. PBL also operates three metropolitan and one regional television licenses (Cassar 2003). Australian television is dominated by three free-to-air commercial services which in mid-April 2003 accounted for 77.4 percent of prime time audiences, and more than two-thirds of all viewing (source: OzTAM in Jackson 2003c). Channel 7 (controlled by Kerry Stokes) and Channel 10 (the Canadian conglomerate CanWest) each has about a quarter of the free-to-air audience and a fifth of all television audiences. PBL and News Limited share equally a half stake in the main paid-for television supplier, Foxtel, and PBL has a 33 percent share of News' subscription service, Sky News (Given 2000: 43–5; Cassar 2003). In 2003, pay-TV had about 13 percent of the 24-hour viewing audience (Murphy 2003b). The ABC, based on the BBC model, and the Special Broadcasting Service, a public service oriented multicultural and multilingual broadcaster introduced in 1980, share about a fifth of prime-time television audiences (16 percent and 4 percent respectively), and 17 percent of the 24-hour audience. This situation has provoked some to ask whether public service television in Australia is "an endangered species" (Jacka 2000).

Eighty percent of Australians get their news from television, and more from the Channel 9 network than any other source (Flew 2002: 177). Editions of *National Nine News* regularly head the ratings (with audiences of around 2 million), and the *60 Minutes* current affairs program is routinely in the top 10.

Nevertheless, since the late 1980s there has been "a major and potentially catastrophic decline in network news and current affairs audiences" (Turner 2001: 56). These shows have been positioned as commercial "flagship formats" built on prioritizing the credibility of personality presenters rather than investments in news gathering, and on tabloidization (Turner 2000: 91–2). All the same, there is evidence that crises (such as the invasion of Iraq) temporarily boost ABC news viewing (Tiffen 1991: 10–11; Jackson 2003c).

Radio

The main owners control more than three-quarters of radio broadcasting over 250 commercial stations (Miller and Turner 2002: 145). Austereo, the largest commercial radio broadcaster in Australia operating two national networks each with five stations, is also the biggest outside the US (see www.austereo.com.au). The British newspaper and broadcast company, DMGT, has 63 radio stations in Australia (see www.dmgt.co.uk), while the Australian Radio Network (12 stations) is part of APN (see www.apn.com.au). All three have various partnership arrangements with the US Clear Channel company. The conglomerates have been heavily criticized for cutting costs, cutting jobs, and cutting news to the extent of sacrificing "public interest objectives [such] as plurality, diversity and competition [which are essential] in order to ensure a free, vigorous and independent media sector" (IRB 1999). Music formats predominate, but "talkback" radio has considerable currency: journalists and news producers rank it among the four most important news and current affairs services—in part because it is viewed as "a broader litmus test of community opinion" (Pearson and Brand 2001). Attempts to dismantle the ABC's radio news and current affairs service failed in the late 1990s (Miller and Turner 2002: 144). In 2003 ABC operated a range of about 50 national, regional, and local stations, including Radio National and NewsRadio (Dunn 2001).

Magazines

The five largest magazine publishers control more than 80 percent of audited sales; the top two alone nearly 70 percent. PBL, through its subsidiary Australian Consolidated Press, has 45 titles with sales of more than 53 million—nearly 50 percent of the market. Stokes' Pacific Publications (9 titles) accounts for 21.5 percent. The smallest of the "big five," Murdoch Magazines (3 titles) has a 2.4 percent share (Jackson 2003e).

In sum, the mainstream Australian mediascape amounts to a carve-up, favoring a small coterie of commercial operators. Griffen-Foley (2003) in particular has traced a close, at times corrupt, relationship between Australian politicians and the country's powerful patrician commercial media. This situation has been characterized by a general, and perhaps unsurprising, lack of journalistic independence, or editorial vigor—the modest supposed exceptions being a brief, and ultimately largely unsuccessful, attempt between the late 1960s and the mid-1970s to assert "professional standards of integrity" over the growing partisanship and self-interestedness of the less than a handful of key media proprietors, and a more vigorous pursuit of "the Fourth Estate role of the news media" between 1980 and the mid-1990s (see also Schultz 1998: 195–229). Of all the media, newspapers seem to exercise the most influence on public views of politics with television some way behind, and talkback radio a further distance off. Surveying so-called Middle Australia, Pusey (2003: 127–32) concluded that media audiences were more or less polarized between those who valued a critical, independent Fourth Estate operating in the public realm, and those who turned to the media for projections of their own social prejudices, resentments, and private anxieties. Responding to suggestions that politicians had lied to justify the invasion of Iraq, a British correspondent wrote that Australians preferred "to concentrate on their desire for good times" (Fickling 2003b).

Journalism's performance during the Iraq invasion

These factors suggest at least a partial dissolution of the traditional role of journalism in Australia from primarily agenda-setting into a "smiling profession" (Hartley 1992: 119–39; Hartley 2000: 44–5). Yet journalists have generally found it difficult to acknowledge that they share a "common moral nexus" with not only a public whose access to and controls over social communication have increased but also with the now ubiquitous public relations industry (Hargreaves 2003: 204). To mainstream journalists, PR is a duplicitous way of, at best, wrapping the truth in a "bodyguard of lies," at worst, brutalizing through propaganda (Rampton and Stauber 2003). In this context, the invasion of Iraq could be couched in terms of a PR exercise pursued by the government (Spearritt 2003)—even "a propaganda game" (Pilger 2003), in which military misinformation tactics were cynically deployed (*Media Watch* 2003i). Set against the backdrop of an oligopoly of commercial media ownerships with a uniform ideological agenda, the State's news management strategies, and governmental and military impediments to information gathering, journalists were constrained to privilege only one, jingoistic version of events, predominantly "channelling and echoing . . . the official viewpoint" (Borman cited in Franklin 2003). Only three of the 12 national and metropolitan daily newspapers (the *West Australian*, *Canberra Times* and *Sydney Morning Herald*) countenanced any opposition editorially to the invasion (*Media Watch* 2003d).

That charge had been leveled at the commercial media during the previous US-led invasion of Iraq in 1991, in which Australian forces had also participated (Tiffen 1992a: 114). Indeed, in this regard, the events of 2003 were something of a re-run of those of 12 years before. On both occasions accusations of bias—in these instances *against* the coalition—were made against the ABC, too (Tiffen 1991; Uechtritz 2003a, 2003b). Perhaps having learnt from their experiences in 1991, the media seemed less inclined to sanitize armed conflict, however, by masking human suffering—at least to the extent that the Australian government felt that media coverage in 2003 had dwelt too much on "the awfulness of the war" (Dodson 2003b). One commentator observed that "nearly non-stop live television of a kind never seen before" was delivering "footage . . . of the battle for Iraq [which] is so pore-close, graphic and in-spite-of-yourself compelling it has been dubbed 'war porn'" (Jackson 2003b). Events in 2003, no less and possibly more, than in 1991, were subjected to "saturation coverage"—from SMS text news messages supplied to mobile phones by Channel 9 to the post-war recollections of The (Melbourne) Age newspaper's journalistic team published as a colour supplement. In the first four days of fighting, Channel 9 aired 56 hours of coverage, and the ABC 41 hours (Agenda 2003; Media Watch 2003c). Several newspapers published special editions, the Sydney Daily Telegraph, for one, even temporarily resurrecting its otherwise defunct afternoon edition (Meade and Brook 2003).

Viewerships for television news reportedly rose immediately on the afternoon of March 20 by between 22 percent (ABC) and 196 percent (SBS) over the previous week. Channels 9 and 7 posted 64 percent and 58 percent rises respectively, although their prime time evening newscasts had more modest increases of 12–13 percent. SBS's evening bulletin audiences rose by 15 percent and 30 percent and those for the morning shows the following day (Sunrise on Channel 7 and Today on Channel 9) by 30 percent combined. However, the stations began to return to their normal schedules after the first week of fighting, and most of the gains were lost, except by the ABC (Murphy 2003a). Tens of thousands of extra copies of the major newspapers were printed during the opening days of the conflict, but it was difficult to determine whether these captured additional readers: over the 12-month audit period including March and April, readerships remained mostly static (Jackson 2003d). By early April, 62 percent of a sample of the Australian population surveyed felt that there had been too much media coverage, and only 3 percent that there had been too little (Dodson 2003b).

Debates about the quantity of journalism are almost inextricably tied, however, to both assessments of the quality of journalism and to the technologies of news. Tiffen (1992a: 139) makes the point that the earlier military action in Iraq represented something of a turning-point in these respects in Australia as the ADF had not been in combat since the Vietnam War. Satellite communications, allied to intense market competition, among other factors, made feasible in 1991 on-demand "real time" broadcasting from multiple locations and sources. The same combination of factors which enhanced journalists' capacities to monitor governments also increased the cost advantages of relying on generic, pre-packaged internationally syndicated feeds, however. The system of "pooling" enforced by the US in 1991 angered many journalists, and excluded all those from Australia (Tiffen 1992a: 117ff; Miskin, Rayner, and Lalic 2003). Similar anxieties were expressed about the system of embedding journalists with US military units in 2003, and the role of the Doha media centre, which Australian correspondents nicknamed Operation Mushrooms because they suspected that its real purpose was to keep them in the dark (Callinan 2003). Australian journalists working outside closely accredited assignments (known colloquially as "unilaterals") were far more numerical—and more vulnerable in what was described as a conflict that was of greater danger to journalists than it was to soldiers (Byrne 2003). The camera operator Paul Moran, working for the ABC, was killed on March 23 in northern Iraq in a bomb attack. News Limited's correspondent Ian McPhedran was later expelled from Baghdad by the Iraqis. McGeough reflected that the Pentagon, too, did not "like the foreign press being in Baghdad. They spoke about us quite contemptuously as 'the independents'" (*The Media Report* 2003).

These factors appear to be constitutive of a longer-term trend evident in Australian journalism, in which reporting from the field, especially overseas, has been in decline in favor of informed analysis and comment, often originated domestically and produced locally (Tiffen 1992a: 119, 139). Notwithstanding general continuing developments in these areas (notably, but not exclusively, digitization), it may be conjectured that as far as Australian journalism was concerned, the changes apparent in 2003, compared to 1991, were fewer, and less significant, than those which Tiffen noted occurred between 1965 and 1991. Both the scope and scale of journalism produced in March and April 2003 are far too great to sample comprehensively with any degree of reliability at this temporal proximity. Nevertheless, some aspects of the coverage may be gauged from a more or less impressionistic snapshot analysis of the main newspapers, television, and radio.

Television not only made extensive use of satellite-based communications (notably the videophone) for "live" reporting feeds, wholesale news exchanges, and studio links (Jenkins 2003; Wilson 2003), but also broadcast direct and sometimes uninterrupted the output of a variety of American and British news organizations, such as the BBC, ITN, Sky, PBS, NBC, and CNN, piggybacking on the greater US and UK news investments. Australian news organizations also made considerable use of the Internet, trawling the Web chiefly to check on what other media around the world were publishing and broadcasting (Vermeer 2003). The reporting of the relatively small number of Australian journalists in the field was thus heavily supplemented by material emanating from the far larger corps of American and British journalists and crews assigned to the story worldwide, but captured and/or edited locally. At the same time, ABC's *Lateline* program particularly, but not exclusively, utilized satellite links for extended studio-based analyses and commentaries. Media demand for expert domestic input was at times "almost unquenchable" with the Strategic and Defence Studies Centre at the Australian National University holding briefings daily for the first 16 days of the conflict and more intermittently thereafter. "We were essentially shaping the news," said the organizer (Hull 2003). In this way, major international events were substantively domesticated.

Even so, the demand for actuality of Australian involvement on the ground was so great that it offered the Defence Ministry opportunities to "spin" misleading coverage. SBS, Channel 7 and Channel 10, as well as the *Daily Telegraph*, reproduced Ministry images of Australian commandos "deep behind enemy lines"

(Channel 7), which turned out to have been from a photo-shoot staged during preparations three days before the invasion began (*Media Watch* 2003f). Such duplicity was occasionally matched by the media themselves: *Media Watch* (2003g) reported that the Channel 7 current affairs show *Today Tonight* edited stock footage from Iraq with a report by correspondent David Richardson to purport to show him having penetrated "into the unknown" when he had merely walked ten metres into the demilitarized zone on the Kuwaiti border. Later both the *Daily Telegraph* and the weekly news magazine *Bulletin* held to the story that an American flag wrapped by US Marines around a statue of Saddam Hussein in Baghdad had been recovered from the debris of the Pentagon following the terrorist attack of 9/11, when it had been purchased for $9 US from the US Senate gift shop (*Media Watch* 2003j, 2003k).

Tabloidization

Debates about both the processes and effects of tabloidization have been a feature of and around the Australian media for about 20 years (see Turner 2001). A sample of the presentation of the opening days of the conflict in a number of newspapers provides a sense of how the Australian press negotiated the challenges of engaging their audiences. On March 21 (the first full day of the invasion in Australian time), the tabloid-sized, but otherwise "serious," *Australian Financial Review* wrapped its usual Monday–Friday five-column, type-dominated front page with a poster "lift-off" showing gun-carrying troops silhouetted against a fiery orange and yellow sky. The main headline was simply "WAR." The tabloid *Daily Telegraph*, identifying for its readers the "MOMENT THE WAR BEGAN," published a similar poster front page of a photograph of a missile exploding over Baghdad above the headline "GET SADDAM." On March 23, the tabloid Brisbane *Sunday Mail* used a double-page poster wrap around the newspaper to carry a picture of the presidential palace in Baghdad erupting in flames "as cruise missiles find their target with deadly accuracy." The headline was "AWESTRUCK." The following day, in a "SPECIAL WAR EDITION" the front page of the broadsheet *Australian* was dominated by a half-page photograph of a British marine firing a guided missile at an Iraqi position. The rest of the page was taken up by text, and the main headline was a more sober "IRAQ FIGHTS BACK." In Broinowski's view (2003: 111–12), however, the otherwise measured *Australian* approached the invasion with a surprising degree of zealotry. Other News Limited papers offered readers facilities for sending messages to "our troops": the Brisbane *Courier-Mail's* service remained available on the paper's website in early October (www.couriermail.news.com.au). On the other hand, tabloidization also provided occasional relief from the chorus: on the day the rest of the press reported the attack on Baghdad, the main story in the *Northern Territory News* in Darwin was "Topless woman attacks picnic" (*Media Watch* 2003h).

The use of "our" (usually in conjunction with "troops") was commonplace in television, especially on Channels 7 and 10. The ABC's Geoff Thompson apologized for using "we" while reporting on US forces (Meade and Brook 2003). The executive producer of Channel 9's *Sunday* program acknowledged that "News judgments may occasionally have been skewed by the desire to support 'our troops'" (Rice 2003: 12). Giving the news a distinctive Australian slant was taken to be a high priority in television—even at SBS. Iraq's time zone meant that many events were better scheduled for the lighter morning news shows, however. Substantial numbers of Australians used pay-TV services, with BBC World, CNBC, Sky News, CNN, and Fox News audience levels doubling or more (Matthew 2003). Giving Australian journalism a "distinction" grade, Rice (2003: 12) nevertheless indicated the traps into which television coverage could—and sometimes did—fall:

> What passes for reportage is more often live-action commentary over near-raw footage, interspersed by dubious military claims and unsourced rumours. We're hypnotized by fuzzy images of armoured columns racing across the desert; by green-hued firefights that deliver plenty of muzzle-flash but no blood; by video-phone links that promise reality but deliver a strangely disconnected view of the war. If the purpose of journalism is to give context, then this is its antithesis.

The way in which the invasion was handled by the ABC's major networked radio news program AM raised the most visible debate. The Communications Minister Richard Alston (2003a) produced a 68-point document detailing complaints against the program which included allegations of exaggeration, "gratuitous barbs," jumping to negative conclusions, mockery, dismissiveness, trivialization, cynicism, put-downs, "putting the boot in," taking sides, "immature and irrelevant abuse," "unreasonableness, scoffing, making furious attacks," sarcasm, derision, vitriol, contempt, and using "strong and pejorative" language—all directed against the US and the coalition. The corporation's head of news and current affairs had referred to the military as "lying bastards" during an international conference eight months previously (Alston 2003b). The Media, Entertainment, and Arts Alliance, which includes the Australian Journalists' Association, condemned Alston for trying to influence news coverage (ABC Online 2003a). An internal inquiry by the ABC, while admitting that in two instances AM reports had been sarcastic and "excessive," generally cleared the program of bias. "Overall, I believe our coverage of the conflict was balanced and delivered in a professional manner upholding the standards of objective journalism," the ABC's managing director said (News.com.au 2003).

War correspondence and Australian identity

On March 27, the regional daily *Gold Coast Bulletin* devoted its front page to a single orange-hued photograph of out-of-focus and unidentifiable soldiers, with the headline "Diggers in hand-to-hand combat." Readers were referred to a hazy account on page 7 supposedly of Australian SAS troops in combat. The term "digger," meaning a soldier, was applied to members of the Australian New Zealand Army Corps (ANZAC) of World War I. A mythology surrounding the ANZACs arose out of the landings on the Gallipoli Peninsula in Turkey on April 25, 1915, which "helped to provide Australians with a new sense of identity and their place in the world" (ANZAC Commemoration Committee 2003). A military blunder which claimed thousands of lives, the landings were seen as a proving-ground for "the ideals of courage and sacrifice and the principles of mateship that distinguish and unite all Australians" (Veterans Support and Advocacy Service 2003). This interpretation remains current chiefly through the annual commemoration of Anzac Day as "Australia's sacred day." The term "digger" draws on a conceptualization of the typical Australian as a bushman (a native-born pastoral worker in the physically huge and often environmentally hostile and isolated hinterland), which was "embalmed as a national myth" during the closing decades of the nineteenth century, and transferred to Australia's citizen-soldiers in World War I (Ward 1958: 196, 212–20). "The Anzacs . . . were portrayed as belonging to a new, vigorous race from the Great South Land, grown strong through generations of combat with the Australian bush" (Gerster 1987: 2).

Mediation was crucial to the process through, initially, the reporting of war, and subsequently the remembrance of war in photographs, memorials, fiction, painting, poetry, art, ephemera, public lectures, and both oral and written histories, and in determining the connections with the bushman image, and the establishment of the Federal State of Australia in 1901 and of Australian identity (Gerster 1987; Vidal nd). Journalists were key figures in creating war narratives; not only reporting from the battlefields, but also collecting and shaping the recollections of soldiers, producing histories, and fictionalizing accounts of war.

> the stories we have told each other about Australians at war are powerful and resonant. They endure in the national mind. And they were, in the main, first told by war correspondents.
>
> There is no permanent archive or exhibition in any Australian institution which does justice to the extraordinary record of this distinguished band of Australians whose contribution to understanding our history goes far beyond their dispatches from the front.
>
> . . . Few other countries can boast news men and women of such renown who have involved themselves in reporting war to the world and have, at the same time, exerted such a singular influence on their own country's political, cultural and literary traditions.
>
> (Rees 2002)

While this tradition can be traced back at least to the work of A.B. "Banjo" Paterson, a notable devotee and promoter of the bush who reported on the Boer War for two Australian newspapers (Gerster 1987: 17–18), two journalists stand out in this regard. C.E.W. Bean, as Australia's first official war correspondent, accompanied the ANZACs to Gallipoli. Following the evacuation, he compiled *The Anzac Book* from soldiers' writings and illustrations. He later supervised the publication of *The Official History of Australia in the War of 1914–18*, writing six volumes himself, and he was instrumental in the establishment of the national war memorial in Canberra. Bean is widely credited with having created the ANZAC "digger" myth (see *The Media Report* 2002). George Johnston, a corre-spondent during World War II, helped construct a similar, linked, if somewhat weaker, mythology around the Australian defence along the Kokoda Trail in New Guinea through not only his reporting but also his non-fictional *Australia at War* (1942) and his novel *My Brother Jack* (Sekuless 1999: 91–3). This novel was not published until 1964; it was almost immediately made into a television drama series by the ABC, by which time Anzac Day was beginning to look like an anachronism. In the 1960s, Alan Seymour's play *The One Day of the Year* was intended to demonstrate "the essential hollowness of the Anzac Day maunder-ings": one of its main characters dismissed the commemoration as "a great meaningless booze-up" (Stewart 2001; Henderson 2002). Starting with the 75th anniversary of the Gallipoli landings in 1990, however, successive Australian governments have consciously revalidated the ANZAC myth (Kirk 2000).

During the referendum on republican status in 1999, one monarchist govern-ment minister invoked "the Crown which was with us at Gallipoli, the Crown which was with us at Kokoda" (Zin and Campbell 1999). When in 2001 Aus-tralia celebrated the centenary of its federation, attempts were made to cement strong links with the "digger" myth (Irving 2001). The government commis-sioned an eight-part television series, *Australians at War*, shown on ABC, and the Channel 10 television network broadcast a remade serialization of *My Son Jack*. In 2002 and 2003 two new popular accounts of *The Spirit of Kokoda* and *The Spirit of the Digger* written by the former journalist Patrick Lindsay were published. This version of the Anzac myth has not been uncontested, however: it has been denounced as "an historical hypocrisy" in its affirmation of a sectarian (white, European) racist construct (Clark 2002). Nevertheless, by April 2003 a revised "contemporary meaning of the Anzac legend" seemed to have emerged (Hender-son 2003). In many respects, this reflected the original, pre-ANZAC orientation of Australians, when in 1901 "Newspaper reports [from the Boer War] of heroism, danger, and loyalty captured the imagination . . . in a manner that the federation issue never could" (Fitzgerald 2002: 34). Military adventures overseas, it has been argued, have tended to galvanize Australians as politics at home have not (Reynolds 1999: 180–2). Given these circumstances, Australian journalists have been made aware of the critical importance of adopting "the appropriate emo-tional tone and orientation of war reporting" (Tiffen 1992b: 47).

Conclusion

Since the 1990s politicians have contested the right to lay claim to "the Aus-tralian legend with its working-class roots in egalitarianism, mateship, the fair go and practical improvisation" embedded in the ANZAC myth (Kelly 2003). In April 2003, trying to counteract opposition to Australia's participation in the invasion of Iraq, Howard again appealed to this collective memory. As one of Australia's leading political journalists observed, "The focus is purely the love and pride Australian have for the military men and women who have in the past created the Anzac spirit, the Gallipoli legend and, more than anything else, framed our national identity" (Dodson 2003a). Journalism and the media appear to have been crucial in substantiating this. For example, tracing the performance of New Zealand television in recording and interpreting the 85th anniversary of Gallipoli, Hoar (2000) found a privileging of traditional versions of the story, of continuity in constructions of national identity, of evocative imagery, and of an emotional style of presentation.

This suggests that the cooptation of journalism, including war reporting, on behalf of the imagined nation of "diggers," and the historical and cultural power ascribed to such "first brush stokes of history," may have done more to shape representations of Australian involvement in the invasion of Iraq than even the muscle of media moguls, or the media management practices of government alone. If that is so, then the importance of the Australian military effort lay not in its meagre material presence but in its symbolic aura, and the ways in which journalism and the media could be relied on to invoke and evoke in response the myth of the "digger" as a potentially universal rallying-point for Australians.

Notes

1 Figure published by the CEW Bean Foundation.
2 During the invasion of Iraq weblogs were used by some military personnel to post public communication on the worldwide web, and more utilized email for private correspondence. Because of the sheer volume of the material, this chapter does not address either blogs or websites.
3 Accurate statistics on military deployments in and around Iraq in 2003 were notoriously difficult to come by. The Australian government always used the word "about" as a qualifier. The figures used here are the most reliable available, but should still be approached with caution. See the Defence Ministry (2003) Web pages devoted to Operation Falconer.
4 Estimates varied from 70 Australian troops on the ground in Iraq to 800 stationed in the region in August 2003 (see Banham 2003).
5 Australian news workers also continued to die. At the beginning of July the Australian sound recordist for the US television network NBC, Jeremy Little, was wounded in a grenade attack in Fallujah. He died in hospital in Germany just over a week later (*The Mercury*, 2003).
6 Marr and Wilkinson (2003) trace the censorship, secrecy, and misinformation originating with the Australian government associated with the so-called Children Overboard affair in 2001.

References

ABC Online (2003a) "MEAA condemns Alston's 'intimidation' of ABC" (nd), posted at www.abc.net.au/news accessed October 6, 2003.

ABC Online (2003b) "Most Australians feel misled on Iraq: poll" (September 24), posted at www.abc.net.au/news/ accessed September 24, 2003.

Agenda (2003) "Iraq: stories from the front line," *The Age* (June), pp. 1–7.

Alston, R. (2003a) Minister for Communications, Information Technology and the Arts, media release (May 28), posted as "Alston seeks urgent investigation into AM's Iraq coverage" at www.dcita.gov.au accessed October 6, 2003.

Alston, R. (2003b) "'Analysis of the AM program's Iraq coverage" (May 30), posted as "Alston attacks ABC coverage of Iraq war," AustralianPolitics, at www.australianpolitics.com.au/news accessed October 6, 2003.

ANZAC Commemoration Committee (2003) "Gallipoli," posted at www.anzacday.org.au accessed June 13, 2003.

Banham, C. (2003) "Security force lifts troop numbers to 1000," *Sydney Morning Herald* (May 2), posted at www.smh.com.au accessed August 22, 2003.

Blumler, J. and Gurevitch, M. (1996) "Media, change and social change: linkages and junctures" in J. Curran and M. Gurevitch (eds) *Mass Media and Society*, 2nd edition, London: Arnold, pp. 127–8.

Bowman, D. (2003) "The Fourth Estate: war and moral courage," Australian Policy Online (January 1), posted at www.apo.org accessed September 29, 2003.

Broinowski, A. (2003) *Howard's War*, Melbourne: Scribe Books.

Byrne, C. (2003) "Watchdog condemns Iraq deaths," *The Guardian* (May 2), posted at www.media.guardian.co.uk accessed September 9, 2003.

Callinan, R. (2003) "Secret service," *The Australian Media* (April 3–9), p. 4.

Cassar, E. (2003) "Government granting content control to media proprietors," Guidomedia.com at www.guidomedia.com.au/erincassar.html accessed November 5, 2003.

Clark, A. (2002) untitled, "The first annual Dymphna Clark lecture," Manning Clark House (March 2), posted at www.manningclark.org/papers/DClecture-2002.html accessed November 7, 2003.

Cohen, D. (2003) "Look back in wonder," *The Walkley Magazine*, vol. 22, p. 40.

Crikey.com (2003) "Australian journalists in the war zone" (March 24), posted at www.crikey.com.au/media accessed September 10, 2003.

Day, M. (2003) "Lies, damn lies and governments," *The Australian Media* (June 5–11), p. 6.

Deacon, D. and Golding, P. (1994) *Taxation and Representation: the Media, Political Communication and the Poll Tax*, London: John Libbey.

Defence Ministry (2003) *Disarmament of Iraq: Operation Falconer*, posted at www.defence.gov.au/opcatalyst accessed September 30, 2003.

Dodson, L. (2003a) "Uniting Australia, the PM's greatest challenge," *The Age* (March 21), posted at www.theage.com.au accessed June 19, 2003.

Dodson, L. (2003b) "Howard doesn't like what the media shows us," *The Age* (April 4), posted at www.theage.com.au/articles accessed September 1, 2003.

Dunn, A. (2001) "What have you done for us lately?: public service broadcasting and its audiences" in M. Bromley (ed.), *No News is Bad News: Radio, Television and the Public*, Harlow: Longman, pp. 210–18.

Ferguson, P. (2003) "Our busiest soldiers," *The Australian Business* (June 21), p. 27.

Fickling, D. (2003a) "Australia criticised for troops pullout," *The Guardian* (April 18), posted at www.guardian.co.uk accessed September 15, 2003.

Fickling, D. (2003b) "Spinning out of control," *The Guardian* (June 16), posted at www.guardian.co.uk accessed September 15, 2003.

Fitzgerald, R. (2002) *The Federation Mirror: Queensland 1901–2001*, St Lucia: University of Queensland Press.

Flew, T. (2002) "Television and pay TV" in S. Cunningham and G. Turner (eds), *The Media and Communications in Australia*, St Leonards NSW: Allen and Unwin, pp. 173–87.

Franklin, M. (2003) "Foreign correspondent's view of Iraq," posted at www.reportage. uts.edu.au accessed September 29, 2003.

George Munster Forum (2002) "Did September 11 dull journalists' critical faculties?" Australian Centre for Independent Journalism, University of Technology, Sydney (October 8), posted at http://journalism.uts.edu.au/acij/forums accessed October 23, 2002.

George Munster Forum (2003) "Reporting the *symbolic war*: intelligence sources and journalists," Australian Centre for Independent Journalism, University of Technology, Sydney (September 19). Broadcast in *Big Ideas*, ABC Radio National (September 28), posted at www.abc.net.au/rn/bigidea/stories/s951897.htm accessed September 29, 2003.

Gerster, R. (1987) *Big-noting: the Heroic Theme in Australian War Writing*, Melbourne: Melbourne University Press.

Given, J. (2000) "Commercial networks: still the ones?" in G. Turner and S. Cunningham (eds), *The Australian TV Book*, St Leonards, NSW: Allen and Unwin, pp. 35–51.

Greenslade, R. (2003) "Their master's voice," *Media Guardian* (February 17), posted at www.media.guardian.co.uk accessed September 15, 2003.

Griffen-Foley, B. (2003) *Party Games: Australian Politicians and the Media from War to Dismissal*, Melbourne: The Text Publishing Company.

Hargreaves, I. (2003) *Journalism: Truth or Dare?*, Oxford: Oxford University Press.

Hartley, J. (1992) *The Politics of Pictures: the Creation of the Public in the Age of Popular Media*, London: Routledge.

Hartley, J. (2000) "Communication democracy in a reactional society: the future of journalism studies," *Journalism: Theory, Practice and Criticism*, vol. 1, no. 1, pp. 39–48.

Henderson, G. (2002) "Anzac Day: an unfinished story," *The Age* (April 23), posted at www.theage.com.au accessed October 8, 2003.

Henderson, G. (2003) "Crean runs afoul of new patriotism," The Sydney Institute (April 29), posted at www.thesydneyinstitute.com.au accessed October 9, 2003.

Hilmer, F. (2001) "The media industry in Australia: public policy choices," A.N. Smith Memorial Lecture, University of Melbourne (October 30). Excerpts posted at www.fxj.com.au accessed November 4, 2002.

Hoar, P. (2000) "Live from Chunk Bair: new media/old media and Gallipoli mythology," posted at www.greatwar.org.nz accessed June 19, 2003.

Hull, C. (2003) "Thirst for information," *Quarterly Bulletin*, vol. 4, no. 2, Research School of Pacific and Asian Studies, Australian National University, posted at htpp//: rspas.anu.edu/qb/articles accessed September 1, 2003.

IRB (1999) submission by the Australian Association of Independent Regional Broadcasters (IRB) to the Productivity Commission Broadcasting Inquiry.

Irving, H. (2001) "Tragic choice for a national myth," *The Australian* (April 27), posted at www.theaustralian.news.com.au accessed June 19, 2003.

Jacka, E. (2000) "Public service TV: an endangered species?" in G. Turner and S. Cunningham (eds), *The Australian TV Book*, St Leonards, NSW: Allen and Unwin, pp. 52–68.

Jackson, S. (2003a) "Pushing their opinions," *The Australian Media* (February 27–March 5), pp. 4–5.

Jackson, S. (2003b) "'War porn' obscures the gruesome truth," *The Australian Media* (April 3–9), p. 5.

Jackson, S. (2003c) "ABC news wins the viewing war," *The Australian Media* (April 10–16), p. 12.

Jackson, S. (2003d) "News posts best readership gains," *The Australian Media* (August 28–September 3), p. 12.

Jackson, S. (2003e) "The top five magazine groups increase their dominance," *The Australian Media* (November 6–12), p. 10.

Jenkins, C. (2003) "Real-time view from the eye of the storm," *The Australian Media* (April 3–9), p. 6.

Keeble, R. (1997) *Secret State, Silent Press*, Luton: University of Luton Press.

Kelly, P. (2003) "How PM stole a legend," *The Australian* (August 9), posted at www.theaustralian.news.com.au accessed October 9, 2003.

Kirk, A. (2000) "John Howard to visit Gallipoli," AM, ABC local radio (April 22), transcript posted at www.abc.net.au/am accessed October 9, 2003.

Lewis, K. (2001) "Pluralism in the Australian print media," *AsiaPacific Media Educator*, vol. 11, pp. 100–12.

McCrum, R. (2001) "War without witnesses," *The Observer* (October 28), posted at www.guardian.co.uk accessed November 5, 2003.

McGeough, P. (2003) *In Baghdad: a Reporter's War*, Crows Nest, NSW: Allen and Unwin.

Marcus, J. (2003) "Analysis: Australia's military role in Iraq," BBC News (March 14), posted at http://news.bbc.co.uk accessed September 30, 2003.

Marr, D. and Wilkinson, M. (2003) *Dark Victory*, Crows Nest, NSW: Allen and Unwin.

Matthew, P. (2003) "Of war and media," posted at www.bandt.com.au/ articles/ f1/ 0c0158f1.asp accessed October 5, 2003.

Meade, A. and Brook, S. (2003) 'Deadly theatre of war," *The Australian Media* (March 27–April 2), pp. 4–5.

The Media Report (2001) "How well are we served by foreign correspondents?," ABC Radio National (November 1), posted in transcript at www.abc.net.au/rn/talks accessed September 6, 2002.

The Media Report (2002) "Frontline to the front page," ABC Radio National (April 25), posted in transcript at www.abc.net.au/rn/talks accessed October 2, 2003.

The Media Report (2003) "What happened to the war?", ABC Radio National (May 15), posted in transcript at www.abc.net.au/run/talks accessed June 19, 2003.

Media Watch (2003a) "Where are our troops?," ABC Television (March 24), transcript posted at www.abc.net.au/mediawatch accessed May 13, 2003.

Media Watch (2003b) "Embedded truth," ABC Television (March 24), transcript posted at www.abc.net.au/mediawatch accessed May 13, 2003.

Media Watch (2003c) "A new national broadcaster?" ABC Television (March 24), transcript posted at www.abc.net.au/mediawatch accessed May 13, 2003.

Media Watch (2003d) "The moment of truth," ABC Television (March 24), transcript posted at www.abc.net.au/mediawatch accessed May 13, 2003.

Media Watch (2003e) "Pilots lite," ABC Television (March 31), transcript posted at www.abc.net.au/mediawatch accessed May 13, 2003.

Media Watch (2003f) "4RAR poses," ABC Television (March 31), transcript posted at www.abc.net.au/mediawatch accessed May 13, 2003.

Media Watch (2003g) "Sluggo in Baghdad tonight," ABC Television (March 31), transcript posted at www.abc.net.au/mediawatch accessed May 13, 2003.

Media Watch (2003h) "*NT News* boycotts war," ABC Television (March 31), transcript posted at www.abc.net.au/mediawatch accessed May 13, 2003.

Media Watch (2003i) "Propaganda and the *Tele*," ABC Television (April 7), transcript posted at www.abc.net.au/mediawatch accessed May 13, 2003.

Media Watch (2003j) "Saddam falls," ABC Television (April 14), transcript posted at www.abc.net.au/mediawatch accessed May 13, 2003.

Media Watch (2003k) "Blair is toppled," ABC Television (May 5), transcript posted at www.abc.net.au/mediawatch accessed May 13, 2003.

The Mercury (2003) "Wounded Australian newsman dies' (July 7), posted at www.themercury.news.com.au accessed September 9, 2003.

Miller, T. and Turner, G. (2002) "Radio" in S. Cunningham and G. Turner (eds), *The Media and Communications in Australia* St Leonards, NSW: Allen and Unwin, pp. 133–51.

Miskin, S., Rayner, L., and Lalic, M. (2003) *Media Under Fire: Reporting Conflict in Iraq*, Current Issues Brief 21, Parliament of Australia, Department of the Parliamentary Library, posted at www.aph.gov.au/library accessed May 13, 2003.

Morrison, D. and Tumber, H. (1988) *Journalists at War*, London: Sage.

Mottram, M. (2003) "Australia left in the dark, say reporters," *The Age* (March 25), posted at http://new.theage.com.au accessed September 10, 2003.

Murphy, K. (2003a) "Viewers turn on the news as bombs blast Baghdad," *The Australian Media* (April 3–9), p. 12.

Murphy, K. (2003b) "Hewitt helps Seven back into play," *The Australian Media* (September 25–October 1), p. 12.

News.com.au (2003) "ABC denies bias in Iraq coverage' (July 21), posted at www.news.com.au accessed October 6, 2003.

Pearson, M. and Brand, J. (2001) *Sources of News and Current Affairs*, Sydney: Australian Broadcasting Authority, vol 1, pp. 5, 6.

Phillips, M. (2003) "Ministers' advice bill hits $20m," *Courier-Mail* (September 23), p. 2.

Pilger, J. (2002) "Journalism in Australia has a courageous history, but Murdochism has turned it into a disgrace," *New Statesman* (February 21), posted at http://pilger.carlton.com accessed November 18, 2002.

Pilger, J. (2003) untitled talk at John Pilger Forum, Australian Centre for Independent Journalism, University of Technology Sydney (March 28), transcript posted at http://acij.uts.edu.au/seminars/2003pilger.html accessed September 10, 2003.

Pusey, M. (2003) *The Experience of Middle Australia: the Dark Side of Economic Reform*, Cambridge: Cambridge University Press.

Putnis, P. (1996) "Producing overseas news for Australian television," *Australian Journal of Communication*, vol. 23, no. 3, pp. 1–22.

Radio 4BC (2003), John Howard interview with John Miller and Ross Davie (June 12), transcript posted at www.pm.gov.au/news/interviews accessed September 11, 2003.

Rampton, S. and Stauber, J. (2003) *Weapons of Mass Deception: the Uses of Propaganda in Bush's War on Iraq*, New York: Jeremy P. Tarcher/Penguin.

Rees, J. (2002) "Foundation origins," CEW Bean Foundation, posted at www.npc.org.au/CEWbean/foundation_origins.htm accessed September 10, 2003.

Reynolds, H. (1999) *Why Weren't We Told?: a Personal Search for the Truth about Our History*, Ringwood, Victoria: Viking.

Rice, S. (2003) "The charge of the lite brigade," *The Walkley Magazine*, vol. 21, pp. 10–12.

Schultz, J. (1998) *Reviving the Fourth Estate: Democracy, Accountability and the Media*, Cambridge: Cambridge University Press.

Sekuless, P. (1999) *A Handful of Hacks*, St Leonards, NSW: Allen and Unwin.

Simms, M. (2002). "The media and the 2001 election: Afghans, asylum seekers and anthrax" in J. Warnhust and M. Simms (eds), *2002: The Centenary Election*, Brisbane: University of Queensland Press.

Spearritt, P. (2003) "Unfriendly fire: Australia and the war on Iraq," Brisbane Institute (April 2), posted at www.brisinst.org.au accessed September 1, 2003.

Stewart, C. (2001) "The legend that must not die," *The Weekend Australian* (April 26), posted at www.theaustralian.news.co.au accessed October 8, 2003.

Tiffen, R. (1991) "The second casualty: the ABC and the Gulf War," *Current Affairs Bulletin*, vol. 67, no. 11 (April), pp. 10–18.

Tiffen, R. (1992a) "News coverage" in M. Goot and R. Tiffen (eds), *Australia's Gulf War*, Carlton, Victoria: Melbourne University Press, pp. 114–39.

Tiffen, R. (1992b) "Marching to whose drum?: media battles in the Gulf War," *Australian Journal of International Affairs*, vol. 46, no. 1 (May), pp. 44–60.

Turner, G. (2000) "Television news and current affairs: 'Welcome to *Frontline*'" in G. Turner and S. Cunningham (eds), *The Australian TV Book*, St Leonards, NSW: Allen and Unwin, pp. 89–102.

Turner, G. (2001) "Sold out: recent shifts in television news and current affairs in Australia," in M. Bromley (ed.), *No News is Bad News: Radio, Television and the Public*, Harlow: Longman, pp. 46–58.

Uechtritz, M. (2003a) "On balance, ABC news coverage is not biased," *The Australian Media* (June 5–11), p. 7.

Uechtritz, M. (2003b) "Complaints, Minister?," *The Walkley Magazine*, vol. 22, p. 5.

Van Druten, R. (2003) "Neo-fire fighter: a new profile for the international news correspondent," BA (Hons) thesis, Brisbane: Queensland University of Technology.

Vermeer, T. (2003) untitled talk, Australian Centre for Independent Journalism, University of Technology Sydney (April 4), transcript posted at http://acij.uts.edu.au/seminars/2003vermeer.html accessed October 5, 2003.

Veterans Support and Advocacy Service (2003), posted at www.ausvets.com.au/tradition.htm accessed June 12, 2003.

Vidal, G. (nd) "War, seen through photographs darkly: visual traces and interpretive possibilities in the photographic representation of Gallipoli," posted at www.arts.monash.edu.au/history/events/genidwar/papers/callister.html accessed May 14, 2003.

Ward, R. (1958) *The Australian Legend*, Melbourne: Oxford University Press.

Wilson, P. (2003) "Ingenuity that delivers pictures on demand," *The Australian Media* (April 3–9), p. 6.

Wright, T. (2003) "Fog of war," *The Bulletin*, vol. 121, no. 13) posted at http://bulletin.ninemsn.co.au/bulletin accessed September 10, 2003.

Zin, C. and Campbell, D. (1999) "Queen of Australia looks set to survive historical vote," *The Guardian* (November 6), posted at www.guardian.co.uk accessed October 9, 2003.

Part 3

REPORTING THE IRAQ WAR

13

MILITARIZED JOURNALISM

Framing dissent in the Persian Gulf wars

Stephen D. Reese

War has become an increasingly common tool of US national policy. Rather than Congressionally declared states of war periodically punctuating otherwise harmonious periods of peace, military conflict has become a condition of modern life. Now the National Security Strategy of the United States has formalized the case for pre-emptive unilateral military action, a policy of great significance for international relations. This plan, advocated for years by neo-conservatives who ascended to key positions in the latest Bush administration, was put into practice most recently in Afghanistan and Iraq, and even contemplated with respect to Iran and Syria. Advocating overwhelming US world military superiority to prevent the emergence of rivals follows in line with other administration steps away from multilateral international agreements on arms control, the environment, and other issues. This unilateralism of military force is rationalized by its architects as "power that can be trusted" (e.g., Armstrong 2002). Although anti-war voices have been at work, American military action has taken place largely against a backdrop of public support, or at least acquiescence. To understand how this support is developed and sustained we look to the relationships among the military, state, and media.

At a basic operational level, many analysts have looked at specific media censorship, public relations, and other manipulatory actions taken by military and administration officials in shaping media coverage. At a broader systemic level, others have considered how the ideological leadership of the media serves the interest of the US "empire." It is helpful, however, to combine these insights to examine from a sociological perspective specifically how news organizations enter into routinized relationships with military and other newsmakers, and how news of conflict is placed into particular frames of reference, which serve to anchor war in familiar cultural terms. These "routinized frames" are revealed through the recurring combination of visual and verbal elements within media coverage, showing what organizing principles are at work in the decisions of news managers and news sources. In this way, we may better see how the media perform their jobs in communicating news of war, national policy, and public debate over it.

247

US media performance in this arena becomes ever more crucial given the country's lone super-power status, and the administration's decision to act alone if need be in wielding military force. Of course, the attacks of 9/11 in New York and Washington launched a new "war on terrorism," a loaded and elastic frame used to help justify and fast-track the new unilateralist foreign policy. Patriotic post 9/11 television news graphics provided short-hand labels describing how "America strikes back" quickly mutating into "America's new war," with that "war" invoked as a main justification for the 2003 American invasion of Iraq. That is why implying the dubious connection of Saddam Hussein to those attacks was so strategically important in justifying military action against him. To the extent they can help examine such claims and facilitate reasoned discussion of these policies, the American news media have major implications for the rest of the world.

Chapter purpose

In this chapter I return to the Desert Shield/Desert Storm operation in the Persian Gulf War of 1990/1991 (Gulf War I) and consider how specific frames within news coverage at the local level create an implicitly pro-policy position, delegitimating, and marginalizing dissent.[1] The structured routines of newswork give rise to certain predictable ways of making sense of military conflict, particularly in the public debate that follows. We need to understand coverage of front-line conflict, but a broader "war at home" takes place away from the scene of actual combat as the government tries to build support for the policy behind it and policy opponents attempt to mount their challenges. These two processes are carried out in large part via the media. Although most analysis of the news media in wartime has focused on the front-line war, these actions are connected to and color the coverage of the domestic front. Thus it is important to consider how these two wars are organized for public consumption by the news media, how one feeds the other, and how that coverage works to advance or prevent a healthy public debate.

I focus here specifically on a local television news station as a lens into how coverage of the conflict in 1991, even far away from the front-line, created a no-win situation for the anti-war position. In Gulf I, the local community was an important site of public debate, including rallies for and against the war and the ubiquitous yellow ribbons. Although the national debate and network level media drew much of the scholarly analysis, people found support for and gave voice to their opinions in local schools, churches, and locally organized political speech. Furthermore, local television showed the commercial imperative of audience appeal writ large, which highlighted the processing by which news converts military action into an audience-friendly story line. Of course, this happened at the national level too, but within a single community the news organization's decision-making in connection to specific events, relationships with sources, and the resulting coverage can be easily explored. Entertainment values too make this analysis even more relevant. In the recent 2003 war in Iraq, stories such as the

"Rescue of Private Jessica Lynch" were packaged for cross-platform promotion in news, talk-shows, magazines, and books, becoming stories that were mutually beneficial to both the military for its image management and to news organizations seeking drama for audience appeal.[2]

Some of the more telling examples of framing in local news coverage show the powerful ideological domestication of dissent when military logic is combined with cultural patriotism—a phenomenon just as relevant to understanding the more recent war in Iraq (or Gulf War II).[3] I have defined "frames" as "organizing principles that are socially shared and persistent over time, that work symbolically to meaningfully structure the social world" (Reese 2001: 11). Taking this sociological approach involves examining the responses of newsworkers, media texts, and cultural context to determine how these principles manifest themselves in issue discourse. In my analysis here, a close look at language in news reports shows how concepts and cultural elements are linked together into frames, which are significant in shaping the "definition of the situation" and subsequent audience understandings. Thus, in reviewing this case in one community, we can see how military logic reaches far beyond the front lines to color the entire public discourse.

Military logic: from Gulf War I to the war on terrorism

War does not stand alone, but becomes interpreted within local idioms, community structures, national myths, and routine journalistic frames for making sense of the world. There was an "illusory" quality to Gulf War I, which others have examined in detail (Gerbner 1992; Graubard 1992; Kellner 1992; Smith 1992). To understand this illusion requires that we focus on how it emerged from the routine workings of the press. In Stuart Hall's terms, the media's power lies not in transmitting unchallenged government propaganda but in rooting those definitions in culture, drawing from it and reinforcing consensual norms, adding to their "taken for granted" quality in a "spiral of amplification" (Hall *et al.* 1978). "The troops," for example, became an irresistible underpinning to the Gulf War I conflict, especially given that news organizations needed a human face and a mythical story line that appealed to commercial values and community interest. This helped to integrate the logic of military conflict into the society, making it difficult to separate out the merits of the larger policy which became hopelessly woven into the larger story. Embedded journalists in Gulf War II highlighted even further the human US and UK face of troops, to add to the face of leadership more narrowly available in Gulf War I in the persons in particular of Generals Norman Schwarzkopf and Colin Powell. To the extent that military logic became the prevailing way of making sense of world relationships, a large part of public debate was limited. The naturalization of the military option was advanced when familiar cultural myths were invoked, as the tendency to set deadlines for enemies like Saddam, which encouraged likening the president to actor Gary Cooper in the movie *High Noon*.

The strength of military logic in the broader conflicts of recent years, particularly post 9/11, is undeniable. Since Gulf War I, the more formalized conflict of armies from that war has been supplanted by asymmetric warfare, yet with the same premises and approaches applied to this more fluid conflict in which the "enemy" does not agree to play by the rules of traditional combat. The "war on terrorism" frame for this new condition carries in its terminology a traditional Defense Department solution, which, although it may be partly accurate, overshadows other interventions in this jointly sociological, economic, political, and religious issue. (The "war on drugs" worked similarly, privileging military and law enforcement solutions to an issue that was also a public health matter. The two became linked when government officials argued that using illegal drugs helped provide revenue for terrorists.) Military logic becomes mapped onto every other discussion, becoming the dominant organizing principle and short-circuiting debate. The success of military action as a policy response may, as a result, be said to be determined through criteria of the military's own choosing.

The dominance of this military logic frame was aptly illustrated in President Bush's famous photo-op jet landing on the aircraft carrier *Abraham Lincoln* last May 2003 off the coast of San Diego. Changing out of his flight suit, he addressed the cameras with a banner behind him, "Mission accomplished." The clear message was that in the military completing its major combat operations, the president's national mission had been effectively completed too—one being conflated with the other in this mediated imagery and symbolism. Though the military branch was an instrument of national political policy, the president wearing a flight suit visually overrode this distinction.[4] The power of this "war on terrorism" and its associated "axis of evil" was further illustrated by the fact that the majority of Americans were reported to hold Saddam Hussein responsible for the 9/11 World Trade Center attack, even though no evidence supported such a link. He was also implicitly linked by his inclusion in the "axis," against which the war on terrorism was arrayed. As mentioned earlier, this framing cast a preemptive strike national policy into a self-defense context, making it more intuitively palatable to most Americans.

The routines of newswork draw attention to the structured ways that journalists enter into relationships to obtain desirable goals (Shoemaker and Reese 1996). In front-line coverage these routines are often clearly delineated; military officials desire positive accounts of their activities, to "get their story out," and to simply accommodate the demands of the many news organizations seeking access to the story. Systems are developed to meet those needs. Journalists, of course, want the most exciting material possible that will be of interest to their organizations and audiences. The Vietnam-era memory of these relationships, particularly among military officers of that generation, is adversarial, with journalists "not on the team." The more typical modern characterization of this relationship is symbiotic, and a perceived anti-military attitude risks a journalist being excluded from interview opportunities and other desired access. These routine structures impose their own logic, working against alternative frameworks of interpretation.

In the case of war reporting, they contribute to what Kellner (1992) called the "militarization of consciousness." Law enforcement and military institutions are particularly important agents of social control in society and act as "primary definers," on which journalists have come to rely heavily for sources or news. Hall *et al.* (1978) argue that the media stand in structured subordination to these institutions which in the case of the military, is able to exert great definitional power—not only on its own realm but also in a way that carries over into others.

The post-Vietnam image of the military emerged with damage but was gradually rehabilitated both in the political and wider cultural spheres (Baritz 1985). President Reagan's policies emphasized a greater ideological justification for using the military and a willingness to deploy it in tune-up conflicts like Grenada. In popular culture, movies such as *Rambo* and *Missing in Action* carried a revisionist version of Vietnam history, advancing the notion that the military was undermined by spineless politicians and forced to fight with "one hand tied behind its back." As the Rambo character said at the end of *First Blood*, "I did what I had to do to win, but somebody wouldn't let us win!" President Nixon had been able to distract attention from the unpopular southeast Asia policy by focusing public attention on the prisoners of war issue, a matter in which there was much more fervent and exploitative strategic government gamesmanship than evidence (apart from Chuck Norris movies) for POWs still behind enemy lines (Franklin 1992). With the advent of Gulf War I, national officials were able to draw on this restored image of American forces to engage public support. The potency of this focus was seen in its power to invert one post-Vietnam principle of military policy. Before Gulf War I, officers like Colin Powell advocated building public support before any large-scale commitment of troops; paradoxically, however, the US administration showed that by committing the troops they could engage the public. Once significant forces had been deployed in Saudi Arabia and a January deadline set ("showdown") for Hussein to leave Kuwait, the "support the troops" motif exploited a powerful cultural value, which found its way into news framing. They, the troops, engaged support precisely because they were there, effectively obliterating any challenge to the policy that got them there.

Framing dissent: Gulf War I

Through two major frames a coherent body of local coverage emerged implicitly supportive of the government's policy, which I label "conflict" and "consensus." Dissent was managed through the conflict frame by pitting two non-equivalent sides against each other: anti-policy and pro-troops. This frame, rooted in the news routine of "balance," ostensibly protected the reporter from charges of bias but worked against the dissenting position by contrasting it against the pro-troops, "patriotic" side. Local news, and particularly television, strove to adopt the voice of the community and be its supportive advocate. The consensus frame led reporters to emphasize community solidarity.[5]

The quotations below were all taken from transcripts of news stories broadcast by KVUE-TV, which at the time was the ratings leader in Austin, Texas. Interviews were conducted with station producers and reporters, and raw footage of several community public demonstrations was also examined. Anchor introductions to stories were emphasized because these lead-ins displayed the most obvious encapsulation of the frame by compressing the essence of the story into a few attention-getting words.

Conflict

In 1991, a variety of public protests and demonstrations were going on throughout the community. Once the January 15, 1991, deadline for Saddam Hussein set by President George Bush (Bush senior) arrived, public opposition to the conflict was framed to domesticate its focus. The language in news reports clearly worked to downwardly adjust perceptions of anti-war protest strength. Indeed, anti-war protest was probably more vocal in this relatively liberal city, making the framing job perhaps more clearly necessary. (My italics are added below for emphasis.)

January 16

Reporter: (on anti-war protest at the University of Texas) . . . Protestors outnumbered those supporting the war by 2 to 1, *but supporters say that's only because the anti-war folks are more vocal.*

January 17

Anchor: . . . Even though anti-war protesters outnumbered Bush supporters two to one, conservatives say they are tired of staying silent.

January 17

Reporter: Anti-war protesters have demonstrated almost continuously since yesterday evening and conservatives felt it was time to defend themselves.

Other references upgraded the pro-policy position, treating it respectfully.

January 16

Anchor: There are many, many Austin residents who support President Bush's decision to bomb Iraq and they say they want to be heard. They plan a candle-light vigil in Waterloo Park tonight.

January 20

Anchor: . . . In the beginning pro-war forces were relatively quiet, *now they are gaining in momentum* . . . [after shots of rally, in conclusion] . . . Later the pro-war group was confronted by those opposed to the US presence in the Persian Gulf region.

January 17

Anchor: A stark contrast tonight to the overwhelming crowds that have gathered recently to protest the war. Tonight about 30 people stood by in City Park . . . a quiet candlelight vigil to support President Bush. They were small in number *but their feelings were just as strong* . . . Those in attendance had to dodge rain showers, *but that didn't dampen their spirits.*

Other reports presented a less positive view of dissenters, calling attention to disruptions, minimizing their strength, and challenging their symbolism.

January 17

Anchor: At the State Capitol today, anti-war protesters were *anything but peaceful.*

January 19

Anchor: Police and war protesters had estimated that a peace rally at the State Capitol this afternoon would reach some 20,000. Instead 1,500 to 2,300 showed up, *far short of the anticipated crowd.*

January 26

Anchor: . . . Anti-war protesters carried flag-draped caskets symbolizing war dead . . . But [notes the anchor] so far, US military officials say one American serviceman has been killed in combat.

This attempt by the anchor to "correct" the symbolism of the protesters, which presumably referenced deaths on both sides, implicitly restricted war dead to American casualties.

Station officials reported that audience complaints often made them sensitive to airing footage of protest, arguing that it allowed them to "consider all sides." One producer said, "The people who supported the troops were a kind of silent majority." Thus, in this case the opposing sides became the anti-war position, on the one hand, and the "support the troops" position, on the other—not an anti-policy and pro-policy side. Examining the linguistic composition of these frames shows how strongly intertwined the "pro-troops" position and the related stance of "get behind the president" became in coverage.

January 23

Anchor: 150 demonstrators *supporting the war effort* demonstrated at the University of Texas and listened to people *speak about patriotism.* As a counterpoint, these five protesters at the State Capitol are all who are on hand for a war protest that began on the 15th.

In a story from an area public school, the reporter even overtly made a point to separate policy and troops before implicitly joining them again.

January 16

Reporter: [about school kids' reaction] . . . In the meantime the students are following through on their commitment to support not the war itself but rather the Americans in the Middle East *fighting for peace.*

This distinction between troops and policy is further eroded, with local officials adding their voice of support—again implicitly joining the two.

January 23

Anchor: Austin County Commissioners came out in support of American men and women serving in the Middle East and against the actions of Saddam.

Most reports of public expression continued to focus on the "pro-troops" position and families.

January 23

Reporter: . . . There are others who say they don't necessarily want to fight in a war either but will do whatever it takes to *protect their country's interests.*

January 17

Anchor: . . . The peace protests are hard for families whose loved ones are in the Persian Gulf. One military wife says she can handle the stress and anxiety of knowing her husband is in the thick of things, but it's harder when she's confronted by scenes of angry protesters demonstrating against the war.
Woman: There are lots of families hanging on to every word that the news is putting out and I think it's really destructive to them.

January 17

Anchor: . . . The anti-war sentiment is unsettling for families whose loved ones are involved in Operation Desert Storm *and for those who back President Bush's decision to go to war.*

Later reporting further served to reinforce this clear pitting of the anti-policy stance against the pro-troops/patriotism position in a binary opposition.

January 19

Anchor [over shots of protesters]: People converge on the State Capitol shouting their pleas for peace while a *patriotic group* of small town residents sing their support for American soldiers at war.

January 24

Anchor [over video of veterans rally]: The US must show 100 percent support for our troops in the Middle East. That's the message from veterans who say they are upset over the number of anti-war protests. They say it sends a bad message to the troops in the Middle East, that we don't support them.

January 24

Wife of serviceman: It's time for all Americans to unite behind the young men and women who are serving their country.
Anchor: . . . Many are upset over the number of anti-war protests and say they should stop.

Of course, in the aftermath of 9/11, patriotism took on new significance in the culture, but looking back on this reporting reveals how actively local reporters worked to link patriotism with the troops, especially in the highlighting of community patriotic rallies.

January 19

Reporter [over pictures of flag-waving rally in adjoining town]: They are the images of Americana . . . The pictures of heartfelt pride and support for soldiers in the Middle East. The war in the Middle East has revived patriotism here.

January 20

Anchor: As the battlefield gets more intense, more Americans are working to show their support for the troops who are under attack in Saudi Arabia.

The distortion of "balance"

A closer look at one particular story showed how a stronger anti-war protest was neutralized by its juxtaposition with a pro-troops, "patriotic" activity—following the "objectivity" routine in creating what could be considered a "false balance," given the disparity of 10 to 1 in attendance at the two events. This story was aired on January 17, based on events at the University of Texas. The final story was examined against the original raw footage.

Reporter: On one side of the UT campus, several hundred people who are opposed to the war carried on a protest that began last night.

Anti-war speaker: During the war in Vietnam we lost over 58,000 young American lives.

Pro-war speaker: The legacy of Vietnam will die with this conflict.

Reporter: A few feet away supporters of the President held their own rally.

Same person: Because Iraq is not Vietnam.

Reporter: It was smaller *but feelings ran just as strong.*

Chanting males: USA, USA.

Student: How many troops do they have compared to ours?

Reporter: With two groups so close together there was inevitably conflict.

Students: [unintelligible argument]

Student: The sheep can preach the virtues of vegetarianism until hell freezes over, but the wolf isn't listening. You've got to deal with people in a language they're capable of understanding and Saddam Hussein only understands violence.

The reporter moved from this bi-polar pairing of positions to reach and conclude with a consensual, but ultimately "pro-troops," and therefore "pro-policy," theme.

Reporter: Some who came here were motivated by a deeper feeling, a sense of commitment. [Said over shots of anthem and flag to a woman who has a brother in the Gulf.]

Woman: When your family's over there all you know is to support them.

Reporter: Students raised during a time of peace are now debating their generation's war [over shots of signs, peace signs]. Some of the slogans have changed, some haven't. But the emotions raised by patriotism and violence [Saddam Hussein's?] run just as strong.

Thus, again the anti-war position was pitted against the high ground of those with a "deeper commitment." Indeed, opposing the war was tantamount to opposing the woman interviewed and her family. But this framing was part of a routine package that made it possible for news organizations to handle protest stories easily and with a minimum of audience complaint. Reporters were not expected to have expertise in the policy issues. They were able to present the "form" of balance as an easily followed format, which would then yield a consensual "patriotic" middle ground.

Consensus

The "support the troops" concept became a crucial element in the conflict and consensus frames and a way to manage public dissent over government policy. Particularly with regard to local television, Kaniss (1991) argued that, given the

256

nature of the large and fragmented audiences, stations are driven to find unifying symbols and themes, such as sports franchises, which help to promote a sense of community solidarity.[6] Thus, the "support the troops" message was tailor-made for news coverage seeking to restore a community threatened by the divisive disputes over war policy. Frames derive their power in large part because they are internalized "organizing principles" that news workers can apply routinely. Interviews with station reporters showed how this occurred for the pro-troops element. As one admitted:

> Look, almost everyone had strong feelings about the war . . . not like they were "pro-war" but that everyone backed the troops. They wanted the troops not to get hurt over there. No one wanted them hurt. I have to admit maybe I was too close to the story. I had relatives—close relatives—over there fighting.

"The troops" became the nation's home-town team, indeed the consensual glue used by reporters to symbolically hold the community together, especially when trying to frame expressions of conflicting public opinion.

January 22

Anchor: . . . Although both sides of the war issue are still battling back and forth, one thing seems to hold the factions together: support for the men and women in Saudi Arabia . . . [Referring later to flag sales] Although everyone may not choose to show their support in the same way, at least for some, the support for the troops is there no matter what the belief about the war itself.

January 22

Anchor: . . . People may be divided about how they feel about US involvement in the Middle East, but one feeling seems to be shared by everyone: support for the troops who are over there now.

News routines show that not all stories require balanced voices. According to Hallin (1986), those stories that deal with subjects within either the sphere of deviance or sphere of consensus are by their nature not ones that require even treatment. Those, however, within the "sphere of legitimate controversy" do. Thus, as a consensual story, "support the troops" stories came to no longer require balance, as in this report on efforts at a local school.

January 23

Anchor: . . . Those who support the American forces in the Persian Gulf War are trying to make themselves more visible . . . Among other things, the students signed a huge Happy Valentine's card to be sent to the troops and passed out yellow ribbons.

Of course, there was no shortage of stories from the community and surrounding areas that served to exemplify traditional values: placement of yellow ribbons, rallies, flag-flying, and veterans meetings. Even the veterans themselves were processed through the consensus frame to eliminate any troubling qualms about war in general. As one veteran was quoted as saying:

January 16

"War produces dead bodies. Let's hope this one's over quickly. War is hell . . . it's just you can't describe it."

The reporter, given this threatening notion of war's consequences, quickly reassured the audience:

Despite the knowledge of how horrible war can be, for every ounce of fear among members of this group, *there's still a ton of patriotism* . . . These men have been there . . . They know first hand the turmoil, the desperation of war . . . But all are very proud tonight and holding their heads up high.

With military success, the pro-troops element soon morphed into the "heroes of Desert Storm," a label that continued linking the troops to the policy. A reporter's January 18 story glorified local Bergstrom Air Force Base reconnaissance pilots as the "unsung heroes of the war." The characterization suggests one who embarks on a worthy undertaking, so it is difficult to celebrate the heroes without also endorsing the mission on which they were sent. This theme was a valuable resource for routine story construction by providing an easily constructed story-line, drama, and meaning to the conflict.

In this chapter I have largely centered my attention on how war and its public debate were handled within a specific geographical community. The routinized structure of media/military relationships rooted conflict in frames of reference that held audience appeal and accessible cultural meaning. Coverage of this conflict as seen in the first Gulf War was closely related to coverage of dissent at home within an overall military logic, finding particular expression in support for "the troops." During the interval between this Gulf conflict and that which followed, the local community was superseded in many ways by global public communities, which had implications for public support for military action.

Conflict and dissent in the global community: Gulf War II

In the years since Gulf War I, the previously-existent community focus in news was increasingly intertwined with the changing patterns of news and its changing audiences. With greater competition among US cable news networks, ; more forceful patriotic voice of Fox News, national news became more aligned with the commercial imperatives of local television. Indeed, the trau of 9/11 drove news to appeal to the same sense of one community in the name of national solidarity that was typical of local news. This had an impact on the extent to which conflicts were easily framed within military logic and dissent was marginalized. The local/national, "vertical" frames of reference came into increasing tension with more globalized, multi-level "horizontal" orientations of world news gathering. Global communities, if not supplanting local ones, certainly added an important layer to the public sphere. The current Bush administration took an active role in framing national policy very explicitly in the shape of the "war on terrorism" and the "axis of evil." These perspectives became more pointed and publicly resonant than the vague, negatively connotated sense of a "new world order," employed by the earlier Bush administration in Gulf War I. But they were also more open to contestation. How might we compare the potential for framing dissent, as we reflect on differences between Gulf War I and Gulf War II? Although it is difficult to visualize a public sphere projected globally, some suggestive anecdotal outlines emerge in the way that world publics react and interact through the media.

In many respects, a globalized public opinion came of age following the attacks of 9/11 and the subsequent US efforts to engage militarily in Afghanistan and Iraq. Public protests around the world on February 15, 2003, were a particular watershed event, which created a boundary-spanning anti-war movement acting in its various locations but in a simultaneous global arena, supported by transmission of global news and other communication (from email to CNN, weblogs, news sites, etc.). The national media continued to cater to the parochial views of their officials and mass audience, and local media were still limited to covering locally based public protest actions. Global elites, however, increasingly took into account world opinion, driven by alternative sources of information to any specific locally based channels. Dissent was not so easily marginalized in this more diffused media environment.

The new ability of citizens to mount a globally coordinated expression of opposition produced corresponding political consequences. Thus, compared to the first Gulf War of 1990 and 1991, the US administration had much greater difficulty operating free of constraint in implementing what amounted to a preemptive strike national security policy in the 2003 Iraq invasion (it is, of course, true that the international community was more unified behind Gulf War I). An anti-war public in many countries made it politically treacherous for national leaders to support the Bush administration. Media and public opinion, particularly as seen recently in Europe, were less apt to follow government policy. Forging multilateral agreement for a unilateral policy came with greater difficulty in a world with global communication supporting different dimensions of public opinion, and where the purported rationale for policy was subjected to world scrutiny, helping expose disconnects between surface discourse and underlying strategic motives. The Qatar-based Al-Jazeera television news organization, for example, was increasingly in position in Palestinian territory, Afghanistan, and Iraq to show the aftermath of bombing and the resulting effects on civilian populations (e.g., el-Nawawy and Iskandar 2002). Compared to the relatively more sanitized view of Gulf War I, CNN was joined by a host of international 24-hour news channels and many other news sources on the scene to show the wider "reality" of war.

Certainly, the military will continue to work to control access to the battlefield and manage the coverage that results. The US and British defense officials' plans to incorporate some 600 reporters within individual military units clearly gave greater access to the battlefield than was ever provided in the tightly restricted journalistic environment of Gulf War I. In retrospect, this "embedding" of assigning journalists to military units was a brilliant strategy—from the standpoint of the military. These attached reporters were inevitably drawn into the perspective of the soldiers with whom they traveled, and the dramatic, if often blurred and grainy, images from the scene gave a vivid impression from the point of view of the troops. Journalists shared the perspective and tactical emphasis of the units they accompanied, and their group solidarity ("going native") affected their independence. This "routinized" perspective was not new and can be seen in other settings where journalists effectively take the perspective of police, by using, for example, television footage shot from the police side of an altercation or, in the case of reality-based programming like Fox's "cops," following agents into homes and through neighborhood backyards.

For US news organizations, embedding met professional needs for access to the story and, from their standpoint, was a step forward compared to Gulf War I. Although BBC news executives had been distrustful of the program, they later regretted that some of their top journalists had missed out on the main action (Byrne 2003). Although the view from the military units was not the only part of the larger story, its historic immediacy, technology-enhanced drama, and first-hand vantage point gave embedded reports a quality that overwhelmed other perspectives. As a matter of framing emphasis alone, the war on terrorism became a military conflict with Iraq, which became ultimately the story of individual units seeking their objectives: immediate tactical details of casualties, speed, and logistics. Nevertheless, the multinational character of the embedded journalists gave insights into the depth of the American national frame of reference. That embedding was to a large extent an image-management strategy was seen in the exclusion from desirable assignments of reporters from countries regarded as unfriendly to the "policy," such as France and Germany (two major German television news organizations were "offered" the same assignment to an aircraft carrier far from the front; they refused). Non-US journalists observed that the Americans seemed "completely signed up" to "America, Inc.," with little critical distance.

This perspective, however, allowed the American journalists to work in relative harmony with their units and for American officers to make assumptions about their coverage (while obliging them to monitor more closely the work of non-US journalists—particularly, for example, from countries such as Abu Dhabi). Ted Koppel of ABC News Nightline was unable to resist seeking an embedded position (an enhanced one attached to the division commander) and prefacing one report with ominous heroic imagery from Shakespeare ("Unleash the dogs of war!"). An embedded reporter from the *Atlanta Journal-Constitution* exhibited this professional ease with the heroic theme by presenting a photographic retrospective of his work following his assignment, accompanied by an arrangement of Samuel Barber's sublime "Adagio for Strings" (also used in the movie *Platoon*).[7] Indeed, I would argue that the unilateralist policy that got the troops to Iraq made this perspective even more necessary, for it was a policy, after all, predicated on the assumption that US military superiority would be used wisely and was "power that can be trusted." Thus, perhaps it was not surprising that American journalists internalized this assumption and that non-US journalists were more likely to at least make a distinction between taking the perspective of the unit and the side of "the American war machine."[8] Thus, although the embedding program worked to reinforce a military logic and a heroic frame, within the still emerging global norms of newsgathering there was evidence of a fault line between a nationalistic unilateralism and a multilateral world.

Thus, embedding was a form of control that created a strong dependency relationship between journalists and their units (not only for getting the story but for protection in a dangerous place). Even the training supervised by the military for aspiring embeds underscored the premise that "we know what we're doing, and you don't." Nevertheless, on the ground of military conflict, it became more difficult to manage information in an environment more fluid and porous than just 12 years prior, with satellite phones and other technologies making communication easier and quicker. In some ways, this more fluid communication field made controlling the "story line" more crucial, with the Pentagon and the US administration seeking foremost to frame the story as "mission accomplished." The availability of satellite phones, for example, made it possible for many more journalists to instantly transmit their first-hand observations to editors anywhere in the world. Peter Arnett was alone in transmitting via satellite phone from Baghdad in 1991; reporting from the same city in 2003 he noted far greater competition, with 200 to 300 such phones in the city and a dozen video uplinks and video phones (Blumenthal and Rutenberg 2003). In the first Gulf War, restricted coverage led many viewers to give little consideration to civilian suffering, while during that later war reporters had greater access to the impact of the conflict.

In the current Iraq conflict of Gulf War II, even the powerful "support the troops" component within the frames of dissent cuts both ways, that is, with dual and contrary consequences. On the one hand, the media dynamic remained similar today, with news organizations clearly "on board" with the policy. A recent report from NBC Nightly News, for example, documented the hospital rehabilitation efforts of American soldiers wounded in Iraq. The account of men with missing limbs learning to walk again easily leads viewers to question the wisdom of the policy behind their suffering, but anchor Brian Williams worked to block this possibility in his studio conclusion: "If you're looking for anti-war spirit you won't find it in this (hospital) ward. These men are anxious to get back to their unit" (October 31, 2003). On the other hand, soldiers had families at home who, as the engagement lengthened, became increasingly unhappy. Unlike in Gulf I, they were able to email and communicate their own impressions of the conflict in ways that their organization found difficult to control. A quick and decisive conflict with few military casualties allowed the "support the troops" atmosphere to work unchallenged by qualms over policy. But as they remained vulnerable in a protracted struggle, as rationales for the war became increasingly questioned and undermined, then the troops engaged a counter-dynamic at home, leading their communities to question the policy putting them at risk.

The work of unembedded "unilateral" journalists remains important, and their work is more globally available than ever before. Supported by technology, journalist Robert Fisk, for example, was able to base himself in Lebanon, reporting for a London newspaper, *The Independent*, with many more readers around the world via the Internet. Although his ideological stance gained him a wide audience on the left and critics within the profession, reporters like him remained valuable for their first-hand accounts on the ground of world hot spots. These first-hand perspectives supported a broader perspective by readers who otherwise would not have had much available beyond their own narrow national frames of reference articulated, in particular, by network and local television.

In addition to the freer information environment, and the associated link-ups of world publics around issues, casting the public sphere globally made it less susceptible to control and cooptation by a single "state." State-controlled propaganda in the traditional sense was less viable when the global public had alternative sources of news beyond their national organs and could coordinate their efforts across international boundaries. Bill Dutton of the Oxford Internet Institute, for example, argued that "The most obvious thing that the web provides is access to a greater diversity of viewpoints and a more international viewpoint." Adam Porter, of the British on-line current affairs quarterly, *Year Zero*, said,

> It's really patronizing to assume, as the mainstream media often does that ordinary people don't talk about Iraq, asylum or economics down the pub. You can go all around the world and find similar things and it's the web that's bringing them together.
>
> (*Media Guardian* 2003)

Issues as important as war must be understood beyond a single national context. Thus, it is natural that the public actively seeks a globally oriented perspective. One example may be seen in US audiences tracking European news sites more closely for alternative points of view concerning the war in Iraq. According to Croad (2003), "Much of the US media's reaction to France and Germany's intransigence on the Iraqi war issue has verged on the xenophobic, even in the so-called 'respectable' press." As a result, she observed that the feedback to these European websites suggested that people no longer rely only on their own national media, exercising instead their need for information on a global scale. Web-based autonomous media emerged such as Indymedia.org, a collective of independent media organizations and journalists, that provided a critique of war coverage in the mainstream press, reframed issues away from military strength to diplomatic relationships and, as it reported, promoted "global citizenship." So, information globalization means that citizens have access to the policy record in a way never possible before, and other countries have access to well-informed points of view around the world. Thus, greater transparency has developed concerning US policy objectives, even if not from the government itself, making it harder for national leaders to "go it alone" with the expectation that the world public will fall in line.

As a globalized public sphere becomes more complex and interconnected, it will become important to theorize the implications for public support for military conflict. Local news organizations during Gulf War I effectively structured support for the policy as they applied a military logic to local debates. As these debates over military conflict become globalized and denationalized, beyond the scope of any single local community, there remains the hope that these policies can be debated clearly through a more multilateral cultural media lens.

Notes

1 A fuller analysis is contained in a previous article (Reese and Buckalew 1995).
2 Lynch was an American soldier captured and taken to an Iraqi hospital, where by all accounts she was treated humanely before being retrieved in what was hailed at the time as a heroic special rescue operation. The Pentagon has denied staging the rescue as a media event, but it provided to the media its video footage of the operation, acted no doubt as the source of many details in news accounts attributed to anonymous sources, and failed to later correct erroneous details that didn't conform to the story line (Lynch was captured without resistance, although early reports had her emptying her gun at the enemy before being overcome).
3 I understand that in the Arab world this most recent Iraq war is Gulf War III, with the Iraq–Iran war being the first.
4 News stories in November 2003 at this writing discuss the White House's attempts to distance the president from the "mission accomplished" banner, a jarring symbolic memory given the ongoing presence of US forces in Iraq. The president has blamed the navy for posting the banner, but the administration's skill in framing visual backdrops for his speeches and controlling every other aspect of media interaction casts doubt on this innocence. What appeared to be a classic presidential photo opportunity and a golden opportunity for campaign advertising now ironically may be just that, for the opposition that is.
5 In the original study, another frame, "control," was also explored. It emerged from the tight relationship between local news organizations and law enforcement, making it easy to slip into a "police work" perspective and cast public dissent as a threat to

social control. Dissent, as a result, was often treated as a matter of police work, keeping unruly crowds in check and focusing on procedures in place to manage public gatherings.

6 This interlock with sports continues on a national level, as seen, for example, in the National Football League promoting its "Intrepid fallen heroes fund" meant to support the families of military personnel "who have given their lives in the current operations in defense of our country" (www.nfl.com/heroesfund, November 10, 2003). My point is certainly not to diminish the loss of these individuals but to suggest how deeply ingrained the troops are in the national psyche, reinforced in this case by initiatives supported by commercial enterprises. The frequent analogies of sports to war and vice versa is another lengthy subject.

7 My observations from this section are drawn from various comments at recent professionals' meetings. Insights into the foreign press are from the Newsworld International meeting for news professional in Dublin (October 20–3, 2003). The Koppel and Atlanta details are from a symposium on war reporting at the University of Texas at Austin (November 4–5, 2003).

8 The latter view was expressed by BBC correspondent David Loyn at the same Newsworld meeting referenced above (October 21, 2003).

References

Armstrong, D. (2002) "Dick Cheney's song of America," *Harper's Magazine*, October, vol. 305.

Baritz, L. (1985) *Backfire: American Culture and the Vietnam War*, New York: Ballentine.

Blumenthal, Ralph and Rutenberg, Jim (February 18, 2003) "Journalists are assigned to accompany US troops," *The New York Times*, p. A12.

Byrne, C. (October 22, 2003) "BBC was 'distrustful' of embedding," *The Guardian*.

Croad, Elizabeth (February 27, 2003) "US public turns to Europe for news," *dot.journalism*, www.journalism.co.uk/news/story576.html.

el-Nawawy, M. and Iskandar, A. (2002) *Al-Jazeera: how the Free Arab News Network Scooped the World and Changed the Middle East*, Cambridge, MA: Westview.

Franklin, H. (1992) *M.I.A: Mythmaking in America*, Brooklyn: L. Hill Books.

Gerbner, G. (1992) *Persian Gulf War: the Movie* in H. Mowlana, G. Gerbner, and H. Schiller (eds), *Triumph of the Image: Persian Gulf War in Global Perspective*, Boulder, CO: Westview, pp. 243–65.

Graubard, S. (1992) *Mr Bush's War*, New York: Hill and Wang.

Hall, S., Critcher, C., Jefferson, T., Clarke, J., and Roberts, B. (1978) *Policing the Crisis: Mugging, the State, and Law and Order*, London: Macmillan.

Hallin, D. (1986) *The "Uncensored" War: the Media and Vietnam*, Berkeley, CA: University of California Press.

Kaniss, P. (1991) *Making Local News*. Chicago, IL: University of Chicago Press.

Kellner, D. (1992) *The Persian Gulf TV War*, Boulder, CO: Westview.

Media Guardian (February 17, 2003) "Spin caught in a web trap." Media.Guardian. co.uk/ iraqandthemedia/story/0,12823,897330,00.html

Reese, S. (2001) "Framing public life: a bridging model for media research" in S. Reese, O. Gandy, and A. Grant (eds), *Framing Public Life: Perspectives on Media and Our Understanding of the Social World*, Mahwah, NJ: Erlbaum.

Reese, S. and Buckalew, B. (1995) "The militarism of local television: the routine framing of the Persian Gulf War," *Critical Studies in Mass Communication*, vol. 12, pp. 40–59.

Shoemaker P.J. and Reese S.D. (1996) *Mediating the Message: Theories of Influences on Mass Media Content*, New York: Longman.
Smith, J. (1992) *George Bush's War*, New York: Holt.

14

WAR OR PEACE?

Legitimation, dissent, and rhetorical closure in press coverage of the Iraq war build-up

Nick Couldry and John Downey

The global space within which much news and media comment are produced and circulate has never been clearer than in the contentious build-up to the recent UK/USA war in Iraq. As disputes within and between national governments over the very *definition* of the issues at stake intensified, the global circulation of critical perspectives on the expected war was striking and cut across the divisions between official government positions. Whatever the local tendencies toward closure of the issues from a specific national perspective (and as the war began in the UK, those tendencies intensified), in order to understand the conflict fully, it is essential to comprehend the global character of dissent and opposition. The global nature of elite media and political discourse was matched by the globalization of opposition to a UK/USA invasion of Iraq. On February 15 over 8 million people marched in five continents to express their dissent (although the large majority of them marched through the streets of major cities in western and southern Europe). The analysis of both media discourse and popular dissent as a consequence demands a cosmopolitan approach (Beck 2000). In this chapter we will focus on press discourse in the UK but we see this very much as a contribution to a broader cosmopolitan project that does not, however, overlook national specificities.

There are good reasons to focus on the UK beyond the limitations of the authors and their circumstances. Not only was the UK America's closest ally, diplomatically and militarily, but the UK government was renowned for its public relations, having won two landslide elections in 1997 and 2001 with apparent ease, leaving the major opposition party in disarray. Moreover, it was unusual that a supposedly left-of-centre government, unlike other European social democratic parties, should support a neo-conservative US Republican executive and that consequently the two major UK political parties were united in their support for the USA. Despite this, only 38 percent of the British population surveyed in an opinion poll supported a "unilateral" war (a war without UN sanction) against Iraq immediately before the outbreak of war. (After the advent of war there was a dramatic shift in favor of military action.) The low point in terms of support for the war was between mid-January and mid-February 2003 when opinion polls revealed that only 30 percent and 29 percent of representative samples of the British population supported war (*The Guardian*, ICM). On February 15 an unprecedented one and a half million people marched through the streets of London to voice their dissent. The numbers took most people by surprise. Only a few days before the march newspapers were predicting 500,000 demonstrators but it was clear that a momentum was developing. A march organizer commented that week: "it's a new movement, out of anyone's control. It's like a tidal wave. The people organizing it are not in control. It has its own momentum" (Burgin, *The Guardian*, December 2, 2003: 6).

We will analyze the reporting of the conflict by seven national newspapers during a key week of this low point in support for war. The first day of analysis coincides with the publication of the Blix Report on January 27. George Bush delivered his second State of the Union speech to Congress on January 28. Tony Blair travelled to Camp David for "a council of war" at the end of the week (at which time journalists were presented with copies of a new intelligence dossier quickly dubbed the "dodgy dossier" by most of the British media because of its extensive plagiarism of dated academic work downloaded from the Internet and passed off as based on new intelligence sources). It was thus a key week for newspapers to take their position with regard to the possibility of war.

The degree of dissent from the pro-war position of the UK government and official opposition poses an interesting but welcome problem for critical media researchers. It has become the received wisdom among critical media scholars that the mainstream media generally act as handmaidens to the public relations state in the manufacture of consent. Whether or not this describes accurately the normal relationship of media and state, it is clear that, during the early months of 2003 at a time of geopolitical crisis, relations between some sections of the mass media and state were and indeed remain severely strained. The degree of media dissent may have also helped to legitimate and mobilize popular dissent, although we also argue that the narrow terms on which some of that dissent was drawn may, in the longer-term, have contributed to the fragility of the anti-war majority. The relationship between media dissent and popular dissent is, of course, complex and multi-causal, and requires, ideally, an holistic approach, both to media (texts, production, and consumption) and to broader social and cultural change, beyond that which we can attempt here.

Theoretical and methodological background

Jurgen Habermas (1996) sets himself a similar problem to the one we address: to explain how in certain crisis situations, generally neglected actors in civil society can assume "a surprisingly active and momentous role" (1996: 380). What interests Habermas is how poorly resourced and institutionally powerless groups and movements can throw a spanner into the workings of the public sphere dominated normally by the interests of the economically and politically powerful. This is a key question for understanding how social change occurs in complex, mediated societies and is essential for assessing the prospects of democratization. Echoing the work of Alberto Melucci (1996) and others, Habermas argues that the great issues of the last decades—feminism, ecology, nuclear disarmament, and global poverty—have all been raised initially by new social movements and subcultures who through effective dramatization (for example, by non-violent symbolic acts of civil disobedience) of their concerns have persuaded the mass media to place the issues on the "public agenda." Of course, while opposition to the war was surprising and momentous, it prevented neither the UK's participation in the war nor a sudden shift in public opinion in favor of war in March and April 2003.

While Habermas' account (1996) possesses a certain plausibility, it needs to be supplemented by considering how these groups may penetrate the confines of the public sphere. Habermas seeks to explain this largely in terms of the mass media's self-understanding in liberal democratic societies (rightly or wrongly) as objective observers of society. However, the ability of counter-publicity groups to make their voices heard in the mass media depends not only on this self-understanding but also on the existence of crisis in the public sphere, manifested through mediated disagreement and controversy within economic, political, and cultural elites. The destabilization of the public sphere is both a top-down (centre–periphery) and a bottom-up (periphery–centre) process whose dimensions may be mutually reinforcing. It follows that, to understand both the generation and outcomes of crisis, one must grasp the dynamic relationship within and between elite and popular discourses, and between actors in the mass media public sphere and in the counter-public sphere (Downey and Fenton 2003). Indeed, this is an essential and overlooked task if we wish to understand social change in global modernity (Fenton and Downey 2003).

We are interested primarily in three broad processes: the construction of *consensus* (and dissent), the construction of *authority* (specifically authority to represent the reality of what is happening in the world), and the *naturalization* of facts or frameworks of interpretation (Potter 1996).

Taking these in turn, the build-up to a major international war is, obviously, a time when many actors are intensely concerned with the representation, or construction, of consensus around that war; what was immediately striking, however, from the early days of the Iraq war build-up, was the degree to which consensus *against* the war was also being constructed not just by media, but also by elements within the military, diplomatic, political, and cultural elites. This was why we chose the representation of consensus and dissent as our principal focus from the outset. Consensus is however never just consensus; it is used, rhetorically, as a warrant of truth (Potter 1996: 117). Hence the importance of the second theme: the construction of particular actors as "entitled to know particular sorts of things [so that] . . . their reports or descriptions may thus be given special credence" (Potter 1996: 114), against which there is the equally important construction of other actors as having a "stake" in this or that statement which disqualifies them as credible sources (Potter 1996: 124–5). The construction of consensus and authority occur within a third and wider construction, more difficult to detect: what Potter calls "constructing out-thereness," that is, the construction of certain claims "as *not* being constructed' (Potter 1996: 151, added emphasis).

This is a complex process: certain major explicit claims are presented as simply factual (and therefore beyond contestation) on the basis of other claims that are left implicit (but whose obviousness is assumed). The selection of background and foreground "facts" is obviously crucial to what forms part of the apparently natural "surface" of events and what does not. During the Iraq war build-up the relative exclusion of certain issues from the frame of possible discussion (for example, perspectives which challenged the relevance and justification of the US timetable toward war) was important if other claims and statements (specifically US and UK claims about what was happening) were to appear as "just" facts. This complex process of light and shade is what Steve Woolgar has called "ontological gerrymandering" (quoted in Potter 1996: 183–4). There was a lot of it around in the early months of 2003.[1]

Our analysis focuses on press articles from the six days beginning January 27, 2003.[2] Seven newspapers were chosen (the four broadsheet dailies—*Daily Telegraph, Times, Guardian, Independent*—and the top three tabloid dailies in terms of circulation—*Sun, Daily Mirror, Daily Mail*) to represent broadsheet and tabloid opinion in the UK. All war-related articles were analyzed (the initial selection used the Lexis-Nexis database and contained 955 articles), from which articles (news items, but also editorial and "independent" comment columns) were chosen for a more detailed discourse analysis on the basis of being broadly representative either of the discourse positions and/or rhetorical strategies of newspapers. A full list of the latter articles is contained in Appendix 1. Our analysis does not, therefore, pretend to be an exhaustive study of the full range of comment present (or absent) during this period (this would have required a much more extensive study that would have also considered images as well as written texts), but rather an indicative analysis of certain key discourse positions that seem to us significant in the broader construction of the crisis. Different discourse positions could be found within the same newspaper during the Iraq crisis. This is indicative in itself of both crisis and flux in the mass media public sphere concerning the then impending invasion of Iraq.

The construction of consensus

The most unambiguous support for the UK/USA position was granted by the *Times*. In contrast to other newspapers that backed the UK/USA position, the *Times* supported both policy and rhetoric, at times appearing to see itself as coach of a somewhat disorganized team. The editorial of January 30 assumes both the existence of WMD under the control of Saddam and an Iraq invasion's justification, with or without the support of the UN Security Council, as a means of protecting international security; there are no covert reasons for going to war (for example, to secure access to oil supplies). Indeed the editorial, published on the same day as a letter signed by eight European leaders in support of the US's stance, even holds out the prospect of constructing a united European–US position. The chief stumbling block to this, of course, was the Franco-German position that the UN inspectors should be given more time to complete their work and that war should be contemplated only as a last resort. The predicational strategy of the *Times* is illuminating. Jacques Chirac is accused of "posturing." This implies that his present opposition is not sincere, calculated in order to bring about certain effects that would be to the advantage of France, and that France's opposition will be reversed once suitable accommodations could be found. Schroeder is accused of "strategic pacifism." Given that Germany under Schroeder took part in the Kosovo conflict (its first military engagement since the end of World War II), it is somewhat curious to accuse Schroeder of pacifism. Of course, the charge of pacifism means that one can both explain and dismiss Germany's opposition by reference to this principle without having to justify the present conflict by reference to the principle of a "just war." The *Times* not merely misrepresents the German position but also attempts to dispel pacifism's positive connotations by suggesting Schroeder's was not a principled pacifism but adopted for strategic reasons. Without claiming the Franco-German position was somehow interest-free, our point is the *Times*' contrast between the "universal" interests represented by the UK/USA position (international security) and the "particular" interests ascribed to the Franco-German position.

This editorial position had been developed in a comment article by Daniel Finkelstein on January 28. Finkelstein supports war, with or without the UN's resolutions. Finkelstein adopts a Kantian-sounding moral vocabulary that gives the impression of possessing some intellectual authority. We have, according to Finkelstein, a moral duty or obligation to maintain international security and this demands that we should support the invasion of Iraq whether it has the sanction of the UN or not. Whereas the UK/USA is presented as obeying a Kantian categorical imperative and as acting selflessly, the UN as an institution is brought into question: "the Security Council is not a panel of disinterested philosophers. Its decisions all too often are based on national prejudice, imperial adventurism, the vanity of individuals, and the murderous impulses of dictators." This juxtaposition of the UK/USA and the Security Council is contradictory and rather ironic bearing in mind that the UK and USA are two of its five permanent members and thus are presumably as interested as other members. The article's clear strategy is to remove the argument from matters of fact (whether or not Iraq possesses WMD and poses an imminent threat to the world) and, assuming that "fact" as widely recognized, to convert the argument to one about morality. The moral case for war is wrapped in a pseudo-Kantian vocabulary and presented as a contrast between the dutiful and selfless UK/USA (going to war to protect the universal good of international security) and the war's immoral opponents.

The editorial of the *Daily Telegraph* "Why Britain should fight" on the day of the publication of the Blix Report (January 27: p. 21) admitted that three-quarters of the British public were opposed to war and argued this was because anti-war campaigners were presenting the better argument; Tony Blair by pursuing a "narrow legal" case for war against Iraq (i.e. via UN resolutions) had left the majority of the public confused as to "what they are fighting for." The only way to overturn the anti-war consensus, the editorial argues, is to invoke the national interest irrespective of the reports of the UN inspectors; not only is the regime of Saddam a military threat to the UK but also "let us not be shy of saying that it is in no one's interest for the [sic] some of the world's key oil supplies to be in the hands of an unstable dictator." Ultimately, then, the war is about "who is the boss." An Anglo-American hegemony would also be good for Iraq, the region, and the world.

The *Daily Telegraph* is here arguing for a new era of imperialism based on liberal representative democracy and free trade under the auspices of the benign powers of the UK/USA. The account that it provides is strikingly similar to the radical critique of the war aims. Of course, what is different is the evaluation of the outcome. *Prima facie*, the *Daily Telegraph*'s assumption that, once anti-war campaigners' diagnosis of the war rationale is admitted, the majority of public opinion will switch from being anti- to pro-war, is paradoxical; the paradox disappears, however, if one assumes a natural consensus in favor of that rationale, once directly stated.

While the *Daily Telegraph*'s assessment may indeed have been close to the unofficial government reasons for going to war, the open espousal of such a position hardly helped Blair who at this stage was relying on winning UN Security Council support for a war to win over public opinion and, therefore, emphasizing the supposed threat of Saddam rather than the benefits of "regime change." Not only therefore was there no consensus for war but also no consensus among the war's supporters about how to wage the rhetorical battle for public opinion. Indeed the clear anti-war consensus meant that assorted supporters of the UK government felt at liberty to advocate various rhetorical repair jobs, thus adding to the sense of confusion concerning the war's justification and the impression that the official justification was a screen to cover imperial ambitions. (In this context, the contradiction between the *Daily Telegraph*'s claim that the UN inspectors were irrelevant on January 27 and its editorial (January 28: 21) the day after the Blix report's publication stating the "case for war [was] still strong" seems less surprising.)

The *Daily Telegraph*'s discourse position was consistently adopted across genres (news reports, comment columns, and editorials). Even the devastating and surreal comment article by comedian Armando Iannucci, that offered an immanent critique of the UK/USA attitude toward the authority of the UN and the notion of a pre-emptive self-defense, may be seen as consistent with the newspaper's stress on *realpolitik* (the overwhelming importance of projecting Anglo-American power in oil rich regions of the world).

Whereas the *Daily Telegraph* clearly supported a war against Iraq if not entirely for the reasons used by the UK Government, the *Daily Mail* came out against the war in editorials on January 27 and 28 (p. 10 on both occasions), stating that the UK and USA had failed to provide evidence that Iraq was an "imminent threat" and consequently the war was not justified. The *Daily Mail's* doubts went beyond the evidential, however. Rather than sharing the *Daily Telegraph's* judgment that a post-Saddam Anglo-American empire would be good for UK and global interests, the *Daily Mail*, after noting the great likelihood of conflict, comments: "at what cost to the Middle East, world oil supplies, the war against terrorism, the Western alliance and the public's trust in the prime minister remains to be seen" (January 27: 10). It is not that the *Daily Mail* is against an Anglo-American empire, just that it believes that this enterprise is likely to backfire. The *Daily Telegraph* and *Daily Mail* agree on the criteria by which the world should be judged but have radically different projections of the consequences of war.

Whereas the *Daily Telegraph* was consistent in its discourse position, the *Daily Mail* adopted a number of positions across different genres. Its columnists, for example, ranged from the skeptical (in line with the editor: for example Peter McKay January 27: 13; Keith Waterhouse January 27: 14) to that of Melanie Phillips (January 27: 10) who bolted a "clash of civilizations" thesis between the "West" and Islam onto a "decline of European civilisation" argument, reaching general conclusions about Islam from the activities of neofundamentalist groups and distinguishing liberal Europe (unwilling to defend itself, therefore likely to be crushed by the "Islamist tiger") from the USA (strongly nationalist, deeply religious, and prepared to fight). The meaning of Phillips' argument is clear: Europe's survival is dependent upon becoming more like the USA and rejecting liberalism in all shapes and forms.

Despite an editorial line that was skeptical of the UK/USA position, *Daily Mail* news journalists accepted the UK/USA framing of the conflict. Thus coverage written by David Hughes of the Blix report claimed the report exposed Iraq's "charade" (adopting uncritically the phrase of Jack Straw), so that "the countdown to war quickened last night" (January 28: 4–5). The illogical idea of a countdown quickening (rather than, say, being continued or interrupted) is a strategy of intensification taken from the UK/USA. The elision of the actors (the people setting up the "countdown") serves to make conflict appear an unavoidable, natural process rather than a humanly constructed, and thus entirely mutable, series of events. The same journalist employs the same strategies a day later when writing of the "looming conflict" (January 29: 15) as though the conflict had a life of its own, beyond human control.

The Independent adopted a consistently anti-war position across genres with Robert Fisk spearheading its coverage and analysis of the conflict. Fisk used the occasion of the day of the Blix Report to launch a broadside against UK/USA "deceptions" (January 27: 5). The first "deception" is that Saddam is a dictator who poses an imminent threat to the region and the world in the manner of Hitler's Germany in the 1930s, making the anti-war position one of "appeasement." Not only was this Saddam/ Hitler elision intended to bring the conflict closer to home, thereby making the threat appear more real, but it also borrowed World War II's legitimacy for the present conflict while intimating a successful conclusion. This was a key strategy of the UK/USA because it provided the moral justification for war and was an argument designed to appeal to liberals, leftists, and pacificists by questioning the morality of their moral opposition to the present conflict. The difficulty in disrupting this analogy lay, Fisk argued, in the obviously brutal character of Saddam's regime. The easier task was to disrupt the idea that Saddam posed the same threat to the world after a crushing military defeat in the 1991 Gulf War and 12 years of sanctions and containment as Hitler did in the 1930s after the German annexations and invasions of Czechoslovakia and Poland. That is, of course, why the issue of "weapons of mass destruction" was crucial. Fisk asks whether "we are prepared to pay the price of so promiscuous a war" and points to the likelihood that thousands of Iraqis will die and that the UK/USA will be seen as an occupying power that will strengthen support for neofundamentalist groups. The second deception, Fisk argued, was that the war was not about oil. While the UK/USA insisted that the war was exclusively about WMD, the Iraqi regime and protesters insisted that the war was about the imperial control of Iraq's oil and that the issue of WMD was a rhetorical fig leaf to cover naked ambition and self-interest. This was the central argument of more radical anti-war protesters for whom the UN "weapons inspections" were a public relations charade. This radical position seemed to win widespread support in everyday life in the weeks leading up to the war. Even many war supporters did not believe the UK/USA official version of the war.

Fisk presents the UK/USA as relatively isolated: "The only other nation pushing for war—save for the ever-grateful Kuwait—is Israel." This serves of course to emphasize the lack of consensus in favor of war internationally and to damn the UK/USA through association with an already occupying power. Domestically the populations of the UK/USA, despite "being told to go to war by their newspapers and television stations and politicians," are becoming increasingly skeptical of the claims of their governments. Indeed, the "popular" consensus in Britain is anti-war. What Fisk does not explain, however, is how this might be so: is this popular anti-war consensus generated from the periphery? Does Fisk overstate the elite consensus? Or do both play a role in the generation of popular dissent? In any case, it is this "popular" consensus for which Fisk claimed to speak.

A striking feature of press coverage in this period, notwithstanding this significant dissent about the ends and means of war, was the *de facto* consensus constructed around the time-frame of the UK/USA war build-up. The dominant *news*-frame almost everywhere was the momentum building toward war around the UK/USA diplomatic agenda. Turning to the three remaining papers in our sample, this was virtually the only perspective referred to in the *Sun* and it also dominated the news coverage in the *Guardian*; only in the *Daily Mirror* did other perspectives contribute to news reports, and then always within a context determined by the UK/USA official agenda.

Since the *Sun* has been the most belligerent UK newspaper, its construction of national and international consensus for its position was hardly surprising. This was expressed not only in terms of UK "hearts and minds" (January 30: 9) but also in terms of a broad coalition of "the West v the Rest" (headline January 30: 9)

273

and even "the world" being on course for war (January 28: 8). There were other more disturbing aspects to this construction of consensus: the denigration of Islam and asylum-seekers set up a situation where Muslims were seen as the "enemy within." Where dissent from this "consensus" was mentioned, it was always in disparaging terms: unspecified "anti-war campaigners" (January 28: 8), "rebel lefties" and the "loopy left" (January 30: 9).

Since the *Guardian* was the newspaper whose editorial opposition to war was most predictable from its general discourse, its reproduction of the momentum for war in its lead news items is more surprising: for example, the suggestion of a diplomatic "consensus" after the Blix report that Iraq was not cooperating (January 28: 1); in addition, the isolation of France implied by its comment (after the Blair/Bush summit on January 31) that, while the UK and US were seeking to convince "the international community," Blair felt increasing "frustration with the French" (who, however, would have "the squeeze" put on them) (February 2: 1).[3] The significance of these suggestions in *Guardian* news reports emerges more clearly when we look later at their close reliance on UK and US diplomatic agendas; for now, we should just note that it was at odds with the *Guardian*'s clear editorial position (January 28, January 30) against the war.

In contrast, the *Mirror* followed its editorials' anti-war position into its news articles, interpreting diplomatic reactions after the Blix report as a consensus *against* war that left the US isolated (January 28: 4) and mocking Blair's January 29 House of Commons performance as "My war against the world" (headline, January 30: 2). Here there was an overlap with the editorials, if not the news coverage, of the *Guardian* which argued (January 28: 21) that the UK/USA reaction to the Blix report "will not be how most of the world views" that report and (January 30: 23) insisted that Blair should overturn his existing pro-war, pro-Bush policy and instead "speak *for* this nation." The idea that, far from war tapping into a national consensus, war went directly against the national consensus (noted already in Robert Fisk's writing for *The Independent*) was developed later in the week by the *Daily Mirror* (January 31: 6), reporting its commissioned YouGov poll that showed 75 percent currently against the war and, more strikingly, only 2 percent believing that the war would make them safer from terrorist attack. The resulting image of Blair as the isolated leader battling against the tides of popular opinion remained, however, ambiguous, as we note below.

To sum up, the *Times*, *Daily Telegraph* and *Sun* (the two biggest circulation broadsheet papers and the biggest tabloid) supported the UK/USA war at this stage but the last two used arguments for war (for example, control over oil, the West versus the rest) that were antithetical to the official UK/USA position. These arguments presumably only helped to confirm popular doubts about the truthfulness of the official line. Only the *Sun* claimed an international and domestic consensus existed in favor of war. The other newspapers clearly recognized and commented upon both the international and domestic absence of such a consensus, even if in more subtle ways they generally reinforced, rather than challenged, the event-frame assumed by the UK/USA position. The four newspapers that took anti-war editorial stances did so for contrasting reasons. While the *Daily Mail* was simply concerned about whether the national interest would be served by war, the *Independent*, *Guardian*, and *Daily Mirror* raised moral objections concerning the consequences of war.

Media elites, then, were split not only in terms of which action would further national interests but also of which actions were moral. The confusion between the two in anti-war positions is one explanation why, once the war started, some newspapers and some of the public swung in behind the UK/USA position. It was not that they supported the war but that once the war which appeared irreversible had started, apparently consensual appeals to "the nation" (for example, the call to support "our" armed forces) trumped prior doubts concerning whether the war was, in fact, in the national interest.[4]

The uses of authority

Max Weber (1968) argued that modern societies have developed three types of authority: rational–legal, traditional, and charismatic. Rational–legal authority is developed from impersonal rule-based institutions and practices, traditional authority from historical continuities of institutions and practices, and charismatic authority rests on the force of personality of protagonists.

During the period of our analysis the UK/USA were attempting to develop an international rational–legal justification for war through the United Nations Security Council. As the possibility of this receded in February and March, there was a concerted attempt to question both the authority of the UN and that of the governments of anti-war states (most notably, the French President, Jacques Chirac). The failure to win international rational–legal authority meant that such a justification had to be produced nationally (via a vote in the House of Commons and the Attorney-General's opinion on the legal basis for war) but such an enterprise was hindered by the obvious failure to secure an international agreement. In such circumstances, the attempt to build support for war drew increasingly heavily upon the charismatic authority of Tony Blair.

A striking feature of the early articles we analyzed was the limited range of interpretative sources that were treated as credible. All newspapers reproduced extensive quotations from official speeches by US and UK politicians, the obvious "primary definers" in the build-up to war (Hall *et al.* 1978). Also universally cited was Hans Blix himself, as the UN weapons inspector more inclined toward the UK/USA position (note that the *Sun* never referred *at all* to Mohammed al-Baradei, the head of the Atomic Weapons Authority, who reported alongside Blix that the possibility of Iraq's nuclear weapons could be eliminated in months). More significant are differences in how other sources were treated. UK intelligence sources played a significant part in the week's events, with the announcement late on January 26 (the day before the Blix report) that the UK government had handed a "dossier" reporting Saddam's breaches of cooperation with the UN inspectors. The *Sun* reported these intelligence claims directly as fact ("Saddam is using guerrilla tactics to sabotage the hunt for his doomsday weapons, it emerged last night," January 27: 2); in the *Guardian* (January 27: 1) the story was the fact of the intelligence briefing itself and its diplomatic significance, although there was little reference in its main news report to alternative interpretations of the claims in the briefing. Only in the *Mirror* was there substantial skepticism, with its sub-headline "War in weeks as Blair gives 'evidence' for attack" (January 27: 4).

Similar differences were played out in news treatment of diplomatic sources. While the *Sun* presented UK and US diplomatic sources without any suggestion of distance from them, the *Guardian* on occasion indicated skepticism (for example in noting (January 28: 1) the difference between the UK Foreign Secretary's "bellicose" interpretation of the Blix report and the UK ambassador to the United Nations' more cautious interpretation). On other occasions, however, it is striking how close the *Guardian's* news reports stayed to the interpretation that the UK and US administrations were encouraging; its front page February 1 report on the Blair/ Bush Washington summit read more like a Whitehall press release ("Mr Blair impressed on the Americans . . . Mr Blair secured support [from the US]," and so on). The implication—one that UK diplomats no doubt encouraged—was that the summit was about *diplomacy* (Blair restraining Bush from war) even though, as the same report made clear, Blair had already secured Bush's support on the need for a second UN resolution by phone on the evening *before* the summit. Why then the time and expense of Blair's transatlantic visit? The reason, already anticipated in media comment earlier that week, emerged clearly in the *Sun's* news report, but was fudged in the *Guardian*: "The President and the PM thrashed out final details for an onslaught beginning in mid-March—as exclusively revealed in yesterday's Sun." So much for diplomats' claim (reported by the *Guardian* without demur) that the summit was a "council of diplomacy"! Only the *Mirror* kept a more consistent distance from official UK/USA sources.

A quite different issue of authority concerned Blair's own standing as prime minister. Some personalization of the war build-up is hardly surprising. The personalization, however, that really mattered for the British public's perception of the issues at stake concerned Blair himself. A theme, more dominant in press coverage nearer to the outbreak of war, was the presentation of Blair as the lone leader, bravely opposing the skepticism of his people at considerable personal cost. It is worth noting the assumptions about the credibility of Blair's self-representation as a man of "ideals" upon which this depended. Possibly the strongest attack on Blair's policy during the week we analyzed came in a *Guardian* editorial (January 30: 23), which argued that his policy would have results directly at odds with his ideals (of "global justice" and so on). Even this criticism already conceded that the prime minister was motivated by "ideals," rather than, say, by a calculation of Britain's strategic interests; yet this was a reading of Blair's actions and motives on which he later played himself when under maximum pressure just before war started. We see how, behind the surface of dissent from the British government's position, there were significant limits to that dissent.

While pro-war reports tended to personalize the war by focusing on Saddam—contrasting him with Bush and Blair, comparing him to Hitler—thereby creating the impression that the war was not against Iraq but against Saddam, the *Daily Mirror* resolutely referred to the "war on Iraq." The contrasting referential strategies are designed to connote different types of conflict—one limited and precise with few casualties, the other widespread with many casualties. This counter-personalization strategy was accompanied by a re-personalization strategy. January 31 was an excellent example. The *Mirror's* front page carries the story of a Nelson Mandela speech in Johannesburg criticizing the UK/USA position and ties this in to the anti-war petition organized by the newspaper. This is followed by a longer news story relating to the speech (pp. 4 and 5). Also on page 5 is an article relating to two popular Labour politicians' (Claire Short and Tony Benn) criticism of the UK/USA position. This is followed on page 6 by an editorial supporting Mandela. On pages 8 and 9 there is a list of celebrities, politicians, and war heroes who have signed the paper's anti-war petition. The global meaning of "Mandela" is that of selfless and ultimately victorious struggle against oppression. The *Daily Mirror* (January 31: 6) editorial asks Blair (and by extension the British people) to choose between Mandela, "symbol of honour, principle and commitment to justice" and Bush, "the warmongering president."

The reliance on charismatic authority, rather than legal–rational and traditional authority, to legitimate *dissent* at this time needs to be understood both in terms of the discourse strategies and the character of British society. The UN's rational–legal authority, for example, was ambiguous from the point of view of the anti-war movement, since accepting the UN's authority could have undermined the anti-war movement if the UK/USA had in fact persuaded the Security Council to back war. Traditional authority figures were also rarely used to legitimate dissent. Anti-war religious leaders, for example, were given a much lower profile in the UK than in Germany and Italy. The *Daily Mirror* clearly judged that the oppositional opinion of pop stars would do more for the anti-war cause than that of the Pope, the Archbishop of Canterbury, or leading British Muslim clerics.

Closing down/opening up the argument

We now look more specifically at how press coverage naturalized certain frameworks of interpretation of great relevance to the official UK/USA position on events. We have already seen how the UK press gave credence to UK/USA intelligence and diplomatic sources in ways that were at least open to question. The broad UK/USA policy framework (that the war was "to disarm" Iraq) and its inherent military momentum (in relation to which the UN inspections were merely a "delay") was naturalized right across the British press. It was uncommon to find dissenting opinion reflected, or even acknowledged, in the news articles we analyzed; even in the comment columns, dissenting opinion was often surprisingly uncritical on this crucial point with the exception of some columnists writing for the *Daily Mirror*, *Independent*, and *Guardian* who directly raised oil resources as a key reason lying behind the UK/USA drive to war.

The naturalization of the UK/USA perspective took the form, first, of constant references to "time running out" for peace. This was, of course, the stated UK/USA position, but it became naturalized when, for example, UN inspectors were described as having "earned themselves" a few further weeks, whereas the UK had "nudge[d] back Bush's decision to go to war" (*The Guardian*, January 28: 1); or when the UK's release of "intelligence" information just before Blix's report was described as if it were a disinterested speeding-up of the weapons inspections: "Britain is aiming to prevent the process from dragging on indefinitely, by handing over and publicizing sensitive intelligence which allegedly shows that Iraq is flouting the UN" (January 1: 1). The word "allegedly" hardly counters the naturalizing force of that apparently neutral phrase "the process." "The process" is not the UN inspections as such, but those inspections as interpreted by the US and UK (as "delay" to their underlying war timetable; otherwise how could a few months' inspections be seen as "dragging on indefinitely"?). The *Guardian's* editorial (January 28: 23) made a concerted effort to dislodge this naturalization, by arguing that it was the inspections process that was "natural" and should be left undisturbed: "if the Bush administration and its admirers wish to curtail or cancel this UN process, after a mere two months or so, it is up to them to explain why. They have not done so to date . . . " Yet this fundamental point failed to influence the *Guardian's* own news reports later in the week, most importantly in its reports of the Blair/ Bush summit (see above).

It is worth noting what metaphors came to dominate in newspapers' coverage of the war build-up. We might have expected the metaphor of war as something to fear (*Mirror*, January 27), although in fact it was surprisingly rare; we might also have expected the *Sun's* celebration of Blair confronting his critics in the House of Commons on January 29 as a man of action: "the Prime Minister raised the stakes . . . [he] was stung into action . . . under fire from all sides . . . it was the first time he had lined up Stalinist tyrant Kim Jong II for a possible military strike." With an image of a watchful rifle-carrying UK soldier above the article, and a comic-book picture of the globe with members of the "axis of evil" named within jagged balloons (like mini-explosions), it was almost as if the war had begun (*Sun*, January 30: 8). Less expected, however, was the way that this "Boy's Own" picture of Blair—as the isolated, embattled, but brave quasi-military leader—circulated beyond the pages of the *Sun* and into articles elsewhere that *prima facie* were strongly critical of the Prime Minister (for example, the columnist Jackie Ashley's article: *The Guardian*, January 30: 21).

Such an idea of Blair as the embattled leader was however double-edged, as became clear in the article published in the *Mirror* the next day (January 31: 6) by Ashley's fellow *Guardian* columnist, Jonathan Freedland, headed "A leader who has left behind his people." This article analyzed the devastating findings of that day's YouGov poll (referred to above) and concluded that Blair was isolated from his people as never before. However:

. . . that is not, by itself, a reason to condemn him. On the contrary, it can be a mark of greatness for a politician that he dares to lead, rather than follow his people. We always say we want someone who is prepared to trust his own convictions rather than merely obey opinion polls. Well now we have one.

Not surprisingly, this was a line used to great effect by Blair's supporters (and even some of his formal Conservative opponents) later in the war build-up. The article concluded:

How will historians look back at this solo stance by Tony Blair? That depends on the outcome of the coming war. But they will either say this was his defining act of great statesmanship—or the decision that ultimately led to his downfall.

Naturalized here are a number of assumptions: first, that the war was inevitable (remember this "critical" piece was written a full two weeks *before* the largest of the global anti-war protests on February 15); second, that Blair's position was dictated solely by a sense of what is right (otherwise, how can the mere success of the war be grounds for attributing his stance to "statesmanship," rather than, say, lucky miscalculation?); third, that Blair will survive, if he does, because his policy proves a success, rather than because his opponents fail to oppose him (much closer to the truth, as we write); and finally, and most obviously, that if the war is a "success" on UK/USA terms, it will be impossible to interpret otherwise than to Blair's credit, which precisely reproduces the UK/USA framework for interpreting the build-up to war as "inevitable."

If the image of Blair, the isolated leader, rose to prominence, it is worth asking what other themes (less favorable to the UK/USA position) received less prominence in UK press coverage. A minimal list would be:

- the arguments behind the French, German, Russian, or Chinese positions against the war, let alone those of Arab or Latin American countries, who faced acute risks in opposing the US;
- the range of dissent (both popular and elite) within the US (it was *Le Monde* which reported the *Washington Post* anti-war article by the US's Supreme commander in Gulf War I, Norman Schwarzkopf: *Le Monde*, January 31: 15);
- underlying concerns whether a war was likely to increase Britain's risk of being a target for "terrorist" attack (mentioned for example in Freedland's article, but rarely referred to in news coverage);
- the opinions on the war of Britain's ethnic minorities, especially its Muslim population (to its credit, the *Guardian* later began a comment column which tried to cover this, but this was the exception, not the rule).

Yet it must also be noted that, in contrast to this naturalization of the UK/USA framework for interpreting the coming war, the *Mail*, *Guardian*, *Independent*, and *Mirror* began to give the anti-war movement greater prominence, especially in the period directly after our sample week. The *Mirror* was the most campaigning anti-war paper, urging its readers to sign a petition (by February 15 it claimed to have collected 195,000 signatures) and also sponsoring the "Stop the war coalition" march on February 15. On the morning of the march the *Mirror* headline read "The world against the war" with the contents devoted to details of the globalization of the anti-war protests and accounts of the preparations for the London deomonstration. The *Guardian* and *Independent* ran stories about first-time "ordinary" protesters. The *Mail* provided a map for its readers wishing to join the march. The anti-war movement, if only for a while, cut across ethnic, class, religious, and political boundaries, as newspapers helped to construct as well as simply reflect the diverse character of the movement.

Conclusion

How are we to make overall sense of this complex picture? The fundamental point is that elite media and political discourse concerning the waging of a war against Iraq in the UK was deeply divided. Opinion was divided concerning whether war was in the national interest and/or right morally. Generally speaking right-wing papers (*Times*, *Telegraph*, *Sun*, *Mail*) either supported or opposed the war along lines of perceived national interest whereas liberal and left-of-centre newspapers (*Mirror*, *Independent*, *Guardian*) employed arguments questioning the morality of the UK/USA position. Divisions within elite media discourse and the consequent legitimation of dissent helped to establish the preconditions for a successful mobilization of one and a half million people on the streets of central London in winter. To understand this mobilization fully, one must acknowledge not only the legitimacy crisis in the public sphere but also the creative disobedience of counter-public spheres and alternative media in encouraging such a display of public opposition.

Of course, public opposition to the war did not prevent it taking place (for reasons which we have also explored) and, when the war started, media representations and public opinion shifted to being pro-war. In the longer term, as the memory of "liberation" fades in the face of the realities of occupation, critical media voices are returning and popular disaffection is growing. In the post-war situation, there is no naturalized "timetable" on which the UK/USA position can rely to close down popular dissent. On the contrary, the situation in Iraq, the UK, and the US is open-ended and uncertain. It remains to be seen what consequences the long-term legacy of dissent from the war at all levels will have for national and international politics.

Notes

1 Nor of course, in the UK, was it unique to this period: compare Fairclough's analysis of New Labour language in relation to "the international community" during the Kosovo war (Fairclough 2000, p. 152–3).
2 Sunday papers were excluded since the principal war-related events (Blix report, State of Union address, Blair–Bush summit) all occurred during Monday to Friday.
3 The same article's sub-headline was "Blair gains extra time to win over *waverers*."
4 There were other reasons for this shift: the limitations inherent in the framework of mediated dissent (see next two sections) and probably a general fatalism (cf Croteau 1995, p. 115).

References

Beck, Ulrich (2000) "The cosmopolitan perspective: sociology of the second age of modernity," *British Journal of Sociology*, vol. 51, no. 1, pp. 79–105.

Chiapello, Eve and Fairclough, Norman (2002) "Understanding the new management ideology: a transdisciplinary contribution from critical discourse analysis and new sociology of capitalism," *Discourse and Society*, vol. 13, no. 2, pp. 185–208.

Croteau, David (1995) *Politics and the Class Divide*, Philadelphia, PA: Temple University Press.

Downey, John and Fenton, Natalie (2003) "New media, counter publicity and the public sphere," *New Media and Society*, vol. 5, no. 2, pp. 185–202.

Fairclough, Norman (1995) *Media Discourse*, London: Arnold.

Fairclough, Norman (2000) *New Labour, New Language*, London: Routledge.

Fairclough, Norman and Wodak, Ruth (1997) "Critical discourse analysis" in T. Van Dijk (ed.), *Discourse as Social Interactions*, London: Sage, pp. 258–84.

Fenton, Natalie and Downey, John (2003) "Counter public spheres and global modernity," *Javnost*, vol. X, no. 1, pp. 15–31.

Habermas, Jurgen (1996) *Between Facts and Norms*, Polity: Cambridge.

Hall, S., Critcher, C., Jefferson, T., Clarke, J., and Roberts, B., (1978) *Policing the Crisis: Mugging the State, and Law and Order*, London: Macmillan.

Melucci, Alberto (1996) *Challenging Codes*, Cambridge: Cambridge University Press.

Potter, Jonathan (1996) *Representing Reality*, London: Sage.

Wodak, Ruth and Meyer, Michael (eds) (2001) *Methods of Critical Discourse Analysis*, Sage: London.

Appendix 1

List of 2003 articles chosen for detailed analysis:

January 27

The Daily Telegraph, editorial, p. 21
Daily Mail, editorial, p. 10
Daily Mail, comment, Peter McKay, p. 13
Daily Mail, comment, Keith Waterhouse, p. 14
Daily Mail, comment, Melanie Phillips, p. 10

The Independent, comment, Robert Fisk, p. 5
The Guardian, lead story, Wintour/Watt/Younge, p. 1
The Sun, lead story, Wooding, p. 2
The Mirror, Hardy article, pp. 4–5

January 28

The Daily Telegraph, editorial, p. 21
Daily Mail, editorial, p. 10
Daily Mail, news, David Hughes, pp. 4–5
The Times, comment, Daniel Finkelstein
The Guardian, lead story, Borger/White/Macaskill, p. 1
The Sun, Kavanagh/Flinn article, pp. 8–9
The Mirror, Wallace article, pp. 4–5
The Guardian, editorial, p. 21
The Sun, editorial, p. 8
Mirror, editorial, p. 6

January 29

Daily Mail, news, David Hughes, p. 15

January 30

The Times, editorial
The Guardian, lead comment, Jackie Ashley, p. 21
The Sun, lead comment, Kavanagh, p. 9
The Mirror, lead story, Hardy, plus Routledge comment, p. 2
The Guardian, editorial, p. 23
The Sun, editorial, p. 8

January 31

The Guardian, lead story, Wintour/Campbell, p. 1
The Sun, lead story, Pascoe-Watson, p. 2
The Mirror, lead comment, Jonathan Freedland, p. 6
The Mirror, pp. 1–9

February 1

The Guardian, lead story, Wintour/Borger, p. 1
The Sun, lead story, Pascoe-Watson, p. 2
The Mirror, news article, Roberts, pp. 4–5

15

HOW BRITISH TELEVISION NEWS REPRESENTED THE CASE FOR THE WAR IN IRAQ[1]

Justin Lewis and Rod Brookes

Introduction

There has been much interest in whether there has been a fundamental transformation in governments' attempts to manage news coverage of international conflict in the post-Cold war era (Thussu and Freedman 2003). The effects of globalization and technological development on the production, distribution, and consumption of the media have been seen as crucial: the proliferation of new sources of information (Allan 2002); the emergence of transnational, 24-hour rolling news channels (Thussu 2003); the uncertain future of state-owned and public broadcasters in the context of deregulation, privatization, and the growth of transnational entertainment-based, mainly US-owned media conglomerates; and the development of transnational media services such as Al-Jazeera serving diasporic communities that transcend national boundaries (Miladi 2003). The events of September 11, 2001 and the adoption by the US government of policies based on pre-emptive military intervention have given urgency to this discussion (Zelizer and Allan 2002; Thussu and Freedman 2003).

Two key aspects of the British news media's role in covering the war in Iraq in the UK cut across most of these themes. The first was an attack led by the British government on the role of particular news organizations in undermining its case for the war: its targets being Al-Jazeera and other Arabic media, and, most significantly, the BBC.[2] The second was a debate about the implications of the Pentagon-led policy of embedded reporting. Purportedly an exercise in facilitating access for news organizations to the frontline (enabled by the development of portable communications technology), the policy had attracted criticism for encouraging a sense of identification among reporters with the military units on whom they were dependent for everyday survival.

Contributions to these two debates have often focused on particular episodes. The most notable was BBC Radio 4 *Today* correspondent Andrew Gilligan's report that members of the British security services were unhappy that the government's dossier on Iraqi WMD had been "sexed up" by 10 Downing Street. In many quarters, this single episode was held up as symptomatic of the BBC institutional anti-war bias. In this article we take a broader view in order to test competing claims over different broadcasters' coverage of the case for the war. Our analysis is based on an extensive content analysis of weeknight bulletins by the most-watched UK television news providers during the war itself.

In the six months leading up to the beginning of the war, opinion polls suggested that public opinion was divided. Those in support of a war against Iraq to remove Saddam varied between 30 percent and 40 percent throughout those six months.[3] Support for the war with Iraq rose significantly on two conditions: first, if it could be shown that Iraq possessed WMD, or second, if the war had the approval of the United Nations. In an ICM poll for the *Guardian*, for example (September 20–2, 2002), only 37 percent approved of a military attack to remove Saddam Hussein, as opposed to 46 percent against. However the number approving if the government provided evidence that Saddam possessed WMD rose to 65 percent. Conversely, polls indicate that even with evidence that Saddam possessed WMD about a quarter of the population were still against a war. The polls therefore indicated that there was a significant group who could be won over to either side (Kellner 2003).

Three arguments were central to the case for war: the assertion that Iraq possessed—and might use—WMD; the brutality of the Saddam Hussein regime; and the notion that an invasion was in support of (and supported by) the Iraqi people themselves.

In the ensuing battle for public opinion, a significant shift occurred during the war itself, when polls suggested support for the war—*without* the two conditions having been met—rose to high enough levels for the government to be able to claim majority (though by no means overwhelming) support. Research suggests that this was partly a function of a residual feeling of patriotism—once war began, some people felt it was important to put aside doubts and support the mission of the British armed forces.[4] But we were also interested to see how the government's case for war was presented during the conflict.

Methodology

We carried out a content analysis of the four main British television news sources during the Iraq war in order to examine the patterns of coverage and to assess the degree to which the government's case for war was validated or undermined by that coverage. We chose *BBC News at Six*; *ITV Evening News* at 6:30 p.m.; *Channel 4 News* at 7 p.m. and *Sky News at Ten*. The early evening news programs on BBC and ITV were chosen because they are generally the most popular, and because they were more consistent in terms of time slot and length throughout the war than the late evening bulletins.

Each news bulletin was broken down into discrete units of analysis—something increasingly difficult to do in contemporary styles of broadcasting, especially when one news event dominates the news bulletin, and various reports flow into one another. In this study a "report" involved an identifiable, authored segment of the news program: a news anchor's introduction—if it contained substantive information in its own right—and a correspondent's report would typically be coded as two discrete reports.

The sample consisted of 1,534 reports, all of which were coded by type/authorship. This allowed us to look at the overall shape of news coverage in order to see which part of the news operations were important in relaying information to viewers. The main categories of authorship used in our analysis were as follows:

- Embedded reporter
- Baghdad reporter
- Qatar reporter
- unilateral reporter
- available footage
- studio analysis
- interview with reporter
- interview with expert(s)
- anchor.

Methodologically the task of differentiating between categories of news reporting proved difficult. This problem was, in itself, revealing about the character of television news coverage of the 2003 Iraq war, whereby it was often hard to identify the origins of a report. There were a substantial number of reports sent back by front line correspondents clearly showing the correspondent embedded with their unit. Reports filed by Baghdad-based reporters were also relatively easy to identify, at least until the arrival of embedded and unilateral correspondents after the US forces entered the city. There were, however, a large number of reports whose origin was unclear.

Some of these were edited by correspondents embedded with the Ministry of Defence's Forward Transmission Unit (known as the FTU), based initially in north Kuwait and, a week into the war, six miles north of the Iraqi border (Franks 2003). These correspondents were intended to form the "hub," their role to edit reports sent back from front-line embedded correspondents or "spokes" (whose reports were pooled) in an attempt to convey a broader picture of the war in a way that the embeds could not (see Lewis *et al.* 2003 for a detailed analysis of the hub and spokes system). Reporters at the hub also had access to other footage—from a range of sources—which were inserted to accompany the reporter's narration. Thus while a report's voiceover might have been an embedded reporter, the footage came from a range of (embedded and non-embedded) sources whose origin was difficult to identify.

Where we could not positively identify the origins of stories as filed by any of the above types of correspondent we coded these under the category "available footage." This category could include footage from embedded reporters and unilaterals from the same news organization or others through pools, news agencies, news exchanges as well as footage from the Pentagon and the Ministry of Defence (MoD).

Stories filed by embedded reporters, Baghdad-based unilaterals, roving unilaterals and Doha-based correspondents, were coded thus when they were clearly marked as such. Two-ways between anchors and correspondents in the region were coded under the category of reporter they were with, on the basis that it was the correspondent who provided most of the information during the exchange. Some reporters—notably political correspondents—delivered much of their reports during two-ways with anchors, and these were categorized as "interviews with reporters."

The first stage of analysis gave us a broad picture of how the war was covered. The second stage of analysis focused on the three main themes central to the case for war:

1   Iraq had a program of WMD which constituted a threat;
2   Saddam was an evil and brutal dictator;
3   his regime repressed an Iraqi people who would welcome liberation through US/UK military intervention.

We explored the presence and treatment of these themes during the war, in order to see the extent to which broadcasters embraced or rejected the government's case.

Theme 1: Iraqi WMD capability

These were references that alluded to the Iraqi possession of WMD. This included footage of the US/UK forces' discovery of facilities suggesting evidence of WMD capability, stories in which US/UK forces or correspondents donned gas masks or chemical protection suits (thus implying the clear and present threat of Iraqi deployment of chemical or biological weapons), and speculation about Iraq's WMD capability.

We coded assessments of Iraqi WMD under two broad headings: those references that asserted or implied the possible or likely presence of chemical/biological weapons, and those references that either cast doubt or denied Iraqi WMD capability.

Theme 2: rescuing the Iraqi people

While the presence of WMD—and the threat they posed—constituted the legal basis of the government's case for invading Iraq, war supporters also stressed the moral basis of intervention, as the only way in which the Iraqi people could be liberated from Saddam's oppressive regime. Critical to this argument was the idea that the Iraqi people would welcome liberation, and that civilian casualties could be kept to a minimum.[5] We therefore coded every reference to the condition and attitude of the Iraqi people in order to see whether they were represented as supporting and celebrating the invasion, or as suspicious, angry, or hostile. We also coded every reference to news of Iraqi casualties (although it would be a mistake to assume that news of civilian casualties was necessarily a problem for the government's case, as the numbers reported in these cases were usually quite small, which could be interpreted as supporting the idea that casualties were minimal).

Theme 3: the depravity of the Iraqi regime

A significant moment in the media coverage of the war was the broadcast by Al-Jazeera of footage showing two dead British soldiers. On March 27, during a press conference with George Bush, Tony Blair seized on these photographs, asserting (incorrectly, as it transpired) that these soldiers were executed POWs. In a condemnation shown on all the British news channels, he claimed that "if anyone needed further evidence of the depravity of Saddam's regime, this atrocity provides it." We coded all such references as indicative of the depravity of the Saddam Hussein regime—a list which included visual footage of UK/US forces' discoveries of torture chambers or morgues, condemnations of Iraqi propaganda, and pictures indicating the decadence of Saddam's palaces with their expensive, and extravagant nouveau riche fittings.

Finally, we coded each report which included one of these three themes in order to establish the nature and type of source used to justify claims being made.

How the war was reported

It would be wrong to draw conclusions *only* from the percentages expressed in Table 15.1, as our method takes no account of the widely varying length of different types of discrete stories, or the significance of their position in the running order. However, it does indicate that, while this was perhaps the most televised war to date, edited packages delivered by anchors in the studio remained central to the coverage. What is perhaps surprising here is that Sky, as the one rolling news channel, carried more reports by news anchors than the other broadcasters.

The coverage of the war against Iraq in 2003 differed fundamentally from the previous Gulf War and other conflicts because of the practice of deploying "embedded reporters," a phrase which had entered common currency only a few months before.[6] Although reports had been "embedded" in previous conflicts, the Pentagon saw its implementation in 2003 as marking a new approach to combat news management. Embed opportunities were assigned to news organizations centrally by the Pentagon and by the MoD, giving certain reporters privileged and protected access to the front line.

This is clearly manifested in our analysis: after news anchors, embedded reporters were responsible for the largest identifiably authored form of reportage.

Table 15.1 Types of news report, by percentage

	BBC	ITV	C4	Sky	Total[7]
Embedded reporter	6.3	13.0	10.5	6.7	9
Baghdad reporter	6.9	6.6	5.9	4.1	6
Qatar reporter	2.7	7.0	3.9	1.8	4
Unilateral	1.8	2.3	0	0.2	1
Available footage	17.1	19.9	12.9	13.1	15
Studio analysis	8.4	2.3	3.7	1.0	4
Interview with reporter	6.6	3.7	3.9	9.2	6
Interview with expert(s)	0.3	3.9	8.0	1.4	3
Anchor	45.6	39.9	43.9	57.1	48
Other	4.5	3.3	7.3	5.3	5

If we exclude reports by anchors, reports from embeds constituted 17 percent of the coverage—notably more than any other form of reporting from the region. Embeds also produced much of the material for the sizeable "available footage" category, as well editing and/or providing voiceovers for the footage compiled under this heading.

The size of this miscellaneous category should, perhaps, give us pause. It is worth noting here that if we, as analysts, had difficulty identifying the origins of many news reports without background knowledge—what chance did the viewer have? Most journalists would agree, for example, that footage should be attributed, so that the viewer is aware of its origin. And yet some of the footage used in these news reports came from Pentagon and MoD camera crews, which was mixed in with other images but *not* attributed (MoD footage of Iraqi's surrendering, for example, was used by ITV and Channel 4 news on March 21 with no indication of its origin).

Correspondents based in Baghdad (under the supervision of the Iraqi military) were also prominent in the coverage—providing 11 percent of the non-anchor based reports. The UK and US governments, while happy for reporters to be reporting from the US and British troops' point of view (in a literal rather than necessarily a figurative sense), had expressed opposition to the deployment of journalists in Baghdad, reporting, as it were, from the perspective of the "enemy." While the US television networks caved into this pressure and pulled their journalists from Baghdad, the British broadcasters felt that this was an important side of the story to cover, and they remained there throughout the war. Indeed, it is notable that the BBC, at least in the formal terms of this analysis, was especially assiduous in balancing reports from embeds with reports from Baghdad.

In previous conflicts, military briefings have been a prominent information source for reporters. Indeed, during the previous Gulf War, broadcasters were heavily dependent on such briefings, as well as on the footage supplied by the military at such briefings. In this conflict, the main US/UK news management operation was based at Central Command in Doha, Qatar, where UK correspondents were largely dependent on US military press conferences and unofficial UK military briefings as their only sources of news.

On this occasion, there was widespread reported dissatisfaction among UK journalists about the paucity and low quality of the information provided at Doha and, while reports from these briefings punctuated the coverage, they were, in this conflict, very much overshadowed by journalists filing reports closer to the action.

The other main contrast with the 1991 conflict was the comparative absence of the "armchair generals," experts brought in to provide commentary on the progress of the conflict. The only channel to use interviews with experts in any significant number was Channel 4, and many of these provided non-military expertise.

In sum, it is fair to say that the presence of embedded reports, and, to a lesser extent, reporters in Baghdad, made this a very different kind of television war, with far more testimony from the "front lines" than hitherto. We will explore the controversy about embedded reporting shortly, but it is worth noting that without the embeds, broadcasters would have been much more dependent upon information from military briefings, and far less able to provide independent testimony of what was occurring.

As our findings imply, the bulk of the coverage during the war focused on the progress of the war itself. Apart from, to a small extent, Channel 4's coverage, very little space was made available for discussion of wider issues. While this might seem, on the surface, an ideologically neutral position for broadcasters to adopt, it did mean that the central question about the merits of war was eclipsed by more pragmatic questions about the outcome of the war. In this context, the narrative shifted very much onto the US and British governments' terrain. In brief, political and moral questions were replaced by military ones—which, given the overwhelming strength of US-led forces, were always going to be answered on a triumphant note.[8]

Reporting the government's case for the war

Sources

While the bulk of the coverage focused on the progress of the war, of the 1,534 reports we looked at, over a third (36 percent) contained references to (at least) one of the three themes central to the government's case.[9] Of these, the most common were references to the condition/attitude of the Iraqi people, found in 25 percent of all the reports in the sample (see Table 15.2). We found reports containing references to Iraqi WMD capability in just over 8 percent of the sample, and reports referring to the theme of the depravity of the Iraqi regime in a little over 7 percent of the sample.

The BBC was, by comparison with the other broadcasters, more reluctant to engage in (generally highly speculative) coverage of WMD. Sky, by contrast, was

Table 15.2 Number of stories including one or more reference to themes relevant to the government's case[10]

	BBC	%	ITV	%	C4	%	Sky	%	Total	%
WMD	15	4.5	20	7	43	10.5	49	10	127	8
Iraqi people	83	25	90	30	109	27	101	21	383	25
Regime depravity	21	6	28	9	28	7	33	7	110	7

a little less likely to concern itself with the state of the Iraqi people, while ITN was more likely than any other channel to run stories on the themes of the Iraqi people and the depravity of the Iraqi regime.

We then looked at who was used as the source of claims about these issues. This includes all sources shown directly (i.e. through coverage of press conferences, in interviews, etc.) as well as where such claims are attributed to a particular source verbally by anchors or correspondents or visually through graphics. Obviously any content analysis is limited in its ability to account for journalists' use of sources in that it cannot account for unattributed use of sources, unofficial briefings, or off-screen use of official briefings. Nevertheless such an analysis indicates which sources were given the opportunity to present their version of events as authoritative.

We identified 185 instances of where on-screen sources were used to back up claims related to the case for the war. Given that there were 549 reports that included one or more reference to these claims, it is striking how sparing was the use of identifiable sources overall. We are left with the conclusion that the claims made in the vast majority of the stories were not backed up by an attributable source. Overall, Channel 4 was the most likely to attribute claims: of the four broadcasters in our sample, Channel 4 accounted for 40 percent of our total number of sources identified.

Table 15.3 shows that of the sources used, most were, fairly predictably, official US/UK government or military (48 percent), followed by official Iraqi sources (30 percent). This almost certainly underestimates the importance of British or US military sources, however, as many claims that came from military sources were not attributed. So, for example, when we analyzed the television coverage of four stories that came from military sources—all of which turned out to be unfounded[11]—we found that nearly half the claims made were unattributed (Lewis *et al.* 2003).

What is notable from Table 15.3 is that, despite allegations that the BBC's coverage was anti-war, the BBC made more use of British/US government and military sources than any other, outnumbering the use of Iraqi sources by more than 2 to 1. Channel 4's coverage, by contrast, struck the closest balance between US/UK and Iraqi sources.

Other types of sources were used sparingly. Iraqi citizens were not often used

Table 15.3 Use of on-screen sources

	BBC	ITV	C4	Sky	Total
UK/US gov. and military	56	50	42	48	46
Official Iraqi sources	26	22	37	27	30
Other media	11	8	3	4	5
Iraqi citizens	0	11	5	8	7
Other e.g. Red Cross	7	8	15	13	12

as sources—indeed, in our sample the BBC did not use Iraqi citizens as sources at all. Thus while a number of claims were made about the mood of the Iraqi people, these tended to be made on their behalf. Other types of source were also used—spokespersons for non-governmental organizations (NGOs) such as the Red Cross—but these amounted to only 12 percent of occasions, with Channel 4 accounting for half of these.

These data confirm the extent to which the coverage focused on the war itself, the majority of sources identified being government or military sources. Those who might have shed light on the validity of this case as the war progressed—whether NGOs, weapons inspectors, academics, or experts on and in the Arab world—played very little part in the story told by television news.

Weapons of mass destruction

The presence (or absence) of WMD became a significant issue after the war, as the US-led forces failed to uncover any evidence of WMD, undermining the claims made by the US and British governments in seeking a legal and "national security" justification for the use of force. But, during the war, broadcasters seemed to broadly accept the claims made about WMD. Overall, 91 percent of the reports we examined contained references to WMD that suggested that Iraq had or could have such weapons, while only 15 percent contained references which raised doubts about their existence or possible use (Table 15.4).[12]

Of the four channels, Sky was most likely to run stories including references that supported the argument that Iraq possessed WMD—96 percent of all its stories on this theme did so—and least likely to cast doubt on their existence. The BBC, who were less likely to include speculation about WMD one way or the other, were the most cautious, a third of their reports on this issue casting a note of doubt.

This suggests that broadcasters were, on the whole, persuaded by the government that Iraq probably possessed WMD, and that those—such as Robin Cook—who cast doubt on these claims before the war were deemed less credible. Indeed, it could be argued that it was an adoption of such an unquestioning stance that made post-war allegations that the public had been misled on this issue—by reporters such as Andrew Gilligan—so controversial.

Table 15.4 Number of stories including one or more references to Iraqi WMD capability

	BBC	ITV	C4	Sky	Total
Implying capability	87	85	91	96	91
Doubting capability	33	20	19	4	15

The mood of the Iraqi people

It was, of course, difficult to know how most Iraqis felt about the invasion—Iraqis living in Britain embraced a range of views, and, even so, it was unclear how representative they were of the Iraqi population. Most considered analysis suggested that views were decidedly mixed, as did the first post-war survey to test Iraqi opinion in Baghdad, conducted by YouGov, which suggested that most people were happy to see the end of Saddam Hussein but unhappy about the US occupation and cynical about its motives.[13]

While the impression created by television news was similarly mixed, it erred heavily—by around 2 to 1—on the side of the government's claims that the Iraqi people would welcome the US-led "liberation." Thirty-nine percent of reports referring to the Iraqi people showed or suggested the Iraqi people welcoming the invasion or the overthrow of Saddam Hussein[14] (Table 15.5)—with the common use of words like "joy" and "celebration"—compared with only 22 percent of reports referring to Iraqis as unhappy, angry, upset or merely suspicious. Sky was, once again, the most likely channel to reflect the pro-war view (47 percent to 19 percent), with only Channel 4 showing "liberated" and "invaded" Iraqis in roughly equal number (33 percent to 28 percent). Again, there is no evidence here to suggest the BBC erred in favor of anti-war assumptions.

This is not to say that television news ignored the negative effects of war on the Iraqi people—42 percent of reports about Iraqi people concerned the injury or death of Iraqi citizens. Channel 4 was, again, the most likely news bulletin to refer to Iraqi casualties (55 percent of its reports representing the Iraqi people mentioned casualties, as opposed to 33 percent on the BBC and 32 percent on ITV).

Other stories referring to the Iraqi people were, in terms of the case for war, ambiguous—whether it was Iraqis going about their everyday lives in a market in Baghdad, or Iraqis looting from presidential palaces. Stories including these types of references—representing the Iraqi people in ways which neither demonstrably supported nor opposed the government's case—amounted to about a third (34 percent) of the number of stories on the Iraqi people.

The picture that emerges from this analysis is one in which we were much more likely to see or hear about Iraqis feeling liberated rather than invaded. Our finding therefore suggests that the weight of coverage of the Iraqi people was

Table 15.5 Number of stories containing one or more reference to the theme of the state of the Iraqi people

	BBC	ITV	C4	Sky	Total
Iraqis welcoming liberation	39	40	33	47	39
Iraqis opposing invasion	21	21	28	19	22
Iraqi casualties	33	32	55	44	42
Other	39	34	28	37	34

more likely to support the government's case than undermine it. And since much of the pro-invasion imagery happened toward the end of the war—with a great deal of coverage given to the "celebrations" and "joy" of Iraqis tearing down statues of Saddam Hussein in Baghdad and Kirkuk—it could be argued that the lasting impression was of a people happy to be free of Saddam Hussein, and less of a people disgruntled about being invaded and occupied.

The depravity of the regime

Although the least referred to of the government's themes, 7 percent of the reports in our sample contained references to evidence suggesting the depravity of the regime. These reports were most likely to feature the mistreatment of US/UK POWs (35 percent) or the manipulative nature of Iraqi propaganda (34 percent) (see Table 15.6). A number of reports—20 percent—referred to the decadent nature of the regime—usually signified by journalists' discovering the opulence of Saddam Hussein's palaces,[15] 16 percent involved the discovery of torture or surveillance facilities, and 8 percent were reports of atrocities committed against Iraqi people.

The BBC was proportionately more likely to run stories on the mistreatment of US/UK POWs—52 percent of all BBC stories on the theme of the depravity of the Iraqi regime were in this category, as opposed to 32 percent on Channel 4. This may be because of Tony Blair's allegations on this issue—the BBC being more likely than the other broadcast news channels to use British government or military sources.

Few would argue, in this instance, against the idea that the Saddam Hussein regime was brutal and self-serving. It is worth noting, however, that while most of these reports contained ample evidence of the depravity of the Iraqi regime, we found no attempt to situate it within the broader context of the abuse of human rights by many other dictatorial regimes worldwide. Without such a context, it could be argued that the Iraqi regime was represented as exceptional in its abuse of human rights, bolstering the government's case that military intervention was justified.

Table 15.6 Number of stories including one or more references to the theme of Iraqi
regime depravity

	BBC	ITV	C4	Sky	Total %
Discovery of torture facility	19	25	4	18	16
Regime decadence	19	25	18	18	20
Propaganda/state media	24	32	40	36	34
Atrocities against Iraqis	5	11	11	9	8
Mistreatment of POWs	52	29	32	30	35

Embeds or in-beds?

We cross-tabulated the types of news reports against the number of stories including references that supported the government's case for war, in order to explore a number of key questions. Did the practice of "embedded reporters" result in news coverage that was more sympathetic to the government's case for war than types of reports that used different newsgathering methods? Did the deployment of correspondents under Iraqi government supervision in Baghdad lead to stories about the public mood of Iraqi citizens as more hostile than the government's case suggested, or to more stories about Iraqi citizen injuries or deaths?

We tabulated the stories including references supporting the government's case on the existence of WMD according to type of news report, and compared the results with the overall distribution of our sample according to type of news report (Table 15.7). So, for example, reports including references supporting the government's case on WMD were most likely to come from anchors (24 percent) but, given that anchor reports dominate our overall sample (48 percent) this suggests that anchors were proportionally less likely to refer to such claims. This is indicative of the fact that the WMD story tended not to make headline news (which, given none were found, is hardly surprising).

Perhaps more significant is that reports from embedded correspondents were also less likely to contain references supporting the government's case on WMD. By contrast, reports supporting the government's case on WMD were more likely to come from correspondents based at the official military briefings in Qatar.

The fact that embedded reporters were less likely than most other forms of reportage to imply the presence of WMD would seem to go against the idea that embedded reporters were more likely to reproduce government and military claims. Indeed, had broadcasters been more reliant upon military briefings, it seems likely that assertions about Iraqi WMD would have been more widely repeated. This suggests that, while embedded reporters will inevitably be presenting a limited view of war, their reports are more likely to be independent than information coming from military briefings.

More significant, in our view, is the breakdown of representations of the Iraqi

Table 15.7 Stories including one or more reference to the theme of Iraqi WMD capability, tabulated against type of news report

	Implying capability	% of reports	Doubting capability	% of reports	% of total news reports
Embedded reporter	6	5	1	5	9
Baghdad reporter	5	4	0	0	6
Qatar reporter	10	9	1	5	4
Unilateral	1	1	0	0	1
Available footage	23	20	6	32	15
Studio analysis	10	9	4	2	4
Interview with reporter	11	10	0	0	6
Interview with expert(s)	9	8	3	16	3
Anchor	27	23	4	21	48
Other	14	12	0	0	5

people. Table 15.8 indicates that, whereas the ratio between stories portraying the Iraqi people as welcoming liberation as opposed to antagonistic to invasion in our total sample was nearly 2 to 1 (151 to 85) in favor of the government's case, reports by embeds were much more balanced. Embedded reporters were, in other words, notably more likely than news reports in general to portray the Iraqi people as antagonistic to or suspicious of US/UK military action. Put another way, out of the 85 stories which included references representing the Iraqi people as unenthusiastic about or hostile toward the invasion, 32 percent were based on embedded reports (remembering that embedded reports constituted only 9 percent of our total sample).

More predictably, reports from correspondents based in Baghdad were also as likely to include references to the Iraqi people opposing US/UK intervention as they were to welcoming it (by 19 to 16). This type of report accounted for nearly a quarter of all the reports including references suggesting that the Iraqi people opposed US/UK military intervention.

By contrast, in reports by anchors the ratio between stories including references to the Iraqi people welcoming compared to opposing US/UK military intervention was almost 7 to 1 (34 stories as opposed to 5). It would seem that the account of the war given by television news anchors, highly trusted by the public according to surveys, was overwhelmingly more likely to give the impression that the Iraqi people welcomed US/UK military intervention.

While we would not want to draw too much from this, the picture presented here is an interesting one. We have found no evidence that embedded reporters were more likely to cover issues critical to the government/military case sympathetically. On the contrary, they tended to be more balanced than other kinds of reporters. The distinction implied by Table 15.8 is not between embedded reporters and those based in Baghdad—who both gave a similarly balanced account, but *between reporters on the ground* and scripts written for

Table 15.8 Number of stories with references to the state of the Iraqi people, against type of news report

	Iraqis welcoming liberation	Iraqis opposing invasion	Iraqis as casualties	Other
Embedded reporter	29	27	29	17
Baghdad reporter	16	19	21	25
Qatar reporter	3	0	4	2
Unilateral	0	2	2	3
Available footage	54	25	31	47
Studio analysis	2	2	3	1
Interview with reporter	8	1	8	2
Interview with expert(s)	2	3	1	2
Anchor	34	5	56	32
Other	1	1	4	3
Total	151	85	160	131

anchors in London. In short, while reporters in the region told a fairly nuanced story about the reaction of the Iraqi people, the editorial line in London echoed the government's position. If there was bias here, in other words, it was in spite of rather than because of the embedded reporters.

Use of on-screen sources

The use of sources does differ according to which aspect of the government's case is being covered. Table 15.9 indicates that US/UK government and military sources were often used to support the government's case. Conversely, Iraqi sources were used only four times and other types of sources (NGOs, academics, etc.) were used on only seven occasions. During the course of the war UK news broadcasters appear to have given official US/UK government and military sources carte blanche to make assertions about the likelihood of Iraqi WMD capability with little attempt made to balance these claims.

This suggests that, on this issue, broadcasters had decided that Iraqi officials—in contrast to US and British officials—were of so little credence as to be not worth reporting. This judgment now looks somewhat premature.

Official Iraqi sources occur almost exclusively in stories relating to the Iraqi people: on 51 out of 55 occasions. And out of those 51 occasions, 48 referred to Iraqi casualties—an area where there were few alternate sources of information (US and UK forces rarely commented on Iraqi casualties). Thus while official Iraqi sources appear to have constituted 30 percent of the sources used overall, they were really only used as a source of information by UK/US news broadcasters on the issue of the number of deaths and injuries sustained by Iraqi citizens.

Table 15.9 Number of on-screen sources tabulated against theme

	UK/US government and military	Official Iraqi	Other media	Iraqi citizens	Other	Total
WMD	53	4	0	0	7	64
Iraqi people	20	51	6	7	13	97
Regime depravity	10	0	4	5	2	21
Total	83	55	10	12	22	182

The performance of different news organizations

As we noted in the introduction, the BBC has been singled out by the UK government and by antagonistic newspapers as more critical of the government's message than other UK news broadcasters. Our evidence suggests that the argument that BBC news was institutionally more critical of the government's case for the war than its competitors is difficult to sustain. The BBC (along with Sky) was more likely to run stories simply reporting the progress of the war, rather than the case for the war, than either ITV or Channel 4. On the BBC, the balance between Iraqis happy or unhappy about the US/UK military intervention was about average for the four channels, although its reporting of Iraqi citizen casualties was much less than average (33 percent as opposed to an average of 42 percent).

In terms of the use of on-screen sources on subjects relevant to the government's case, the BBC was marginally *more* likely to use official US/UK government/military sources (56 percent of its sources used were of this type, compared to an average of 48 percent). And while all broadcasters were sparing in their use of Iraqi citizens, we could not identify a single case on the BBC reports in our sample where Iraqi citizens were used as a source.

The only instance where the BBC was less likely to report the government's case was on WMD. The BBC was half as likely to cover the WMD issue than either Channel 4 or Sky and, when it did, it was a little more likely to challenge the idea of Iraqi WMD capability. Even so, the BBC was much more likely to accept the government line than not.

Our figures would suggest that the BBC's coverage of the war would be better characterized as a mix of caution in covering contentious issues, and trust in UK government and military sources. The indicators that any news organization might have been adopting an anti-war stance, such as the disproportionate use of sources expressing skepticism about Iraqi WMD capability or the validity of US/UK military intervention, and disproportionate reporting of civilian casualties compared to other news organizations, could not be applied to the BBC.

If there was one broadcaster more likely to feature reports about the Iraqi people that could be seen as critical of the government's case for war, it was Channel 4. A greater percentage of Channel 4 stories on the Iraqi people featured Iraqis demonstrating opposition to the UK/US invasion: 28 percent as opposed to an average for all four broadcasters of 22 percent. Channel 4 ran more stories including reports of Iraqi casualties: 55 percent of stories on the Iraqi people featured reports of casualties as opposed to an average of 42 percent. Embedded correspondents for Channel 4 were more likely to report Iraqi opposition to US/UK intervention and Iraqi citizen casualties than the other channels. Finally, Channel 4 was least likely to use official UK/US government or military sources than other broadcasters: 42 percent of all its sources as compared to the average for all four broadcasters of 46 percent.

It should still be noted that, while our analysis seems to indicate that Channel 4 news was relatively more critical of the government's case for the war than the other news broadcasters, overall *all* broadcasters were significantly more sympathetic to the government's case than they were critical.

Our analysis suggests that the most pro-war broadcaster, by these measures, was Sky, which was most likely to portray Iraqis as welcoming the invasion and was most likely to suggest the presence rather than the absence of WMD. Again, we should not exaggerate this, as Sky and Channel 4 represent opposite ends of a fairly small spectrum.

Conclusion

While British broadcasters clearly did not submit to the kind of cheerleading that characterized much of the US network coverage, our research suggests that the wartime coverage was generally fairly sympathetic to the government's case. This manifested itself in various ways, notably: the focus on the progress of war to the exclusion of other issues, the tendency to portray the Iraqi people as liberated rather than invaded, the failure to question the claim that Iraq possessed WMD, and the focus on the brutality or decadence of the regime without putting this evidence in a broader historical and geopolitical context.

This is not to say that all the coverage was sympathetic—but we can see how the *overall weight* of the coverage *might* have encouraged some hitherto unconvinced people to support the war. Opinion polls during the war indicated support increased from 54 percent at the beginning to 63 percent in the days following the destruction of Saddam's statue in Baghdad.[16]

As for concerns that embedded reporting would result in more sympathetic coverage toward the case for the war, we found, on one level, no evidence to support this. Rather, reports filed by embedded correspondents were a major source of information suggesting Iraqi citizens had mixed feelings about US/UK military intervention. Whereas reports by Baghdad-based unilateral correspondents accounted for a significant proportion of the coverage, the tiny amount of reports filed by roving unilateral correspondents suggests that the Pentagon's attempt to replace independent reporting with embedded reporting was largely successful.

What the embedded reporters did do, however, was help to make the main narrative a simple story of the progress of a war. It is in this context that the debate about embedded reporting—and media coverage of war generally—needs to move away from simple notions of censorship toward a more complex under-standing of the media–military relationship. The Pentagon's embed strategy was ingenious because it *increased* rather than *limited* access to information. By giving broadcasters access to highly newsworthy action footage from the front line, they were encouraging a focus on the actions of US and British troops, who would be seen fighting a short and successful war. The story was thus all about winning and losing, rather than a consideration of the context in which the war was fought.

Notes

1 We are indebted to our research assistant Kirsten Brander for her work on this part of the project.

2 In a widely reported interview with the Australian Broadcasting Corporation (G. Jones, "Blair calls for claims to rebut 'negative' Arab media," *Daily Telegraph*, April 1, 2003). Downing Street Director of Communications Alastair Campbell expressed dismay at the reporting of allegations of atrocities committed by UK/US forces by Arabic television and newspapers, and announced that as a result, Downing Street was setting up an "Islamic media unit" to rebut claims allegations raised in the Arab media. In the context of this attack on the Arab media, Campbell also attacked the Western media for allowing dictatorships to exploit what they see as the weaknesses of democratic media systems, by which he implied that media organizations were allow-ing dictatorships to exploit their freedom to report claims critical of the conduct of the war. The BBC had already been attacked by a number of columnists working for news-papers widely recognized as editorially antagonistic to the BBC: the *Sun's* Richard Littlejohn had accused the BBC of treating "statements by coalition spokesmen . . . with scepticism bordering on cynicism, while any old drivel put out by Baghdad is taken as gospel" (R. Littlejohn, opinion, *Sun*, March 28, 2003).

3 ICM conducted a regular poll for *The Guardian* asking the question "would you approve or disapprove of a military attack on Iraq to remove Saddam Hussein?" between August 23–5, 2002, and April 11–13, 2003, at variable intervals (www.icmresearch.co.uk).

4 Our own survey of opinion before, during, and after the war suggested that much of the shift to a pro-war stance was based on a desire to support the troops—see Lewis *et al.* 2003.

5 The reporting of civilian casualties became a major issue in debates around US tele-vision news coverage of the war in Afghanistan. US television news channels tended to minimize the reporting of such figures—partly because of lack of access—and some channels (CNN) issued guidelines indicating that reporting of civilian casualties should be accompanied by a reminder of how many US citizens died on 9/11.

6 A search of the Lexis-Nexis Executive database for the term "embedded reporters," conducted on August 29, 2003, revealed only five articles before January 1, 2003, as compared to 914 articles for the first quarter of 2003; 1,457 articles for the second.

7 Percentages have been rounded up, and thus add up to 101 percent.

8 Many journalists found it hard not to get carried along with this shift, hence the moment of victory was interpreted by many as a vindication of the war (such as Andrew Marr on the BBC), even though few advancing the anti-war case did so on the basis that the US-led forces would lose the war.

9 This percentage is lower than the figure derived from adding the three categories in Table 15.2, as some reports contained references to more than one theme.

10 The percentages here refer to the proportion of reports in which these themes were covered as a percentage of all reports broadcast during the war.

11 These involved unfounded claims that Iraq had fired Scud missiles at Kuwait; of a pop-

ular uprising against Saddam Hussein in Basra, a large tank column leaving Basra, and premature claims of the capture of Umm Qasr.

12 These add to more than 100 percent, as some reports contained *both* claims and counter claims about WMD.

13 "What Baghdad really thinks," poll conducted for the *Spectator*/Channel 4 News, July 8–10, 2003, www.YouGov.com

14 These two things are, of course, quite separate, although they tended to get lumped together in much of the coverage.

15 The tone of condemnation adopted by many journalists at this lavish lifestyle was, in some ways, curious, given the wealth of Britain's royal family in a country that has, by European standards, a conspicuously large disparity between rich and poor.

16 ICM *Guardian* polls March 21–3 and April 11–13, 2003; YouGov polls taken at the same time are very similar: 53 percent (March 20) rising to 66 percent (April 10) agreed with the statement that the US and UK were right to take military action (Kellner 2003, p. 13).

References

Allan, S. (2002) "Reweaving the Internet: online news of September 11" in B. Zelizer and S. Allan (eds), *Journalism after September 11*, London: Routledge.

Bennett, W.L. and D.L. Paletz (1994) *Taken by Storm: the Media, Public Opinion and Us Foreign Policy in the Gulf War*, Chicago, IL: University of Chicago.

Franks, T. (2003) "Not war reporting—just reporting," *British Journalism Review*, vol. 14, no. 2, pp. 15–19.

Glasgow University Media Group (1985) *War and Peace News*, Milton Keynes: Open University Press.

Hallin, D. (1986) *The Uncensored War—the Media and Vietnam*, Berkeley, CA: University of California.

Kellner, D. (1992) *The Persian Gulf TV War*, Boulder, CO: Westview.

Kellner, P. (2003) *Iraq—the Public and the War: a Report on YouGov Opinion Surveys before, during and after the Conflict*, www.yougov.co.uk

Lewis, J., Brookes, R., Mosdell, N., and Threadgold, T. (2003) "Embeds or in-beds?" BBC/Cardiff School of Journalism.

Miladi, N. (2003) "Mapping the Al-Jazeera phenomenon" in D.K. Thussu and D. Freedman (eds), *War and the Media*, London: Sage.

Thussu, D.K. (2003) "Live TV and bloodless deaths: war, infotainment and 24/7 news" in D.K. Thussu and D. Freedman (eds), *War and the Media*, London: Sage.

Zelizer, B. and S. Allan (eds) (2002) *Journalism after September 11*, London: Routledge.

16

EUROPEAN NEWS AGENCIES AND THEIR SOURCES IN THE IRAQ WAR COVERAGE

Terhi Rantanen

After September 2002, when US President George W. Bush told a UN General Assembly session to confront the "grave and gathering danger" of Iraq or stand aside as the United States acted, it became clear that preparations were being made to declare war at any moment. When the first US missiles hit targets in Baghdad on March 20, 2003 and the war started, followed by US and British ground troops entering Iraq,[1] the news war that had started long before became an actual war. World opinion was divided: several countries, including France, Germany, and Russia, condemned the war. People voted with their feet: millions of people all over the world marched against the war. In conflict situations where world public opinion is divided, news becomes even more important than usual. The question "whose news?" is suddenly raised loudly again. As Lewis *et al.* (2003) note, what made the war in Iraq different from other wars was the scale of the exercise, the changes in technology which made live or near-live television war reporting from the battlefield possible for the first time, and also, perhaps, the level of political controversy about the war itself and whether it was justified. Despite the fact that the two countries which invaded Iraq are considered the most powerful media empires of the world, they did not succeed in convincing millions of people of the rightness of their actions. If people who opposed the war were not pleased with the news that was available they turned to alternative sources, increasingly through the Internet. Many people, dissatisfied with the news they received from their national media, turned to the media of other countries using the access provided by the Internet. They also visited the websites of anti-war organizations.

However, it is to their national media that most people still turn for news. The national media indigenize global news by translating it into national languages. They also frame this news by situating it within a national framework. They offer complementary news, locating the global news, which often comes from a distance, by the addition of national actors. In short, the national media make sense of global news by transforming it into national news. They also measure its importance by giving it a certain amount of space in relation to domestic, local, and other foreign news. Increasingly, because of the growing availability of global news, national media start increasing the number of news items on a conflict even if their country is not directly involved. This is the power of global news: to set the agenda for news around the world.

In a conflict, there are at least two sides. In the war against Iraq, the media in Iraq and in other Arab countries were much less prepared for the news war, which had already begun before the actual war. According to the news criteria commonly accepted as ideal in Western countries, news should be neutral, impartially covering different stances. In the war against Iraq, the biased structure of news machinery inevitably favored the USA and the UK simply by the sheer amount of news coming from their national media. The Arab media, however, have not adopted Western news criteria, but operated on a different basis, not setting out to construct the news in a similar way to Western media. Those Western media which sought to present a balanced picture about the conflict found themselves in a situation where there were either no sources available to cover both sides equally or, if there were, these sources were not equal in number, style, or level of professionalism. Despite the discrepancy in resources, a conflict like the war against Iraq also reveals the vacuum, the non-existence, of non-Western global media. It thus provides an opportunity for new players, if they are able to provide news that is sought after.

The success of Al-Jazeera, the 24-hour pan-Arabic satellite news channel established in November 1996 in Doha, Qatar, and providing the Arab perspective, is a living example. Al-Jazeera has 630 members of staff, more than 50 correspondents working in 31 countries worldwide, 27 bureaus spread across major Arab states and major world capitals—Washington, New York, London, Paris, Brussels, Moscow, Jakarta, and Islamabad (Teh 2002). It has not only become a major source of news in the Arab world (el-Nawawy and Iskander 2002: 33) but also a source for Western media. As Miladi (2003: 149) writes, it was from the coverage of the 1991 Gulf War that CNN became the "eyes and ears of the world." In a similar fashion, Al-Jazeera ascended to the world stage after September 11, 2001 through the exclusive coverage of the war in Afganistan. Today Al-Jazeera is available to most of the world's 310 million Arabs, with a regular audience of 35 million (Miladi 2003: 150).

The importance of sources

In this war the sources of news come under particular scrutiny. As is commonly known, the sources of news available to any medium have an effect on *what* is covered and *how* it is covered. As Sigal (1986: 15) famously put it, "news is not what happens, but what someone says has happened and will happen." This was one of the findings of the *news flow* studies (International Press Institute 1953; Kayser 1953; Schramm 1960; Sreberny-Mohammadi *et al.* 1985) which focused on sources of news. These studies revealed that *news agencies* played a significant role as sources of news for the media. This, in turn, resulted briefly in an increasing scholarly interest in news agencies and their critical evaluation (the UNESCO New World Information and Communication Order debate in the 1970s and early 1980s)—this has now almost completely disappeared.

Much of the earlier research took the form of quantitative content analysis, untheorized or under-theorized (Boyd-Barrett and Rantanen 1998: 2–3). Most studies were based on a mechanistic model of a communication chain leading back to news agencies as primary sources of news. Metaphors of "flows" or "chains" were frequently employed to describe a one-way dissemination of news from powerful *international* agencies to *national* agencies, and from national agencies to national and local media. The "flow" metaphor was not foreign to early models of communication, which depicted linear processes of message transmission from senders to receivers without much reciprocity. As Galtung and Ruge (1965: 64) wrote in their classic study "The structure of foreign news," in which they analyzed the presentation of the crises in Congo, Cuba, and Cyprus in four Norwegian newspapers,

> we shall treat the news media as non-personal invisible entities and not distinguish between the journalist in the field in the news-sending country, the local press agency bureau, the district bureau, the central bureau of the press agency, the district bureau on the receiving end, the local bureau in the news receiving country, the news editor in the receiving paper, the layout man [*sic*] and what not—to indicate a *chain* with seven or eight steps in it [emphasis added].

Much has changed both theoretically and empirically in the almost 30 years since Galtung and Ruge published their study. The division between wholesalers and retailers of news is no longer entirely valid; increasingly traditional wholesalers (news agencies) find themselves in competition with retailers such as CNN and the BBC, or with their own media clients who either directly subscribe to global news sources or even compete themselves with national agencies. News agencies have also themselves become retailers by delivering news on the Internet. As Gurevitch *et al.* (1991: 197) argue, the institutional arrangements for transmitting and exchanging news materials spawned by the availability of new technology have transformed the global structure of news dissemination around the world toward a greater decentralization of news. According to Gurevitch *et al.*, we have also entered a relatively new stage, the *globalization of news* (see also Boyd-Barrett and Rantanen 1998).

The globalization of news challenges earlier seven- or eight-step chain models. We now live in a largely convergent media environment in which simple chain models leading to a single source are no longer valid. It is now time to start re-theorizing the global news system as a complex network of different media where every medium both receives and transmits news. We need to bear in mind, however, that there are still some clusters which are significantly larger and more important than others. Equally, it is important to understand that this network is not stagnant, but that relationships among clusters do change and new clusters do appear.

News agencies as sources

The most recent research (Boyd-Barrett and Rantanen 1998; Boyd-Barrett and Rantanen 2000; Rantanen and Boyd-Barrett 2004) has shown that some global news agencies have already partly lost their previous power, and that they—like many national news agencies—struggle with financial difficulties and competition from other media. Instead of five international news agencies, we now have three *global* agencies, namely the British Reuters, the US Associated Press (AP) and the French Agence France-Presse (AFP). Even these agencies have faced severe financial difficulties. Reuters' loss was £493 million in 2002, the biggest in its history and the first since its listing in 1984 (Cassey 2003). In 2000 AP was forced to break its cooperative ownership tradition dating from 1848, when it began selling news to non-members. The move allowed AP to keep costs down and fund new services for members; it also blunted the competitive edge between AP members and other news providers.[2] As a result, AP now profits from providing information to third-party subscribers such as state governments and private corporations. With revenue from newspapers representing less than 40 percent of the total, AP cannot thrive and remain stable on their custom alone.[3] AFP has secured its financial position by continuing reliance on the state.

The state subsidy is in the order of 50 percent. AFP accounts are not presented in a way that enables one to distinguish profits or losses, at least officially. In late 2003, AFP was in the throes of a crisis about attempts to balance the books and plan forward expected sources of income. Its accumulated losses had reached already the amount of €66 million (with a budgeted turnover for 2004 of €251.1 million and a budgeted loss of €5.8 million).[4] In the field of news agency television news, there are only two significant contenders left: Reuters Television News and Associated Press Television News (the result of a merger between AP's APTV and Disney's WTN), both headquartered in London (Boyd-Barrett 1998).

The traditional wholesale media news agencies now also compete with global broadcasting companies, such as the US CNN and the British BBC World, which operate both as wholesalers and retailers. Tunstall (1999: 77) writes that we now live under a *world news duopoly*, where the British Reuters and BBC, the US AP and CNN, and the French AFP dominate the world's news market. Tunstall groups the French and UK organizations as one. In his view, western Europe now offers serious competition to the USA for the title of world news leader. In this new world duopoly situation, most European media thus face a choice between US and western European news sources.

There are, however, significant differences between European agencies in terms of size and wealth (Boyd-Barrett and Rantanen 2000: 89). Those agencies with significantly above average turnover have larger and thus wealthier markets and even operate globally. The largest of these is AFP (France) with a turnover of €195 million. It is followed, by dpa (Germany) at €99.8 million, ANSA (Italy) at €91.6 million, the PA (UK) at €87 million and EFE (Spain) at €70.6 million. At the other extreme is one of the smallest European agencies, ANA (Greece) at €6.6 million. The average turnover for these agencies is €16.5 million.

Two very strong national agencies, the German dpa and the Spanish EFE, increasingly operate as global agencies. So far, although many national agencies face severe financial difficulties, news is primarily still exchanged between global and national players. In most European countries there is one national news agency, which serves most of the media in that country, although it often finds itself in competition with its own clients or with the global media. The situation is much more complicated than it used to be, but national news agencies are still important sources, especially of foreign news for small and medium-sized national and local media which cannot afford to maintain their own foreign correspondents or other direct sources. With the collapse of Communism and thus of the position of the Soviet TASS, there is no longer a clear difference between, on the one hand, western and, on the other hand, central and eastern European media in terms of the sources they use. All central and eastern European media now increasingly use Western sources.

Hence news agencies maintain their importance, even if they are no longer the only sources of foreign news, especially in times of crisis such as international conflicts when the costs of sending and maintaining one's own correspondents can become very high. We do not have accurate data on the number of news stories coming from different sources during the Iraq war. The study by Lewis *et al.* (2003) of British television news states that 48 percent of reports were delivered by anchors in the studio, while nearly one in five (19 percent) were edited packages or studio-based analysis. A high percentage of this news probably came from agency sources. The number of news stories in other media, especially local media, coming from agency sources is even higher. As a rule of thumb, the smaller the medium, the higher the percentage of foreign news which comes from agencies.

It seems more than reasonable to study how European news agencies covered the beginning of the war in Iraq in the first part of 2003. This is an especially interesting object of study since, although the conflict is outside Europe, the two countries which invaded Iraq, the USA and the UK, are also the home countries of the world's news duopoly. Their governments and military forces also waged a news war, which was probably more carefully planned than any previous news war. The second European player in the world news duopoly is AFP in France, where the government took a very different stance to the war than the UK and US governments, and opposed their military actions. In general public opinion in the EU was very divided, with huge anti-war demonstrations taking place around Europe. So, what sources did the European agencies turn to in this situation?

The results presented here are based on a questionnaire, which I sent to the members of the European Alliance of News Agencies (EANA) in July 2003. The

French AFP, the German dpa, and the Spanish EFE are all members of EANA, along with small national agencies which operate mainly inside their own countries. The British Reuters, however, is not a member. Nineteen out of 28 member agencies returned questionnaires. They were AA (Turkey), AFP (France), ANA (Greece), ANP (Netherlands), ANSA (Italy), APA (Austria), ČTK (Czech Republic), dpa (Germany), EFE (Spain), HINA (Croatia), Itar-TASS (Russia), LUSA (Portugal), MTI (Hungary), NTB (Norway), Ritzau (Denmark), Rompress (Romania), STT-FNB (Finland), SDA-ATS (Switzerland), and STA (Slovenia). The respondents were mostly chief editors or foreign news editors.

Golding and Elliot (1979: 92) divide the production cycle of newsmaking into four stages: planning; gathering; selection; and production. The questionnaire focused mostly on the first two stages, since I was mainly interested in their use of sources. This is different from earlier research, which saw news agencies solely as the *source* of news, without realizing that they, like any other media, are dependent both on each other and on other media, i.e. they use each other as sources. Furthermore, I did not study the content of news, i.e. what sources they actually used, but instead tried to find out what they thought about the different sources they subscribed to. My main research questions were:

1 What measures did the agencies take to cover the war?
2 What sources did they use in covering the war?
3 How did the agencies evaluate their sources?

The questionnaire sent to the agencies included four kinds of questions:

1 Factual general questions about their operations (resources, number of correspondents, their locations, sources subscribed) before the war started;
2 Factual questions about the measures the agencies took before and during the war (changes in resources, correspondents, and their locations, timing, in their routines);
3 Evaluation questions about the value of different sources (what were the sources they thought they used most/least; which one they would give up first/last, what they considered the most reliable/least reliable sources);
4 Open-ended questions where the respondents themselves could write in their own words how they experienced various issues (any difference from earlier war coverage, any lessons learned from this war).

1 What measures did the agencies take to cover the war?

Early preparation

Often war is understood as something which takes place unexpectedly and has to be covered instantaneously without long-term preparations. Modern wars, and especially the war in Iraq, are anticipated and thus give time for the media to prepare their coverage. Approximately half of the agencies started their planning as early as the autumn of 2002, and the other half in January or February 2003. Many agencies sent correspondents to Iraq and neighboring countries early in 2003. There were only a couple of agencies which made no advance preparations. These were smaller agencies, often with a small corps of correspondents.

Number of correspondents uneven

One of the striking features of the war coverage is the variability of the resources the agencies had available. The biggest agency in the alliance is AFP, with an editorial staff of 1,250 in 165 countries, in a league of its own comparable in Europe only to Reuters. AFP phased in the deployment of around 80 special correspondents and photographers to destinations including Baghdad (6), Kuwait (9), Qatar (5), Jordan (5), Kurdistan (4), Dubai (5), Turkish border (4), Tel Aviv (1), embedded with US troops (19), Washington (6), and Nicosia (13). The German dpa, the Spanish EFE, the Italian ANSA and the Russian Itar-TASS each had between 50 and 70 foreign correspondents. ANSA formed a task force of 10 (correspondents and roving reporters) who later traveled to cover the war from Iraq, Jordan, Turkey, Abu Dhabi, and Iran. Between March and June EFE deployed 15 journalists from other countries to the conflict area. In January dpa sent two correspondents to Baghdad, one to Kuwait, one to Cairo, and one to Dubai. Itar-TASS had one correspondent in Baghdad and the Middle East before the war and sent no new correspondents when the war started.

In contrast to the mega (AFP) and large agencies, most European national news agencies were unable to send any correspondents to the area, or sent only one. Two of the small national agencies with a small corps of correspondents, the Finnish STT and the Norwegian NTB, each sent one correspondent—the former to Syria and Jordan and the latter to Baghdad and later to Amman. There were also agencies, such as the Austrian APA, the Croatian HINA, the Greek News Agency (ANA), the Portuguese LUSA, the Rumanian Rompress, the Slovenian SPA and the Danish Ritzau, which sent no correspondents to Iraq or to neighboring countries. Hence, many news agencies in Europe were completely dependent in their coverage on other media sources. As one editor put it, "we, as a small national news agency, are totally dependent on the big media and official information."

Working hours extended

Many of the agencies increased the number of staff working or hours worked in the home office, or set up a special Iraq war desk. For many agencies this was the most significant change in their normal routines. Some of them also offered military training to their staff members. AFP organized training for staff in battlefield awareness and first aid, and enrolled 15 staff members in field survival courses offered by the US and French military. It also published and distributed a handbook in French and English for correspondents and photographers in war zones. The Finnish STT sent five of its journalists to a one-day training course at the Finnish Defense Forces International Center, where they learned what to do if wounded or taken hostage.

2 What sources did they use in covering the war?

AFP and Reuters most subscribed services

Apart from those who sent correspondents to Iraq or neighboring countries and/or increased their home desk working hours, most national agencies in Europe did what they have always done: they relied on the sources they already subscribed to. There was no significant change from the European sources they used before the war to those they began using after the war started. All agencies in Europe subscribe to Reuters and AFP.

Most agencies also subscribe to the German dpa and often to agencies in neighboring countries. The Nordic agencies, for example, subscribe to agencies in other Nordic countries, as do central European agencies to agencies in central and eastern Europe. Because of this long-standing principle the Turkish agency AA already subscribed to INA (Iraqi News Agency), QNA (Qatar News Agency) and Kuna (Kuwait News Agency), even before the war broke out, making its situation very different from that of other national agencies. The biggest agencies, AFP, dpa, and EFE, all subscribe to news agencies such as INA, IRNA (Iranian News Agency), and KUNA together with broadcasting companies in the Arab countries.

CNN more popular than AP

In addition to their traditional news agency sources, most news agencies now subscribe to CNN and many to the BBC. The US Associated Press has lost its position in western Europe to CNN, but not in central and eastern Europe, where national agencies still subscribe to the Associated Press. The Austrian APA, the Croatian HINA, the Hungarian MTI, the Russian Itar-TASS, the Turkish AA, the Czech ČTK and the Slovenian STA agencies all subscribe to AP as well as to their western European sources.

Al-Jazeera has achieved a foothold in Europe

In the arena of global news, which has traditionally been dominated by the Western media, Al-Jazeera has now taken a place. At present all the large agencies in Europe (AFP, ANSA, dpa, EFE, and Itar-TASS) subscribe to it. Most national agencies in Europe in turn receive Al-Jazeera's services through these five agencies. There are three national agencies, the Swiss SDA-ATS, the Hungarian MTI and the Czech ČTK which subscribe directly to Al-Jazeera. Use of Al-Jazeera increased after the outbreak of war and it was monitored more closely, even around the clock. As one editor put it:

One ground-breaking aspect of the Iraq war was the emergence of Al-Jazeera and other Arabic-language television stations as major providers of battlefield news. The journalistic community should encourage the development of a pluralistic, indigenous media, coupling it with training programs to foster a more rigorous and objective approach to the news.

AFP and Reuters most used during the war

Since news agencies did not start subscribing to new services, AFP and Reuters, followed by dpa, remained the sources which agencies said they most often used in their war coverage. The only significant change was the increased use of Al-Jazeera and, to a minor extent, of other Arab news agencies and media. The news agencies also considered AFP and Reuters the most important sources. Their position remained unchanged and unchallenged. Reuters' position was not questioned, and it was not considered more biased or less reliable than AFP.

3 How did the agencies evaluate their sources?

Greatest trust in own correspondents

Overall, there was not much diversity in the sources the agencies subscribed to and/or used. There seems to be a shared professional culture (Gurevitch *et al.* 1991: 202) among agencies across Europe of using the same sources. This is also partly related to the resources they have available: roughly, the poorer a national agency is, the fewer sources it has. There was an interesting difference between the sources which the agencies said they used and those they thought were the most important, fastest, most reliable, most comprehensive and objective. While Reuters and AFP were most used, they were appreciated for different qualities. AFP was seen as the most important source, followed by Reuters, but Reuters was seen as the most comprehensive. No one agency was seen as the most reliable and objective source; those agencies which have their own correspondents view these as the most reliable. CNN was considered as by far the fastest source, but was hardly mentioned for any other qualities. CNN was also seen as giving most publicity to material justifying and glorifying the war.

Mistrust in US and Arabic sources

Although news agencies almost unanimously saw their European sources as reliable, they cast doubt on the reliability of the US and Arab sources. AP, Fox, and CNN were given as examples of the least reliable US sources, while Al-Jazeera, INA, KUNA, and Iraqi television were mentioned as the least reliable Arab sources. However, editors were also aware of the imbalance between the resources available to the different parties to the war. One editor wrote that "as always, the actual winners also win the news war." Another noted that, in covering a war where the media capabilities of the two sides are so unequal, the media must make a concerted effort to be balanced and report from both sides of the conflict, including political, economic, and social consequences as well as human interest angles.

Military officials on both sides mistrusted

One source was mistrusted more than any other: the military. It was seen to control information more than in earlier wars. As one editor put it,

> the military can never be considered a trustworthy source of information when they are fighting a war in their national interest. Their reports must be confirmed or offset by independent reporting on the ground and at other news centers such as the Pentagon.

Both US and Iraqi officials were mentioned most often as the least reliable sources. As one editor put it,

> The briefings in Qatar were virtually useless, filled with slogans more than information, as well as disinformation and a lack of explanation. Also absent were the background briefings offered in Riyadh on various aspects of the war, as well as around-the-clock access to the US or British spokesmen's office. The Washington briefings on Iraq, featuring Secretary of Defense Donald Rumsfeld and Chairman of the Joint Chiefs of Staff General Richard Myers, provided more quotable copy but were still full of vagaries and propaganda.

Modern technology seen as both a blessing and a curse

The Iraq war was again a war where visual images played a major role. Many editors felt that television became more and more important for immediate coverage. This is also reflected in the increasing use of CNN. However, as one editor noted, with visual information, manipulation is possible and difficult to identify.

It was generally agreed that "technology makes it a lot easier to do our job," but at the same time it was felt that news was perhaps delivered too fast and was in danger of losing its credibility. It was also noted that US military successes were announced faster than any other news and that these announcements were not always true. As a result, there was a constant need to weigh speed against accuracy, but this was difficult in the news race. "Getting the news out" even faster has become the new parameter for competition among news agencies in the era of the Internet. Some editors even felt that there was too much media coverage and too exclusive a focus on the war.

Journalists with troops increase bias

In the Iraq war, journalists reported from alongside the troops, and from both sides, as has never happened before. The editors were very aware of the advantages and disadvantages of using "embedded" journalists. The positive feature was that this resulted in genuine access to military action on the ground and some unique perspectives. However, many editors noted that reporters who traveled with the troops could hardly be completely unbiased. According to one editor,

> the embedded journalists seemed to be tempted to play a double role, but that fact perhaps made us more aware of possible bias. The result of the embedding was that it provided any one correspondent with a fragmented view of the war in his/her sector, with US officials reluctant to furnish a more strategic overview. But it produced only a fragmented view of the war and fostered in too many journalists an unhealthy identification with coalition troops, consciously or unconsciously engendering a pro-American slant. The embedding process also promoted a sense of identification with the troops and an "us-versus-them," pro-US boosterism among too many of the American media.

This result is very different from those of Lewis *et al.* (2003) in their study of how the British media covered the war. They found no evidence to support the idea that embeds were necessarily "in bed" with the military or the US/British government in the tone of their reporting. They wrote:

> Indeed, our evidence suggests that the embeds provided a much more balanced account of events than some non-embedded reporters—especially studio based anchors, whose scripts could be seen, on some issues, to be inadvertently tilted toward certain pro-war assumptions.

The agencies also faced another problem, which they were fully prepared for. The presence of so many journalists on the ground, whether embedded or not, also made the Iraq war one of the most dangerous for the media, with more than a dozen reporters killed over a relatively short period. This raises the question of journalists' security in war zones and their need for training and protection.

Conclusion

There is no question that news agencies in Europe share a professional journalistic culture which goes beyond national boundaries. They subscribe mainly to the same sources and, even more importantly, also trust the professionalism and integrity of these sources. This shared professional culture does not disappear when war breaks out, even if the government of the country *in* Europe where one

311

agency is located is involved in the war. In the Iraq war, sources *outside* Europe were seen as less reliable and this applied to *both* the US and Arab media.

It is somewhat surprising that US sources were seen as so biased, since US and European media have traditionally shared to a great extent the same journalistic ideology of objective, reliable, and unpartisan news. The fact that the US Associated Press had lost its position in western Europe before the war and been replaced there by CNN indicates that a structural change is taking place. Whether this means that CNN has managed to become a global source able to serve the diversified interests of its clients around the world better than other US media remains, now that the war has ended, to be seen. But CNN has already succeeded in becoming part of the professional journalistic culture in Europe.

It is less surprising that Arabic media are also considered less reliable. They are after all new players with less experience of operating in the global market. They do not share the same Western journalistic culture as other agencies. However, the success of Al-Jazeera cannot be underestimated. It has become a global actor noted and quoted around the world.

The high trust in agencies' own correspondents gives support to what Gurevitch *et al.* (1991: 206) noted already 16 years ago, i.e. how the global is being *domesticated*. Own correspondents were seen as the most reliable, almost covering the war "with our eyes." The trust in them illustrates a situation where there was so much news available that it was difficult to know which source to trust. But very few agencies actually had their own correspondents. What is the next "domesticated" source if you do not have it available in your own country? In the coverage of the war in Iraq, the next trustworthy source was a European source. It did not even matter if the source was located in the UK, a country that was allied with the USA against Iraq, as long as it was a European source.

The trust in European sources can be explained in at least in two different ways. First, one could say that because of the political unification of Europe in the framework of the European Union a new European identity is emerging and that identity is reflected particularly in conflict situations. Second, in more narrow and more professional terms, the fact that the agencies kept on trusting Reuters, something they have done in western Europe for a long time, reveals that they did not see Reuters losing its professional integrity even if the UK was involved in the war.

The evidence is still scarce but indicates that a structural change may take place. Tunstall wrote about the global duopoly that was based on the power of US and British media. However, what we witnessed in the war coverage was a clear drift between western European and US sources where the former were favored over the latter. Of course, this situation is different from normal day-to-day coverage when conflicting interests do not become visible and remain hidden. In this sense, war coverage brings the issues of impartiality again to the surface and under public scrutiny. Most European news agencies were very aware of their responsibility before the public.

Whether the drift between US and western European sources is permanent remains to be seen. But it challenges our previous theorization of the nature of

Western media: we can no longer take for granted that there is a holy alliance between the US and western European media, and that they are the same. We should concentrate more on the differences between the two rather than the similarities. This is even more important when not only the alliance of the US and Western European agencies has become fragile, but also a new global player, Al-Jazeera, has emerged. It still has a different status compared to Western sources and is being viewed critically. Its status is partly based on the conflict between the Western and Arab worlds, to use very crude categories, but its rapid rise shows the niche it has filled. Again, we do not know how permanent the Al-Jazeera phenomenon will be after the day the Iraq war is over. Whether Al-Jazeera becomes today's equivalent of the Cold War Soviet TASS—a global source with a recognized status, but clearly in a different category compared to its Western counterparts—is also something that can only be seen in the daily routines of global news transmission in years to come.

The war against Iraq, like wars in general, not only reveals the existing media structures, but also questions them. As one editor put it, "too many interests collided under the surface of the war, so the spectrum of coverage was far more comprehensive than in the case of an average war, and in a way indicated the birth of a new world order." The old world order of news is still in place, but if one looks carefully at it, one can see fractures that may cause more permanent changes in the future.

The author would like to thank the members of the European Alliance of News Agencies (EANA) for their help.

Notes

1 news.bbc.co.uk/1/hi/world/middle_east/737483.stm, October 3, 2003
2 www.azcentral.com/specials/special50/articles/1016apme-conversation17-ON.html, 16/11/2003
3 www.ojr.org/ojr/workplace/1061417078.php November 16, 2003
4 *Libération*, September 18, 2003

References

Boyd-Barrett, O. (1998) "'Global' news agencies," in O. Boyd-Barrett and T. Rantanen (eds), *The Globalization of News*, London: Sage, pp. 19–34.

Boyd-Barrett, O. and Rantanen, T. (1998) "The globalization of news," in O. Boyd-Barrett and T. Rantanen (eds), *The Globalization of News*, London: Sage, pp. 1–14.

Boyd-Barrett, O. and Rantanen, T. (2000) "European national news agencies—the end of an era or a new beginning?" in *Journalism Theory, Practice and Criticism*, vol. 1, no. 1, pp. 86–105.

Cassey, J. (2003) "The news coming out of Reuters makes for pretty grim reading: agents of its own misfortune," *The Guardian*, February 10.

el-Naway, M. and Iskander, A. (2002) *Al-Jazeera: how the Free Arab News Network Scooped the World and Changed the Middle East*, Cambridge, MA: Westview Press.

Galtung, J. and Ruge, M.H. (1965) "The structure of foreign news", in *Journal of Peace Research*, no. 1, pp. 64–90.

Golding, P. and Elliot, P. (1979) *Making the News*, London: Longman.

Gurevitch, M., Levy, M.R. and Roeh, I. (1991) "The global newsroom: convergence and diversities in the globalization of television news", in P. Dahlgren and C. Sparks (eds), *Communication and Citizenship*, London: Routledge, pp. 195–216.

International Press Institute (1953) *The Flow of News*, Zurich: IPI.

Kayser, J. (1953) *One Week's News: Comparative Study of 17 Major Dailies for a Seven Day Period*, Paris: UNESCO.

Lewis, J., Brookes, R., Mosdell, N., and Threadgold, T. (2003) "The role of embedded reporting during the 2003 Iraq war: summary report," a report commissioned by the BBC: The Cardiff School of Journalism.

Miladi, N. (2003) "Mapping the Al-Jazeera phenomenon," in D.K. Thussu and D. Freedman (eds), *War and the Media: Reporting Conflict 27/7*, London: Sage, pp. 149–60.

Rantanen, T. and Boyd-Barrett, O. (2004) "Global and national news agencies: the unstable nexus", in A.S. de Beer and J. Merrill (eds), *Global Journalism: Topical Issues and Media Systems*, Boston, MA: Allyn and Bacon/Longman.

Schramm, W. (1960) *One Day in the World's Press: Fourteen Great Newspapers on a Day of Crisis*, Stanford, CA: Stanford University Press.

Sigal, L.V. (1986/1999) "Reporters and officials: the organization and politics of news-making", in H. Tumber (ed.) *News: a Reader*, Oxford: Oxford University Press, pp. 212–23.

Sreberny-Mohamamadi, A. with K. Nordenstreng, R. Stevenson, and F. Ugboajah (1985) *Foreign News in the Media: International reporting in 29 countries*, Reports and Papers on Mass Communication, no. 93, Paris: UNESCO.

Teh, K. (2002) "Towards a regional perspective in media and globalisation theories: the rise of regional news," a comparative study on Al-Jazeera and Channel NewsAsia, unpublished honours thesis, University of Cambridge: Fitzwilliam College.

Tunstall, J. (1999) *The Anglo-American Media Connection*, Oxford: Oxford University Press.

17

AL-JAZEERA AND WAR COVERAGE IN IRAQ

The media's quest for contextual objectivity

Adel Iskandar and Mohammed el-Nawawy

Across the world, the word Al-Jazeera has become synonymous with war. Since the station's emergence on the global media scene in 1996, the Qatar-based satellite station has been the go-to channel for conflict coverage from the Middle East. As Al-Jazeera reaffirms its position as a top transnational news organization, its coverage of wars in Afghanistan and Iraq has catapulted it into a prominent position and stirred much international controversy, placing its approach to journalism in the spotlight. Despite having had reporters arrested, licenses rescinded, bureaus closed, and offices bombed, Al-Jazeera's audience figures continue to soar. Why does Al-Jazeera's brand of journalism draw so much attention, debate, and controversy? No evaluation of Al-Jazeera and its operations is coherent or complete without a close look at the media landscape from which the network emerged.

This chapter is a discussion of Al-Jazeera's journalistic model and the network's coverage of the US-led war in Iraq as a case study for thinking about the journalism of conflict. Since most historical landmarks in the development of Arab media relate to conflict coverage, we briefly describe three major stages in the development of journalism in the region and show how they articulate the dilemmas facing journalists, suggesting that the impact of foreign programming and the Arab world's quest for press freedoms have culminated with Al-Jazeera and other satellite news channels. Two contesting forces in war coverage of the region—editorial decision-making and network responsibility to audiences—help explain how Al-Jazeera works, and we describe this tension as *contextual objectivity* and illustrate how it is employed generally by Al-Jazeera and specifically in the case of its coverage of the war in Iraq.

Broadcasting in/to the Arab world

Journalism in the Arab world has been shaped by three major stages of development—the introduction of foreign media and negotiations over a presumed standard of "objectivity"; a gravitation toward "the Voice of the Arabs" as a model for journalism, occasioned by a need to develop a venue for voicing regional concerns; and the "Phoenix of Arab media," by which journalism in the region took on its own autonomous and singular identity. The evolution across these three stages was gradual and occurred in conjunction with larger developments in the region.

The first stage was parallel with the introduction of media more generally. It was in the juvenile days of international journalism that fundamental questions of objectivity, independence, and fairness in the region were first contested and articulated. When the West first considered broadcasting to the developing world with the purpose of influencing public opinion, they came to the Arab world (Boyd 1999). Italian Radio Bari, built primarily to boost Italian influence in the Arab world beyond the colony in Libya, was the earliest Arabic language radio station to go to air in 1934, while a Nazi German broadcast went on air shortly afterwards in the hopes of winning Arab hearts and minds. The Arab world's most influential foreign radio outlet, the British Broadcasting Corporation (BBC), began its programming in Arabic in 1938 with the aim of countering Radio Bari's messages, winning Arab public opinion, and furthering Britain's national interests in an increasingly influential region. Known at first as the Empire Radio, BBC programs were meant to be a "projection of British culture" (Hourani 1988) and a technique of mass persuasion. It was this very mandate that conflicted with the network's journalistic principles and highlighted one of the earliest accounts of media's undeterred pursuit of "objectivity." Soon after its inauguration and within days of its first broadcast, the BBC's editorial policy soon came into question when the story of a Palestinian Arab's execution was featured in the news bulletin. The story cast a dark shadow on the British government's policy in the Palestine mandate and marked the beginnings of tension between BBC broadcasters and the British government. From that point forward, the BBC differentiated its news operations from the empire's policies and recommendations. Other broadcasters, such as the French government-sponsored Radio Monte Carlo Middle East (RMCME) and the Voice of America (VOA), broadcast with a narrower and more contested appeal.

The events of September 11 helped the US government recognize the importance of relaunching its instruments of "public diplomacy" in the Arab world. A complete overhaul of the former VOA, the allocation of millions of dollars to the campaign, the hiring of a larger pool of bilingual staff, and the re-invention of the station's image produced Radio Sawa. Heralded as the single most ambitious project of the kind since Radio Free Europe/Radio Liberty, Radio Sawa's formula is comprised of juxtaposed Arabic and Western pop music presented in disc-jockey style. Its clearly pro-US message is transmitted within the interspersed news bulletins that interrupt the flow of music. Although preliminary surveys point to a rising audience-base for Radio Sawa's edgy music line-ups, there is little concrete evidence that the station's directive messages are affecting impressions of the United States.

Overall, the history of foreign radio programming to the Arab world seems to have gone full circle. Early messages from Italian, British, German, and American stations sought to win Arab popular sentiments. Following World War II, the credibility of a foreign radio broadcast was built on its ability to deliver fair and balanced news to a region that depended on external feeds for uncensored journalism. Once again, the events of September 11, the war in Iraq, the prospects of a protracted conflict between the Palestinians and Israelis, and the threat of an expanded war in the Arab world have redirected foreign media messages back to the mandated agendized "diplomatic" discourses of yesteryear. It is this sidelining of news balance which threatens the perceived credibility of foreign broadcasters, both radio and television, in the Arab world. This first stage of broadcasting is therefore characterized by its marked emphasis on "diplomacy" rather than objectivity.

A second stage signaled the earliest major indigenous experiment in Arab broadcasting, which occurred in Egypt. This venture, which would eventually establish the country as a leader of the Arabist movement and home of the most developed media, film, and theatre industry, was facilitated by Egypt's efforts in being first among the Arab nations to build a high-powered medium-wave and short-wave transmitter for radio broadcasting (Boyd 1999). Built both to reach the indigenous population within the country's borders and to project and dispense the message of pan-Arab nationalism throughout the region, the venture, called "Voice of the Arabs," allowed Arab anti-colonial revolutionaries to use the Egyptian radio service to broadcast dissenting messages to their home states.

Situated as the prescribed vehicle for pan-Arabism in the 1950s and 1960s, "Voice of the Arabs" became immensely popular throughout the Arab world. Nasser's speeches and the late Egyptian singer Um Kalthoum captured and mesmerized audiences across the region through their broadcasts, consolidating Egypt as a leader in the Arab world, both as a political and media power (el-Nawawy and Iskandar 2003). However, "Voice of the Arabs" soon fell from grace in the Arab world, when, during the first few days of the 1967 war, its news bulletins painted a misleading picture of the war, suggesting that Arab armies were successful and neglecting to report casualties and damage in their ranks. The fact that "Voice of the Arabs" had kept a general optimism throughout the war was seen by many Arabs as a betrayal. Though the station was transformed after the war, it was too late to salvage its reputation with its listeners (Boyd 1999). Nonetheless, some characteristics of the nationalistic "Voice of the Arabs" model are still emulated throughout the region. At its side, however, an elaborate printed press in some Arab countries developed a tradition consonant with principles of free discourse. Lebanon and Egypt had for long allowed newspapers with leanings across the political spectrum to publish, and various political publications allowed public discourse to flourish among the literate (Boyd 1999; el-Nawawy and Iskandar 2003). This trend, however, was not consistent throughout the Arab world, with countries applying varying degrees of pressure on opposition press. Furthermore, while some nations in the Arab world had loosened the belt on the print press, until the advent of satellite television, none had allowed this phenomenon to translate to the broadcast media which were virtually all extensions of government.

Until the late 1990s, most Arab countries had a Ministry of Information—formally a regulatory body—which was primarily responsible for monitoring and censoring all mass communication in the nation. That is primarily why foreign broadcasters had initially built such a large audience in the region. The rise of Arab satellite television stations would soon displace Arabic language foreign programming.

A third stage of development began with a chain reaction which followed access to CNN in the Arab world during the Gulf War of 1991 and led to the transformation of the Arab media landscape in the years that followed. It heralded the birth of investigative reporting and war correspondence in the Arab world. The Arab satellite networks' coverage of the war was nothing short of a revolution in the region and amounted to a phoenix rising out of the ashes of previous experiments such as "Voice of the Arabs." The first Arabic station to emulate the CNN formula was the London-based Saudi-funded Middle East Broadcasting Center (MBC). A mixed content station, MBC, offered news, entertainment, sports, and specialty programs. In the 1990s, a new satellite station was launched virtually every year. Over time, there would develop two types of satellite television stations in the region, those that were an extension of the local government's programming, and those considered "offshore"—with little or no "clear" relationship to the government of a particular nation. Most of those listed here are considered "offshore" satellite networks. Other major contenders to MBC that tried to carve a niche for themselves in this domain included the Saudi-owned Arab Radio and Television (ART) and Orbit. While these stations were not directly and overtly connected to particular governments, they were not subject to the work of censors, at least not formally. The Lebanese Broadcasting Corporation (LBC) and Abu Dhabi television were also among the newcomers that made their mark on regional broadcasting and continue to be influential today. However, it was not until Al-Jazeera came on the scene in 1996 that the Arab world had its own 24-hour all-news station with an extensive international bureau system.

A product of the 1996 editorial fallout between the BBC and the Saudi investors in the BBC Arabic Television News Service, Al-Jazeera was the brainchild of Qatar's comparatively progressive emir, Sheikh Hamad bin Khalifa Al-Thani (el-Nawawy and Iskandar 2003). While Saudi investors had pulled the plug on the BBC service after a row over the airing of a documentary on executions in the Saudi Kingdom in 1996, Qatar's emir saw this as a unique opportunity to hire a group of critically minded, independent, and well trained journalists to better represent the interests of the region. The emir and Al-Jazeera's founders recruited the staff of the fallen BBC service and relocated them to Doha to comprise the start-up crew for the first 24-hour Arabic television news channel (el-Nawawy and Iskandar 2003). The differences between the BBC's Saudi funders and Qatar's emir embody the contrasting principles of their respective networks.

Today, Al-Jazeera's headquarters in Doha are filled with professionals from most Arab countries, comprising a demographic microcosm of the 22-nation Arab world. The diverse pan-Arab workforce of 350 journalists in its main office and 35 international bureaus reflects every political leaning, religious affiliation, and educational background in the Arab world. However, as far as funding, Al-Jazeera is exclusively Qatari. The emir provided a start-up fee of $140 million to launch the network and continues to make regular loans (almost $100 million annually) to help sustain the station's operations (el-Nawawy and Iskandar 2003).

While some have called into question Al-Jazeera's financial dependence on the Qatar government (el-Nawawy and Iskandar 2003), it seems that much of the network's editorial policy is independent of direct or indirect governmental control as far as international affairs are concerned. Alternately, we have been critical of Al-Jazeera's negligence toward domestic news in Qatar and have brought forward questions regarding political connections between the network and the Qatari government. This, however, seems to have a marginal impact on coverage of international news (el-Nawawy and Iskandar 2003).

It was not long before Al-Jazeera raised eyebrows with its aggressive investigative reporting style, demonstrating dissent against regional governments, hosting volatile political debate shows, and its journalistic professionalism. The station's news style and political debates have been imitated to varying degrees by a growing number of other channels in the region. The latest members of the now-highly competitive media terrain are Al-Arabiya and the reinvented Abu Dhabi television and Dubai television.

In addition to rattling governments in the region, Al-Jazeera's coverage of wars in Afghanistan and Iraq triggered a global debate about conflict in the media and the nature of "objectivity." The network's immense success, with an estimated audience of 50 million viewers worldwide, has drawn attention to its brand of journalism.

While most Arab news organizations imitate Al-Jazeera's approach and style, the network's global reputation and reach have made it the regional victor. Like news organizations everywhere, these stations all have one thing in common—the pursuit of journalistic integrity. This is notably due to a well articulated journalistic philosophy and a unique way of employing it. The ways in which this philosophy is conceptualized are exemplified by its application during coverage of the recent war in Iraq.

The Minotaur of contextual objectivity

In times of war, journalism comes under increased scrutiny with evaluations and re-evaluations of content to ensure and promote the concept of "objectivity." Public discourse about media content offers assessments of stations' coverage, whether they are CNN, Fox News Channel, or Al-Jazeera. Networks' decisions to include or exclude items from their news bulletins arouse lively and often volatile discussion in the print media and the public sphere. Such discussions ultimately call into question and reflect on journalistic standards, invoking the institutional ideal—"objectivity."

The pursuit of objectivity in journalistic reporting has been a cornerstone of the ideals of news coverage. Every journalism textbook and news reporting course enshrines and standardizes objectivity as the prime responsibility of a keen reporter. Although it seems to have its roots as far back as the 1830s, the notion of "objectivity" became popular following World War I among news organizations as they developed an appreciation for a scientific validation of truths (Schudson 1978).

Mass communication scholars and media critics have also grappled with this concept for decades, articulating its variable contexts and applying multiple philosophical interpretations to it. More recently, the aftermath of September 11 and the war in Iraq have triggered a renewed debate on media's responsibilities, culminating with the conceptualization of objectivity as a media practice of information collection, processing, dissemination, and as an overarching attitude (el-Nawawy and Iskandar 2002; Zelizer and Allan 2002; Tumber and Prentoulis 2003).

The term objectivity itself, when used within the journalistic context, signifies the adoption of a position of detachment, rather than neutrality, toward the subject of reporting. It also suggests the absence of subjectivity, personalized involvement, and judgment. This *ideal* or mirage is one that is particular to the media practitioner and the institution in which she operates. By virtue of her occupational responsibilities as a reporter—and reflected in her training—she is trained to avoid leanings in matters of dispute.

The notion of contextualization offers a corrective to some of the limitations inherent in the notion of objectivity. Contrary to the standard of "objectivity" to which journalists and news organizations aspire, media audiences are opinionated, partial, and highly invested in the news content. Audiences are expected to espouse certain opinions and to express a degree of partisanship. While journalists are trained to excavate the "truths" that lie beyond the "context," audiences are invariably and inevitably contextualized. Contextualization demonstrates a situational position, a way by which collectivism among participants within the same "context"—whether cultural, religious, political, or economic—is realized and engaged. It is precisely this contextualization that aggravates and complicates the pursuit of "objective" coverage within the news media setting.

Contextualization further confuses attempts at even-handedness and efforts to cover all sides of a story. Particularly in times of war, it is the context within which a reporter operates that makes communication with the "enemy" unacceptable. Context may be seen as the reason why dissenting voices in the US during the build-up for war on Iraq were perceived and represented negatively by many policy-makers, the American media, and subsequently by the public. Accordingly, the ratings for networks that demonstrated a predominantly pro-government and pro-war stance, such as the Fox News Channel (the network that offered the most support for military action in Iraq), skyrocketed throughout and during the war—suggesting a growing political "context" in the US. One instance that demonstrated this was a visit by two US senators to Iraq before the war to evaluate the humanitarian crisis caused by United Nations sanctions . The reaction to the visit was swift and intense. Many television commentators and politicians saw this visit as an act of "national betrayal" and defection. Evidently, if politicians were heavily criticized for communicating with the "enemy," then how would the media fare if they did the same?

That is precisely what Al-Jazeera did—communicate with the "enemy." In our discussion of the network's role in the world of post-September 11 journalism, we offered the concept of "contextual objectivity," in an attempt to articulate and capture the eclectic discourse and epistemological tensions between the relativism of message receivers and the empirical positivist attempts of message-builders (el-Nawawy and Iskandar 2002, 2003). Should the media lead the masses or be led by them? "[T]he theory of contextual objectivity—the necessity of television and media to present stories in a fashion that is . . . impartial yet sensitive to local sensibilities—is at work" (el-Nawawy and Iskandar 2003: 54).

Contextual objectivity, the perpetual tension between the decontextualized messages of the news deliverer and the nuanced and colored perceptions of the receiver of news messages, can be witnessed on virtually every news bulletin of war on every media outlet in the world today, not the least CNN and Al-Jazeera. It permeates every story, and has become increasingly emblematic of the struggle for the construction of mediated messages.

We used the Minotaur as a metaphor to describe the contestation forged by the new media to accomplish both seemingly-contradictory duties (el-Nawawy and Iskandar 2002). Like the Minotaur, the Cretan mythological character that bore the head of a bull and the body of a man, contextual objectivity reflects the tensions of the instinctive and rational, the relativist and the positivist. The Minotaur's hybrid identity and the contradictory co-existence of human and beast within the same entity is precisely what makes it a compelling analogy for contextual objectivity. At the root of both the Minotaur's existence and of contextual objectivity is an internal tension and turmoil which facilitates a consensual balance between the two natures, allowing for their cohabitation in the same creature. Both the Minotaur and contextual objectivity represent a balance between two forces, a balance that can tilt either way. On the scale's pivot is the ideal intermediate between context and objectivity—best articulated as fairness and balance. Like the Minotaur who struggles to maintain equilibrium between his beastly and human qualities, the media try to strike the balance between audience appeal and "objective" coverage.

The media have a dual role as both informants and a mirror for society, hence, they are held to a rather stringent policy by their viewers. They must meet their dual duties of being balanced (objectivity) while reflecting the views of their public constituency (contextualization). For instance, American television coverage, under no overt government influence, may reflect the views of mainstream American audiences in the aftermath of the September 11 attacks while, at the same time, creating public opinion.

While most networks engage in contextual objectivity, consciously or otherwise, in their coverage of war, Al-Jazeera is perhaps the first network to articulate this approach as a network philosophy. The channel's mottos, repeated frequently during program intermissions, are operationalizations of contextual objectivity: "The opinion and the other opinion," "Freedom, objectivity, accuracy," and "With all the colours of a rainbow." These slogans demonstrate explicitly the contesting dimensions of "contextual objectivity"—seemingly suggesting that "truth" is the culmination of multiple conglomerated subjectivities. This implies that neither objectivity nor context should be the sole priorities—thereby dismissing the exclusivity of either. Instead, onus is placed on the gray area in-between the two—where fairness and balance are situated. As Al-Jazeera attempts to harness the advantages of both context and objectivity, they represent an experiment that redefines modern journalism. Their attempts at delivering news and commentary that juxtaposes multiple opinions and realities into a single mosaic are a testament to the network's pursuit of contextual objectivity. However, attempts to strike equilibrium between the tensions of context and objectivity have left Al-Jazeera celebrated by admirers and battered by critics (see el-Nawawy and Iskandar 2003 for examples).

Since its conception, reactions to the concept of contextual objectivity within scholarly circles have been generally positive, while the popular press and media appeared more ambivalent about its ability to explain differences in coverage between networks. For example, a review article in the September 7, 2002 issue of *The Economist* characterized the concept of contextual objectivity as a symptom of the "struggle to defend the network [Al-Jazeera] from its detractors," arguing that the concept, which suggests that networks offer news with a particular worldview, was a "dubious" notion, "at best a muddle, at worst, an evasion" ("Island in the sun," 2002). By contrast, an article published in the *Washington Diplomat* in June 2002 included an interview with Robin Wright, the chief diplomatic correspondent at the *Los Angeles Times*, who suggested that covering the Israeli–Palestinian conflict generally emerged from a "set opinion or acceptance of a certain moral value" on the part of reporters, a view in consonance with the notion of contextual objectivity (Beyerle 2002).

When the concept of contextual objectivity is applied to Al-Jazeera, it is obvious that the network faces two major dilemmas: making the news comprehensive and placing the stories within a meaningful historical account. However, the inclusion of context and analysis almost inevitably leads to the encroachment of opinion. For instance, while the network labors to bring forth multiple perspectives on the Palestinian–Israeli conflict, the Arab public's opposition to Israel's occupation of Palestinian territories is a prevailing context that permeates Al-Jazeera's coverage (el-Nawawy and Iskandar 2003: 209).

Much of the controversy and criticism Al-Jazeera has garnered since its inception is a consequence of the station's pursuit of contextual objectivity as a fundamental journalistic standard. In our chronological sketch of Al-Jazeera coverage during the war in Iraq, we concentrate on the kinds of reporting choices that made Al-Jazeera distinctive, and offer some reflection on, consideration for, or demonstration of "context." This is an attempt to showcase the editorial decisions made by one station in the coverage of war. How does Al-Jazeera demonstrate contextual objectivity in its presentation of the war in Iraq?

Al-Jazeera and the early days of the Iraq war

The war in Iraq and the events that ensued in its aftermath have been big news on the American networks, but they have been even bigger news on Al-Jazeera, whose perspective on the war has been called clearly Arab rather than American. The differences in coverage were a reinforcement of the extent of contextualization in the news that ensued.

Al-Jazeera's coverage displayed an invocation of both broader journalistic practices and a clear instance of contextual objectivity. Its reporters engaged in a number of practices that suggested a consonance with its motto—"The opinion and the other opinion," and in many ways these practices paralleled the journalistic routines followed elsewhere. Its reporters covered press briefings by the Iraqi officials in Baghdad as well as war updates from US Central Command (CENTCOM) in Doha, Qatar. Its reporters were interspersed throughout Iraq and one—Amr Al-Kahki—was embedded with the US marines. It had almost a dozen roaming correspondents on the ground in Baghdad and other key Iraqi cities. In a measure of those correspondents' success during the war, US and other Western networks often relied upon them for access to exclusive video from Iraq of the bombing and of breaking news.

At the same time, Al-Jazeera's coverage of the Iraq war and its aftermath displayed a struggle to find a balance that provided its audience with the "truth" that fits its context—the same struggle that other networks, Arab or non-Arab, go through in covering any major conflict. For instance, while the American media showcased US state-of-the-art military machines in action and the high morale of the US troops in what was described as a "war of liberation," Al-Jazeera focused on Iraqi civilian casualties and damage to Iraqi cities in a "war of occupation" (el-Nawawy 2003a).

Because Al-Jazeera had several non-embedded correspondents reporting on the ground from major Iraqi cities where Western correspondents were almost non-existent, they were in a position to investigate US and British assertions about the war or simply outpace information received by American networks. On many occasions, Al-Jazeera's on-the-ground, non-embedded correspondents did provide a corrective to the American official line that the military campaign was, barring occasional resistance, going according to plan.

Similarly, while Al-Jazeera broadcast images reflecting the horror of the bombing campaign on Iraq and demonstrations of Arab people angry with the US decision to launch this war, it also aired documentaries showing the tough living conditions inside Iraqi prisons and the brutality of Saddam's regime. Moreover, despite the fact that the overwhelming majority of Arabs were opposed to the war, Al-Jazeera correspondents went out of their way to interview members of the Iraqi opposition who lived overseas and who supported the war.

In some respects, Al-Jazeera correspondents had an edge over their Western counterparts, owing to the fact that they spoke Arabic and were more familiar with the Iraqi culture. This enabled them to interview average Iraqi citizens on the street and to give their audience an overall sense of the general mood on the Iraqi streets. The following is a report from Al-Kahki (Al-Jazeera's only embedded correspondent), obtained through a direct feed to Al-Jazeera studios in Qatar from Umm Qasr, where he was stationed with the coalition troops on March 27, 2003. Al-Kahki was reporting on the situation inside Umm Qasr, which was surrounded by coalition troops, but was still controlled by the Iraqis. Al-Kahki said:

> The feeling I got from the people in Umm Qasr is that they were "confused" and weren't sure exactly what their legal status was. They didn't know what type of land they were standing on; whether it was controlled by the British/American troops or still under the control of the Iraqi regime. All they said they wanted was living peacefully with food, water, and milk for their children.

Responding to a question from the Doha studio anchor with regard to the general security and the Iraqi resistance in Umm Qasr, Al-Khaki said:

> Regarding the issue of resistance, we cannot predict it, since from time to time we see some pockets of resistance despite the fact that some British troops here have been searching for these pockets everywhere. There is a big void, however, in security and safety in this area. The residents told us about some looting in the warehouses of Umm Qasr. Moreover, the power outage is worsening the situation. People are suffering, and they are living in darkness with hardly any infrastructure.

It was that kind of live reporting on the ground from places that were still inaccessible to Western correspondents that offered audiences a street-level view of the war's impact on Iraqis that made Al-Jazeera a number-one choice for Arab viewers during the Iraq war. Despite hackers' attacks, its battered website continued to top the charts for the most sought-after keyword on the Internet (Schatz 2003). Moreover, Al-Jazeera's subscriptions skyrocketed to four million additional subscribers in Europe during the war (Cozens 2003). Its effort to cover wide-ranging angles of the conflict throughout the war— including the Arab street, Iraqi civilians, embedded reporters with coalition forces, Iraqi press conferences, and US Central Command briefings—also earned Al-Jazeera the respect and admiration of many journalistic media organizations, with favorable articles appearing in numerous American and European newspapers (Faine 2003; Hasso 2003; Steele 2003; Suellentrop 2003; Tahboub 2003, etc.).

In the midst of this publicity, the Al-Jazeera Baghdad bureau was shelled by an American missile on April 8, 2003, leading to the tragic death of one of the network's star reporters, Tareq Ayoub. This happened despite the fact that Al-Jazeera officials informed the Pentagon about the exact location of its bureau in Baghdad three months before the war had started. US Central Command in Qatar said its forces had come under significant enemy fire from the Al-Jazeera building, and had returned fire in self-defense. Although many Arabs accused the Pentagon of intentionally targeting Al-Jazeera (they based their conclusion on the fact that the Al-Jazeera Kabul bureau too was bombed by an American missile during the Afghanistan war in November 2001), Al-Jazeera officials were wise enough not to rush to that conclusion. They held a press conference during which they demanded a thorough investigation by the Pentagon.

The following day, April 9, 2003, was a historic day that witnessed the fall of Baghdad to the coalition troops. Al-Jazeera was there, along with major Arab and Western news organizations, in Firdous Square in the heart of Baghdad transmitting to its audience the toppling of Saddam's statue. During these moments, Al-Jazeera's reporter interviewed some Iraqi civilians, who were celebrating in the square, and he also interviewed a US marine about his feelings.

During the war, Al-Jazeera presented what appeared to be climactic, Hollywoodesque promotions that dramatized the situation on the ground with the intention of attracting and retaining the viewers' attention. One such promotion which aired throughout the duration of the war opened with US President George W. Bush warning former Iraqi President Saddam Hussein of imminent war, followed by a montage of a crying Iraqi child wearing a blood-drenched T-shirt swathed in bandages, burning oil fields, and missiles dropping on buildings. This moving promotion segued to a news anchor at Al-Jazeera headquarters in Doha, Qatar, who proceeded to read the headlines. In Olympic competition style, the background displayed two flags, the American and the Iraqi, draped in juxtaposition.

Since the start of the war, some of the most graphic and gruesome images from Iraq—wounded men carried in bloody blankets to hospitals, toddlers sharing metal shelves at a morgue, seared corpses next to burned cars, and the hail of missiles, bombs, and rockets that fell on the Iraqi capital of Baghdad—were continuously replayed on Al-Jazeera.

Al-Jazeera's frequent emphasis on Iraqi civilian casualties prompted US officials to accuse the network of inflaming the "Arab street," of not just reporting on the war but stirring it up, and of serving as a "propaganda" tool for the Iraqi regime. However, viewed in context, Al-Jazeera was not "out to get Americans"; nor was its reporting of the war any more inflammatory than that of the American networks. Moreover Al-Jazeera did not appear to be aiming to please the Iraqi government, which expelled two of the network's reporters from Baghdad.

(They were allowed to return after Al-Jazeera decided to completely halt all its reporting operations in Iraq.) Al-Jazeera played to the general feelings of Arabs who wanted to see an end to the Iraqi civilians' suffering and who were strongly opposed to a war they deemed unjust.

As disgusting as these gory images were, editors at the station argued that not showing them would have been a denial of the reality witnessed by Arab reporters. Had Al-Jazeera decided not to show these images, it would have risked losing its audience to other Arab networks, such as the brand new Saudi satellite channel, Al-Arabiya, which also showed close-up images of dead and wounded Iraqis (el-Nawawy 2003a).

Al-Jazeera also focused on US losses in the Iraq war. For example, during the early days of the war, Al-Jazeera beamed pictures of Iraqi farmers cheering the downing of a US plane over the Iraqi city of Basra. The network also showed live pictures of hundreds of Iraqis gathered on the banks of the Tigris River in Baghdad, setting fire to cane fields and shooting into the river to flush out US pilots who witnesses said had parachuted from the sky.

Most Arabs who followed these losses on television were pleasantly surprised, perhaps even exhilarated, to see the much weaker Iraqis resist what they considered an "occupying superpower." In a way, there is a desire in the Arab world to support the underdog, and Arab networks, including Al-Jazeera, fed that desire during the war. That was one main reason why US officials appeared dissatisfied with Al-Jazeera's war coverage.

However, it was Al-Jazeera's broadcast on March 23 of video footage (taken from Iraqi television) of American prisoners of war and dead American soldiers that stirred much anger and outrage against Al-Jazeera in the United States. The footage showed dead US soldiers, easily identifiable by the faces. One of them was a young man lying diagonally across the screen, his head in the lower-right hand corner. His eyes were closed, and blood was gushing beneath his head and soaking his T-shirt. The American POWs, who were shown in the same video, were visibly exhausted and somewhat confused. They were interviewed by an unseen speaker, presumably from the Iraqi government or Iraqi state television. The POWs were asked their names and their hometowns.

In a move that was considered a punishment for Al-Jazeera for airing these images, the New York Stock Exchange and Nasdaq ejected Al-Jazeera reporters. (The Al-Jazeera reporters have since been readmitted to the New York Stock Exchange.) Moreover, hackers attacked Al-Jazeera's new English-language website, replacing it with a red, white, and blue US map and the slogan "Let freedom ring."

While some of Al-Jazeera's coverage may be seen as "contextually" objectionable to an American audience, it was appropriate for non-American viewers. Regardless of judgment, the treatment the station received in the US was unwarranted for several reasons. First, some European and American networks showed still pictures from the same footage that was broadcast on Al-Jazeera but were not singled out. Second, it was a dramatic demonstration of how US officials found themselves outpaced by reports and images from the battlefield. Al-Jazeera, by showing these images, placed pressure on the US administration to admit to the capturing of these POWs. On the other hand, most American media showed the faces of Iraqi POWs captured by American troops. Hence, asking Al-Jazeera to refrain from airing footage of American POWs is a double standard.

Third, Al-Jazeera is not watched by most American families, and so the concern, raised by some US officials, that American families might have learned from the media that their sons were captured did not apply to Al-Jazeera. Despite that, Al-Jazeera aired the complete footage of American POWs only once, and then it aired segments of it later on.

Finally, the decision as to whether or not to show these images should be determined by the networks themselves depending on the nature of their audiences. A plethora of wars in the Arab world's contemporary history and the ongoing Palestinian–Israeli conflict have provided Arab audiences with years of gruesome imagery of war casualties. That is why, perhaps, the images of casualties shown on Al-Jazeera were not as shocking to the Arab audiences as they might have been to the American audiences. In this regard, Al-Jazeera, which often bases its editorial decisions on its audiences' sensitivities, was operating, at least in part, on "contextual" market principles, which dictate that content follows audience interest.

> For these reasons, the reaction by which what may be the only independent and uncensored television network in the Arab world was punished because its style of war coverage was seen as unsuitable to certain people seems to have been counterproductive. The question remains whether other nations similarly have the right to ban US media outlets because they disagree with their coverage?
>
> (el-Nawawy 2003b)

On one evening during the second week of the war, Al-Jazeera broadcast a phone interview with Mohammed Saeed al-Sahhaf, the former Iraqi Information Minister. Al-Sahhaf became a media star and a cult figure in the West for insulting the Americans in charming and flowery Arabic, feeding Arab television with misinformation about Iraq's military power, and declaring Baghdad "safe and secure," even when the coalition troops were on the capital's doorsteps. Following the phone interview with the Iraqi official, Al-Jazeera aired a speech by President George W. Bush, and then US Secretary of State Colin Powell came on to give an exclusive interview to the Al-Jazeera anchor, Adnan Al-Sharif, a former employee of Jordanian television and now Al-Jazeera's interim managing director. Powell told Arab audiences that the US wanted this war to end as soon as possible and that American forces had been doing their best to minimize Iraqi civilian casualties. Realizing Al-Jazeera's great popularity among Arab audiences, US officials in Washington have been lining up to get on the network.

Al-Jazeera and the recent stages of the Iraq war

Al-Jazeera's attempt to offer wide-ranging coverage of the Iraq conflict has continued in the more recent stages of the war. In 12 weeks of Al-Jazeera's coverage of the so-called "post-war" period, reporters used field reports and interviews with key Iraqi figures to explain the complexity of the situation after the fall of Saddam, given the various religious, ethnic, and nationalist rivalries among different Iraqi factions.

For example, in late June 2003, Al-Jazeera interviewed Sheikh Mohammed Baqir Al-Hakim, the leader of the Supreme Assembly of Islamic Revolution in Iraq (SAIRI), the largest Shi'ite Iraqi group, who was assassinated later that year, about his position toward the existence of coalition troops in Iraq and his assessment of the political situation in post-Saddam Iraq. The interview with Al-Hakim had special importance because of the tension that has started since the end of the war in the Shi'ite holy city of Najaf, where thousands of Shi'ites had been demonstrating against what they called the "foreign occupation" of their land.

The multiple Iraqi perspectives were not the only ones presented on Al-Jazeera after the war. The American perspective was also presented through interviews with US political strategists working for think tanks in Washington, DC. One of those strategists, Jon Alterman of the Center for International and Strategic Studies, came on Al-Jazeera in July 2003 to comment on the Iraqi resistance to the US troops and the daily violent confrontations between the Iraqi guerrillas and the American soldiers.

Al-Jazeera also included a series of exclusive interviews with key American figures in Iraq. In early July 2003, one of its main reporters in Baghdad, Waddah Khanfar, conducted an interview with Paul Bremer, the top US administrator in Iraq, who addressed the key issues that had been going on in the minds of most Arab people after the situation in Iraq had started to deteriorate. The following is a transcript of part of the interview:

Khanfar: During the past few weeks, there has been an increase in the attacks against the American soldiers. Are you worried that these attacks might include more cities in Iraq?

Bremer: I certainly hope the attacks do not spread. Until now, these attacks are concentrated in the north and the west of Baghdad, and they seem to be individual attempts by Ba'athists from the former regime. We are doing our best to capture all the militants so that we can live in peace.

Khanfar: But sir, a lot of people are now unemployed and you might find them joining the resistance groups.

Bremer: Obviously, senior members of the Ba'ath Party are unhappy since they will not have any role in the new government. This is the most important decision I took for this country. People on the streets thank me for that decision. As for the middle and lower members of the Ba'ath,

328

we are currently preparing them to become civilized members of the society and have jobs.

Khanfar: When will you go home?

Bremer: When my job here is completed. My job here is clear and identified. The Iraqi people need to create their own constitution and interim government. When this is completed, all the coalition forces will leave. We will not stay one more day or one less day. It all depends on the Iraqi people and when they finish writing the constitution.

Such open and frank interviews with US officials were much needed at that point, given a deterioration of the American image in the Arab world since the start of the Iraq war. For American officials to appear on the most popular Arab network and talk face-to-face to members of the Arab audience about issues of concern to them was a vital step in making clear the American point of view.

One of Al-Jazeera's more notable achievements was engaging its audience in an open dialogue, where people from various countries exchanged ideas in the hope of fostering mutual understanding in a constructive and respectful environment. One popular Al-Jazeera program—"Open Dialogue"—allowed for this type of exchange. A recent episode of the live monthly program (all Al-Jazeera's programs are aired live, which does not give room for any kind of censorship or previewing editing) invited students and their faculties from Egypt, Lebanon, and Iraq to engage in a dialogue via direct satellite link about what the Arabs could do to improve the situation in Iraq after the war. The episode was hosted and moderated by Al-Jazeera's veteran correspondent Ghassan bin Jeddo (July 5, 2003).

Although most comments began with students sending regards and wishes for peace, the discussion heated up and included accusations and pleas from all sides. Some members of the Iraqi side accused the Iraqis living abroad of being passive and not helping their country. "Where are the Iraqi professors who are living abroad? Why don't they come back and help their country?" said one Iraqi arts professor in Baghdad. A professor in Beirut said, addressing his words to the Arab leaders, "Please don't turn Iraq into a 'deal' by distributing its wealth among you while the Iraqi people are starving to death." Then a student from Cairo said, "There are lots of reasons that led Iraq through this dark tunnel, but the number one reason are the Arab countries; when I say that I mean the Arab leaders, not the people."

The Iraqi students in the Baghdad studio disagreed among themselves on the way they viewed the resistance movements against the US troops. One Iraqi student said, "I would like to tell everyone in Fallouja [an Iraqi Sunni-dominated city which had witnessed repeated Iraqi attacks against the American troops] please, don't drive the Iraqis into another massacre; we have been through enough already." An Iraqi political science professor interrupted him and said: "The fact that Al-Fallouja is being accused of resistance is an honor for us and for all Iraqis. Any country facing an invasion has the right to resist."

This debate and others like it showed that Al-Jazeera aired commentary and multiple perspectives, and in doing so it broke ground by venturing into the realm of open discussion rarely attempted by other broadcasters in the Arab world.

In the process of presenting pluralistic and open debates, Al-Jazeera also assigned episodes of its key programs to assess the Iraq war coverage by Arab news networks, including, of course, Al-Jazeera itself—an indication that Al-Jazeera welcomed critical analysis of its own coverage. One such episode was aired from a program titled "Behind the Events," a daily program that started airing after the war (May 12, 2003). The episode was hosted by Faisal Al-Kasim, one of the most popular television hosts in the Arab world, who some people call "the Arab Larry King." Al-Kasim's celebrity status came from hosting the popular program "The Opposite Direction," which is the flagship talk show on Al-Jazeera.

Four guests were invited to the "Behind the Events" episode that evening: Jawad Maraka, former president of Qatari television, Asa'ad Abu Khalil, a political science professor at the University of California, Mowafak Harb, director of the American-sponsored Radio Sawa, and Mustafa Bakry, editor-in-chief of a daily Egyptian opposition newspaper. The episode focused on the media revolution caused by the transnational satellite networks in the Arab world and how these networks had affected coverage of the Iraq war. The following is a transcript of part of the show:

Al-Kasim: Now we see Arab news channels are becoming more independent and free while the Western networks have been cheering for the Iraq war; even some American viewers complained that they weren't getting the full picture through their media. What do you think of that phenomenon?

Harb: The Arab media have come a long way over the past few years. They have advanced a lot in terms of technology, ways of obtaining the news, and even in competition with the Western networks. Having said that, I still think that most of the Arab news channels distort reality on purpose because they get their commands from the Arab governments.

Abu Khalil: We cannot look at the Arab media as one entity. There is a difference between print and broadcast and a difference between the media of one country and that of another. This difference was apparent in the Iraq war coverage, where we saw more diversity of opinions in the French and the British media; however, the American media were biased and one-sided although they pretended to be giving a balanced picture. Now, with the American networks, there is hardly any room for the opposite opinion. For example, when Ashleigh Banfield [MSNBC correspondent] tried to criticize the war, she was labeled as a "traitor" and received threat notes. On another note, I believe that Al-Jazeera and Abu Dhabi television did a better job in covering this war than the American media; however, I am against the fact that every time an American official coughs or sneezes, Al-Jazeera broadcasts everything live.

Al-Kasim: The Arab media have been accused of unrealistic reporting and falsely raising the morale of the Arab viewers in the Iraq war. Can I get your opinions on that?

Bakry: I don't believe the Arab media could have been objective in this war, especially when we know that the true motive behind this war was not only to remove Saddam Hussein, but Americanizing everything in the Arab world.

Maraka: During the war, the Arab media made no distinction between the Iraqi citizens and the Iraqi administration. So, they viewed whoever defended the Iraqi citizens as a defender for the Iraqi regime. I also think the Arab media presented more impressionistic, rather than factual information, about the war.

Harb: I think the problem lies in defining the role of the Arab media. In the West, each media outlet has a mission and a strategy; however, we don't find that with the Arab media. They are confused as to whether they are seeking facts or criticizing their governments or advertising for their governments.

Pluralistic dialogues such as this one engaged the viewers and helped them become critical users of their own media. This is especially important in the Arab world, where the viewers had never been exposed to a program discussing the role of the Arab media in covering a major conflict and assessing the strengths and weaknesses of the Arab networks in a free manner without any inhibitions or red lines. In processing what they receive from the media, the onus falls on the audiences to use a critical eye and to be aware of the different factors influencing and biasing the media. In the meantime, media personnel have to be self-critical and have to hold themselves accountable for any clearly partisan or incomplete reporting.

Al-Jazeera's coverage of the Iraq war was not devoid of context. For example, its reporters used the term "martyrs" to refer to the Iraqi civilians killed during the military operations (el-Nawawy 2003a). These leanings often seem inevitable as networks cannot be devoid of perspective, a perspective that produces and reflects context. However, this context's overemphasis ushers in a certain degree of slant. Our monitoring and analysis of the Al-Jazeera coverage suggests that the network labored to present multiple sides of the Iraq conflict, despite strong criticism from and measures taken by both Iraqi and US officials, and that these multiple sides were presented systematically within a larger contextual frame that made sense within the region, if not to the world at large.

To this day, Al-Jazeera continues to be the target of criticism, prosecution, and punishment from many governments around the world, in what may be an inadvertent reaffirmation of the network's success at employing, implementing, and engaging contextual objectivity.

Much like the mythical Minotaur, who was thought to be responsible for climatic changes and seasonal unrest, in its short and notorious history, Al-Jazeera has been no less than a hurricane in the media landscape. On the contrary, unlike the Minotaur, who in the end was slain, there is much reason to believe that Al-Jazeera and its news formula—contextual objectivity—will outlive the criticism and perhaps the network itself. Instead, the Iraq war and its coverage by Al-Jazeera, have helped create an urgent necessity for a meaningful analysis and re-evaluation of war coverage to include an assessment of contextual objectivity as a barometer for fairness and balance in reporting around the world.

References

Beyerle, S. (2002, June) "Al-Jazeera says it tries to cover both sides in the Israeli–Palestinian conflict," *Washington Diplomat*.

Boyd, D. (1999) *Broadcasting in the Arab World: a Survey of the Electronic Media in the Middle East*, 3rd edition, Ames: Iowa State University Press.

Cozens, C. (2003, March 26) "4m in Europe sign up for Al-Jazeera," *The Guardian*.

el-Nawawy, M. (2003a, April 8) "Whose truth is being reported?" *The Christian Science Monitor*, vol. 95, no. 92, p. 9.

el-Nawawy, M. (2003b, April 9) "Al-Jazeera shouldn't be taking US fire," *The Star Ledger*, p. 17.

el-Nawawy, M. and Iskandar, A. (2002) "The Minotaur of 'contextual objectivity': war coverage and the pursuit of accuracy and appeal," *Transnational Broadcasting Studies Journal*, 9 (fall/winter).

el-Nawawy, M. and Iskandar, A. (2003) *Al-Jazeera: the Story of the Network that is Rattling Governments and Redefining Modern Journalism*, Boulder, CO: Westview.

Faine, J. (2003, November 10) "The US media could learn from Al-Jazeera," *The Age*.

Hasso, F.S. (2003, April 17) "Who covered the war best? Try Al-Jazeera," *Newsday*.

Hourani, A. (1988) "Foreword" in P. Partner, *Arab Voices: the BBC Arabic Service 1938–1988*, pp. vi–vii, London: BBC External Services.

"Island in the sun; Arab media," (2002, September 5) *The Economist*.

Partner, P. (1988) *Arab Voices: the BBC Arabic Service 1938–1988*, London: BBC External Services.

Schatz, A. (2003, April 1) "All that Jazeera," *The Lycos 50 Daily Report*, retrieved on November 28, 2003 from http://50.lycos.com/040103.asp

Schudson, M. (1978) *Discovering the News: a Social History of American Newspapers*, New York: Basic Books.

Steele, B. (2003, March 26) "Wall Street attack on Al-Jazeera unwise and unfair," *Poynter-Online*.

Suellentrop, C. (2003, April 3) "Al-Jazeera: it's just as fair as CNN," *Slate*.

Tahboub, D.T. (2003, October 4) "The war on Al-Jazeera," *The Guardian*.

Tumber, H. and Prentoulis, M. (2003) "Journalists under fire: subcultures, objectivity and emotional literacy" in D. Thussu and D. Freedman (eds), *War and the Media*, pp. 215–30, London: Sage.

Zelizer, B. and Allan, S. (eds) (2002) *Journalism after September 11*, London and New York: Routledge.

18

BIG MEDIA AND LITTLE MEDIA

The journalistic informal sector during the invasion of Iraq

Patricia Aufderheide

The brief moment in which the US armed forces with allies destroyed the regime of Saddam Hussein in Iraq in spring and early summer 2003 offered a snapshot view of the US media's performance of the toughest job in democracy: managing public discussion of controversial issues in a way that included significant minority voices. It was not a lovely picture, but it was a provocative one.

Electronic big media were bigger than ever, both domestically and internationally, and along with the big moguls—Murdoch, Berlusconi— there were big and growing corporations such as Disney, Vivendi, and Viacom, and big media mergers, notably that of AOL and Time Warner. At the same time, electronic little media flourished, a myriad grassroots attempt to fuel public opinion with information and attitude—often living, however briefly, in the virtual realm of the Internet. The vast burgeoning of the World Wide Web over the previous decade had transformed the expectations of a generation about their ability both to express their opinions and to reach others. The 1999 anti-globalization demonstrations in Seattle, WA, that pre-empted a meeting of the World Trade Organization (Kidd 2002), which used the Internet to launch do-it-yourself news services and triggered the rise of "indymedia" centers globally, made the possibilities vividly evident within the US. Other global organizations including OneWorld (oneworld.net) had already combined the strength of grassroots expertise with the power of distributed networking.

The invasion of Iraq—that is, the brief period of military conquest ending officially on May 1 when President George W. Bush declared on the flight deck of the USS *Abraham Lincoln* that "the United States and our allies have prevailed"— displayed the spaces in which both big and little media flourished. In particular, it revealed the antic vigor of a journalistic "informal sector." Borrowed from development economics, the term referred to the unofficial, untaxed, unpoliced, and often flourishing underground economy.

Big media had been on a roll in the US since the Telecommunications Act of 1996 had greatly increased concentration of ownership in radio and moderately increased concentration in other areas, including terrestrial television (Aufder-heide 1999). The act, which started out as a revision of telecommunications sector regulation to foster new entrants, competition, and investment, became a lumpy package of legislative gifts to powerful industry players. Major mass media inter-ests, especially radio, had argued that deregulation of ownership limitations was critical to provide incentives for mass media to invest capital in new ventures, and legislators obliged. Concentration of ownership was propelled further by Bush-era enthusiasts at the Federal Communications Commission, which implements telecommunications legislation and was charged under the act with biennial regu-latory reviews. The FCC under the leadership of Michael Powell continued the tradition of permitting owners of large telecommunication networks such as Rupert Murdoch unprecedented waivers, and its Republican majority successfully pursued the goal of further deregulation of anti-concentration measures (US, FCC 2003).

During the invasion of Iraq, quantity became quality in big media. That is, size affected content. Commercial practice—much of it on entertainment media such as music radio or prime-time television that did *not* make claims to be providing news or public affairs—became effective political clout. This happened whether management directed it or not. It happened because big media's bottom-line con-cerns and practices—its sensitivities to ratings and the notorious fickleness of audiences, its currying of advertisers' favor, its support for highly colorful charac-ters whose sensationalism drives up ratings—shaped choices about political coverage and events. These practices became ever more extreme as the channels and alternatives available to people burgeoned. Multichannel cable and satellite radio and television, Web-based information services and the dawn of the per-sonal video recorder (of which the commercial service TIVO was one example) which made it possible to download and replay digitized versions of television programs all intensified commercial practices that drew and held audiences. In assessing media behavior in a political crisis, it is important to look here beyond the headlines of prestige daily journalism, because public opinion is powerfully shaped by the most popular media—the entertainment that pervades daily life.

Big media

Consider four examples, none of them necessarily a demonstration of tendentious ideological behavior on the part of news outlets. Rather, they all demonstrated the consequences of a media entity's size on coverage and the voicing of controversial views. The first example concerned using the commercial airwaves as a platform to rally pro-war demonstrators. As the invasion with Iraq drew close, pro-war demon-strations suddenly started springing up all over the country. Dozens of "Rally for America!" events were held. They were organized by a particular conservative radio talk-show host, Glenn Beck, who positioned himself as someone standing up against liberal media—by which he apparently mostly meant television and which he decried for running footage of anti-war rallies (although most US protesting groups argued that coverage was meager and slighted the numbers). Supporting the "75 to 78 percent in favor of military action,"—he told a group estimated at 20,000 in a Clearwater, Florida, rally to "Begin your day and end your day on your knees . . . Pray for our troops and pray for our president" (Gregoire 2003).

Beck's show, along with those of other conservatives such as Rush Limbaugh, was carried by the gigantic national radio company Clear Channel. Clear Channel used to be a small radio company until the 1996 Telecommunications Act rolled back ownership restrictions on radio. Now it is by far the largest company owning local radio stations in the US, and it lowers costs by sharing programming among its more than 1,200 stations. Glenn Beck was a national voice with an ability to reach into local events planning. Though Clear Channel denied any role in Glenn Beck's call to action, his efforts clearly didn't hurt. Clear Channel, which was in fiscal straits, stood to benefit from a federal government decision to further deregulate radio—eventually made in its favor, although later challenged in Congress (Krugman 2003; Schwartz and Fabrikant 2003).

A second case also concerned Clear Channel which, besides being the biggest radio station owner in the US, was also the largest concert promoter. This incident concerned cross-ownership and control, and it was relayed via actor and movie producer Tim Robbins, who spoke about the incident in Washington, DC, in April 2003, at a press conference he called at the National Press Club. Complaining about the way he and his wife Susan Sarandon had been treated by the National Baseball Hall of Fame, when their invitation to celebrate the 15th anniversary of *Bull Durham* was rescinded because of their dissident views on the invasion, Robbins discussed his isolation within the entertainment community, but also noted that people were secretly cheering him on.

"A famous middle-aged rock-and-roller called me last week to thank me for speaking out against the war," he said, "only to go on to tell me that he could not speak himself because he fears repercussions from Clear Channel. 'They promote our concert appearances,' he said. 'They own most of the stations that play our music. I can't come out against this war'" (Robbins 2003).

Clear Channel corporate spokespeople denied intimidating and suppressing speech in this instance. Of course, as an individual under US law, the corporation does have full-fledged First Amendment rights, and because it is so big, its First Amendment rights have a very big footprint. But the rocker did not say that Clear Channel had denied him speech, like the National Baseball Hall of Fame had done to Tim Robbins. He just said he was afraid. He could not take a commercial risk, not with a company that had the unique power to pull the plug on his concert-driven career.

A third example also demonstrated the power of size to diminish points of view. Cumulus Media, a company that owns 262 stations, refused to carry the music of the country music band Dixie Chicks because the group criticized Bush and the war while touring Europe. The British left-wing newspaper, the *Guardian*, was the first to publish the on-stage comment of Dixie Chicks singer Natalie Maines in London: "We're ashamed that the president of the United States is from Texas"

(Campbell). This remark reverberated across the ocean. Once Cumulus dropped the Dixie Chicks, almost every country music radio station group, including all of those supported by Clear Channel, dropped them during the invasion. Their record sales fell 75 percent the following week, and they suffered a near-blackout of their new album during the invasion. (The sales rebounded after the invasion, though.) The choice to drop the Dixie Chicks was probably a canny market decision since country music listeners skew to the conservative. In fact, Cumulus Media spokespeople argued that the company was just being sensitive to its listeners' viewpoints. Because of consolidation, though, a few decision-makers had a blanketing effect, at least during the invasion (Bishop and Florida 2003; Segal 2003).

A fourth example shows the power of commerce to affect the news judgment of local television stations. Television stations have long been understandably sensitive to ratings because their income from advertisers depends on the number of viewers they get. Local news is an area where local stations keep the money. Frank Magid, one of the most respected and trusted media research firms in US television and known particularly for its consultation with local television stations, told local stations the week after the invasion started that covering anti-war protests could, according to a survey the firm had conducted, affect ratings. The firm's survey of 6,400 viewers showed that anti-war protest information was the topic that tested the lowest, or the least of interest, and was most likely therefore to lead viewers to change channels. Polls by the reputed independent firm Gallup and others showed at that point that 70 percent of Americans were for the war. Covering the opinions of the 30 percent could affect ratings, which would affect profits. It seems that many stations got the message. Anchors were uniformly supportive of the invasion, and station websites were heavy on the "support your troops" weblinks (Farhi 2003).

Big media's downplaying of dissent within the US also generated a counter-effect. It rekindled the never-extinguished coals of customer suspicion and disgruntlement. The bigger big media get, the more easily their customers move from their default stance of cynicism and mistrust to anger and rejection. That is one good part of the reason why big media executives are so very sensitive to majority customer mood. And the more demographically-targeted big media get—a function of increased specialization and multichannelization—the less leeway big media executives have to deviate from a perceived predilection of its demographic.

"Beyond the box"

This time, disgruntlement spilled out into the informal sector of journalism, inhabited by freelancers, moonlighters, activists, angry citizens, and the odd oddball. At the Center for Social Media at American University, a group of students and professors sampled activity in this informal sector, in March and April of 2003.[1] We used Google and scanned news reports and checked in with a range of alternative or independent media organizations ranging from Indymedia to Oneworld to Alternet. We developed a website to share our findings with researchers—a snapshot from the weeks before the invasion began and during the immediate aftermath of the first fighting (http://centerforsocialmedia.org/warbeyondbox/index.htm). We called it "War beyond the box"—"the box" being the commercial mass media (see Figure 18.1).

Our scan of the informal communications environment easily came up with dozens of websites against the war. We found fewer but equally vociferous ones that supported the war. Conservative sites were much more likely to be linked with an explicitly political organization. Many of the informal sites—and they dotted the cyberlandscape—were the work of individuals, of ad hoc groups, or groups that sprung up as part of the anti-war mobilization that used the "viral networking" of the Internet, sometimes to mobilize "smart mobs."

We grouped the behaviors we saw into several categories. While the full list is on the website, they included the following:

Aggregating

Infomediaries abounded, which were established Internet sites that culled both mainstream reporting and material from "alternative" international or specialized presses, and also often encouraged "open publishing" (post your own work or comments on others'), in order to compose a news agenda different from the prestige dailies. These sites acted as semi-open gates for news creators and news seekers. Indymedia, itself a child of 1999 anti-globalization protests, put the emphasis on open publishing, although many sites linked on Indymedia were also infomediaries (Anonymous 2002; Kidd 2002). Some, such as the Information Clearing House ("News you won't find on CNN or Fox Moooo's"), were labors of love, fed intermittently with donations from site visitors (www.informationclearinghouse.info/). Others, such as oneworld.net and opendemocracy.net, were foundation-funded. These latter had different missions. OneWorld hosted a virtual community of nonprofit organizations supporting social justice and human rights. Open Democracy provided a forum for diverse and conflicting opinions on public affairs. Infomediary sites deliberately blurred the line between news providers and news creators. At the same time, they provided a degree of moderating (indymedia.org much less than others), which contributed to reader confidence in the veracity of the material.

Do-it-yourself

We noticed a spontaneous creation of new media, often by activists testifying to a reality that they found obscured in mainstream media and sometimes by people demanding a voice in a time of crisis. Some of it was *email* letters, or petitions, or a forwarded emailed testimony. We called this "electronic samizdat," underground duplication of information sneaked among friends in the tradition of

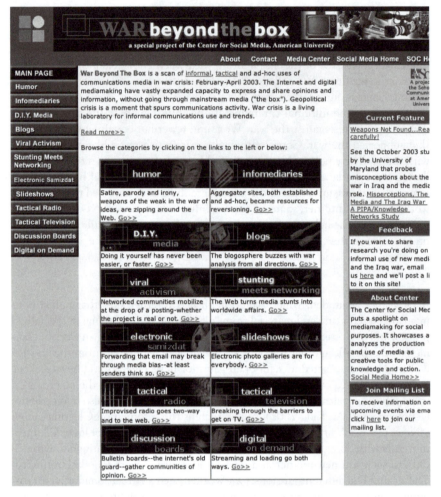

Figure 18.1 "War beyond the box"—this website encapsulated the Center for Social Media's scan of the informal media landscape (courtesy of the American University School of Communication)

illegally reproduced work in the USSR (http://centerforsocialmedia.org/war beyondbox/esamizdat.htm). Some of the DIY work was in the form of Powerpoint-style slideshows—a kind of cyber photograph gallery, on display for anyone who chooses to click (http://centerforsocialmedia.org/warbeyondbox/slideshows.htm). Some of it was websites, where on-the-ground testimony that challenged received wisdom or mainstream reporting was released, such as that by the anti-war group Voices in the Wilderness, which reported its eyewitness experiences in text and images at electroniciraq.org. Some of it drew conclusions from mainstream data, such as the website iraqbodycount.org, which featured a running tally of deaths

in Iraq, providing a data-driven critique of the war (http://centerforsocialmedia.
org/warbeyondbox/infomediaries.htm).

Some of this work was by people creating downloadable documents—poetry
and video and music for friends and sympathizers to download. Some creators,
like the Beastie Boys, who wrote an instant protest song that they made public
domain, were well known; others produced their work as a gift (http://center
forsocialmedia.org/warbeyondbox/digital.htm). And some of it was jokes. One
widely circulated email was the lyrics to the tune of "If you're happy and you
know it," including: "If you never were elected, bomb Iraq / If your mood is quite
dejected, bomb Iraq / If you think Saddam's gone mad/ With the weapons that he
had / (And he tried to kill your dad) / Bomb Iraq." (This was an email received by
one person from another who forwarded it within three minutes of receiving it to
some 15 people, and who promptly sent it forward again to a blind-copy list.)

These works often circulated from email list to email list, among like-minded
friends. Sometimes they were folded into intermediary sites. They made a claim
for attention and confidence on readers and viewers as the work of friends or virtual friends. Their appeal depended in part on a shared sense of having gone
unrepresented in mainstream media, and unheard by government officials. That
shared sense sometimes overrode reader judgment, as people sometimes forwarded petitions that were bogus or outdated (http://centerforsocialmedia.org/
warbeyondbox/viral.htm).

Interactive grassroots journalism

Blogs, hybrid-journalism Internet sites that were part diary and part reporting also
emphasized the interactivity, spontaneity, informality, and community we saw in
other behaviors (http://centerforsocialmedia.org/warbeyondbox/blogs.htm). Some,
such as warblogs.cc, depended on the work of trained journalists (Chris Allbritton had worked at the Associated Press and *The New York Daily News*, for
example). Some were supported by viewers, others by advertisers and sponsors.
Some conducted journalistic investigations, and they generally had a concern,
typical of journalists, for timeliness, accuracy, and accessibility. They usually provided links to mainstream news media. At the same time, their deliberately open
structure undercut assurance. On warblogging (www.warblogging.com), blogger
Nick Paine noted that a longtime blog contributor, "Nick," claimed to be a US
army lieutenant. "I am inclined to believe that Nick is who he says he is . . . It is,
however, up to you to make up your own minds about his veracity," he noted on
the website's front page. Blogs showcased voices underrepresented in mainstream
media, most notably an Iraqi citizen calling himself Salam Pax (http://dear_raed.
blogspot.com/), who created a mini-debate around who he was and even if he
existed. (This comment was accessed October 21, 2003, at which time the blog
continued to flourish.)

Radio and television

Dissenters to mainstream opinion and individuals looking for a way to express themselves found their way to ungatekept spots on the usually tightly patrolled borders of radio and television. We dubbed this "tactical" use of electronic media, acknowledging the traditions of European—especially Eastern European— activists who seized small technological opportunities to break through media blackouts. The Serbian radio station B-92 was one well known example and the term "tactical" is featured in irregular conferences held by the loosely structured Next Five Minutes organization (www.n5m4.org).

People used shortwave radio to create anti-war programs and used unlicensed spectra to link together neighbors on an ad hoc radio network. Creators sought out cable access—first-come-first-serve channels open to the public on many cable services—and made work at community technology centers (CTCs). In at least one case, the CTC distributed the information via broadband Internet. Creators also sought out program services using the public channels on direct-broadcast satellite television. FreeSpeech television and WorldLink both aired programs which were made to respond to the moment. OneWorld's newly launched Internet TV service—actually digitized video cut into short segments—showcased dissident views as well (http://centerforsocialmedia.org/ war beyond box/ tactical radio.htm; http://centerforsocial media.org/warbeyond box/tacticaltv.htm).

We found anti-war sentiment, information, and outrage at both government and media popping up all over in electronic media. We found a frequent resort to humor, and especially satire and parody (http://centerforsocialmedia.org/war beyondbox/humor.htm). Randall Packer's "We the blog" (http://wetheblog.org/), for instance, solemnly proposed a new Bill of Rights appropriate for the Patriot Act era. (This proposal formed part of Packer's larger site, www.usdat.us/, hosting the imaginary US Department of Art and Technology, of which Packer has made himself the Secretary.) Many humor items borrowed from popular culture. Mad magazine's parody of a Star Wars poster, with Bush in the leading role for Gulf War II, was widely circulated (and rarely attributed). Children's toys were featured in a parody of Secretary of State Colin Powell's UN speech, with murky toy soldiers and action figures standing in for Powell's murky, portentous proofs of WMD. Other humor items borrowed jokes from the cyber-universe in which they circulated. At www.coxar.pwp.blueyonder.co.uk/ inattentive viewers might believe they were getting a Microsoft error message—until they tried to click on the Regime change button. This "Weapons of mass destruction 404" page, created by British pharmacist Anthony Cox on a whim (see Figure 18.2), became the topranked website returned when searching the words "weapons mass destruction" on search engine Google, as a result of a myriad of links to it from bloggers worldwide (Cox 2003). The humor turned the tables on the most powerful political and military figures in the world, turning them into figures that you could laugh at from your workstation. This humor employed the familiar weapons of the weak: contempt and ridicule.

Cannot find Weapons of Mass Destruction

 These Weapons of Mass Destruction cannot be displayed

The weapons you are looking for are currently unavailable. The country might be experiencing technical difficulties, or you may need to adjust your weapons inspectors mandate.

Please try the following:

- Click the [⊕] Regime change button, or try again later.
- If you are George Bush and typed the country's name in the address bar, make sure that it is spelled correctly. (IRAQ).
- To check your weapons inspector settings, click the **UN** menu, and then click **Weapons Inspector Options**. On the **Security Council** tab, click **Consensus**. The settings should match those provided by your government or NATO.
- If the Security Council has enabled it, The United States of America can examine your country and automatically discover Weapons of Mass Destruction.
  If you would like to use the CIA to try and discover them,
  click 🔍 <u>Detect weapons</u>
- Some countries require 128 thousand troops to liberate them. Click the **Panic** menu and then click **About US foreign policy** to determine what regime they will install.
- If you are an Old European Country trying to protect your interests, make sure your options are left wide open as long as possible. Click the **Tools** menu, and then click on **League of Nations**. On the Advanced tab, scroll to the Head in the Sand section and check settings for your exports to Iraq.
- Click the 💣 <u>Bomb</u> button if you are Donald Rumsfeld.

Cannot find weapons or CIA Error
Iraqi Explorer
Get the WMD 404 T-shirt.

Figure 18.2 Bloggers' links turned the "Weapons of Mass Destruction 404" parody website into an international favorite (courtesy of Anthony Cox)

These jokes, like the testimonies, slideshows, and websites, fueled an underground current of resistance. Strongly marked by a sense of community, the journalistic informal sector was organized by networks of friends and communities of belief and values. This had implications both for the growth and use of information within that sector, and also for its potential participation in the public opinion-shaping spheres now dominated by professional journalism.

Between branded and uncharted

Certainly this burgeoning of the informal sector does not mean that mainstream media have lost their pride of place. They have hard won reputations for credibility that went to good use on many informal-sector sites. In fact, many sites in the informal sector did much more culling and interpreting of mainstream media than they created or platformed new information. Many blogs were also punctuated throughout the day with links to and reports on gatekept media.

People were able to mobilize others for action more swiftly than ever before, particularly at MoveOn (http://moveon.org/), an organization that used the Internet to build an "electronic advocacy group," as its website declared. Born of liberal outrage at the Clinton impeachment movement and run by brilliant political strategists and tacticians, the core group of which came out of the Democratic Party (Hazen 2003), it had extraordinary success in coalescing hitherto inchoate demands for participation in democratic process. MoveOn mobilized via mass emails (often then propelled via viral marketing to many more friends-and-family lists), which linked to websites loaded with specific actions to take. MoveOn moved into people's intimate lives on screen, supported a widespread sense of alarm and mistrust of government, and connected people to anti-war protests. In fact, MoveOn mobilized many more people—by at least one decimal point—than conservative talk-show host Glenn Beck. But the impact the two had on public opinion was quite different. Beck made a claim about speaking in a public venue; MoveOn showed up in one's office cubicle or home.

What MoveOn could not do was to convince someone who was not in its address book or listserv or interested in Googling it in the first place that its viewpoint was interesting, reasonable or worthy of attention. In his one-to-many environment, Glenn Beck was able to convince people that he warranted attention, regardless of agreement. Speaking to millions at once and touching the button of righteous anger, he generated relatively few demonstrations, but his position as radio host amplified his opinion into that of a demographic. MoveOn remained one's email buddy, while Glenn Beck became one's angry neighbor. What Glenn Beck could do that MoveOn could not was sway and intimidate fencesitters. The clout of Glenn Beck reflected the power of the gatekept journalistic venues for agenda-setting, even more than for information provision.

The burgeoning of the informal sector raised the informational noise level dramatically, adding creatively to public debate, but that conclusion was by no means foretold. The proliferation of opportunities to gather information, in fact, remained a kind of curse for the information end user, without tools to manage information. Our multi-channel, multi-screen world is too full of information. It is even regarded as a kind of pollution, as David Shenk's term "data smog" evokes (Shenk 1997), whereby filters are sought to make sense of it. While mainstream media provided an avowedly public filter, the informal sector so far has filtered information through a lens of domestic life and private judgments, building on common values or friendship links.

Too often during the Iraq invasion that meant choosing between branded info-tainment and an uncharted information environment. Big media continued, during the invasion, to be absolutely critical in establishing what we think is our common reality, because they acted as big filters. The efforts of some sites in the informal sector, such as OneWorld, to moderate information, to host exchanges of viewpoints, and to encourage citizen input within a civil framework are all interesting and encouraging attempts to address that problem.

The invasion of Iraq, in which the US administration so carefully managed mainstream media, created unprecedented media activity among people who insisted upon expression of their views, and who had been developing their digital skills at their workstations, in class, and while producing their family newsletters. On the basis of this activity, viral networks grew and some sites became more established sources of information, investigation, and commentary. Months after the invasion, most of the sites we found and featured on "War beyond the box" were still active, and many were still reporting.

The informal sector's burgeoning activity during the Iraq invasion has prompted a range of responses. Among what *Wired* magazine editors early dubbed the "digerati," some have been inspired to address at least one of the weaknesses in the sector: its dispersion and lack of indexing. The Media Venture Collective,[2] a network of public-interest-oriented digerati, launched an experimental media project related to the 2004 US presidential election. The central element of the project was a repository for affirmatively public domain material (licensed under the terms of the Creative Commons[3]) at the servers of the Internet Archive, a public domain project backed by the dot.com plutocrat Brewster Kahle. It anticipated building relationships with providers of raw material, producers using the material, and distributors—all of which were already in place and used during the invasion of Iraq—to develop an open media network on the model shown in Figure 18.3.

Such a nonpartisan, affirmatively public domain repository for audio-visual material, proposed by project designer Brad DeGraf deliberately as an experiment to test the waters, offers an interesting approach to the challenges of the journalistic informal sector today. It could create clear lines of antecedence and origination, without losing easy access. It could give grassroots-created materials a home, rather than depending on friends, family, Google, and accident to find voices beyond big media. It could offer advantages to both traditional journalists and those arising from the informal sector, in that this kind of central space could permit spontaneity and flexible use of material by commercial and noncommercial users, from both traditional and nontraditional sources and journalists. Functioning as a kind of public library of ephemeral, Web-based, digital information of all kinds, such a service would need some kind of public backing, investment or endorsement, rather than depending on the largesse of dot.com winners. It would need to become a spot on the public media landscape.

Other models to aggregate and share information, already extant during the Iraq invasion, will assuredly also develop. The left-culture indymedia sites, for instance, continue to proliferate worldwide and to draw on the youthful energies

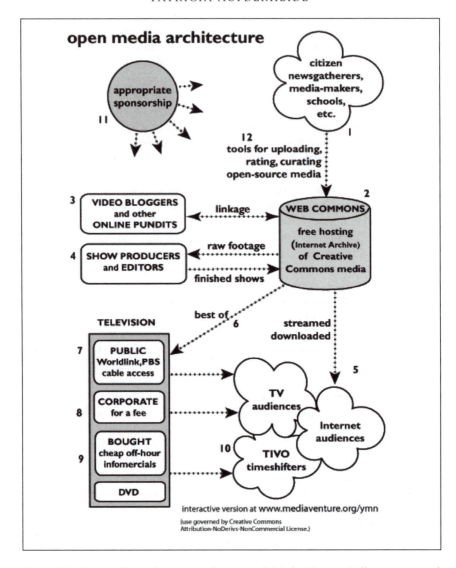

Figure 18.3 Open media architecture—the nonprofit Media Venture Collective proposed a nonpartisan repository for informal media linked to events such as the 2004 US election (courtesy of Media Venture Collective)

of many volunteers, at the same time suffering from bouts of incivility and attempts at sabotage by opposed ideologues. Blogs are becoming a staple journalistic hybrid, both personal and public, with some becoming celebrity sites. Web-based public platforms such as Open Democracy and OneWorld are building in the learning from each experiment in Web-based public discourse, as they develop their interactive, grassroots journalism. Meanwhile, mainstream media,

344

especially in their electronic forms, have been made newly aware of the power of interactivity and the public appetite for it.

The gap between big and little media in the Iraq invasion was enormous, and if the energy released by the informal sector's generating of information and opinion was great, so was the confusion. The contradictions were boldly on display. Minority voices in the US—generally, those opposed to the war—had an unprecedented range of expression open to them at unpredecented low costs. At the same time, these very possibilities were capable of reinforcing paranoia, mistrust, and a sense of embattlement. These new options could spread misinformation as quickly as they could enlightenment, and often did.

The journalistic informal sector continued to grow on the sites we identified on "War beyond the box," as the post-invasion scenario turned into a grinding conflict. It will continue to develop, particularly in times of crisis where distrust of mainstream media turns into action. We may yet get to see the gap between big media and little media become a spectrum, or even a structured network of relationships.

For the effusions of informal journalistic sector to develop into a truly public and participatory sphere of civic engagement as well as discrete communities of belief, sustained public support and scholarly analysis are both important. Public support should entail a revision of the current regulatory permission to media concentration, given the power of highly concentrated media outlets to set agendas and intimidate. It should also acknowledge that ad hoc information sharing in times of crisis indicates the desperate desire of ordinary citizens to contribute to public decision-making. Such desires should be honored with public resources to encourage citizen participation. Among many examples of government fostering of civic informational engagement is the Canadian e-commons project (http://ecommons.net/). Public funding for affirmatively public domain resources, repositories, and for indexing and archiving systems are valuable investments in civic discourse. This informal sector also merits closer academic study—case studies, cultural production studies, textual analysis and reception studies. The powerful claims that journalists have made in the US over the last 50 years for professional journalistic standards and behaviors can become critical principles brought to practices developing today in the informal sector.

Notes

1 Participants included principal investigator Professor Patricia Aufderheide, Project Manager Agnes Varnum, and students Lisa Chan, Aaron Johnson, Navin Kulshreshtha, and Catherine Taylor. Professor B.J. Altschul acted as adviser.

2 The Media Venture Collective (www.mediaventure.org) is, as its website maintains, a "grass roots, non-profit venture fund . . . focused on channeling citizen donations into strategic investments that facilitate media democracy, and thereby maximizing their social change impact."

3 Creative Commons (http://creativecommons.org/) offers licenses that affirmatively assign the default copyright that authors are granted under US law, in graduated terms, ranging from highly conditional use only by certain kinds of parties to unconditional

public domain use. Creative Commons, which exists to facilitate the range of materials available for creators, works with many partners; for instance, the Open Elections Network expects to use Creative Commons licensing.

References

Aufderheide, P. (1999) *Communications Policy and the Public Interest*, New York: Guilford Press.

Bishop, B. and Florida, R. (March 23, 2003) "O, Give me a home where the like-minded roam," *Washington Post*, Outlook edition, p. B5.

Campbell, D. (April 25, 2003) "Dixie sluts fight on with naked defiance," *The Guardian* (London), p. 1.

Cox, A. (July 10, 2003) "The war on the web," *The Guardian* (London), www.guardian.co.uk/online/story/0,3605,994676,00.html, accessed November 12, 2003.

Farhi, P. (March 28, 2003) "For broadcast media, patriotism pays: consultants tell radio, TV clients that protest coverage drives off viewers," *Washington Post*, Style edition, p. C1.

Gregoire, N. (April 6, 2003) "Radio host, Gov. Bush cheered in Clearwater," Tampa *Tribune*, p. 1.

Hazen, Don (February 11, 2003) "Moving on: a new kind of peace activism," Alternet, available www.alternet.org/story.html?StoryID=15163 (accessed October 21, 2003).

Kidd, D. (2002) "Indymedia.org: the development of the communications commons," *Democratic Communiqué*, vol. 18, pp. 65–86.

Krugman, P. (March 25, 2003) "Channels of influence," *The New York Times*, available www.nytimes.com/2003/03/25/opinion/ (accessed April 4, 2003).

Robbins, T. (April 16, 2003) "A chill wind is blowing in this nation . . .," transcript of the speech given by actor Tim Robbins to the National Press Club in Washington, DC on April 15, 2003, CommonDreams.org, available www.commondreams. org/views 03/0416-01.htm (accessed October 28, 2003).

Schwartz, J. and Fabrikant, G. (March 31, 2003) "War puts radio giant on the defensive," *The New York Times*, available www.nytimes.com/2003/03/31/business/media (accessed April 4, 2003).

Segal, D. (April 25, 2003) "Dixie chicks bare their, uh, souls: band counters critics of anti-war remarks," *Washington Post*, Style edition, p. C1.

Shenk, D. (1997) *Data Smog: Surviving the Information Glut*, 1st edition. San Francisco, CA: Harper Edge.

Shepard, B.H. and Hayduk, R. (2002) *From ACT UP to the WTO: Urban Protest and Community Building in the Era of Globalization*, London: Verso.

US Federal Communications Commission. (FCC) (June 2, 2003) "FCC sets limits on media concentration," press release available at www.fcc.gov/ Daily_Releases/ Daily_Business/2003/db0602/DOC-235047A1.pdf (accessed October 21, 2003).

19

THE CULTURE OF DISTANCE

Online reporting of the Iraq war

Stuart Allan

Actually too tired, scared and burnt-out to write anything. Yes, we
did go out again to see what was hit. Yes, everything just hurts . . . I
can't stand the TV or the lies on the news any more. No good news
wherever you look.

Salam Pax, the Baghdad Blogger

Writing in the *London Review of Books* at the time of the British military conflict
with Argentina over the disputed sovereignty of the Falkland/Malvinas Islands,
Raymond Williams (1982) sought to discern how this "unnecessary war," to use
his apt turn of phrase, was being reported. He argued that underlying the typical
sorts of questions that arise when television news reports are examined, such as
"issues of control and independence; of the quality of reporting; of access and balance in discussion," was a deeper problematic. In order to describe it, he coined
the phrase "the culture of distance."

The central technical claim of television, Williams pointed out, is its capacity
to represent distant events. While reminding us that the televisual picture of
the world is a selective one, he argued that "what is much more significant is
the revealed distance between the technology of television, as professionally
understood, managed, and interpreted, and the political and cultural space
within which it actually operates" (1982: 14). Across this distance—via the
conventions of "familiar connections"—the tragic devastation endemic to warfare is recurrently taken-up and re-inflected by television news into an "antiseptic" representation of reality. Not surprisingly for someone who had experienced
conflict first hand, namely as a tank commander in World War II, this problem of
distance was particularly troubling, not least in moral terms. Commenting on the
daily news reporting of the build-up to the seemingly inevitable outbreak of war,
he wrote:

After several days of it, feeling the rhythm soaking in, I happened to pass
a bonfire of rags and oil in the village and suddenly, in an overwhelming

347

moment, I was in a field in Normandy and the next tank, with my friends in it, was burning and about to explode. I think I then understood the professional culture of distance.

(Williams 1982: 17)

Of utmost importance, he believed, was the need to understand the ways in which television news shaped the "representation of spectacular destruction" while, at the same time, serving to "insulate us from reality" as we watch our television screens in our respective households. Hence the urgency of his call for new investigations to be made into this culture of distance, this "latent culture of alienation, within which men and women are reduced to models, figures and the quick cry in the throat" (1982: 21; see also Williams 1958).

In taking Williams' notion of the "culture of distance" as the point of departure for this chapter, it is my intention to help discern the basis for a related line of enquiry into online journalism. Specifically, I want to explore several issues regarding the Web-based mediation of witnessing, in general, and that of the distant suffering of others, in particular. Already the online reporting of the war in Iraq is being lauded—as well as being assailed—for having a formative influence on the perceptions of different publics. "In terms of coverage," Dean Wright, editor-in-chief of MSNBC.com, has observed, "this may well become known as the Internet war, in the same way that World War II was a radio war and Vietnam was a television war" (cited in Hewitt 2003). While it is too early to tell whether this will prove to be the case, this chapter aims to contribute to an evaluative assessment. It begins in the next section with a consideration of the Internet as a news source during the conflict, before proceeding to examine, first, the online reporting of Al-Jazeera (www.aljazeera.net) and, second, the rise of warblogs, such as that belonging to Salam Pax, cited above. Attention will focus throughout on the ways in which online reporting provides alternative spaces for acts of witnessing, a process which will be shown to be uneven, contingent, and frequently the site of intense resistance.

Searching for alternatives

"Day 20 of America's war for the 'liberation' of Iraq," British journalist Robert Fisk reported, "was another day of fire, pain and death." His article, published in the April 9, 2003 edition of The Independent newspaper, continued:

It started with an attack by two A-10 jets that danced in the air like acrobats, tipping on one wing, sliding down the sky to turn on another, and spraying burning phosphorus to mislead heat-seeking missiles before turning their cannons on a government ministry and plastering it with depleted uranium shells. The day ended in blood-streaked hospital corridors and with three foreign correspondents dead and five wounded.

(The Independent, April 9, 2003)

Fisk, well known for his incisive writing style, was clearly aiming to ensure that his eyewitness description of the unfolding events in Baghdad resonated with his readers. His report appeared beneath the day's lead story, "The US advance, street by street," on the front page. In contrast with it, however, Fisk's report provided the kind of personal insight that ordinarily falls outside of the conventionalized strictures of ostensibly objective, hard news reporting. Indeed, his commitment to sustaining a reporter-centered narrative—"The A-10s passed my bedroom window, so close I could see the cockpit Perspex, with their trail of stars dripping from their wingtips, a magical, dangerous performance fit for any air show, however infernal its intent"—presumably would have been particularly valued by many of The Independent's readers, even though the events in question had transpired the day before.

The issue of immediacy is important here. It is altogether likely, of course, that most of these same readers would have been aware of much more recent developments in Baghdad than those described in their newspaper, courtesy of the electronic media. Television, as one would expect, led the way in reporting the battle for control of the city as it unfolded on April 9. While fighting continued in some areas, images of a statue of Saddam Hussein in Firdous Square being pulled from its plinth by a US armored personnel carrier (the bronze head promptly, if only momentarily, draped by a US flag) featured in television newscasts around the globe. In visual terms, the fallen statue promptly assumed a charged symbolic status in some news reports, frequently being held to represent the collapse of the central regime's authority, the power of Saddam broken and removed. This television coverage, it would be later claimed by some commentators, effectively demonstrated the immediacy of real-time reporting and its benefits. No war, they argued, had been better recorded, the sheer volume of words and images offering an unprecedented degree of detail in near-instantaneous time. Citing factors such as improvements in news technologies, as well as the use of reports from "embedded" correspondents, they insisted that many of the criticisms first leveled at 24-hour news in the 1991 Gulf War had been laid to rest.

Meanwhile, observations of a different sort were being made time and again on different Internet websites in response to the day's television reporting (well before newspaper reports covering the events in Firdous Square had gone to press). Across chat rooms, bulletin boards, discussion forums, weblogs, and the like, Internet users gave voice to their points of view about what these events meant to them. Some rejoiced, while others, in sharp contrast, demanded to know what was really happening on the ground in Baghdad. For some, the toppling of the statue appeared to have been almost choreographed for the benefit of the cameras. Awkward questions were posed on various sites about whether it was a spontaneous act (or one organized with US television schedules in mind?), the composition of the "crowd" of onlookers (was their number made to appear more substantial by the camera angles chosen?) and the extent to which these "jubilant" people were actually "celebrating," among other concerns. Many of those writing online posts vented their anger at what they regarded to be the pro-war, even jingoistic stance of mainstream news reports, singling out Fox News for particular criticism owing to its perceived over-reliance on official "propaganda" and "spin." Regardless of differing political perspectives, however, many users simply wanted much more by way of context, critique, and explanation than television news was providing that day, and were too impatient to wait for the next day's newspapers.[1]

Accordingly, news sites—whether "official" ones associated with an established news organization, or "unofficial" ones such as personal blogs—were proving to be indispensable resources. From the moment news of the first attacks launching so-called "Operation Iraqi Freedom" on March 19, 2003 was reported, Internet traffic to online news services surged dramatically. More people than ever, according to companies monitoring Internet traffic such as Hitwise, Nielsen Net Ratings, and the like, were surfing the Internet for news and information.[2] For many Internet commentators, the US-led attack on Iraq represented the "coming of age" of the Internet as a news medium. Regularly singled out for attention was the role of high-speed, broadband Internet access, not least its capacity to enable news sites to offer users live video and audio reports, multimedia slideshows, animated graphics, interactive maps, and so forth. The rapid rise in the number of users availing themselves of the technology—over 70 million people in the US at the time—meant that providers could further enhance existing types of digital reportage accordingly (Kirkpatrick 2003). Moreover, other commentators pointed to the ways in which online news was consolidating its position as a primary news source. Of significance here, for example, was the extent to which users, especially office workers unable to watch television in the workplace, were relying on the Internet for up-to-the-minute news of breaking developments. Research conducted during the first six days of the war by the Pew Internet and American Life Project (2003) indicated that 56 percent of online users in the US had turned to news sites for reports about the conflict. "More than half the people who are online are getting their news online—that's never happened before," Lee Rainie, the project's director, maintained. "It's another milestone moment for online news" (cited in Weaver 2003).

Moreover, this same opinion survey by Pew sought to determine what US citizens thought about the conflict, how they were acquiring their news about it, and what sort of impact developments were having on them.[3] Briefly, its findings suggested that 77 percent of the country's 116 million adult Internet users had been online in connection with the war in Iraq. Their main reasons for turning to the Internet, as one might expect, included searching for information about the war, seeking alternative opinions about the conflict, sending, and receiving emails about pertinent events, and expressing their views and offering prayers. Evidently a relatively small percentage of users were making use of email to mobilize others in efforts to build collective support for their views about the conflict—while 10 percent of users received email from organizations against the war, 7 percent of them received email from pro-war organizations. Approximately one in seven (or 14 percent) of users said that they had been online more frequently than usual because of the news, a tendency judged to be more pronounced among opponents of the war than among its supporters.

Not surprisingly, this study also found that the overwhelming majority of these Internet users—some 87 percent—were relying on television as their main source of news about the war. That said, however, it is noteworthy that some 17 percent of users stated that the Internet was their principal source of information about the conflict, which represents a considerable increase when compared with the results of a similar survey conducted after the September 11 attacks. "At that time," the report declared, "only 3 percent of online Americans said the Internet was their primary source of information about the attacks on the World Trade Center towers and the Pentagon and the aftermath of the attack" (Pew 2003: 2). Moreover, where previous research commissioned by Pew indicated that some 24 to 26 percent of users typically go online to get news, this survey suggested that 37 percent of users were looking for online news in the days immediately before the formal declaration of hostilities. This is a substantial increase, one attributed to factors such as variety and timeliness by users turning to the Internet to keep abreast of developments. And yet, how varied was the range of perspectives on offer online? "Even though a clear majority of Internet users say they value the online environment because they get a *variety* of points of view," the authors of the report wrote, "just 17 percent of Internet users said going online gave them *different* points of view" (2003: 7; emphasis in original). Indeed, some 64 percent of those surveyed said perspectives encountered online were "pretty much the same" as those in newspapers and television (a further 19 percent of respondents did not express an opinion one way or the other). Here it should be noted, though, that the report indicated that more users were going to the websites belonging to US television networks for their online news (32 percent) than any other news source online, with US newspaper sites a close second (29 percent). US government sites were next (15 percent), followed by foreign news organizations (10 percent) and alternative news sites (8 percent).[4]

Bearing in mind the usual sorts of qualifications where opinion surveys are concerned (margins of sampling error, interpretations of question wording, practical difficulties, and so forth), these results need to be treated with due care. Nevertheless, while it would be inappropriate to extrapolate from them to characterize a "typical" user, this type of data usefully underscores an important set of issues. Judging from this evidence, certain celebratory claims about the "global village" engendered by online journalism would appear to ring hollow, at least where US users are concerned in the early days of the invasion. Still, for those users concerned enough about the crisis to look beyond the confines of their country's sites, the sheer diversity of the perspectives available online enabled them to supplement their understanding of alternative, even opposing views. "The new war in Iraq has made world news sources far more important," online writer Stephen Gilliard argued. "While not all news sources are reliable, there is such a gap between the way Americans see the world and the way other people do that it is invaluable to use these resources" (cited in Kahney 2003). Indeed, it was presumably this very gap in perception which motivated many users to look abroad in the first place.

"In the Internet age," as US journalist Elizabeth Putnam (2003) pointed out, "overseas newspapers are a few keystrokes away, making them more available and attractive to people who want to understand why there seems to be so much anti-American sentiment around the world." Nowhere were these sorts of tensions more apparent than with regard to news sites in the Arab world. From the vantage point of most US and UK users, however, no site in the region would attract more intense interest during the Iraq war than Al-Jazeera (www. aljazeera.net).

Al-Jazeera online

Often described as the "CNN of the Arab World," Al-Jazeera (which means "an island" in Arabic) is arguably the region's most influential news organization. Launched in the Qatari capital, Doha, in 1996, the 24-hour satellite television network attracts an audience currently estimated to be about 35 million regular viewers, making it the most widely watched Arab news channel. Available free of charge throughout much of the Arab world, it is typically a pay-television channel in Europe and North America. Although backed financially by the government of Qatar, Al-Jazeera's journalists consistently maintain that their editorial freedom is not compromised as a result. That said, the network's status as an independent voice in the Arab world, encapsulated in its slogan "The opinion and the other opinion," is frequently called into question by its many critics. For some, the network's commitment to providing news coverage from an Arab perspective means that it is ideologically compromised, and as such biased against the US and Israel. Other critics, in contrast, have denounced Al-Jazeera for being a Zionist tool, while still others insist that it is little more than a front for the Central Intelligence Agency (CIA). In any case, above dispute is the fact that its news coverage has recurrently placed a considerable strain on Qatar's relations with other countries in the region, including Bahrain, Jordan, and Saudi Arabia where the network's offices have been closed on different occasions.

No stranger to controversy, Al-Jazeera came to prominence across the global mediascape in the aftermath of the dreadful events of September 11, 2001, owing to its decision to broadcast taped messages attributed to Osama bin Laden (see also Zelizer and Allan 2002; el-Nawawy and Iskandar 2003; Thussu and Freedman 2003). News organizations around the world paid considerable sums to air edited excerpts, much to the consternation of US officials—not least National Security Adviser Condoleezza Rice, for example, who demanded of television network executives that they "exercise judgment" (i.e. censorship) in re-broadcasting the messages. Interestingly, most of the considerable traffic to the network's site (www.aljazeera.net) at the time was from the US, despite the fact that its content was entirely in Arabic. During the subsequent "war on terror" in Afghanistan, attention was once again directed at Al-Jazeera's role in making available reports of the conflict that challenged the preferred definitions of reality set down by military officials. For this reason alone, further controversy erupted in November 2001 when a US "smart" bomb destroyed the network's Kabul offices. Intense speculation ensued that the offices had been deliberately destroyed. For example, Nik Gowing, a presenter on BBC World, stated afterwards that Al-Jazeera's only crime was "bearing witness" to events that the US officials would prefer it did not see. In demanding that the Pentagon be called to account, he pointed out that when the presence of journalists is "inconvenient" they risk becoming "legitimate targets" in the eyes of the military—a charge promptly denied, as one would expect, by a Pentagon spokesperson (see Wells 2001).[5]

Following the start of "Operation Iraqi Freedom," subscriber numbers surged dramatically in response to the intense demand for alternative insights into the conflict. The number of subscribers to the channel in Europe, it was claimed at the time, effectively doubled once the war was underway. The depth of its reporting was recurrently singled out for praise—or condemnation—depending on conflicting perceptions of the relative legitimacy of the war. In addition to reporting from Central Command in Qatar, four of Al-Jazeera's reporters were "embedded" with the US and British military forces. In the main, however, the network ensured that most of its journalists roamed more freely. Together they covered the breadth of Iraq, including areas where Western journalists did not venture. The Al-Jazeera television crews remained in Baghdad throughout the conflict, as well as in other major battlegrounds such as Basra, Mosul, and in Kurdish-controlled northern Iraq. Not surprisingly, a very different kind of coverage ensued. Tarik Kafala (2003), a *BBC News Online* reporter, identified a case in point. "When Western journalists outside Basra were speculating about an uprising on the basis of coalition briefings," he observed, "Al-Jazeera's correspondent inside the city was reporting first hand that 'the streets are very calm and there are no indications of violence or riots.'" This type of disjuncture between the network's reporting and that of its Western rivals attracted considerable comment. US Secretary of State Colin Powell, for example, criticized the coverage, contending that it "magnifies the minor successes of the [Iraqi] regime and tends to portray our efforts in a negative light" (cited in Delio 2003). For others, however, it was the very extent to which Al-Jazeera's reporting called into question the more "sanitized" representations of the conflict that made its presence so important—both on their television screens and, increasingly, on their personal computers (see Gubash 2003).

Prior to the launch of Al-Jazeera's website, Arabic speakers were typically most interested in CNN.com (www.arabic.cnn.com) when looking for news online. Since the September 11 attacks, however, the page views for the Arabic-language site operated by Al-Jazeera reportedly grew from about 700,000 a day to 3 million, with more than 40 percent of visitors logging-on from the US (Ostrom 2003). Indeed, at the outbreak of hostilities in Iraq, aljazeera.net was widely recognized as receiving the most "hits" of any Arabic site in the world. Of critical significance here was its commitment to pushing back the boundaries of Western

definitions of "objective" journalism so as to help give voice to contrary definitions of the world (see also Iskandar and el-Nawawy, chapter 17 of this volume).
In the case of the conflict in Iraq, this meant those of the Iraqi people themselves—victims, in the eyes of the network, both of Saddam Hussein's regime and
the invasion of US and UK forces to destroy it. By including in its reports what
were frequently horrific images of civilian casualties, Al-Jazeera re-inflected familiar notions of "balanced" reporting. It was precisely these images, in the view of
Faisal Bodi (2003), a senior editor for aljazeera.net, that made Al-Jazeera "the
most sought-after news resource in the world." In his words:

> I do not mean to brag—people are turning to us simply because the
> Western media coverage has been so poor. For although Doha is just a
> 15-minute drive from central command, the view of events from here
> could not be more different. Of all the major global networks, Al-Jazeera
> has been alone in proceeding from the premise that this war should be
> viewed as an illegal enterprise. It has broadcast the horror of the bomb-
> ing campaign, the blown-out brains, the blood-spattered pavements, the
> screaming infants and the corpses. Its team of on-the-ground, unembed-
> ded correspondents has provided a corrective to the official line that the
> campaign is, barring occasional resistance, going to plan.
>
> (Bodi 2003)

At no time was this difference in news values cast in sharper relief than on
March 23, the night Al-Jazeera broadcast footage of US casualties, as well as Iraqi
television's interviews with five US prisoners of war. Al-Jazeera's decision to air
the interviews was promptly denounced by US Defense Secretary, Donald Rumsfeld, who alleged that it was a violation of the Geneva Convention protecting
prisoners of war. In reply, the network's London bureau chief, Yosri Fouda, argued
that Western news reports were being constrained to the extent that they failed
to provide accurate coverage. Regarding the Geneva Convention, he insisted
that a double standard was being invoked. "We and other broadcasters were not
criticized for showing pictures of Iraqi dead and captured," he stated, "or those
famous pictures from Guantanamo Bay" (cited in Kafala 2003).

The more heated the ensuing furore became, of course, the more news headlines it generated around the world. The very images deemed by Western news
organizations to be too disturbing to screen were being actively sought out by vast
numbers of people via online news sites. According to figures compiled by popular search engines, such as Google, Lycos, and AltaVista, the term "Al-Jazeera"
was quickly becoming one of the most searched-for-topics on the Web. Figures for
the week in question indicated that the term "Al-Jazeera" (and variant spellings)
was the term that showed the greatest increase on Google, while Lycos reported
that it was the top search term, with three times more searches than "sex" (a
perennial favourite with Web surfers). For Karl Gregory of AltaVista, the popularity of Al-Jazeera's online sites was clear evidence of "people branching out

beyond their normal sources of news" (*BBC News Online*, April 1, 2003). The decision taken at Al-Jazeera to broadcast the images, as well as to display them online, was justified by its spokesperson, Jihad Ballout, as being consistent with its journalistic ethos of reporting the war as it was being fought on the ground. In his words: "We didn't make the pictures—the pictures are there. It's a facet of the war. Our duty is to show the war from all angles" (cited in Whitaker 2003). In the opinion of others, however, the network had become a mouthpiece for Iraqi propaganda. Citing the images, some military officials began ignoring questions from Al-Jazeera's reporters at briefings. At the same time, two of the network's financial reporters were evicted from the floor of the New York Stock Exchange (Nasdaq would follow suit, citing "Al-Jazeera's recent conduct during the war" as the reason), their press credentials revoked. It was in cyberspace, however, that the backlash registered most decisively as various pro-war individuals and groups made clear their intent to make Al-Jazeera a target of retaliation.

News sites of all descriptions are always vulnerable to attack from hackers—typically involving little more than webpage defacements and graffiti—but those directed at Al-Jazeera's sites were remarkably vicious. The "electronic onslaught," as aptly characterized by one Internet commentator, began on March 25, the same day the English-language site, www.english.aljazeera.net, was launched. Two days later, hackers "crashed" both sites, effectively forcing them offline by a "denial of service" or DOS attack. This type of attack aims to close down a targeted site by overwhelming the associated server with so much meaningless data that it can no longer handle legitimate traffic. Few sites have sufficient resources, such as the necessary bandwidth, to withstand millions of simultaneous page impressions. Such was certainly the case with both Al-Jazeera sites. The English-language site was disabled virtually from the outset, while its Arabic-language counterpart struggled—with only limited success—to hold up against the storm. Efforts to restore the sites, which reportedly included re-aligning them with servers in France, encountered fierce resistance by repeated hack attacks. "We come up for five or ten minutes," stated Salah Al-Seddiqi, IT manager at Al-Jazeera, "and then the attacks bring us down again" (cited in Roberts 2003).

Later the same day, even though security protocols had been reinforced for the sites, matters went from bad to worse. Evidently, a pro-war hacker was able to access the servers at Network Solutions Inc., a domain name registration service based in Dulles, Virginia, that operates a database linking addresses (in this case, www.aljazeera.net) with the identification numbers of the servers responsible for maintaining its Web pages. This meant that Al-Jazeera's domain was effectively "hijacked" by the hacker, such that users were pointed to an altogether different site instead. Specifically, traffic was redirected to a pro-war webpage featuring a US flag, together with the messages "Let freedom ring" and "God bless our troops," signed by a self-proclaimed "Patriot." It was quickly determined that this latter site belonged to an Internet provider based in Salt Lake City, Utah, albeit without their knowledge. Hackers calling themselves the "Freedom Cyber Force Militia" had claimed responsibility for the attack, but in any case the registration information provided to establish the webpage proved to be fictitious. Hours later, traffic intended for the Al-Jazeera site was redirected again, this time presenting users with a webpage bearing the message "taken over by Saimoon Bhuiyan." Further attacks continued apace, one of which apparently succeeded in diverting users to a pornography site.

Meanwhile, as Al-Jazeera's technicians scrambled to reinstate the correct addresses for the sites, pressures of a different sort were brought to bear. As a result of the hacker attacks, DataPipe, a US-based hosting company, announced that it was terminating its services to the Qatar-based company that supported Al-Jazeera's sites. In the absence of a detailed explanation for the decision from DataPipe, some commentators speculated that it must have received complaints by other clients concerned that the hacking targeted at Al-Jazeera was harming their sites as well. Others argued that "war sensitivities" were surely involved, once again pointing to the decision to air the controversial images of US soldiers and its alleged pro-Iraqi stance. Al-Jazeera's difficulties were further compounded when Akamai Technologies, brought in to help deal with the increased traffic to the sites and to provide protection against hacking attempts, abruptly cancelled its contract. Akamai, based in the US with clients such as ABC.com, MSNBC.com and Yahoo.com, refused to elaborate on the reasons behind its decision. "It has nothing to do with technical issues," Joanne Tucker, the managing editor of Al-Jazeera's English-language site, argued. "It's non-stop political pressure on these companies not to deal with us" (cited in St John 2003; see also Roberts 2003). Commenting on the repeated hacking, she added: "It's a narrow, pro-censorship attempt to silence a news site."[6]

Indeed, it was the relative ease with which the Al-Jazeera site was effectively silenced that was startling, even for many online commentators at the time. Some proceeded to argue that the attacks on the sites represented the future of political protest, the virtual equivalent of burning books containing heretic viewpoints. By this type of logic, any site providing news or information which called into question the legitimacy of a military campaign could be perceived, in turn, as constituting a threat to the war effort. Hacking thus becomes an insidious form of censorship. Summing up the crisis engendered by the hacking attacks, Hafez Mirazi, the network's Washington bureau chief, commented: "This is very typical of what Al-Jazeera has been through in the Arab world and in many authoritarian regimes. It's just sad that the US and US institutions didn't deal with us any differently than the Iraqi regime did" (cited in Carlson 2003).

Blogs at war

Much of what passes for journalism in the US, in Mediachannel.org editor Danny Schechter's (2003) assessment, "is seen as nothing but propaganda by people in other countries and by an increasing number of Americans, who are turning to international Web sites to find the kind of news they can no longer get here." In addition to international sites such as Al-Jazeera's, however, an altogether different type of site has similarly attracted a remarkable degree of attention during the Iraq conflict. Specifically, news-oriented weblogs achieved widespread public salience, being heralded as a new interactive form of participatory reporting, commentary, and analysis of breaking news. Indeed, by the time of the formal declaration of "Operation Iraqi Freedom" on March 19, 2003, the term "blog" was rapidly being appropriated into the everyday language of journalism.

Weblogs, or blogs for short, may be characterized as diaries or journals written by individuals with net access who are in possession of the necessary software publishing tools (e.g. those provided by sites such as Blogger.com) to establish an online presence. Most bloggers pull together their resources from a diverse array of other sites, thereby situating a given news event within a larger context, and illuminating multiple dimensions of its elements. The apparent facts or claims being collected are usually time-stamped and placed in reverse-chronological order as the blog is updated, making it easier for readers to follow its ongoing narrative. Customarily the sources of the blogger's information are acknowledged explicitly and the accompanying hyperlink enables the user to negotiate a network of cross-references from one blog to the next, or from other types of sites altogether. In principle, the facts or claims presented in any one blog can be subjected to the relentless double-checking of users, some of whom may be even better informed about the events in question than the initial blogger. Any attempt by a blogger to present a partisan assertion as an impartial statement of fact is likely to be promptly recognized as such by other users.[7]

Many news bloggers—a small minority compared to the number of ordinary netizens involved overall—consider themselves to be "personal" journalists, intent on transgressing the border between "professional" and "amateur" reporting. By acting as "unofficial" news sources on the Web, these blogs link together information and opinion which supplements—or, in the eyes of some advocates, supplants—the coverage provided by "official" news outlets. The potential of blogs in this regard was widely recognized during the tragic events of September 11, 2001. In the early hours after the attacks, most of the major news sites in the US, as well as others such as the BBC's site in London, were so besieged by user demand that they were largely inaccessible (see Allan 2002). As one site after the next refused to load properly, users turned elsewhere for news of breaking developments. Hundreds of refashioned websites began to appear over the course of the day, making publicly available eyewitness accounts, personal photographs and in some cases video-footage of the unfolding disasters. Of particular importance here was the crucial role played by blogs in making these forms of "amateur," "guerrilla," or "DIY" (do it yourself) journalism available. "Most of the amateur content," Kahney (2001) remarked at the time, "would be inaccessible, or at least hard to find, if not for many of the Web's outstanding weblogs, which function as 'portals' to personal content." Managers of these blogs spent the day rapidly linking together any and all items of "personal journalism" from "amateur newsies" onto their respective sites. In so doing, they rendered problematic the familiar criteria defining what counted as news—as well as who qualified to be a journalist—thereby throwing into sharp relief the reportorial conventions of the mainstream news coverage.

"The Weblog world before September 11 was mostly inward-looking—mostly tech people talking about tech things," Glenn Harlan Reynolds of the blog InstaPundit.com observed. "After 9/11, we got a whole generation of Weblogs that were outward looking" (cited in Gallagher 2002). Significantly, in the weeks following the atrocity, a new type of blog began to emerge, described by its proponents as a "warblog." Taking as their focus the proclaimed "war on terror," these blogs devoted particular attention to the perceived shortcomings of the mainstream news media with regard to their responsibility to inform the public about possible risks, threats, and dangers. Warbloggers were divided, as one might expect, between those who favored US and UK military intervention in the Middle East, and those who did not. In both cases, however, an emphasis was placed on documenting sufficient evidence to demonstrate the basis for their dissatisfaction with what they deemed to be the apparent biases of the mainstream news coverage of the ensuing conflict in Afghanistan. For pro-war bloggers, a "liberal bias" was detectable in much mainstream journalism, leading them to call into question the patriotism of well known reporters and news organizations. In sharp contrast, bloggers opposed to the war were equally convinced that mainstream journalism, with its over-reliance on sources from the Bush administration, the Pentagon and other military sources, pro-war think tanks, and so forth, was failing to provide fair and balanced coverage. Many were able to show, with little difficulty, how voices of dissent were being routinely marginalized, when they were even acknowledged at all. For warbloggers of either persuasion, then, it was desperately important to seek out alternative sources of information from across the Web in order to buttress their preferred perspective.

Few of these online sources originated in Afghanistan, however, owing to the severity of the official restrictions imposed on journalists, as well as because of the limited availability of telecommunications services (an average of two telephones per 1,000 people). Accordingly, for many in the blogging communities, it was the US-led invasion of Iraq that proved to be the "breakthrough" for this grassroots movement. Steven Levy (2003), writing in a *Newsweek* Web exclusive, suggested that blogs "finally found their moment" as bombs were dropped on the city of Baghdad. The formal initiation of hostilities, he maintained, and "the frustratingly variegated nature of this particular conflict, called for two things: an easy-to-parse overview for news junkies who wanted information from all sides, and a personal insight that bypassed the sanitizing Cuisinart of big-media news editing." In Levy's view, blogs were able to "deliver on both counts." Adopting a similar line of argument were those who pointed to the success of blogs in attracting attention, especially that of individuals largely indifferent to mainstream reporting (here young people are frequently mentioned), by virtue of their shared intimacy. "I think that sort of clarity of voice and immediacy is more possible on Web logs than in any print media," argued Dean Allen of textism.com. "I can't think of another broadcast medium that has such a potential for directness.

Someone reporting live from the battlefield for CNN can't come close" (cited in Allemang 2003). Commenting on this type of "horizontal" communication, Glenn Harlan Reynolds (2003) of InstaPundit.com noted wryly that "the term 'correspondent' is reverting to its original meaning of 'one who corresponds,' rather than the more recent one of 'well-paid microphone-holder with good hair.'"

While it is difficult to generalize, most warbloggers posting from Iraq seemed motivated to share their eyewitness experiences of the conflict so as to counterbalance mainstream news media coverage. The work of CNN correspondent Kevin Sites was a case in point. In addition to filing his television reports, Sites wrote "behind the scenes" features for CNN.com, all the while maintaining a multimedia blog. Published on his own site, Sites' blog provided his personal commentary about the events he was witnessing from one day to the next, along with various photographs and audio reports that he prepared. Perhaps in light of the media attention Sites' blog received, however, CNN asked him to suspend it on Friday, March 21, 2003. A spokesperson for the network stated at the time that covering war "is a full-time job and we've asked Kevin to concentrate only on that for the time being" (cited in Kurtz 2003). Sites agreed to stop blogging, later explaining that "CNN was signing my checks at the time and sent me to Iraq. Although I felt the blog was a separate and independent journalistic enterprise, they did not" (www.kevinsites.net). Reactions from other bloggers were swift. CNN's response, according to Steven Levy (2003) of *Newsweek*, "was seen in the Blogosphere as one more sign that the media dinosaurs are determined to stamp out this subversive new form of reporting."[8]

In contrast, MSNBC's support for blogging meant that three warblogs were focused on war coverage at the height of the conflict. "Weblogs are journalism," argued Joan Connell, one of the site's executive producers. "They can be used to great effect in reporting an unfolding story and keeping readers informed" (cited in Mernit 2003). Nevertheless, while she does not share CNN's stance that blogs lack a sufficiently "structured approach to presenting the news," she does believe that there is a necessary role for an editor in the process. In her words: "Unlike many Weblogs, whose posts go from the mind of the writer straight into the 'blogosphere,' MSNBC's weblogs are edited. Our editors scrutinize our weblogs for accuracy, fairness, and balance, just as they would any news story" (cited in Mernit 2003). Not all bloggers on the front lines were associated with a major news organization, however. Many worked as a "sojo" or "solo journalist," writing and editing their own copy for both online and print or broadcast media. Being almost constantly on the move meant relying on mobile technologies, such as a notebook computer and digital camera, or even a videophone and mini-satellite dish. Still, for these bloggers, their relative freedom of movement enabled them to pursue the stories which mattered most to them—and the readers of their warblog. Herein lay the popularity of the warblogs among users, which in the opinion of journalist Bryony Gordon (2003) was hardly surprising: "if a television reporter's movements aren't subject to Iraqi restrictions, then his [or her] report is likely to be monitored by the Allied Forces. Devoid of such regulations, the Internet is thriving."

Freelancer Christopher Allbritton had announced his intention to be the Web's first independent war correspondent in the months leading up to the invasion. His blog, titled "Back to Iraq. 2.0" (www.back-to-iraq.com), called upon readers to help contribute to the financial support necessary to fund his travel and expenses in Iraqi Kurdistan. "It's a marketplace of ideas," he maintained, "and those who are awarded credibility by their readers will prosper" (cited in Warner 2003). Support was such that his expenses were met by some 320 donors, allowing him to file daily stories from the country using a borrowed notebook computer and a rented satellite phone. As his blog's daily readership grew to upwards of 25,000, he became accustomed to receiving emails which posed questions and suggested story leads, while others provided useful links to online materials. "My reporting created a connection between the readers and me," Allbritton (2003) later observed, "and they trusted me to bring them an unfettered view of what I was seeing and hearing." This involvement on the part of his readers in shaping his reporting worked to improve its quality, in his view, each one of them effectively serving as an editor. "One of the great things about the blogosphere," he maintained, "is that there's built-in fact-checking." Given that so many people will "swarm" over posts, "generally the truth of the matter will come out" (cited in Glaser 2003). Self Righting Principle – Milton

Precisely what counts as truth in a war zone, of course, is very much in the eye of the beholder. Above dispute, in the view of many commentators, was that some of the best eyewitness reporting being conducted was that attributed to the warblog of "Salam Pax" (a playful pseudonym derived from the Arabic and Latin words for peace), a 29 year-old architect living in middle-class suburban Baghdad. Indeed, of the various English language warblogs posted by Iraqis, none attracted a greater following than Salam's "Where is Raed?" (dear_raed.blogspot.com), which had begun to appear in September 2002. His motivation for blogging was later explained as a desire to keep in touch with his friend Raed, who had moved to study in Jordan. In the months leading up to the initial "decapitation attack," to use his turn of phrase, the blog contained material ranging from personal—and frequently humorous—descriptions of everyday life, to angry criticisms of the events around him. It was to his astonishment, however, that he discovered that the international blogging community had attracted such intense attention to his site. As word about "Where is Raed?" spread via other blogs, email, online discussion groups, and mainstream news media accounts, it began to regularly top the lists of popular blogs as the conflict unfolded. For Salam, this attention brought with it the danger that he would be identified—a risk likely to lead to his arrest, possibly followed by a death sentence. At the same time, speculation over the identity of the Baghdad Blogger—and whether or not "Dear Raed" was actually authentic—was intensifying. Some critics claimed that it was an elaborate hoax, others insisted it was the work of Iraqi officials, while still others maintained that a sinister CIA disinformation campaign was behind it. Salam responded to skeptics on March 21, writing: "please stop sending emails asking if I were for real, don't belive [sic] it? then don't read it." Moreover, he added, "I am not anybody's propaganda ploy, well except my own" (cited in *BBC News Online*, March 25, 2003).

Enraged by both Saddam Hussein's Ba'athist dictatorship and George W. Bush's motivations for the invasion, Salam documented life on the ground in Baghdad before and after the bombs began to drop. This was "embedded" reporting of a very different order, effectively demonstrating the potential of blogging as an alternative means of war reporting. His warblog entry for March 23, 8:30 p.m., was typically vivid:

> Today's (and last night's) shock attacks didn't come from airplanes but rather from the airwaves. The images Al-Jazeera are broadcasting are beyond any description. . . . This war is starting to show its ugly face to the world. . . . People (and I bet "allied forces") were expecting things to be much easier. There are no waving masses of people welcoming the Americans, nor are they surrendering by the thousands. People are doing what all of us are doing—sitting in their homes hoping that a bomb doesn't fall on them and keeping their doors shut.
>
> Salam Pax, dear_raed.blogspot.com

Salam's posts offered readers a stronger sense of immediacy, an emotional feel for life on the ground, than more traditional news sites. For John Allemang (2003), writing in *The Globe and Mail*, "what makes his diary so affecting is the way it achieves an easy intimacy that eludes the one-size-fits-all coverage of Baghdad's besieged residents." As Salam himself would later reflect, "I was telling everybody who was reading the web log where the bombs fell, what happened . . . what the streets looked like." While acknowledging that the risks involved meant that he considered his actions to be somewhat "foolish" in retrospect, nevertheless he added: "it felt for me important. It is just somebody should be telling this because journalists weren't" (cited in Church 2003).

Multiple truths

Any bold declaration that online journalism will abolish once and for all the "culture of distance" will invite a more considered response, once it is situated in relation to the sorts of developments discussed above. As has been made apparent, however, these emergent forms of journalism have the capacity to bring to bear alternative perspectives, contexts, and ideological diversity to war reporting, providing users with the means to connect with distant voices otherwise being marginalized, if not silenced altogether, from across the globe. In the words of US journalist Paul Andrews (2003), "media coverage of the war that most Americans saw was so jingoistic and administration-friendly as to proscribe any sense of impartiality or balance," hence the importance of the insights provided by the

ɔf Salam Pax. This "pseudonymous blogger's reports from Iraq," Andrews
͵eved, "took on more credibility than established media institutions." This
͵oint is echoed by Toby Dodge (2003), who argued that Salam managed to post
far more perceptive dispatches than those written by "the crowds of well-
resourced international journalists sitting in the air-conditioned comfort of five
star hotels." Communicating to the world using a personal computer with unreliable Internet access, he reported "the traumas and more importantly the opinions
of Iraqis as they faced the uncertainty of violent regime change."

To close, this chapter has taken as its focus some of the ways in which online
reporting opens up alternative spaces for acts of witnessing. Warblogs—together
with sites such as those of belonging to Al-Jazeera—have been shown to possess
the potential to throw into sharp relief the narrow ideological parameters within
which mainstream news media typically operate. Journalists' routine, everyday
choices about what to report—how best to do it, and why—necessarily implicate
them in a discursive politics of mediation. The very multi-vocality at the heart of
their narrativization of reality renders problematic any one claim to truth, and in
so doing reveals that witnessing is socially situated, perspectival, and thus politi-
cized. Before online reporting can become interactively dialogical in any
meaningful sense of the term, however, it will have to counter the forms of social
exclusion endemic to the culture of distance. A first step in this direction, as this
chapter has sought to demonstrate, is to recognize that the culture of distance is,
simultaneously, a culture of othering. At stake, in my view, is the need to deconstruct journalism's "us and them" dichotomies precisely as they are taken up and
re-inflected in news accounts where the structural interests of "people like us" are
counterpoised against the suffering of strangers. To recast the imperatives of
"here" and "there," and thereby resist the familiar pull of the culture of distance,
it is the corresponding gap between knowledge and action that will have to be
overcome.

Notes

1 To gain a quick sense of these sorts of interventions across the webscape, simply type
   the words "Saddam," "statue," and "blog" into a search engine, such as Google
   (www.google.com). At the time of writing, some 7,830 hits were generated by this
   combination, thereby providing a flavor of the nature of the ensuing discussion and
   debate.
2 In Britain that day, the level of traffic to *The Guardian* newspaper's website soared by
   nearly 30 percent to around 4.5 million impressions. According to Hitwise research,
   The Guardian's site was the leading online newspaper service with a 7.26 percent share
   of the market, followed by *FT.com* (5.17 percent), the *Sun* (3.05 percent), *The Times*
   (2.86 percent), the *Telegraph* (2.24 percent) and the *Independent* (1.51 percent). Of
   the non-print sites, the British Broadcasting Corporation's stand-alone news site was
   ranked highest with a 4.69 percent share. Evidently traffic to this BBC site was up by
   30 to 40 percent for the day, a level of demand which appeared to have caused the service to repeatedly "crash" in the early hours (see Timms 2003). Over the course of the
   days to follow, people going online during office hours appeared to be largely responsible for the surge in traffic to news sites. Many were seeking out alternative news

sources, as well as wanting particular types of perspectives about the factors under-pinning the conflict. "These figures show the desire of British surfers to get a real range of informed opinion on the war," argued Tom Ewing, a Nielsen Net Ratings analyst. "This shows where the Internet comes into its own when fast-moving news stories are involved" (cited by BBC *Online*, April 15, 2003).

In the US, Yahoo.com reported that in the first hour following President George W. Bush's announcement that the conflict had started, traffic levels to its site were three times higher. The volume of traffic to its news section jumped 600 percent the next day (Thursday, March 20) and again the day after. The sites associated with dif-ferent television networks proved particularly popular. On the Thursday, CNN.com evidently secured the highest figures for all news sites with 9 million visitors, followed by MSNBC with 6.8 million (about half of the visitors for both sites were accessing them from their workplaces). Other news sites witnessing a significant rise in demand that day included Foxnews.com (77 percent increase), Washingtonpost.com (29 per-cent increase) and USAToday.com (17 percent). "Without a doubt," stated Daniel E. Hess of ComScore, "people are glued to their Web browsers for virtually minute-by-minute updates of the war as it unfolds" (cited in Walker 2003, see also Richtel 2003).

3 The evidential basis for the study's findings was derived from a daily tracking survey, carried out via telephone interviews among a random sample of 1,600 adults between March 20 and 25, 2003 (999 of whom were Internet users). "For results based on the total sample," the Pew report states, "one can say with 95 percent confidence that the error attributable to sampling and other random effects is plus or minus 3 percentage points. For results based on Internet users (n = 999), the margin of sampling error is plus or minus 4 percentage points. In addition to sampling error, question wording and practical difficulties in conducting telephone surveys may introduce some error or bias into the findings of opinion polls" (Pew 2003: 10).

4 Additional results worthy of attention here include the study's finding that Internet users in the US were likely to support their country's war effort by a 3 to 1 margin. Some 74 percent of users surveyed were found to be backing the war effort in the early days of the campaign, compared with 22 percent who were opposed to it. Still, it appears that in contrast with those who support the war, its opponents "are more polit-ically active online, more anxious to discuss the war, and more likely to seek out a variety of sources of information about the war" (2003, p. 8).

5 Among the dead foreign correspondents mentioned in Robert Fisk's report (discussed above) was an Al-Jazeera reporter, killed by the US air attack on the network's office in Baghdad. "Despite two separate assurances from the American government that Al-Jazeera's base of operations would not be targeted," he wrote, "it was destroyed."

6 Further details regarding who was behind the pro-war hacking attacks against Al-Jazeera have begun to emerge in the months since these events transpired. In June 2003, John William Racine II, a website designer from Norco, California, pleaded guilty to felony charges revolving around the hijacking of the Al-Jazeera site. Evi-dently he had contacted the Federal Bureau of Investigation (FBI) himself on March 26 in order to confess to the "scheme to defraud," which also included inter-cepting some 300 email messages sent to Aljazeera.net (US District Court, California, case no. CR 03-557; filed June 9, 2003).

7 Interestingly, Fisk has seen his surname turned into a verb—"Fisking"—by some blog-gers as a form of shorthand to describe the critical practice of deconstructing a published news item on a point-by-point basis. A somewhat skeptical Brendan O'Neill (2003) comments: "Fisk is now a kind of mythical figure, that strange British journalist who dares to say the unthinkable—a view which, it has to be said, is often out of pro-portion to any biting insight on Fisk's part." Evidently it is fair to say that, for some, Fisking is a way to challenge mainstream journalism's hegemony while, for others, it is little more than an opportunity to engage in a politically partisan rant.

8 Kevin Sites, working as a freelance journalist at the time of writing, is on assignment in Iraq with MSNBC which is allowing him to maintain his personal (non-affiliated) blog. Evidently, MSNBC set down "a few understandable stipulations," which he describes in his blog as: "(1) I'm here because NBC News has hired me to be here, therefore the observations and experiences in Iraq that I relate to you in this blog would probably not happen without them. (2) They have the right of first refusal on anything that I write that relates to this assignment. That means I run it by them and if they want it they will publish it on MSNBC.COM. It will be republished here. (3) If it's something they're not interested in or not directly related to an assignment they've paid me to do—it can appear here first. I think that's fair and bypasses any of the editorial oversight and ownership issues that we encountered in the first run of kevinsites.net."

9 An example of the "corrective power" of the medium's interactivity, to use Allbritton's (2003) phrase, revolved around Fisk's report in The Independent newspaper of an incident where a bomb exploded in a crowded Baghdad marketplace, killing many individuals in the vicinity. In the report in question, Fisk cites the Western numerals painted on a metal fragment found nearby. According to Welch (2003), "Australian blogger Tim Blair, a freelance journalist, reprinted the partial numbers and asked his military-knowledgeable readers for insight. Within twenty-four hours, more than a dozen readers with specialized knowledge (retired Air Force, former Naval Air Systems Command employees, others) had written in describing the weapon (US high-speed antiradiation missile), manufacturer (Raytheon), launch point (F-16), and dozens of other minute details not seen in press accounts days and weeks later. Their conclusion, much as it pained them to say so: Fisk was probably right."

References

Allan, S. (2002) "Reweaving the Internet: online news of September 11," in B. Zelizer and S. Allan (eds), Journalism after September 11, London and New York: Routledge, 119–40.

Allbritton, C. (2003) "Blogging from Iraq," Nieman Reports, Fall, pp. 82–5.

Allemang, J. (2003) "Where everybody is a war reporter," The Globe and Mail, www.globeandmail.com, March 29.

Andrews, P. (2003) "Is blogging journalism?," Nieman Reports, Fall, pp. 63–4.

Bodi, F. (2003) "Al-Jazeera tells the truth about war," The Guardian, March 28.

Carlson, P. (2003) "In the line of fire," The Washington Post, April 3.

Church, R. (2003) "Interview with Salam Pax," CNN International, transcript no. 100302cb.k18, October 3.

Delio, M. (2003) "US tries email to charm Iraqis," Wired News, February 13.

Dodge, T. (2003) "An Iraqi in cyberspace," The Times Literary Supplement, October 24.

el-Nawawy, M. and Iskandar, A. (2003) Al-Jazeera: the Story of the Network that is Rattling Governments and Redefining Modern Journalism, Boulder, CO: Westview.

Gallagher, D.F. (2002) "A rift among bloggers," The New York Times, www.nytimes.com, June 10.

Glaser, M. (2003) "Reading between the lines in Iraqi blogs and newspapers," Online Journalism Review, www.ojr.org, November 7.

Gordon, B. (2003) "The Internet is having a field day—war 'blogs' are everywhere," The Telegraph, www.telegraph.co.uk, April 2.

Gubash, C. (2003) "New Arab TV channels show clout," MSNBC.com, March 31.

Hewitt, G. (2003) "The war on the web," *Cooltech.iafrica.com*, March 25.

Kafala, T. (2003) "Al-Jazeera: news channel in the news," *BBC News Online*, March 29.

Kahney, L. (2001) "Amateur newsies top the pros," *Wired News*, September 15.

Kahney, L. (2003) "Media watchdogs caught napping," *Wired News*, March 17.

Kirkpatrick, D.D. (2003) "War is test of high-speed web," *The New York Times*, March 24.

Kurtz, H. (2003) "'Webloggers,' signing on as war correspondents," *The Washington Post*, www.washingtonpost.com, March 23.

Levy, S. (2003) "Blogger's delight," *Newsweek Web Exclusive*, www.msnbc.com, March 28.

Mernit, S. (2003) "Kevin Sites and the blogging controversy," *Online Journalism Review*, www.ojr.org, April 3.

O'Neill, B. (2003) "Gone to the blogs," Spiked-IT, www.spiked-online.com, January 14.

Ostrom, M.A. (2003) "Net plays big role in war news commentary," *The Mercury News*, February 28.

Pew Internet and American Life Project (2003) "The Internet and the Iraq war," project report, April 1.

Putman, E. (2003) "Foreign news sites a hit as war looms," *Wausau Daily Herald*, February 9.

Reynolds, G.H. (2003) "Weblogs and journalism: back to the future?" *Nieman Reports*, Fall, pp. 81–2.

Richtel, M. (2003) "Visits to web sites surge as war begins, and most are up to task," *The New York Times*, March 23.

Roberts, P. (2003) "Al-Jazeera hobbled by DDOS attack," *Infoworld.com*, March 26.

St John, W. (2003) "Akamai cancels a contract for Arabic network's site," *The New York Times*, April 4.

Schechter, D. (2003) "Blogging the war away," *Nieman Reports*, Summer, pp. 90–2.

Thussu, D.K. and Freedman, D. (eds) (2003) *War and the Media*, London: Sage.

Timms, D. (2003) "News websites see traffic soar," *The Guardian*, March 20.

Walker, L. (2003) "Web use spikes on news of war," *The Washington Post*, March 22.

Warner, B. (2003) "War bloggers get reality check," *MSNBC News*, www.msnbc.com, April 9.

Weaver, J. (2003) "Iraq war a 'milestone' for Web News," *MSNBC.com*, April 1.

Welch, M. (2003) "Blogworld: the new amateur journalists weigh in," *Columbia Journalism Review*, www.cjr.org, 5, September/October.

Wells, M. (2001) "How smart was this bomb?," *The Guardian*, November 19.

Whitaker, B. (2003) "Al-Jazeera cause outcry with broadcast of battle casualities," *The Guardian*, March 24.

Williams, R. (1958) "Culture is ordinary," in R. Gable (ed.) (1989), *Resources of Hope*, London: Verso.

Williams, R. (1982) "Distance," in A. O'Connor (ed.), (1989) *Raymond Williams on Television*, London: Routledge.

Zelizer, B. and Allan, S. (eds) (2002) *Journalism after September 11*, London and New York: Routledge.

INDEX

ABC News (Australia) 226, 227, 229, 230, 231, 232, 233, 235, 237
ABC News (US) 7, 80, 87, 88, 103, 109, 140, 142, 143, 144, 152, 200, 261, 356
Abu Dhabi television 81, 261, 307, 318, 319, 330
Acheson, Dean 37
Adams, Eddie 119, 121, 126
Adie, Kate 3, 5, 11
advertising (influence on reporting) 12, 26, 38, 93, 101, 124, 125, 334, 336, 339
Afghanistan 27, 28, 29, 30, 33, 34, 35, 36, 45, 51, 65, 68, 69, 77, 78, 80, 87, 105, 107, 120, 122, 123, 124, 129, 131, 153, 174, 175, 184, 191, 206, 211, 220, 247, 259, 260, 299, 315, 319, 325, 352, 358
Africa 16, 63, 67, 120, 155–73, 207
Agence France Presse (AFP) 18, 44, 304, 305, 306, 307, 308, 309
agenda-setting 6, 11, 12, 15, 26, 30, 33, 54, 69, 71, 78, 96, 97, 99, 100, 102, 105, 158, 161, 162, 168, 212, 216, 231, 268, 302, 337, 342, 345
Al-Arabiya 81, 326
Albright, Madeleine 164, 176
Al-Jazeera 8, 18, 19, 51, 65, 80, 81, 83, 84, 85, 86, 93, 102, 104, 121, 260, 283, 287, 302, 308, 309, 312, 313, 315–32, 348, 352–6, 361, 362, 363
Al-Kahki, Amr 323, 324
Al-Kasim, Faisal 320, 330, 331
Allbritton, Christopher 339, 360, 364
Allemang, John 361
Allen, Dean 358
Alouni, Tayseer 84, 86, 93
al-Qaeda 9, 45, 62, 64, 65, 66, 69, 70, 71, 77, 86, 90, 93, 107, 110, 155
al-Sahhaf, Mohammed Saeed 44, 327

Al-Seddiqi, Salah 355
AltaVista 354
Alternet 337
Amanpour, Christiane 8, 9, 70, 182
Amnesty International 142
Anderson, Steve 7
Andrews, Paul 361
anthrax 48, 64
anti-war protests 10, 28, 31, 54, 103, 104, 108, 142, 143, 145, 159, 180, 247, 248, 252, 253, 254, 255, 256, 259, 262, 266–82, 299, 301, 305, 334, 336, 337, 340, 342
AOL Time Warner 333
Argentina 191, 347
Arnett, Peter 159, 261
A-shafi, Suleiman 88
Associated Press (AP) 18, 68, 176, 304, 308, 309, 312, 339
asylum seekers 48, 166, 184, 262, 274; see also refugees
Atlanta Journal Constitution 67, 261
Atomic Weapons Authority 275
Atta, Muhammad 90, 91
Auchmutey, Jim 67
Australia 17, 31, 208, 224–43, 299, 364
Austria 306, 307, 308
"axis of evil" 64, 77, 250, 259, 278
Ayoub, Tareq 325
Ayres, Chris 199, 202
Ayyoub, Tayek 51
Aziz, Tariq 8

Baghdad Blogger; see Salam Pax
Bahrain 50, 352
Baker, James A. 149
Balkans 13, 16, 120, 126, 174–89
Ballout, Jihad 355

Bangladesh 214
Barr, Cameron 66
Basque separatism 210
Basra 7, 8, 105, 123, 225, 300, 326, 353
BBC World 10, 235, 304, 354
Beck, Glenn 334, 335, 342
Belgium 27, 141, 152, 168
Bell, Martin 11–12, 159, 182, 184
Benn, Tony 277
Benton, Ross 54
Berlin Wall 63, 129, 181
Berlusconi, Silvio 333
Bernstein, Carl 38
bias (accusations of) 9, 68, 102, 228, 231, 235, 251, 284, 286, 302, 309, 311, 312, 330, 331, 352, 358
bin Laden, Osama 48, 64, 80, 81, 83, 84, 85, 86, 87, 88, 91, 93, 94, 107, 156, 352
biological weapons (threat of) 8, 28, 72, 146, 153, 196, 286
Bishop, Patrick 184, 191
Black Hawk Down 156
Blair, Tony 46, 47, 54, 55, 105, 106, 107, 110, 178, 180, 184, 185, 267, 271, 274, 225, 276, 277, 278, 279, 281, 287, 293
Bleifuss, Joel 141, 152
Blitzer, Wolf 85, 86, 94
Blix, Hans (report of) 18, 267, 270, 271, 272, 274, 275, 276, 278, 281
blog; see weblog
Bodi, Faisal 354
Boer War 25, 236, 237
Borger, Julian 53, 282
Bosnia 35, 72, 126, 175, 181–6, 191
Boston Globe 117, 129
Boston Herald 197
Bourke-White, Margaret 119
Bremer, Paul 328–9
Briganti, Irena 9
British Broadcasting Corporation (BBC) 3, 8, 10, 11, 12, 18, 20, 34, 47, 159, 176, 177, 178, 179, 182, 229, 233, 235, 260, 264, 283–300, 303, 304, 308, 316, 318, 353, 357, 362, 363
Brokaw, Tom 120, 144; see also NBC News
Brown, Tina 8–9, 70
Browne, Malcolm 119, 127
Bull Durham 335
Buoen, Roger 68
Burkeman, Oliver 6
Burns, John 3, 70, 71
Burrows, Larry 119
Burundi 120, 126

Bush (Snr), George H. 15, 27, 33, 63, 72, 142, 149, 150, 151, 153, 184, 252
Bush, George W. 34, 37, 43, 47, 60, 61, 62, 63, 64, 65, 69, 71, 73, 74, 138, 139, 145, 148, 150, 151, 156, 157, 162, 174, 180, 186, 250, 252, 253, 254, 267, 274, 276, 277, 278, 287, 301, 325, 327, 333, 334, 335, 340, 361, 363
Bush administration (George W.) 8, 14, 15, 60, 64, 67, 69, 71, 73, 106, 136, 137, 139, 140, 141, 142, 144, 145, 146, 147, 151, 152, 153, 156, 158, 62, 174, 187, 247, 259, 278, 358

Caldicott, Helen 36
Cambodia 34, 125, 216
Cameron, James 224
Campaign for Peace and Democracy 103
Campbell, Alistair 105, 299
Canadian Broadcasting Corporation (CBC) 4, 20
Capa, Robert 124, 127
Carter, Jimmy 33, 35, 69
cartoons 55, 185, 227, 228
Castro, Luis 51
Catalonia 206, 210
CBS News 7, 85, 86, 88, 103, 143, 144, 152
celebrity 14, 51, 78, 80, 82, 86, 90, 91, 93, 183, 277, 330
censorship 8, 9, 13, 30, 50, 98, 120, 137, 145, 152, 190, 204, 224, 238, 247, 299, 317, 318, 327, 329, 352, 356
Center for Social Media 19, 336, 338
Central Intelligence Agency (CIA) 31, 32, 33, 38, 39, 46, 52, 144, 153, 177, 352, 360
chemical weapons (threat of) 8, 28, 29, 48, 52, 53, 69, 72, 144, 145, 146, 149, 153, 196, 199, 204, 286
Chile 32
China 37, 59, 126, 212, 214, 216, 279
Chirac, Jacques 270, 275
Chomsky, Noam 25, 34, 38, 39, 53, 97, 98, 109, 143
Christian Science Monitor 36, 66
citizenship 5, 20, 28, 136, 207, 259, 263, 336, 343, 345
Civil War (US) 25, 119
Clark, David 107, 110
Clarke, Wesley 176
"clash of civilizations" 56, 181, 272
Clear Channel 230, 335, 336

Clinton, Bill 63, 69, 72, 105, 158, 160, 182, 184, 342
CNN 6–12, 13, 16, 65, 70, 80, 81, 83, 84, 85, 86, 91, 99, 100, 102, 104, 106, 108, 136, 148, 152, 153, 157–63, 164, 166, 182, 199, 233, 235, 259, 260, 299, 302, 303, 304, 308, 309, 310, 312, 318, 320, 321, 337, 353, 359, 363
Cold War 15, 16, 32, 36, 45, 63, 72, 74, 69, 97, 98, 99, 106, 107, 108, 109, 157, 158, 159, 175, 180, 181, 184, 283, 313
Colombia 33
"compassion fatigue" 161
Connell, Joan 359
Conservative Party (UK) 159, 279
Cook, Robin 177, 184, 291
Couso, Jose 51
Croatia 180, 181, 183, 306, 307, 308
C-Span (US) 148
Cuba 36, 303; see also Guantanamo Bay
Czech Republic 306, 308
Czechoslovakia 126, 273

Daily Express 48, 51, 193, 194
Daily Mail 192, 269, 271, 272, 275, 281, 282
Daily Star 52, 194
Daily Telegraph 44, 52, 93, 184, 185, 232, 233, 237, 269, 270, 271, 272, 274, 280, 281, 282, 299, 362
Democratic Party (US) 34, 106, 146, 148, 342
Democratic Republic of Congo 27, 116, 155, 164, 168, 303
Denmark 306, 307
Detroit Free Press 127
digital technology 119, 224, 233, 334, 340, 343, 350, 359
diplomacy 16, 29, 32, 46, 63, 71, 72, 106, 138, 141, 146, 149, 151, 162, 175, 176, 177, 180, 182, 226, 263, 266, 268, 273, 274, 276, 277, 316, 317
disinformation 9, 30, 47, 48, 70, 136, 137–41, 143, 144, 147, 310, 360
Dixie Chicks 335–6
Dodge, Toby 362
Dyke, Greg 10; see also BBC

East Timor 116, 126, 206, 214,
Economist, The (UK) 126, 322
Egypt 11, 93, 94, 307, 317, 329, 330
email 19, 48, 50, 238, 259, 262, 337, 339, 342, 350, 360, 361, 363; see also Internet

embedded reporting 5, 6, 9, 13, 16, 17, 18, 19, 28, 30, 31, 49–50, 70–1, 77, 91, 105, 136, 166, 167, 190, 191, 193, 194–200, 203, 204, 206, 226, 232, 249, 260, 261, 262, 283, 285, 286, 287, 289, 294–6, 297, 298, 299, 307, 311, 323, 324, 349, 353, 354, 361
Ethiopia 63, 165, 210
"ethnic cleansing" 16, 34, 177, 178, 179
Express and Star (Wolverhampton) 194

Fairness and Accuracy in Reporting (FAIR) 143, 145, 152
Falklands/Malvinas conflict 16, 28, 30, 104, 120, 122, 152, 190, 191–4, 199, 201, 202, 203, 204, 225, 347
Federal Bureau of Investigation (FBI) 32, 363
Federal Communications Commission (FCC) 334
Finkelstein, Daniel 270
Finland 36, 152, 306, 307, 308
Firdous Square 43, 101, 117, 298, 325, 349
First Blood 251
Fisk, Robert 51, 117, 211, 262, 272, 273, 274, 282, 348, 349, 363, 364
flak (criticisms of reporting) 38, 97, 98, 99, 102, 109
Fletcher, Kim 51
Foot, Paul 51
Fouda, Yosri 354
Fox News 6, 7, 8, 9, 10, 11, 50, 93, 235, 259, 260, 309, 320, 321, 350, 363
framing 13, 17, 18, 29, 31, 52, 53, 55, 63, 64, 72–4, 77, 85, 88, 89, 97, 99, 104, 105, 106, 107, 117, 126, 130, 136, 139, 143, 144, 152, 161, 163, 183, 219, 247–65, 268, 269, 272, 273, 274, 277–80, 301
France 176, 260, 263, 270, 274, 275, 279, 301, 302, 304, 305, 307, 316, 330, 355
Freedland, Jonathan 180, 278, 279, 282
freelance journalism 336, 360, 364
Friedman, Tom 73
"friendly fire" 13, 44, 54, 146, 204

Gellhorn, Martha 20
genocide 16, 61, 69, 72, 155, 157, 160, 161, 163, 164, 165, 166, 168, 169, 179, 183
Germany 12, 119, 124, 127, 144, 152, 176, 178, 179, 181, 185, 187, 199, 238, 260, 263, 270, 272, 273, 277, 279, 301, 305, 306, 307, 308, 316, 317

Gibbs, Phillip 50
Gillan, Audrey 50, 55, 127, 179
Gilligan, Andrew 20, 47, 283, 291
Girard, Renaud 176, 187
globalization 46, 102, 103, 169, 221, 259, 263, 266, 280, 283, 303, 333, 337
Globe and Mail 361
Goldenberg, Suzanne 54
Google search engine 336, 340, 343, 354, 362
Gordon, Bryony 359
Gowing, Nik 108, 157, 160, 162, 163, 183, 353
Gralnick, Jeff 195–6
Greece 305, 306, 307
Greenslade, Roy 46, 227
Gregory, Karl 354
Grenada 28, 30, 45, 152, 251
Guantanamo Bay 354
Guardian, see The Guardian
Guatemala 31
Gulf War; *see* Persian Gulf War (1991)
Gupta, Sanjay 199, 200

hacking (online) 324, 326, 355–6, 363
Haeberle, Ron 119
Haiti 190
Hari, Johann 180
Harper's magazine 142
Hastings, Max 202
Heller, Jean 140
Herbert, Gerald 96, 197, 202
Herman, Edward 25, 38, 39, 45, 97, 98, 109, 175
Heyward, Andrew 85, 86
High Noon 249
Hindustan Times 212
Hiroshima 35, 224; *see also* Nagasaki; World War II
Hitler, Adolph 52, 85, 141, 152, 272, 273, 277
Holbrooke, Richard 176
Hollywood cinema 4, 29, 55, 149, 156, 166, 204, 249, 325, 335; *see also* individual film titles
Holocaust 91, 126, 179, 183, 185; *see also* World War II
Hoon, Geoff 50
Howard, John 225, 226, 237
Hughes, David 272, 282
human rights 16, 31, 51, 56, 72, 73, 74, 142, 150, 168, 174, 175, 184, 185, 186, 187, 206, 216, 217, 218, 293, 337

humanitarian intervention 106, 157, 158, 159, 186, 187
Humphrey, Hubert 34
Hungary 117, 306, 308
Hurd, Douglas 159
Hussein, Saddam 11, 29, 43, 47, 48, 52–3, 54, 55, 65, 66, 69, 73, 77, 85, 94, 96, 101, 105, 107, 117, 129, 138, 139, 144, 149, 150, 152, 153, 198, 199, 234, 248, 249, 250, 252, 254, 256, 269, 271, 272, 273, 275, 276, 277, 284, 286, 287, 292, 293, 298, 299, 300, 324, 325, 328, 331, 333, 339, 349, 354, 362
Hutton inquiry 10, 20, 47

Ignatieff, Michael 72, 159, 168, 174, 175, 183, 185, 186, 187
immediacy 11, 100, 160, 260, 349, 358, 361
In These Times 140, 141, 151, 152, 153
Independent 46, 48, 51, 54, 180, 181, 185, 262, 269, 272, 274, 275, 278, 280, 282, 348, 349, 362, 364
Independent Television News (ITN) 50, 233, 289
India 17, 127, 206–23
Indian Express 212
Indonesia 31, 32, 36, 126
Indymedia 263, 333, 337, 343
infotainment 19, 101, 202, 248, 343
Institute for Policy Studies 143
intelligence dossier 20, 48, 267, 275, 284
International Monetary Fund (IMF) 31, 34, 169
Internet 19, 87, 92, 96, 99, 100, 102–4, 118, 119, 150, 233, 262, 267, 301, 303, 310, 324, 333–46, 347–65; *see also* email; online news
Intifada 126, 127; *see also* Palestinians
IRA 67, 79, 84, 92
Iran 29, 33, 35, 45, 50, 52, 69, 123, 139, 149, 152, 153, 247, 263, 307, 308
Iraqi News Agency (INA) 308
Isaacson, Walter 65
Islam 65, 84, 105, 181, 184, 208, 213, 216, 272, 274, 299, 302, 328
Israel 27, 33, 64, 65, 66, 68, 69, 77, 84, 88, 89, 92, 93, 126, 127, 136, 144, 145, 273, 307, 317, 322, 327, 352
Italy 79, 277, 305, 306, 307, 316, 317
ITV News Channel 7, 10

Japan 27, 35, 37, 214, 216, 224; *see also* Hiroshima; Nagasaki

Jennings, Peter 200; *see also* ABC News
Johnson, Peter 71
Johnson, Scott 88, 93
Johnston, George 237
Jordan 50, 93, 141, 307, 327, 352, 360
Jukes, Stephen 68

Kabul 129, 174, 325, 353
Kafala, Tarik 353, 354
Kashmir 17, 206, 209, 210, 212–21
Keegan, John 44, 181
Kelly, David 20, 47
Kennan, George 37, 158, 159
Kennicot, Philip 83
Kenya 162, 167
Khanfar, Waddah 328–9
Kissinger, Henry 37
Knightley, Phillip 25, 34, 35, 46, 47, 50,
    56, 119
Koppel, Ted 261, 264
Korean War 45, 119, 122, 224; *see also*
    North Korea
Kosovo 16, 34, 35, 102, 104, 105, 129, 168,
    175, 176, 177, 178, 179, 180, 184, 185,
    186, 187, 191, 206, 270, 281
Kross, Kathryn 9
Kurdish crisis 50, 52, 54, 127, 129, 148,
    150, 157, 161, 307, 353, 360
Kurtz, Howard 10, 65, 68, 359
Kuwait 8, 11, 50, 52, 137, 138, 139, 140,
    141, 142, 144, 149, 150, 200, 210, 234,
    251, 273, 285, 300, 307, 308

Labour Party (UK) 277, 281
Lake, Anthony 158
Lange, Dorothea 118
Laos 33, 34
Laqueur, Walter 66
Le Monde 279
Le Nouvel Observateur 178
Lebanon 118, 262, 317, 318, 329
Leibovich, Mark 71
Levy, Steven 358
Liberia 116, 155, 164, 175
Libya 45, 47, 316
Limbaugh, Rush 50, 335
Little, Allan 182
Little, Jeremy 238
Littlejohn, Richard 299
Lloyd, Terry 50–1
London Review of Books 179, 347
Los Angeles Times 60, 85, 86, 93, 149, 153,
    180, 322

Lule, Jack 44
Lycos 354
Lynch, Jessica 8, 29, 44, 55, 105, 249, 263

MacArthur, Brian 50
MacArthur, John 142
McCullin, Don 118
McFarlane, Robert 139
McGhee, Ralph 31
McGowan, Robert 193
McGrory, Mary 138
McKay, Peter 272
McNeil-Lehrer (PBS) 139
Maddocks, Melvin 66, 69
Madrid (bombings, 2004) 122
Madsen, Wayne 27
Mandela, Nelson 166, 277
"manifest destiny" 61, 70, 74
Media Research Center (US) 93
memory (collective) 124, 143, 199, 209,
    236, 237, 238, 250, 263, 280
Mexico 100
MI5 46, 47
MI6 46, 47, 49
Microsoft 340; *see also* MSNBC
Middle East Broadcast Center 318
militarism 4, 44–6, 56
Miller, John 87–8, 93
Minneapolis Star Tribune 68
Mirazi, Hafez 356
Mirror (UK) 51, 52, 54, 192, 269, 273, 274,
    275, 276, 277, 278, 280, 282
Missing in Action 251
Moldovia 126
Montenegro 178, 181
Morgan, Piers 51; *see also Mirror*
Moussaoui, Zacarias 90
MoveOn 342
MSNBC 7, 9, 86, 330, 348, 356, 359, 363,
    364; *see also* Microsoft; NBC News
Murdoch, Rupert 7, 17, 31, 51, 227, 228,
    230, 333, 334; *see also* ownership
museums (in Iraq) 123
Muslims 17, 91, 126, 181, 182, 183, 184,
    208, 213, 214, 216, 219, 274, 279
Myers, Richard 49, 310

Nagasaki 35; *see also* Hiroshima
Nasdaq 326, 355
National Public Radio (NPR) 67
NATO 16, 34, 35, 51, 53, 106, 168, 175,
    176, 177, 178, 179, 180, 183, 184, 185,
    186, 188

NBC News 7, 103, 143, 144, 152, 196, 233, 238, 261, 364; *see also* MSNBC
Netherlands 306
New York Daily News 339
New York Stock Exchange 102, 326, 355
The New York Times 3, 7, 62, 65, 67, 69, 70, 73, 80, 85, 86, 88, 90, 92, 93, 120, 121, 123, 126, 129, 142, 152, 158, 174, 186, 187, 219
New Zealand 236, 238
news agencies 18, 286, 301–14
news photographs 15, 44, 54, 55, 88, 89, 115–35, 140, 142, 156, 191, 196, 197, 204, 225, 234, 235, 236, 261, 287, 307, 338, 357, 359
news values 16, 85, 193, 202, 203, 207, 208, 303, 354
Newsweek 88, 90, 91, 94, 126, 130, 140, 152, 358, 359
Nicaragua 33, 63, 204
Nightline (ABC) 261
9/11 14, 60, 64, 65, 66, 68, 73, 74, 155, 174, 175, 234, 248, 250, 259, 358; *see also* September 11, 2001; World Trade Center
Nixon, Richard 34, 108, 251
Normandy 348
Norris, David 192
North Korea 26, 45, 66, 200; *see also* Korean War
Northern Ireland 206, 210
Norway 306
nuclear technology 26, 28, 35, 36, 47, 48, 55, 64, 72, 149, 196, 275
Nunberg, Geoff 67

O'Sullivan, John L. 61, 62, 74
objectivity 6, 7, 13, 16, 19, 49, 92, 159, 191, 193, 194, 201–4, 221, 255, 315–27, 332
Observer, see The Observer
Official Secrets Act 46
Omaar, Rageh 11
Omar, Mullah 85, 90
Oneworld 333, 337, 340, 343, 344
Open Democracy 337, 344
Orwell, George 49, 53
ownership of news organizations 17, 38, 98, 108, 211, 228, 229, 231, 304, 333, 334, 335, 364

Pakistan 93, 196, 210, 212, 213, 219
Palestinians 64, 65, 66, 68, 69, 77, 79, 84, 88, 89, 92, 93, 126, 127, 260, 316, 317, 322, 327
Panama 28, 30, 33, 36, 45, 152
"parachute journalism" 165
Parry, Gareth 192
patriotism (impact of on news coverage) 4, 5, 7, 8, 9, 10, 13, 17, 18, 26, 28, 50, 51, 55, 68, 74, 78, 85, 91, 92, 97, 98, 115, 125, 144, 145, 149, 192, 201, 249, 251, 253, 254, 255, 256, 258, 259, 284, 358
PBS (US) 139, 150, 233
Pearl, Daniel 88, 92, 196
Pearl Harbor 35, 64, 68, 127; *see also* World War II
Pentagon 6, 15, 29, 30, 331, 35, 36, 53, 65, 70, 71, 136, 137, 139, 140, 141, 143, 144, 145, 146, 151, 153, 180, 191, 195, 196, 203, 233, 234, 261, 263, 283, 286, 287, 288, 298, 299, 310, 325, 351, 353, 358
Persian Gulf War (1991) 6, 15, 17, 25, 28, 30, 35, 36, 37, 43, 44, 47, 49, 53, 54, 55, 97, 104, 105, 119, 120, 125, 130, 136–54, 157, 191, 224, 225, 247–65, 273, 279, 287, 288, 302, 318, 340, 349
"personal journalism" 357
Pew Research Center 350, 351, 363
Philadelphia Inquirer 121, 123, 127
Philippines 36
Phillips, Melanie 226, 272, 282
photojournalism: *see* news photographs
Pilger, John 31, 32, 34, 39, 44, 46, 51, 228, 231
Platoon 261
Platt, Spencer 197
Poland 273
polls 47, 108, 143, 146, 148, 150, 153, 226, 266, 267, 274, 278, 279, 284, 298, 299, 300, 363; *see also* public opinion
pool system 28, 30, 49, 104, 136, 137, 142, 145, 148, 152, 190, 225, 232, 285, 286
Portugal 306, 307
Powell, Colin 48, 174, 249, 251, 327, 340, 353
Powell, Michael 334
press briefings 30, 101, 104, 105, 141, 162, 191, 227, 233, 276, 288, 289, 290, 294, 310, 323, 324, 353, 355
Preston, Peter 6
Prime Time Live (ABC) 140
prisoners of war (POWs) 116, 145, 146, 147, 148, 251, 287, 293, 326, 327
professionalism 15, 16, 17, 18, 26, 30, 78,

81, 82, 83, 84, 85, 86, 87, 91, 118, 121,
  159, 165, 190, 192, 193, 200, 201, 202,
  203, 206, 208, 209, 221, 225, 231, 235,
  260, 261, 302, 309, 311, 312, 319, 341,
  345, 348, 357
propaganda 8, 13, 16, 25, 31, 34, 35, 38–9,
  50, 52, 53, 54, 82, 85, 102, 136, 137,
  139, 141, 142, 143, 144–6, 147, 148,
  160, 165, 174, 176, 179, 180, 206, 231,
  249, 262, 287, 293, 294, 310, 325, 350,
  355, 356, 361; see also spin
Protsyuk, Tara 51
psychological warfare 30, 44, 190, 206, 225
public opinion 6, 15, 18, 19, 96, 99, 103,
  137, 143, 148, 150, 151, 153, 180, 190,
  207, 252, 257, 259, 268, 271, 280, 284,
  301, 305, 316, 322, 333, 334, 341, 342;
  see also polls
public relations (PR) 6, 18, 97, 104, 136,
  141, 174, 225, 231, 247, 266, 267, 273
public sphere 18, 100, 101, 102, 103, 131,
  207, 259, 262, 263, 267, 268, 269, 280,
  320
Purdum, Todd 66, 69

Qatar 50, 105 204, 227, 260, 285, 288, 294,
  295, 296, 302, 307, 308, 310, 315, 318,
  319, 323, 324, 325, 330, 352, 353, 356

radio 100, 137, 151, 165, 226 230–1, 233,
  235, 283, 316, 317, 318, 330, 333, 334,
  335, 340–1, 342, 348
Radio Free Europe 316
Radio Sawa 316, 330
radioactivity 35, 36
Rambo 250
Rather, Dan 120, 144; see also CBS News
Reagan, Ronald 33, 39, 47, 140, 142, 149,
  151, 153, 184, 251
Red Brigades 79
Red Cross 162, 174, 178, 183, 291
Reeves, Cris 44
refugees 123, 129, 142, 155, 161, 164, 166,
  177, 178, 179, 184
Republican Party 9, 27, 34, 148, 174, 266,
  334
Reuters 18, 51, 67, 68, 128, 162, 304, 306,
  307, 308, 309, 312
Reynolds, Glenn Harlan 358, 359
Rice, Condoleezza 69, 85, 352
Ridge, Tom 71–2
Ritter, Scott 29
Robbins, Tim 335

Robertson, George 177, 178
Rokke, Doug 35
rolling news 6–12, 13, 165, 283, 287; see
  also 24-hour news and individual
  networks
Romania 306
Rosenthal, A.M. 67
Rubin, James 176, 178, 180
Rumsfeld, Donald 29, 48, 66, 310, 354
Rushdie, Salman 67
Russia 25, 34, 35, 67, 126, 279, 301, 302,
  306, 307, 308
Rutenberg, Jim 7, 261
Rwanda 16, 27, 69, 72, 120, 126, 155–7,
  160–9

Said, Edward 56, 143
St Petersburg Times 140
Salam Pax 19, 339, 347, 348, 360–2
sanitization of reality 28, 104, 144, 231,
  260, 347, 353, 358
satellite technology 11, 19, 55, 81, 96, 100,
  102, 136, 140, 141, 148, 151, 160, 232,
  233, 261, 302, 315, 318, 326, 329, 330,
  334, 340, 352, 359, 360
Saudi Arabia 93, 137, 138, 139, 140, 141,
  143, 144, 145, 147, 148, 152, 251, 255,
  257, 318, 326, 352
Saving Private Ryan 55
Schechter, Danny 30, 31, 356
Schmemann, Serge 65
Schroeder, Gerhard 270
Schwarzkopf, Norman 141, 142, 150, 249,
  279
Seamark, Mick 192
Security Council 18, 27, 36, 191, 269, 270,
  271, 275, 277; see also United Nations
September 11, 2001 14, 30, 37, 45, 48, 61,
  63, 65, 66, 67, 69, 73, 77, 78, 80, 81, 83,
  85, 86, 91, 92, 93, 106, 120, 124, 127,
  140, 155, 207, 208, 211, 283, 302, 316,
  317, 320, 321, 322, 351, 352, 253, 357,
  358; see also 9/11; Twin Towers; World
  Trade Center
Serbia 34, 45, 51, 53, 106, 168, 176, 177,
  178, 179, 180, 181, 183, 340
Shnev, Ismail Abu 88
Short, Claire 277
Sierra Leone 155, 164, 169
Silva, Victor 51
Simpson, John 8, 9, 183; see also BBC
Sirota, David J. 7
Sites, Kevin 359, 364

60 Minutes 80, 200, 229; *see also* CBS News

Sky News 7, 8, 10, 12, 18, 44, 81, 109, 229, 233, 235, 284, 287, 288, 289, 290, 291, 292, 293, 294, 297, 298

Slovenia 180, 181, 306, 307, 308

Smith, W. Eugene 127, 128

Snow, Jon 11

Solana, Javier 177

Somalia 16, 45, 72, 106, 108, 116, 125, 129, 130, 155, 156, 157, 158, 160, 161, 162, 163, 164, 184, 191

Sorenson, Erik 7, 93

Soviet Union 31, 35, 38, 45, 63, 126, 129, 140, 144, 181, 211, 305, 313

Sowcroft, Brent 200

Spain 51, 124, 210, 305, 306, 307

Spanish-American War 36, 119, 122

Spanish Civil War 25, 124

spectacle (war as) 14, 15, 43, 45, 47, 49, 55, 90, 136, 149, 150, 161, 186, 348

"spin" 8, 14, 60, 71, 98, 104, 158, 198, 225, 233, 350; *see also* public relations

Stalin, Joseph 117

stereotypes 63, 165, 185

Stockholm Syndrome 195

Stop the War Coalition 103, 280

Straw, Jack 12, 272

Sudan 116, 155, 161, 162

Sun (UK) 48, 52, 53, 54, 55, 179, 185, 269, 273, 274, 275, 276, 278, 280, 282, 299, 362

Sunday Times (UK) 177, 179, 184

Swain, Jon 11

Switzerland 36, 306

Sydney Morning Herald 227, 228, 231

Syria 35, 45, 247, 307

tabloidization 228, 230, 234–5

Taliban 33, 51, 65, 73, 93, 107, 211; *see also* Afghanistan

Tanner, Marcus 185

Tanzania 164

Tears of the Sun 166

The Australian 31, 226, 228

The Chicago Tribune 123, 124

The Guardian 9, 39, 46, 50, 51, 53, 54, 55, 69, 70, 90, 100, 174, 183, 184, 192, 208, 262, 267, 269, 273, 274, 275, 276, 278, 280, 282, 284, 299, 335, 362

The Hindu 212

The Nation 151

The Observer 46, 53, 54, 120, 191

The Statesman 212

The Times (UK) 50, 54, 143, 147, 269, 270, 274, 280, 282, 362

The Times of India 210, 212, 217, 219

think tanks 31, 37, 207, 328, 358

Tianenmen Square 126

Time magazine 126, 129, 152

torture 142, 145, 146, 287, 293, 294

trauma 77, 86, 259, 362

Tucker, Joanne 356

Turkey 220, 236, 306, 307, 219

20/20 (ABC) 142

24-hour news 6–12, 96, 99–101, 104, 108, 119, 158, 229, 260, 283, 302, 349, 352; *see also* rolling news; individual networks

Twin Towers; *see* World Trade Center

Tyler, Patrick 138, 139

Uganda 27, 161

Umm Qasr 8, 105, 194, 300, 324

unilateral reporting 13, 50, 195, 204, 233, 262, 285–8, 295, 296, 298; *see also* embedded reporting

United Nations (UN) 28, 29, 52, 60, 66, 88, 96, 103, 142, 143, 156, 159, 160, 161, 169, 175, 177, 178, 179, 183, 187, 211, 266, 270, 271, 273, 275, 276, 277, 278, 284, 301, 303, 321, 340; *see also* Security Council

United Press International (UPI) 71, 196

US Central Command 50, 105, 227, 288, 323, 324, 325, 353, 354

US News and World Report 152

USA Patriot Act 340

USA Today 9, 71, 152

USS Abraham Lincoln 71, 250, 261, 263, 333

Uzbekistan 73

Viacom 333; *see also* ownership

videophone 233, 359; *see also* satellite technology

Vietnam 25, 31, 34, 47, 50, 53, 63, 72, 73, 79, 97, 98, 107, 108, 118, 119, 121, 122, 125, 125, 126, 127, 129, 143, 150, 157, 159, 160, 190, 195, 224, 232, 250, 251, 256, 348

Village Voice 151

Vivendi 333; *see also* ownership

Voice of America 316

Waas, Murray 149, 153

Walker, William 176

Wall Street Journal 152, 196

Wallace, Mike 200; *see also* CBS News
Walt Disney Co. 304, 333; *see also* ownership
Walton, Jim 9
"War beyond the box" 337–45
"war on drugs" 25, 32, 33, 250
"war on terrorism" 14, 15, 16, 32, 45, 49, 59–74, 107, 156, 174, 175, 186, 187, 248, 249, 250, 259, 260, 352, 358
warblogs 19, 339, 348, 358–61, 362; *see also* weblogs
Washington Diplomat 322
Washington Post 68, 71, 83, 93, 97, 110, 138, 139, 152, 279
Washington Times 196, 197, 202
weapons of mass destruction (WMD) 8, 9, 18, 29, 43, 48, 49, 64, 70, 71, 72, 83, 96, 104, 105, 107, 174, 180, 226, 269, 270, 273, 284, 286, 289. 290, 291, 292, 294, 295, 296, 297, 298, 300, 304, 341
weblogs 19, 151, 238, 259, 339, 340, 341, 342, 344, 347, 348, 349, 350, 356–62, 363, 364; *see also* Internet; warblogs
Wells, Matt 11, 353
Williams, Brian 262
Wilson, Joseph 138, 139

Wilson, Woodrow 36, 67, 106
wire services 39, 68, 138; *see also* news agencies
Wolff, Michael 50
Woodruff, Judy 139
Woodward, Bob 139, 140–1
World Trade Center 64, 65, 68, 77, 82, 127, 156, 250, 351; *see also* 9/11; September 11, 2001
World Trade Organization 333
World War I 12, 25, 50, 122, 124, 141, 224, 236, 320
World War II 12, 25, 27, 34, 38, 43, 47, 55, 63, 64, 66, 119, 124, 127, 190, 199, 214, 224, 237, 270, 272, 317, 347, 348; *see also* Holocaust
Wright, Dean 348
Wright, Robin 74, 322

Yahoo.com 356, 363
Year Zero 262
Yugoslavia 16, 25, 35, 161, 175, 187

Z Magazine 151
Zaire; *see* Democratic Republic of Congo
Zelnick, Bob 139